The CD that accompanied this book has been replaced by a web site that can be found at the following address: http://www.phptr.com

Note that all references to the CD in the book now pertain to the web site.

Understanding SNMP MIBs

David Perkins

and

Evan McGinnis

To join a Prentice Hall PTR internet mailing list, point to:
http://www.prenhall.com/register

Prentice Hall PTR
Upper Saddle River, New Jersey 07458
http://www.prenhall.com

Editorial/production supervision: *Camille Trentacoste*
Manufacturing manager: *Alexis R. Heydt*
Acquisitions editor: *Mary Franz*
Editorial assistant: *Noreen Regina*
Cover design: *Design Source*
Cover design director: *Jerry Votta*
Marketing Manager: *Dan Rush*

Upper Saddle River, NJ 07458

The publisher offers discounts on this book when ordered in bulk quantities.
For more information, contact:

Corporate Sales Department
Prentice Hall PTR
One Lake Street
Upper Saddle River, New Jersey 07458

Phone: 800-382-3419, Fax: 201-236-7141
E-mail: corpsales@prenhall.com

Printed in the United States of America
10 9

ISBN 0-13-437708-7

Prentice-Hall International (UK) Limited, *London*
Prentice-Hall of Australia Pty. Limited, *Sydney*
Prentice-Hall of Canada, Inc., *Toronto*
Prentice-Hall Hispanoamericana, S. A., *Mexico*
Prentice-Hall of India Private Limited, *New Delhi*
Prentice-Hall of Japan, Inc., *Tokyo*
Prentice-Hall Asia Pte. Ltd., *Singapore*
Editora Prentice-Hall do Brasil, Ltda., *Rio de Janeiro*

Contents

Foreword

It is a pleasure to introduce the reader to "Understanding SNMP MIBs" and its authors David Perkins and Evan McGinnis.

David has long been one of the early implementors of SNMP MIB technology. His tireless work on the premiere reference implementation for MIB compilers, SMIC, has advanced both the state of the art and the state of the industry. Not only have his efforts have shown what works (and what doesn't), thereby improving the quality of the SNMP standards, but they also form the basis for various commercial and private deployments of SNMP technology.

Evan has also been involved in SNMP technology, writing both agents and applications in addition to SNMP MIBs. Although Evan's name isn't as widely known, he has been on the front lines of delivering SNMP technology to anxious users who need to manage their networks with products that provide actual solutions.

In this book, David and Evan use their experience to provide a readable explanation for both the MIB reader and the MIB writer. The MIB reader benefits because they explain the myriad of nuances that go into interpreting a MIB module. The MIB writer also benefits because they explain all of the "tricks of the trade" used by the folks who've written MIBs to model everything from toasters to launch delivery systems!

David and Evan are also not shy about giving their opinions about "the good, the bad, and the ugly" of SNMP. Whilst I may not agree with all of these opinions, their positions all come from their voluminous experience as two of the field officers in the SNMP calvary!

Dr. Marshall T. Rose
former IETF Area Director for Network Management
November, 1996

Preface

The Berkeley California philosopher Ashleigh Brilliant once wrote, "The world is controlled by a small, evil group to which no one I know belongs." If it seems that the rules and subtleties of writing an SNMP MIB are controlled by the same secretive group, you're not alone. Until now there has been little guidance provided on how to write, read, and use MIBs.

In a nutshell, MIBs are specifications containing definitions of management information so that network systems can be remotely monitored, configured, and controlled.

The standards bodies involved have formal documents that state the set of rules which must be followed in writing MIBs. The rules are written in an adapted sub-set of an obsolete version of a specification language called Abstract Syntax Notation One (ASN.1). These documents are almost unreadable, since the ASN.1 language is intended more for machine processing than human comprehension. Also, no one has yet provided a style guide for MIB writers, or an answer book for MIB readers. The unfortunate result has been that understanding MIBs often comes down to learning the oral folklore, or worse, reading the endless stream of email on a large number of IETF mailing lists. Unfortunately, much of this email and other information made available on the Internet is not quite correct.

As a result, many MIB writers end up reinventing the wheel, using conflicting techniques, simply because the authors didn't know about a precedent in another MIB, or writing incorrect MIBs. Thus, understanding MIBs requires careful and detailed reading to determine the intent of the author.

There has been enormous growth in recent years in the development of SNMP-based management stations, as well as a flood of MIBs from both vendors and international standards bodies. These MIBs are the language of network and applications management.

Whether you are a network manager trying to manage devices from numerous vendors, a test engineer putting together a test plan, or a product manager writing a data sheet, it may indeed seem as if all MIBs were written by a small, evil group of which you're not a part. If you are going to be involved with network management anywhere along the chain, understanding MIBs is quickly becoming a requirement. Whether you are a designer or user of MIBs, this book was written so you, too, can get some real work done, and not waste time learning the initiation rites of this small, evil group.

The Scope Of This Book

There are a number of excellent books already in print that attempt to provide an overview of the entire Network Management universe; there are also several excellent texts specifically focusing on the Simple Network Management Protocol (SNMP) in all of its deceiving simplicity.

This book is different, in that it focuses on the key aspects of SNMP-based management that you must know to allow you to first, read and understand existing MIBs, and then (if you are so inclined) design, define, and write useful, compliant MIBs for your own devices or applications.

The process of understanding MIBs is often confused with understanding the protocol. Naturally, the two are related, but understanding a MIB doesn't require that you have detailed knowledge of the inner workings of the protocol. Its definition and operation are fixed and can be treated as a "black box." Understanding MIBs requires only a high level understanding and not in-depth knowledge of the protocol. This book gives you enough of an introduction to SNMP that you can understand what will be going on with the protocol, and how it relates to good MIB design.

Also confused with writing a MIB are the tasks of writing the code that makes available, or uses, specific instances of management information defined in a MIB. These are separate tasks, which may be performed by the same individual. This book introduces the concepts needed for development of an agent or management application, but is not a tutorial on these tasks. That information is provided by vendors of agent and management application development systems.

A summary of all the elements of SNMP is provided as appendices so you will have one reference source for what you need to know to do useful work.

Who Should Read This Book

This book was written with three main audience groups in mind:

- *Network administrators* (and end-users), who cannot change the network information that is available to them, but would like to be able to read and understand the manageable aspects of their network.
- *Personnel of network component vendors* (which includes agent and application developers, test engineers, and product managers), who must be able to define and create software based on the management aspects specified in existing MIBs, create

new MIB specifications for management elements that have not yet been standardized, test that the implementations are compliant, and find creative ways to differentiate products that are based on standardized specifications.
- *Students*, who can use this book to complement introductory texts on SNMP, or as the primary source in a project-oriented class to apply network management.

Typographical Conventions

Icons

We have written this book using facts and our experiences. We have found problems with the SNMP definitions. Some of these cause SNMP to be limited. Some of these are the result of contradictory, ambiguous, incomplete, and incomprehensible text in the SNMP definitions. Where there is a problem, we use a *caution* or an *our opinion* icon to bring this point to the attention of the reader.

We use this icon to emphasize a particularly important point or one that has tripped up those trying to understand or use SNMP.

Our Opinion

We use this icon to express a strong conviction that we have, which may be counter to the conventional wisdom or practice.

Notation for Syntax Descriptions

This book describes the language used to write MIB modules. We use an extended form of the BNF notation to specify this language. The rules for this notation are shown below:

- Literal values are specified in quotes, for example **"BEGIN"**
- Replaceable items are surrounded by less than (<) and greater than (>) characters, for example **<oidValue>**
- Defined items are specified without surrounding quotes or less than and greater than characters, for example **lcName**
- A vertical bar (|) is used to indicate a choice between items, for example **<synType> | <tcType> | <seqEnum> | <seqBits>**
- Ellipsis are used to indicate that the previous item may be repeated one or more times, for example **<importsFrom>...**
- Square brackets are used to enclose optional items, for example **["DISPLAY-HINT" chrStr]**
- Curly braces are used to group together items, for example **{ "OBJECT" "IDENTIFIER" }**
- An equals character (=) is used to mean "defined as," for example **<mibFile> = <mibModule>...**

An example of a combined usage of several rules is the following:

<importsFrom> = <importsName> ["," <importsName>]... "FROM" <moduleIdent>

This example uses an equals character to specify that an *<importsFrom>* item is defined as the list of items to the right of the equals character. The square brackets are used to indicate that a comma followed by an *<importsName>* item is optional. The ellipsis are used to indicate that the preceding item, that is *["," <importsName>]*, may be repeated. The text *FROM* is in quotes to indicate that it is a literal value.

Notation for Examples

Many example MIB fragments are specified throughout the book. These fragments are formatted with a fixed width font. The examples may also contain text that is proportionally spaced. This text is a comment to explain the example, and would not typically be used in an actual MIB module. The following example shows the use of the two fonts:

```
-- This module is for company BigCo and contains the top level (or root)
-- definitions for the OID sub-tree allocated to BigCo.
BIGCO-ROOT-MIB DEFINITIONS ::= BEGIN
-- rest of module would go here
END

-- This module is for industry consortium ERV (Ethernet Repeater Vendors)
-- and contains extensions to the IETF's Ethernet repeater MIB for
-- topology determination.
ERV-ETHTOP-MIB
DEFINITIONS ::= BEGIN
-- rest of module would go here
END
```

Our Credo

This book contains facts, our experiences, and our beliefs tempered by the comments of our reviewers. A primary result of our experiences in network management is the following belief, which we call the Fundamental Axiom of Technology, and is our credo.

> *The impact of learning about a technology must be minimal, and must not stand in the way of applying the technology.*

We believe the burden of communicating the concepts and applications of a technology should be on the creators and proponents of the technology and not on the users of the technology. Please let us know how we did after you have read the book.

Acknowledgments

The technical review by the following colleagues from the SNMP community was greatly appreciated: Maria Greene, Jeff Johnson, Bob Natale, Randy Presuhn, Cliff Sojourner, Bob Stewart, Kaj Tesink, David Waitzman, James Watt, and Chris Wellens. Double thanks go to Maria and Randy who read much of the book several times.

Lastly, without the assistance from Sandy Perkins, Ron Milbank, and the production staff at Prentice Hall the book would have never been completed.

CHAPTER 1

An Introduction to SNMP-based Management

This book explains how to read and understand an existing Simple Network Management Protocol (SNMP) Management Information Base (MIB), and then design and/or update useful and compliant MIBs for your own devices or applications.

> *MIBs are specifications containing definitions of management information so that networked systems can be remotely monitored, configured, and controlled.*

The rules for writing MIBs are defined in a collection of documents called the Structure of Management Information (SMI).

In general, the term MIB has different meanings depending on the context in which it is used. Sometimes there is a distinction made between a single specification, called *a MIB*, and the union of all specifications, called *the MIB*. Finally, the term MIB is also used to mean the actual values of management information in a system. (See Figure 1–1)

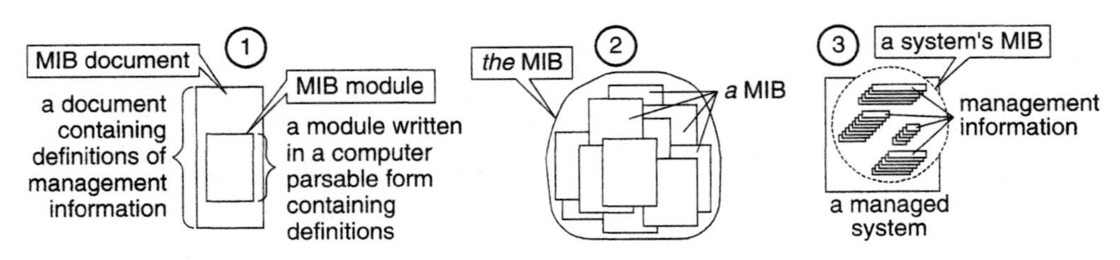

Figure 1–1 Uses of the term MIB

We assume that you're not reading this book for fun and that your real goal is to learn what you need to know about MIBs using SNMP as quickly as possible and get on with whatever task is at hand. We don't want to slow you down, but we need to introduce some basic concepts and terminology definitions that are used throughout this book.

This chapter begins with a description of the model of an SNMP-based managed network. Next specified is the definition of the SNMP-based management framework, including lists of defining documents. The chapter concludes with a short history of the evolution of SNMP-based management.

We encourage you to read through this chapter, even if you already have a familiarity with SNMP. The terminology that we define is consistent with the latest usage. It is somewhat different from that used in older versions of SNMP. Also, if you are familiar with other management systems, please note that while the same words may be used, they may be used for different purposes. All of the terms introduced in this chapter are found in the glossary and index. Please note that the information in this chapter should be viewed as clarification and not as a definitive tutorial.

1.1 Introduction

The genesis of SNMP-based management is the Internet Engineering Task Force (IETF), an open organization to create standards for the Internet. The initial targets for this effort were TCP/IP routers (also called gateways) and hosts (i.e, computer systems). However, the SNMP-based management approach is inherently generic so that it can be used to manage many types of systems. This approach can be used with computer data networks, automotive traffic networks, heating and cooling control networks, irrigation networks, or chemical plants. Thus, you can see that almost any real-time system consisting of a collection of independent communicating elements can use SNMP.

1.2 IETF Terminology

A member of the IETF organization is anyone who participates in the IETF activities, either in person at meetings or through email. This seemingly chaotic group of people is organized and has accomplished much. The top-level managing body of the Internet community is the Internet Society (ISOC). Under it comes the Internet Architecture Board (IAB), which provides technical and process oversight of the IETF. Technical guidance and administration of IETF processes is provided by the Internet Engineering Steering Group (IESG). It consists of the chair of the IETF and the directors of the functional areas of IETF activities. (The SNMP-related activities are within the network management area.)

In each area, working groups (WGs) are chartered to complete specific tasks, after which the working group is disbanded. Working group membership is open to anyone. Members are expected to assist in completing the working group's charter.

The output from a WG is one or more documents. A document that is made generally available for review, but is not yet published, is called an internet-draft (ID). It is a work in progress. An ID may range from a "rough draft" to a "final draft" before being published by the IETF. When published, a document may be on the standards track, or may be given the status of *Informational* or *Experimental*. The first rung on the standards ladder is the status of *Proposed*. This is followed by the status of *Draft* and finally the status of *[Full] Standard*. A document that is replaced by an updated version is given the status of *Obsolete*. A document that is retired is given the status of *Historic*.

Published documents are assigned an *RFC number* and made available in an on-line archival system. (The term RFC is an acronym for Request for Comments.) These documents are easily accessed via a connection to the Internet. The document titled INTERNET OFFICIAL PROTOCOL STANDARDS, which is published approximately quarterly, specifies the current status of published documents. (See the section on obtaining RFCs in Appendix "Guide to MIB Resources.")

There has been much confusion between the status of *Draft* and the status of *internet-draft*. Don't be confused between the two. A document that is available from the internet-drafts directory is a "work in progress." A document that has been published as an RFC and is on the IETF standards track may be designated as a Draft standard.

1.3 The Model of an SNMP-based Managed Network

The SNMP model of a managed network (see Figure 1–2) consists of the following elements:

- one or more managed nodes, each containing a processing entity called an agent
- at least one management station containing one or more processing entities called management applications (or managers)
- optionally, processing entities able to perform in both manager and agent roles called dual-role entities
- management information in each managed node, which describes the configuration, state, statistics and which controls the actions of the managed node
- a management protocol, which the managers and agents use to exchange management messages

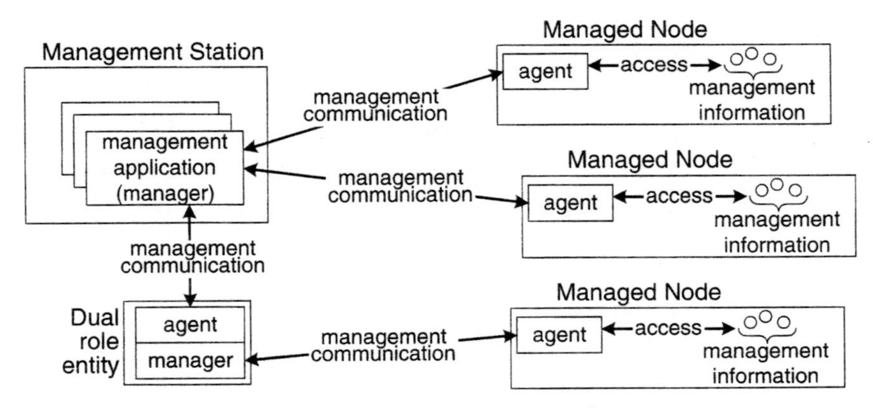

Figure 1–2 The SNMP model of a managed network

This model of management can be applied to computer data networks where the managed nodes are hosts (i.e., workstations, PCs, mini and mainframe computers), routers, bridges, printers, and terminal servers. Also, the model can be applied to automotive traffic networks where the managed nodes are traffic signals, vehicle detectors, message boards, and changeable lanes. Or the model can be applied to heating and cooling systems where the nodes are temperature sensors, flow meters, vent controllers, compressors, and furnaces

1.4 The Definition of SNMP-based Management

The SNMP-based management approach is defined by a collection of documents. (See Table 1–1, Table 1–2, Table 1–3, and Table 1–4 for the names of the documents.) These documents define a management framework consisting of four major components. These are:

- a management protocol
- a definition of management information and events
- a core set of management information and events
- a mechanism and approach to manage the use of the protocol including security and access control

The text that follows describes each component of the management framework, and includes a list of documents containing definitions for that component.

Our Opinion

We believe that the RFCs defining SNMP contain definitions that are ambiguous, incomplete, internally inconsistent, incomprehensible, or are in conflict with accepted usage. Throughout this book, we will point out these areas. Even though these problems exist, we believe that the SNMP-based management approach is easier to understand, develop, and use than the competing management approaches.

1.4.1 A Management Protocol

The first component of the framework is a management protocol. It defines the format and meaning of the management communications (the so called bits-on-the-wire) between the SNMP processing entities. There are two major versions of the SNMP protocol. The first version is now called SNMPv1 and the second version is called SNMPv2. (There was also an experimental version of the protocol called Secure SNMP. It is no longer used.) Unfortunately, the second version of the protocol did not gain market acceptance, even though it contained significant improvements over SNMPv1. Several proposals have been made that modify aspects of the SNMPv2 protocol to gain market approval.

Table 1–1 RFCs Defining the SNMP Protocol

Description	Published	RFC	Status
SNMPv1 Protocol	Aug. 1988	1067	Obsoleted by 1098
SNMPv1 Protocol (republished)	Apr. 1989	1098	Obsoleted by 1157
SNMPv1 Protocol (republished)	May 1990	1157	Full Standard
Secure SNMP Protocol	July 1992	1352	Historic
SNMPv2 Protocol Operations	May 1993	1448	Obsoleted by 1905
SNMPv2 Transport Mappings	May 1993	1449	Obsoleted by 1906
SNMPv2 Protocol Operations (updated)	Jan. 1996	1905	Draft
SNMPv2 Transport Mappings (updated)	Jan. 1996	1906	Draft

The following is a list of aspects of any version of the protocol:

SNMP Operations

The operations in SNMP are limited to retrieving the value of management information, modifying the value of management information, and reporting an event. Each class (or type) of management information is assigned a unique identity. An instance from a class of management information is called a variable. Each variable is given a unique identity based on the identity of its class and its identification within its class. Each class (or type) of event is assigned a unique identity.

There is one modification operation, which is called a SET. The operand to a SET is a list of pairs. Each pair consists of the identity of a variable and its desired value. SET operations are used to configure and control a managed system.

There are two types of retrieval operations. Both retrieve the value of variables. For both, the result is a list of pairs, where each pair consists of the identity of a variable and its current value. Both types have as operands a list of identities. The first type of retrieval operation requires that the identities are those that match exactly the identity of returned variables. This retrieval operation is used when the identity for each variable is known. There is a single operation of this type, called GET. The second type of retrieval operation uses each identity in a request as an approximation of the identity for a variable. Each returned identity is the one assigned to the first accessible variable whose identity is greater than the given identity. There are two operations of this type, called GETNEXT and GETBULK. These operations are used when the identity for a class of management information is known, but the identity for each accessible instance within that class is not known. Also, these operations may be used to determine each class of management information containing accessible instances. The GET, GETNEXT, and GETBULK operations are used to monitor a managed system.

There are two event-reporting operations, called TRAP and INFORM. Each specify an event and a list of pairs. A pair consists of the identity of a variable and its value. These operations are used to report the occurrence of events on a managed system to a list of managers configured to receive events for that managed system.

SNMP Messages

SNMP operations occur through message exchange over a message transport service. (See Figure 1–3) The format of messages is defined using a sub-set of the Abstract Syntax Notation One (ASN.1) language. This format, called an abstract syntax, is independent of the representation of data on any particular system. To transmit a message, it must be first converted into a string of octets (bytes). A transfer syntax specifies the format of converted data. SNMP uses a sub-set of the Basic Encoding Rules (BER) to define the format of encoded (or serialized) messages.

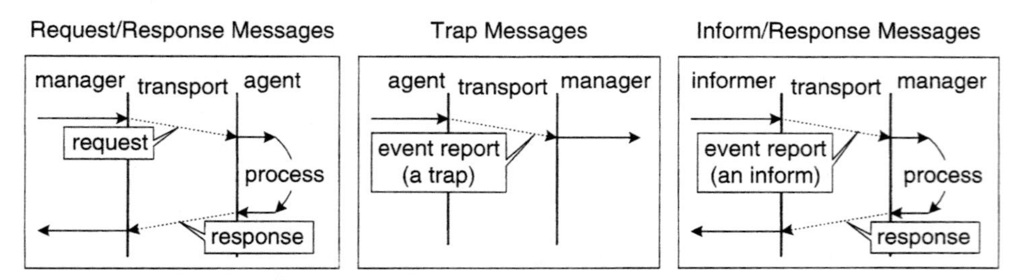

Figure 1–3 SNMP Message Exchange

The retrieval and modification operations require two messages. The first is a *request* and the second is a *response*. There are two event report operations. The first uses a single message, which is called a *trap*. The second uses two messages. The first is an *inform* and the second is a *response*.

A message contains administrative information and an SNMP Protocol Data Unit (PDU). The PDU type identifies the type of the message. The contents of a PDU are control fields, which are dependent on the message type, and an array of pairs. The first element of each pair is used to identify management information and the second element is used to specify the value of management information.

SNMP Entity

Messages are exchanged between processes called SNMP entities. An entity may be designed to process only one message at a time (i.e., be implemented as single-threaded), or may be designed to process multiple messages concurrently (i.e., be implemented as multi-threaded). An entity plays one of three roles during message exchange. The role is determined by the message type and message originator.

SNMP Manager

An entity that assumes the operational role to generate requests to retrieve and modify management information, receive the response to requests, or to receive event reports is called an SNMP manager. This role is assumed by (or on behalf of) an SNMP management application.

SNMP Agent

An entity that assumes the operational role to receive, process, and respond to requests, and to generate event reports is called an SNMP agent. An agent must have access to network management information to respond to requests, and must be notified of internal events to generate reports.

SNMP Informer

An entity that assumes the operational role to generate informs and receive responses to informs is called an SNMP informer. An informer must have access to network management information from an agent, and informs a manager of an event using this information.

We made up the term *SNMP informer*, since the SNMP WG cannot decide what type of entity sends informs.

Dual-Role Entity

An entity may assume the operational role of both an agent and a manager (and possibly an informer). This is called a dual-role entity. However, in describing SNMP message exchange, an entity must perform either as a manager, or as an agent, or as an informer for a particular message. Dual-role entities are typically used to forward SNMP messages (an SNMP proxy), or to consolidate and synthesize information from many systems and make that information available to a higher-level manager (a mid-level manager).

Client-Server

In other message-based systems, the terms *client* and *server* are used to designate the roles played in the message exchange. (These terms are not typically used to describe SNMP. Generally, a *client* is an SNMP manager and a *server* is an SNMP agent.)

SNMP Message Exchange

Message exchange requires only a simple connectionless (i.e., datagram) transport service. Examples include the User Datagram Protocol (UDP) from the Internet protocol suite, the Connectionless-mode Transport Service (CLTS) from the OSI protocol suite, the Datagram Delivery Protocol (DDP) protocol from the AppleTalk protocol suite, the Packet Exchange Protocol (PEP) from the Novell IPX protocol suite, or any form of an interprocess communication message within a single system. The SNMP protocol is stateless. That is, the protocol does not keep information about or for the entities after an operation has been performed. Any such information must be kept by the entities themselves. Fortunately, such information is quite small, with the burden being on the manager entity.

SNMPv1 and SNMPv2 Message Exchange

The message formats of SNMPv1 and SNMPv2 protocols are similar, but not interoperable. The format of the PDUs inside a message are identical with the exception that SNMPv2 contains a few additional PDU types and doesn't use one of the types from SNMPv1. Thus, SNMPv1 entities cannot directly exchange messages with SNMPv2 entities.

However, this lack of direct interoperation can be overcome by use of entities that implement both protocols (which are called bilingual entities), or by use of an intermediary that translates between the two message formats (which is called a translating proxy).

1.4.2 A Definition of Management Information and Events

The second component of the framework is a definition of management information and events. This includes the model of management information, the allowed data types, and the rules for specifying classes (or types) of management information. Also included is the model for events and the rules for specifying classes (or types) of events. All of these definitions were originally specified in a single document called the Structure of Management Information (SMI). Currently, this information is specified in several documents with the main one called the SMI. (Thus the term SMI is used to mean a particular document and the set of rules defining management information and events.)

A system is managed by retrieval and modification of management information. Each class (or type) of management information is called an *object* or *object type*. A specific instance from a class of management information is called an SNMP *variable* or an *object instance*. The definition of an object type includes its data type, the maximal allowed access, its assigned identity, how instances are identified, and its semantics (or behaviors).

Table 1–2 RFCs Defining Management Information and Events

Description	Published	RFC	Status
SMIv1	Aug. 1988	1065	Obsoleted by 1155
SMIv1 with typos fixed	May 1990	1155	Full Standard
SMIv1 Concise MIB format	Mar. 1991	1212	Full Standard
SMIv1 Trap formats	Mar. 1991	1215	Informational[a]
SMIv2	May 1993	1442	Obsoleted by 1902
SMIv2 Textual Conventions	May 1993	1443	Obsoleted by 1903
SMIv2 Conformances	May 1993	1444	Obsoleted by 1904
SMIv2 (updated)	Jan. 1996	1902	Draft
SMIv2 Textual Conventions (updated)	Jan. 1996	1903	Draft
SMIv2 Conformances (updated)	Jan. 1996	1904	Draft

a. This document was not included on the standards track where it functionally belongs.

SNMP uses an identification scheme found in ASN.1 to uniquely identify items for all space and time. An identifier in this scheme is called an *object identifier* (or OID). The permanent assignment of an OID value, an identity, to an item is called *registration*. Once a registration has been performed, no other item may be registered with the same OID value, the characteristics of the registered item may not be changed, and the registered item may not be deleted. SNMP uses OIDs to identify many types of items.

The term *object identifier* (OID) is not limited to application with only SNMP objects. An OID value can be used to identify any type of item. For example, an OID value can be used to identify a document. Also, an OID value could be assigned to each person who ever lived, and to each future person at birth. There is no limit to the number of OID values.

Besides the data types and rules for specifying management information, the SMI also includes some administrative assignments. These are used to organize the definitions of management information into those targeted for the IETF standards track, experimental ones within the IETF, and proprietary ones developed by vendors of SNMP-based managed systems. Finally, the SMI contains rules for specifying implementation compliance requirements; and actual implemented characteristics of agents.

Definitions for related management information, events, and associated implementation compliance requirements are specified in documents called Management Information Base (MIB) specifications. These specifications include prose descriptions and computer-readable descriptions. The computer-readable descriptions, called MIB information modules (or just MIB modules), are written in an *adapted* sub-set of the Abstract Syntax Notation One (ASN.1) language. The definition of the SNMP MIB module language comes from ASN.1 modules defining macros, from textual descriptions modifying and qualifying the macros and elements of the ASN.1 language, and from common usage. (See Figure 1–4) Computer programs that parse the MIB module language are called MIB compilers.

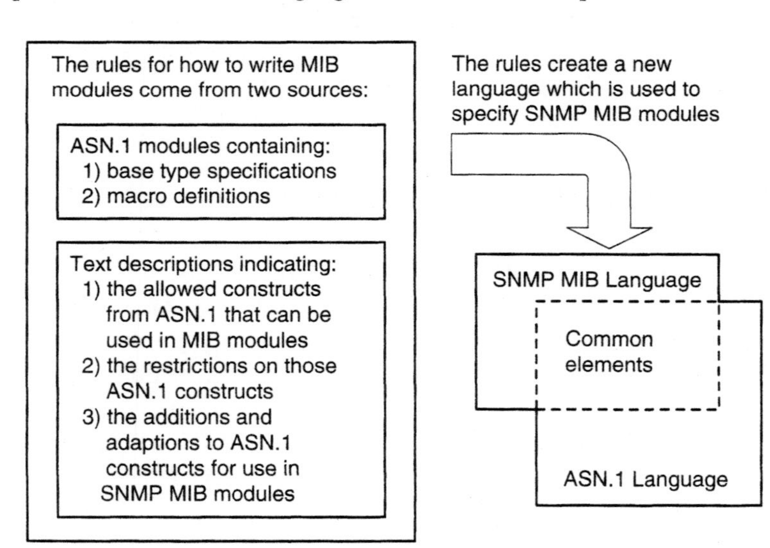

Figure 1–4 Rules for writing MIB modules

The ASN.1 language is used in SNMP for two different purposes. The first is to define the abstract syntax of SNMP messages. In this application, a "pure" sub-set of ASN.1 is used. This application of ASN.1 is a good match of its designed use. The second use of ASN.1 is to specify the format of MIB modules. In this application, an adapted sub-set of ASN.1 is used. This application of ASN.1 is a poor match of its designed use and has resulted in much confusion to those learning how to read MIB modules. For your benefit, we do not use ASN.1 in this book to specify the format of MIB modules!

The SMI has changed over time to expand the language for SNMP MIB modules. The original version of the SMI for SNMPv1 required some information to be specified in prose and other information to be specified in the computer-readable language. Unfortunately, much information was redundantly specified in both the prose and the computer-readable format. This resulted in MIB specifications twice the size they needed to be, and was the source for many errors made updating the specifications. (Each change had to be made in two places instead of one and generally one change was forgotten or done incorrectly.) The language for MIB modules was extended by two RFCs to eliminate the redundant prose and increase the information specified in computer-readable form.

The original version of the SMI for SNMPv2 included several small updates to the language and several large changes that allowed implementation conformance requirements, actual implemented characteristics of agents, and other descriptive items to be specified in a computer-readable format. It also added some new data types for management information. The primary goal of this SMI version met with much success. Unfortunately, the secondary goal of supporting new data types caused compatibility problems with SNMPv1. All except one type was removed in an update to the SMI for SNMPv2.

1.4.3 A Core Set of Management Information

SNMP-based management requires that each conforming agent provide access to a small common set of management information. (See Table 1–3) The original SNMP WG defined a core set of standard management information for systems implementing the Internet protocol suite. This specification is called MIB-I. The WG focused on items available in all systems for configuration and fault management. The number of items was kept small. There were no implementation-specific items or ones that would significantly affect the performance of a managed device.

A few years later, after implementation experience, the SNMP WG created an extended and refined version called MIB-II. Both of these specifications include definitions for management information in the following areas:

- system — characteristics of the system
- interfaces — characteristics of the network interfaces
- protocol — characteristics of various components of the Internet protocol including IP, TCP, UDP, ICMP, and EGP

Table 1–3 RFCs Defining the Core Set of Management Information

Description	Published	RFC	Status
MIB-I	Aug. 1988	1066	Obsoleted by 1156
MIB-I with typos fixed	May 1990	1156	Obsoleted by 1158
MIB-II	May 1990	1158	Obsoleted by 1213
MIB-II updated to the concise format	Mar. 1991	1213	Full Standard
Interfaces MIB	Jan. 1994	1573	Proposed
SNMPv2 Core	May 1994	1450	Obsoleted by 1907
SNMPv2 Core (updated)	Jan. 1996	1907	Draft

As the SNMP-based management approach has broadened from managing computer data networks using the Internet protocol suite to managing any network (i.e., those using different data network protocol suites, and other types of networks such as automotive traffic, or irrigation) the core set of management information has shrunk. That is, management information for members of the Internet protocol suite are no longer required members of the core set. This has resulted in the SNMP WG reorganizing the definitions contained in MIB-II and spliting them into separate MIB specifications.

1.4.4 Managing the Use of the SNMP Protocol

Use of SNMP-based management itself needs to be monitored, configured, and controlled. This area is called the SNMP administration framework. This area can be small or quite large, depending on the services that it provides. SNMPv1 has a simple usage model based on *communities*. The first definition of SNMPv2 has a much richer usage model based on *parties*. The revised version of SNMPv2 does not yet have a standards track usage model defined. Several models have been proposed, but none are on the standards track.

Caution

In late 1994 and through 1995, the SNMP WG reviewed the party mechanism and concluded that it was fatally flawed. Unfortunately, a replacement could not be found that satisfied all members of the WG. Currently, no complete set of definitions for the SNMPv2 administrative framework is contained in documents on the IETF standards track.

The mechanisms of the usage models in any SNMP protocol version could potentially be managed by SNMP. Management through SNMP is accomplished by retrieving and modifying the management information corresponding to the mechanisms of the SNMP administrative framework or (frameworks) in a managed system. Monitoring the number of messages received and transmitted, and the type of errors that have occurred is straightforward. (The documents defining the management of SNMP are listed in Table 1–4.)

Table 1–4 RFCs Defining the Management of SNMP

Description	Published	RFC	Status
Admin Model for Secure SNMP	July 1992	1351	Historic
Security Protocols for Secure SNMP	July 1992	1352	Historic
Secure SNMP parties	July 1992	1353	Historic
Admin Model for SNMPv2	May 1993	1445	Historic
Security Protocol for SNMPv2	May 1993	1446	Historic
Party MIB for SNMPv2	May 1993	1447	Historic
SNMPv2 Core	May 1994	1450	Obsoleted by 1907
SNMPv2 Core (updated)	Jan. 1996	1907	Draft

On the other hand, using SNMP to manage security aspects of an SNMP administrative framework has been quite difficult for the SNMP WG to develop workable approaches. Security aspects are:

- authentication: includes mechanisms to determine if a message originated from its claimed originator; if a message is unaltered; and if a message is timely (that is, not saved and replayed)
- privacy: includes mechanisms to keep the contents of messages from being disclosed
- authorization: includes mechanisms to define collections of management information (a collection is called a view); mechanisms to specify unrestricted or read-only access to items in a collection (a pairing of a view and access is called a profile); and mechanisms to specify which profiles may be used (the rules are called an access policy)

SNMPv1 Administration Services

An SNMPv1 *community* contains one agent and one or more managers, and is named by a string of octets. Each SNMPv1 message contains the name of a community, which is called a *community string*. There are no standard mechanisms in SNMPv1 for verifying that a message originated from a member of the named community, keeping the contents of a message private, or for determining if a message has been modified or replayed.

The description in the SNMPv1 protocol specification of the administration services using a community string has confused many. Unfortunately, many developers and users of SNMPv1 believe that the community string is a field to specify a password for read-only access or another for read-write access. However, its interpretation is not that simple. The community string field was designed to serve several purposes simultaneously! Without clarification on how this could be accomplished, the objectives were not achieved. One of the proposals for a replacement of the original SNMPv2 mechanisms is based on clarifying how the community string field can be used to provide authentication, privacy, and authorization services.

SNMPv1 Usage Management

MIB-I for SNMPv1 contains no definitions to allow management of the community mechanisms. MIB-II for SNMPv1 added definitions for management information which consists of counts of SNMPv1 message types and error codes, and control of the generation of authentication failure event reports. No other definitions were specified in IETF documents to allow the community mechanisms to be managed through SNMPv1. Thus, vendors of SNMPv1 products either hard-coded the community mechanisms, created proprietary definitions of SNMP management information to manage all or part of the community mechanisms, or used some other management approach such as configuration files or back-door access (such as a local terminal) to the agent to manage the community mechanisms.

SNMPv2 Administration Services

The abandoned Secure SNMP framework specified the first version of the *party* mechanisms, which were reworked for the now historic, first version of the SNMPv2 framework. An SNMPv2 party identifies an SNMPv2 entity. The change from the SNMPv1 community mechanisms to the party mechanisms allows more sophisticated security approaches. Also enhanced was the criteria for selecting items in a view, and the access privileges that can be paired with a view. Each first-version SNMPv2 message contains the source and destination parties for the message. Also contained in each message is a selector of management information called the *context*, and if needed, information specific to the security mechanism being used.

Three security levels are defined with the party approach. These are *noAuth*, *auth*, and *priv*. There are no security services provided at the noAuth level. The auth-level service includes data integrity, data origin authentication, and delay or replay detection services. The priv-level service includes all the auth-level services and data confidentiality service.

This party-based model was found too difficult to deploy in operational networks. The SNMPv2 WG believed that a model based on users could be deployed and tried to layer such an approach on top of the mechanisms used for parties. The result, while potentially deployable, was much too complex for SNMP technology developers. The SNMP WG broke into two major factions as to how to best re-engineer administration services for SNMPv2.

SNMPv2 Usage Management

The now historic SNMPv2 administration framework based on parties included definitions of management information so that all aspects could be managed via SNMP. There is currently no standards track document defining SNMPv2 administration. However, the MIB module defined in RFC 1907 includes counts of SNMP messages sent and received, and counts for a limited number of errors.

1.5 A Short Pictorial History of SNMP

SNMP-based management incorporates ideas found in other management approaches, adds a few unique touches, and has gone through two major versions and incremental refinements. The first version is called the SNMPv1 framework, the second is the SNMPv2 framework. These frameworks are quite similar. The combination is called the SNMP-based management framework. (Between these two versions there was a short-lived version called Secure SNMP.)

At the time that the SNMP-based management framework was first being developed, there also were two other management frameworks in development. The first of the two is the High-level Entity Monitoring System (HEMS). It was withdrawn for consideration by the authors in early 1988. The other one is CMIP[1] on TCP/IP, which is called CMOT. It has not seen widespread support. It is still lingering and being used by researchers. Figure 1–5 shows the competing management protocols from the IETF and their ancestry.

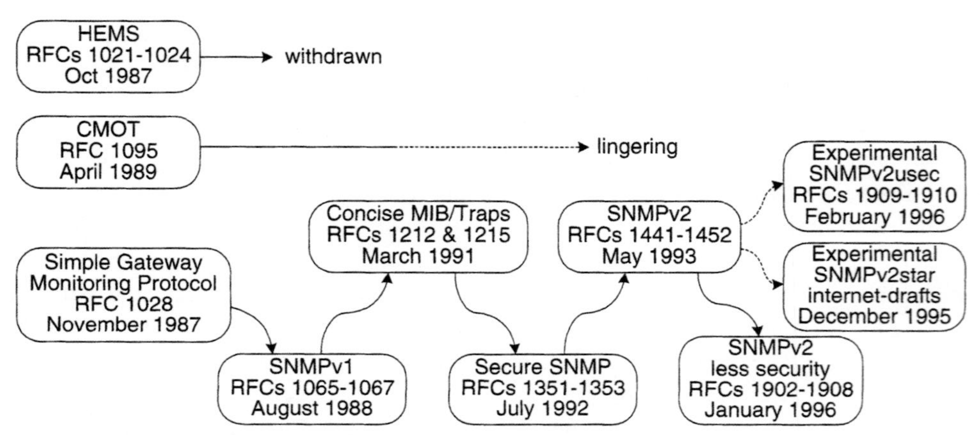

Figure 1–5 Pictorial History of SNMP

1.6 A Categorization of IETF MIB Modules

The IETF organization defines standards for computer data networks. The focus has been on networking protocols and networking infrastructure services for the Internet protocol suite. So far, MIB modules developed by IETF working groups have been to manage IETF defined protocols and services, and the common aspects of hardware and environments on which these protocol and services execute. When other organizations such as the IEEE or ANSI have developed management standards, IETF WGs have used them to create SNMP MIB specifications. Examples include IEEE-802.3 (ethernet), IEEE-802.5 (token ring), and ANSI FDDI. Only timing and availability of qualified personnel have so far limited the formation of additional IETF WGs to create SNMP MIB specifications for standards developed by other organizations.

There are three categories of systems on a data network running the Internet protocol suite. These are end systems (i.e., hosts), intermediate systems (i.e., routers), and media devices (i.e., repeaters and bridges). End systems originate and receive application-level data. Routers forward network-level data. Media devices forward data-link and physical-level data. All of these systems have one or more data network interfaces.

1. The Common Management Information Protocol (CMIP)-based management framework was developed by the ISO community to manage OSI-based networks.

There are many types of transmission technology used in data networks. These are generally categorized as either local-area or wide-area transmission technologies. On the same physical network interfaces and physical interconnections there may be one or more protocol suites that are running concurrently. Besides the Internet protocol suite, typical suites are Digital Equipment Corporation's DECnet Phase IV, Novell's IPX, Apple Computer's AppleTalk, IBM's SNA, and ISO's OSI. Each of these protocol suites may contain several protocols. For example, the Internet protocol suite contains the ICMP, UDP, TCP, RIP, OSPF, EGP, and BGP protocols. Using the lower-level protocols are communicating applications which use application protocols. Some of the applications are part of the data network infrastructure and others just use the data network as a mechanism to communicate with other applications. For example, the domain name server protocol, the telnet protocol, the FTP protocol, and the SNMP protocol are part of the network infrastructure. Protocols used for email, for hypertext (WEB), and database access use the network for communication but are not typically required for the network to operate. Figure 1–6 shows a typical computer data network. In even small networks there can be found many different types of devices and networking protocols.

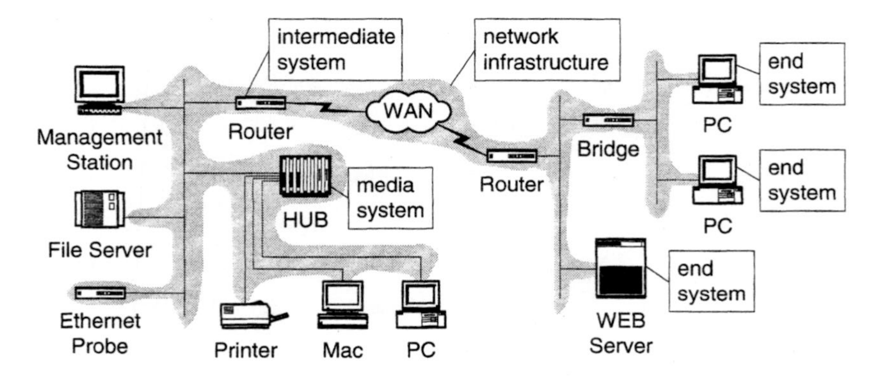

Figure 1–6 Example of a Computer Data Network

The Internet technology has advanced so rapidly that it is difficult to keep up with all the changes. There are several thousand objects that have been defined by IETF WGs. Table 1–5 gives a list of the standards-track RFCs containing MIB modules.

Table 1–5 IETF Standards-Track MIB Modules, in July 1996

RFC	Module Name	Description	SMI	Objects	Events
1213	RFC1213-MIB	Core management information	v1	190	0
1215	RFC1215-TRAP	The "generic" traps for SNMPv1	v1	0	6
1285	RFC1285-MIB	FDDI SMT v6.2	v1	93	0
1315	RFC1315-MIB	Frame Relay	v1	35	1
1354	RFC1354-MIB	IP Forwarding table	v1	18	0

Table 1–5 IETF Standards-Track MIB Modules, in July 1996 (Continued)

RFC	Module Name	Description	SMI	Objects	Events
1381	RFC1381-MIB	X.25 LAPB	v1	54	0
1382	RFC1382-MIB	X.25 Packet layer	v1	160	0
1406	RFC1406-MIB	DS1/E1 Interface	v1	99	0
1407	RFC1407-MIB	DS3/E3 Interface	v1	90	0
1414	RFC1414-MIB	Identification Protocol	v1	7	0
1461	MIOX25-MIB	Multi-protocol interconnect over X.25	v1	34	0
1471	PPP-LCP-MIB	PPP Link Control Protocol (LCP)	v1	39	0
1472	PPP-SEC-MIB	PPP Security Protocols	v1	15	0
1473	PPP-IP-NCP-MIB	PPP IP Networks Control Protocol	v1	11	0
1474	PPP-BRIDGE-NCP-MIB	PPP Bridge Network Control Protocol	v1	23	0
1493	BRIDGE-MIB	Transparent Bridge	v1	56	2
1512	FDDI-SMT73-MIB	FDDI SMT 7.3	v1	120	0
1513	TOKEN-RING-RMON-MIB	Token Ring Extensions to RMON	v1	181	0
1514	HOST-RESOURCES-MIB	Host Resources	v1	83	0
1515	MAU-MIB	IEEE 802.3 Medium Attachment Unit	v1	28	0
1516	SNMP-REPEATER-MIB	IEEE 802.3 Repeater	v1	52	3
1525	SOURCE-ROUTING-MIB	Source Routing Bridge	v1	28	0
1559	DECNET-PHIV-MIB	DECnet phase IV Protocol	v1	221	0
1565	APPLICATION-MIB	Network Services Monitoring	v2	24	0
1566	MTA-MIB	Mail Transport Service Monitoring	v2	41	0
1567	DSA-MIB	X.500 Directory Service Monitoring	v2	39	0
1573	IANAifType-MIB and IF-MIB	Network Interface Types and Interface Monitoring	v2 v2	0 62	0 2
1595	SONET-MIB	SONET/SDH Interface Type	v2	105	0
1604	FRNETSERV-MIB	Frame Relay Service	v2	74	1
1611	DNS-SERVER-MIB	DNS Server	v2	63	0
1612	DNS-RESOLVER-MIB	DNS Resolver	v2	76	0
1628	UPS-MIB	Uninterruptible Power Supply	v2	67	4
1643	EtherLike-MIB	Ether-Like Interface Type	v1	20	0
1657	BGP4-MIB	BGP version 4	v2	53	2
1658	CHARACTER-MIB	Character Device	v2	36	0

Table 1–5 IETF Standards-Track MIB Modules, in July 1996 (Continued)

RFC	Module Name	Description	SMI	Objects	Events
1659	RS-232-MIB	RS-232 Interface Type	v2	49	0
1660	PARALLEL-MIB	Parallel Printer Interface Type	v2	19	0
1666	SNA-NAU-MIB	SNA NAU	v2	126	4
1694	SIP-MIB	SMDS Interface Protocol (SIP) Interface Type	v2	58	0
1695	ATM-MIB	ATM	v2	96	0
1696	Modem-MIB	Modems	v2	69	0
1697	RDBMS-MIB	Relational Database Management System	v2	73	2
1724	RIPv2-MIB	RIP version 2	v2	28	0
1742	APPLETALK-MIB	AppleTalk Protocol	v1	254	0
1747	SNA-SDLC-MIB	SNA DLC	v2	136	2
1748	TOKENRING-MIB	IEEE 802.5 Token Ring Interface Type	v2	46	0
1749	TOKENRING-STATION-SR-MIB	IEEE 802.5 Station Source Routing	v2	6	0
1757	RMON-MIB	Remote Network Monitoring	v1	203	2
1759	Printer-MIB	Printer Device	v2	179	1
1850	OSPF-MIB and OSPF-TRAP-MIB	OSPF protocol and events for OSPF	v2 v2	139 4	0 16
1907	SNMPv2-MIB	Core SNMP definitions	v2	47	3

CHAPTER 2

SNMP Management Information

This chapter presents the SNMP model of management information. Also included is an explanation of the system used to assign identities to items such as objects.

2.1 The Model

SNMP views management information as variables and their values. SNMP operations retrieve or modify the value of variables. A class (or type) of management information is called an *object* or *object type*. A specific instance from a class of management information is called an SNMP *variable* or an *object instance*. The OBJECT-TYPE construct is used in MIB modules to define each class of management information and specifies an object's data type, the maximal allowed access, its assigned identity, how instances are identified, and its semantics (or behaviors). An object may be defined to have exactly one instance, or may be defined to have multiple instances. A *scalar object* has exactly one instance. A *columnar object* has zero, one, or more instances at any point in time. (See Figure 2–1)

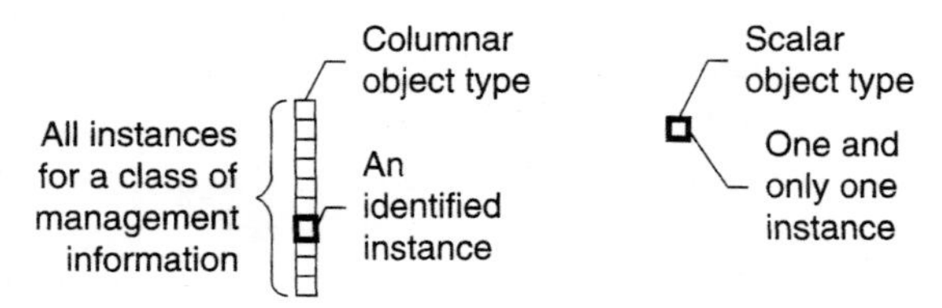

Figure 2–1 Columnar and Scalar Objects

To be consistent with columnar objects, all scalar objects use a mechanism to identify the one instance in each class. The mechanism is identical for all scalar objects. An example of a scalar object is the location of a managed system, since a system has exactly one location. An example of a columnar object is the state of a TCP connection. There may be zero, one, or more TCP connections to a system at any point in time. Each TCP connection that exists has a state.

The SMI requires columnar objects to be organized into *conceptual tables*. All the columnar objects in a conceptual table must use the same mechanism for identifying instances within their class. The mechanism is called the *indexing scheme*. Instead of specifying the indexing scheme for each columnar object, the OBJECT-TYPE construct is used to define a *row object,* where the indexing scheme is defined. Also, the OBJECT-TYPE construct is used to define a *table object,* to group the definitions of the row and columnar objects. There is no special construct to organize a collection of scalar objects. (However, section 2.4.1 shows how the identity assigned to each object can be used to informally organize scalar objects.) The informal term *group* is used to reference a collection of scalar objects and/or a collection of columnar and scalar objects. (See Figure 2–2)

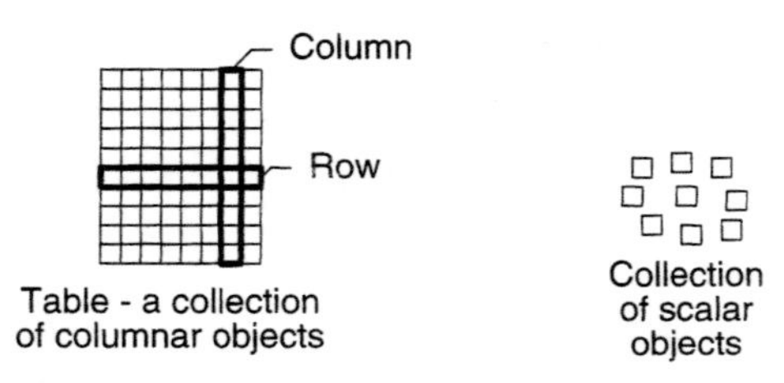

Figure 2–2 Organizational models for management information

The operands (the inputs) of SNMP-based management operations are the identities (or approximations) of SNMP variables. (The operands to the GETNEXT and GETBULK operations are approximations of a variable's identity.) There are no SNMP operations where the result is the identity of a table, row, or column. Only identities of variables are results. The term *conceptual* is used in front of the term *table* by many in the SNMP community to emphasize this point. However, the term *table* is perfectly acceptable and usable without being qualified with the term *conceptual.*

Use of the OBJECT-TYPE construct to define tables and rows is an artifact from the early goal of trying to specify one set of rules to define management information that could be used for both SNMP-based management and CMIP-based management.

Before we can complete a description of the SNMP model of management information, we need to first take a look at the identification scheme used in SNMP.

2.2 Object Identifiers

An identification scheme from ASN.1 is used throughout SNMP to uniquely identify items for all space and time. An identifier in this scheme is called an *object identifier* (or OID) and the identity of an item is determined by its OID value. The permanent assignment of an OID value, an identity, to an item is called a *registration*. Once a registration has been performed, no other item may be registered with the same OID value, the characteristics of the registered item may not be changed, and the registered item may not be deleted. SNMP uses OIDs to identify many types of items.

This Is Repeated From The First Chapter For Emphasis.
The term object identifier (OID) is not limited to application with only SNMP objects. An OID value can be used to identify any type of item. For example, an OID value can be used to identify a document. Also, an OID value could be assigned to each person who ever lived, and to each future person at birth. There is no limit to the number of OID values.

An OID value is an ordered sequence of non-negative integers, written from left to right, containing at least two elements. This scheme was created by the ISO and CCITT (now the ITU) organizations. OID values are organized like a hierarchical file system and the IETF's domain name system (DNS). (Note that a fully qualified domain name is written with the most significant part on the right, where OID values are written with the most significant part on the left.) Administration of assignments is delegated. The top level assignments are controlled by the ISO and ITU organizations, which put restrictions on the first two numbers in the sequence. Lower level assignments are delegated and may also be sub-delegated. Each number in the sequence is assigned by the administrator of the number that immediately precedes it.

A rooted tree (as shown in Figure 2–3) is often used to illustrate the numbers in the sequences that correspond to OID values. Each vertex in the tree is labelled with a number,

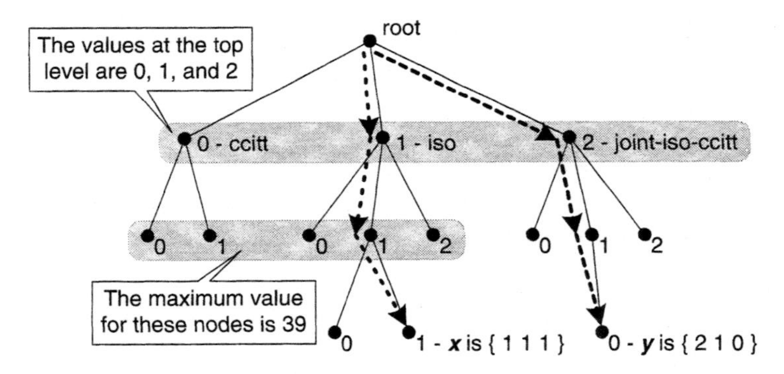

Figure 2–3 Object Identifier tree

such that a path from the root to the vertex corresponds to the sequence of numbers that is the OID value for the vertex. In Figure 2–3, the vertex labelled ***x*** has the OID value of { 1 1 1 }, and the vertex labelled ***y*** has the OID value of { 2 1 0 }, since their OID values correspond to the sequence of numbers from the vertices on a path from the root to these vertices.

The maximum length of any path from the root of the tree to a leaf node is not bounded in ASN.1. Also, the maximum value of any number (other than those on the top two levels) is not restricted by ASN.1. However, SNMP imposes a restriction on the maximum length of any OID value to 128 numbers in the sequence. Also, SNMP restricts the maximum value of a number to 2^{32}-1 (4294967295 decimal). Each number in the sequence is called an object identifier *component* in ASN.1 and a *sub-identifier* in the SNMP SMI. The values of the vertices at the top level are defined by ISO and ITU to be 0, 1, and 2. ISO and ITU also restrict the maximum value of the vertices at the second level under top vertices of 0 and 1 to 39. (These restrictions are necessary due to the BER encoding of OID values.)

2.2.1 Specifying OID Values

The syntax for specifying an OID value in an SNMP MIB module is the following:

```
-- There are four formats for Object identifier values.
-- (Note that a value has at least two components.)
<oidValue>
        = "{" <wellKnownName> <oidCompVal>... "}"
        | "{" <oidCompVal> <oidCompVal>... "}"
        | "{" <oidValRef> <oidCompVal>... "}"
        | <oidValRef>

-- SNMP recognizes only a sub-set of the well-known names from
-- ASN.1. They can only be used for the head of an OID value.
-- (Note that "itu" is not a well-known name!)
<wellKnownName> = "ccitt" | "iso" | "joint-iso-ccitt"

-- An OID value reference is the OID value of an item
-- defined in or imported into the MIB module which has
-- an OID value. In the rule that follows, ucName is a
-- MIB module name and lcName is the identifier for an item.
<oidValRef> = [ ucName "." ] lcName

-- The value of a component (or sub-identifier) in an OID value
-- may optionally be qualified by a label, lcName in the rule below.
-- That optional label is purely commentary and has no significance!
<oidCompVal> = number | lcName "(" number ")"

where:
        lcName is a name starting with a lowercase letter;
        ucName is a name starting with an uppercase letter; and
        number is a non-negative integer
```

Outside an SNMP MIB module, an OID value is usually written as a sequence of numbers separated by a dot (.) and optionally labelled. This format is for ease in specifying values. The syntax for this format is shown below:

```
-- There are two formats of a dotted object identifier value.
<dottedOidValue>
        = <wellKnownName> { "." <oidCompVal> }...
        | <oidCompVal> { "." <oidCompVal> }...
```

OID values in SNMP MIB modules are usually written with the following syntax, which is a sub-set of the complete syntax for OID values:

```
-- There is a single format for specifying a "conventional"
-- object identifier value. Note that lcName in the rule is the
-- identifier for an item defined in or imported into the MIB
-- module which has an OID value.
<convOidValue> = "{" lcName number "}"
```

2.2.2 Example of OID Values

Shown below are examples of OID values written in a MIB module and the same values written as they would appear in a document or a management application:

```
-- these are not dependent on other definitions
{ iso org(3) dod(6) internet(1) } is 1.3.6.1
{ 0 0 }, { ccitt 0 }, and { z(0) z(0)} are all 0.0
{ 1 3 6 1 mgmt(2) mib(1) 2 } is 1.3.6.1.2.1.2

-- in a MIB module where system is defined with value { 1 3 6 1 2 1 1 }
{ system 1 } is 1.3.6.1.2.1.1.1

-- in a MIB module where internet is defined with value { 1 3 6 1 }
{ internet 4 } is 1.3.6.1.4

-- in a MIB module where item commonName has been assigned
-- value { 1 3 6 1 }, and imported from module MOD1. Note that
-- SNMP requires that another item with identifier commonName
-- must be defined in the same module or imported from another module
-- before the "module-name.item-name" syntax is allowed.
{ MOD1.commonName 4 } is 1.3.6.1.4
```

2.2.3 IETF OID Assignments for SNMP

The SMI contains administrative assignments for use in developing SNMP MIB modules by IETF working groups, researchers, and vendors. The following administrative areas are currently assigned:

- internet — top of the administrative domain managed by the IETF
- mgmt — area for items defined in standards track documents
- mib — primary area for definitions of SNMP management information
- experimental — area for IETF experimental items
- enterprises — area for delegation of subtrees to other organizations
- private — area for delegation of subtrees to enterprises, that is, anyone who asks for an *enterprise number*
- snmpv2 — area for items that are related to managing SNMPv2 agents

Figure 2–4 shows an OID tree with the IETF administrative assignments highlighted.

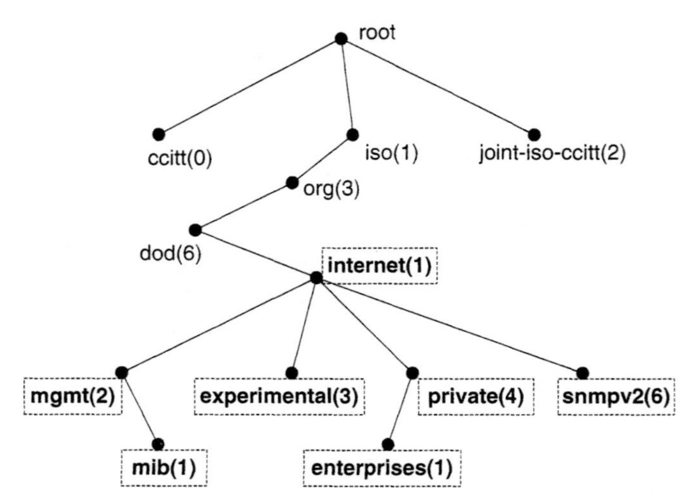

Figure 2–4 OID tree with IETF OID assignments for SNMP

2.2.4 Object Identifier Summary

The following are the key points about OIDs:

- SNMP uses OIDs to identify items
- once a permanent assignment, called a registration, has been made it cannot be taken back or reused for a different purpose
- the characteristics of an item cannot be changed once it has been registered
- OID values are organized into a hierarchical tree

2.3 Instances of Management Information

Now that object identifiers have been defined, we can take a closer look at SNMP variables. Remember, a specific instance of management information is a variable. The identity for a variable is based on the identity of its class and its identification within its class. (See Figure 2–5)

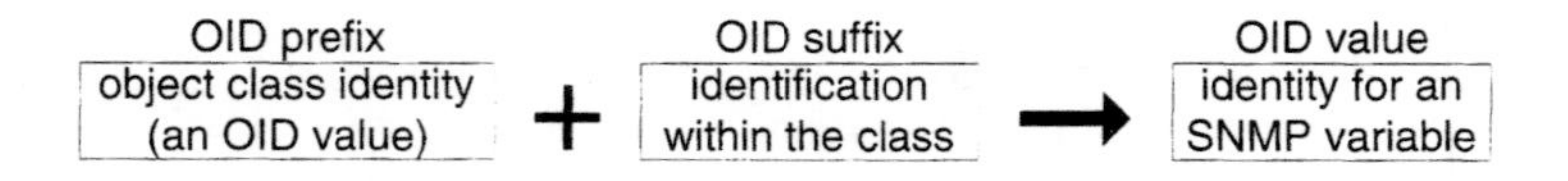

Figure 2–5 Identity of an SNMP variable

The identity of an object class (or type) is an OID value. For example, the identity of object class sysLocation, a scalar object, is OID value { 1 3 6 1 2 1 1 6 }; the identity of object class ifOperStatus, a columnar object, is OID value { 1 3 6 1 2 1 2 2 1 8 }; and the identity of object class tcpConnState, a columnar object, is OID value { 1 3 6 1 2 1 6 13 1 1 }.

Identity of Scalar Objects

The identity of the single instance of management information for any scalar object is an OID value whose prefix is the OID value of the object and whose suffix is the number zero. Thus, the OID value for the single instance of sysLocation is { 1 3 6 1 2 1 1 6 0 }, which is commonly written as *sysLocation.0*. (See Figure 2–6)

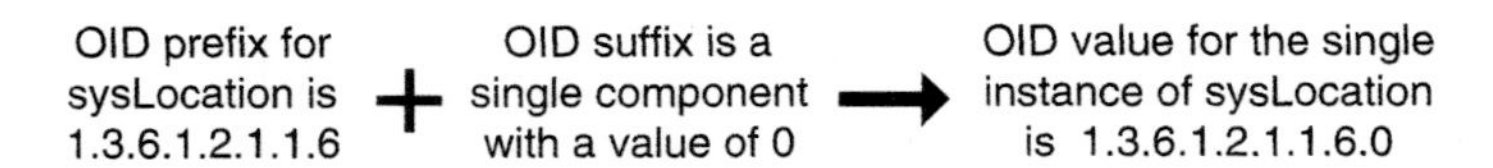

Figure 2–6 Identity format of variable for sysLocation

Identity of Columnar Objects

The rules for identification of instances of columnar objects, the *indexing scheme*, can be simple or quite complex. The indexing scheme must uniquely identify each instance. For example, ifOperStatus is identified by the value of a single integer index. Object tcpConnState is identified by four indices, which are two IP addresses and two port numbers.

The indexing scheme for columnar objects is specified by an INDEX or AUGMENTS clause on the OBJECT-TYPE construct for a row object of the table containing the columnar objects. (See Figure 2–7) The indexing scheme applies to all columnar objects in the table.

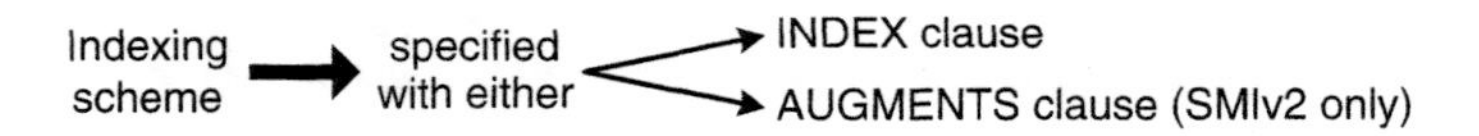

Figure 2–7 Specification of indexing scheme for columnar objects

The AUGMENTS clause, available only in SMIv2, specifies another row object. This indicates that the same indexing scheme is used on the current table as the one containing the specified row. Most indexing schemes are specified with an INDEX clause, which specifies a list of objects. (In SMIv1, the INDEX clause may alternatively specify data types. However, this usage is not widely supported in SNMPv1 MIB compilers, and it is not allowed in SMIv2.) Each object specified is called an *index* for the table. For example, the table object containing columnar objects for network interfaces is called *ifTable*. The row object for this table is called *ifEntry*, and has INDEX clause *INDEX { ifIndex }*. The table of TCP connections is called *tcpConnTable*, with row called *tcpConnEntry*, and INDEX clause *INDEX { tcpConnLocalAddr, tcpConnLocalPort, tcpConnRemAddres, tcpConnRemPort }*.

There is no explicit limit on the number of indices. However, the number of indices and the encoding of their values must not cause an SNMP variable to exceed the 128 component (also called sub-identifier) limit in an OID value. The data type of each index determines how the value(s) that identify an instance are encoded. Table 2–1 shows the encoding rules for each base data type and result of encoding typical values of that data type. Finally, an OID suffix is constructed by concatenating the OID fragments created by encoding the value(s) that identify an instance.

Table 2–1 Index Value Encodings

Index Data Type	Encoding	Examples
Integer (must be non-negative)	a single component containing the value	- value 0 is encoded as .0 - value 10 is encoded as .10
Fixed length string and varying length string with implied length	"n" components, one for each octet in the string	- value '01020304'h is encoded as .1.2.3.4 - value "012" is encoded as .48.49.50 (note: the decimal value of "0" is 48)
Varying length string	"n+1" components, the first has the length of the string and the remaining are one for each octet in the string	- value '01020304'h is encoded as .4.1.2.3.4 - value "012" is encoded as .3.48.49.50 (note: the decimal value of "0" is 48) - value "" (a zero length string) is encoded as .0
OID without implied length	"n+1" components, the first has the number of components in the value and the remaining are the components of the value	- value 1.3.6.1 is encoded as .4.1.3.6.1 - value 0.0 is encoded as .2.0.0
OID with implied length	"n" components, one for each component of the value	- value 1.3.6.1 is encoded as .1.3.6.1 - value 0.0 is encoded as .0.0
NetworkAddress (SNMPv1)	5 components, the first has the value of 1, the next four are the octets of an IP address in network byte order	- value 1.2.3.4 (an IP address) is encoded as .1.1.2.3.4 (an OID suffix) - value 105.179.99.1 (an IP address) is encoded as .1.105.179.99.1

The data type of object *ifIndex* is integer, thus all the columnar objects in the interfaces table have a single OID component in their OID suffix. (See Figure 2–8) The columnar objects in the TCP connection table use the encoding of the data types of four indices. The data type for *tcpConnLocalAddr* is IP address (a string with fixed length of 4), for *tcpConnLocalPort* is integer, for *tcpConnRemAddres* is IP address (a string with fixed length of 4), and for *tcpConnRemPort* is integer. Thus, all the columnar objects in the TCP connection table have 10 OID components in their OID suffix. (See Figure 2–8)

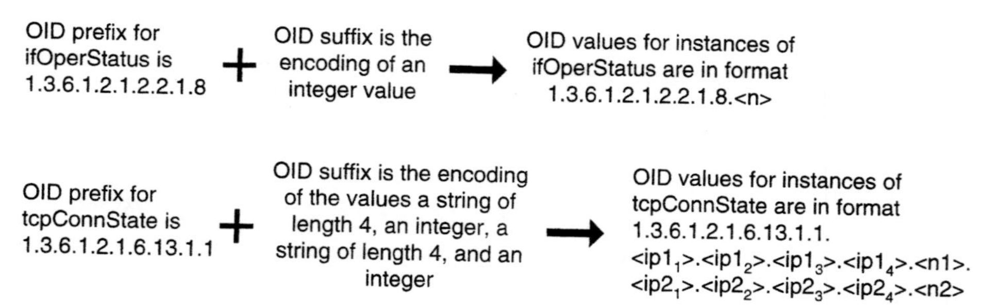

Figure 2–8 Identity format of variables for ipOperStatus and tcpConnState

The instances of columnar objects are ordered by the ascending value of the encoding of the values of their indices. For example, if a table has a single integer index with the values

5, 6, 3, and 2, then the sorted order of the encoded values is 2, 3, 5, and 6. Consider a table with two indices, where the first is a fixed length string of size 3, and the second is an integer. For this table, the following is an example of instance values in sorted order: ("abc", 2), ("bbb", 1), ("bbb", 9), and ("stu", 2). In this case, and in general, the sorted order is that which one would expect for integers, fixed length strings, varying strings with implied length, and OIDs with implied length. However, varying length strings and OIDs seem to be sorted somewhat "unnaturally" at first glance. For a table with a single varying length string index, the values "aa", "b", "z", "abc", and "az" are sorted as "b", "z", "aa", "az", and "abc". This is due to the encoding of varying length strings, including the length in the encoding of the value! The following is the sorted list with the length shown as a number in "<" and ">": "<1>b", "<1>z", "<2>aa", "<2>az", "<3>abc". OIDs also include their length in determining the sorted order. The following is a sorted list of OID values with the length shown as a number in "<" and ">": <2>2.19, <3>0.0.0, <3>1.2.3, and <4>1.2.1.8.

2.4 Relationships between Objects

There are several methods that can be used to show relationships between objects. Unfortunately, most relationships can only be described with prose in descriptions of objects and not in a format parsable by a MIB compiler. We will briefly describe the most common relationships in this section and leave examples of their application to Chapters 8 and 9.

2.4.1 OID Assignments and Identifier Spellings

The most basic relationship between objects is that they represent related aspects of a managed system. By convention, definitions of related objects are grouped together using the OID assignments and by the spelling of their identifiers. Figure 2–9 shows a portion of the OID tree with assignments for related scalar objects.

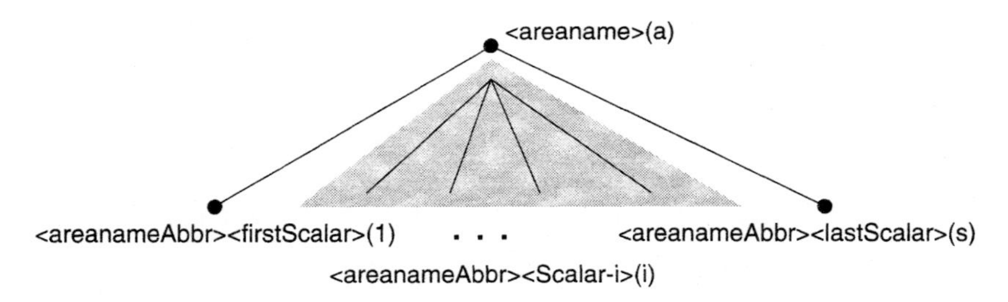

Figure 2–9 Typical OID values and identifier spellings for scalar objects

The identifiers for scalar objects, by convention, consist of a prefix, which is typically an abbreviation of the area, and a suffix, which describes the object. Historically, areas have been called groups. Objects that report counts are typically given an identifier that is a plural spelling. For example, object *ipInReceives* reports the count of received IP datagrams. The core set of SNMP object definitions include attributes of a system. This area is called *system*. The scalar objects in this area use the abbreviation *sys* in the spelling of their identifiers. Examples include *sysDescr*, *sysLocation*, *sysContact*, and *sysUpTime*.

Strongly related columnar objects are required to be organized in a table. The SMI requires the OID assignments as shown in Figure 2–10 for table, row, and columnar objects.

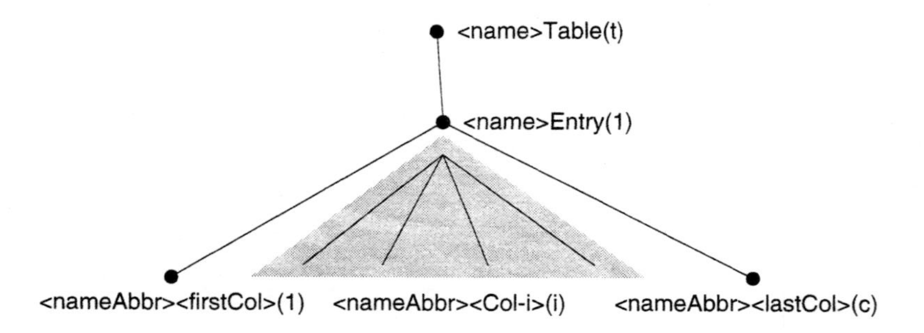

Figure 2–10 Typical OID values and identifier spellings for table, row, and columnar objects

The identifiers for table, row, and columnar objects follow a strong pattern. This pattern for the spelling of these identifiers is followed religiously by MIB designers. However, it is not a requirement of the SMI. The spelling of the identifier for a table consists of a prefix describing the table, and a suffix of *Table*. For example, the identifier for the table of information about network interfaces is *ifTable*. The spelling of the identifier for the row consists of the same prefix as the table, and a suffix of *Entry*. For example, the row for table *ifTable* is *ifEntry*. Columnar objects in the table, by convention, use a spelling for their identifiers that consists of a prefix, which is typically an abbreviation of the table, and a suffix, which describes the object. For example, columnar objects in the interfaces table have a prefix of *if*. Examples include *ifDescr*, *ifOperStatus*, *ifInOctets*, and *ifOutOctets*.

2.4.2 Sharing Existence Within a Table

Besides sharing a common indexing scheme, columnar objects in the same table share existence. That is, each instance of all columnar objects in a table share a common fate.

Simple Fate Relationship

Most columnar objects in a table have a simple fate sharing relationship, of or not existing. For this type of relationship (see Figure 2–11), any existence of an instance in one col-

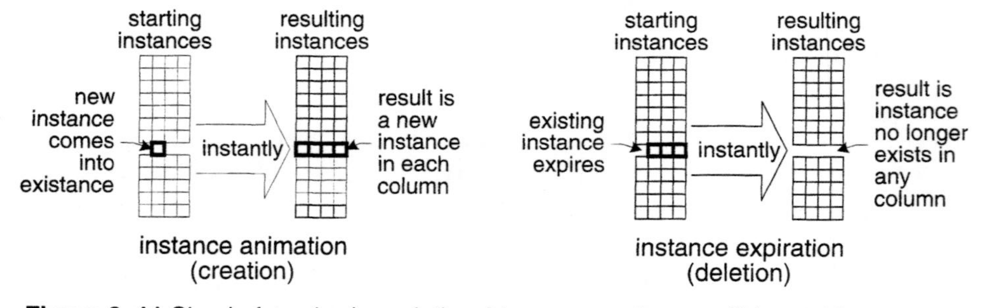

Figure 2–11 Simple fate sharing relationship among columns within a table

umn means that the same instance exists for all other columns in the table. Any expiration of an instance means that the same instance expires for all other columns in the table. Early SNMP MIB designs only contained tables with this simple fate sharing relationship.

As experience was gained with MIB design, the simple fate sharing relationship was found to be inadequate for creation of new instances of management information through SNMP. Remember, instances of management information in a managed system allow resources in that system to be monitored, configured, and controlled. New instances of management information come and go, tracking the fate of resources in a system, without interaction of an SNMP agent in that system. However, with proper MIB design, SNMP SET operations can be used to create and delete instances of resources in a managed system. Tables based on a simple fate sharing relationship require that the creation via an SNMP SET operation of an instance of any columnar object results in the animation of instances of the other columnar objects, and deletion via an SNMP SET operation of an instance of any columnar object results in the deletion of the other columnar objects in the table.

Complex Fate Relationships

The next step in the evolution of MIB design added a columnar object to tables to report and control the fate of the other columnar objects in the table. First attempts defined such columnar objects to have two values. The first value was "valid" and the second value was "invalid" (or "delete"). An SNMP SET of value "valid" created a row in the table, and an SNMP SET of value "invalid" deleted the row. An SNMP retrieval operation returned a value of "valid" if the instance existed. This approach was found to be too limited in many cases and was advanced to a mechanism first published in the RMON MIB specification. The early attempts did not support environments where more than one management application was simultaneously accessing an agent, and did not support tables where the necessary data values for all needed columns could not fit within one minimal sized SNMP message. The approach specified in the RMON MIB specification addressed these deficiencies. Rows using this mechanism are in one of three states: "not existing," "under creation," or "valid." The state of a row is reported and controlled by one column. (See Figure 2–12) The relationships

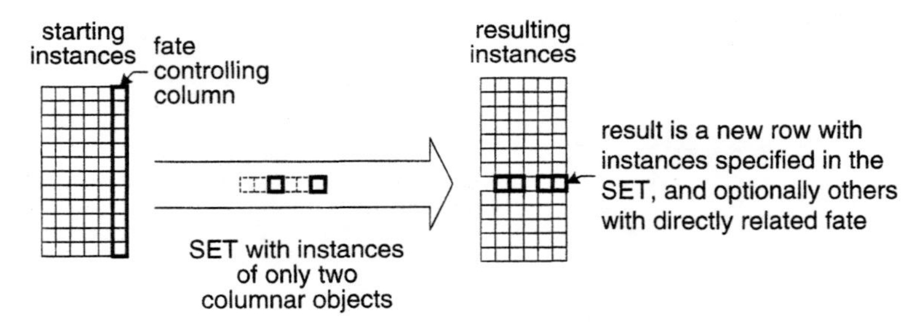

Figure 2–12 Complex fate sharing of columns within a table

between the other columns in the table and the fate controlling column are implied by the allowed maximal access, data type, and specified "default value" and specified in descriptive text in the definitions of the objects. The fate relationships between columns could be simple or complex as chosen by the MIB designer. Unfortunately, these relationships could not be determined by a MIB compiler, but only by human readers of the definitions

During development of SMIv2, the RMON mechanism was reviewed and further improved. The improvements provided finer control and better feedback to management applications during row creation. A detailed presentation of the RMON mechanism, called EntryStatus, and the SMIv2 mechanism, called RowStatus, can be found in Chapter 8. Unfortunately, the current SMI format has no mechanism to completely describe the fate relationships between columns in a table which can be determined by a MIB compiler. This aspect is important for two reasons. The first is for precise communication between MIB designers and MIB users, such as agent and management application developers. The second is to be able to generate code for agents, management applications, test scripts, etc., after parsing a MIB without additional information.

Our Opinion

We believe that the SMI needs to be extended so that fate relationships between columns in a table are parsable by MIB compilers. We believe that this is an important area for the SNMP WG and researchers to investigate and resolve.

2.5 Fate Relationships between Tables

Besides fate sharing between columnar objects in a table, there can be fate sharing between tables. Table fate sharing means that there is a relationship between the existence of a row in one table and a row in another table. The SMI allows some of these relationships to be described with parsable constructs, but most relationships must be fully described with textual descriptions. It was briefly mentioned earlier that an AUGMENTS clause can be used to specify the indexing scheme for a table. It is also possible to specify a hint of a fate relationship through the INDEX clause.

2.5.1 One-to-One Dependent Relationship

The AUGMENTS clause is used when there is a *one-to-one dependent* relationship between rows in one table and rows in another table. One table is designated the *base* table, and the other the *augmenting* table. This relationship is shown in Figure 2–13. The fate of the

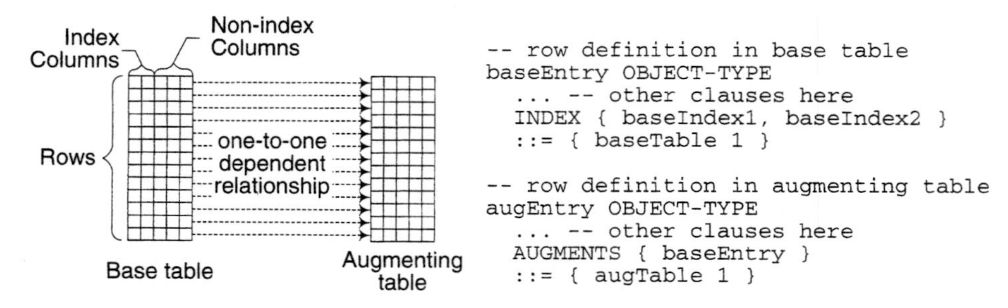

Figure 2–13 One-to-one dependent relationship indicated with an AUGMENTS clause

rows in an augmenting table match the fate in the base table. That is, when a row comes into existence in a base table, it must also come into existence in the augmenting table. Likewise, when a row expires in the base table, it also expires in the augmenting table. Chapter 10 describes situations where this type of relationship is used in some standards-track MIBs.

2.5.2 Sparse Dependent Relationship

A *sparse dependent* relationship exists between two tables when the first table may have more rows than the second table, but instances in the two tables use the same indexing scheme. The tables still have a fate relationship, but it is more complex. For example, a table of statistics for ethernet interfaces is dependent on the table of network interfaces. (See Figure 2–14) There are network interface types other than ethernet. Thus, the number of rows in the table of statistics for ethernet interfaces is equal to the number of rows in the network interface table where the type is ethernet. The fate of rows in the dependent table still tracks that of rows in the base table. The second table may not use an AUGMENTS clause, but should use an INDEX clause containing the same objects specified in the INDEX clause of the first table. Unfortunately, the SMI does not have a parsable method to specify the criteria for inclusion of rows in the dependent table. This must be specified in description text. Chapter 10 describes situations where this type of relationship is used.

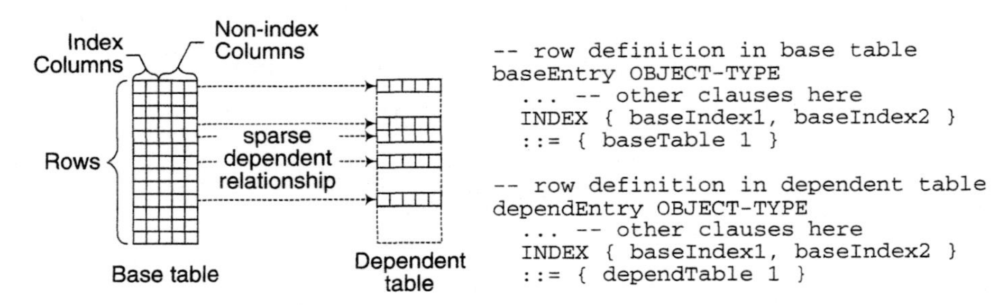
Index Columns
Non-index Columns
Rows
sparse dependent relationship
Base table
Dependent table
-- row definition in base table
baseEntry OBJECT-TYPE
... -- other clauses here
INDEX { baseIndex1, baseIndex2 }
::= { baseTable 1 }
-- row definition in dependent table
dependEntry OBJECT-TYPE
... -- other clauses here
INDEX { baseIndex1, baseIndex2 }
::= { dependTable 1 }

Figure 2–14 Sparse dependent relationship indicated with an INDEX clause

2.5.3 Expansion Relationship

An *expansion* relationship exists between two tables when the second table extends the indexing mechanism of the first table. (See Figure 2–15) This is shown by the INDEX clause

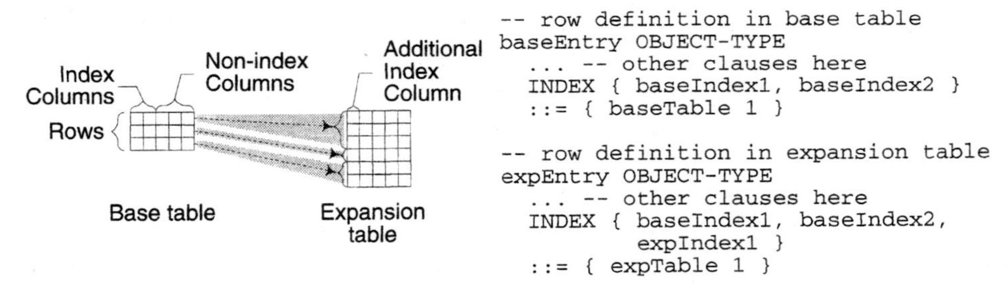
Index Columns
Non-index Columns
Additional Index Column
Rows
Base table
Expansion table
-- row definition in base table
baseEntry OBJECT-TYPE
... -- other clauses here
INDEX { baseIndex1, baseIndex2 }
::= { baseTable 1 }
-- row definition in expansion table
expEntry OBJECT-TYPE
... -- other clauses here
INDEX { baseIndex1, baseIndex2,
expIndex1 }
::= { expTable 1 }

Figure 2–15 Expansion Relationship indicated with an INDEX clause

of the row for the second table containing all the index items of the first table and additional index items. An extension capability is used to specify a list of information for an instance in the base table. There may be zero, one, or more elements of the list for each instance in the base table. The SMI does not have parsable method to specify when elements should be added or removed from the expansion table. This must be specified in the DESCRIPTION clause of the second table. Also, the elements in the expansion table for an instance in the base table expire when that instance expires. Chapter 10 describes situations where this type of relationship is used.

2.5.4 Re-ordering Relationship

Two tables may describe the same information, but each is ordered so that the data may be retrieved in an order that is convenient to a management application. Such tables have a *re-ordering* relationship. Consider a table containing statistics about messages between systems. The columnar objects for such a table would be the source system, the destination system, and the statistics. Instances are identified by source and destination systems. The order of the objects in the INDEX clause determine the ordering of the instances in a table. Thus, two tables are needed to be able to access the information by (source, destination) and by (destination, source). (See Figure 2–16) Neither table is dependent on the other. Both are dependent on the same management information. The fate of rows in such tables track the management information and are thus identical. Unfortunately, there is not a method in SNMP to describe this relationship between the tables with a parsable construct. The relationship must be completely documented with textual descriptions.

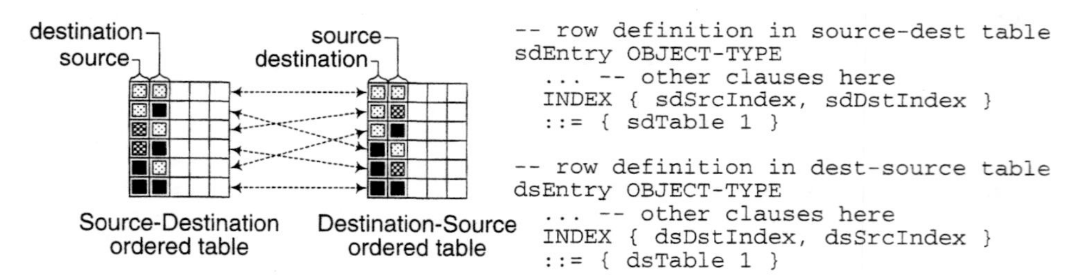
destination
source
source
destination
Source-Destination ordered table
Destination-Source ordered table
-- row definition in source-dest table
sdEntry OBJECT-TYPE
... -- other clauses here
INDEX { sdSrcIndex, sdDstIndex }
::= { sdTable 1 }
-- row definition in dest-source table
dsEntry OBJECT-TYPE
... -- other clauses here
INDEX { dsDstIndex, dsSrcIndex }
::= { dsTable 1 }

Figure 2–16 Re-ordering relationship between two tables

2.5.5 Complex Relationships

There may be fate relationships between tables that are quite complex. The SMI offers little assistance in describing these. These relationships must be documented with descriptive text.

Our Opinion

We believe that the SMI needs to be extended so that fate relationships between tables are parsable by MIB compilers. We believe that this is an important area for the SNMP WG and researchers to investigate and resolve.

2.6 Events

The event reporting mechanism, specification, and control is one of the weaker areas of SNMPv1-based management. The SNMP operations TRAP (in SNMPv1) and TRAPv2 (in SNMPv2) report the occurrence of an event.

2.6.1 Event Identification

The construct to define events is called TRAP-TYPE in SMIv1 and NOTIFICATION-TYPE in SMIv2. The operations and event definitions are identical, except for how events are identified. In SNMPv2, events are identified by an OID value, and specific instances by a timestamp. In SNMPv1, events are identified by the combination of three fields, which are called:

- *enterprise*, a field whose value is an object identifier
- *generic-trap*, a field whose value is an enumerated integer from the list of coldStart(0), warmStart(1), linkDown(2), linkUp(3), authenticationFailure(4), egpNeighborLoss(5), enterpriseSpecific(6)
- *specific-trap*, a field whose value is a non-negative integer

Unfortunately, the names of the fields do not express their meaning. The following is the algorithm that must be used to interpret the value of these fields:

1. Examine the value of field *generic-trap*.
2. If the value is not one of the enumerations, then the identity cannot be determined.
3. If the value is *enterpriseSpecific*(6), then the combination of the value of the fields *enterprise* and *specific-trap* identify the event.
4. Otherwise, the event is identified by the enumerated value from the *generic-trap* field, and the *enterprise* and *specific-trap* fields are not used to identify the event.

Specific instances of SNMPv1 traps are also identified by a timestamp. For both SNMPv1 and SNMPv2, the definition of the event may specify variables to return with their values as operands of an event report. SNMP allows additional pairs of "variable and value" to be returned in the event report. However, neither SMIv1 or SMIv2 provide a mechanism to describe the meaning and use of any extra information. Thus, an agent designer must describe this information in private communication to management application designers for this information to be used.

Our Opinion We believe that the SMI should be extended to allow this extra information to be identified and described.

2.6.2 Use of Events

Event reports, which are called traps in SNMP, are used to reduce the length of time between when an event occurs and when it is noticed by a manager. This time is called the event reaction latency. The SNMP model of management has managers in the roll of deciding what data is needed and how often it needed. Agents provide the specified data only when requested by managers. The periodic gathering of data is called *polling*. From analyzing the data, a manager can determine if a device (and network) is functioning properly and make adjustments, if needed. This approach is called a *pull model*, since a manager is responsible for gathering the information. (See Figure 2–17)

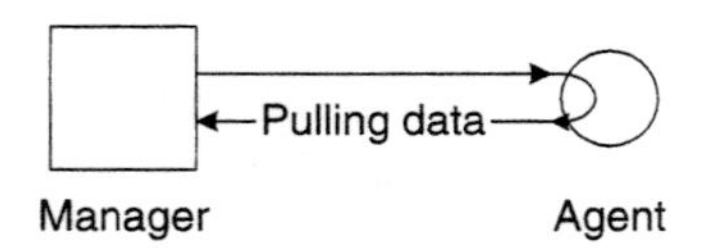

Figure 2–17 Pull model

Another model of management is based on agents in managed systems sending data to configured managers describing events and exceptions which the agents are programmed to believe are significant. In this model, a manager configures agents of interest and waits for data from agents. If there are changes in the managed system, then the manager will (in theory) be told about it and make adjustments, if needed. This approach is called a *push model*, since the agents send data to configured managers without the data being requested. (See Figure 2–18)

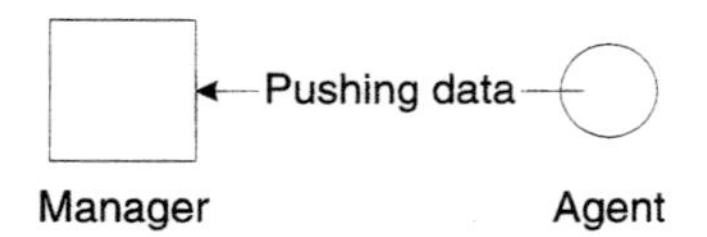

Figure 2–18 Push model

The designers of SNMP were also users of networks with much operational experience. They knew from using and running networks that most serious network errors were communication failures due to physical failure of network interfaces, devices, or the connecting wires (or cables); misconfigured routing tables; or network congestion (too much network traffic). Thus, during a communication failure when a manager wanted to know there was a problem, an event report would never reach a manager. Even worse, many event reports of the same problem would increase network traffic and potentially increase congestion.

On the other hand, a manager using polling will soon determine that a communication failure has occurred. However, it may be some time before a manager realizes that an error condition or important event has occurred. (See Figure 2–19) This amount of time between an event and a manager realizing that an event has occurred is called the event reaction latency. The average latency with a manager only polling is one half the poll interval.

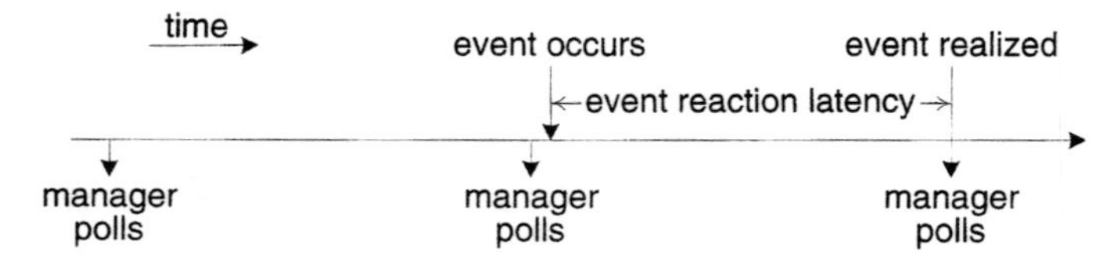

Figure 2–19 Event reaction latency

The poll interval can be reduced to reduce the latency, but this will consume additional network resources that could be used by network applications. This would also reduce the maximum number of agents that a manager can poll, since a manager has a maximum number of messages and responses that it can generate and process. The SNMP solution to this dilemma is called "trap directed polling." In this model, event reports are used to provide "hints" to a manager to modify its polling schedule, and event reports are not used as the primary method to transfer data from agents to managers. Figure 2–20 shows the poll cycle of a manager being accelerated in response to an event report.

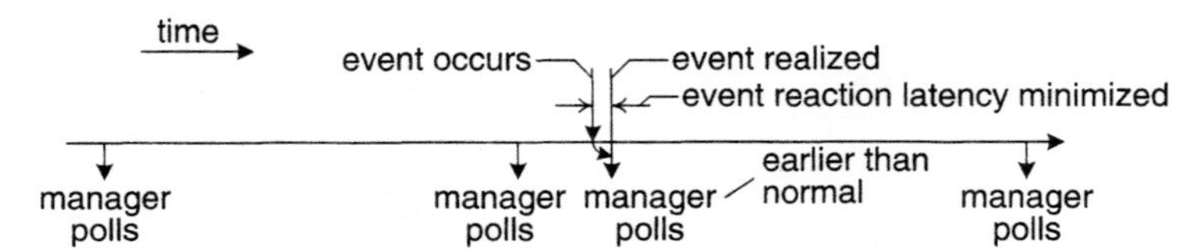

Figure 2–20 Reduced event reaction latency via trap directed polling

The trap directed polling is a combined approach using the best aspects of the pull and push models.

2.6.3 Event Triggering

There are two models for deciding when an event has occurred. (See Figure 2–21) In the first, an event occurs when a monitored value first enters a range. This type of event is called "edge triggered." The monitored value must then enter a potentially different range before the event may occur again. (This is called rearming the trigger.)

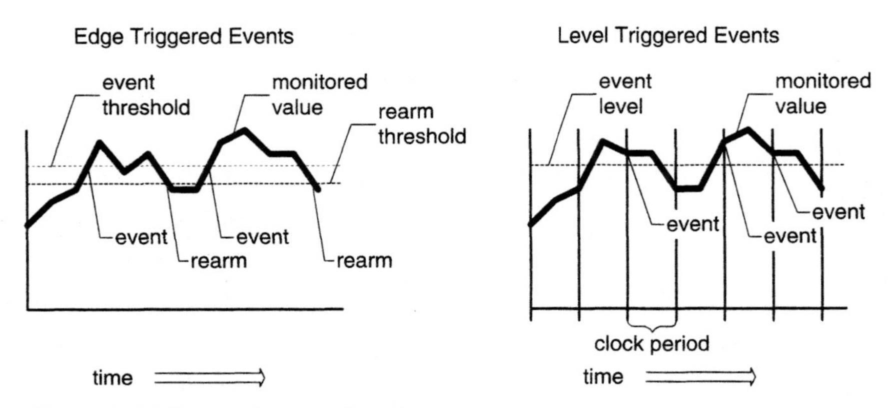

Figure 2–21 Types of event triggering

Alternatively, an event can be defined to occur when a monitored value is inside a range at the start of each periodic time interval. This type of event is called "level triggered." The event may "occur" only at each periodic interval. The DESCRIPTION clause must describe the modeling of the event. If the event is "edge triggered," the description must specify how the event is throttled or turned off so to keep from flooding network managers with event reports.

2.7 Data Types for Management Information

Much, if not all, data can be described as being one of the following types: integer, floating point, octet string, and unique identifier. Computation occurs on these types. Any restrictions on values, grouping, and permitted operations are based on the information represented by the data. These restrictions are called *behaviors* or *semantics* of the information. New, higher level data types can be created by using previously defined data types. These new types represent information having behaviors that can be more restrictive than that for the types on which they were built.

The ASN.1 language was designed to specify complex types and values. Each type is identified with a tag. A companion to ASN.1 is the Basic Encoding Rules (BER) specification, which defines how values are encoded into a string of octets. Encoding a value is called *serialization*. The basic encoding rules specify encodings as consisting of a tag, length, and value (TLV). A tag for a type is identical to the tag specified in the ASN.1 definition of the type. The length specifies how many octets are needed for the encoded value. This is needed, since BER compresses integer, floating point, and unique identifier (OID) values. For example, integers are compressed so that values 0 to 127 are encoded in a single octet, values 128 to 32767 are encoded in two octets, values 32768 to 8388607 are encoded in three octets, values 8388608 to 2147483647 are encoded in four octets, and so on.

The basic ASN.1 types (also called the UNIVERSAL types) are either simple types or structured types. Instead of restricting the simple types to just integer (called INTEGER), floating point (called REAL), octet string (called OCTET STRING), and unique identifier (called OBJECT IDENTIFIER), ASN.1 additionally has the BOOLEAN, BIT STRING, ENUMERATED, NULL, and eight different representations of character strings. Note that all of these additional types could be layered on top of INTEGER or OCTET STRING. The structured types consist of an unordered list (called a SET), multiple occurrences of a SET (called a SET OF), an ordered list (called a SEQUENCE), multiple occurrences of a SEQUENCE (called a SEQUENCE OF), a selection of one from a list (called a CHOICE), and a placeholder for any type (called ANY).

The designers of SNMP wisely chose to use only a sub-set of the ASN.1 simple types to use as the data types for management information. (None of the ASN.1 structured types are allowed for the data type of management information.) The chosen types are INTEGER, OCTET STRING, and OBJECT IDENTIFIER. Unfortunately, they chose to create the following ASN.1 types for use in SNMP: Gauge, Counter, TimeTicks, IpAddress, NetworkAddress, and Opaque. These new types (called APPLICATION types), are assigned a unique tag, but are really just restricted versions of the INTEGER and OCTET STRING types.

Not until the first update of SNMP was it realized that the addition of new types would cause non-interoperation of old and new implementations of the protocol! This was quite unfortunate, since few, if any, changes were planned for the protocol, but many additions of new types were anticipated as new MIB modules were defined. The outcome of this situation was a break with the ASN.1 approach of creating new types, and the invention of what is now called a *textual convention*.

A textual convention allows additional restrictions to be specified on an existing type, but does not actually create an ASN.1 type with a new tag. In SMIv1, a textual convention is defined with an ASN.1 type assignment (the syntax will be shown in the next section). Textual conventions proved popular, so in SMIv2 a new construct (called TEXTUAL-CONVENTION) was created so that key information about a definition could be specified in a format parsable by MIB compilers. In general, textual conventions look and function as new data types.

There is one more kind of type, which is called *pseudotype* (a word we made up). Currently there is a single member, which is BITS. Pseudotypes look and function like ASN.1 types and textual conventions, but they are different.

In SNMP, the combination of the allowed types from ASN.1, the ASN.1 types created for use by SNMP, and the SNMP pseudotypes are called *SNMP base types*.

ASN.1 allows restricting the range of integer types and the size of string types. This is called *sub-typing*. SNMP uses ASN.1 sub-typing and textual descriptions to specify the behaviors (or semantics) of types.

Three types were allowed in the original version of SMIv2, but were removed in an update. They seemed like a good idea during WG discussion, but they proved to be problematic, since they were incompatible with SMIv1. Thus, they were removed. We have included them (see Table 2–2) in case you run into them in MIB modules written using the first version of SMIv2.

Table 2–2 Historic Types

SNMP Base Type Name	ASN.1 Type	Description
UInteger32	[APPLICATION 7] IMPLICIT INTEGER (0..4294967295)	unsigned integer
NsapAddress	[APPLICATION 5] IMPLICIT OCTET STRING (SIZE (1 | 4..21))	NSAP address
BIT STRING	BIT STRING	labelled bits

In summary, the kinds of data types for management information are:

- ASN.1 UNIVERSAL types — those types created as part of the definition of ASN.1, and restricted by the SMI to INTEGER, OCTET STRING, and OBJECT IDENTIFIER
- SNMP ASN.1 APPLICATION types — those types created as part of the definition of SNMP's SMI. SMIv1 has Gauge, Counter, TimeTicks, IpAddress, NetworkAddress, and Opaque. SMIv2 has Integer32, Unsigned32, Gauge32, Counter32, Counter64, TimeTicks, IpAddress, and Opaque
- SNMP Pseudotypes — items that look and function like a type, but due to ASN.1 rules are not really a type. There is only one, which is BITS in SMIv2
- Textual Conventions — ASN.1 type assignments where additional restrictions are added to existing data types
- Sub-types — restrictions on the range of integer types or sizes of string types

A description of each SNMP base type (see Table 2–3) follows:

Table 2–3 Base Data Types for Management Information

SNMP Base Type Name	ASN.1 Type	Description	In v1	In v2
INTEGER	INTEGER (-2147483648..2147483647)	signed integer	yes	no
Integer32	INTEGER (-2147483648..2147483647)	signed integer	no	yes
INTEGER	INTEGER	enumerated integer	yes	yes
Unsigned32	[APPLICATION 2] IMPLICIT INTEGER (0..4294967295)[a]	unsigned integer	no	yes
Gauge	[APPLICATION 2] IMPLICIT INTEGER (0..4294967295)	gauge	yes	no
Gauge32	[APPLICATION 2] IMPLICIT INTEGER (0..4294967295)	gauge	no	yes
Counter	[APPLICATION 1] IMPLICIT INTEGER (0..4294967295)	counter	yes	no
Counter32	[APPLICATION 1] IMPLICIT INTEGER (0..4294967295)	counter	no	yes
Counter64	[APPLICATION 6] IMPLICIT INTEGER (0..18446744073709551615)	large counter	no	yes
TimeTicks	[APPLICATION 3] IMPLICIT INTEGER (0..4294967295)	elapsed time	yes	yes
OCTET STRING	OCTET STRING	bytes	yes	yes
OBJECT IDENTIFIER	OBJECT IDENTIFIER	unique identification	yes	yes
IpAddress	[APPLICATION 0] IMPLICIT OCTET STRING (SIZE (4))	IPv4 Address	yes	yes
NetworkAddress	CHOICE { internet [APPLICATION 0] IMPLICIT OCTET STRING (SIZE (4)) }	union of network addresses	yes	no
Opaque	[APPLICATION 4] IMPLICIT OCTET STRING	encapsulation of ASN.1 BER	yes	yes
BITS	OCTET STRING	labelled bits	no	yes

a. This type is the same ASN.1 type as the Gauge/Gauge32 type.

2.7.1 INTEGER and Integer32

The INTEGER(SMIv1) and Integer32(SMIv2) types are used to specify a value whose range may include both positive and negative numbers. No minimum or maximum values are specified for the range in SMIv1. However, SMIv2 restricts the minimum and maximum values to -2147483648 (-2^{31}) and 2147483647 ($2^{31}-1$), respectively. When used, a range (or ranges) of values should be specified that makes sense architecturally, and not just to specify the current implementation limits.

Syntax

```
<signedIntegerV1> = "INTEGER" [<rangeSpec>]
<signedIntegerV2> = "Integer32" [<rangeSpec>]

-- range specification
<rangeSpec> = "(" <rangeItem> [ "|" <rangeItem> ]... ")"

-- individual range
<rangeItem>
            = "-" number
            | <intVal>
            | "-" number ".." "-" number
            | "-" number ".." <intVal>
            | <intVal> ".." <intVal>

-- integer value
<intVal> = number | binStr | hexStr

where:
        number is an unsigned integer;
        binStr is a binary string; and
        hexStr is a hexadecimal string
```

Range

v1/v2 -2147483648 to 2147483647

Examples

v1 INTEGER -- this is ambiguous, since the range is not specified in V1
v1 INTEGER(0..65535) or INTEGER(0..'ffff'h) -- corresponds to an unsigned 16-bit int
v1 INTEGER(-128..127) -- corresponds to a signed char
v1 INTEGER(-2147483648..-1 | 1..2147483647) -- all values except zero
v1 INTEGER(0..10 | 15 | 25 | 100..500) -- only the values in the specified ranges
v1 INTEGER(-2147483648..2147483647) -- corresponds to a signed 32-bit int

v2 Integer32 --corresponds to a signed 32-bit int
v2 Integer32(0..65535) or Integer32(0..'ffff'h) -- corresponds to an unsigned 16-bit int
v2 Integer32(-128..127) -- corresponds to a signed char
v2 Integer32(-2147483648..-1 | 1..2147483647) -- all values except zero
v2 Integer32(0..10 | 15 | 25 | 100..500) -- only the values in the specified ranges
v2 Integer32(-2147483648..2147483647) -- same as Integer32

Behavior

There are no behaviors associated with this type.

2.7.2 Enumerated Integer Construct

The enumerated integer construct is used to specify a list of labelled integer values. (Technically, this is not a new ASN.1 type. Actually, enumerated integers are the same ASN.1 type as INTEGER and Integer32. However, from a look-and-feel and usage standpoint, enumerated integers are effectively another type.) In SMIv1 the values must be greater than zero. (In practice, many MIB modules were written that included the value zero.) In SMIv2 the values are allowed to be any in the range from -2147483648 (-2^{31}) to 2147483647 ($2^{31}-1$).

The labels for the values consist of 1 to 64 letters, digits, and hyphens (only in SMIv1). The initial character must be a lowercase letter. A hyphen may not be the last character. A hyphen may not be immediately followed by another hyphen. Each label in the list of integer values must be unique. (There is no requirement that the labels be unique within a MIB module.)

Our Opinion We believe that the change between SMIv1 and SMIv2 to disallow hyphens from labels was unnecessary, and has far greater costs than benefits. We believe that this change should be "undone."

Originally, the usage of this type was to create labelled values that started at one and were consecutive up to the maximum value. However, the usage has been liberalized so that the values are not required to be consecutive, nor required to start at one.

Syntax

```
<enumeratedInteger> = "INTEGER" "{" <enumItem> [ "," <enumItem> ]... "}"

-- v1 enumerated item, with label lcName
<enumItem> = lcName "(" number ")"

-- v2 enumerated item, with label lcName
<enumItem> = lcName "(" <enumVal> ")"

--enumerated value
<enumVal> = binStr | hexStr | [ "-" ] number
```

where:

number is an unsigned integer;
binStr is a binary string;
hexStr is a hexadecimal string; and
lcName is a name starting with a lowercase letter

Range

v1 1 to 2147483647
v2 -2147483648 to 2147483647

Examples

```
v1/v2  INTEGER { true(1), false(2) }
v1/v2  INTEGER { up(1), down(2), testing(3), offline(4) }
```

```
v1/v2   INTEGER { b110(110), b300(300), b1200(1200), b2400(2400) }
v2      INTEGER { lessThan(-1), equal(0), greaterThan(1) }
v2      INTEGER { red('001'b), blue('010'b), green('100'b), white('111'b),
                  black('000'b), yellow('110'b), orange('011'b), purple('101'b) }
```

Behavior

There are no behaviors associated with this type.

2.7.3 Unsigned32

The Unsigned32 type is used to specify a value whose range includes only non-negative integers. The values range from zero to 4294967295 (2^{32} - 1). This type is actually identically encoded as Gauge (from SMIv1) and Gauge32 (from SMIv2). When used, a range (or ranges) of values must be specified that makes sense architecturally, and not just to specify the current implementation limits.

Syntax

```
<unsignedIntegerV1> = -- does not exist directly
<unsignedIntegerV2> = "Unsigned32" [<rangeSpec>]

-- range specification
<rangeSpec> = "(" <rangeItem> [ "|" <rangeItem> ]... ")"

-- individual range
<rangeItem> = <intVal> | <intVal> ".." <intVal>

-- integer value
<intVal> = number | binStr | hexStr
```

where:

number is an unsigned integer;
binStr is a binary string; and
hexStr is a hexadecimal string

Range

```
v2      0 to 4294967295
```

Examples

```
v2      Unsigned32 -- corresponds to an unsigned 32 bit int
v2      Unsigned32(0..65535) -- corresponds to an unsigned 16 bit int
v2      Unsigned32(0..255) -- corresponds to an unsigned char
v2      Unsigned32(0..10 | 15 | 25 | 100..500) -- only the values in the specified ranges
v2      Unsigned32(0..4294967295) -- same as Unsigned32
```

Behavior

There are no behaviors associated with this type.

2.7.4 UInteger32

The UInteger32 type was created in the original version of SMIv2. However, this new type resulted in incompatibility between SNMPv1 and SNMPv2. Thus, the UInteger type was removed in an update of SNMPv2 and replaced by the Unsigned32 type. These two types are encoded differently and not interchangeable, thus the name of the type had to be changed. (The removal of this type was approved since it was not allowed in any IETF WG created MIBs.) The replacement type, Unsigned32, uses the same encoding as the Gauge and Gauge32 types. The Unsigned32 type allows interoperation between SNMPv1 and SNMPv2.

The UInteger32 type must not be used, since it is no longer available and it is not compatible with SNMPv1 or SNMPv2.

2.7.5 Gauge and Gauge32

The Gauge and Gauge32 types are used to specify a value whose range includes only non-negative integers. The values range from zero to 4294967295 (2^{32} - 1).

Syntax

```
<gaugeV1> = "Gauge" [<rangeSpec>]
<gaugeV2> = "Gauge32" [<rangeSpec>]

-- range specification
<rangeSpec> = "(" <rangeItem> [ "|" <rangeItem> ]... ")"

-- individual range
<rangeItem> = <intVal> | <intVal> ".." <intVal>

-- integer value
<intVal> = number | binStr | hexStr
```

where:

number is an unsigned integer;
binStr is a binary string; and
hexStr is a hexadecimal string

Range

v1/v2 0 to 4294967295

Examples

```
v1    Gauge -- corresponds to an unsigned 32 bit int
v1    Gauge(0..65535) -- corresponds to an unsigned 16 bit int
v1    Gauge(0..255) -- corresponds to an unsigned char
v1    Gauge(100..200) -- range does not have to start at zero
v1    Gauge(0..10 | 15 | 70..100) -- only the values in the specified ranges are reported
v1    Gauge(0..4294967295) -- same as Gauge

v2    Gauge32 -- corresponds to an unsigned 32 bit int
```

v2 Gauge32(0..65535) -- corresponds to an unsigned 16 bit int
v2 Gauge32(0..255) -- corresponds to an unsigned char
v2 Gauge(100..200) -- range does not have to start at zero
v2 Gauge32(0..10 | 15 | 70..100) -- only the values in the specified ranges are reported
v2 Gauge32(0..4294967295) -- same as Gauge32

Behavior

These types have the behavior such that the reported value is always within the specified range even when the actual value is outside the specified range. For example, a thermometer may be able to display a temperature only within a particular range. When the temperature is outside the range, the value displayed would be the highest (or lowest) possible for the thermometer.

There is much folklore associated with the behavior of the Gauge type due to its definition from RFC 1155 and shown below:

3.2.3.4. Gauge

This application-wide type represents a non-negative integer, which may increase or decrease, but which latches at a maximum value. This memo specifies a maximum value of 2^32-1 (4294967295 decimal) for gauges.

The term *latches* in the definition has confused many readers. The diagram shown in Figure 2–22 illustrates the intent of the authors. (Remember a thermometer — when the actual tem-

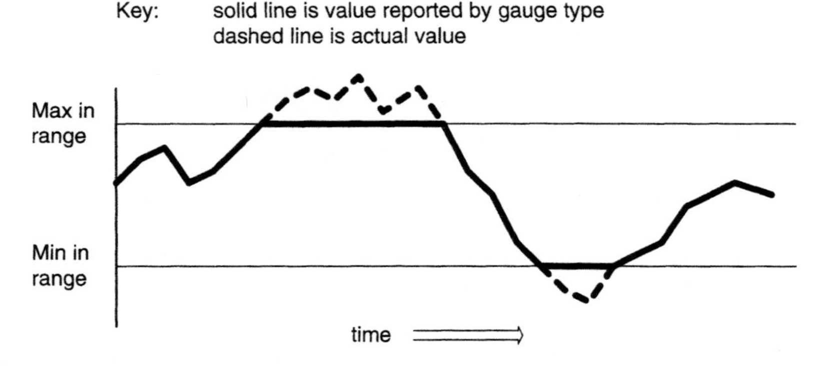

Figure 2–22 Example of gauge latching

perature is higher or lower than what can be reported, the thermometer reports its highest or lowest value respectively.)

The gauge type allows multiple ranges to be specified, and objects defined with this type may allow modifications.

2.7.6 Counter and Counter32

The Counter and Counter32 types are used to specify a non-negative value whose range includes only non-negative integers.

Syntax

<counterV1> = "Counter"
<counterV2> = "Counter32"

Range

v1/v2 0 to 4294967295

Example

v1 Counter -- this is the only format
v2/v2 Counter32 -- this is the only format

Behavior

The reported value for objects of this type is a count, modulo 2^{32} (4294967296 decimal), of the occurrence of an event or the measure of a flow. The starting value of a counter is undefined unless specified where the type is used. An example of an event is a packet sent by a network interface. An example of a flow measurement is the number of bytes in good packets received on an interface.

The values reported by counters are not absolute, since the count is not required to start at zero and the count may roll over. A counter has a maximum value of 4294967295 and thus a large number of events or quantity of flow will cause the actual value to overflow. When this occurs, the reported value wraps (i.e., starts over at zero) just like an odometer on an automobile. (See Figure 2–23)

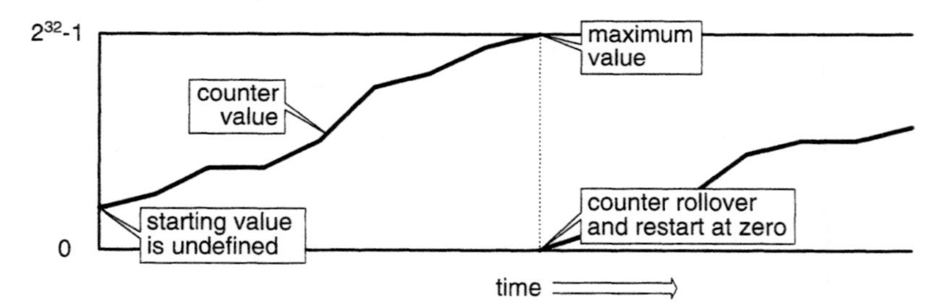

Figure 2–23 Counter behaviors

Counters are used by obtaining a value, v_0, at a base time, t_0, and then later obtaining a value, v_1, at time t_1. The difference between v_1 and v_0 is the count over the time period. That is, the count for period i, C_i, is v_i minus v_0 (i.e., $C_i = v_i - v_0$). (See Figure 2–24)

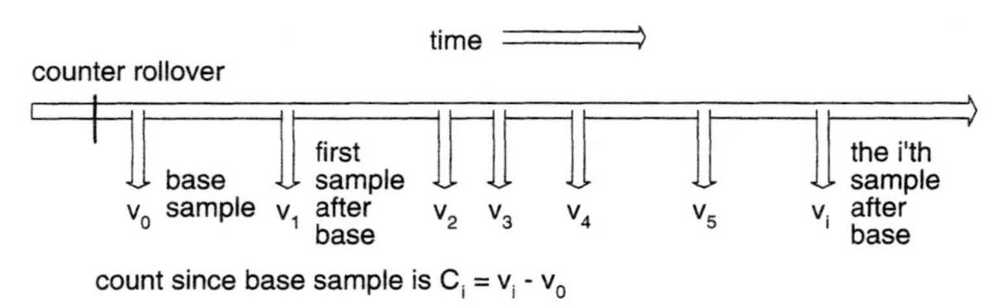
case 1: no counter rollover during sampling (and total count during sampling less than counter max)
time
counter rollover
base sample
first sample after base
the i'th sample after base
v0 v1 v2 v3 v4 v5 vi
count since base sample is Ci = vi - v0

Figure 2–24 Counter with no rollover

However, the reported value may have wrapped. This must be taken into account when computing the difference. This is done by checking if v_0 is greater than v_1. If so, the count for period i, C_i, is computed by subtracting v_i from v_0, subtracting the result from 4294967295, and adding one (i.e., $C_i = (4294967295 - (v_0 - v_i)) + 1$). (See Figure 2–25)

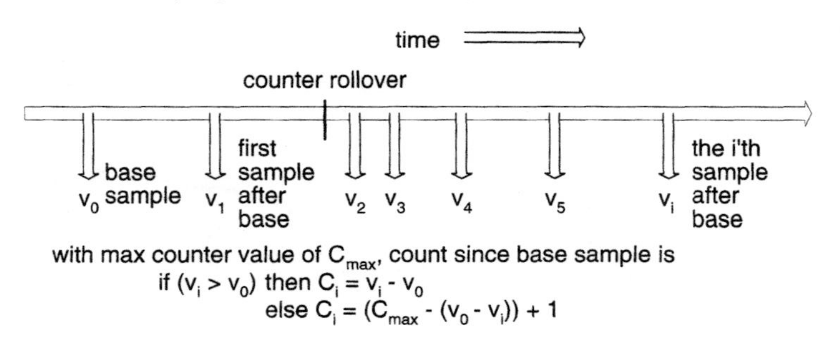
case 2: counter rollover during sampling (and total count during sampling less than counter max)
time
counter rollover
base sample
first sample after base
the i'th sample after base
v0 v1 v2 v3 v4 v5 vi
with max counter value of Cmax, count since base sample is
if (vi > v0) then Ci = vi - v0
else Ci = (Cmax - (v0 - vi)) + 1

Figure 2–25 Counter with rollover

During a time interval, a counter may have been disabled and then re-enabled. When a counter is re-enabled, its initial value is undefined, and may be the last value that was reported, or an unpredictable value.

An analogy is the odometer in your automobile breaking and being replaced by a used one. The value on the replacement odometer will be unpredictable. If before a trip you had written down the value on the odometer, and had planned to take the value at the end of your trip so you could compute the distance of the trip, a change of odometers during the trip would result in an invalid distance computation.

A counter becoming disabled and re-enabled is called a *counter discontinuity*. To be able to detect discontinuances, each use of a counter type must have an associated time-related indication of when the last counter discontinuity occurred. The time indication must be used to determine if the base count is still valid. Further information about time indicators is presented in Chapter 8.

A periodic sampling of counter values may be converted into a rate by dividing each difference in counter values by the length of the sample period. (See Figure 2–26)

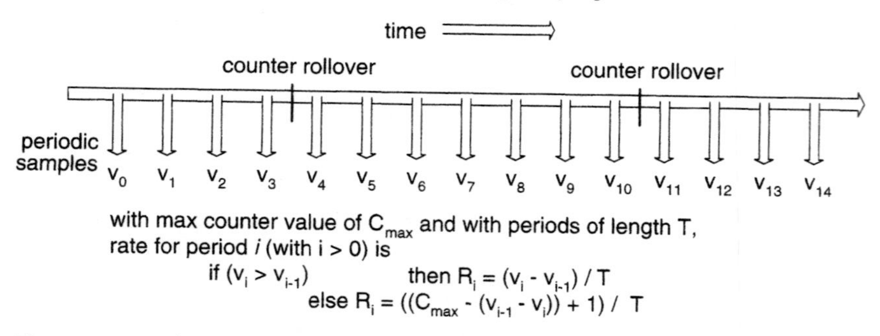

Figure 2–26 Using a counter to compute a rate

Figure 2–27 shows a strip graph of a counter value and the computed rate. Note that the value is sampled only periodically, and thus the rollover of the counter appears as its value decreasing. The rollover (and any counter discontinuities) must be compensated for in the use of a counter.

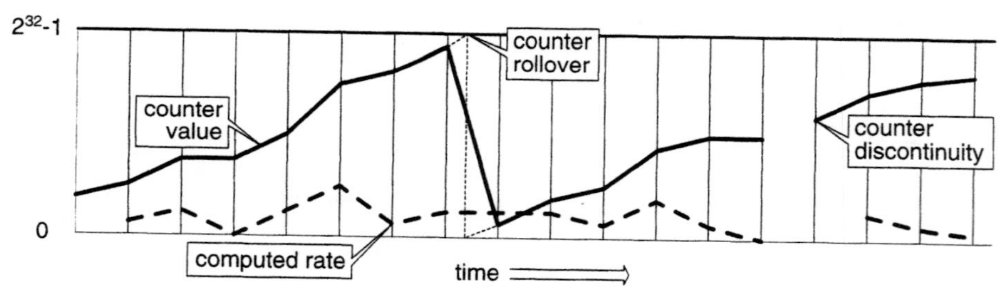

Figure 2–27 Strip chart of a counter and computed rate

The last concern when using the counter type is the minimum time for a rollover to occur. If the time between obtaining two values of a counter is greater than the time for a counter to rollover, then it is impossible to determine the actual difference between the two recorded values.

2.7.7 Counter64

The Counter64 type is used to specify a non-negative value whose range includes only non-negative integers

Syntax

<counter64V1> = -- does not exist
<counter64V2> = "Counter64"

Range

v2 0 to 18446744073709551615

Example

v2 Counter64 -- this is the only format

Behavior

The reported value for objects of this type is a count, modulo 2^{64} (18446744073709551616 decimal), of the occurrence of an event or the measure of a flow. The starting value of a counter is undefined unless specified where the type is used. An example of an event is a packet sent by a network interface. An example of a flow measurement is the number of bytes in good packets received on an interface. This type may only be used when a 32-bit counter rollover could occur in less than an hour. Otherwise, the Counter32 type must be used. This type is not available in SNMPv1 and may only be used when backwards compatibility is not a requirement. (See the description of Counter and Counter32 for details of the behavior of this type.)

2.7.8 TimeTicks

The TimeTicks type is used to specify a non-negative value whose range includes only non-negative integers.

Syntax

<timeTicks> = "TimeTicks"

Range

v1/v2 0 to 4294967295

Example

v1/v2 TimeTicks -- this is the only format

Behavior

The reported value of objects of this type is an elapsed time, modulo 2^{32} (4294967296 decimal), in units of hundredths of a second between two events (or epochs). Use of this type must describe those events. The length of time between rollovers (4294967296 hundredths of seconds) is approximately 497 days.

2.7.9 OCTET STRING

The OCTET STRING type is used to specify octets (eight-bit bytes) of binary or textual information. There is no limit to the maximum number of octets in a value of this type specified in SMIv1. However, SMIv2 specifies a limit of 65535 (2^{16} - 1) octets. SMIv2 contains a caution that there may be implementation and interoperability problems for sizes greater than 255 (2^8 - 1) octets. A size may be specified which can be fixed, varying, or multiple ranges.

Syntax

```
<octetString> = "OCTET" "STRING" [ <sizeClause>]

-- size clause
<sizeClause> = "(" "SIZE" <rangeSpec> ")"

-- range specification
<rangeSpec> = "(" <rangeItem> [ "|" <rangeItem> ]... ")"

-- individual range,
<rangeItem> = number | number ".." number
```

where:

number is an unsigned integer

Size

v1/v2 0 to 65535

Examples

v1/v2 OCTET STRING -- varying in length from 0 to 65535 bytes
v1/v2 OCTET STRING (SIZE(0..255)) -- varying in length from 0 to 255 bytes
v1/v2 OCTET STRING (SIZE(4)) -- fixed in length of exactly 4 bytes
v1/v2 OCTET STRING (SIZE(0 | 4 | 6)) -- varying with length 0, 4, or 6 bytes
v1/v2 OCTET STRING (SIZE(4 | 6..12)) -- varying with length 0 or 6 to 12 bytes

Behavior

There are no behaviors associated with this type. Textual conventions may be created using this base type which specify required behavior or values. For example, the DisplayString textual convention requires that the values be characters from a specified character set. The PhysAddress textual convention requires the value to be a media- or physical-level address.

2.7.10 OBJECT IDENTIFIER

The OBJECT IDENTIFIER type is used to uniquely identify an item that has an assigned object identifier value. SMIv1 has no restrictions on the number of components (sub-identifiers) in an OID value, nor the maximum value of any component (after the first two). SMIv2 limits OID values to a maximum of 128 components, and limits OID component values to less than or equal to 4294967295 (2^{32} - 1). Also, just like in SMIv1, an OID value must have at least two components. The first component must have a value of 0, 1, or 2. The second component when the first component is either 0 or 1 must have a value less than 40.

Syntax

```
<objectIdentifer> = "OBJECT" "IDENTIFIER"
```

Example

v1/v2 OBJECT IDENTIFIER -- this is the only format

Behavior

There are no behaviors associated with this type. Textual conventions may be created using this base type which specify required behavior or values. For example, the VariablePointer textual convention requires that the values be the identity of an SNMP variable.

2.7.11 IpAddress

The IpAddress type is used to specify a string of four octets.

Syntax

```
<ipv4Address> = "IpAddress"
```

Example

```
v1/v2   IpAddress -- this is the only format
```

Behavior

A value of this type is an IPv4 address. A value is encoded as 4 bytes in network byte order. This type is available in SMIv1 and SMIv2. However, it is being phased out to be replaced with a general solution.

2.7.12 NsapAddress

The NsapAddress type was created for the original version of SMIv2. However, this new type resulted in incompatibility between SNMPv1 and SNMPv2. It was removed in an update to SMIv2, since its use was not allowed in IETF-developed MIB modules. Also, another approach was created that allows backwards compatibility and allows new network address types to be easily added. Thus, the type NsapAddress must not be used, since it is no longer available and it is not compatible with SNMPv1 or SNMPv2.

2.7.13 NetworkAddress

The NetworkAddress type is used to specify a string of four octets.

Syntax

```
<unionOfNetworkAddressTypesV1> = "NetworkAddress"
<unionOfNetworkAddressTypesV2> = -- does not exist
```

Example

```
v1      NetworkAddress -- this is the only format
```

Behavior

A value of this type is an IPv4 address. A value is encoded as 4 bytes in network byte order. This type is available in only in SMIv1. It was designed to allow a network address of any type to be specified. However, this type is now obsolete. Its fatal flaw is that it requires specifications and code in deployed systems to be changed for each addition of a new kind of network address. Since this union has only one member, which is the IpAddress type, there is support for this type in SMIv2 via the IpAddress type.

2.7.14 Opaque

The Opaque type is used to specify octets (eight bit bytes) of binary information. There is no limit to the maximum number of octets in a value of this type specified in SMIv1. However, SMIv2 specifies a limit of 65535 (2^{16} - 1) octets. SMIv2 contains a caution that there may be implementation and interoperability problems for sizes greater than 255 (2^8 - 1) octets. A size may be specified which can be fixed, varying, or multiple ranges.

Syntax

```
<opaque> = "Opaque" [ <sizeClause>]

-- size clause
<sizeClause> = "(" "SIZE" <rangeSpec> ")"

-- range specification
<rangeSpec> = "(" <rangeItem> [ "|" <rangeItem> ]... ")"

-- individual range
<rangeItem> = number | number ".." number

where:
        number is an unsigned integer
```

Size

v1/v2 0 to 65535

Examples

v1/v2 Opaque -- varying in length from 0 to 65535
v1/v2 Opaque (SIZE(0..255)) -- varying in length from 0 to 255 bytes
v1/v2 Opaque (SIZE(4)) -- fixed in length of exactly 4 bytes
v1/v2 Opaque (SIZE(0 | 4 | 6)) -- varying with length 0, 4, or 6 bytes
v1/v2 Opaque (SIZE(0 | 6..12)) -- varying with length 0 or 6 to 12 bytes

Behavior

A value of this type must be an encapsulation of an ASN.1 BER encoded value. This can be used as a backward-compatible method to extend SNMP base types, or to create new private types. The values are effectively double-wrapped. (See Figure 2–28) Creating new types by

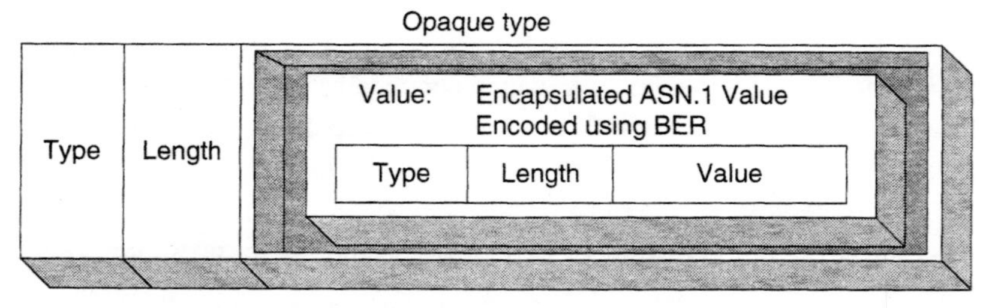

Figure 2–28 Double wrapping a value by using Opaque type

using the Opaque type is strongly discouraged. The correct way to add additional semantics (or behaviors) to an existing type is through creating a textual convention. Use of the Opaque type to add new base types is meant primarily for extending the SMI, such as for adding a floating point type. When new types are added, their encapsulation in an Opaque type can be hidden with a textual convention.

Our Opinion

We believe that the Counter64 type should be removed from SMIv2 and replaced by a textual convention of an Opaque type wrapping the 64-bit counter. This would allow 64-bit counters in SNMPv1! We also believe that this approach should be used to add single and double precision floating point numbers to SNMP.

The following is an example of a textual convention to support 64-bit counters encoded as Opaque type:

```
C64 TEXTUAL-CONVENTION
    STATUS  current
    DESCRIPTION
        "A 64-bit counter which monotonically increases until it
        reaches a maximum value of (2^64)-1 (18446744073709551615
        decimal), when it wraps around and starts increasing again
        from zero. Counters have no defined 'initial' value, and thus,
        a single value of a counter has (in general) no information
        content. Discontinuities in the monotonically increasing
        value normally occur at re-initialization of the management
        system, and at other times as specified in the description
        of an object-type using this textual convention.
        If such other times can occur, for example, the creation of
        an object instance at times other than re-initialization,
        then a corresponding object should be defined with a SYNTAX
        clause value of TimeStamp (a well-known textual convention)
        indicating the time of the last discontinuity.
        The value of the MAX-ACCESS clause for objects
        with a SYNTAX clause of this textual convention
        must be either 'read-only' or 'accessible-for-notify'.
        A DEFVAL clause is not allowed for objects using
        this textual convention.
        The value is restricted to the BER serialization of
        the following ASN.1 type:
            COUNTER64 ::= [118] IMPLICIT Counter64
        (note: the value 118 is the sum of '30'h and '46'h)
        The BER serialization of the length for values of
        this type must use the definite length, short
        encoding form.
        For example, the BER serialization of value 56782 of
        type COUNTER64 is '9f760300ddce'h.  The BER serialization
        of value '9f760300ddce'h of type Opaque is
        '44069f760300ddce'h."
    SYNTAX      Opaque (SIZE(4..12))
```

2.7.15 BIT STRING

The BIT STRING type from ASN.1 was allowed in the original version of SMIv2. However, this new type resulted in incompatibility between SNMPv1 and SNMPv2. It was replaced in an update to SMIv2, since its use was not allowed in IETF-developed MIB modules with the pseudotype BITS. This was done to create backwards compatibility with SNMPv1. Thus, the type BIT STRING must not be used, since it is no longer available and it is not compatible with SNMPv1 or SNMPv2.

2.7.16 BITS Pseudotype

The BITS pseudotype is used for a collection of labelled bits. This pseudotype was introduced in an update of SMIv2 as a mechanism that allowed bits to be labelled, and which was also backwards compatible with SNMPv1. The BITS type is not a new ASN.1 type, but is actually the OCTET STRING type with a way to label individual bits.

Bits are numbered starting at zero and must be contiguously numbered up to the last bit. Each bit is also labelled. The labels consist of 1 to 64 letters and digits. (The SMI does not allow hyphens!) The initial character must be a lowercase letter. Each label in a collection of bits must be unique. (Note: there is no requirement that the labels be unique within a MIB module). There is no restriction specified on the maximum number of bits that can be specified. SMIv2 contains a caution that there may be implementation and interoperability problems when the number of bits is greater then 127.

Our Opinion We believe that SMIv2 should allow hyphens in labels. It this change is made, a hyphen cannot be the last character in a label. Also, a hyphen cannot be immediately followed by another hyphen.

Syntax

<bitsV1> = -- does not exist
<bitsV2> = "BITS" "{" <bitItem> ["," <bitItem>]... "}"

-- bit item, with label *lcName*
<bitItem> = lcName "(" number ")"

where:
number is an unsigned integer

Range

v2 0 to 65535

Examples

v2 BITS { red(0), green(1), blue(2) }
v2 BITS { monday(0), tuesday(1), wednesday(2), thursday(3), friday(4), saturday(5), sunday(6) }

Behavior

Values for the BITS pseudotype are encoded as values for the ASN.1 OCTET STRING type, with the bits packed 8 per octet. (See Figure 2–29) Bits are numbered by their position, starting at zero. Position zero is the high order (or left-most) bit in the first octet of the string. Position 7 is the low order (or right-most) bit of the first octet of the string. Position 8 is the high order bit in the second octet of the string, and so on. When the number of bits is not a multiple of eight, then there will be remaining bits in the final octet. When a value of the pseudotype BITS is encoded, the remaining bits, if any, of the final octet are set to zero. On decoding a value of the pseudotype BITS, the remaining bits, if any, of the final octet are ignored. The bit values are grouped eight per octet (8-bit byte). There are no operations in SNMP to retrieve or modify individual bits within a collection. There are no other behaviors associated with this type.

Encoding of "n" bits, numbered 0 to n-1 in (n+7)/8 octets
note: any remaining bits in the last octet are not used

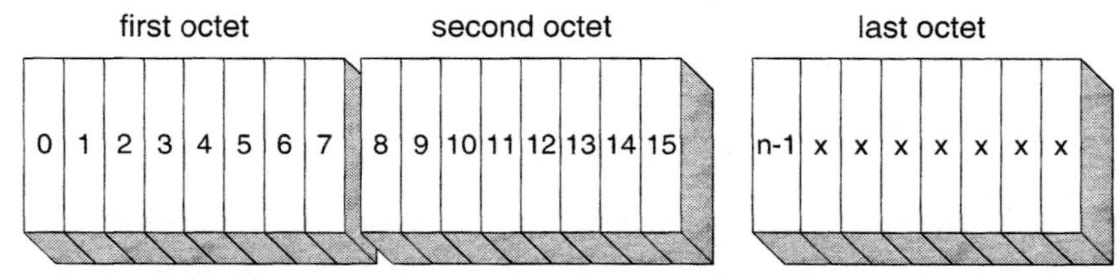

Figure 2–29 Encoding of bits in octets

2.8 Well-Known Textual Conventions

During development of MIB modules using SMIv1, there was no well-defined place to define generally useful textual conventions. They were defined in the modules where they were first needed. During development of SMIv2, the currently existing textual conventions were cleaned up, if needed, and defined in a single MIB module, named SNMPv2-TC. Listed in Table 2–4 are the textual conventions found in that module when this book was written.

Table 2–4 Well-Known Textual Conventions

Name	Syntax	Description
DisplayString	OCTET STRING (SIZE(0..255))	The printable ASCII characters and a few of the control characters
PhysAddress	OCTET STRING	A media- or physical-level address
MacAddress	OCTET STRING (SIZE(6))	An IEEE 802 MAC address in canonical order
TruthValue	INTEGER { true(1), false(2) }	A boolean value
TestAndIncr	Integer32(0..2147483647)	A service number to mediate between competing management applications

Table 2–4 Well-Known Textual Conventions (Continued)

Name	Syntax	Description
AutonomousType	OBJECT IDENTIFIER	The identity of an item
VariablePointer	OBJECT IDENTIFIER	The identity of an SNMP variable
RowPointer	OBJECT IDENTIFIER	The identity of an SNMP variable that is also the first accessible columnar object of a table
RowStatus	INTEGER {active(1), notInService(2), notReady(3), createAndGo(4), createAndWait(5), destroy(6) }	The values for the columnar object controlling the fate of a row in a table
TimeStamp	TimeTicks	The value of object sysUpTime when an event occurred
TimeInterval	Integer32(0..2147483647)	A period of time measured in hundredths of seconds
DateAndTime	OCTET STRING (SIZE (8 | 11))	A date/time specification, optionally including time zone offset
StorageType	INTEGER { other(1), volatile(2), nonVolatile(3), permanent(4), readOnly(5) }	Status and control values for storage of data in a row of a table
TDomain	OBJECT IDENTIFIER	A kind of transport address
TAddress	OCTET STRING (SIZE (1..255))	A transport address

CHAPTER 3

MIB Module Syntax

This chapter walks you through the elements of an SNMP MIB module.

3.1 SNMP MIB Specifications

SNMP MIB specifications are documents containing three sections. The first contains prose descriptions, the next consists of one or more MIB modules, and the last section contains references to other documents. (See Figure 3–1) MIB specifications developed by IETF working groups are published as RFCs. Most vendors either do not produce MIB specifications in such a form, make them available only for internal use, or choose another approach to publish this information. The section containing prose descriptions is quite important for

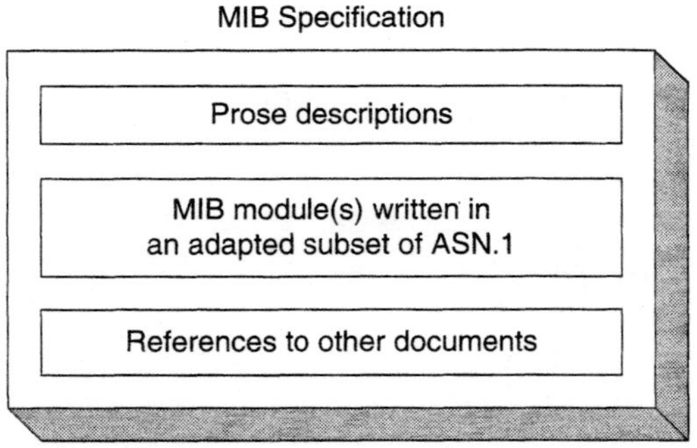

MIB Specification

Prose descriptions

MIB module(s) written in
an adapted subset of ASN.1

References to other documents

Figure 3–1 Contents of a MIB specification

agent developers, management application developers, test engineers, and network operators. Before a device or software can be managed, it must be understood. A MIB specification is not the document to provide the information necessary to understand the device or software. That information is typically provided in architecture and implementation documents, or in "functional specification" documents for the device or software that is being managed. However, the prose descriptions in a MIB specification are needed to map between the managed device or software and the definitions of the management information contained in the MIB module. Also, the prose descriptions are needed to explain interactions between items in a complex MIB module. The reference section completes a MIB specification by providing a list of all the sources used or which can provide additional information to understand the item being managed.

3.2 SNMP MIB Modules

SNMP MIB modules are written in an adapted sub-set of ASN.1. (ASN.1 is a specification language originally designed to specify network protocols.) SNMP MIB modules are meant to be read by people as well as be read by programs. These programs are called MIB compilers. The result of having a specification meant for both people and programs is that the specification is difficult for people to read and for programs to parse and use.

The language used to define items within a MIB module consists of constructs taken directly from ASN.1 and constructs created for SNMP through use of the ASN.1 macro facility. (ASN.1 macros are a mechanism to extend what can be specified in ASN.1 modules. To a user of the ASN.1 language, the macros appear to augment the language with additional constructs.) There are two ASN.1 macros defined in SMIv1. These are the OBJECT-TYPE and TRAP-TYPE macros. In SMIv2 there are nine macros defined. The macros are used to define SNMP management information, SNMP events, administrative assignments, describe SNMP MIB modules, group management information and events, specify the requirements for conformance, and specify implementation characteristics.

Our Opinion

We believe that defining the MIB module language with ASN.1 macros was a poor decision. We believe that the MIB module language is better specified and will be better understood without using ASN.1 macro notation.

Throughout this book, we will not use the term "ASN.1 macro," but will use the term "construct" in describing the statements found in the MIB module language.

Before showing the details for each of the constructs, we have provided an example SNMPv1 MIB module and SNMPv2 MIB module. Both of these MIB modules are trivial, but complete.

3.2.1 Example SNMPv1 MIB module

```
    -- the name of the MIB module is MIBS4YOU-XYZ-MIB
MIBS4YOU-XYZ-MIB DEFINITIONS ::= BEGIN
    -- The imports section specifies items defined in
    -- other modules and referenced in this module.
    -- Note: the imports section must precede the definitions.
```

```
    IMPORTS
        OBJECT-TYPE
            FROM RFC1155-SMI
        m4yXyz
            FROM MIBS4YOU-ROOT-MIB;

-- MIB module for enterprise MIBs4You
-- for management of XYZ.
m4yXyzBase OBJECT IDENTIFIER
    -- base XYZ objects
    ::= { m4yXyz 1 }

m4yXyzArea1 OBJECT IDENTIFIER
    -- objects in area 1 of XYZ
    ::= { m4yXyz 2 }

  -- a definition of management information
m4yXyz01 OBJECT-TYPE
    SYNTAX       INTEGER (1..50)
    ACCESS       read-write
    STATUS       mandatory
    DESCRIPTION
        "The ... "
    ::= { m4yXyzBase 1 }

  -- the rest of the module would go here

END
```

3.2.2 Example SNMPv2 MIB module

```
  -- the name of the MIB module is MIBS4YOU-XYZ-MIB
MIBS4YOU-XYZ-MIB DEFINITIONS ::= BEGIN
  -- The imports section specifies items defined in
  -- other modules and referenced in this module.
  -- Note: the imports section must precede the definitions.
    IMPORTS
        MODULE-IDENTITY, OBJECT-TYPE, Integer32
            FROM SNMPv2-SMI
        m4yModules, m4yXyz
            FROM MIBS4YOU-ROOT-MIB;

  -- SMIv2 requires that an SNMP MIB module contain exactly
  -- one module identity definition that must precede all other
  -- definitions in the MIB module.
  --
  -- The module identity construct specifies the revision history of the
  -- MIB module, the owner/creator of the MIB module, contact information,
  -- and a description of the MIB module.
```

```
mibs4youXyzModule MODULE-IDENTITY
    LAST-UPDATED "9512210000Z" -- December 21, 1995
    ORGANIZATION "MIBs4You"
    CONTACT-INFO
        "        support@mibs4you.xxx

         Postal: MIBs4You
                 1234 Any Street
                 Anytown, XX"
    DESCRIPTION
        "Objects for management of XYZ."
    REVISION    "9512210000Z" -- December 21, 1995
    DESCRIPTION
        "The initial version."
    ::= { m4yModules 10 }

m4yXyzBase OBJECT IDENTIFIER
    -- base XYZ objects
    ::= { m4yXyz 1 }

m4yXyzArea1 OBJECT IDENTIFIER
    -- objects in area 1 of XYZ
    ::= { m4yXyz 2 }

  -- a definition of management information
m4yXyz01 OBJECT-TYPE
    SYNTAX      Integer32 (1..50)
    MAX-ACCESS  read-write
    STATUS      current
    DESCRIPTION
        "The ... "
    ::= { m4yXyzBase 1 }

  -- the rest of the module would go here

END
```

3.3 MIB Module Layout and Elements

MIB modules consist of an outer wrapper which names it and delimits it from other MIB modules. Inside the wrapper is a linkage section, called the IMPORTS section, that specifies items defined in other modules and used in the current module. After the IMPORTS section and before other definitions, SNMPv2 MIB modules are required to define the identity of the MIB module using a MODULE-IDENTITY construct. The remaining contents of a MIB module are definitions. (See Figure 3–2)

There are no constraints on the ordering of these definitions in a MIB module. However, some MIB compilers may require an ordering so that there are no forward references to items.

SNMPv1 MIB Module

<moduleName>
DEFINITIONS ::= BEGIN

<importedItems>

<definitions>

END

SNMPv2 MIB Module

<moduleName>
DEFINITIONS ::= BEGIN

<importedItems>
<moduleIdentityDefinition>

<definitions>

END

Figure 3–2 Layout of an SNMP MIB module

3.4 Lexical Rules for SNMP MIB Modules

An SNMP MIB module is contained in one ASCII file. More than one MIB module may be contained in the same file. The ASCII file consists of a stream of printable characters and line terminators. A file is terminated by an end of file (EOF). The characters form a stream of *tokens*. The tokens are identifiers, keywords, literals (i.e., constants), punctuation, and white space. White space consists of space characters, line terminators, tab characters, and comments. White space is ignored other than for use to separate otherwise adjacent identifiers, keywords, and literals. If the input has been parsed into tokens up to a given character, the next token is the longest string of characters that could possibly constitute a token. For example, if the next part of the input is the string of characters:

```
SYNTAX OFFERTYPE -- a comment
```

then the next tokens are keyword "SYNTAX", white space, identifier "OFFERTYPE", and white space. The identifier "OFFERTYPE" starts with the letters "OF", which happen to be a keyword. However, parsing of input characters for the token does not stop until the white space after "OFFERTYPE" is read.

3.4.1 Comments

Two adjacent hyphens (--) start a comment, which is terminated by a line terminator or two adjacent hyphens. (This duplicates the lexical rules for comments in ASN.1.) However, many MIB compilers only allow comments to be terminated with a line terminator, and a few MIB compilers allow the user to select how comments should be terminated. The hyphens starting the comment and the characters up to and including the first pair of adjacent hyphens or the line terminator are treated as "white space".

Two adjacent hyphens terminating a comment have been a constant source of errors in writing MIB modules.

The problems caused by comments being terminated with a pair of hyphens show up in unexpected places. One common occurrence is during MIB development, when definitions in a MIB module are "commented out." Instead of just prefixing each line in the section to be "commented out" with a pair of hyphens, each existing pair of hyphens that start comments in the commented out section must be changed. Otherwise, these hyphens end a comment, and will cause a syntax error.

```
    -- The following definition is commented out.
    -- The comment on the SYNTAX clause had to be modified
    -- so that it would not cause an error. The two hyphens were
    -- changed to an asterisk and hyphen (*-).
--m4yXyz01 OBJECT-TYPE
--      SYNTAX       Integer32 (1..50)   *- a comment
--      MAX-ACCESS   read-write
--      STATUS       current
--      DESCRIPTION
--          "The ... "
--      ::= { m4yXyzBase 1 }
```

Another situation that can be irritating occurs when a line of hyphens is used to separate a section of a MIB module. If the number of hyphens in the line is 5, 9, 13, etc. (i.e., is a multiple of 4 plus 1), then the last hyphen is not in a comment, and most likely will cause a syntax error. A similar situation occurs when hyphens are used in comments for ASCII drawings such as boxes.

Our Opinion We believe that all of these problems would be eliminated by changing the rule to be that only an end of line terminates a comment.

3.4.2 Identifiers

An identifier consists of 1 to 64 letters, digits, and hyphens. (Note that SMIv2 has restrictions on the use of hyphens.) The initial character must be a letter. A hyphen cannot be the last character of an identifier. A hyphen cannot be immediately followed by another hyphen in an identifier. (NOTE: ASN.1 has no limit on number of characters in an identifier. Otherwise, the lexical rules for identifiers are identical.) There are two types of identifiers which are distinguished by the case of the initial letter. (This classification comes from ASN.1 and is followed in SNMP.) Even though identifiers up to a length of 64 are allowed in SNMP MIB modules, lengths greater than 24 may cause compatibility difficulties with tools that process MIB modules. A sequence of characters that conforms to all the rules for identifiers, except the length is greater than 64 characters is called an "invalid identifier" token. Some MIB compilers treat such tokens as errors and stop parsing input. Others produce a warning and continue parsing as if the token was an identifier.

Caution

In SMIv1, there are no formal rules specified for identifiers in MIB modules. Thus, the rules from ASN.1 were followed (mostly). In SMIv2 the rules were specified. They are a sub-set of the rules from ASN.1. In particular, the maximum length is restricted to 64 characters and hyphens are disallowed in identifiers (except in module names and keywords). The maximum length was chosen by looking at all the existing IETF standards-track MIB modules from RFCs and picking a length greater than any identifier found. The rule to disallow hyphens was added to allow ease of writing tools that used MIB modules as input and generated programming language code, such in C, as output. Unfortunately, there are existing standards track MIB modules written in the SMIv1 format containing identifiers using hyphens. And there are even new standards track MIB modules written in the SMIv2 format containing identifiers using hyphens. The result is that SMIv2 explicitly disallows hyphens in identifiers, yet standard practice allows them.

Our Opinion We believe that the rules should reflect common practice, and thus should be changed to allow hyphens in identifiers.

Some MIB compilers allow an underscore (_) in identifiers. This is not valid in ASN.1 modules or in MIB modules. Underscores versus hyphens for use in identifiers is an old issue in programming language design.

Our Opinion We believe that it is too late to replace hyphens with underscores. However, we believe that the rules should be changed to allow underscores in identifiers.

3.4.3 Keywords

Some identifiers are reserved for use as keywords. This aspect of the language for MIB modules is not explicitly specified in SMIv1 or SMIv2. If the rules from ASN.1 are followed, then only the identifiers explicitly listed in the ASN.1 specification are keywords. However, the common practice in current SNMP MIB compilers is to treat the identifiers used in the SNMP constructs (macros) as keywords and to allow the ASN.1 keywords not used in the SNMP MIB module language to be treated as identifiers. Table 3–1 lists ASN.1 and SNMP keywords and specifies for each its source and usage.

Table 3–1 SNMP and ASN.1 Keywords

Keyword	Source	In ASN.1	In v1	In v2
ABSENT	ASN.1 keyword not used in SNMP	yes	no	no
ACCESS	v1-OBJECT-TYPE construct and v2-AGENT-CAPABILITIES construct	no	yes	yes
AGENT-CAPABILITIES	v2-AGENT-CAPABILITIES construct name	no	no	yes
ANY	ASN.1 keyword not used in SNMP	yes	no	no
APPLICATION	ASN.1 keyword not used in SNMP	yes	no	no
AUGMENTS	v2-OBJECT-TYPE construct	no	no	yes
BEGIN	ASN.1 keyword	yes	yes	yes
BIT	ASN.1 keyword	yes	no	no[a]
BITS	v2-pseudotype	no	no	yes
BOOLEAN	ASN.1 keyword not used in SNMP	yes	no	no
BY	ASN.1 keyword not used in SNMP	yes	no	no
CHOICE	ASN.1 keyword not used in SNMP	yes	no	no
COMPONENT	ASN.1 keyword not used in SNMP	yes	no	no
COMPONENTS	ASN.1 keyword not used in SNMP	yes	no	no
CONTACT-INFO	v2-MODULE-IDENTITY construct	no	no	yes
CREATION-REQUIRES	v2-AGENT-CAPABILITIES construct	no	no	yes
Counter	v1-SMI	no	yes	no
Counter32	v2-SMI	no	no	yes
Counter64	v2-SMI	no	no	yes
DEFAULT	ASN.1 keyword not used in SNMP	yes	no	no
DEFINED	ASN.1 keyword not used in SNMP	yes	no	no
DEFINITIONS	ASN.1 keyword	yes	yes	yes
DEFVAL	v1-OBJECT-TYPE construct, v2-AGENT-CAPABILITIES construct, v2-OBJECT-TYPE construct	no	yes	yes

Table 3–1 SNMP and ASN.1 Keywords (Continued)

Keyword	Source	In ASN.1	In v1	In v2
DESCRIPTION	v1-OBJECT-TYPE construct, v1-TRAP-TYPE construct, v2-AGENT-CAPABILITIES construct, v2-MODULE-COMPLIANCE construct, v2-MODULE-IDENTITY construct, v2-NOTIFICATION-GROUP construct, v2-NOTIFICATION-TYPE construct, v2-OBJECT-GROUP construct, v2-OBJECT-IDENTITY construct, v2-OBJECT-TYPE construct, v2-TEXTUAL-CONVENTION construct	no	yes	yes
DISPLAY-HINT	v2-TEXTUAL-CONVENTION construct	no	no	yes
END	ASN.1 keyword	yes	yes	yes
ENTERPRISE	v1-TRAP-TYPE construct	no	yes	no
ENUMERATED	ASN.1 keyword not used in SNMP	yes	no	no
EXPLICIT	ASN.1 keyword not used in SNMP	yes	no	no
EXPORTS	ASN.1 keyword not used in SNMP	yes	no[b]	no
EXTERNAL	ASN.1 keyword not used in SNMP	yes	no	no
FALSE	ASN.1 keyword not used in SNMP	yes	no	no
FROM	ASN.1 keyword	yes	yes	yes
GROUP	v2-MODULE-COMPLIANCE construct	no	no	yes
Gauge	v1-SMI	no	yes	no
Gauge32	v2-SMI	no	no	yes
IDENTIFIER	ASN.1 keyword	yes	yes	yes
IMPLICIT	ASN.1 keyword not used in SNMP	yes	no	no
IMPLIED	v2-OBJECT-TYPE construct	no	no[c]	yes
IMPORTS	ASN.1 keyword	yes	yes	yes
INCLUDES	ASN.1 keyword not used as intended in SNMP, v2-AGENT-CAPABILITIES construct	yes	no	yes
INDEX	v1-OBJECT-TYPE construct, v2-OBJECT-TYPE construct	no	yes	yes
INTEGER	ASN.1 keyword	yes	yes	yes
Integer32	v2-SMI	no	no	yes
IpAddress	v1-SMI, v2-SMI	no	yes	yes

Table 3–1 SNMP and ASN.1 Keywords (Continued)

Keyword	Source	In ASN.1	In v1	In v2
LAST-UPDATED	v2-MODULE-IDENTITY construct	no	no	yes
MANDATORY-GROUPS	v2-MODULE-COMPLIANCE construct	no	no	yes
MAX	ASN.1 keyword not used in SNMP	yes	no	no
MAX-ACCESS	v2-OBJECT-TYPE construct	no	no	yes
MIN	ASN.1 keyword not used in SNMP	yes	no	no
MIN-ACCESS	v2-MODULE-COMPLIANCE construct	no	no	yes
MINUS-INFINITY	ASN.1 keyword not used in SNMP	yes	no	no
MODULE	v2-MODULE-COMPLIANCE construct	no	no	yes
MODULE-COMPLIANCE	v2-MODULE-COMPLIANCE construct name	no	no	yes
MODULE-IDENTITY	v2-MODULE-IDENTITY construct name	no	no	yes
NOTIFICATION-GROUP	v2-NOTIFICATION-GROUP construct name	no	no	yes
NOTIFICATION-TYPE	v2-NOTIFICATION-TYPE construct name	no	no	yes
NULL	ASN.1 keyword not used in SNMP	yes	no	no
NetworkAddress	v1-SMI	no	yes	no
NsapAddress	v2-SMI	no	no	no[d]
OBJECT	ASN.1 keyword, v2-MODULE-COMPLIANCE construct	yes	yes	yes
OBJECT-GROUP	v2-OBJECT-GROUP construct name	no	no	yes
OBJECT-IDENTITY	v2-OBJECT-IDENTITY construct name	no	no	yes
OBJECT-TYPE	v1-OBJECT-TYPE construct name, v2-OBJECT-TYPE construct name	no	yes	yes
OBJECTS	v2-NOTIFICATION-TYPE construct, v2-OBJECT-GROUP construct	no	no	yes
OCTET	ASN.1 keyword	yes	yes	yes
OF	ASN.1 keyword	yes	yes	yes
OPTIONAL	ASN.1 keyword not used in SNMP	yes	no	no
ORGANIZATION	v2-MODULE-IDENTITY construct	no	no	yes
Opaque	v1-SMI, v2-SMI	no	yes	yes
PLUS-INFINITY	ASN.1 keyword not used in SNMP	yes	no	no
PRESENT	ASN.1 keyword not used in SNMP	yes	no	no

Table 3–1 SNMP and ASN.1 Keywords (Continued)

Keyword	Source	In ASN.1	In v1	In v2
PRIVATE	ASN.1 keyword not used in SNMP	yes	no	no
PRODUCT-RELEASE	v2-AGENT-CAPABILITIES construct	no	no	yes
REAL	ASN.1 keyword not used in SNMP	yes	no	no
REFERENCE	v1-OBJECT-TYPE construct, v1-TRAP-TYPE construct, v2-AGENT-CAPABILITIES construct, v2-MODULE-COMPLIANCE construct, v2-NOTIFICATION-GROUP construct, v2-NOTIFICATION-TYPE construct, v2-OBJECT-GROUP construct, v2-OBJECT-IDENTITY construct, v2-OBJECT-TYPE construct, v2-TEXTUAL-CONVENTION construct	no	yes	yes
REVISION	v2-MODULE-IDENTITY construct	no	no	yes
SEQUENCE	ASN.1 keyword	yes	yes	yes
SET	ASN.1 keyword not used in SNMP	yes	no	no
SIZE	ASN.1 keyword	yes	yes	yes
STATUS	v1-OBJECT-TYPE construct, v2-AGENT-CAPABILITIES construct, v2-MODULE-COMPLIANCE construct, v2-NOTIFICATION-GROUP construct, v2-NOTIFICATION-TYPE construct, v2-OBJECT-GROUP construct, v2-OBJECT-IDENTITY construct, v2-OBJECT-TYPE construct, v2-TEXTUAL-CONVENTION construct	no	yes	yes
STRING	ASN.1 keyword	yes	yes	yes
SUPPORTS	v2-AGENT-CAPABILITIES construct	no	no	yes
SYNTAX	v1-OBJECT-TYPE construct, v2-OBJECT-TYPE construct, v2-AGENT-CAPABILITIES construct, v2-MODULE-COMPLIANCE construct, v2-TEXTUAL-CONVENTION construct	no	yes	yes
TAGS	ASN.1 keyword not used in SNMP	yes	no	no
TEXTUAL-CONVEN-TION	v1-TEXTUAL-CONVENTION construct name	no	no	yes
TRAP-TYPE	v1-TRAP-TYPE construct name	no	yes	no
TRUE	ASN.1 keyword not used in SNMP	yes	no	no

Table 3–1 SNMP and ASN.1 Keywords (Continued)

Keyword	Source	In ASN.1	In v1	In v2
TimeTicks	v1-SMI, v2-SMI	no	yes	yes
UInteger32	v2-SMI	no	no	no[e]
UNITS	v2-OBJECT-TYPE construct	no	no	yes
UNIVERSAL	ASN.1 keyword not used in SNMP	yes	no	no
Unsigned32	v2-SMI	no	no	yes
VARIABLES	v1-TRAP-TYPE construct	no	yes	no
VARIATION	v2-AGENT-CAPABILITIES construct	no	no	yes
WITH	ASN.1 keyword not used in SNMP	yes	no	no
WRITE-SYNTAX	v2-AGENT-CAPABILITIES construct, v2-MODULE-COMPLIANCE construct	no	no	yes

a. existed in the original version of SMIv2

b. the SMI was silent on whether it could or could not be used

c. provided in SMIC/SMICng MIB compiler for compatibility between SMIv1 and SMIv2

d. existed in the original version of SMIv2

e. existed in the original version of SMIv2

3.4.4 Punctuation

The following is a list of single characters used as punctuation tokens in SNMP MIB modules:

```
{ left curly brace
} right curly brace
( left parenthesis
) right parenthesis
; semicolon
, coma
- hyphen (dash)
. period
| vertical bar
```

The following is a list of character combinations used as punctuation tokens in SNMP MIB modules:

```
.. two periods
::= two colons and an equal sign
```

(NOTE: ASN.1 has additional single character punctuation tokens which are not used in SNMP MIB modules.)

Any character or sequence of characters from the ASCII character set not defined elsewhere in this section on lexical rules is called an "invalid punctuation" token. Some MIB compilers treat such tokens as errors and stop parsing input. Others produce a warning and continue parsing as if the token was white space.

3.4.5 Literals

The literals (or constants) in SNMP MIB modules are unsigned numbers, character strings, hexadecimal strings, and binary strings. (NOTE: the literals in ASN.1 are defined quite differently.) The description of each SNMP literal follows:

Unsigned numbers

Unsigned numbers consist of one or more digits. Leading zeros are not allowed. The value of an unsigned number ranges from zero to 4294967295. An unsigned number with one or more leading zeros, an unsigned number with a value greater than 4294967295, or a sequence of one or more digits followed by a letter with no separating white space or punctuation is called an "invalid number" token. Some MIB compilers treat such tokens as errors and stop parsing input. Others produce a warning and continue parsing as if the token was a number.

```
Example unsigned numbers:
    0 - valid
    01 - invalid (leading zero)
    56 - valid
    4294967296 - invalid (value too large)
    34Alert - invalid (digits must be separated from letters
                by white space or punctuation)
```

Character Strings

Character strings are started with a leading quote (") and are terminated with a trailing quote ("). A character string may not contain a quote. A string may be continued across multiple lines and contains the embedded line separators. (A line separator is encoded in a quoted string token as the newline, the '\n', character.))

The maximum number of characters in a character string is not restricted in SMIv1 or SMIv2.

A reasonable value of 8192 or fewer characters should be observed for maximum interoperability. (NOTE: the leading quote and trailing quote are not characters in the string.) A string containing more than the maximum number of characters (i.e., 8192) or a string terminated by the end of file is called an "invalid character string" token. Some MIB compilers treat such tokens as errors and stop parsing input. Others produce a warning and continue parsing as if the token was a string. Note: MIB compilers have much difficulty trying to recover from errors caused by missing quotes around strings.

```
Example character strings:
    "example string" - valid
    "a 'quoted' item" - valid (apostrophes are allowed in strings)
    "a "quote" example" - invalid (quotes are not allowed in strings)
```

```
"a ""quote"" example" - invalid (quotes are not allowed in
                         strings and two quotes cannot
                         be used to specify a quote)
"a multi-line
string is just fine" - valid
```

Hexadecimal Strings

Hexadecimal strings are started by an apostrophe (') and terminated by an apostrophe followed by the letter "H" written in upper or lower case. The content of the string is zero, one, or several characters from the digits, and the letters "A" through "F" written in upper or lower case. The leading apostrophe and trailing apostrophe (and letter "h") are not included in the string. The maximum number of digits in a hexadecimal string is not restricted in SMIv1 or SMIv2. However, a reasonable value of 128 or fewer digits should be observed for maximum interoperability. A hexadecimal string containing invalid characters, having a length longer than the maximum (i.e., 128), or terminated by the end of file is called an "invalid hexadecimal string" token. Some MIB compilers treat such tokens as errors and stop parsing input. Others produce a warning and continue parsing as if the token was a hexadecimal string. (NOTE: hexadecimal strings in ASN.1 may use only uppercase letters and must be terminated with an apostrophe followed by an uppercase letter "H". Also, ASN.1 imposes no maximum length.)

```
Example hexadecimal strings:
        '1A3B5C'H - valid
        '1a3b5c'h - valid
        '23jk'h - invalid (only digits and letters a thru f)
        'ab123' h - invalid (no space allowed between ' and h)
        "9872"h - invalid (must use ' and not ")
        0x4578 - invalid (the format used in C is not valid)
        '02345h - invalid (missing final ')
```

Binary Strings

Binary strings are started by an apostrophe (') and terminated by an apostrophe followed by the letter "B" written in upper or lower case. The content of the string is zero, one, or more zero (0) or one (1) digits. The leading apostrophe and trailing apostrophe (and letter "b") are not included in the string. The maximum number of digits in a binary string is not restricted in SMIv1 or SMIv2. However, a reasonable value of 128 or fewer digits should be observed for maximum interoperability. A string containing invalid characters, having a length longer than the maximum (i.e., 128), or terminated by the end of file is called an "invalid binary string" token. Some MIB compilers treat such tokens as errors and stop parsing input. Others produce a warning and continue parsing as if the token was a binary string. (NOTE: binary strings in ASN.1 must be terminated with an apostrophe followed by an uppercase letter "B". Also, ASN.1 imposes no maximum length.)

```
Example binary strings:
    '000110'B - valid
    '000110'b - valid
    '123'b - invalid (only digits 0 and 1)
    '01100' b - invalid (no space allowed between ' and b)
```

```
"1100"b - invalid (must use ' and not ")
'011b - invalid (missing final ')
```

3.5 Constructs in MIB Modules

The constructs in a MIB module consist of the IMPORTS statement, followed by definitions. The IMPORTS statement specifies items that are defined in other MIB modules and used in the current MIB module. The definitions are either ASN.1 "type assignments" to define textual conventions and sequences, or ASN.1 "value assignments" to define all other items in a MIB module.

Textual conventions are defined in SNMPv1 using an ASN.1 type assignment written as "<TCidentifier> ::= <type>", where <TCidentifier> is the identifier for a textual convention, which starts with an uppercase letter, and <type>, which may be optionally sub-typed, is an SNMP basic type or a previously defined textual convention. In SMIv2, textual conventions may additionally be defined with the TEXTUAL-CONVENTION construct, which includes several clauses to specify information in parsable formats. The pattern for the construct is:

```
<TCidentifier> "::=" "TEXTUAL-CONVENTION"
        <clauses>
        "SYNTAX" <type>
where
      <type> is basic SNMP type or a previously defined textual convention
```

Sequence definitions are also an ASN.1 type assignment and written as "<SeqIdentifier> ::= SEQUENCE { <seqMembers> }". Item <SeqIdentifier> is an identifier, starting with an uppercase letter, and <seqMembers> is a list of members of the sequence.

There are two types of value assignments. The first is an OID value assignment. The format is "<OIDvalueIdentifier> OBJECT IDENTIFER ::= <OIDvalue>", where <OIDvalueIdentifier> is the identifier for the OID value and <OIDvalue> is an OID value. The second type is used for all other value assignments. The pattern for the construct is:

```
<identifierForValue> <constructName>
        <clauses>
        "::=" <value>
where
      <identifierForValue> is the identifier for the item that is being defined
      <constructName> is one of constructs such as OBJECT-TYPE,
          TRAP-TYPE, MODULE-COMPLIANCE, OBJECT-IDENTITY, etc.
      <value> is an integer for the TRAP-TYPE construct, and an
          OID value for all other constructs
```

Table 3–2 lists the constructs that are used to define items in SNMP MIB modules.

Table 3–2 Constructs used to Define Items in SNMP MIB Modules

Construct	Description	In ASN.1	In v1	In v2
OID value assignment	Names an OID value. Note: this is not a registration of the OID value	yes	yes	yes
Textual Convention assignment	Names a type and may specify constraints on the values	yes	yes	yes
TEXTUAL-CONVENTION definition	Defines a type and may specify constraints on the values	no	no	yes
OBJECT-TYPE definition	Defines management information and registers it with an OID value	no	yes[a]	yes
TRAP-TYPE definition	Defines an event and identifies it with two numbers and an OID value	no	yes	no
SEQUENCE definition	Specifies the columns in an SNMP table	yes	yes	yes
MODULE-IDENTITY definition	Specifies information about an SNMP MIB module and registers the module with an OID value	no	no	yes
OBJECT-IDENTITY definition	Defines a unique item and registers it with an OID value	no	no	yes
NOTIFICATION-TYPE definition	Defines an event and registers it with an OID value	no	no	yes
OBJECT-GROUP definition	Groups management information and registers that grouping with an OID value	no	no	yes
NOTIFICATION-GROUP definition	Groups events and registers that grouping with an OID value	no	no	yes
MODULE-COMPLIANCE definition	Specifies requirements for compliance and registers that requirements specification with an OID value	no	no	yes
AGENT-CAPABILITIES definition	Specifies implementation characteristics and registers that implementation specification with an OID value	no	no	yes

a. Even though the name is the same, the clauses of the OBJECT-TYPE construct are quite different in SNMPv1 from those in SNMPv2

3.6 MIB Module Names

The outer wrapper of a MIB module contains its name, which is an identifier with hyphens allowed. SMIv2 requires that all standards-track MIB modules have unique names. It also requires that different versions of the same MIB module have the same name. The SMIv2 required MODULE-IDENTITY construct, which specifies revision information, can be used to distinguish between versions of the same MIB module. SMIv1 provides no guidance on this subject. Thus, the original MIB modules in RFCs were named based on the RFC number.

As a MIB module was updated and republished with a new RFC number, its name was also changed. This caused problems with the linkage between MIB modules. The practice was changed and a rule specified in SMIv2 that module names are not modified when a module is republished.

Now, by convention, IETF MIB modules are named by the subject of the MIB module in uppercase letters with a suffix of "-MIB". For example, the following are names of MIB modules: EtherLike-MIB (an exception to the convention), APPLETALK-MIB, and RMON-MIB. The names of MIB modules must follow the rules for identifiers in MIB modules with the initial character restricted to an uppercase letter and hyphens allowed. There are no length restrictions on the name of a MIB module specified in the SMI. However, for the greatest interoperability, MIB module names should be limited to 16 characters or less. (Some MIB tools assume that the ASCII file containing a MIB module has the same name as the MIB module plus an extension. For these tools, long MIB module names may run into filename length restrictions of the operating system where the tools are running.)

Caution

The IETF and other standards organizations sometimes forget that they are not the only standards organization. With module naming, a better convention for naming might have been names prefixed with "IETF-", then followed by the subject of the MIB module, and finally a suffix of "-MIB". For example, RMON-MIB would be named IETF-RMON-MIB. Without such naming conventions, there is a high probability that another organization will create modules using names that are already in use. This will result in much confusion.

SMIv2 disallows the ASN.1 syntax of specifying an OID value between a module name and the keyword "DEFINITIONS". Some MIB tools require this syntax. However, it has never been used in IETF-standard track MIB modules and SMIv2 prohibits it.

Syntax

```
-- a file containing one or more MIB modules
<mibFile> = <mibModule>...

-- a MIB module, with name ucName
<mibModule> =
        ucName "DEFINITIONS" "::=" "BEGIN"
        [ "IMPORTS" <importsFrom>... ";" ]
        [ <definition> ]...
        "END"
```

where

ucName is an identifier that starts with an uppercase letter (and usually contains no lowercase letters);

<importsFrom> is a list of items and the module where they are defined; and

<definition> is the construct for a definition.

Examples

```
-- Note that the name of the module should include the name (or an abbreviation)
-- of the enterprise (or organization) creating the module, and a
-- functional description of the contents of the module.

-- Example showing the typical style.
-- This module is for company BigCo and contains the top level (or root)
-- definitions for the OID sub-tree allocated to BigCo.
BIGCO-ROOT-MIB DEFINITIONS ::= BEGIN
-- rest of module would go here
END

-- Example showing another style.
-- (Note that some MIB tools may not function correctly when the
-- module name and the tokens "DEFINITIONS ::= BEGIN" are
-- on separate lines. However, there is no requirement that they
-- be on the same line.)
-- This module is for industry consortium ERV (Ethernet Repeater
-- Vendors) and contains extensions to the IETF's Ethernet repeater
-- MIB for topology determination.
ERV-ETHTOP-MIB
DEFINITIONS ::= BEGIN
-- rest of module would go here
END
```

3.7 IMPORTS Construct

The IMPORTS construct is used to specify items used in the current MIB module which are defined in another MIB module or ASN.1 module. The IMPORTS construct contains one or more <importsFrom> clauses. Each <importsFrom> clause contains a list of items and the name of the module where they are defined. A module may be specified in only one <importsFrom> clause. The <importsFrom> clauses may be arranged in any order.

All items defined in the current MIB module must use a unique identifier. However, items from another module may be defined with the same identifier as an item defined in the current module. This is allowed in ASN.1 modules and allowed in non-standards-track MIB modules. (However, SMIv1 and SMIv2 require all identifiers used for items defined in standards-track MIB modules to be unique.) When an item that has been imported is referenced in a MIB module, just the identifier is used unless another imported item or item defined in the MIB module uses the same identifier. In this case, the imported item is referenced by specifying the module name and the identifier for the item, separated by a period.

Syntax

```
<imports> = "IMPORTS" <importsFrom>... ";"

-- an "imports from" sub-clause
<importsFrom> =
```

```
    <importsName> [ "," <importsName> ]...
        "FROM" <moduleIdentifier>

-- name of imported item, lcName is an item defined with an OID value
-- and ucName is a textual convention
<importsName> = lcName | ucName | <snmpConstructOrTypeName>

-- identifier of a module, ucName is the name of a module
<moduleIdentifier> = ucName [<oidValue>]
```

where:

lcName is an identifier that starts with a lowercase letter;
ucName is an identifier that starts with an uppercase letter;
<snmpConstructOrTypeName> is the name of an SNMP type or construct defined in one of the SMI MIB modules; and
<oidValue> is an OID value.

Examples

```
  -- a typical IMPORTS construct found in a SNMPv1 MIB module
IMPORTS
    Counter, Gauge
        FROM RFC1155-SMI
    DisplayString
        FROM RFC1213-MIB
    OBJECT-TYPE
        FROM RFC-1212
    TRAP-TYPE
        FROM RFC-1215;

  -- a typical IMPORTS construct found in a SNMPv2 MIB module
IMPORTS
    OBJECT-TYPE, MODULE-IDENTITY, NOTIFICATION-TYPE,
    Counter32, Gauge32
        FROM SNMPv2-SMI
    MODULE-COMPLIANCE, OBJECT-GROUP, NOTIFICATION-GROUP
        FROM SNMPv2-CONF
    TEXTUAL-CONVENTION, DisplayString, TimeStamp
        FROM SNMPv2-TC;

  -- An unusual IMPORTS construct found in a SNMPv2 MIB module.
  -- This example is unusual because it includes an OID value to identify
  -- a MIB module. This is needed because the names of the two
  -- MIB modules are the same! If MIB modules are named by
  -- specifying the name of the enterprise (or organization) and
  -- functional area of the MIB module, then the probability of
  -- name conflicts is greatly reduced.
IMPORTS
    OBJECT-TYPE, MODULE-IDENTITY, Counter32, Gauge32
```

```
        FROM SNMPv2-SMI
    MODULE-COMPLIANCE, OBJECT-GROUP
        FROM SNMPv2-CONF
    bigcoModules
        FROM BIGCO-ROOT-MIB
    itemA
        FROM BIGCO-D1A-MIB { bigcoModules 1 }
    itemB
        FROM BIGCO-D1B-MIB { bigcoModules 99 };
```

An OID value is only needed (and may only be used) to identify a module when items from two different MIB modules are imported and those MIB modules have the same name. This may happen when MIB modules are created in two separate organizations, and these organizations do not choose unique prefixes for their MIB module names. In this case, one (or both) of the MIB modules must be specified with a name that is unique within the MIB module containing the IMPORTS construct. The OID value from the MODULE-IDENTITY construct in the referenced MIB module is used to identify the MIB module in the IMPORTS construct.

Example

```
  -- This example is for SMIv2, since the MODULE-IDENTITY
  -- construct does not exist in SMIv1.

  -- first module named BIGCO-D1-MIB
BIGCO-D1-MIB DEFINITIONS ::= BEGIN
  -- IMPORTS construct not shown

  -- module identity construct is required to use a unique OID value
bigcoD1Module MODULE-IDENTITY
    -- clauses of MODULE-IDENTITY construct not shown
    ::= { bigcoModules 1 }

  -- rest of MIB module
END

  --second module named MY-D1-MIB
BIGCO-D1-MIB DEFINITIONS ::= BEGIN
  -- IMPORTS construct not shown

  -- module identity construct is required to use a unique OID value
bigcoD1Module MODULE-IDENTITY
    -- clauses of MODULE-IDENTITY construct not shown
    ::= { bigcoModules 99 }

  -- rest of MIB module
END
```

```
    --another module which needs to reference items defined in both
    -- of the identically named modules
BIGCO-D2-MIB DEFINITIONS ::= BEGIN
IMPORTS
    bigcoModules
        FROM BIGCO-ROOT-MIB
    a, b FROM
        BIGCO-D1A-MIB { bigcoModules 1 }
    b, c FROM
        BIGCO-D1B-MIB { bigcoModules 99 }
    -- rest of IMPORTS construct

    -- References to 'a' specify only 'a' since no other item that
    -- is defined or imported use 'a' for its identifier.
a2 OBJECT IDENTIFIER ::= { a 1 }

    -- References to 'b' must include the module as named in
    -- the IMPORTS construct since there is more than one
    -- item using identifier 'b' within the module.
b2a OBJECT IDENTIFIER ::= { BIGCO-D1A-MIB.b 1 }
b2b OBJECT IDENTIFIER ::= { BIGCO-D1B-MIB.b 1 }

    -- If an item is defined with identifier 'c', then imported
    -- item with identifier 'c' must specify the module name
    -- when it is referenced.
c OBJECT IDENTIFIER ::= { BIGCO-D1B-MIB.c 2 }

    -- rest of MIB module

END
```

Caution

The examples clearly show how messy and confusing that naming can become when poor choices are made for module names and for the items defined in the modules. Also, most MIB compilers and other tools which process SNMP MIB modules cannot cope with duplicate names used together in a single MIB module. So be cautious with your naming.

The IMPORTS construct specifies indirectly which type of MIB module is being defined, that is, whether the MIB module is written using the rules from SMIv1 or SMIv2. All imported SNMP constructs and types must originate from modules from the same SMI version. Only textual conventions or items defined with an associated OID value which are defined in one MIB module may be imported into another MIB module. (Note: the MIB modules do not have to be written using the same SMI version.) Note that neither sequences nor events defined with the TRAP-TYPE construct may be imported.

Most MIB compilers do an incomplete job of correctly processing the IMPORTS construct. The support ranges from requiring that no IMPORTS be specified; to checking whether it is present and skipping over it; to searching for specific items or module names such as DisplayString, RFC1155-SMI, or OBJECT-TYPE; and to fully checking the items in the IMPORTS construct for existence and valid usage.

Our Opinion

The IMPORTS construct is taken directly from ASN.1. It is difficult for MIB compiler writers to implement it, and it causes problems for MIB authors. The IMPORTS construct is quite different from linkage in programming languages. We believe that MIB modules would be much easier to write, read, and maintain if the IMPORTS construct was replaced with another mechanism for linkage.

3.8 Common Clauses

Many of the MIB constructs have identical clauses. These are the STATUS clause to specify the status of the definition, the DESCRIPTION clause to provide a textual description of the item being defined, and the REFERENCE clause to specify the source of the definition (such as a document from another standards organization, or an architectural document for a proprietary system). Instead of duplicating the descriptions of these clauses, all of these clauses are shown below:

Syntax for STATUS Clause

```
<statusClauseV1> = "STATUS" <statusV1>
<statusClauseV2> = "STATUS" <statusV2>

-- SMIv1 values for status. NOTE that these are not reserved keywords
<statusV1> = "mandatory" | "optional" | "deprecated" | "obsolete"

-- SMIv2 values for status. NOTE that these are
-- not reserved keywords
<statusV2> = "current" | "deprecated" | "obsolete"
```

Syntax for DESCRIPTION Clause

```
<descriptionClause> = "DESCRIPTION" chrStr
```

where

chrStr is a quoted character string which may span multiple lines

Syntax for REFERENCE Clause

```
<referenceClause> = "REFERENCE" chrStr
```

where

chrStr is a quoted character string which may span multiple lines

STATUS Clause

The use and values of the STATUS clause have changed between SMIv1 and SMIv2. In SMIv1 the STATUS clause is used to specify two attributes of definitions. The first attribute is the validity of the definition, that is, whether the definition is well conceived, replaced with another, flawed, or no longer relevant. The second attribute is the level of need for the definition, that is, whether support for the definition is required or is optional. These two attributes are combined into one set of values for the STATUS clause for SMIv1. This approach caused confusion, and thus the usage of the STATUS clause was changed in SMIv2 to specify only the validity of a definition, and not the conformance requirements. With the change of usage, the value "optional" was eliminated and the value "mandatory" was replaced by "current". The conformance aspect of a definition is specified with the MODULE-COMPLIANCE construct in SMIv2. A valid definition has the following properties:

- It is well conceived. The definition is precise, unambiguous, complete, and applicable across a wide scope.
- It is relevant. It is useful and has been used (or soon will be used) for implementation.

On the other hand, an invalid definition has the following properties:

- It is flawed. This can be due to technical inaccuracies or to an extremely limited scope of applicability.
- It is no longer relevant. The definition was redundant with another, never implemented, or its implementation provided little or no benefit.

Table 3–3 contains the definition for each of the values of the STATUS clause.

Table 3–3 Values for the STATUS clause

Value	Description	In v1	In v2
mandatory	The definition is valid and implementation is required for conformance.	yes	no
current	The definition is valid.	no	yes
optional	The definition is valid, however implementation is not required for conformance. NOTE: there has been much confusion as to the exact meaning and allowed usage of this value. The mainstream view is that a value of optional is not allowed in SNMP MIB modules.	yes	no
deprecated	The definition is valid in limited circumstances (and in SMIv1, implementation is required for conformance), but has been replaced by another. The new definition typically encompasses a wider scope, or has been changed to ease implementation.	yes	yes
obsolete	The definition is not valid. It was found to be flawed; could not be implemented; was redundant or not useful; or was no longer relevant. The definition may, but need not be, replaced with another.	yes	yes

The value *deprecated*, which was added in an update to SMIv1 and carried forward in SMIv2, has caused confusion to authors and users of MIB modules. This value was added to clearly document that a definition from the core IETF MIB definitions (i.e., the address translation table in MIB-II) had been found to be limited in scope. The management information was implemented in systems and useful, but it could not be extended to support network protocols other than IP. A new table, the IP network to media table, was created for the IP protocol, and instructions were given for other protocols to create similar tables. At this point, you may wonder, "why not just fix a flawed definition or expand a definition with limited scope?" The problem is that once a definition has been published and an OID value registered to it, the definition may not be changed. It is quite difficult to determine the users of the definition and get them to use a replacement. The lowest cost approach, and the one required in ASN.1 modules and SNMP MIB modules, is to create a new definition that corrects the flaws or expands the scope and register it with a new OID value. There is one rule of MIB design which may not be broken. It is the prime directive for MIB designers:

> *New versions of MIB modules may:*
> *1) change the status of object types to obsolete (if necessary), but may not delete their definitions;*
> *2) define new columnar object types for an existing table; or*
> *3) define entirely new object types.*
>
> *New versions may not:*
> *1) change the semantics of any previously defined object type.*

Caution

The STATUS clause appears to be quite simple in concept and specification. However, its definition and usage have not been clearly specified in SMI documents, and its definition has been somewhat trivialized in the SNMP community. The following text from "The Simple Book" defines each status value:

> **current**, *indicates that the definition is current*
> **deprecated**, *indicates that the definition will soon be made obsolete and need no longer be implemented*
> **obsolete**, *indicates the managed nodes shouldn't implement this object*

These values are often quoted, and unfortunately do not tell the complete story. (See Table 3–3)

MIB modules are designed, reviewed, published, implemented, and maintained. The prime directive for MIB design requires that once a definition has been published, that its semantics cannot be changed and that it cannot be "removed." For the IETF, published means posted as an RFC. Posting a work-in-progress in the internet-drafts directory does not qualify as being published. The IETF standards process requires that standards-track documents be reviewed at each level before advancement. At each review, definitions are checked to determine if they have been implemented and are useful. If not, then a new and better definition is created, or the definition is retired. The following diagram (Figure 3–3) shows the life cycle of definitions:

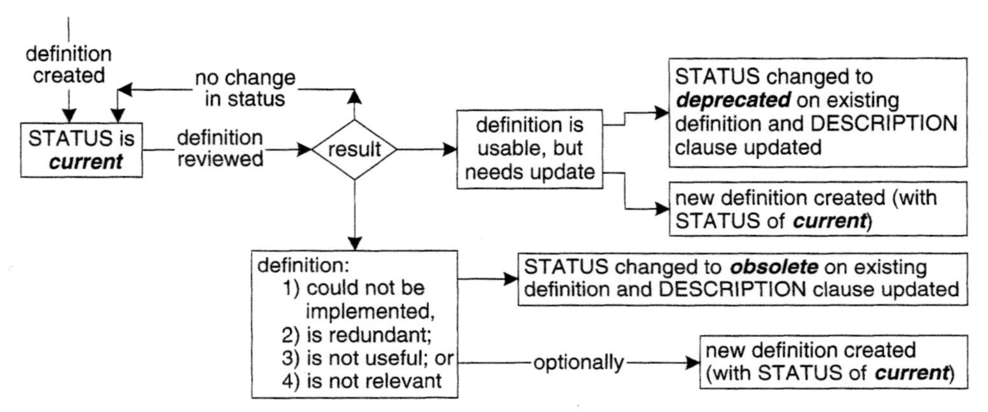

Figure 3–3 Life cycle of Definitions in a MIB module

MIB designers try to accomplish conflicting goals in creating definitions in a MIB module. The definitions must describe a current system implementation of a technology, but must also try to anticipate future implementations and changes in the technology. If definitions map too tightly to current implementations, then any additions or modifications will most likely break the mapping, resulting in the definitions becoming useless. However, if the definitions are too abstract or too broad in scope, they may not be understood or used correctly. Also, extensive definitions will be more costly to implement and test.

Development and use of products containing implementations of definitions from MIB modules happens over time. Usually, managed systems containing agents that support the definitions are fielded three to nine months (or more) before sophisticated management applications. Management capabilities must be used to learn which parts are useful.

Experience has shown that MIB designers cannot always get all definitions right at the time the MIB is first published. Also, different sets of agent and management application developers use the definitions in a MIB module at different points in the life cycle of the MIB module. For example, "bleeding edge" developers may be the designers of the original MIB module. Developers of mass market products may not develop implementations until after the MIB module has reached "Full Standard" status.

Table 3–4 contains the actions that should be followed by agent and management application developers for changes of STATUS. (Note that when the status of a definition is changed, SMIv2 requires that the text of the DESCRIPTION clause be updated.)

Table 3–4 Actions on change of STATUS

Change	Action for Agent Implementors	Action for Management Application Implementors
object created with STATUS of **mandatory** or **current**	should implement the object if the resource modeled by the definition is present on the system	can use the object, if needed, by the application
object created with STATUS of **optional** *(not valid in standards track MIBs)*	should treat the object as if the definition had a STATUS of current. Whether the object is implemented depends on the requirements.	should not use the object, since it probably is not well conceived and probably not widely implemented
object has current STATUS of **deprecated**	should treat the object as if the definition had a STATUS of current. Whether the object is implemented depends on the requirement for compatibility with existing management applications. The replacement object should be implemented if the deprecated object is implemented.	should treat the object as if the definition had a STATUS of current. The object should not be used as the primary access to the management information. Instead, the replacement object should be used. However, if compatibility is required with existing agents, then the application should first try to access the replacement object, and only if it is not implemented, should the application try to access the object whose definition has a STATUS of deprecated.
STATUS changed to **deprecated**	should implement the replacement object for the next released version of the agent. Whether the object whose STATUS is deprecated should be removed depends on the resources needed to support it and the requirement for compatibility with existing management applications.	should implement the replacement object for the next released version of the application. The primary access to the management information should be changed to use the replacement object. However, if compatibility is required with existing agents, then the application should first try to access the replacement object, and only if it is not implemented should the application try to access the object whose definition had its STATUS changed to deprecated.
object has current STATUS of **obsolete**	should not implement the object. If a replacement object has been defined, it should be implemented if applicable.	should not use the object.
STATUS changed to **obsolete**	may remove the object. If a replacement object has been defined, it should be implemented if applicable.	should remove use of the object in applications and review their application for proper design assumptions.

Below are a few examples that show the result of changing the status of a definition:

```
-- The status of an object changed from "current" to "deprecated"

atNetAddress OBJECT-TYPE
  SYNTAX  NetworkAddress
  ACCESS  read-write
  STATUS  deprecated
  DESCRIPTION
    "The NetworkAddress (e.g., the IP address)
    corresponding to the media-dependent `physical'
    address.
    **NOTE: this object is deprecated and replaced by
    ipNetToMediaNetAddress from table ipNetToMediaTable
    and by similar objects in protocol specific tables."
  ::= { atEntry 3 }

-- The status of an object changed from "current" to "obsolete"

ospfAuthType OBJECT-TYPE
  SYNTAX   Integer32
  MAX-ACCESS   read-create
  STATUS   obsolete
  DESCRIPTION
    "**NOTE: this object is obsolete.  Authentication is done
    on each interface.  See table ospfIfTable and object
    ospfIfAuthType."
  REFERENCE
    "OSPF Version 2, Appendix E Authentication"
  DEFVAL { 0 }         -- no authentication, by default
  ::= { ospfAreaEntry 2 }
```

The "obsolete" value is meant to document the existence of a retired definition. However, it can be observed (and even in IETF standards track MIB modules) that these definitions have been removed in updated versions of the containing document. This is bad, and also is counter to the prime directive for MIB design. No definitions may ever be removed from published MIB modules!

Of course, it is possible to create a new MIB module to contain obsolete definitions. For example, RFC 1232 contains a MIB module for managing DS1 interfaces. It was replaced by RFC 1406, which replaced all definitions in RFC 1232. The items defined in RFC 1232 were not included in RFC 1406 and marked as "obsolete." Thus RFC 1406 is not in compliance with the prime directive for MIB design. The action by the WG was an exception case. There were approximately 50 objects in RFC 1232 that were made obsolete by the publishing of RFC 1406. Including the definitions for them in the MIB module in RFC 1406 may have obscured replacement definitions or confused the document readers. These problems should have been addressed by either ordering the definitions in the MIB module so that the obsolete ones were placed after the current ones, or preferably, the obsolete definitions moved to another MIB module (contained in RFC 1406). Either one of these approaches would be compliant to the prime directive for MIB design.

3.9 UTC Time Format

Several of the MIB constructs require that a date and time be specified. The format used is a restricted version of the UTC (coordinated universal time) time format from ASN.1. A time value is a quoted character string consisting of 10 digits that specify the date and time followed by the uppercase letter Z. The digits have the following format:

Format of UTC time

YYMMDDHHmmZ

where:

YY is the last two digits of the year;
MM is the month (01 through 12);
DD is the day (01 through 31);
HH is the hour (00 through 23);
mm is the minute (00 through 59); and
Z is the uppercase letter "Z" which denotes Greenwich Mean Time (GMT).

Examples

```
"9601020812Z" represents 8:12am GMT on January 2, 1996

"9509131455Z" represents 2:55pm GMT on September 13, 1995

"9507220000Z" represents midnight(12am) GMT on July 22, 1996
```

3.10 MODULE-IDENTITY Construct

The MODULE-IDENTITY construct is used to specify information about SNMP MIB modules. This includes the revision history, the name of the organization that has authority over the definitions created, a contact for technical queries, and a high-level description of the module. A MODULE-IDENTITY construct must be specified exactly once and must be the first item defined in an SNMPv2 MIB module. (This construct is not present in SMIv1.)

Syntax

```
-- MODULE-IDENTITY definition, with identifier lcName
<MIdefinition> =
            lcName "MODULE-IDENTITY"
                   "LAST-UPDATED" <UTCtime>
                   "ORGANIZATION" chrStr
                   "CONTACT-INFO" chrStr
                   "DESCRIPTION" chrStr
```

[<revItem>]...
"::=" <oidValue>

-- revision item for MODULE-IDENTITY
<revItem> =
"REVISION" <UTCtime>
"DESCRIPTION" chrStr

where

lcName is an identifier that starts with a lowercase letter;
<UTCtime> is a date and time expressed in UTC time;
<oidValue> is an object identifier value; and
chrStr is a quoted character string which may span multiple lines.

Examples

-- The following example shows a style typical for an organization.
-- Some items of distinction include:
-- 1) the identifier used for the construct uses the organization's
-- name to increase the probability that the identifier will be unique.
-- 2) the identifier is a simple transformation of the MIB module name
-- by removing hyphens, using upper- and lowercase letters, and
-- by replacing "MIB" by "Module".
-- 3) a support group, and not an individual, is specified
-- as the technical contact.
-- 4) the description is used to specify a copyright notice
-- and grants a license to use the MIB module (and of course, you
-- should consult your legal counsel for advice, since the text below
-- is only for illustration).
-- 5) the MIB module is maintained in a source control system and
-- the REVISION/DESCRIPTION clause is used to store the source control
-- system information.

```
bigcoRootModule MODULE-IDENTITY
    LAST-UPDATED "9512201200Z"
    ORGANIZATION "BigCo, Inc."
    CONTACT-INFO
        "Contact: Customer Support Group

          Postal: BigCo, Inc.
                  Customer Support Group
                  P.O. Box 8143
                  Santa Clara, CA 95052-8143
                  US

             Tel: +1 (408) 555-1212
             Fax: +1 (408) 555-2512

             WEB: http://www.bigco.org/
```

```
          email: support@bigco.org"
      DESCRIPTION
          "The root MIB module for BigCo, Inc.

          Copyright 1996 BigCo, Inc. All rights reserved
          Reproduction of this document is authorized on the
          condition that the foregoing copyright notice is
          included.

          This SNMP MIB module (Specification) embodies
          BigCo's proprietary intellectual property.
          BigCo retains all title and ownership in the
          Specification, including any revisions.

          BigCo grants all interested parties a
          non-exclusive license to use and distribute an
          unmodified copy of this Specification in connection
          with management of BigCo products, and without
          fee, provided this copyright notice and license
          appear on all copies.

          This Specification is supplied 'AS IS,' and
          BigCo makes no warranty, either express or
          implied, as to the use, operation, condition, or
          performance of the Specification."

      REVISION     "9512201200Z"
      DESCRIPTION
          "  Rev 1.1    20 Dec 1995 12:00 mibadmin
            Added branch for sprinklers MIB."

      REVISION     "9507011500Z"
      DESCRIPTION
          "  Rev 1.0    01 Jul 1995 15:00 mibadmin
           Initial version of MIB module BIGCO-ROOT-MIB"
      ::= { bigcoModules 1 }
```

-- The following example shows a style typical for an IETF working group.
-- Some items of distinction include:
-- 1) the identifier used for the construct uses 'IETF' as a
--   prefix to increase the probability that the identifier will be unique.
-- 2) the identifier is a simple transformation of the MIB module name
--   by removing hyphens, using upper- and lowercase letters, and
--   by replacing “MIB” by “Module”.
-- 3) the working group email address, the WG chair, and the MIB editor
--   are specified as technical contacts.
-- 4) the description is used to specify abbreviations for references and
--   terms that are used throughout the MIB module.
-- 5) the MIB module has been previously published as an RFC and

```
--    (is currently published as an RFC). The REVISION/DESCRIPTION
--    clause is used to store this history.
-- 6) any revision history that occurred when the MIB was posted as an
--    Internet-draft (a work in progress) has been removed before the
--    MIB was published as an RFC.
ietfXyzModule MODULE-IDENTITY
    LAST-UPDATED "9512201200Z"
    ORGANIZATION "IETF xyz Protocol MIB Working Group"
    CONTACT-INFO
        "     WG: xyzmib@ietf.org

           Chair: Joe B. Cool

          Postal: mibs4you, Inc.
                  P.O. Box 8143
                  Santa Clara, CA 95052-8143
                  US

             Tel: +1 (408) 555-1212
             Fax: +1 (408) 555-2512

          email: jcool@mibs4you.org


          Editor: Al E. Gator

          Postal: SwampProdCo, Inc.
                  3096 Twin Lakes Road
                  Gotha, FL 32837
                  US

             Tel: +1 (407) 555-1212
             Fax: +1 (407) 555-2512

          email: agator@theswamp.com"
    DESCRIPTION
        "Objects and notifications for the xyz protocol.

        The following references are used throughout
        this MIB module:

        [XYZ Architecture]
            refers to the latest version of the
            Architecture Specification for
            protocol XYZ.

        [XYZ Implementation]
            refers to the latest version of the
            Implementation requirements for
            protocol XYZ.
```

```
            The following terms are used throughout this
            MIB module:

            XYZism - something to do with XYZ

            WQRish - something like a WQR"

        REVISION     "9512201200Z"
        DESCRIPTION
            "Published as RFC nnnn
            Obsoleted table xyzFwdTable and replaced
            with table xyzFwd2Table."

        REVISION     "9507011500Z"
        DESCRIPTION
            "Published as RFC nnnn
            Initial version of MIB module IETF-XYZ-MIB"
        ::= { ietfMibModules 97 }
```

As shown in the examples, the LAST-UPDATED clause is used to specify the date and time the module was created or last modified. (The date and time must be identical to the first date and time from the first REVISION/DESCRIPTION clause, if present.) The ORGANIZATION clause specifies the name of the organization that has authority over the definitions created in the MIB module. The CONTACT-INFO clause specifies contact points for technical information. For enterprise MIBs, this could include a support group. For IETF working groups, the technical contacts should include the working group mailing list, the chair, and the editor.

The DESCRIPTION clause describes the MIB module. It is a useful location to specify a copyright and grant of use license in MIB modules from enterprises. It is also useful to specify abbreviations for references and defined terms used throughout a MIB module. The paired REVISION/DESCRIPTION clauses are optionally used to specify information about the creation and each revision of the MIB module in reverse chronological order.

3.11 OID Value Assignment and OBJECT-IDENTITY Construct

The OID value assignment and OBJECT-IDENTITY constructs are used to assign an OID value to an identifier in the MIB module. The OBJECT-IDENTITY construct, which was added in SMIv2, also registers the OID value and provides information in a parsable format. Registration is done for values that are used to identify an item. For example, OID values can be used to identify chip sets created by various vendors which are used in network interface products. The DESCRIPTION and REFERENCE clauses of the OBJECT-IDENTITY construct can be used to specify any information that needs to be recorded.

Another typical example for use of the OBJECT-IDENTITY construct is to specify the contact information for a sub-tree of OID values delegated to another organization or project.

Syntax

```
-- OBJECT IDENTIFIER value assignment, with identifier lcName
<OVAdefinition> =
        lcName "OBJECT" "IDENTIFIER" "::=" <oidValue>

-- OBJECT-IDENTITY definition, with identifier lcName
<OIdefinition> =
        lcName "OBJECT-IDENTITY"
               "STATUS" <statusV2>
               "DESCRIPTION" chrStr
               [ "REFERENCE" chrStr ]
               "::=" <oidValue>

-- status of definition
<statusV2> = "current" | "deprecated" | "obsolete"
```

where:

lcName is an identifier that starts with a lowercase letter;
chrStr is a quoted character string which may span multiple lines; and
<oidValue> is an object identifier value.

Examples

```
  -- Examples of an OID value assignments (which are available
  -- in both SMIv1 and SMIv2)

  -- The OID value is specified from the root of the OID tree.
  -- Note that this format of an OID value may cause interoperability
  -- problems with some MIB compilers.
mgmt OBJECT IDENTIFIER
    -- network management area
    ::= { iso org(3) dod(6) internet(1) 2 }

  -- The OID value is specified as relative to another OID value which is defined
  -- or imported into the same MIB module as the OID value assignment.
mgmt OBJECT IDENTIFIER
    -- network management area
    ::= { internet 2 }

  -- Examples of an OBJECT-IDENTITY constructs which are available
  -- only in SMIv2.
  -- These are used to register an item.

  -- An example to show delegation of authority, or to specify use for
  -- a sub-tree of OID values.
mgmt OBJECT-IDENTITY
    STATUS       current
```

```
    DESCRIPTION
        "The root of the OID sub-tree reserved for IETF
        standards-track definitions in the network
        management area.

        Values are assigned by the Internet Assigned
        Numbers Authority (IANA)."
    REFERENCE
        "See the latest revision of the ASSIGNED NUMBERS RFC"
    ::= { iso org(3) dod(6) internet(1) 2 }

  -- An example to show delegation of authority, or to specify use for a sub-tree of
  -- OID values in a MIB module created for an enterprise with multiple product lines.
bigCoSprinklers OBJECT-IDENTITY
    STATUS      current
    DESCRIPTION
        "The root of Big Company, Inc's OID sub-tree reserved
        for definitions of sprinkler-related items.

        Values in the sub-tree are assigned by the
        MIB Administrator in the sprinkler area of
        Big Company, Inc.
        email: mibadmin@sprinklers.bigco.com."
    ::= { bigcoProds 35 }

  -- An example to show universal identification of an item created by
  -- an enterprise in an enterprise MIB module.
bigCoValveStyle04578 OBJECT-IDENTITY
    STATUS      current
    DESCRIPTION
        "A valve used for precise flow control from
        0 to 10 gallons per minute flow in increments
        of tenths of a gallon. The valve has two female
        3/4 inch connectors with normal threads. The
        valve is all brass construction."
    REFERENCE
        "See the latest version of the Sprinkler
        Division's Specification Book."
    ::= { bigCoValveStyle 4578 }
```

These two constructs are simple to use and understand. However, there has been much mystery associated with OIDs and OID values in the SNMP community. Many MIB compilers do not consider correct all forms of OID values. (See Chapter 2 for the definition of valid forms of OID values.) The difference between OID value assignment and registration, and the required checking for registrations are not correctly implemented in many MIB compilers.

OID value assignments are used to define a shorthand to reference an OID value within a MIB module. A registration of an item with an OID value gives that item a universal identification for all space and time. No other item may be registered with the same OID value. A complete and valid implementation of a MIB compiler must check that there are no duplicate registrations of an OID value, and must impose no restriction on one or more OID value assignments to the same OID value. The following shows examples of valid and invalid use of these constructs:

```
    -- OID value assignments are not registrations. Thus, several assignments
    -- can be made using the same OID value. For example, the following
    -- assignments in a MIB module are valid and should not cause a
    -- MIB compiler to generate an error or warning:
    -- ** valid usage **
oidVal1 OBJECT IDENTIFIER ::= { iso org(3) dod(6) internet(1) }
oidVal2 OBJECT IDENTIFIER ::= { iso org(3) dod(6) internet(1) }

    -- An OBJECT-IDENTITY construct performs a registration (a permanent
    -- assignment) of an OID value. An OID value can be registered to a
    -- single item. (Note that the OBJECT-TYPE, NOTIFICATION-TYPE,
    -- OBJECT-GROUP, NOTIFICATION-GROUP, MODULE-IDENTITY,
    -- MODULE-COMPLIANCE, and AGENT-CAPABILITIES constructs
    -- also perform registration.) The following example shows an illegal
    -- registration of an OID value, since the OID value is already registered.
    -- ** invalid usage **
oidReg1 OBJECT-IDENTITY -- this one is valid
    STATUS      current
    DESCRIPTION
        "Example valid registration"
    ::= { oidNode 1 }

oidReg2 OBJECT-IDENTITY -- this one is invalid
    STATUS      current
    DESCRIPTION
        "Example invalid registration, since OID value
        has already been used in another registration."
    ::= { oidNode 1 }

    -- Since an OID type assignment does not perform a registration,
    -- the OID value assigned may be the same as one used with
    -- a registration.
    -- ** valid usage **
oidReg1 OBJECT-IDENTITY
    STATUS      current
    DESCRIPTION
        "Example valid registration"
    ::= { oidNode 1 }

oidVal1 OBJECT IDENTIFIER ::= { oidNode 1 }
```

3.12 Type Assignment and TEXTUAL-CONVENTION Construct

The "type assignment" and TEXTUAL-CONVENTION constructs are used to create a "new" type. This is done by adding constraints to an existing base type or a previously created type. The constraints may be a reduction in range for numbers or a reduction in length for strings. Also, the constraints may describe required behavior or allowed values. Note that these constructs do not create a new SNMP base type, that is no new ASN.1 tag, to be assigned for the new type.

The type assignment construct, which is a part of the ASN.1 language, proved not to be sufficient in describing new types in SNMP MIB modules. The TEXTUAL-CONVENTION construct was added in SMIv2 to allow created types to be well documented. It should be used to define textual conventions. The ASN.1 language allows types to be further refined by reducing the range of integers or the size of strings. However, the ASN.1 language provides no mechanism to document behaviors of new types, such as the behavior of the gauge type. The TEXTUAL-CONVENTION construct provides a mechanism to specify the behavior.

The TEXTUAL-CONVENTION construct contains the STATUS clause to specify the status of the definition, and the optional DISPLAY-HINT clause to specify a hint for displaying a value and/or describing sub-structuring of the value. Note that ASN.1 requires the identifier for types to start with an uppercase letter.

Syntax

```
-- Type assignment (or textual convention assignment) definition
-- for SMIv1, with identifier ucName.
<TCAdefinitionV1> =
            ucName "::=" <simpleOrEnum>

-- Type assignment (or textual convention assignment) definition
-- for SMIv2, with identifier, ucName.
-- (It is preferred to use a TEXTUAL-CONVENTION construct.)
<TCAdefinitionV2> =
            ucName "::=" <simpleEnumOrBit>

-- TEXTUAL-CONVENTION type definition (only in SMIv2),
-- with identifier ucName
<TCTdefinition> =
            ucName "::=" "TEXTUAL-CONVENTION"
                    [ "DISPLAY-HINT" chrStr ]
                    "STATUS" <statusV2>
                    "DESCRIPTION" chrStr
                    [ "REFERENCE" chrStr ]
                    "SYNTAX" <simpleEnumOrBit>

-- status of definition
<statusV2> = "mandatory" | "deprecated" | "obsolete"
```

-- SMIv1 does not have a bit string construct
<simpleOrEnum> =
<simpleSyntax> |
"INTEGER" "{" <enumItem> ["," <enumItem>]... "}"

-- simple syntax, enumerated integer, or BITS pseudotype.
<simpleEnumOrBit> =
<simpleSyntax> |
"INTEGER" "{" <enumItem> ["," <enumItem>]... "}" |
"BITS" "{" <bitItem> ["," <bitItem>]... "}"

-- base syntax types (and textual conventions)
<simpleSyntax> =
<synType> |
<tcType>

where
ucName is an identifier that starts with an uppercase letter;
chrStr is a quoted character string which may span multiple lines;
<enumItem> is a labelled value in an enumeration;
<bitItem> is a labelled bit;
<synType> is a base syntax type with possible sub-typing; and
<tcType> is a textual convention with possible sub-typing.

Examples

-- Examples of type assignments (or textual convention assignments)
-- available in SMIv1.

-- An assignment to limit values of an OCTET STRING type to the printable
-- 7-bit ASCII character set and a few well-defined control characters.

```
DisplayString ::=
    -- values must conform to the NVT ASCII character set
    -- which consists of the 7-bit ASCII displayable
    -- characters and a few control characters as defined
    -- in RFC 854
    OCTET STRING (SIZE (0..255))
```

-- An assignment to limit displayable characters to uppercase letters

```
UcDisplayString ::=
    -- values must be uppercase letters only
    DisplayString
```

-- Assignments to limit the range of an integer

```
Int8 ::= INTEGER (-128..127)
Int16 ::= INTEGER (-65536..65535)
Int32 ::= INTEGER (-2147483648..2147483647)
```

```
Uint8 ::= Gauge (0..255)
Uint16 ::= Gauge (0..65535)
Uint32 ::= Gauge (0..4294967295)

  -- An assignment to 'create' a new type
TruthValue ::=
    -- a boolean value
    INTEGER { true(1), false(2) }


  -- The same examples using the TEXTUAL-CONVENTION construct which is
  -- available only in SMIv2.

  -- An assignment to limit values of an OCTET STRING type to the printable
  -- 7-bit ASCII character set and a few well-defined control characters.
  -- (Note that a description of the DISPLAY-HINT clause follows
  -- these examples.)
DisplayString ::= TEXTUAL-CONVENTION
    DISPLAY-HINT "255a"
    STATUS      current
    DESCRIPTION
        "The value must conform to the NVT ASCII character
        set which consists of the 7-bit ASCII displayable
        characters and a few control characters as defined
        in RFC 854."
    SYNTAX      OCTET STRING (SIZE (0..255))

  -- An assignment to limit displayable characters to uppercase letters.
UcDisplayString ::= TEXTUAL-CONVENTION
    DISPLAY-HINT "255a"
    STATUS      current
    DESCRIPTION
       "The value must consist of only uppercase letters."
    SYNTAX      DisplayString

  -- Assignments to limit the range of an integer.
Int8 ::= TEXTUAL-CONVENTION
    STATUS      current
    DESCRIPTION
        "An 8 bit signed integer."
    SYNTAX      Integer32 (-128..127)

Int16 ::= TEXTUAL-CONVENTION
    STATUS      current
    DESCRIPTION
        "A 16 bit signed integer."
    SYNTAX      Integer32 (-65536..65535)

Int32 ::= TEXTUAL-CONVENTION
```

```
    STATUS       current
    DESCRIPTION
        "A 32 bit signed integer."
    SYNTAX       Integer32 (-2147483648..2147483647)

Uint8 ::= TEXTUAL-CONVENTION
    STATUS       current
    DESCRIPTION
        "An 8 bit unsigned integer."
    SYNTAX       Unsigned32 (0..255)

Uint16 ::= TEXTUAL-CONVENTION
    STATUS       current
    DESCRIPTION
        "A 16 bit unsigned integer."
    SYNTAX       Unsigned32 (0..65535)

Uint32 ::= TEXTUAL-CONVENTION
    STATUS       current
    DESCRIPTION
        "A 32 bit unsigned integer."
    SYNTAX       Unsigned32 (0..4294967295)

  -- An assignment to 'create' a new type.
TruthValue ::= TEXTUAL-CONVENTION
    STATUS       current
    DESCRIPTION
        "A boolean value."
    SYNTAX       INTEGER { true(1), false(2) }
```

The optional DISPLAY-HINT clause can be used to specify a hint as to how to display a value of the type, and as a side-effect, to describe sub-structuring of the value. It can only be specified for types that are based on integer or octet string. When the type is integer based, the hint is formed with the integer-formatting rules. Otherwise, the hint is formed with the octet-formatting rules. The integer-formatting rules are quite simple and are shown below:

Syntax for Integer-formatting Rules

```
-- Display hint for integers
<intDisplayHint>
        = "d" [ "-" number ] -- display value in decimal with optional
                             -- decimal point placement
        | "b" -- display value in binary
        | "o" -- display value in octal
        | "x" -- display value in hexadecimal

Where
    number is an unsigned integer
```

Examples of Integer Formatting

```
DISPLAY-HINT "d" for value 143 renders 143
DISPLAY-HINT "d-2" for value 143 renders 1.43
DISPLAY-HINT "b" for value 143 renders 100001111
DISPLAY-HINT "o" for value 143 renders 217
DISPLAY-HINT "x" for value 143 renders 8F
```

The octet-formatting rules are quite a bit more complex. A format consists of one or more specifications, each consisting of five parts. Each part uses or removes zero or more octets from the value and generates zero or more characters of the rendering (i.e., output). The octets of the value are processed from the most significant to the least significant. The octet-formatting rules are shown below:

Syntax for Octet-formatting Rules

```
-- Display hint for octet strings
<octetDisplayHint> =
            <octDisplaySpec>...

<octDisplaySpec> =
             number <displayFormat> [ <sepChar> ] |
            "*" number <displayFormat> [ <sepChar> [ <repTermChar> ] ]

<displayFormat>
            = "d" -- display value in decimal
            | "b" -- display value in binary
            | "o" -- display value in octal
            | "x" -- display value in hexadecimal
```

Where

number is an unsigned integer

<sepChar> is the separator character, which may be any character other than a decimal digit or "*"

<repTermChar> is the repeat terminator character, which may be any character other than a decimal digit or "*"

Examples of Octet Formatting

```
DISPLAY-HINT "255a" for value "aBc" renders "aBc"
DISPLAY-HINT "1a:" for value "aBc" renders "a:B:c"
DISPLAY-HINT "1d:" for value "aBc" renders "97:66:99"
-- "a" is 97 decimal, "B" is 66, and "c" is 99
-- "a" is '01100001'b, "B" is '01000010'b, and "c" is '01100011'b
-- "a" is '141'o, "B" is '102'o, and "c" is '143'o
-- "a" is '61'h, "B" is '42'h, and "c" is '63'h
DISPLAY-HINT "1b:" for value "aBc" renders
        "01100001:01000010:01100011"
DISPLAY-HINT "1o:" for value "aBc" renders "141:102:143"
DISPLAY-HINT "1x:" for value "aBc" renders "61:42:63"
```

```
DISPLAY-HINT "2d-1d-1d,1d:1d:1d,1a1d:1d" for value
        '07CB09150D3520032D0700'H renders
        "1995-9-21,13:53:32.3,-7.0"
DISPLAY-HINT "0aH0ae0al0al0ao0a 1a" for value "World"
        renders "Hello World"
DISPLAY-HINT "*0aA*0aB*0aC*0aD1a" for value '030800023C'H
        renders "AAABBBBBBBBDD<"
```

The parts of an octet format specification include:

- the repeat indicator, which is optional. An asterisk (*) indicates that the current octet of the value is the repeat count for the specification. The repeat count is an unsigned integer (zero to 255) which specifies the number of times to apply the remainder of the specification. The repeat count is one if the repeat count is not present in the format specification.
- the number of octets from the value. An unsigned integer in the range of zero to 65535. The lesser of this value and the number of octets remaining are used.
- the display format. The formats are "a" for ASCII, "d" for unsigned decimal, "x" for hexadecimal, and "o" for octal. Numeric formats interpret the octets of the constituting value in network byte order (big-endian encoding).
- the display separator character, which is optional. This character may be any other than an asterisk (*) or a digit. When present, this character is rendered after each application of the previous specification part, except for two cases. The first is when it would be followed by the repeat terminator character. The second is when it would be the last character rendered.
- the repeat terminator character, which is optional. This character may be any other than an asterisk (*) or a digit. This part may only be present when both the repeat indicator and the display separator character are also present. When present, this character is rendered after repeated applications of the second and third parts, unless it would be the last character rendered.

Rendering continues until all octets in a value are exhausted. Any excess octet-formatting specifications are ignored. The last octet-formatting specification is reused repeatedly if the specification string is exhausted before the value has been completely exhausted.

Caution

The DISPLAY-HINT has a limited range of applicability. It can be used for many types, but not all

The DISPLAY-HINT is one of those ideas that seems good at first, but as you try to apply it, it just doesn't measure up. For any type, there are four conversions that need to be specified for values. These conversions are:

1. from transfer format to internal format
2. internal format to transfer format
3. internal format to display format
4. display format to internal format

Note that a type, such as that used for date/time, may sub-structure its values into fields such as the year, month, day, hour, minute, and second. Also, a type may sub-structure its values based on a leading selector field, such as address type, or sub-structure its value based on a selector that is the value of another object.

Our Opinion We believe that a general solution is needed to specify the conversions between the display formats and internal formats for types, that is based on functions from a programming language such as C, TCL, or Perl.

3.13 OBJECT-TYPE Construct

The OBJECT-TYPE construct is used to define an *object type*. An object type is either a class of management information or a mechanism to organize related object types. The majority of the definitions in a MIB module are for management information and use the OBJECT-TYPE construct to define table, row, columnar, and scalar objects.

The OBJECT-TYPE construct exists in both SMIv1 and SMIv2. In general, it provides the same capabilities and has the same look. However, some clauses have been renamed, and some clauses have been added. Also, not all clauses can be used for definitions of table, row, columnar, and scalar objects. Table 3–5 lists the clauses of the OBJECT-TYPE construct and indicates for each clause whether it is available in the SMIv1 or SMIv2. Also indicated is whether the clause is optional or required for table, row, columnar, and scalar objects.

Table 3–5 Allowed clauses of the OBJECT-TYPE construct

Clause	Example	In v1	In v2
SYNTAX	SYNTAX Counter	required for all	required for all
UNITS	UNITS “inches”	not available	optional for columnar and scalar objects
ACCESS	ACCESS read-only	required for all	uses MAX-ACCESS
MAX-ACCESS	MAX-ACCESS read-only	uses ACCESS	required for all
STATUS	STATUS mandatory	required for all	required for all
DESCRIPTION	DESCRIPTION “The distance covered.”	optional for all	required for all
REFERENCE	REFERENCE “ZXY Spec.”	optional for all	optional for all
INDEX	INDEX { ifIndex }	required for row objects	required for row objects if AUGMENTS is not used
AUGMENTS	AUGMENTS { bcoValveEntry }	uses INDEX	required for row objects if INDEX is not used
DEFVAL	DEVAL { 3 }	optional for columnar objects	optional for columnar objects

For management information organized in a table, the following pattern of three definitions is required. The first definition is for a table object using the OBJECT-TYPE construct. A special value for the SYNTAX clause indicates that a table object is being defined. The second definition is for a row object using the OBJECT-TYPE construct. A special value for the SYNTAX clause and the presence of the INDEX clause indicate that a row object is being defined. The third definition is for a sequence using the SEQUENCE construct from ASN.1. After these definitions, the OBJECT-TYPE construct is used repeatedly to specify each column in the table. There is no requirement in ASN.1 or in the SNMP SMI that the definitions be specified in this order. However, most MIB compilers will only accept definitions specified in this order. Most, if not all, readers of MIB modules would be quite confused if this order was not followed. (See Figure 3–4)

Table - with OBJECT-TYPE construct
Row (instance identification) - with OBJECT-TYPE construct
List of columns in table - with SEQUENCE construct

Column 1 - with OBJECT-TYPE construct
Column 2 - with OBJECT-TYPE construct

. . .

Column N - with OBJECT-TYPE construct

Figure 3–4 Pattern of definitions for tabular information

3.13.1 Table Objects

The OBJECT-TYPE construct is used to specify a definition for a table object. An SNMP table contains rows and columns. A table cannot be an operand or result of an SNMP operation.

By convention, the identifier used for a table ends with the suffix "Table." The argument of the SYNTAX clause for a table must be a "SEQUENCE OF <sequence>" construct. By convention, the identifier of the sequence is identical to the identifier for the row except for the first character. The identifiers for a table and row must start with a lowercase letter. The identifier for a sequence must start with an uppercase letter. For example, the identifier for the sequence for table fooTable is FooEntry.

Finally, the value for the ACCESS or MAX-ACCESS clause for a table must be *not-accessible,* since a table cannot be accessed with SNMP operations.

Syntax for Tables

```
-- v1 OBJECT-TYPE definition for a table, with identifier lcName
<OTtableDefinitionV1> =
        lcName "OBJECT-TYPE"
                "SYNTAX" "SEQUENCE" "OF" <SequenceIdentifier>
                "ACCESS" "not-accessible"
                "STATUS" <statusV1>
                [ "DESCRIPTION" chrStr ]
                [ "REFERENCE" chrStr ]
        "::=" <oidValue>
```

```
-- SMIv1 status of definition
<statusV1> = "mandatory" | "deprecated" | "obsolete"


-- v2 OBJECT-TYPE definition for a table, with identifier lcName
<OTtableDefinitionV2> =
        lcName "OBJECT-TYPE"
               "SYNTAX" "SEQUENCE" "OF" <SequenceIdentifier>
               "MAX-ACCESS" "not-accessible"
               "STATUS" <statusV2>
               "DESCRIPTION" chrStr
               [ "REFERENCE" chrStr ]
        "::=" <oidValue>

--SMIv2 status of definition
<statusV2> = "current" | "deprecated" | "obsolete"
```

where

lcName is an identifier that starts with a lowercase letter;
chrStr is a quoted character string which may span multiple lines;
<oidValue> is an OID value; and
<SequenceIdentifier> is the identifier for the sequence associated with the table.

Example Table Specifications

-- In the examples for tables, notice that the text for the DESCRIPTION
-- clause specifies two important pieces of information. The first is a
-- general description of the information in the table or use of the table.
-- The second is an estimate of how many entries (or rows)
-- would be expected in the table. A MIB module is much easier to
-- read when this is consistently provided in the DESCRIPTION
-- clause for each table.

-- example of a table definition in SMIv1

```
ifTable OBJECT-TYPE
    SYNTAX       SEQUENCE OF IfEntry
    ACCESS       not-accessible
    STATUS       mandatory
    DESCRIPTION
        "A table of managed network interfaces and interface
        sub-layers on a system. The number of entries is
        related to the number of sub-layer interfaces below
        the internetwork-layer interfaces on the system and
        the number of physical network interfaces. The
        current number of entries is specified by ifNumber."
    ::= { interfaces 2 }
```

```
-- example of same table defined using SMIv2
ifTable OBJECT-TYPE
    SYNTAX       SEQUENCE OF IfEntry
    MAX-ACCESS   not-accessible
    STATUS       current
    DESCRIPTION
        "A table of managed network interfaces and interface
        sub-layers on a system. The number of entries is
        related to the number of sub-layer interfaces below
        the internetwork-layer interfaces on the system and
        the number of physical network interfaces. The
        current number of entries is specified by ifNumber."
    ::= { interfaces 2 }

-- example of a table definition in SMIv1
etherStatsTable OBJECT-TYPE
    SYNTAX       SEQUENCE OF EtherStatsEntry
    ACCESS       not-accessible
    STATUS       mandatory
    DESCRIPTION
        "A table of statistics for each monitored ethernet
        network interface on a system. The number of entries
        depends on the configuration of the system. The
        maximum number of entries is implementation dependent."
    ::= { statistics 1 }

-- example of same table defined using SMIv2
etherStatsTable OBJECT-TYPE
    SYNTAX       SEQUENCE OF EtherStatsEntry
    MAX-ACCESS   not-accessible
    STATUS       current
    DESCRIPTION
        "A table of statistics for each monitored ethernet
        network interface on a system. The number of
        entries depends on the configuration of the system.
        The maximum number of entries is implementation
        dependent."
    ::= { statistics 1 }
```

One practice we strongly recommend is to consistently use the DESCRIPTION clause for tables to document two important pieces of information. The first is a general description of the information in the table or use of the table. The second is an estimate of how many entries (or rows) would be expected in the table, the maximum number of rows, and any scalar objects whose value is associated with the table. The size estimates should be architectural, and not implementation values. For example, if the table contained information about cards in a chassis, the estimate on the maximum number rows should be based on what makes sense architecturally, and not for a particular product (such as the first).

3.13.2 Row Objects

The OBJECT-TYPE construct is used to specify a definition for a row object. A row consists of columns. A row cannot be an operand or result of an SNMP operation. An SNMP GET, GETNEXT, or GETBULK (in v2) operation may be used to retrieve the values of specified columnar objects of a particular row.

By convention, the identifier used for a row is its containing table's identifier with the suffix "Table" replaced by suffix "Entry." For example, if the identifier for a table was "fooTable," then the identifier for its row would be "fooEntry." The argument of the SYNTAX clause for a row must be an identifier for a sequence. By convention, the identifier for the sequence is identical to the identifier for the row except for the first character. The identifiers for a table and row must start with a lowercase letter. The identifier for a sequence must start with an uppercase letter. For example, the identifier for the sequence for row fooEntry is FooEntry.

The value for the ACCESS or MAX-ACCESS clause for a row must be *not-accessible* since a row cannot be accessed with SNMP operations. The value specified for the STATUS clause must be identical to the value in the STATUS clause for the table. The INDEX clause or the AUGMENTS clause (available only in SMIv2) specifies information that determines how rows (or more precisely, instances of columnar objects) in the table are identified.

The SMI requires that the OID value assigned to the row must be the same as the OID value assigned to the table containing the row, with the addition of a single component with a value of one. This is specified as the identifier for the table followed by the digit one inside curly braces. For example, if the identifier for the table is fooTable, the OID value that must be specified for fooEntry is { fooTable 1 }.

Syntax of Rows

```
-- v1 OBJECT-TYPE definition for a row, with identifier lcName
<OTrowDefinitionV1> =
            lcName "OBJECT-TYPE"
                    "SYNTAX" <SequenceIdentifier>
                    "ACCESS" "not-accessible"
                    "STATUS" <statusV1>
                    [ "DESCRIPTION" chrStr ]
                    [ "REFERENCE" chrStr ]
                    "INDEX" "{" <indexItemV1> ["," <indexItemV1> ]... "}"
            "::=" "{" <tableIdentifier> "1" "}"

-- SMIv1 status of definition
<statusV1> = "mandatory" | "deprecated" | "obsolete"

-- item in index sub-clause, with ucName as the identifier for a MIB module
-- and lcName as the identifier for an object
<indexItemV1> =
            [ ucName "." ] lcName |
            -- caution, the following are valid, but not generally supported
```

```
            -- and are eliminated in SMIv2
            "INTEGER"  |
            "OCTET" "STRING"  |
            "OBJECT" "IDENTIFIER"  |
            "NetworkAddress"  |
            "IpAddress"


-- v2 OBJECT-TYPE definition for a row, with identifier lcName
<OTrowDefinitionV2> =
            lcName  "OBJECT-TYPE"
                    "SYNTAX" <SequenceIdentifier>
                    "MAX-ACCESS" "not-accessible"
                    "STATUS" <statusV2>
                    "DESCRIPTION" chrStr
                    [ "REFERENCE" chrStr ]
                    <indexOrAugments>
            "::=" "{" <tableIdentifier> "1" "}"

--SMIv2 status of definition
<statusV2> = "current" | "deprecated" | "obsolete"

-- index or augments sub-clause
<indexOrAugments> =
            "INDEX" "{" <indexItemV2> ["," <indexItemV2> ]... "}" |
            "AUGMENTS" "{" <baseRow> "}"

-- item in index sub-clause, with ucName as the name of the module and
-- lcName as the identifier
-- Note that the IMPLIED qualifier may only be specified on the
-- last index item in the list.
<indexItemV2> = [ "IMPLIED" ] [ ucName "." ] lcName

-- the row from the base table, with ucName as the name of the module
-- and lcName as the identifier
<baseRow> = [ ucName "." ] lcName
```

where

ucName is an identifier that starts with an uppercase letter;
lcName is an identifier that starts with a lowercase letter;
chrStr is a quoted character string which may span multiple lines;
<tableIdentifier> is the identifier for the table associated with the row; and
<SequenceIdentifier> is the identifier for the sequence
associated with the row.

Example Row Specifications

```
-- In the examples for rows, notice that the text for the DESCRIPTION
-- clause specifies two important pieces of information. The first is
-- a short description of the table associated with the row. The second
-- is an indication if rows can be created or deleted via SNMP operations
-- on columns of the table, and if so, then what is required for this to occur.
-- A MIB module is much easier to read when this is consistently provided
-- in the DESCRIPTION clause for each row.

-- example of a row definition in SMIv1
ifEntry OBJECT-TYPE
    SYNTAX      IfEntry
    ACCESS      not-accessible
    STATUS      mandatory
    DESCRIPTION
        "An entry in the table of network interfaces on
        a system. A row in this table cannot be created
        or deleted by SNMP operations on columns of the
        table."
    INDEX       { ifIndex }
    ::= { ifTable 1}

-- example of same row defined using SMIv2
ifEntry OBJECT-TYPE
    SYNTAX      IfEntry
    MAX-ACCESS  not-accessible
    STATUS      current
    DESCRIPTION
        "An entry in the table of network interfaces on
        a system. A row in this table cannot be created
        or deleted by SNMP operations on columns of the
        table."
    INDEX       { ifIndex }
    ::= { ifTable 1}

-- example of a row definition in SMIv1
etherStatsEntry OBJECT-TYPE
    SYNTAX      EtherStatsEntry
    ACCESS      not-accessible
    STATUS      mandatory
    DESCRIPTION
        "An entry in the table of statistics for each monitored
        ethernet network interfaces on a system. A row in this table
        is created by setting the value of etherStatsStatus to
        'createRequest', and setting the appropriate values for
        etherStatsDataSource and etherStatsOwner. A row in this table is
        deleted by setting the value of etherStatsStatus to 'invalid'."
    INDEX       { etherStatsIndex }
    ::= { etherStatsTable 1 }
```

```
-- example of same table defined using SMIv2
etherStatsEntry OBJECT-TYPE
    SYNTAX      EtherStatsEntry
    MAX-ACCESS  not-accessible
    STATUS      current
    DESCRIPTION
        "An entry in the table of statistics for each monitored
        ethernet network interfaces on a system. A row in this table
        is created by setting the value of etherStatsStatus to
        'createRequest', and setting the appropriate values for
        etherStatsDataSource and etherStatsOwner. A row in this table is
        deleted by setting the value of etherStatsStatus to 'invalid'."
    INDEX       { etherStatsIndex }
    ::= { etherStatsTable 1 }
```

One practice that we strongly recommended is to consistently use the DESCRIPTION clause for rows to document two important pieces of information. The first is a short description of the table containing the row. The second is an indication whether rows can be created or deleted via SNMP operations using columns of the table, and if so, then what is required for this to happen. There are several models of row creation and deletion commonly used in SNMP MIB modules. However, there are no create or delete operations in SNMP. Creation and deletion of rows via SNMP is accomplished as a side-effect of setting values to one or more columns in row. Some of these models are covered in Chapter 8.

Our Opinion

Row creation and deletion has been an area of controversy in the SNMP community for many years. We have views in this area. However, regardless of our views, we do believe that the existing practices must be documented. Clarity allows understanding and interoperation. We believe that a new clause should be added to the OBJECT-TYPE construct for rows to specify whether creation or deletion is possible, and if so, then what must be done.

INDEX and AUGMENTS Clause for Row Objects

The INDEX and AUGMENTS clauses specify how rows are indexed in a table. The INDEX clause lists the ordered index items for a table. There is no direct limit on the number of indices for a table. Typically, the index items are names of columns in the table. Both SMIv1 and SMIv2 allow named items to be any columnar or scalar object type.

SMIv1 also allows a few SNMP base types to be specified. However, no IETF standards track MIB module uses this mechanism. This mechanism is not included in SMIv2. When the index items are columns in the table, SNMP tables appear identical to traditional databases. Many generic SNMP management systems assume that all SNMP tables are indexed only by columns in the table. This assumption is incorrect! The SMI allow columns from an existing table to be specified as the indices for a new table.

Figure 3–5 shows two examples of table indexing. In the first example, the indices are columns from the table. The second example contains two tables. The indices of the second table in the second example are a column from the first table and a column from the second table.

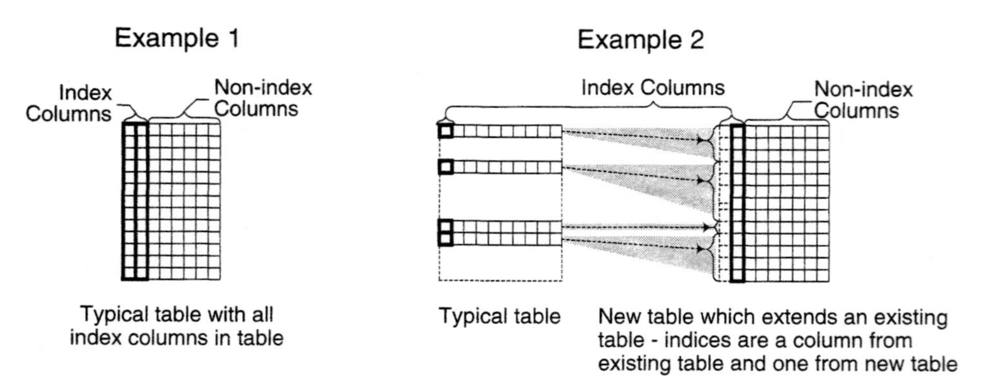

Figure 3–5 Table indexing examples

One example, which occurs quite often, consists of creating object type definitions for the following data structure from the C programming language:

```
typedef struct portInfo_t {   /* info for a port */
    int      iPortType;           /* port type */
    int      iPortStatus;         /* port status */
} PortInfo;
#define MXPORTS 20 /* max number of ports per board */
typedef struct boardInfo_t { /* info for a board */
    int      iBoardType;          /* board type */
    int      cPorts;              /* number of ports on board */
    PortInfo aPortInfo[MXPORTS];/* port info for board */
} BoardInfo;
#define MXBOARDS 6 /* max number of boards in system */

BoardInfo boards[MXBOARDS]; /* info for boards in system */
```

These data structures from C could be represented by two SNMP tables. For this example, the first table is indexed by an integer corresponding to the index of the slot containing the board. This table is given identifier *bcBoardInfoTable* in the MIB module and indexed by the column with identifier *bcBoardInfoBoardIndex*. Since the SMI has no construct to directly represent the array aPortInfo within table bcBoardInfoTable, another table needs to be defined in the MIB module. This table is given identifier *bcPortInfoTable* and indexed by bcBoardInfo-BoardIndex from table bcBoardInfoTable and by column with identifier *bcPortInfoIndex* from table bcPortInfoTable. The index for table bcPortInfoTable corresponds to a port on a board. Numbering for ports starts at one and corresponds to the top most (or left-most) port on the card. Shown below are the two tables written in SMIv2.

```
-- The following are the definitions for the table and row constructs
-- for the first table.
bcBoardInfoTable OBJECT-TYPE
    SYNTAX      SEQUENCE OF BcBoardInfoEntry
    MAX-ACCESS  not-accessible
    STATUS      current
    DESCRIPTION
        "A table of ... "
    ::= { bcHwInfo 4 }

bcBoardInfoEntry OBJECT-TYPE
    SYNTAX      BcBoardInfoEntry
    MAX-ACCESS  not-accessible
    STATUS      current
    DESCRIPTION
        "An entry in the table of ... "
    INDEX       { bcBoardInfoBoardIndex }
    ::= { bcBoardInfoTable 1 }

-- The following are the definitions for the table and row constructs
-- for the second table.
bcPortInfoTable OBJECT-TYPE
    SYNTAX      SEQUENCE OF BcPortInfoEntry
    MAX-ACCESS  not-accessible
    STATUS      current
    DESCRIPTION
        "A table of ... "
    ::= { bcHwInfo 5 }

bcPortInfoEntry OBJECT-TYPE
    SYNTAX      BcPortInfoEntry
    MAX-ACCESS  not-accessible
    STATUS      current
    DESCRIPTION
        "An entry in the table of ... "
    INDEX       { bcBoardInfoBoardIndex,
                  bcPortInfoPortIndex }
    ::= { bcPortInfoTable 1 }
```

The last object specified in an INDEX clause may be qualified with the IMPLIED modifier under certain conditions. For example, the following shows the use of IMPLIED — "INDEX { bigcoDivIndex, IMPLIED bigcoProdSerialNo }".

The IMPLIED modifier may only be specified if the base type for the object is a varying length string (i.e., OCTET STRING and Opaque) or OID. As specified earlier, rows in the table are ordered by the value of the table's indices. However, the values of types "varying length strings" and OIDs have their length specified first. Thus, the varying length strings "bg", "ab", "abc", and "z" are ordered "z", "ab", "bg", and "abc"; and not "ab", "abc", "bg", and "z". The ordering appears as if the values are preceded by their length such as "<1>z",

"<2>ab", "<2>bc", and "<3>abc". The IMPLIED modifier specifies that the ordering should not be based on the length.

Note that SMIv1 does not include the IMPLIED modifier, and thus MIB modules created following SMIv2 rules cannot be converted to equivalent modules written following the SMIv1 rules. However, quite a few agent implementors did not understand the ordering requirements for tables indexed by varying length strings or OIDs. Thus, there are existing MIB modules written with SMIv1 rules which don't match their implementation. Also, some MIB compilers support the IMPLIED modifier in SMIv1 MIB modules.

Our Opinion

We believe that the SMIv1 rules and SMIv2 rules should be aligned as much as possible, so that it is easy to convert a MIB module from the SMIv2 format to the SMIv1 format. Thus, we believe that the SMIv1 should be updated.

Restrictions for Index Items

There are a few restrictions that apply to index items. Some of these have already been covered. However, for completeness, they are specified below:

- The encoding of the values of all the index items for a table may not cause SNMP variables to contain more than 128 components (sub-identifiers).
- The value of index items with base type of integer may not be negative.
- The range of values of index items with a base type of integer should normally start at one and not zero. The value zero should be avoided, except in special cases.
- The IMPLIED modifier may only be specified on the last item in the index list.
- The IMPLIED modifier may only be specified on items that have base type of OID or base type of varying length string. When the type is a varying length string, the string may not allow a size of zero.
- The values of all the items specified in the INDEX clause, taken together, must unambiguously identify rows in the table.
- When the index items specified in the INDEX clause are not columns in that table, the DESCRIPTION clause for the row must be used to uniquely identify rows in the table.

AUGMENTS Clause

The AUGMENTS clause was added to SMIv2 to document one particular special relationship between two tables. The syntax of an AUGMENTS clause is "AUGMENTS { <baseRow> }". The item specified in an AUGMENTS clause is the identifier for a row of another table. The other table is called the *base table*. The table using the AUGMENTS clause in its row definition is called an *augmenting table* of the base table. The AUGMENTS clause may only be used when for every row in the base table there corresponds a row in the augmenting table which is identified by the same indices, and the number of rows in the augmenting table is identical to the number of rows in the base table. A base table may have multiple tables that augment it. An augmenting table may not also be a base table. When rows are created or deleted in a base table, the same rows must also be simultaneously created or deleted in all augmenting tables. The rows in the base table are said to be mapped one-to-one to the rows in each augmenting table. An augmenting table must have a status which is consistent with the status of the base table. That is, if the status of a base table is obsolete, then an augmenting table must also have a status of obsolete. If the status of the base table is deprecated, then the status of the augmenting table may be deprecated or obsolete. The example below shows definitions for a base table and an augmenting table.

```
    -- The following are the definitions for the table and row constructs
    -- for the base table.
tcpConnTable OBJECT-TYPE
    SYNTAX       SEQUENCE OF TcpConnEntry
    MAX-ACCESS   not-accessible
    STATUS       current
    DESCRIPTION
        "A table of ... "
    ::= { tcp 13 }

tcpConnEntry OBJECT-TYPE
    SYNTAX       TcpConnEntry
    MAX-ACCESS   not-accessible
    STATUS       current
    DESCRIPTION
        "An entry in the table of ... "
    INDEX        { tcpConnLocalAddress, tcpConnLocalPort,
                   tcpConnRemAddress, tcpConnRemPort }
    ::= { tcpConnTable 1 }

    -- The following are the definitions for the table and row constructs
    -- for the augmenting table.
bcTcpConnTable OBJECT-TYPE
    SYNTAX       SEQUENCE OF BcTcpConnEntry
    MAX-ACCESS   not-accessible
    STATUS       current
    DESCRIPTION
        "A table of ... "
    ::= { bcTcp 1 }

bcTcpConnEntry OBJECT-TYPE
    SYNTAX       BcTcpConnEntry
    MAX-ACCESS   not-accessible
    STATUS       current
    DESCRIPTION
        "An entry in the table of ... "
    AUGMENTS     { tcpConnEntry }
    ::= { bcTcpConnTable 1 }
```

Choosing INDEX or AUGMENTS

The INDEX clause must be used when there is not a one-to-one mapping between two tables, such as when the number of rows in a second table is less than the number of rows in the first table. In this situation, the second table is said to have a sparse dependent relationship with the first table. A row defined with the AUGMENTS clause written in SMIv2 may be converted to SMIv1 by replacing the AUGMENTS clause with a copy of the INDEX clause from the base table. (See Figure 3–6)

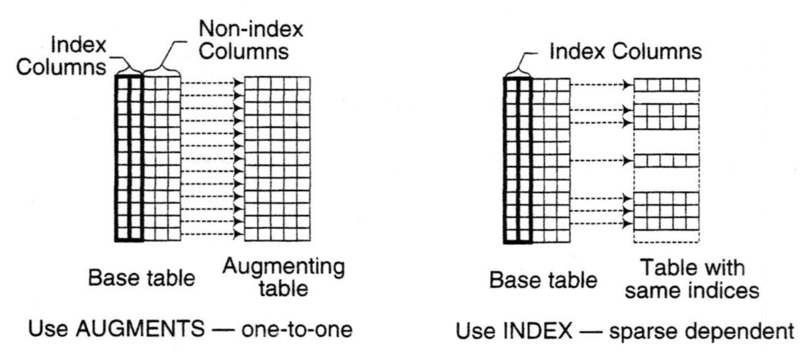

Figure 3–6 AUGMENTS and INDEX

Final Word on Indexing

In SMIv2, there is no explicit prohibition from specifying arbitrary columnar or scalar objects in an INDEX clause. However, the intent is certainly clear that the index items should be chosen to show the relationship between tables. When a choice is being considered, the bias should be to use columnar objects from the table instead of from another table. Using arbitrary columns or scalars makes a table harder to understand and can result in maintenance problems when a MIB module is updated. Using indexing to show fate relationships between tables can improve the understanding.

Our Opinion

There are existing MIB specifications on the standards track where the authors have used scalar items and arbitrary columns as index items. We cannot tell if this approach is due to carelessness, a misunderstanding of the SMI, a lack of understanding of the SMI, an attempt to conserve definitions of index items, or some other reason. First, there is no shortage of resources needed to define index items, and secondly, we hope that by studying this work that future authors of MIB specifications will have no misunderstandings or lack of understanding of the SMI. We believe that the SMI should be changed to restrict which items can be specified as indices for a row of a table.

The columnar objects that are specified as index items for a row of a table and are also defined within that table are called *auxiliary* objects. The rules from SMIv1 required that these objects be accessible, that is, they must have value for the ACCESS clause of *read-only*. Many people from the SNMP community opposed this rule, since the values for these columnar objects are redundant. For example, the value for instance *i* of the columnar object that indexes a row of a table is *i*. The rules were changed in SMIv2 so that auxiliary objects should normally not be accessible, that is, they should have value for the MAX-ACCESS clause of *not-accessible*. The exceptions to this rule are the following:

- a MIB module originally written using SMIv1 rules may not change the access of columnar objects used for indexing from *read-only* to *not-accessible* when converted to SMIv2
- a table that consists solely of columnar objects used for indexing must have at least one which has value for MAX-ACCESS clause of *read-only*

3.13.3 Columnar and Scalar Objects

The OBJECT-TYPE construct is used to specify definitions of columnar and scalar object types, which are also called *leaf object types*. The pairing of the identity of a leaf object and the value to identify an instance of that leaf object is called an SNMP variable. SNMP variables (or approximations of them for the GETNEXT and GETBULK operations) are the operands and results of SNMP operations.

The identifier for all the columnar objects of a table is typically prefixed with a portion of the table's identifier, or an abbreviation of the table's identifier. This approach helps with reading MIB modules. Related scalar objects are typically defined in an area or group. The identifier for a scalar object is typically prefixed with a portion of the group's identifier, or an abbreviation of the group's identifier.

The argument of the SYNTAX clause is any base data type or textual convention, and may be sub-typed if allowed by the base type or textual convention. SMIv2 allows an optional UNITS clause which is used to specify a textual description of the units associated with the data type.

ACCESS and MAX-ACCESS Clauses

The ACCESS clause in SMIv1 specifies the allowed access to the leaf object. There has been confusion within the SNMP community on the use of the clause, and even the allowed values. This is due in part to conflicting specifications. In SMIv1, the values are specified as "read-only", "read-write", and "write-only". However, the SNMP protocol definition allows retrieval operations on object types with access specified as "write-only". (See Table 3–6)

Table 3–6 Values for the ACCESS clause in SMIv1

Value	Description
not-accessible	Not allowed for scalar or columnar object types.[a]
read-only	The object type may be an operand in only retrieval and event report operations.
read-write	The object type may be an operand in modification, retrieval, and event report operations.
write-only	The object type may be an operand in modification, retrieval, and event report operations. However, the result is undefined. Note: this value should not be used, since it is obsolete.

a. This should be allowed for object types as indices. See **Our Opinion** on this issue.

Also, there has been confusion over whether the access specified for a leaf object was the minimal needed for conformance, or the maximum allowed. The rules for SMIv2 clarify the intent of this clause by changing the name to MAX-ACCESS and specifying that the value specified is the one that makes "protocol sense" and not a value for conformance. Another mechanism (the MODULE-COMPLIANCE construct) is provided in SMIv2 to specify conformance, and yet another (the AGENT-CAPABILITIES construct) to document implementation.

In SMIv2, the access values for leaf object are "accessible-for-notify", "read-only", "read-write", and "read-create". (See Table 3–7) Additionally, a columnar object which is also an index for the table may have access value of "not-accessible". Such columnar objects are called *auxiliary objects.*

Table 3–7 Values for the MAX-ACCESS clause in SMIv2

Value	Description
not-accessible	The object type is a column in a table used as an index and may not be used as an operand in any operation.
accessible-for-notify	The object type is a special operand for event report operations.
read-only	The object type may be an operand in only retrieval and event report operations.
read-write	The object type may be an operand in modification, retrieval, and event report operations.
read-create	The object type may be an operand in modification, retrieval, and event report operations. And the object type may be an operand in a modification request that creates a new instance of the object type.

A value of "accessible-for-notify" indicates that instances of the leaf object are only available as operands in event report operations. This value was added to support the special objects which are operands in all event report operations and not to be used for new definitions of leaf objects.

The "read-only" value indicates that an instance of the leaf object may never be an operand to an SNMP modification operation. The "read-write" value indicates that an instance of the object type may be an operand to an SNMP modification, retrieval, and event report operations. However, new instances of the leaf object may not be created via SNMP modification operations.

The "read-create" value indicates that an instance of a columnar object may be created with an SNMP modification operation, and that an instance of the columnar object may be an operand to an SNMP modification, retrieval, and event report operation. If any columnar object in a table has MAX-ACCESS value of "read-create", then no columnar object in the table may have a value of "read-write" for MAX-ACCESS. That is, if row creation is allowed, then "read-create" must be specified for all writable columnar objects, otherwise, "read-write" must be specified.

This requirement for row creation also applies to columnar objects in augmenting tables. That is, if a base table allows row creation, then "read-create" must be specified for all writable columnar objects in an augmenting table for the base table. Otherwise, when a base table does not allow row creation, then "read-write" must be specified for all writable columnar objects in an augmenting table for the base table.

Our Opinion

One small but significant difference between SMIv1 and SMIv2 is the accessibility of indices. SMIv1 requires that indices be accessible, and SMIv2 prefers that they are not accessible. This means that indices written using SMIv2 rules cannot be legally converted to the SMIv1. (Note that it is not valid to just change the value of the MAX-ACCESS clause from "not-accessible" to the value of "read-only" for the SMIv1 ACCESS clause.) This difference is a real incompatibility between SMIv1 and SMIv2. This needs to be resolved, by either changing SMIv1 to allow indices to have an access value of "not-accessible", or to change SMIv2 to require that indices have an access value of "read-only".

STATUS Clause

The value of the STATUS clause for a columnar object must be consistent with the value of the STATUS clause of the containing table. That is, if the status of the containing table is "obsolete", then all the columnar objects must have status of obsolete. If the status for the containing table is "deprecated", then the columnar objects of the table may have status of "deprecated" or "obsolete". There is one further consistency requirement. The columns which are indices for a table must have a status value which is identical to that for the table. (See Table 3–8)

Table 3–8 Consistent STATUS values for Columnar Objects

Value for Containing Table/Row	Allowed values for Index Columnar Objects	Allowed values for Non-Index Columnar Objects
mandatory in SMIv1	mandatory in SMIv1	mandatory, deprecated, or obsolete in SMIv1
current in SMIv2	current in SMIv2	current, deprecated, or obsolete in SMIv2
deprecated	deprecated	deprecated or obsolete
obsolete	obsolete	obsolete

DEFVAL Clause

The DEFVAL clause for a columnar object specifies an acceptable value which may be used when an instance of a row is created via an SNMP modification request and the columnar object is not specified as an operand of the request. Of course, no DEFVAL clause may be specified for the columnar objects which are also the indices of the table, nor may a DEFVAL clause be specified for scalar objects. Also, for some columnar objects there is no one default value that is acceptable for all possible situations. Either a value must always be specified to create an instance, or there are multiple situations and the columnar object has an appropriate default value which is different from others for each situation. These types of columnar objects may not have a DEFVAL clause specified. Instead, these columnar objects must have their default value specified in their DESCRIPTION clause.

In SMIv2 MIB modules, only columnar objects with access of read-create may include a DEFVAL clause. In SMIv1 MIB modules, only columnar objects with access of read-write and which are from tables allowing row creation may include a DEFVAL clause.

The value specified in the DEFVAL clause must conform to the format of values for the "resolved base type" for the columnar object and must conform to restrictions, if any, for values of the syntax specified in the SYNTAX clause for the columnar object. For example, if the value specified for the SYNTAX clause is DisplayString, a textual convention with resolved base type of OCTET STRING (SIZE(0..255)) and with the octets in the string restricted to 7-bit ASCII characters, then the value specified for the DEFVAL clause must be specified in the format of OCTET STRING values and must contain octets with the restricted values. Table 3–9 shows the format of values for each of the base data types.

Table 3–9 Format of Values for DEFVAL Clause

<table>
<tr><th>Base Data Type</th><th>Description</th><th>Syntax and Examples</th></tr>
<tr><td>INTEGER (in SMIv1) and
Integer32 (in SMIv2)</td><td>signed integer
(Note that binary and
hexadecimal values are
always unsigned)</td><td>binStr | hexStr | ["-"] integer,
DEFVAL { 34 }, DEFVAL {'22'h },
DEFVAL {'100010'b}</td></tr>
<tr><td>INTEGER</td><td>label of an enumeration</td><td>lcName, DEFVAL { blue }</td></tr>
<tr><td>Unsigned32 (in SMIv2)</td><td>unsigned integer</td><td>integer | binStr | hexStr,
DEFVAL { 91 }, DEFVAL {'5b'h },
DEFVAL {'01011011'b }</td></tr>
<tr><td>Gauge (in SMIv1) and
Gauge32 (in SMIv2)</td><td>unsigned integer</td><td>integer | binStr | hexStr,
DEFVAL { 578 }, DEFVAL {'242'h },
DEFVAL {'001001000010'b }</td></tr>
<tr><td>Counter (in SMIv1),
Counter32 (in SMIv2), and
Counter64 (in SMIv2)</td><td>no DEFVAL allowed</td><td></td></tr>
<tr><td>TimeTicks</td><td>unsigned integer</td><td>integer | binStr | hexStr,
DEFVAL { 132 }, DEFVAL {'84'h },
DEFVAL {'10000100'b }</td></tr>
<tr><td>OCTET STRING</td><td>character string, binary
string, or hexadecimal
string</td><td>chrStr | hexStr | binStr,
DEFVAL { "aB" },
DEFVAL {'6142'h }, or
DEFVAL {'0110000101000010'b }</td></tr>
<tr><td>OBJECT IDENTIFIER</td><td>identifier of an item
with an OID value, and
additionally in SMIv1
an OID value</td><td>[ucName "."] lcName,
DEFVAL { bcoValve23 }
Additionally, in SMIv1 <oidValue>,
DEFVAL { { 0 0 } }</td></tr>
</table>

Table 3–9 Format of Values for DEFVAL Clause (Continued)

Base Data Type	Description	Syntax and Examples
IpAddress	the value zero or a hexadecimal string of 8 hex digits (4 octets)	"0" | hexStr, DEFVAL { 0 }, DEFVAL {'00000000'h }, or DEFVAL {'a5e30246'h } (i.e., 165.227.2.70)
NetWorkAddress (in SMIv1)	the value zero or a hexadecimal string of 8 hex digits (4 octets)	"0" | hexStr, DEFVAL { 0 }, DEFVAL {'00000000'h }, or DEFVAL {'a5e30246'h } (i.e., 165.227.2.70)
Opaque	hexadecimal string (must be valid BER)	hexStr, DEFVAL {'4403460101'h }
BITS (in SMIv2)	list of bit lablels	"{" [lcName ["," lcName]] "}", DEFVAL { { } }, DEFVAL { { blue } }, DEFVAL { { blue, red, green } }

OID values for Leaf Objects

The OID value assigned to each scalar or columnar object has the following restrictions.

- The final component (or sub-identifier) value of the OID may not be zero.
- No other item may be assigned an OID value which is an extension of an OID value assigned to a scalar or columnar object.
- The OID value for columnar objects must be the object identifier value of the row for the table with an additional component (or sub-identifier).
- By convention, the values of the last component for the OID values assigned to the set of columnar objects for a table start at one, and are consecutively numbered. (See Figure 3–7)
- The OID values assigned to scalar objects generally follow the same pattern with all related scalar objects grouped together under one parent in the OID tree. (See Figure 3–8)

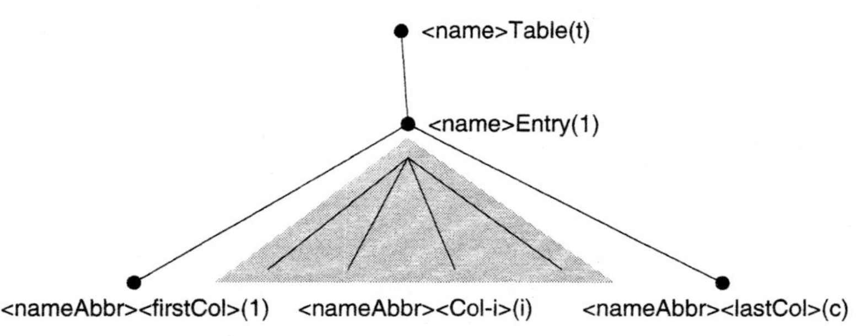

Figure 3–7 OID value assignments for columnar objects

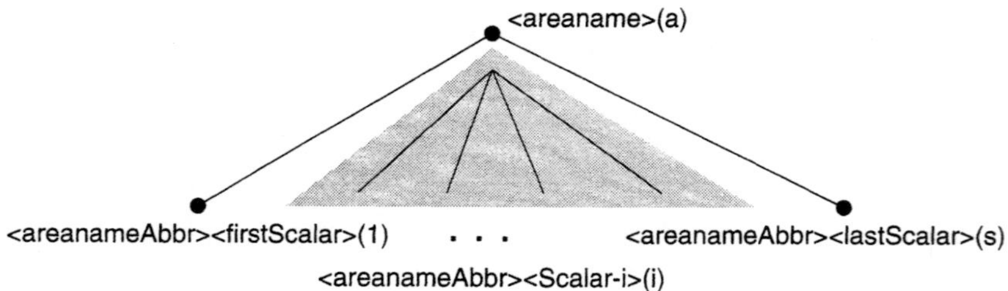

Figure 3–8 OID value assignments for scalar objects

Syntax for Columnar and Scalar Objects

```
-- v1 OBJECT-TYPE definition for a columnar or scalar object,
-- with identifier lcName
<OTdefinitionV1> =
        lcName "OBJECT-TYPE"
              "SYNTAX" <simpleOrEnum>
              "ACCESS" <accessV1>
              "STATUS" <statusV1>
              [ "DESCRIPTION" chrStr ]
              [ "REFERENCE" chrStr ]
              [ "DEFVAL" "{" <defvalV1> "}" ]
        "::=" <oidValue>

-- SMIv1 allowed access
-- note that "write-only" is not valid
<accessV1> = "read-only" | "read-write"

-- SMIv1 status of definition
<statusV1> = "mandatory" | "deprecated" | "obsolete"

-- SMIv1 values for DEFVAL clause
<defvalV1>
        = chrStr
        | binStr
        | hexStr
        | number
        | "-" number
        | [ ucName "." ] lcName
        | <oidValue>


-- v2 OBJECT-TYPE definition for a columnar or scalar object,
-- with identifier lcName
<OTdefinitionV2> =
```

```
                lcName  "OBJECT-TYPE"
                        "SYNTAX" <simpleEnumOrBit>
                        [ "UNITS" chrStr ]
                        "MAX-ACCESS" <accessV2>
                        "STATUS" <statusV2>
                        "DESCRIPTION" chrStr
                        [ "REFERENCE" chrStr ]
                        [ "DEFVAL" "{" <defvalV2> "}" ]
                "::=" <oidValue>

-- SMIv2 allowed access
<accessV2> = "not-accessible" | "accessible-for-notify" |
                        "read-only" | "read-write" | "read-create"

-- SMIv2 status of definition
<statusV2> = "current" | "deprecated" | "obsolete"

-- SMIv2 values for DEFVAL clause
<defvalV2>
        = chrStr
        | binStr
        | hexStr
                | number
                | "-" number
                | [ ucName "." ] lcName
                | "{" [ lcName ["," lcName ]... ] "}"


-- SMIv1 value for SYNTAX clause allows base data types, textual conventions,
-- and enumerated integers.
<simpleOrEnum> =
                <simpleSyntax> |
                "INTEGER" "{" <enumItem> ["," <enumItem> ]... "}"

-- SMIv2 value for SYNTAX clause allows base data types, textual conventions,
-- enumerated integers, and the BITS pseudotype.
<simpleEnumOrBit> =
                <simpleSyntax> |
                "INTEGER" "{" <enumItem> ["," <enumItem> ]... "}" |
                "BITS" "{" <bitItem> ["," <bitItem> ]... "}"

-- base syntax types (and textual conventions)
<simpleSyntax> =
                <synType> |
                <tcType>
```

where

lcName is an identifier that starts with a lowercase letter;
ucName is an identifier that starts with an uppercase letter;
chrStr is a quoted character string which may span multiple lines;
binStr is a binary string;
hexStr is a hexadecimal string;
<oidValue> is an object identifier value;
<enumItem> is a labelled value in an enumeration;
<bitItem> is a labelled bit;
<synType> is a base syntax type with possible sub-typing; and
<tcType> is a textual convention with possible sub-typing.

Example Columnar and Scalar Object Specifications

```
-- In the examples, notice that the text for the DESCRIPTION clause
-- specifies the behavior of semantics of the management information.
-- The REFERENCE clause is used to provide a "pointer" to a source
-- document, if available, where the details are provided.

-- example of a scalar object in SMIv1
sysName OBJECT-TYPE
    SYNTAX      DisplayString (SIZE (0..255))
    ACCESS      read-write
    STATUS      mandatory
    DESCRIPTION
        "An administratively-assigned name for the
        managed system.  By convention, this is the node's
        fully-qualified domain name.  If the name is
        unknown, the value is the zero-length string."
    ::= { system 5 }

-- example of same scalar object written in SMIv2
sysName OBJECT-TYPE
    SYNTAX      DisplayString (SIZE (0..255))
    MAX-ACCESS  read-write
    STATUS      current
    DESCRIPTION
        "An administratively-assigned name for the
        managed system.  By convention, this is the node's
        fully-qualified domain name.  If the name is
        unknown, the value is the zero-length string."
    ::= { system 5 }


-- example of a columnar object in SMIv1
bcoSchedStartTime OBJECT-TYPE
    SYNTAX      INTEGER (0..1439)
    ACCESS      read-write
```

```
    STATUS      mandatory
    DESCRIPTION
        "The starting time in minutes past midnight when
        the sprinkler system schedule starts. A value of
        zero is midnight, and a value 720 is noon."
    DEFVAL      { 360 } -- 6:00am
    ::= { bcoSchedEntry 4 }

  -- example of same columnar object written in SMIv2
bcoSchedStartTime OBJECT-TYPE
    SYNTAX      Integer32 (0..1439)
    UNITS       "minutes"
    MAX-ACCESS  read-create
    STATUS      current
    DESCRIPTION
        "The starting time in minutes past midnight when
        the sprinkler system schedule starts. A value of
        zero is midnight, and a value 720 is noon."
    DEFVAL      { 360 } -- 6:00am
    ::= { bcoSchedEntry 4 }
```

3.14 SEQUENCE Construct

The SEQUENCE construct is used to specify the columnar objects in a row of a table. This construct is an artifact from the original version of an SMIv1, which was supposed to be able to describe management information for both SNMP-based management and CMIP-based management. It is now pretty useless and is a source of the largest number of trivial errors in SNMP MIB modules.

The identifier for a sequence must start with an uppercase letter. This is required by ASN.1. By convention, the identifier used for a sequence is the same as the identifier for the row of the table that uses it, except for the first letter, which is changed from lowercase to uppercase.

The elements of a sequence are pairs of identifier and data type. Each identifier is the same as an identifier for columnar object in the associated table. The data type paired with the identifier is a simplified version of the data type for the columnar object. The following are the simplifications made to the data type of columnar objects:

- no sub-typing is specified — for example Integer32(1..20) is simplified to Integer32
- no enumerated values are specified — for example INTEGER { weekday(1), weekendDay(2)} is simplified to INTEGER
- no named bit values are specified — for example BITS { blue(0), red(1), green(2) } is simplified to BITS

The simplification may not be a change of the data type for the columnar object. For example, if a columnar object had data type "DisplayString" specified for the SYNTAX clause, it would be incorrect to specify "OCTET STRING" as the data type in the sequence definition.

A sequence is used with one-and-only-one table. A sequence may not be imported into a MIB module.

Our Opinion

We believe that the SEQUENCE construct should be eliminated from the grammar for writing SNMP MIB modules. It, along with the table and row constructs, should be combined into one simple construct. A new construct can be created that would not cause any change of current or future assignments of OID values or "bits on the wire."

Syntax

-- SEQUENCE definition, with identifier *ucName*
<SEQdefinition> =
    ucName "::=" "SEQUENCE" "{" <seqMember> ["," <seqMember>]... "}"

-- member of a sequence, with identifier *lcName*
<seqMember> = lcName <seqDataType>

-- Data types for sequence that, by convention, are simplifications of
-- the data types of columnar objects.
-- Note that <seqBits> is not allowed in SMIv1 MIB modules
<seqDataType>
        = <synType>
        | <tcType>
        | <seqEnum>
        | <seqBits>

where

lcName is an identifier that starts with a lowercase letter;
<synType> is a base syntax type with possible sub-typing not specified;
<tcType> is a textual convention with possible sub-typing not specified;
<seqEnum> is the construct for enumerated integers with the list of enumerations not specified (i.e. "INTEGER"); and
<seqBits> is "BITS" with the list of labelled bits not specified;

Example

-- In the example, the table, row, and columnar objects associated with
-- the sequence are also shown.

-- table associated with the sequence

```
exmplTable OBJECT-TYPE
    SYNTAX       SEQUENCE OF ExmplEntry
    MAX-ACCESS   not-accessible
    STATUS       current
    DESCRIPTION
        "A table of ... "
    ::= { exmpl 23 }
```

```
  -- table associated with the sequence
exmplEntry OBJECT-TYPE
    SYNTAX       ExmplEntry
    MAX-ACCESS   not-accessible
    STATUS       current
    DESCRIPTION
        "An entry in the table of ... "
    INDEX        { exmplIndex }
    ::= { exmplTable 1 }

  -- Example sequence.
  -- Notice that the items in the sequence are all of the columnar objects
  -- in the table, and that the data type is a simplification of that specified
  -- in the SYNTAX clause for the columnar objects in the table.
exmplEntry ::= SEQUENCE {
        exmplIndex Unsigned32,
        exmplWeekDay INTEGER,
        exmplColors BITS,
        exmplTemp Gauge32,
        exmplDescr DisplayString,
        exmplPart OBJECT IDENTIFIER
        }

  -- the sub-typing on Unsigned32 below is left off in the sequence
exmplIndex OBJECT-TYPE
    SYNTAX       Unsigned32 (1..255)
    MAX-ACCESS   not-accessible
    STATUS       current
    DESCRIPTION
        " ... "
    ::= { exmplEntry 1 }

  -- the list of enumerated integers that are specified below are left
  -- off in the sequence
exmplWeekDay OBJECT-TYPE
    SYNTAX       INTEGER {
                  monday(1),
                  tuesday(2),
                  wednesday(3),
                  thursday(4),
                  friday(5),
                  saturday(6),
                  sunday(7)
                  }
    MAX-ACCESS   read-only
    STATUS       current
    DESCRIPTION
        " ... "
```

```
    ::= { exmplEntry 2 }

  -- the list of named bits that are specified below are left off in the sequence
exmplColor OBJECT-TYPE
    SYNTAX       BITS {
                  red(0),
                  blue(1),
                  green(2)
                  }
    MAX-ACCESS   read-only
    STATUS       current
    DESCRIPTION
        " ... "
    ::= { exmplEntry 3 }

  -- the sub-typing on Gauge32 below is left off in the sequence
exmplTemp OBJECT-TYPE
    SYNTAX       Gauge32 (80..115)
    MAX-ACCESS   read-only
    STATUS       current
    DESCRIPTION
        " ... "
    ::= { exmplEntry 4 }

  -- the sub-typing on DisplayString below is left off in the sequence
exmplDescr OBJECT-TYPE
    SYNTAX       DisplayString (SIZE(0..80))
    MAX-ACCESS   read-only
    STATUS       current
    DESCRIPTION
        " ... "
    ::= { exmplEntry 5 }

  -- the value for the SYNTAX clause is identical to that in the sequence,
  -- since data type "OBJECT IDENTIFIER" cannot be simplified
exmplPart OBJECT-TYPE
    SYNTAX       OBJECT IDENTIFIER
    MAX-ACCESS   read-only
    STATUS       current
    DESCRIPTION
        " ... "
    ::= { exmplEntry 6 }
```

3.15 TRAP-TYPE Construct

The TRAP-TYPE construct is used in SNMPv1 MIB modules to specify the events that an agent can report to SNMP managers.

Caution

The event reporting mechanisms, specification, and control is one of the weaker areas of SNMPv1-based management. Due to political pressure in the SNMPv1 WG, the rules for defining events reports (which are called traps) are specified in an RFC that is labelled *Informational*. That is, the TRAP-TYPE construct is defined in a document (RFC 1215) that is not on the IETF standards track! However, event reports are an important part of SNMP-based management, even if obscurely specified. Additionally, a poor design choice was made in identifying traps. This poor choice was made worse by an inadequate description of the TRAP-TYPE construct in RFC 1215. The combination of these factors (i.e., an obscure document, a poor design choice in identifying events, and an inadequate description) has resulted in poor understanding and specification of events in SMIv1 using the TRAP-TYPE construct.

An SNMPv1 event report message, a trap, is identified by the values of fields *enterprise*, *generic-trap*, and *specific-trap*. However, the TRAP-TYPE construct has only two places to indicate the values of these three fields. How this is done is explained in the next paragraph, but first we need a quick overview of the TRAP-TYPE construct. The construct looks like many of the other constructs used in SNMP MIB modules. It starts with an identifier, has the keyword "TRAP-TYPE" which is followed by several clauses (ENTERPRISE, VARIABLES, DESCRIPTION, and REFERENCE), and the construct is finished with the "::=" punctuation. However, the value that follows the "::=" is not an OID value, but a non-negative integer. This value is the one to be used in either the *generic-trap* or the *specific-trap* field depending on the value of the ENTERPRISE clause.

When the value specified for the ENTERPRISE clause is snmp (i.e., iso(1).org(3).dod(6).internet(1).mgmt(2).mib(1).snmp(11)), then the value is for the *generic-trap* field. Otherwise, the value is for the *specific-trap* field. All so-called "generic traps" have been defined and no new ones are possible. There are exactly six events that are defined as "generic traps." All other events are defined as "specific traps."

Our Opinion

We believe that much confusion could be eliminated if the TRAP-TYPE construct could be redefined with three places to specify the three fields of the event report message, and the clauses had names other than ENTERPRISE, SPECIFIC, and GENERIC.

There is no STATUS clause in the TRAP-TYPE construct. The status of a definition should be indicated by text in the DESCRIPTION field.

The optional VARIABLES clause of the TRAP-TYPE construct is used to specify one or more scalar or columnar objects whose value describes the event. A single instance of each object type (and its value) specified in the VARIABLES clause is returned in an event report message. There is no sub-clause to specify which instance of a columnar object to return. The DESCRIPTION clause must be used for this purpose. Unfortunately, many events have been defined that show a poor choice of object types specified in the VARIABLES clause. These definitions generally lack adequate description in the DESCRIPTION clause of which instance of a columnar object to return in the event report.

The most frequent mistake (or misunderstanding) is to specify in the VARIABLES clause columnar objects that are also an index for a table. These object types, in most cases, are poor choices, since the value that is returned is identical to the object's instance. A better choice to be returned is a status columnar object from the table. For example, the generic traps "linkUp" and "linkDown" both contain a VARIABLES clause that has object type ifIndex. This object is the index for its containing table. A better choice for inclusion in the VARIABLES clause are object types ifAdminStatus, ifOperStatus, and ifLastChange. These columnar objects specify the desired state of the interface, the current state of the interface, and the time when the interface entered its current state.

Syntax

```
-- TRAP-TYPE definition, with identifier lcName
<TTdefinition> =
        lcName "TRAP-TYPE"
                "ENTERPRISE" [ ucName "." ] lcName
        [ "VARIABLES" "{" <varItem> [ ","<varItem> ]... "}" ]
        [ "DESCRIPTION" chrStr ]
        [ "REFERENCE" chrStr ]
        "::=" number

-- object type, with module name ucName, and lcName as the
-- identifier for the object
<varItem> = [ ucName "." ] lcName
```

where

lcName is an identifier that starts with a lowercase letter;
ucName is an identifier that starts with an uppercase letter;
chrStr is a quoted character string which may span multiple lines; and
number is a non-negative integer.

Examples

```
-- a "generic trap," which is indicated by the value "snmp" for the
-- ENTERPRISE clause
-- (Note: all of the "generic traps" are already defined)
coldStart TRAP-TYPE
    ENTERPRISE  snmp
    DESCRIPTION
        " ... "
    ::= 0
```

```
   -- an OID value assignment, so snmpDot3RptrMgt can be used
   -- in the TRAP-TYPE construct
snmpDot3RptrMgt OBJECT IDENTIFIER ::= { mib-2 22 }

   -- an "enterprise specific trap," which is indicated by a value other
   -- than "snmp" for the ENTERPRISE field
   -- (Note: this format is used to define all events other than
   -- the six generic traps)
rptrResetEvent TRAP-TYPE
    ENTERPRISE  snmpDot3RptrMgt
    VARIABLES   { rptrOperStatus }
    DESCRIPTION
        " ... "
    REFERENCE
        " ... "
    ::= 3

   -- This example shows the information that should be included
   -- in the DESCRIPTION clause to describe which instances of
   -- the specified object types to be returned.
   -- The description also specifies whether the event is
   -- "edge-triggered" or "level-triggered".
bcoBrSpEv TRAP-TYPE
    ENTERPRISE  bcoSprinklerEvents
    VARIABLES   { bcoSprActFlow, bcoSprSetFlow,
                  bcoSchedStartTime }
    DESCRIPTION
        "A sprinkler is not operating correctly for
        a sprinkler schedule. The variables are:
          bcoSprActFlow - the actual flow for the
               sprinkler with the instance identifying
               the index of the sprinkler;
          bcoSprSetFlow - the flow that was set for
               the sprinkler with the instance
               identifying the index of the sprinkler; and
          bcoSchedStartTime - the starting time of the
               schedule containing the sprinkler with
               the instance identifying the index
               of the schedule.

        This event is generated at most once per sprinkler
        per operation of a schedule when the event is first
        observed."
    ::= 24
```

Agent developers have not always implemented traps correctly. One reported problem is to return the OID for each object type in the variable-bindings list instead of the OID for each SNMP variable. (An SNMP variable is the OID for the object type and one or more OID components to identify the instance of the object.) Besides being incorrect, the particular instance columnar objects cannot be determined. The other reported problem is for agent developers to return the wrong value in the enterprise field of a trap message. An agent may always return the value of sysObjectID, even when the trap is not a generic-trap. If so, identification of events may not be possible.

3.16 NOTIFICATION-TYPE Construct

The NOTIFICATION-TYPE construct is used in SNMPv2 MIB modules to specify the events which can be reported to SNMP managers. The event reporting mechanisms and specifications were completely reworked in SNMPv2. There are many improvements over SNMPv1, with the greatest being event identification.

In SNMPv2, events are identified by an OID value. A value can be chosen for the OID so that the event's identity can be mapped between the OID value and the SNMPv1 identification, using an OID value and two integers. The mapping is quite simple. The SNMPv1 "generic traps" have one mapping. The SNMPv1 "specific traps" are mapped to an OID value by using the OID value from the ENTERPRISE clause of the TRAP-TYPE construct, adding an OID component value of zero, and adding a final OID component value which corresponds to the value assigned to the event.

For example, if "bcoBrSpEv" is the identifier for a trap, with bcoSprinklerEvents specified for the value of the ENTERPRISE clause, and the integer 24 assigned to the trap, then the OID value would be specified in the MIB module as { bcoSprinklerEvents 0 24 }.

The optional OBJECTS clause of the NOTIFICATION-TYPE construct is used to specify one or more scalar or columnar objects whose values describe the event. A single instance of each object type (and its value) specified in the OBJECTS clause is contained in an event report message. There is no sub-clause to specify which instance of a columnar object to return. The DESCRIPTION clause must be used for this purpose.

Event definitions translated from SMIv1's TRAP-TYPE construct to SMIv2's NOTIFICATION-TYPE construct will carry forth any poor choices made for the object types. (See the discussion in Section 3.15 about proper choice of object types to associate with an event.)

The status of the object types specified in the OBJECTS clause must be conforming with the status of the event definition. That is, if the event definition has status of "current", then all object types in the OBJECTS clause must also have status of "current". If the event definition is "deprecated", then object types may be "deprecated" or "current". If the event definition is "obsolete", then the object types may be "current", "deprecated", or "obsolete".

The SNMPv2 event definition with the NOTIFICATION-TYPE construct has been designed for two uses. The first use is to define events reported by an agent to a manager. This is identical to the usage of the TRAP-TYPE definition in SMIv1, that is for an SNMP agent to report an event to an SNMP manager, which may trigger some special processing. The other use of the event definition is to define events that one SNMP manager reports to another. This reporting occurs when the first manager notices an event concerning an SNMP agent and reports it to a second manager. The details for this type of event reporting have not yet been completely refined, but may provide some exciting opportunities for developers of distributed management applications.

Our Opinion

SNMPv2-based management does not contain a "confirmed event report" mechanism. This is one of the capabilities found in other management systems which is not present in SNMPv2-based management. When this protocol operation is added, the NOTIFICATION-TYPE construct can do double duty to specify events that can be sent with an unconfirmed report, or with a confirmed report. We believe that the name of this construct poorly describes the use of the construct. We believe that a much more appropriate name would be EVENT-TYPE. In general, events noticed by an agent can be discarded, logged locally, and/or reported to one or more managers.

Syntax

```
-- NOTIFICATION-TYPE definition, with identifier lcName
<NTdefinition> =
            lcName  "NOTIFICATION-TYPE"
                    [ "OBJECTS" "{" <varItem> [ "," <varItem> ]... "}" ]
                    "STATUS" <statusV2>
                    "DESCRIPTION" chrStr
                    [ "REFERENCE" chrStr ]
                    "::=" <oidValue>

-- object type, with module name ucName, and lcName as the
-- identifier for the object
<varItem> = [ ucName "." ] lcName

-- SMIv2 status of definition
<statusV2> = "current" | "deprecated" | "obsolete"
```

where

lcName is an identifier that starts with a lowercase letter;
ucName is an identifier that starts with an uppercase letter;
chrStr is a quoted character string which may span multiple lines; and
<oidValue> is an object identifier value.

Examples

```
-- The SNMPv1 "generic traps" that have been converted to SMIv2 do not
-- follow the suggested format of the OID value to assign to event
-- definitions. Translations between SNMPv1 event reports and SNMPv2
-- event reports have to "special case" these events.

-- the root of the sub-tree of OIDs used to identify events which are
-- translations of the SNMPv1 "generic traps"
snmpTraps OBJECT IDENTIFIER ::= { snmpMIBObjects 5 }

coldStart NOTIFICATION-TYPE
    STATUS      current
    DESCRIPTION
        " ... "
    ::= { snmpTraps 1 }

-- the following shows the conversion of an "enterprise specific trap" from a
-- standards track SNMPv1 MIB module

-- the root of the sub-tree of OIDs used to identify events and object types
-- in the MIB module
snmpDot3RptrMgt OBJECT IDENTIFIER ::= { mib-2 22 }

-- The following is an "enterprise specific trap" that has been converted to an
-- SNMPv2 event definition.
-- Note the OID value which is the value of the ENTERPRISE clause from the
-- TRAP-TYPE definition, a zero, and the value assigned to the SNMPv1 trap.
rptrResetEvent NOTIFICATION-TYPE
    OBJECTS     { rptrOperStatus }
    STATUS      current
    DESCRIPTION
        " ... "
    REFERENCE
        " ... "
    ::= { snmpDot3RptrMgt 0 3 }

-- The above could have also been written slightly different to work around a
-- limitation that some MIB compilers have for the format of OID values.
-- This work-around is shown below:

-- First, define OID value so format is { <name> <number> }.
snmpDot3RptrMgt OBJECT IDENTIFIER ::= { mib-2 22 }
snmpDot3Events OBJECT IDENTIFIER ::= { snmpDot3RptrMgt 0 }

-- Now, the definition is changed so the OID value is expressed
-- in format of { <name> <number> }.
rptrResetEvent NOTIFICATION-TYPE
```

```
    OBJECTS      { rptrOperStatus }
    STATUS       current
    DESCRIPTION
        " ... "
    REFERENCE
        " ... "
    ::= { snmpDot3Events 3 }
```

-- This example shows the information that should be included in
-- the DESCRIPTION clause. It describes which instances of the
-- specified object types to be returned and specifies whether
-- the event is "edge-triggered" or "level-triggered".

```
bcoSprBrEv NOTIFICATION-TYPE
    OBJECTS      { bcoSprActFlow, bcoSprSetFlow,
                   bcoSchedStartTime }
    STATUS       current
    DESCRIPTION
        "A sprinkler is not operating correctly for
        a sprinkler schedule. The variables are:
          bcoSprActFlow - the actual flow for the
               sprinkler with the instance identifying
               the index of the sprinkler;
          bcoSprSetFlow - the flow that was set for
               the sprinkler with the instance
               identifying the index of the sprinkler; and
          bcoSchedStartTime - the starting time of the
               schedule containing the sprinkler with
               the instance identifying the index
               of the schedule.

        This event is generated at most once per sprinkler
        per operation of a schedule when the event is first
        observed."
    ::= { bcoSprinklerEvents 0 24 }
```

3.17 OBJECT-GROUP Construct

The OBJECT-GROUP construct is used in SNMPv2 MIB modules to define a collection of related object type definitions. This grouping is done by the MIB module author to show the logical grouping of object types to help agent and management application developers. Systems usually consist of one or more core sub-systems, and zero, one, or more optional sub-systems. The OBJECT-GROUP construct assists the MIB module author in grouping object types to show their correspondence to sub-systems.

Every object type with a value for the MAX-ACCESS clause other than "not-accessible" must be a member of at least one object group. (The constructs that specify requirements for conformance, and the implementation details for agents specify object groups. Object types not specified in an object group cannot be specified in a requirements construct.) Only the object types defined in the same MIB module as the definition for the object group may be members of that group. An object type may be a member of more than one object group.

The status of the object types specified in the OBJECTS clause must be conforming with the status of the object group definition. That is, if the object group definition has status of "current", then all object types in the OBJECTS clause must also have status of "current". If the object group definition is "deprecated", then object types may be "deprecated" or "current". If the object group definition is "obsolete", then the object types may be "current", "deprecated", or "obsolete".

The DESCRIPTION and REFERENCE clauses describe the object group and any relationship, such as dependencies, that the object group has with others. No implementation requirements for conformance are specified in the DESCRIPTION or REFERENCE clause. All compliances are specified with the MODULE-COMPLIANCE construct.

The value assigned to an object group is an OID which uniquely identifies it.

Syntax

```
-- OBJECT-GROUP definition, with identifier lcName
<OGdefinition> =
            lcName  "OBJECT-GROUP"
                    "OBJECTS" "{" <ogObject> [ "," <ogObject> ]... "}"
                    "STATUS" <statusV2>
                    "DESCRIPTION" chrStr
                    [ "REFERENCE" chrStr ]
                    "::=" <oidValue>

-- An object, with identifer lcName
<ogObject> = lcName

-- SMIv2 status of definition
<statusV2> = "current" | "deprecated" | "obsolete"
```

where

lcName is an identifier that starts with a lowercase letter;
chrStr is a quoted character string which may span multiple lines; and
<oidValue> is an object identifier value.

Example

```
-- Usually all the scalar objects directly defined under the same
-- sub-tree are put into the same object group.
-- Also, usually all of the accessible columnar objects for a table
-- are put into the same object group.
-- However, both scalar and columnar objects may be members
-- of the same object group.
ipGroup OBJECT-GROUP
    OBJECTS     { ipForwarding, ipDefaultTTL, ipInReceives,
                  ipInHdrErrors, ipInAddrErrors,
```

```
                ipForwDatagrams, ipInUnknownProtos,
                  <rest of items>
                 }
    STATUS      current
    DESCRIPTION
        " ... "
    ::= { ipMIBGroups 1 }
```

3.18 NOTIFICATION-GROUP Construct

The NOTIFICATION-GROUP construct is used in SNMPv2 MIB modules to define a collection of related event definitions. This grouping is done by the MIB module author to show the logical grouping of events as a hint for agent and management application designers and/or developers.

Systems usually consist of one or more core sub-systems, and zero, one, or more optional sub-systems. The NOTIFICATION-GROUP construct assists the MIB module author in grouping events to show their correspondence to sub-systems. Every event defined in a MIB module must be a member of at least one event group. (The constructs that specify requirements for conformance, and the implementation details for agents specify event groups. Events not specified in an event group cannot be specified in a requirements construct.) Only the events defined in the same MIB module as the definition for the event group may be members of that group. An event may be a member of more than one event group.

The status of the events specified in the NOTIFICATIONS clause must be conforming with the status of the event group definition. That is, if the event group definition has status of "current", then all events in the NOTIFICATIONS clause must also have status of "current". If the event group definition is "deprecated", then events may be "deprecated" or "current". If the event group definition is "obsolete", then the events may be "current", "deprecated", or "obsolete".

The DESCRIPTION and REFERENCE clauses describe the event group and any relationship, such as dependencies, that the event group has with others. No implementation requirements for conformance are specified in the DESCRIPTION or REFERENCE clause. All compliances are specified with the MODULE-COMPLIANCE construct.

The value assigned to an event group is an OID which uniquely identifies it.

Syntax

```
-- NOTIFICATION-GROUP definition, with identifier lcName
<NGdefinition> =
            lcName "NOTIFICATION-GROUP"
                   "NOTIFICATIONS" "{" <ngEvent> [ "," <ngEvent> ]... "}"
                   "STATUS" <statusV2>
                   "DESCRIPTION" chrStr
                   [ "REFERENCE" chrStr ]
                   "::=" <oidValue>
```

-- An event, with identifier *lcName*
<ngEvent> = lcName

-- SMIv2 status of definition
<statusV2> = "current" | "deprecated" | "obsolete"

where

lcName is an identifier that starts with a lowercase letter;
chrStr is a quoted character string which may span multiple lines; and
<oidValue> is an object identifier value.

Example

-- an event group

```
bcoSprinklerEventGroup NOTIFICATION-GROUP
    NOTIFICATIONS { bcoSprBrEv, bcoSprPrEv }
    STATUS      current
    DESCRIPTION
        " ... "
    ::= { bcoSprinklerGroups 7 }
```

3.19 MODULE-COMPLIANCE Construct

The MODULE-COMPLIANCE construct is used in SNMPv2 MIB modules to define implementation requirements specifications for agents. One or more requirements specifications may be defined within a MIB module. A requirements specification may reference items defined in the containing MIB module and/or in other MIB modules. A requirements specification names groups of object types and/or events to be implemented. (The term "implemented" for a group means that all of the items within the group are implemented.) The groups can be specified as unconditionally required, or as conditionally required, and if so, the conditions that cause each group to be required must be specified in a textual description clause.

There may also be exceptions specified for the behaviors that need be implemented for individual object types. Otherwise, the term "implemented" for an object type or event means that all defined behaviors are present. For example, if an object type is defined with access of "read-write", then an agent which implements that object type must allow retrieval and modification operations to the management information characterized by that object type. An exception may be specified so that the agent needs to provide only retrieval operations. The exceptions are only for object types. The exceptions can specify the minimal access requirements, the minimal range of values for retrieval and/or modification operations, and the minimal overall behaviors.

Currently, the primary use for the MODULE-COMPLIANCE construct is to allow the MIB module author to specify the minimal list of object types and events defined in the containing MIB module that an agent developer must implement. An agent that implements all of the requirements specified in the MODULE-COMPLIANCE construct is said to "implement the MIB module." However, this terminology is not correct. Strictly speaking, an agent's implementation either meets (or does not meet) a requirements specification. In other words, an agent is compliant (or is not compliant) to a requirements specification, since a requirements specification may specify items from more than one MIB module.

For example, the MODULE-COMPLIANCE construct can be used to specify the management information that a management application must access for it to perform a management task. A MODULE-COMPLIANCE construct can be used in a request for quote (RFQ) for networking equipment to make sure that the equipment has the needed network management capabilities.

Our Opinion

We believe the name "MODULE-COMPLIANCE" is a poor choice for the construct to define a requirements specification. Much better names are "AGENT-REQUIREMENTS" and "IMPLEMENTATION-REQUIREMENTS" since they provide a better label for what is being defined.

A requirements specification using the MODULE-COMPLIANCE construct can be quite difficult to read since it is easy to misread the nesting. The construct consists of a header, followed by a list of MIB module requirements specifications. Within a MIB module requirements specification is a list of groups which are unconditionally required, followed by a list of conditionally required groups and exception specifications. (See Figure 3–9)

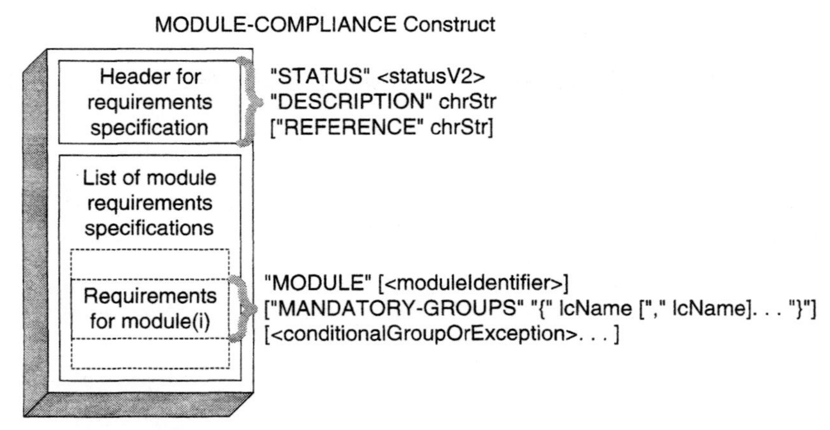

Figure 3–9 Elements of a MODULE-COMPLIANCE construct

There are many consistency dependencies within a MODULE-COMPLAINCE construct. However, unlike the OBJECT-GROUP and NOTIFICATION-GROUP constructs, the value of the STATUS clause is independent of the status value of any group or item specified within a MODULE-COMPLIANCE construct. That is, a requirements specification with a status value of "current" may specify groups or items with status value of "deprecated" or "obsolete". (A requirements specification can be absolutely valid, even though it calls for use of old definitions!)

The dependencies for other clauses follow normal expectations. For a "module requirements" section, all the groups or items must be defined in that module. A group cannot be listed as unconditionally required and conditionally required. (A group which is defined in a MIB module, but which is not specified as unconditionally required or conditionally required is said to be "unconditionally optional." A MIB module in a standards-track MIB specification must not have any unconditionally optional groups. Such groups are those that the MIB author defined, but did not specify conditions for which the group should be required!) An item specified as an exception must be defined in the MIB module, and must be a member of a unconditionally required or conditionally required group specified for the module requirements.

The values specified in the clauses for an item's exceptions must be a sub-set of those in the item's definition. That is, the values cannot be identical, nor may they change the behaviors of the item. They can only sub-set the behaviors. For example, an object type defined with data type of "Integer32 (1..100)" could not have the data type changed to, say, "Gauge32", but could specify that the values were in the range 10 to 20 instead of 1 to 100.

Each requirements specification is assigned an OID value which uniquely identifies it.

Syntax

```
-- MODULE-COMPLIANCE definition, with identifier lcName
<MCdefinition> =
            lcName  "MODULE-COMPLIANCE"
                    "STATUS" <statusV2>
                    "DESCRIPTION" chrStr
                    [ "REFERENCE" chrStr ]
                    [ <mcModule> ]...
                    "::=" <oidValue>

-- SMIv2 status of definition
<statusV2> = "current" | "deprecated" | "obsolete"

-- module for MODULE-COMPLIANCE
<mcModule> =
            "MODULE" [<moduleIdentifier>]
            [ "MANDATORY-GROUPS" "{" lcName ["," lcName ]... "}" ]
            [ <conditionalGroupOrException> ]...

-- a conditional group or exception
<conditionalGroupOrException> =
            <conditionalGroup> |
            <exception>

-- a conditional group
<conditionalGroup> =
            "GROUP" lcName
            "DESCRIPTION" chrStr
```

```
-- an exception for an object type
<exception> =
            "OBJECT" lcName
            [ "SYNTAX" <simpleEnumOrBit> ]
            [ "WRITE-SYNTAX" <simpleEnumOrBit> ]
            [ "MIN-ACCESS" <minAccess> ]
            "DESCRIPTION" chrStr

-- minimal required access for an object type
<minAccess>
            = "not-accessible"
            | "accessible-for-notify"
            | "read-only"
            | "read-write"

-- SMIv2 value for SYNTAX clause allows base data types, textual conventions,
-- enumerated integers, and in SMIv2 the BITS pseudotype
<simpleEnumOrBit> =
            <simpleSyntax> |
            "INTEGER" "{" <enumItem> ["," <enumItem> ]... "}" |
            "BITS" "{" <bitItem> ["," <bitItem> ]... "}"

-- base syntax types (and textual conventions)
<simpleSyntax> =
            <synType> |
            <tcType>
```

where

lcName is an identifier that starts with a lowercase letter;
chrStr is a quoted character string which may span multiple lines;
<moduleIdentifier> is the identification of a module;
<oidValue> is an object identifier value;
<enumItem> is a value in an enumeration;
<bitItem> is a named bit;
<synType> is a base syntax type with possible sub-typing; and
<tcType> is a textual convention with possible sub-typing.

Example

```
-- The following is a requirements specification used to specify
-- only what must be implemented in the current MIB module.
-- Note that there is exactly one MODULE clause and the name of the
-- module is not specified, which is used to specify the current module.
-- Also note that the identifier specified for the MODULE-COMPLIANCE
-- should be related to the name of the MIB module.
```

```
   -- outside wrapper for module
BCO-SPRINKLER-MIB DEFINITIONS ::= BEGIN
IMPORTS
       -- rest of IMPORTS construct not shown

   -- module identity construct
bcoSprinkerModule MODULE-IDENTITY
       -- rest of MODULE-IDENTITY construct not shown

   -- module compliance construct
bcoSprinklerComplV01 MODULE-COMPLIANCE
    STATUS      current
    DESCRIPTION
        " ... "
    MODULE
        MANDATORY-GROUPS { bcoSprValueGroup,
                    bcoSprSchedGroup, bcoSprEventGroup }
        GROUP { bcoSprAdvValueGroup }
            DESCRIPTION
                " ... "
        OBJECT bcoSprValveSetRate
            MIN-ACCESS  read-only
            DESCRIPTION
                " ... "
        OBJECT bcoSprValveActRate
            DESCRIPTION
                " ... "
    ::= { bcoSprinklerCompliances 1 }

END -- module BCO-SPRINKLER-MIB

   -- The following is a requirements specification used to specify the
   -- needed network management capabilities in an agent for a network
   -- management application. Note that this requirements specification
   -- includes multiple MIB modules and that the MIB module containing
   -- this MODULE-COMPLIANCE specification contains no other
   -- definitions (other than the required module identity definition).

   -- a MIB module containing definitions of requirements
XYZ-SPRINKLER-APP-MIB DEFINITIONS ::= BEGIN
IMPORTS
       -- rest of IMPORTS construct not shown

   -- module identity construct
xyzSprinkerAppModule MODULE-IDENTITY
       -- rest of MODULE-IDENTITY construct not shown
```

```
  -- module compliance construct
zyxSprinklerAppReqV01 MODULE-COMPLIANCE
    STATUS      current
    DESCRIPTION
        " ... "
    MODULE IP-MIB
        MANDATORY-GROUPS { ipGroup, icmpGroup }
    MODULE SNMPv2-MIB
        MANDATORY-GROUPS { snmpGroup, systemGroup,
                           snmpBasicNotificationsGroup }
    MODULE UDP-MIB
        MANDATORY-GROUPS { udpGroup }
    ::= { bcoSprinklerCompliances 1 }
    MODULE BCO-SPRINKLER-MIB
        MANDATORY-GROUPS { bcoSprValueGroup,
                  bcoSprSchedGroup, bcoSprEventGroup }
        GROUP { bcoSprAdvValueGroup }
            DESCRIPTION
                " ... "
    ::= { zyxSprinklerAppReq 1 }

END -- module zyxSprinklerAppReqV01
```

3.19.1 Conditional Groups

The GROUP clause is used to specify a conditionally required object or notification group. The DESCRIPTION clause, which is paired with the GROUP clause, specifies the conditions when the group is required. For example, a MODULE-COMPLIANCE specification could be written to indicate that if the managed system implemented the TCP protocol, then the objects associated with the TCP protocol must be implemented by the agent to be compliant to the requirements specification. A group may not be specified in the MANDATORY-GROUPS clause and in a GROUP clause. Also, a group may not be specified in two different GROUP clauses.

3.19.2 Exceptions

The OBJECT clause and its associated clauses specify reductions in required behaviors of an object to meet a requirements specification. This is typically used to specify that an implementation of a table need not support row creation to meet a requirements specification, even though the definition of the table defines row creation. This is accomplished by specifying that the minimum required value for access is either *read-write* or *read-only* instead of *read-create* in the MIN-ACCESS clause. The MIN-ACCESS clause can also be used to specify that an object in an object group need not be implemented. This is done by specifying the value of *not-accessible* for the MIN-ACCESS clause. The value of *accessible-for-notify* is used to indicate that an object need only be present to return an instance in an event.

The purpose of the SYNTAX and WRITE-SYNTAX clauses are to allow a reduction in the behavior of an object to be specified. The values specified for these clauses must be a reduction of the value for the SYNTAX clause in the object's definition. These clauses work in simple cases, such as a reduction in the values for an enumerated integer, but don't really work for slightly more complex cases. The fall back is to use the associated DESCRIPTION clause to specify the reduction in required behaviors.

The MODULE-COMPLIANCE construct has seen quite limited usage and is poorly documented as to how it should be used. We can't help you out with all the answers, since there is no large knowledge or experience base we can tap.

3.20 AGENT-CAPABILITIES Construct

The AGENT-CAPABILITIES construct is used in SNMPv2 MIB modules to specify implementation characteristics of an SNMP agent sub-system with respect to object types and events. The term "implement" means that the agent provides all defined behaviors of these items unless documented by exception clauses in the AGENT-CAPABILITIES construct.

One or more AGENT-CAPABILITIES constructs may be used to completely describe the implementation characteristics of an agent. Whether one, two, or more AGENT-CAPABILITIES constructs are used is the choice of the agent developer. Usually, an AGENT-CAPABILITIES construct is contained in a MIB module with no other constructs other than the required IMPORTS and MODULE-IDENTITY construct. Multiple implementation characteristics specifications may be defined within the same MIB module.

The AGENT-CAPABILITIES construct consists of a header that is followed by a list of implementation specifications. (See Figure 3–10) Each implementation specification lists groups, and optionally objects and events defined within one MIB module. The header con-

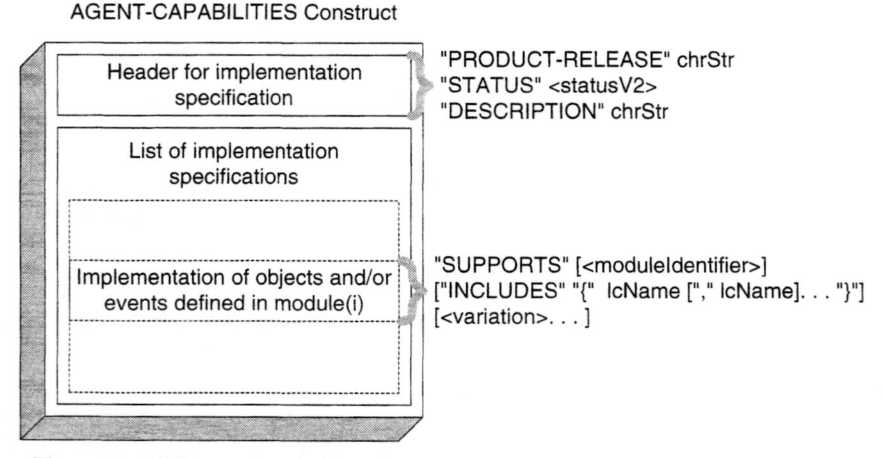

Figure 3–10 Elements of a AGENT-CAPABILITIES construct

sists of the PRODUCT-RELEASE, STATUS, and DESCRIPTION clauses. The PRODUCT-RELEASE clause is meant to describe the product release which includes the implemented capabilities. There are many consistency dependencies within an AGENT-CAPABILITIES construct. Unlike the OBJECT-GROUP and NOTIFICATION-GROUP constructs, the value of the STATUS clause is independent of the status value of any group or item specified within an AGENT-CAPABILITIES construct. That is, an implementation specification with a status value of "current" may specify groups or items with a status value of "deprecated" or "obsolete". (An implementation specification can be absolutely valid even though it specifies that an agent implements old definitions!) The dependencies for other clauses follow normal expectations. For a "supported" module, all the specified groups or items must be defined in that module. An item specified as an exception (or variation) need not be a member of one of the groups listed in the INCLUDES sub-clause for a module. The values specified in the sub-clauses for items must be a sub-set of those in the item's definition. That is, the values cannot be identical, nor may they change the behaviors of the item. They can only sub-set the behaviors. For example, an object type defined with data type of "Integer32 (1..100)" could not have the data type changed to, say, "Gauge32", but could specify that the values were in the range 10 to 20 instead of 1 to 100.

Caution

The PRODUCT-RELEASE clause as currently defined seems somewhat misplaced. This is due to several factors. The AGENT-CAPABILITIES construct has gone through a shift of its meaning. Originally, a single AGENT-CAPABILITIES construct was supposed to completely specify the implementation characteristics of an agent. This has been changed so that an AGENT-CAPABILITIES construct now can be used to describe only a portion of an agent. The clause name, "PRODUCT-RELEASE", seems to associate a date and/or a version of an agent to an AGENT-CAPABILITIES construct. However, an agent may be updated (and given a new version) without changing its management capabilities, as well as an agent may be used on different hardware without changing its management capabilities. For these reasons, the meaning of the PRODUCT-RELEASE clause has lost its precision and, thus, we believe that it needs to be replaced or be redefined.

Each implementation specification is assigned an OID value which uniquely identifies it.

Syntax

```
-- AGENT-CAPABILITIES definition, with identifier lcName
<ACdefinition> =
            lcName "AGENT-CAPABILITIES"
                   "PRODUCT-RELEASE" chrStr
                   "STATUS" <statusV2>
```

```
                    "DESCRIPTION" chrStr
                    [ "REFERENCE" chrStr ]
                    [ <acModule> ]...
                    "::=" <oidValue>

-- SMIv2 status of definition
<statusV2> = "current" | "deprecated" | "obsolete"

-- module for AGENT-CAPABILITIES
<acModule> =
            "SUPPORTS" <moduleIdentifier>
            "INCLUDES" "{" <group> ["," <group> ]... "}"
            [ <variation> ]...

-- an object or event group, with identifier lcName
<group> = lcName

-- variation in AGENT-CAPABILITIES, with identifier lcName
-- (used for both object types and events, with some clause
-- not always appropriate)
<variation>
            "VARIATION" lcName
            [ "SYNTAX" <simpleEnumOrBit> ]
            [ "WRITE-SYNTAX" <simpleEnumOrBit> ]
            [ "ACCESS" <capAccess> ]
            [ "CREATION-REQUIRES" "{" lcName ["," lcName ]... "}" ]
            [ "DEFVAL" "{" <defval> "}" ]
            "DESCRIPTION" chrStr

-- access for object type or event in AGENT-CAPABILITIES
<capAccess>
            = "not-implemented"
            | "accessible-for-notify"
            | "read-only"
            | "read-write"
            | "write-only"

-- SMIv2 value for SYNTAX clause allows base data types, textual conventions,
-- enumerated integers, and in SMIv2 the BITS pseudotype
<simpleEnumOrBit> =
            <simpleSyntax> |
            "INTEGER" "{" <enumItem> ["," <enumItem> ]... "}" |
            "BITS" "{" <bitItem> ["," <bitItem> ]... "}"

-- base syntax types (and textual conventions)
<simpleSyntax> =
```

<synType> |
<tcType>

where

lcName is an identifier that starts with a lowercase letter ;
chrStr is a quoted character string which may span multiple lines;
<moduleIdentifier> is the identification of a module;
<oidValue> is an object identifier value;
<enumItem> is a value in an enumeration;
<bitItem> is a named bit;
<synType> is a base syntax type with possible sub-typing;
<tcType> is a textual convention with possible sub-typing;
<defVal> is a default value which matches the type of the item.

Example

```
  -- an implementation specification
bcoAgentBaseV01 MODULE-COMPLIANCE
    PRODUCT-RELEASE
        " ... "
    STATUS      current
    DESCRIPTION
        " ... "
    SUPPORTS IP-MIB
        INCLUDES { ipGroup, icmpGroup }
        VARIATION ipForwarding
            ACCESS  read-only
            DESCRIPTION
                " ... "
    SUPPORTS SNMPv2-MIB
        INCLUDES { snmpGroup, systemGroup,
                   snmpBasicNotificationsGroup }
        VARIATION coldStart
            DESCRIPTION
                " ... "
    SUPPORTS UDP-MIB
        INCLUDES { udpGroup }
    ::= { bcoAgentBase 1 }

  -- If the capabilities are changed then a new version of the
  -- implementation specification must be defined which has
  -- a different identifier and different OID value, but is quite similar.
  -- For this example, this new version has all behaviors are implemented,
  -- so there are no VARIATION clauses.
bcoAgentBaseV02 MODULE-COMPLIANCE
    PRODUCT-RELEASE
        " ... "
    STATUS      current
```

```
DESCRIPTION
    " ... "
SUPPORTS IP-MIB
    INCLUDES { ipGroup, icmpGroup }
SUPPORTS SNMPv2-MIB
    INCLUDES { snmpGroup, systemGroup,
               snmpBasicNotificationsGroup }
SUPPORTS UDP-MIB
    INCLUDES { udpGroup }
::= { bcoAgentBase 2 }
```

3.20.1 INCLUDES clause

The INCLUDES clause specifies object and event groups that an agent implements. Unless specified in a VARIATION clause, an agent fully implements all of the behaviors specified in the definitions of the objects and/or events that are members of the groups in the INCLUDES clause.

3.20.2 Event Variations

The VARIATION clause may be used to specify a change of behavior of an event, or to specify that an event is not implemented. The ACCESS clause with a value of *not-implemented* is used for the latter case. This is the only clause other than DESCRIPTION that may be specified for an event variation. The DESCRIPTION clause may be used to document all other changes of behaviors.

3.20.3 Object Variations

The VARIATION clause may also be used to specify a change of behavior of an object, to specify that an object is not implemented, or to specify implementation limitations such as the maximum number of rows in a table. This clause and associated clauses document actual implementation characteristics. The ACCESS clause is used to specify the implemented access when it is less than specified in an object's definition, or to specify that an object is not implemented.

The purpose of the SYNTAX and WRITE-SYNTAX clauses is to specify a reduction in the implemented behavior of an object. The values specified for these clauses must be a reduction of the value for the SYNTAX clause in the object's definition. These clauses work in simple cases, such as a reduction in the values for an enumerated integer, but don't really work for slightly more complex cases. The fall back is to use the associated DESCRIPTION clause to specify the reduction in required behaviors.

The CREATION-REQUIRES clause is used to document the objects that are required in a single SET operation to create an instance of a row in a table. The DEFVAL clause specifies a different default value that an agent will use when an instance of a columnar object is created, instead of that specified in the definition of the object.

The AGENT-CAPABILITIES construct has seen quite limited usage and is poorly documented as to how it should be used. We can't help you out with all the answers, since there is no large knowledge or experience base we can tap.

CHAPTER 4

Applying the SNMP-based Management Model

This chapter takes a closer look at the SNMP model of a managed network and how it is applied.

4.1 Management Domains

All management models have assumptions for how that model should be used and which items are included in the model. The application of a model to a specific real-world situation is called a *management domain.* This term is an abstract notion based on administrative and physical bounding conditions. Domains may be overlapping or contained in other domains. Elements may be contained in more than one management domain. (See Figure 4–1)

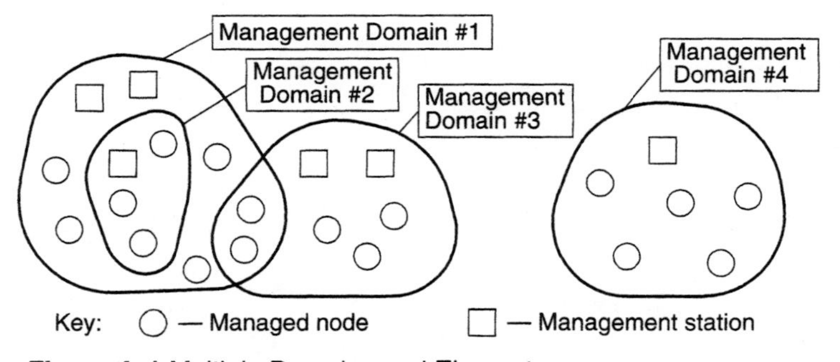

Figure 4–1 Multiple Domains and Elements

As was shown earlier, elements of the SNMP model of a managed network are one or more managed nodes; at least one management station; optional dual role entities; management information in each managed node; and a management protocol. These can be combined and configured in quite complex and unusual configurations. An analysis of management domains is needed to understand real-world complex systems.

For example, consider an organization that has two computer networks, which are not connected. One is used for traditional "back-office" computing, such as accounts receivable and payroll applications. The other is used by the engineering department for development of new products. Since the networks are not physically connected, each network must be in a separate domain.

If the networks were connected together, but the devices in each network used different network management protocols, then each network would still be in a separate management domain. If mechanisms were added that translated between the different network management protocols, then the networks could be in one combined domain. However, for robustness of the network, or to distribute the control, administrative policies could be put in place to create several overlapping management domains. The policies could be based on classes of users such as "engineering network administrator," "engineering network user," "office network administrator," "office network user," and "organization network administrator." The policies could also be based on the actual identities of the users of the network. For each class or individual, the policies could control the allowed access to management information for each managed element.

In summary, management domains are defined by physical boundaries such as network connectivity and implemented protocols, and by administrative policy based on organizational objectives such as cost, responsiveness, or security.

4.2 Extending Management Domains

There are many situations where a management domain is desired, but there exists no communications between a management station and nodes in the network. This can occur for the following reasons:

- no transport-level connectivity
- too high communications costs
- inadequate performance
- no compatible management protocol
- no agent in the network node

4.2.1 Transport-level Connectivity

A manager and an agent will not be able to communicate when they are using different transport protocols. The preferred one is UDP from the Internet protocol suite. However, the SNMP framework includes other transport mappings such as CLTS from the OSI protocol suite, DDP from the AppleTalk protocol suite, and PEP from the Novell IPX protocol suite.

Multiple Transport Protocol Suites

The difference can be resolved by the management station adding support for multiple protocol suites and the management applications running on that station being modified to use these stacks. (See Figure 4–2) This approach can be difficult (if not impossible) when the applications are written by independent vendors. This approach can also be costly to test the different combinations.

Instead of changing the applications, the agents can be modified to support multiple transport protocols. This will increase the memory resources needed by the agent, which is typically not desirable. However, network nodes and their agents can be designed to support only the protocol (or small number of protocols) needed for the environment in which they are used. For example, a managed node could support either the IP or IPX protocol based on how it was configured to be used.

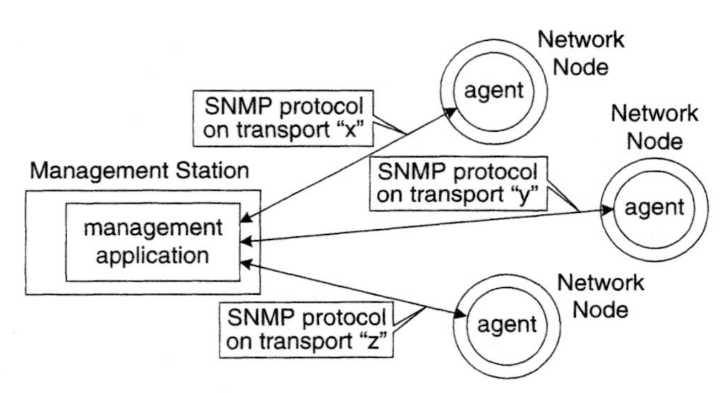

Figure 4–2 SNMP protocol over multiple transports

Transport Bridging Proxy

Alternatively, a transport bridging proxy may be used to forward messages between the management applications on the management station and the agent on each managed node. This approach has the advantage of not requiring a change to management applications, but has the cost of either doubling management traffic on the network, or increased processing if the proxy agent is implemented on the management station. (See Figure 4–3)

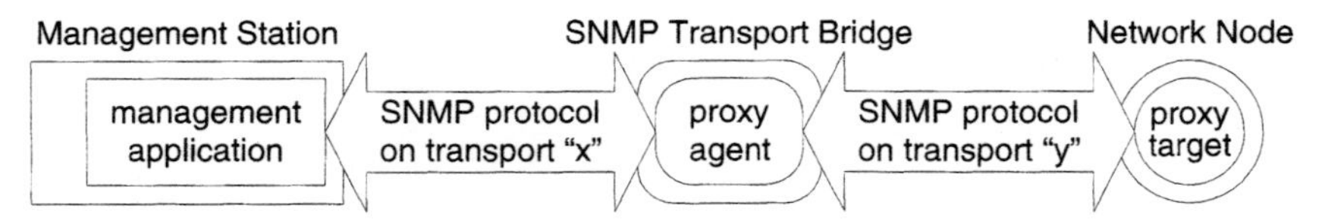

Figure 4–3 SNMP transport bridging proxy

4.2.2 Compatible Management Protocol

A manager and agent will not be able to communicate when they are using different management protocols, or incompatible versions of a management protocol. The preferred one is SNMPv1, since it is a Full Standard. However, the SNMPv2 protocol includes new operations and error codes, which improve performance and ease development of management applications. Also, there are existing network nodes that cannot be updated to support SNMP.

Multiple Management Protocols

The difference can be resolved by the management applications being modified to use multiple management protocols. For example, a high level interface can be developed which insulates the applications from the details of the management protocol. This approach has been tried, but has seen limited success due to the differences in operations and modelling of management information. (See Figure 4–4) Also, this approach can be difficult (if not impossible) when the applications are written by independent vendors.

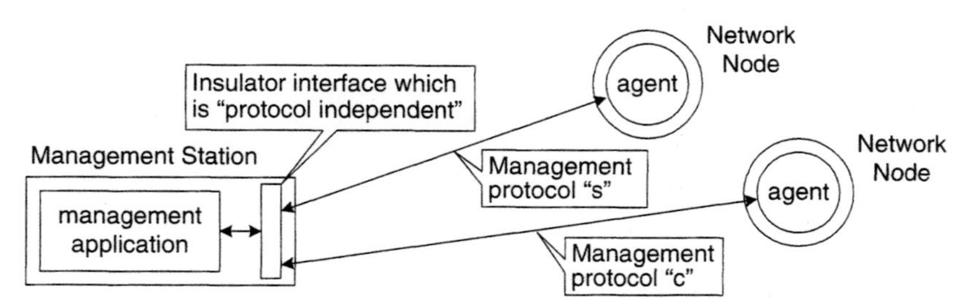

Figure 4–4 Multiple management protocols supported by insulating interface

Instead of changing the applications, the agents can be modified to support multiple management protocols or network nodes can support multiple agents. This will increase the memory and processing resources needed for managing the network node, which is typically not desirable. Figure 4–5 shows a network node that supports two agents. Each communicates to managers using a different management protocol. The two protocols will typically identify and group management information differently. The figure shows an attempt to isolate management information from the details of the protocol. This approach is quite attractive to hardware component manufacturers who want to limit their exposure to management protocols. However, by isolating the details and making the interfaces protocol neutral, any resulting agent implementation is more costly than one developed specifically for a single protocol (or family of protocols).

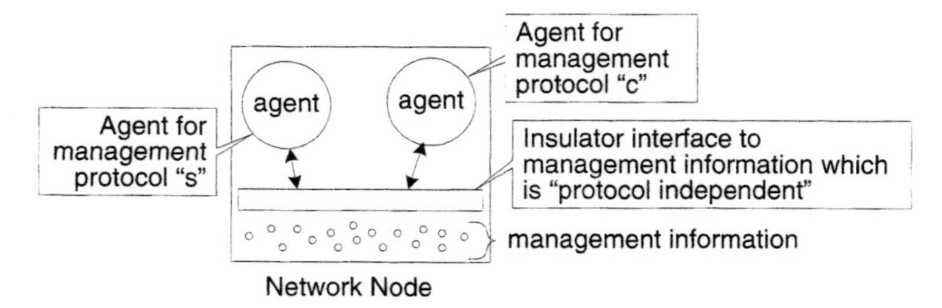

Figure 4–5 Multiple management protocols supported by insulating interface

Translating Proxy

Alternatively, a translating proxy may be used to translate and forward messages between the management applications on the management station and the agent on each managed node. This approach has the advantage of not requiring a change to management applications, but has the cost of either doubling management traffic on the network, or increased processing if the proxy agent is implemented on the management station. (See Figure 4–6) Also, this approach may be quite difficult, or impossible, to design due to large differences in the management protocols. Typically, the proxy must be hand crafted to support each management object (i.e., there is no generic translation unless one protocol is a version of the other).

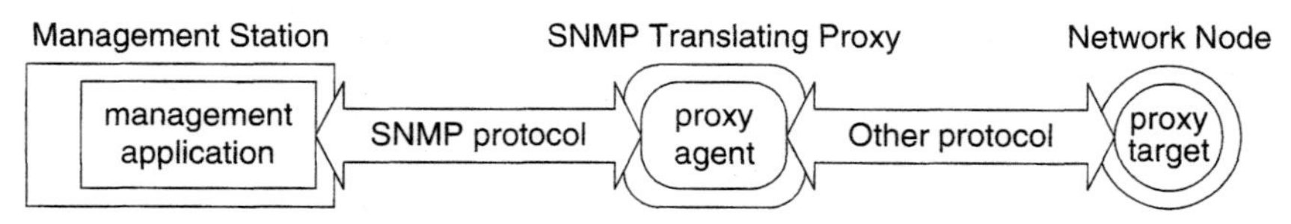

Figure 4–6 SNMP translating proxy

A particularly "ugly" version of a translating proxy is one that does *screen scrapes*. (See Figure 4–7) Many older devices are manageable only through a locally attached ASCII terminal. Commands are entered on the keyboard, and results are shown on the display. There may also be a mode in which many status and statistics variables are continuously displayed. To make this device manageable via SNMP, a proxy must be written to communicate over a serial line to the device as if the proxy was an ASCII terminal. The proxy must convert "screen output" to SNMP management information.

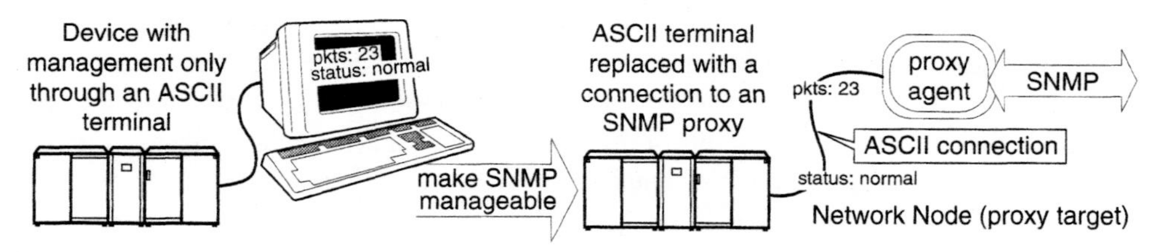

Figure 4–7 SNMP screen scrape version of translating proxy

4.2.3 No agent in the network node

Some systems do not contain an agent and do not have a terminal interface that can be used to gather useful information about the system. Another approach that can be used is to monitor the network traffic of the system and deduce the operation of the system. Also, most networking protocol suites have a mechanism to check if the system is "still alive." For example, the Internet protocol suite contains a mechanism to ask a system to echo the contents of a message. The program (or command) on many systems that is used to request a system to echo the contents of a message is named Ping. A combination of this technology, and monitoring a network for traffic from a system, can be used to synthesize the status of a system without an agent. (See Figure 4–8)

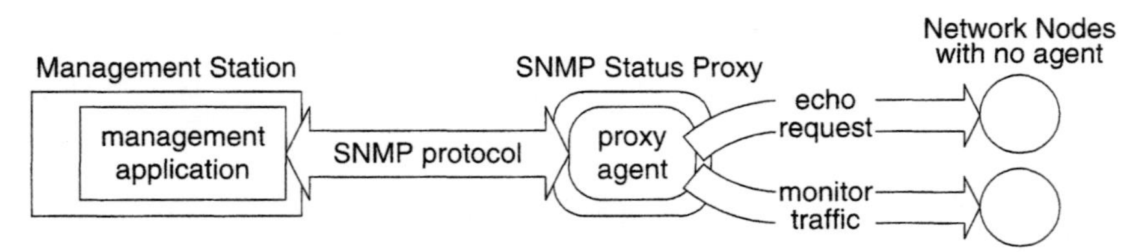

Figure 4–8 SNMP status proxy

4.2.4 Inadequate Performance or High Communications Cost

A domain may be limited in size due to the inability of a single management station to manage a large number of network nodes, or due to the high communications costs of managing systems in sub-networks remote from the manager.

Intermediate Managers.

These entities use a management protocol to gather management information from other managed elements and provide new types of *higher level* management information which is an aggregation, consolidation, or synthesis of the original *low level* management information. (See Figure 4–9) This approach is useful when the number of managed elements is quite large. The "big picture" of the status for management domain can easily be obtained by the highest level manager by consulting lower level intermediate managers. Without intermediate managers, the single manager would need to communicate with every managed device to obtain the "big picture" status of the domain. With intermediate managers, the communications burden is spread and management can scale as the size of a domain grows. This approach works well in helping the personnel managing the network to respond to areas requiring human decision making, and not to be overwhelmed with details.

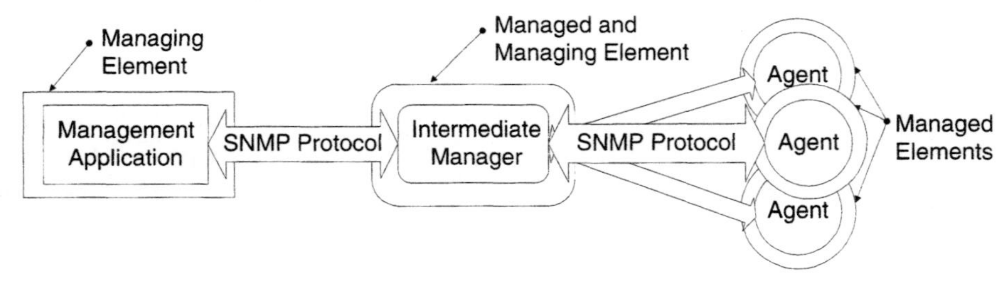

Figure 4–9 Intermediate manager

This approach also works well to reduce the communications costs where the managed systems are located on sub-networks remote from the manager. (See Figure 4–10) Intermediate managers can be located on each remote sub-network. Each intermediate manager manages the systems on their remote sub-network and can provide high level (consolidated) information to the manager for the whole network.

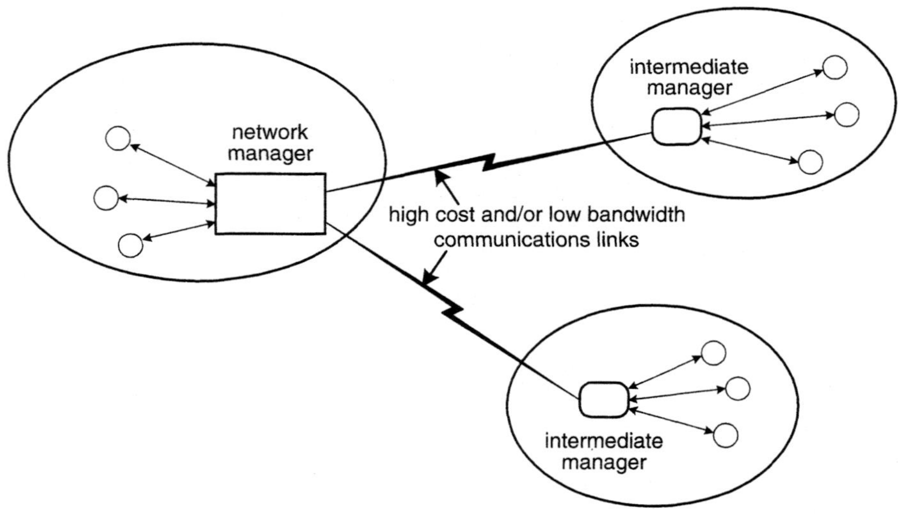

Figure 4–10 Multiple Intermediate managers

4.2.5 Summary

A management domain can be extended by proxy agents and by intermediate managers. Table 4–1 shows a complete list of proxy types.

Table 4–1 Types of Proxy Agents

Type	Use
Administrative firewall	authenticate and authorize access
Caching firewall	minimize access burden
Protocol translation	translate between different management protocols used by a manager and target elements
SNMP message translation	translate between SNMPv1 and SNMPv2 message formats
Transport bridging	provide end-to-end message delivery when no transport path exists between a manager and target elements
Local multiplexing	easy mechanism to share a transport address among agents in a single managed element

4.3 SNMP Management Platforms

In large sites, a central room or rooms may be used to house the network management stations and personnel managing the network. This facility is called the network operations center (NOC) and the personnel managing the network are called the network management operators or network administrators. (See Figure 4–11)

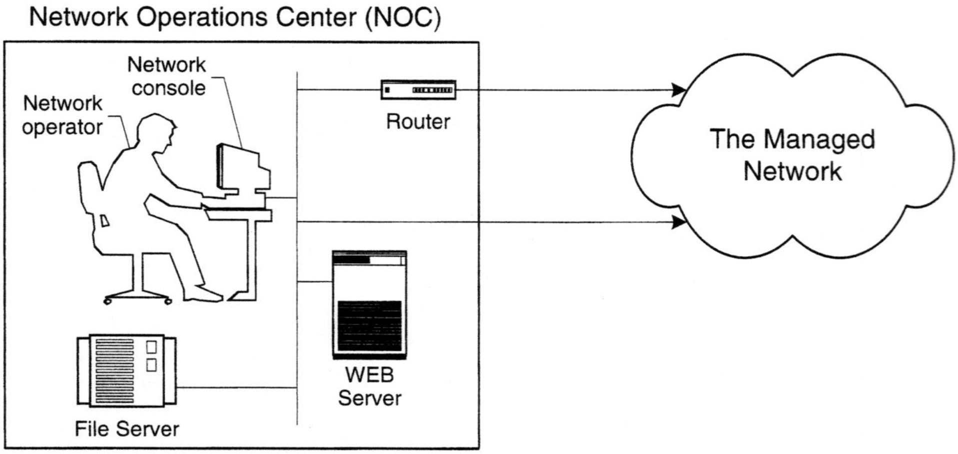

Network Operations Center (NOC)

Network console
Network operator
Router
The Managed Network
WEB Server
File Server

Figure 4–11 Network Operations Center

Typically, a network management station is a high-performance workstation with a large graphical display, one or more network interfaces, and data storage capacity. Some large organizations use a model for managing their networks and computer resources that looks somewhat like a water or power distribution system. In this approach, the "network group" designs and manages the network infrastructure "behind" the ports on devices in wiring closets. It also will typically manage the infrastructure computing resources such as email and directory (name service).

A central group at an organization's headquarters would manage the campus network and WAN connections up to hubs in wiring closets which would be co-managed by the departments connected to the network infrastructure. Department level administrators would have the responsibility to manage network and computer resources needed to provide the services for the department. (See Figure 4–12)

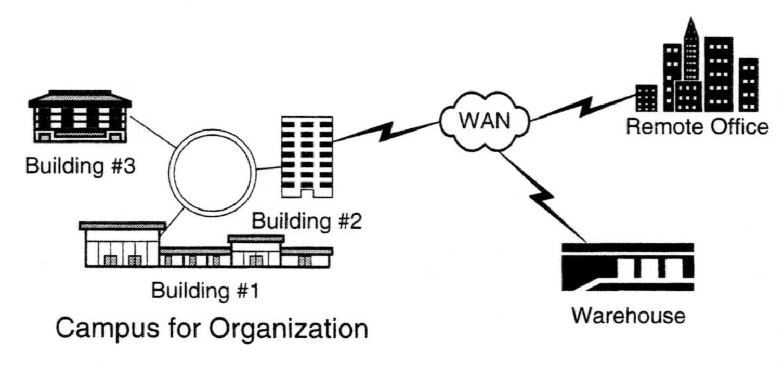

Figure 4–12 Example of a large network with management from a central site of connections to departments and remote locations

4.4 Aspects of Network Management

Management can be characterized in many different ways. One method developed by ISO for the OSI management approach categorizes network management into the following five functional areas:

- Configuration Management — management of the names and configuration for all network elements. Also, the monitoring of the state of network elements and their components. This includes the information needed so that network maps, and exploded diagrams of element components can be drawn by network management applications.
- Performance Management — determines the effective utilization of the network, and the services provided and consumed by elements on the network. Also included are availability, response time, and throughput.
- Fault Management — the detection, isolation, and correction of network problems.
- Security Management — the control of access and protection of information on the network from disclosure or modification.
- Accounting — the measurement of usage and computation of costs based on specified policies.

These functional areas are just one way to categorize network management. The same management information may be used in network management applications from different categories.

4.5 Hoopla

SNMP-based management, like all new technologies, has received much hoopla in the press and by vendors of products supporting SNMP. This has set some high expectations for users of network management. By itself, SNMP-based management does not provide solutions for all aspects in each of the five functional areas. These must be provided by equipment vendors, independent software developers, and by management station platform vendors. Networking and SNMP-based management are quite new technologies that are still evolving. However, the SNMP-based management approach and framework has proved to be stable, relatively easy to understand, and applicable to many areas. Thus, it has experienced significantly greater growth and has a larger installed base than any other standards-based management approach.

The management framework remains unchanged as SNMP is used in new areas. The framework has built into it a method for adding new uses. This portion is the SMI, which specifies the rules for creation of new management information definitions.

4.6 New Management Information Definitions

Creating new management information definitions is an ongoing task as new technologies are invented and experience is gained using existing technologies. Product features can be driven by technology and by customer needs. Definitions of new types of management information can be created by the engineers that created the technology, by engineers writing the applications managing the technology, and by marketing product managers who represent the needs of the purchasers (and users) of the product. A definition is successful if it sees widespread deployment and provides value to managing systems. Time has shown that success must include the following ingredients:

- The definition must be written and made widely available at an insignificant cost.
- It must be implementable by agent developers.
- It must be implementable by management application developers.
- The implementations of agents and applications must be interoperable with each other.
- The results from the application must have a much greater value than the cost of the system (and network) resources needed to run the application.

To meet these requirements, the person or team writing the definitions must have an extensive set of skills and experiences. These include:

- Knowledge of how to write valid definitions.
- Knowledge of the technology to be managed.
- Understanding of how the technology needs to be managed.
- Understanding of the implementation costs of various techniques used to write definitions in both agents and management applications.
- The ability to concisely and precisely write the definitions so that they will be interpreted with the same meaning by an overwhelming majority of the readers of the definitions.
- The ability to write the definitions at a level of abstraction so that they can be extended and applied to unanticipated areas, and yet at an abstraction level that can be efficiently understood and applied to the present generation of technology.

CHAPTER 5

Inside an SNMP-managed System

This chapter provides an overview of the characteristics of systems, requirements for SNMP-management, the functional areas of an SNMP agent, and a comparison of monolithic and extensible agents. This background is relevant, since it affects the design of MIB modules. In this chapter, for each new term, it is formally defined and then examples are given to show how it is used.

5.1 System Types

The term *system* is used loosely throughout the book. For this chapter, we need to present a few formal definitions, starting with system.

A system is any collection of interacting and interrelated items forming a more complex whole. A system may be an abstraction or a physical manifestation.

A constituent item of a system is called a sub-system or component.

Each sub-system forming a system may itself be viewed as a system composed of a collection of items.

In describing the management of systems, it doesn't matter if a system is an abstraction or a physical manifestation. (See Figure 5–1) Unfortunately, some of the biggest controversies that occur when designing MIBs are due to different views (or models) of systems. Typically, the users of a system tend to model it as being composed of sub-systems which correspond to the functions and/or services provided by the system. However, the designers of the hardware of a system tend to model it as being composed of sub-systems which correspond to separable hardware items in the system. The conflict develops when both approaches are forced into one model with one side losing and the other side winning, or both sides winning with the resulting model being unusable. However, there is need for both models. Each should be simple and describe the aspects of their model of the system that need to be managed!

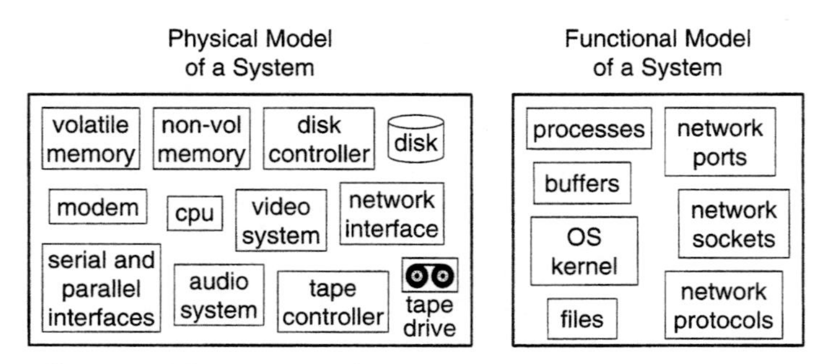

Figure 5–1 Two models of a system

All systems perform some function and/or provide some service without a sub-system (and/or component) that allows management from external sources. After SNMP-based management has been added, a system must still be able to perform its function and/or provide its service. The addition of external (or remote) management must add value to the system for it to be useful. For example, having the ability to remotely monitor, configure, and control a networking device housed in a wiring closet saves the time of a network administrator from going to the wiring closet to perform management on the device. The wiring closet may be at a remote location, or it may be environmentally sealed and be costly to open and then reseal. Also, the use of a standards-based management approach that enjoys widespread popularity typically yields integration of the management of many systems and lowers costs. (See Figure 5–2)

Figure 5–2 Adding value to a system with external SNMP-based management

There are many characteristics that can be used to classify systems. There are three primary ones that affect SNMP management. These are:

- Dedicated versus general purpose
- Open versus closed
- Managed versus unmanaged

A description for each of these characteristics follows. Even though each of these characteristics are independent, most *dedicated* systems are *closed* and most *general purpose* systems are *open*. That is, of the four combinations, the predominate ones are dedicated-and-closed and general purpose-and-open. Those are the system types that we will focus on. (See Figure 5–3)

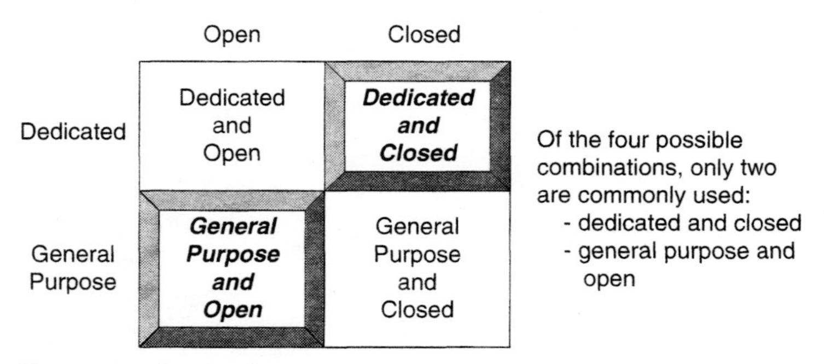

Figure 5–3 Predominate system types

5.1.1 Dedicated and General Purpose Systems

A system designed for a specific purpose is called a dedicated system.[1] Conversely, a system designed to be configured for many different purposes is called a general purpose system. Systems that provide high performance network infrastructure functions such as routing or bridging are typically implemented as dedicated (and closed) systems. Systems that connect to a network to consume or provide services such as workstations, personal computers, mini-computers, or mainframes are typically implemented as general purpose (and open) systems.

5.1.2 Open and Closed

The terms *open* and *closed* are meant to characterize the degree to which other vendors can supply additional hardware and software sub-systems (or components) to the base system. A completely closed system restricts additional components to only those available from the system's vendor. A completely open system uses well-defined and published interfaces so that components may be obtained from any vendor that conforms to those interfaces. (See Figure 5–4) The characterization of closed or open is not binary. Different aspects of a system can vary between the two poles of the spectrum. This characterization is important in several areas.

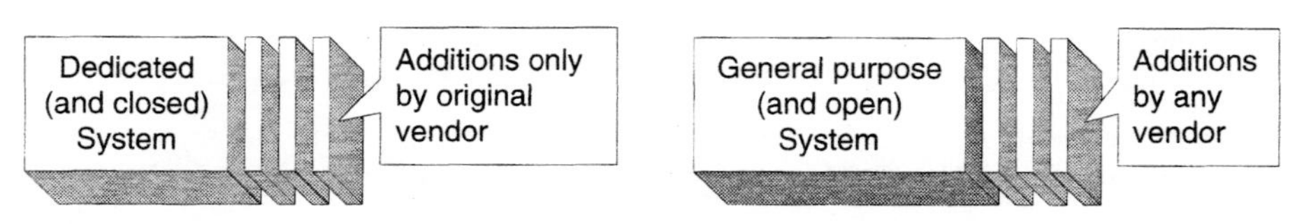

Figure 5–4 Additions to the predominate system types

1. Dedicated systems typically use similar or identical software technology as that found in embedded real-time systems.

First, SNMP-based management allows the opening up of a closed system in a way so that its vendor does not lose control of the potential revenue from future direct additions of hardware and software to the system. If a vendor chooses, the original system can still be closed, while allowing management of the system to be open. This can be advantageous to both the system vendor and the system purchaser (and user). The vendor can focus on the system and allow others to provide management of the system. The system user now gets a managed system with a choice of vendors for management of the system.

Secondly, using SNMP-based management also saves the system vendor the costs of developing a custom management framework and gains the leverage of existing experienced developers, industry knowledge, tools, and utility programs developed for generic SNMP-based management. This really does save costs over the lifetime of systems and families of systems, such as those whose members are different physical realizations that provide the same function but with different price, performance, or expansion characteristics. System users see commonality of management among systems from a vendor. There is a larger pool of knowledge and experience in using a standards-based management approach. Systems from different vendors, even if not identically managed, can be integrated together on a single management platform. This can be quite difficult when proprietary management approaches are used.

Finally, SNMP-based management allows a consistent management interface in an open system consisting of the integration of sub-systems (or components) provided by different vendors. The integration can occur if the sub-systems consist primarily of hardware, software, or a combination of both. For example, different types of network interfaces can be added to an open system. Other examples include service programs such as a relational database server, a mail server, or a directory server.

In a general purpose system, it is important that the SNMP-based management mechanisms in the base system allow the easy addition of management by the sub-system (or component) vendor with the addition of each new sub-system (or component). This requires that the SNMP-based management mechanisms be as open as the mechanisms that allow the addition of the sub-system (or component). On the other hand, in dedicated (and closed) systems the SNMP-based management mechanisms are typically closed to all except the original vendor.

5.1.3 Unmanaged and SNMP-managed Systems

The terms *managed* and *unmanaged* indicate if a system uses SNMP for external (or remote) management. (See Figure 5–5) Even without external (or remote) management, a system may have existing internal and/or proprietary management mechanisms. Each sub-system (or component) may also have management mechanisms. These may not be integrated to form a consistent management interface for the system. Adding SNMP-based management provides external (or remote) access that is integrated and standards based. When SNMP-based management is added, a system must still be able to perform as it had before.

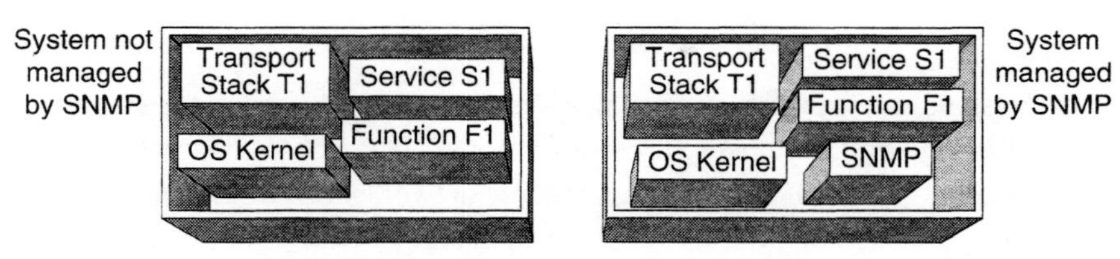

Figure 5–5 A system without SNMP management and one with SNMP management

5.2 System Requirements for SNMP-based Management

SNMP-based management requires message exchange between a processing entity called a manager and one called an agent, which must be able to access management information. The following is a list of requirements for a system to be directly managed by SNMP:

- an SNMP agent
- a datagram transport stack
- sub-systems containing management information
- translators between SNMP and sub-systems definitions of management information
- access to management information in sub-systems and a mechanism for the managed sub-systems to post notification of events to the agent

Of these, a transport stack and manageable sub-systems are typically already present and do not need to be added. However, an SNMP agent, translation and access to management information will need to be added to the system to allow it to be managed via SNMP. Also, work may be needed in the sub-systems to measure and retain the value of management information for access via the SNMP agent. Figure 5–6 shows a system with the additions needed for it to be managed by SNMP.

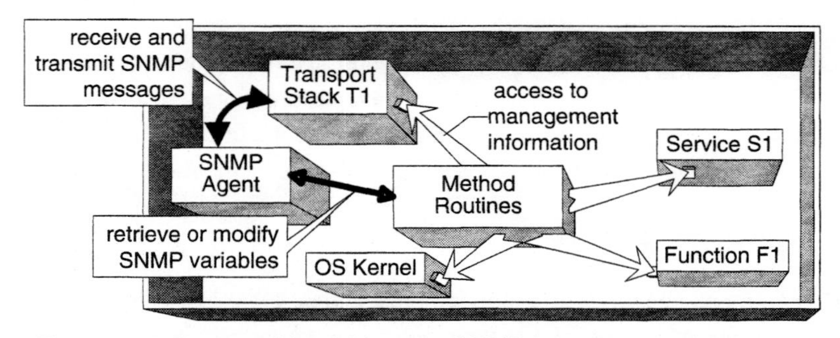

Figure 5–6 System with additions for SNMP-based management

5.2.1 SNMP Agent

All systems directly managed by SNMP contain a processing entity called an agent. It receives SNMP messages to retrieve and/or modify management information and sends responses to those messages. The entity must also be capable of sending SNMP messages to report events.

5.2.2 Datagram Transport Stack

An agent requires a datagram transport stack for message exchange with a manager. One or more stacks can be used.

Using the same stack and/or network in a system for normal and for management operations is called *in-band* management. The path for message exchange is called the *in-band* management channel. Using a separate stack and/or network only for management is called *out-of-band* management. The path for message exchange is called the *out-of-band* management channel.

SNMP typically imposes a light load on a transport stack and thus in-band management is cost efficient and typically provides high performance. However, if the transport path between the agent and manager is not operational, it can be difficult to diagnose and recover from a problem without external intervention (such as by a human). With an out-of-band channel for management, a manager may be able to communicate with an agent and thus diagnose and possibly recover from a problem without external intervention.

The major factor keeping management from always being performed on an out-of-band channel is cost. However, in those environments where out-of-band management is needed for critical situations, a low speed switched (or dial-up) channel is typically used.

An agent may support one or more transport protocols. The preferred protocol is UDP of the internet protocol suite. A preferred transport protocol was selected by the SNMP community to increase the likelihood of a compatible protocol and, thus, interoperation between any manager and agent.

5.2.3 Management Information

A sub-system is manageable if it contains management information which can be accessed by the agent. SNMP operations are limited to a manager retrieving or changing the value of management information accessible by an agent, and an agent reporting an event to a manager. There are no operations in SNMP such as *action, create, or delete* which are found in other management frameworks. However, even with just operations to retrieve and modify management information, SNMP managers still have all the power needed to monitor, control, and configure managed systems. The simplification of the protocol does require that care is used in defining management information, so that all management can be accomplished by reading and/or writing values. Following are examples of management information for each SNMP manager-initiated operation:

- *monitor* — management information which is typically only readable, that provides the changing values of items such as status indicators, counters, or gauges
- *control* — management information that must be writable, and for which a change of value initiates some action to occur, such as start a self-test or terminate a session
- *configure* — management information that is readable and possibly writable, which is used to specify a desired setting or arrangement on the managed system, or to determine the settings or inventory on the managed system

The organization, identification, data type, and behavior of management information is defined in SNMP MIB modules. The mechanisms that implement the management information on a managed system are called *management instrumentation.* The resources to build instrumentation are currently the largest single cost component in building a managed system. This results from the instrumentation being all custom developed. Most of the other functional areas are available from SNMP technology vendors directly, or generated partially or completely by the tools from these vendors. Semi-conductor manufacturers have recently started supplying chips that have built into them management instrumentation corresponding to the function provided by the chips. This can ease, but not eliminate, the cost of building instrumentation required for SNMP management.

5.2.4 Translators between Management Information Definitions

There are many approaches to identify, structure, specify allowed operations, and assign data types for management information. Typically, systems are designed with little consideration for SNMP manageability or were designed before SNMP manageability became a requirement. This can result in differences between the definitions of management information (and allowed operations) found in SNMP MIB modules and those implemented on a system. *Method routines* translate between the identification, structuring, operations, and data types for management information defined by the SNMP management framework and those used internally by a sub-system. The details of this translation is outside the scope of the SNMP-management framework. That is, the SNMP-management framework provides no definition of how this translation is to occur. A method routine may perform the translation for one or more related types and/or instances of management information (and events). The approach to construct method routines varies greatly with different SNMP agent designs. Much of the translation can be performed using code or tables generated from the definitions of management information contained in MIB modules. Additional information is usually needed to complete the translation. Older approaches require most of the translation to be custom written without assistance. Contemporary approaches use tools to generate some skeleton code that then requires some customization to complete. Future approaches will most likely eliminate customizing in most cases and reduce the amount in the remaining cases.

5.2.5 Access to Management Information

An SNMP agent must be able to access management information in a sub-system for it to be managed. An SNMP agent (via the method routines) must be able to access management information on the system, and must be able to receive notifications of events that have occurred on the system. Each managed sub-system must include for the agent an *access mechanism* to *management instrumentation* contained in the sub-system. (See Figure 5–7)

Figure 5–7 Additions to sub-systems for SNMP-based management

The instrumentation is the "extra" hardware or software that must be added to the sub-system to measure and retain the value or act on a changed value of management information. Many sub-systems may be able to perform their function or provide service without this instrumentation. Also, a sub-system may already have some instrumentation, but it may not match that required for compliance with definitions found in a MIB module.

The interface between an agent and the management information in a sub-system is outside the scope of the SNMP-management framework. That is, the SNMP-management framework provides no definition of an interface to access management information. Shown are the additions to a single sub-system for it to be managed by SNMP. In new sub-systems it is straightforward to design an interface for SNMP access. In older sub-systems, or in sub-systems that are controlled by a vendor not interested in adding SNMP management, existing mechanisms which were designed without concern for the SNMP management model must be adapted for use by SNMP agent access. This may require the method routines to perform much work to map between the differences. For example, management information definitions in a MIB module may model the information with an ordering (or identification) different from that used by the sub-system containing the management information. In this case, the method routine for that management information may need to implement a sophisticated mechanism to mediate the differences and/or caching to provide access performance.

5.3 Functional Areas of an SNMP Agent

There are many different approaches to building an agent. For all approaches, an agent must consist of the following functional areas:

- access to one or more transport stacks
- a protocol engine (which includes security)
- a dispatch table to method routines

5.3.1 Transport Stack

An SNMP agent uses a transport stack to receive and transmit messages. An SNMP agent typically uses a well-known transport selector to receive messages. For example, in the Internet protocol suite, UDP port 161 is used as the transport selector with an IP address of the system containing the agent to form the transport address. The interface between an agent and a transport stack is outside the scope of the SNMP-management framework. There are existing well-defined interfaces, such as the *sockets* interface, which may be available for use by an agent. Besides use by an agent to transmit and receive messages, the protocol stack is one of the primary areas of network management interest in a managed system. The protocol stack must include instrumentation and access interfaces for method routines at all layers for the management information in the protocol stack to be accessible by the agent. This is not always possible when the providers of a protocol stack do not themselves provide instrumentation and access, nor make available the source code to others.

5.3.2 Protocol Engine

The part of an agent that receives an SNMP message, decodes it, implements the checks of the administration framework, looks up mappings in the dispatch table, calls method routines, and encodes and sends a response message is the *protocol engine*. It also receives notifications of events within the system and generates SNMP event reports. There are commercial vendors of this technology as well as freely available source code. There is little, if any, reason to re-implement this code from scratch. Once developed, it does not need to be changed for changes in management information accessible by an agent. However, the one-time job of building and verifying that a protocol engine is compliant with the SNMP-management framework (including the administration framework) is a significant undertaking. (See Appendix B for a summary of the format of SNMP messages, and the behavior of SNMP protocol engines.)

5.3.3 Dispatch Table

The dispatch table contains mappings to method routines based on management information identity and selector. SNMP messages received or generated by an agent, contain the identity of management information (or approximations of the identity of management information in messages for the GETNEXT and GETBULK operations). The identity of an instance of management information consists of two parts. The first is the type of management information, and the second specifies an individual (or *instance*) of that type. SNMP messages also contain a selector which is used to qualify the identities in that message. In SNMPv1, the selector is the *community string* field[2] in a message. In SNMPv2, the selector is the *context* field in a message. For each management information identity in a message, an agent must use the selector from that message, and both parts of the identity to access the management information. An identity and selector must also be specified in requests through a local interface, if this is supported by the agent. The implementation details of this table (and local interface) are outside the scope of the SNMP-based management framework. However, it is important to understand this aspect of an agent since it can affect the definitions in MIB modules. Many older implementations of agents required that this table be designed without aid of automation. Most, if not all, contemporary agent implementations have tools to automate the generation of these tables. Older implementations had these tables built as part of the compiling and linking process of an agent. Some contemporary agent implementations allow new entries to be created and removed during agent execution. Adding a new mapping is called *registration*. Deleting a mapping is called *deregistration*.

5.4 The MIB Myth

Many people who have first started learning about SNMP have come to the mistaken belief that a managed system contains a database containing management information. And they believe that this database is "the MIB" on that managed system. (See Figure 5–8) The truth is that no such database is needed or exists. Management information exists in the man-

2. The community string is used concurrently as selector and authenticator.

aged sub-systems, if it exists at all. Some management information is an abstraction, which is only generated when it is requested by a management application. Other management information is used as the argument to initiate an action in a managed sub-system.

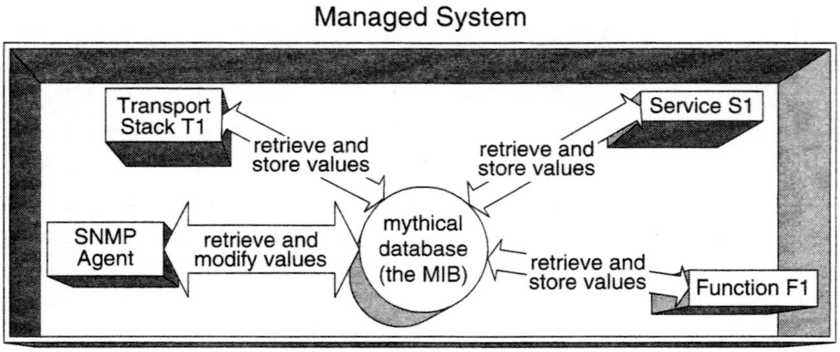

Figure 5–8 The MIB as a database myth

If management information was contained in a database, then designing MIBs and implementing agents would be an easy task. However, the managed system would most likely have much higher memory and processing requirements! All information that has changing values, such as counters and gauges, would be constantly causing the database to be updated. These updates would occur whether or not any management application was accessing their value. (These updates would be a waste of the processing resources.) Additionally, many values would need to be kept locally in the managed sub-systems, as well as in the database. (This would increase the storage requirements for the system.)

In summary, it is a myth that management information is stored in an actual database on a managed system. (Don't take literally those diagrams you might see elsewhere.)

5.5 Agent Diagrammed

There are many approaches that can be used to partition the functional areas of an agent. Some of these approaches may bundle with the agent the other additions needed for management, such as the method routines and even parts of the instrumentation. Shown in Figure 5–9 is an example agent where each of the functional areas is cleanly separated. That is, an agent containing only a protocol engine (including security), a dispatch table, access to a transport interface, access to method routines (including registration and deregistration), and a local interface to access management information via the agent.

In actual implementations, the functional areas of an agent and the additions to satisfy the requirements needed for SNMP-based management are not so cleanly separated. The factors that affect the choices are the following:

- who is responsible for adding management
- the amount of the software in the system
- whether the system uses a single processor or multiple processors
- whether the configuration of the system is static or dynamic

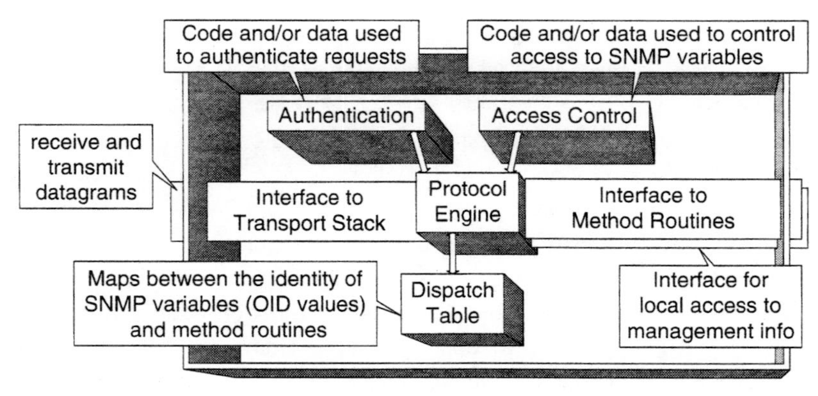

Figure 5–9 Functional areas of an SNMP Agent

The first two factors relate to how software for the system is developed. In a small dedicated (and closed) system, a single person or group may be responsible for adding SNMP-based network management capabilities. The interfaces in a system typically match the communications structures of the development group.[3] In this environment, "the agent" will typically include all of the method routines and perform much mapping between the SNMP model for management information and the model used in each sub-system. In larger projects (including the second or third generation of a small agent), in multi-processor systems, and dynamically configurable systems the method routines tend to be implemented separately from "the agent." This simplifies an agent, allows an agent to be modified independently of the sub-systems, and allows new management information to be added in existing or in new sub-systems without changing the agent.

5.6 Monolithic and Extensible Agent Structure

There are two predominate approaches that have been used to implement agents. In small dedicated (and closed) systems a *monolithic* approach is typically used. This is the approach where the agent, method routines, and much of the instrumentation is combined together. This is a good choice when all the software sub-systems are known and combined together at agent (and typically system) compile and/or link time.[4] In general purpose (and open) systems an *extensible* approach is typically used. This approach keeps separate an agent and method routines. This approach delays linkage of the agent and method routines

3. Conway, M. E., "How do committees invent?" Datamation, 14, 4 (April, 1968), pp. 28-31.

4. A note on terms: "Compile time" refers to the time when a program (or module) is compiled; "Link time" refers to the time when all modules are combined to form an executable unit; "Load time" refers to the time when an executable unit is loaded by the operating system to begin execution; "Initialization time" is the beginning execution phase of a program when any "one time" allocation of resources or processing occurs; "Run time" is the execution phase of a program after initialization, but before termination; "Termination time" is the ending execution phase of a program where any "one time" freeing of resources or processing occurs.

until load time, initialization time, or run time. This is more complex and can be slightly slower in performance and larger in size than a monolithic approach. However, an extensible approach is preferred for multi-processor systems, and those systems that support dynamic addition and removal of managed software sub-systems, such as open and general purpose systems.

For a simple dedicated managed system, there may be one executable code image that contains a small real-time operating system kernel, an agent, a transport stack, services, and functions. In this case, there may be no visible separation and interfaces between each sub-system. This monolithic system is typically built and integrated by one engineer. A more complex dedicated system typically requires several engineers to work together to design and integrate it. There tends to be clearer lines of separation and well-defined interfaces in these systems. Even in this environment, a monolithic agent may still be used. Coordination between the engineers is required to create the system executable code image.

Quite complex systems can be developed with this approach. Many large chunks of the software can be purchased or licensed from technology vendors. The engineers for the final product integrate and customize the purchased technology for the system. It may seem puzzling how software components provided by other vendors could be managed. However, this is possible since usually the engineers on dedicated systems have control of much of the software and access to much of the source code for the software used to build the system. Also, the purchased software is almost always designed to be easily customized. Note that care must be used in customization to allow bug fixes and upgrades to purchased or licensed software.

On the other hand, engineers of managed systems based on general purpose computers typically have very little control of the many sub-systems that make up the system. Unless the manufacturer of the system has well-defined interfaces for SNMP-based management, and providers of sub-systems have developed matching interfaces, then the resulting managed system will be a patchwork of management with some areas fully managed, other areas partially managed, and others not manageable by SNMP.

Several techniques have been proposed and used with varying levels of success for extensible agents. The leading approaches are SMUX, which is defined in RFC 1227 (a non-standards track document); DPI, which is defined in RFCs 1228 & 1592 (non-standards track documents); and EMANATE from SNMP Research, whose definition is not freely available. There are also some published and unpublished variations on SMUX and DPI, and some other approaches whose definition is not freely available. There was a large call within the SNMP community in 1994 for a single approach to be standardized within the IETF. However, the then network management area director ruled that such an effort was not appropriate to be done within an IETF working group. He proposed that such an effort should be taken on by a group whose focus is on programming interfaces. Some initiatives were started in late 1994, but were put on hold when the SNMPv2 WG was reactivated to consider changes in the SNMPv2 framework. In December of 1995, a WG called "AGENTX" was started to tackle this problem and has shown much progress.

In summary, monolithic and extensible agents are two different approaches to implementing SNMP-based management of a system. An SNMP manager should not be able to determine how an SNMP agent has been implemented. No matter what the implementation strategy, a manager should see one agent per managed system and the same management information. These requirements can be met in dedicated (and closed) systems, but are quite difficult and currently economically infeasible in general purpose (and open) systems.

5.7 Other Approaches

It is desirable for there to be a single point of contact on a managed system for which complete and consistent information can be obtained. This simplifies management of the system, but requires all the sub-systems to depend on the same mechanism. In general purpose (and open) systems, there has not been to date an economically feasible method to allow all sub-systems to be managed through a single SNMP-based agent. The following describes a few of the approaches.

5.7.1 Encapsulation

This approach uses an encapsulating agent to "contain" (or front-end) one or more closed or monolithic agents. It requires that the closed or monolithic agents use a different transport address and the encapsulating agent use the standard transport address (or addresses) for the system. (See Figure 5–10)

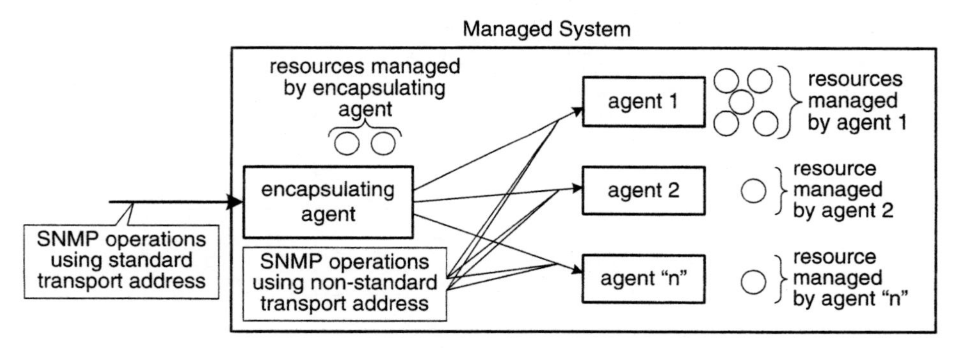

Figure 5–10 Use of an encapsulating agent

The "perfect" implementation of this approach results in managers not being able to determine that this approach is being used. A manager should be able to perform operations that access management information managed by any of the encapsulated agents in the same request. Also, the management information should be consistent between the encapsulated agents. Both of these requirements are difficult, if not impossible, in the general case, when no constraints are placed on the management information made accessible by the encapsulated agents or on the requests.

An encapsulating agent performs the following tasks for each SNMP request message received:

- checks authentication
- splits the list of management information to be accessed into sub-lists, one for each encapsulated agent
- for each non-empty sub-list, performs one or more operations on the associated encapsulated agent
- integrates the responses from the encapsulated agents and sends a single response to the original message

These steps may require that the values and/or identification of management information be modified in the operations between the encapsulating agent and the encapsulated agents to bring about the appearance that the management information is consistent. For example, each encapsulated agent implements the managed object *sysUpTime*, which is the time in hundredths of seconds that the encapsulated agent has been running. The value of *sysUpTime* is used as a time stamp value for other objects. For these objects, the encapsulating agent must adjust their value so that the value of all the time-related objects appear to be using the same clock.

Using the encapsulated approach will most likely not result in a managed system that passes all SNMP tests for correct implementation. However, the results from this approach are generally workable, and allow a general purpose (and open) system to increase the number of managed sub-systems without a large economic burden.

5.7.2 Nonstandard Transport Address

This approach eliminates the requirement of using a single point of contact for all management information on a system. (See Figure 5–11) The philosophy behind this approach is

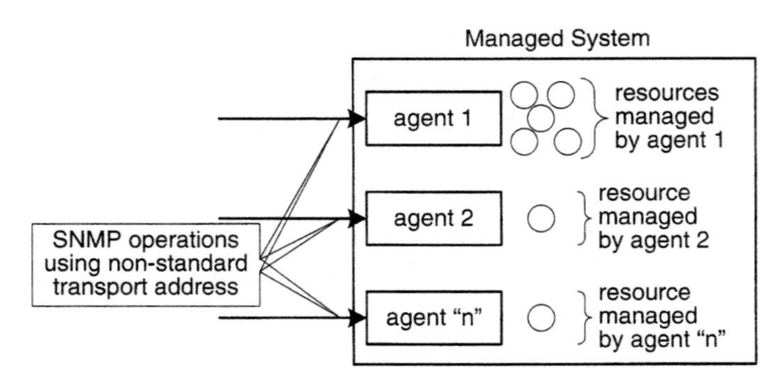

Figure 5–11 Use of non-standard transport addresses

to let the burden of integration (if even needed) be carried by the manager instead of the managed system. A manager (and management applications) must keep track of all agents on a system, and determine which transport address is used by each, and determine which management information is accessible by each. With this approach, management applications must integrate the information from each agent on a managed system to develop a consistent view of management information. An advocated benefit with this approach is that any problems or unusual situations can be pin-pointed and resolved, since the manager has greater knowledge of the implementation of management on the managed system.

This approach has several problems that result in it not being used except in special situations. The biggest problem is that management platforms are not currently designed to work with this approach. They associate one transport address with each managed system and expect there to be a single agent that provides access to all management information on the system. The generic tools provided with management platforms are also built around these assumptions. Also, no management applications for specific tasks are currently designed to allow management information to be arbitrarily partitioned among agents on a system.

5.8 Summary

This chapter was included to provide you with an overview of how agents are implemented. A MIB module can be designed which is not completely implementable. Understanding and appreciating the environment in which an SNMP agent must be implemented will allow you to design MIB modules that are easier to implement by agent engineers.

CHAPTER 6

SNMP Operations

A brief overview of SNMP operations is presented in this chapter to help you understand SNMP MIBs.

6.1 SNMP Operations and Messages

The operations available in SNMP are quite limited, and yet quite powerful. A manager can retrieve or modify the value of management information accessible by an agent, an agent can report an event to a manager, and a manager can inform another manager of the value of management information on an agent. Using the retrieval and modification operations, a manager can cause an agent to perform an action or execute a command. Also with these operations, a manager can create new and delete existing instances of management information.

SNMP operations occur through message exchange over a transport mechanism. (See Figure 6–1 for each type exchange.) The retrieval and modification operations require two messages. The first is a *request* and the second is a *response* message. The event report operation uses a single *event report* message, which is called an SNMP *trap*. The inform operation uses an *inform* and a *response* message.

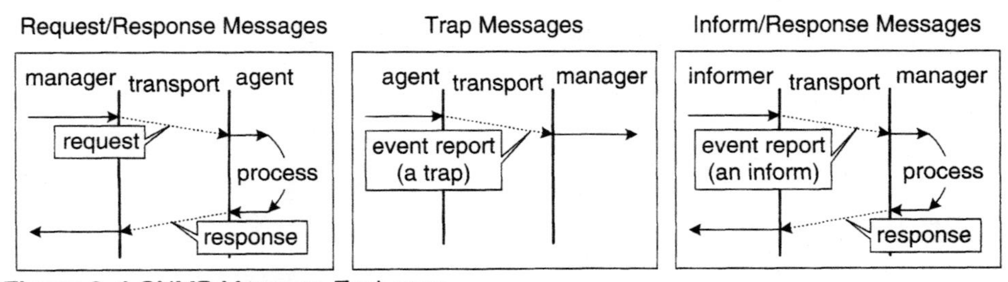

Figure 6–1 SNMP Message Exchange

SNMP messages and their contents are encoded with a *tag*, *length*, and *value*. The *tag* specifies the data type of the *value*, and the *length* specifies the size of the *value* in octets. The *value* may be elementary or may itself consist of a sequence of fields, each with a tag, length, and value. (Note that there may be zero, one, or more fields in a sequence.) The format of *tag*, *length*, and *value* is presented in Appendix A. An understanding of their encodings is not needed to understand SNMP MIBs, so we will skip over encodings.

The *value* of an SNMP message consists of a sequence of fields. (See Figure 6–2) The first few fields specify administrative information, such as the version of the protocol, and that needed for security. A detailed understanding of these fields is not needed to understand MIBs, so we will skip over them and look at the last field in an SNMP message, the *SNMP PDU*.

The tag of this field identifies the SNMP message type. (See Table 6–1 for messages for each operation.) The *value* of SNMP PDU field is a sequence of fields, which are the operands or results of an SNMP operation. The first few fields specify control information and vary based on the message type. The last field is an array of zero, one, or more pairs. The first element of a pair is the identity (or the approximation of the identity) of a specific instance of management information. The second element of the pair is a value of management information (or a place holder for a value). (See Figure 6–2)

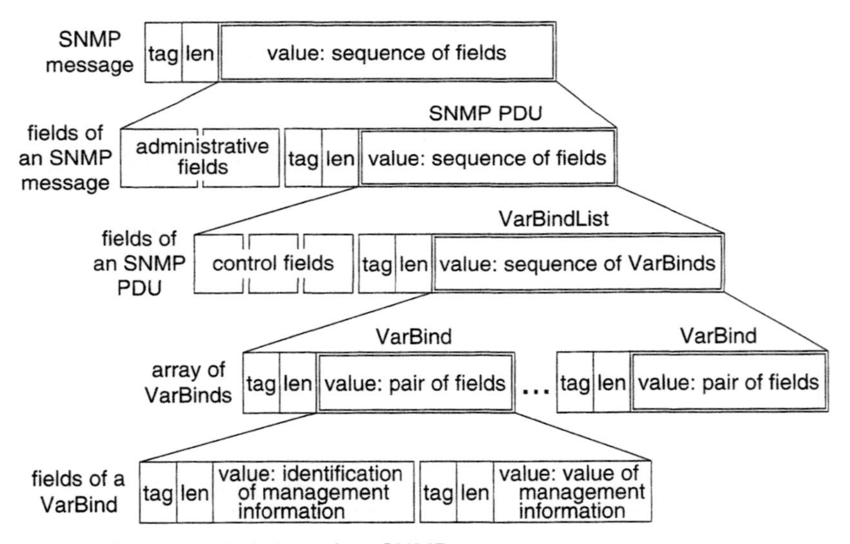

Figure 6–2 Exploded view of an SNMP message

The remainder of this chapter describes each SNMP operation. We will focus on the information that you need to know to understand MIBs and skip the details not needed to understand MIBs. (See Appendix B for details.) Table 6–1 lists each SNMP operation and specifies the messages that are sent to perform that operation.

Table 6–1 SNMP Operations

Operation and Description	From/To	First Message	Second Message
GET: retrieve the value of management information. One or more items can be retrieved in a single message.	Manager/ Agent	get-request	get-response(v1) or response(v2)
GETNEXT: retrieve the value of management information whose identification follows after the approximation of the identification given. One or more items can be retrieved in a single message.	Manager/ Agent	get-next-request	get-response(v1) or response(v2)
GETBULK: extends the functionality of GETNEXT by allowing multiple values to be returned for selected items in the request.	Manager/ Agent	get-bulk-request(v2)	response(v2)
SET: modify the value of management information. One or more items can be modified in a single message.	Manager/ Agent	set-request	get-response(v1) or response(v2)
TRAP: report an event on a managed system. The report is not confirmed.	Agent/ Manager	trap(v1) or snmpV2-trap(v2)	— no message —
INFORM: an unsolicited report of the value of management information. One or more items can be specified in a single message.	Informer/ Manager	inform-request(v2)	response(v2)

6.2 Control Fields

Each type of SNMP message contains control fields as elements of an SNMP PDU. Many of these fields are common between the SNMP message types. Each field is briefly described in Table 6–2. Additional usage information will be provided, if needed, in the descriptions of the operations which follow the table.

Table 6–2 Control Fields

Field	Used In	Description
request-id	get-request get-next-request get-bulk-request(v2) set-request snmpV2-trap(v2) inform-request(v2) get-response(v1) response(v2)	The value is chosen by the sender of a request, inform, or v2Trap, and returned in a response. This value is used by the sender to pair a response with a request or inform. This is needed when the sender does not wait for a response before sending another request or inform.

Table 6–2 Control Fields (Continued)

Field	Used In	Description
error-status	get-request get-next-request set-request snmpV2-trap(v2) inform-request(v2) get-response(v1) response(v2)	The value is not used in a request, inform, or v2Trap, but should be set to zero by the sender. In responses the value indicates the result from processing the request or inform.
error-index	get-request get-next-request set-request snmpV2-trap(v2) inform-request(v2) get-response(v1) response(v2)	The value is not used in a request, inform, or v2Trap, but should be set to zero by the sender. In responses the value is either zero, or the one-based index of a pair in the VarBindList array. A non-zero value is used to provide additional information for some error results.
non-repeaters	get-bulk-request(v2)	The value is the number of pairs in the VarBindList array for which a single instance should be returned.
max-repetitions	get-bulk-request(v2)	The value is the maximum number of repetitions to return.
enterprise	trap(v1)	The value identifies the system type for generic traps and partially identifies the event that occurred for specific traps.
agent-addr	trap(v1)	Originally defined to specify the network address of an agent, but recent interpretations specify that the value should be zero.
generic-trap	trap(v1)	A value of zero to five to identify a generic trap, or the value of six to identify a specific trap. A generic trap is one of six events defined in the original SNMP definitions.
specific-trap	trap(v1)	The value is not used when the trap is a generic trap, but should be set to zero. The value, along with the value of the enterprise field, is used to identify an event when the value of the generic-trap field is six.
time-stamp	trap(v1)	The value of variable sysUpTime when the event occurred.

6.3 Retrieval Operations

There are three operations that a manager can use to retrieve the value of management information. They are GET, GETNEXT, and GETBULK. The last, GETBULK, is available only in SNMPv2. It is an optimization of the GETNEXT operation.

6.3.1 GET Operation

The GET operation retrieves the value of one or more instances of management information. In a *get-request* message, each VarBind element of array VarBindList specifies the identity of an instance of management information. The value of management information in a VarBind element is a placeholder and is not used by agents, but should be set to the special value NULL. In SNMPv1, when no error occurs processing the request, a *get-response* message replaces the place holder values with the actual values of management information for each instance of management information. Also, the error-status and error-index fields are set to a value of zero to indicate success in processing the request. (See Figure 6–3)

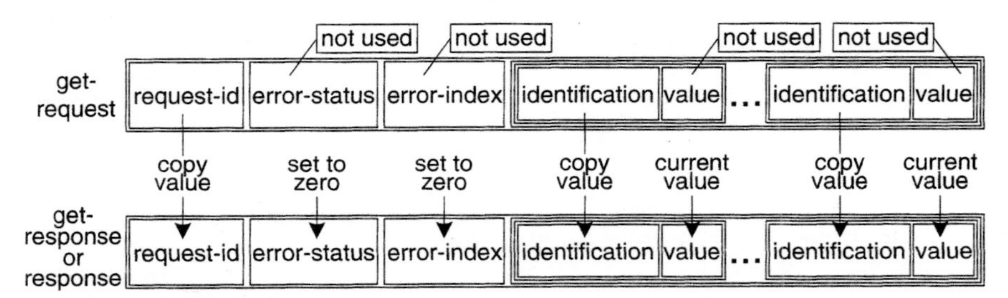

Figure 6–3 An SNMPv1 get-response or SNMPv2 response with no error

In SNMPv1, when one or more errors occur processing a request, a *get-response* message returns the identical value for all fields other than for error-status and error-index. (See Figure 6–4)

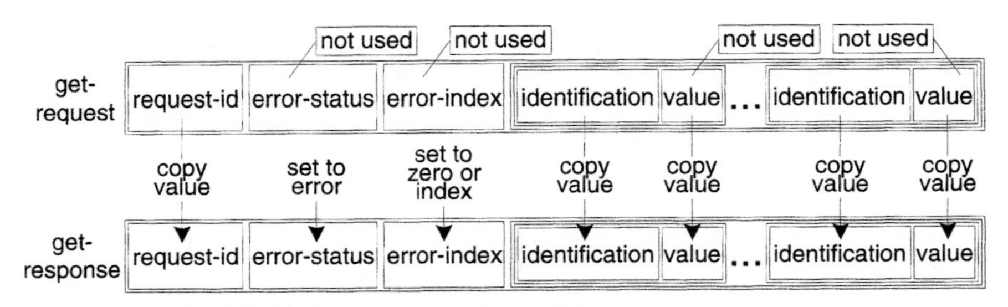

Figure 6–4 An SNMPv1 get-response specifying an error

On error, one of the following values is returned in the error-status field:

- tooBig — the size of the response would exceed a local limitation (and the error-index field has no additional information).
- noSuchName — a specified instance of the management information is not available to be accessed (and the error-index field has the one-based index of the element from array VarBindList). Management information may not be available due to access control settings, the particular instance not existing, or the agent not supporting the type of management information specified.
- genErr — a specified instance of the management information is not available due to some other reason (and the error-index field has the one-based index of the element from array VarBindList).

Since only one error indication is returned in a *get-response* message and each identified instance of management information in the request can cause an error, a manager may have to try the GET operation many times before a *get-response* message is returned with no error. (See Figure 6–5)

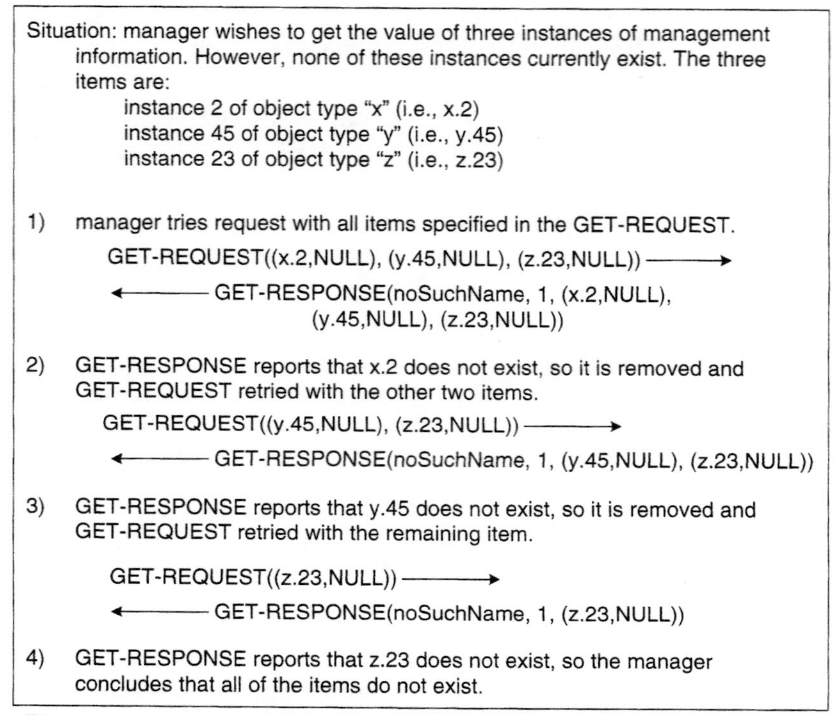

Figure 6–5 Multiple GET-REQUESTS in SNMPv1 to determine all errors

In SNMPv2, the two most typical errors are returned as special exception values in *response* messages. (See Figure 6–6) Instead of the value of management information of the instance specified, one of the following exception values are returned:

- noSuchObject — either the type of object cannot be accessed due to access control settings or the agent does not support the type of management information.
- noSuchInstance — either the instance of the object cannot be accessed due to access control settings or the instance does not currently exist.

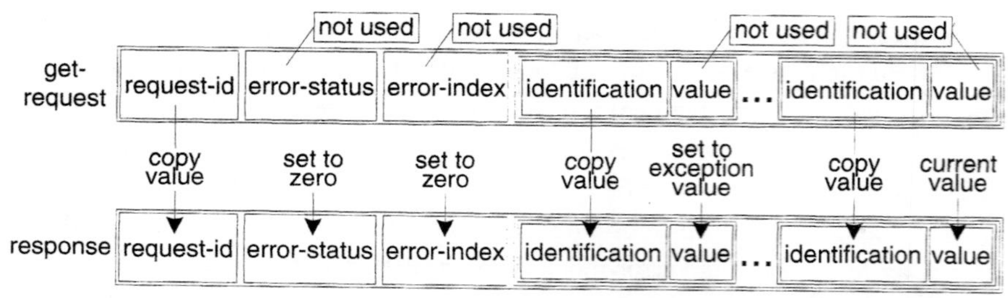

Figure 6–6 An SNMPv2 response with no error, but with an exception value

With the exception values, multiple error indications may be returned in a single SNMPv2 *response* message. Thus, the steps to determine all errors are much shorter with SNMPv2. (See Figure 6–7)

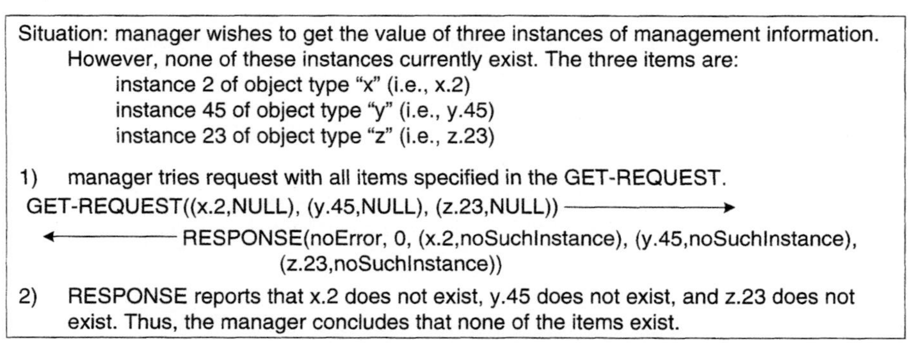
Situation: manager wishes to get the value of three instances of management information.
However, none of these instances currently exist. The three items are:
instance 2 of object type "x" (i.e., x.2)
instance 45 of object type "y" (i.e., y.45)
instance 23 of object type "z" (i.e., z.23)
1) manager tries request with all items specified in the GET-REQUEST.
GET-REQUEST((x.2,NULL), (y.45,NULL), (z.23,NULL))
RESPONSE(noError, 0, (x.2,noSuchInstance), (y.45,noSuchInstance), (z.23,noSuchInstance))
2) RESPONSE reports that x.2 does not exist, y.45 does not exist, and z.23 does not exist. Thus, the manager concludes that none of the items exist.

Figure 6–7 A single GET-REQUEST in SNMPv2 to determine all errors

In summary, the GET operation is used when the identification of the instance of management information is already known. Examples include scalar objects and columnar objects that are long lived. The major difference between SNMPv1 and SNMPv2 is that multiple error indications may be returned in SNMPv2, where in SNMPv1 at most one error may be returned. Also, no values are returned when an error occurs in SNMPv1, but values are returned (for other variables) when an exception value is returned in SNMPv2.

6.3.2 GETNEXT and GETBULK Operations

The GETNEXT and GETBULK operations retrieve the value of one or more instances of management information. In a *get-next-request* or *get-bulk-request* message, each VarBind element of array VarBindList specifies the approximation of the identity of an instance of management information. The value of management information in a VarBind element is a placeholder and is not used by agents, but should be set to the special value NULL.

In both SNMPv1 and SNMPv2, when no error occurs processing the request, a response is returned where the approximations are replaced with actual identities of instances of management information and the placeholder values are replaced with actual values of management information. Also, the error-status and error-index fields are set to a value of zero to indicate success in processing the request. (See Figure 6–8)

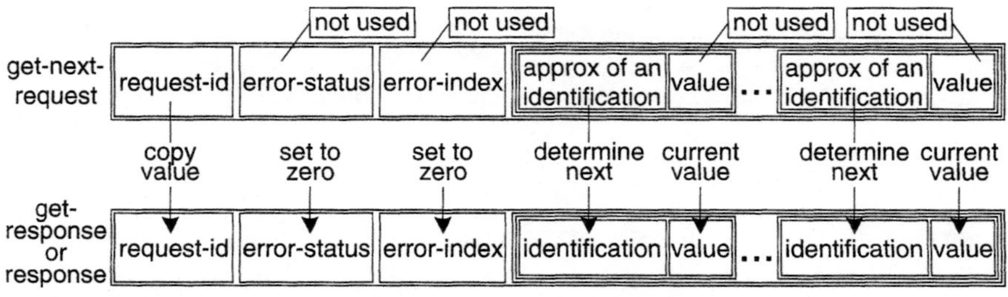
not used
not used
not used
not used
get-next-request
request-id
error-status
error-index
approx of an identification
value
...
approx of an identification
value
copy value
set to zero
set to zero
determine next
current value
determine next
current value
get-response or response
request-id
error-status
error-index
identification
value
...
identification
value

Figure 6–8 An SNMPv1 get-response or SNMPv2 response for a get-next-request

In SNMPv1, when there is no management information with identity greater than that specified for any of the elements of the VarBindList, then a noSuchName error is returned. (See Figure 6–9)

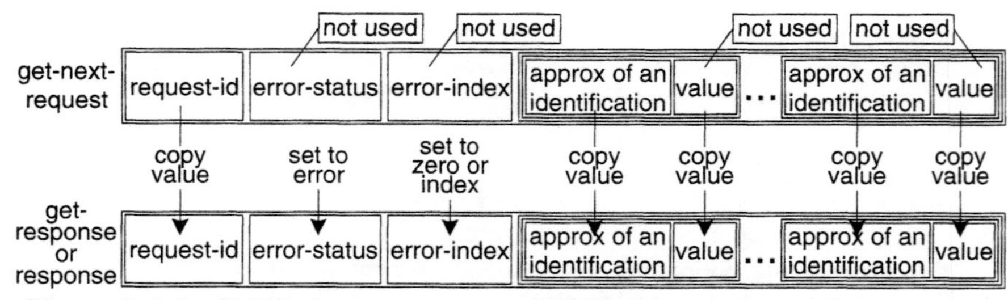

Figure 6–9 An SNMPv1 get-response or SNMPv2 response specifying an error

The following is a complete list of errors that can be returned in SNMPv1:

- tooBig — the size of the response would exceed a local limitation (and the error-index field has no additional information).
- noSuchName — no instance of the management information is available to be accessed that has an identification greater than the approximation specified in at least one element of the array VarBindList. The error-index field has the one-based index of an element from the array. Note that management information that is not available due to access control settings is skipped.
- genErr — an instance of the management information is not available due to some other reason (and the error-index field has the one-based index of the element from array VarBindList).

In SNMPv2, the special exception value of *endOfMibView* is returned instead of the error noSuchName. This allows efficient processing of instances of management information implemented in an agent whose identity has the largest lexicographical value. (See Figure 6–10)

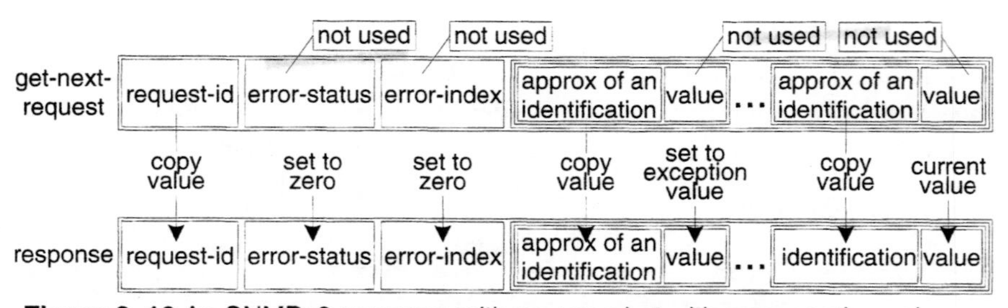

Figure 6–10 An SNMPv2 response with no error, but with an exception value

Uses of GETNEXT and GETBULK

The GETNEXT and GETBULK operations are used for two purposes. The first and primary purpose is to retrieve all instances of management information of a specific class (or type) when the identity of the instances are not already known. This means simply to retrieve rows from a table when the index values (or row keys) are not already known. If already known, then the GET operation can be used.

The other use of the GETNEXT and GETBULK operations is for "discovering" management information that can be accessed by a manager. The process of retrieving all instances of management information with GETNEXT or GETBULK operations is called "doing a MIB walk" on an agent. This probing of an agent is done when trying to determine what classes of management information are available when there is no description of the agent. MIB walks are also performed on agents as part of agent testing, to determine if an agent has been correctly implemented.

In both uses of the GETNEXT and GETBULK operations, instances of management information are returned in lexicographical order. This means that the identity of the instance of management information returned, which is an OID value, is lexicographically greater than the approximation of an identity of an instance of management information, which is also an OID value, specified in *get-next-request* or *get-bulk-request* messages.

Example MIB Walk

Figure 6–11 shows a "GETNEXT walk" through a portion of the instances of management information implemented by an agent. Each item on the path is discovered by a GETNEXT operation with a single element in the VarBindList array. The circles in the figure represent OID values. Columnar objects xyzC1 through zyxC2 and scalar objects stuS1 through stuS3 are classes (or types) of management information. Scalar objects have a single instance as represented by a rectangle in the figure. Columnar objects may have zero, one, or more instances. In the figure, there are four instances of each columnar object.

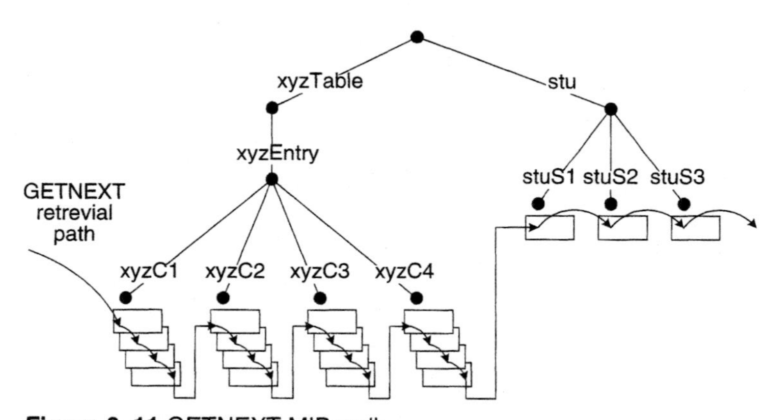

Figure 6–11 GETNEXT MIB walk

The GETNEXT MIB walk starts with an approximation of the identity of the first instance of columnar object xyzC1. The result of the *get-next-request* message is the identity of the first instance of xyzC1 and its current value. The next *get-next-request* message uses the identity of the first instance of xyzC1 to approximate the identity of the second instance of xyzC1. The MIB walk continues with the identity returned for previous operation as the approximation for the identity of management information in the next operation. For example, a *get-next-request* message with the identity of the fourth (and last) instance of xyzC1 returns the identity of the first instance of xyzC2.

Example Table Retrieval

Figure 6–12 shows the GETNEXT operation used to retrieve management information organized in a table, one row at a time. The initial GETNEXT operation specifies as operands, approximations of the first instances of columnar objects xyzC1, xyzC2, xyzC3, and xyzC4. The approximations are simply the identities, that is, the OID values of the columnar objects. Four additional GETNEXT operations are then required to retrieve all rows and to realize the end of the table. The results from the last GETNEXT operation are instances of management information from different columnar or scalar objects as specified in the request. This is how the end of a table is determined.

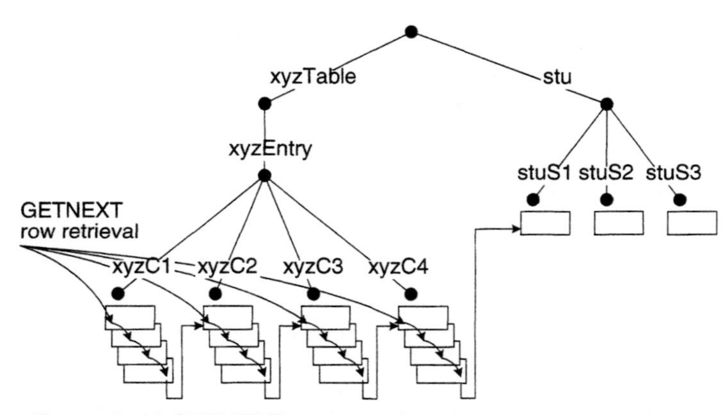

Figure 6–12 GETNEXT retrieval of a table, one row at a time

Figure 6–13 shows the same retrieval of the rows in table xyzTable expressed as *get-next-request* and *response* messages. Only the approximations of the identity of instances of management information and the actual identities (and no values) are shown in the messages. In the last response, identities are returned for instances of objects xyzC2, xyzC3, xyzC4, and stuS1 instead of objects xyzC1, xyzC2, xyzC3, and xyzC4. The change of object class is how a manager determines that the end of a column has been reached.

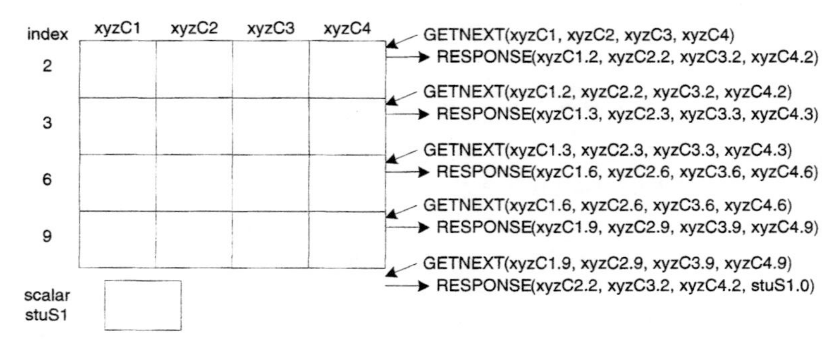

Figure 6–13 GETNEXT operands and results

Results from Empty Tables and Access Control

In general, managers don't always know the number of rows in a table and, thus, cannot know ahead of time how many GETNEXT operations are needed to retrieve all rows. For example, consider management information that is the status of a network connection and whose instances are identified by a pair of transport end-point addresses. Instances of connections come and go, shadowing the fate of the connections. Only the GETNEXT and GETBULK operations can retrieve the status of all the current connections, since they can be used without prior knowledge of the number or identification of the current instances.

Additionally, a table may be empty (i.e., currently have no rows in the table) or a manager may not have access to all objects. In both of these cases the result of a GETNEXT or GETBULK operation is the first present and accessible object instance (or instances) whose identity is lexicographically greater than the approximation of an identity specified in the request. Figure 6–14 shows a GETNEXT walk through the same portion of object classes (or types) implemented by an agent as shown in Figure 6–11.

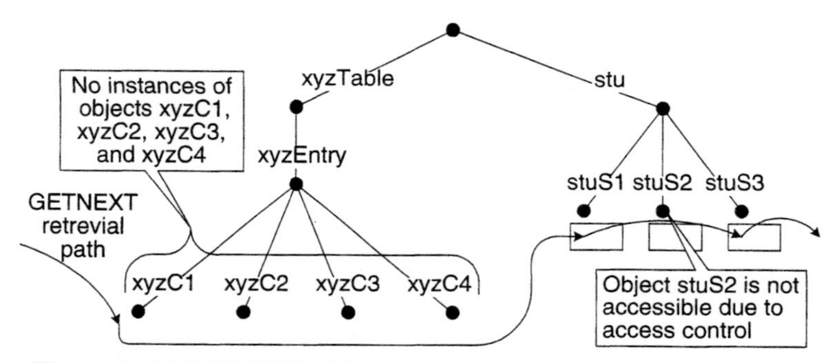

Figure 6–14 GETNEXT with no rows in table, and no access of scalar objects due to access controls

The results from these two GETNEXT walks are different. The second walk does not return any instances of columnar objects xyzC1, xyzC2, xyzC3, or xyzC4, since there no rows presently in the table. Also, the instance of scalar object stuS2 is not returned in the second walk even though it exists. It is skipped due to access control changes between the first and second GETNEXT walks.

Sparse Tables

It is possible that due to access control, limitations in the agent implementation, or design of a MIB that not all columns in a table have an instance in a row. In this situation, GETNEXT operations skip over the non-existing instances (or "holes") in the table. The unfortunate result for a manager is that additional checking is required on the results. Figure 6–15 shows table xyzTable containing four rows. However, columnar object xyzC3 does not have instances in rows 2 and 3, and columnar object xyzC4 does not have instances in rows 3 and 4.

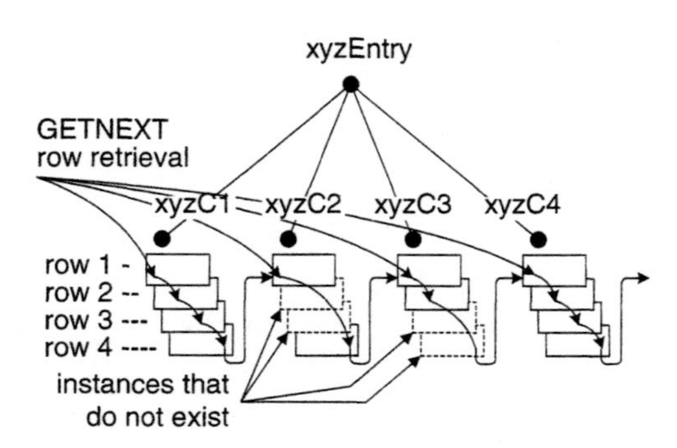

Figure 6–15 Example of a sparse table

Selective Retrieval of Table Information

The GETNEXT and GETBULK operations can also be used to retrieve a portion instead of all the rows and columns of a table. For example, if only columns xyzC1 and xyzC2 were of interest, then only these columns would be specified in GETNEXT and GETBULK operations. If only rows with index values greater than ten were of interest, then the operations could be started with the identity of the columnar objects for the row with an index of ten. The first operation would return the first present and accessible row with an index greater than ten. Also, if rows with an index value greater than 100 were not of interest, then retrieval of the table can be terminated early before the table's end is reached.

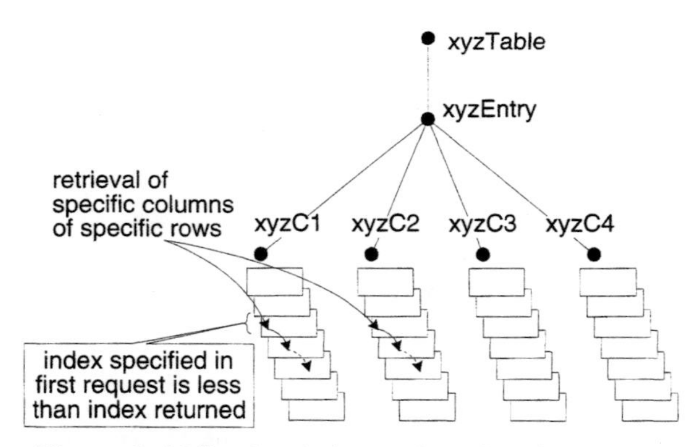

Figure 6–16 Retrieval of a portion of a table

Figure 6–16 shows retrieval of only two columns of table xyzTable starting at a row indexed below the row of interest, and continuing until a row not of interest is retrieved. (The retrieval would also be terminated if the end of the table was encountered.)

GETBULK Operation

The GETBULK operation is an optimization of the GETNEXT operation, which allows multiple instances of objects to be returned instead of just one when the GETNEXT operation is used. The *get-bulk-request* message uses the *non-repeaters* and the *max-repeti-*

tions fields, which are in the same location as the error-status and error-index fields, to control its operation. (See Figure 6–17)

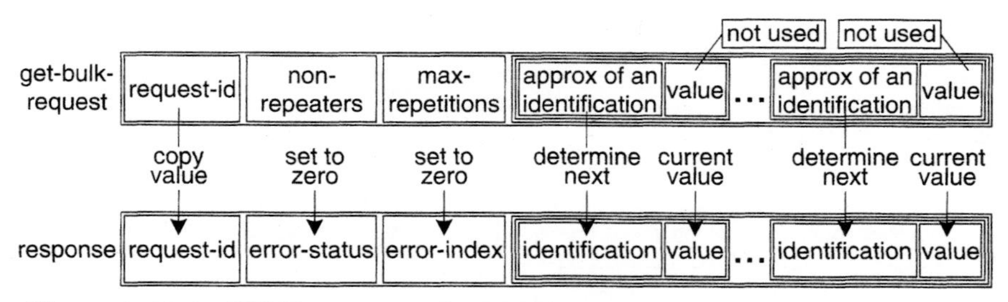

Figure 6–17 An SNMPv2 successful GETBULK operation

The *non-repeaters* field is the number of elements from the beginning of the VarBindList array for which a single instance should be returned. The *max-repetitions* field is the maximum number of instances to return for the remaining elements in the VarBindList array. However, only the elements that will fit in a response will be returned. Also, if the value for all elements is the special exception value *endOfMibView*, then these repetitions are returned and no more. (See Figure 6–18)

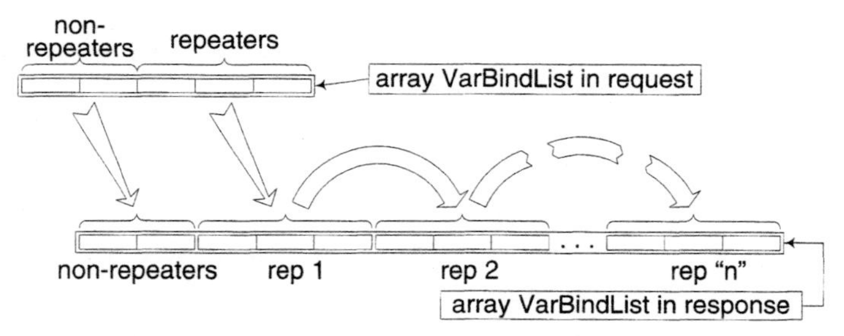

Figure 6–18 Array VarBindList in request and response of a GETBULK operation

The typical use of GETBULK is to retrieve zero or a small number of scalar objects as the "non-repeaters" and specify columnar objects as the repeaters. In this way, the GETBULK operation reduces the number of GETNEXT operations to retrieve a table by the "packing factor." The packing factor is the number of rows that will fit in a single response message. Figure 6–19 shows a table being retrieved by GETBULK operations. Note that the figure shows the values for the non-repeaters and max-repetition fields in the GETBULK request message.

In Figure 6–19, up to four rows of the table are retrieved by each GETBULK operation and, thus, a speedup of up to a factor of four should be observed using GETBULK instead of GETNEXT operations to retrieve rows from the table. However, note that the GETBULK operation does not terminate at the end of the table and, thus, the last response returns values from the beginning of the table and instances of columnar or scalar objects that lexicographically follow the table. Also note that sparse tables cause extra processing for management applications.

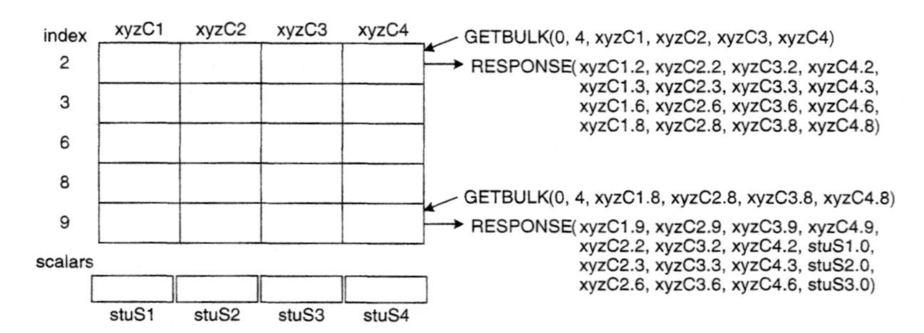

Figure 6–19 Using GETBULK to retrieve all rows in a table

Our Opinion

While the GETBULK operation does improve the performance of retrieving all the rows in a table, we believe that the GETBULK operation does not boost performance high enough. Also, we don't believe that GETBULK does quite the right job. We believe that a better version of GETBULK is required that is much more space efficient, stops at the end of a table, and reduces the amount of extra processing for sparse tables.

Summary of GETNEXT and GETBULK

In summary, the GETNEXT operation is primarily used in SNMP to retrieve the rows from a table. It can be used to retrieve all columns and rows, or selected columns and rows. The GETBULK operation, which is available only in SNMPv2, is an optimization of GETNEXT.

6.4 Modification Operations

The SET operation modifies the value of one or more instances of management information. Also, the operation can create new instances and delete existing instances of management information. Note however, values of management information are also modified, and instances created and deleted through normal operation of the managed system without interaction with the SNMP agent for the system. In a *set-request* message, each VarBind element of array VarBindList specifies the identity of an instance of management information. The value of management information in a VarBind element is the value for the modification request.

In both SNMPv1 and SNMPv2, the contents of the array VarBindList are copied to the response. The error-status and error-index fields are set to zero to indicate success, or to appropriate values on error. (See Figure 6–20)

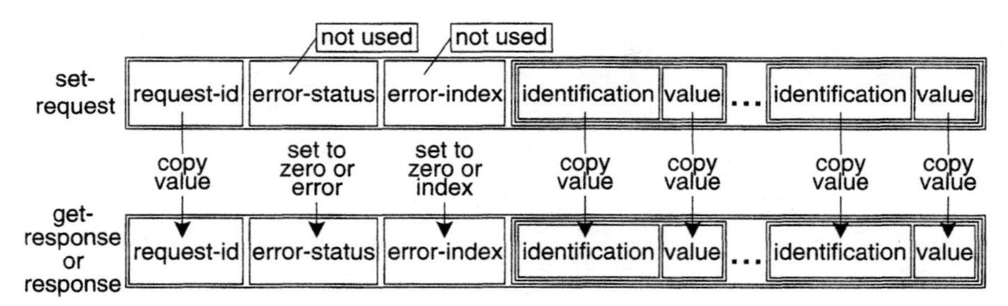

Figure 6–20 A SET operation with no error

If the operation can be carried out, then all changes must be done as if they were done simultaneously. If the operation cannot be carried out, then no changes may be done. That is, if the first two elements in a VarBindList array specify valid modifications, but the third element specifies an invalid modification, then an error must be returned and no modifications may be performed. In SNMPv1, there are four errors that can be returned. In SNMPv2, there are seventeen errors that can be returned. (See Appendix B for a listing of the errors.) Of these errors, the following are the ones that are most likely to occur (and the one-based index of the element from the VarBindList array is returned in the error-index field):

- noSuchName(v1) — either the type or instance of the management information cannot be accessed due to access control settings, the agent does not support the type of management information, or the object is only readable.
- badValue(v1) — either the value does not match the type, range or size specified in the MIB module specification, or the value is not consistent with the value of other instances of management information in the *set-request* message or on the managed system.
- genErr(v1/v2) — the agent could not perform the operation for some other reason.
- noAccess(v2) — the type or instance of the management information is not accessible due to access control settings.
- inconsistentName(v2) — the instance of the management information does not currently exist and could not be created in the request since its identification or value is not consistent with other instances of management information in the *set-request* message or on the managed system.
- inconsistentValue(v2) — the value is not consistent with the values of other instances of management information in the *set-request* message or on the managed system.
- resourceUnavailable(v2) — modification of the value requires a resource that is not currently available.

The SET operation can be quite difficult, if not impossible, to implement correctly in an agent. Or, the SET operation may be quite easy to implement. It all depends on the design of the definitions of management information!

Since there are no CREATE, DELETE, or ACTION operations in SNMP, the SET operation must be used to provide that capability. There are no restrictions on the order of elements in the VarBindList array. Elements in the array can refer to managed objects in unrelated subsystems. Multiple instances can be created in the same SET operation that compete for the same resources. However, designers of MIB modules can specify a list of items which must be included in a single SET operation to create a new instance of a row in a table, but they cannot restrict the SET operation from containing other items.

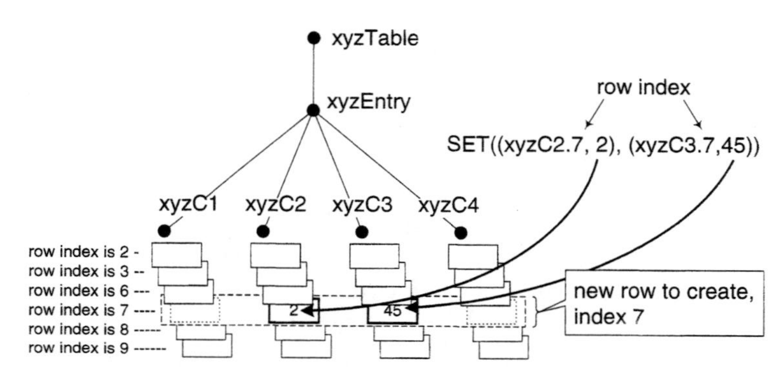

Figure 6–21 A SET operation to create a row in a table

Figure 6–21 shows a SET operation to create a new row in table xyzTable. The row has an index of seven, which corresponds to the instances specified in the set request (i.e., xyzC2.7 and xyzC3.7). Columnar objects xyzC1 and xyzC4 are not specified in the request. They may be read-only, or may not be required for row creation, since the agent may be able to use a default value.

In summary, the SET operation is used to control and configure a managed system. The multiple uses and power of the SET operation requires careful design of definitions of management information. For a SET operation to succeed, all the items in the request must be modified, or created and set to the corresponding value specified. If this cannot be done, then no value may be changed, nor a new instance created. Also, the operation must appear to affect all items in the request simultaneously. There can be no requirement for ordering of items in the request, nor can there be a requirement that all items be processed by the same method routine. Meeting these requirements in all cases can be quite difficult (or impossible) or quite easy based on the approaches and techniques used for the definitions of management information.

6.5 Event Reporting Operations

There are two operations that send unsolicited management information to a manager. These are TRAP and INFORM. The TRAP operation reports the occurrence of an event on a system and may provide the value of one or more instances of management information. An agent sends to a manager a *trap* message in SNMPv1, and a *snmpV2-trap* message in SNMPv2. No response is returned to either message, and thus reception of the message cannot be assumed. The formats of these two messages are quite different. However, the information contained in these messages is essentially identical. The major difference between the two message formats are how events are identified.

On receiving an event report message, a manager chooses how to process it. Typically, a manager creates a new entry in an event log containing the event report. Also, the manager may signal or distribute the event report message to processes on the management system. These processes may query the agent for additional information, or may try to correlate the event report with other reports and status information to determine a network-wide event, such as a power outage. For example, when a widespread power outage occurs, a manager would receive many reports that a loss of power has occurred and critical devices are switching to a backup power source. Other devices without a backup power source would cease to respond to management requests. When the power was restored and devices restarted, they would generate an event report indicating this condition. A less catastrophic event such as the power outage of a single router or the congestion of a single line could also cause many event report messages.

The other operation, available only in SNMPv2, is INFORM. This operation, sent by an SNMP "informer" entity, advises an SNMP manager of an event on a system and may provide the value of one or more instances of management information on that system. Remember, we made up the term "informer," since the SNMP WG cannot decide if agents or managers send INFORMs. This operation is not currently well defined, and no further information is provided about it. It could be modified to function as a confirmed event report, but currently it is defined as "something else."

Our Opinion

We believe that one of the most glaring deficiencies in the SNMP protocol is the lack of a "confirmed event report." Other management systems are built around confirmed events, and for users of these systems to move to SNMP requires that SNMP support this capability. A solution can be direct by adding a new operation, or may be indirect via additional GET and SET operations. There are benefits and costs with either approach. However, we believe that choosing an approach soon is critically important for the future of SNMP. Progress has been blocked so far by leaders in the SNMP community who do not believe that event driven approaches are workable. We believe that these leaders should step out of the way and allow confirmed event reporting to be added to the framework.

The area of event reporting has been one of the most controversial topics on SNMP. It is second only to the topic of security.

6.6 Summary

The reader may be somewhat surprised at the small number of operations in the SNMP management framework. However, this simplicity has been one of the reasons that SNMP has been so widely deployed. Having just a few simple operations has allowed the implementations of the protocol engines to be quite small and require fewer resources to develop, as compared with other management protocols. Also, the protocol is easy to understand. Unfortunately, the reduction of complexity of the protocol has resulted in some increase in complexity of MIB understanding and design. Some of the trade-offs in MIB design require you to understand the protocol. But now, having completed this chapter, you are on the way to becoming a master of designing SNMP MIB modules.

CHAPTER 7

Object Modelling

Producing a well-organized, easy to implement, easy to read MIB is a relatively straightforward task if the proper planning has been done up front. In this chapter, we will discuss how to go about analyzing systems and services with SNMP in mind, and how to translate that analysis into a MIB. We will not produce complete MIBs yet, but the work we do here will make that task quite easy.

7.1 Introduction

Before we begin, we should be clear on one important point: we will be discussing object analysis in this chapter, not object-oriented analysis. The intent of this chapter is to outline the process and procedures used in analyzing a complex system, and to break down that system into manageable objects you can then use within a MIB. Object-oriented analysis, on the other hand, is a related, but decidedly different procedure. It is tempting at first glance to look at a MIB hierarchy and declare it to be object-oriented. Externally, it certainly looks that way: we have generalized groups that contain more specific groups, and we have what roughly appears to be an inheritance tree. This last attribute is where the problem lies. SNMP MIBs are not really object-oriented, as there is no concept of *inheritance*. Inheritance is a key concept in most object-oriented systems that allows for objects in a system to retain characteristics and behaviors of their predecessors. An object-oriented system typically demonstrates these relationships using a tree structure, so confusing the tree structure of a MIB and the tree structure of an object system is a common mistake. The tree structure used by a MIB is merely a very convenient registration system for groups of related parameters, and has no real impact on the semantics of objects found there. In this chapter we won't really be concerned with object-oriented modelling, but the modelling of MIB objects. Hopefully, the differences between these two will be apparent soon. To design an effective MIB, the entire system must be systematically decomposed into specific categories and organized into a registration tree. This process of decomposition is not always obvious, although it does get much easier with practice.

Just as few programmers would not simply sit down at a workstation and begin writing code when asked to write a word processor, MIB writers should not immediately start laying out MIB modules when beginning to model a system. The single most critical element of work done by a MIB writer is design, so the more attention paid to this phase of development, the more useful and robust your MIB will turn out. The MIB model development phase is also a good time to bring in the experts, on a particular topic, who may not even have specific knowledge of SNMP or MIBs.

7.2 Categories of the Model

When first approaching a new MIB design problem, we need to keep several categories of objects in mind so that we can tackle the problem in an organized way:

- Actions — control a system. Action objects are used to accomplish a well-defined task, such as: reboot a device or stop providing a network service.
- Statistics — provide us with useful information about what a system has been doing since the start of some time interval. Statistics might include such items as: the number of packets transmitted by a network interface card or the number of times a user has logged on to a machine.
- State — indicates the current condition of a system. State might include such items as: a board is initializing or a fan in failure mode.
- Components — aid in describing the collections of logical and physical devices or services which are under the control of an SNMP agent. These might describe the physical boards in a multi-slot chassis or contain the names of the services active on a file server.
- Attributes — are the properties of a modelled object which describe relatively static things about a device or service: the number of slots in a 802.3 repeater, the person to call when this device misbehaves, or the type of CPU on board.

All of the items we will model in a MIB fall into one of these categories, and recognizing what type of object we are working with is the first step in placing it into a MIB. In this chapter, we will concentrate on these five aspects of a manageable system and examine examples of what each category entails.

7.3 Components

Components are perhaps the most difficult of the categories to model. In describing components, we are attempting to reveal the logical or physical containments that exist in a device or service. Physical containments might be relationships, such as a list of boards contained in a chassis or a list of batteries in an uninterruptable power supply. Logical containment is a bit more unclear — this can be anything from a list of systems for which a device is a proxy manager to a list of services provided by a network server. The good news is that humans have a natural classification ability; the bad news is that the complex systems we engineer often have murky relationships between groups in a system.

No matter the complexity of the system, the approach is the same. Starting at the top level (the item being modelled), what does it contain? For each of those items, what do they contain? This process continues for each level of the object. The answer to the question "*what does it contain?*" is easier asked than answered. We probably want the answer to be as general as possible at first, and more specific later. As an example, let's look at an automobile. It contains:

- an engine
- a powertrain
- a chassis
- a passenger compartment
- an electrical system
- a climate control system

There are probably a great many more sub-systems, but these are the major ones we will concern ourselves with for now. Taking each of these systems in turn, what do they contain?

Engine

- block
- pistons and cylinders
- spark plugs
- turbo charger

Powertrain

- transmission
- drivetrain

Chassis

- doors
- windows

Passenger compartment

- seats
- dashboard/instrument panel
- air bag(s)

Electrical system

- starter
- lights

Climate control system

- compressors
- heaters
- ductwork

Continuing this process until each bolt, washer, and fastener is listed would probably be pointless. We are interested in the major systems and the controllable aspects of each. As with actions, it is not always clear where to start and stop decomposing systems into sub-systems, nor is it always apparent where a component really resides. In this quick example, there are actually two types of containment described: physical (the passenger compartment) and logical (the electrical system). The logical components may reside in one of the three major compartments (engine, passenger, and trunk), but it seems appropriate to group them together. Components at the "edge" of a sub-system may not always seem to fall neatly into one category — are the fuel injectors in a car part of the fuel system or the engine?

Alternatively, we can break down this system based on strict adherence to physical containment and arrive at a breakdown which looks like:

Engine compartment
- engine
- transmission
- climate control system
- turbo charger

Passenger compartment
- seats
- dashboard/instrument panel

Chassis
- suspension system
- doors

This approach aids in correlating components with their physical containers, but may prove to be a bit inflexible where there are not clear locations for an object. Typically, the best solution is a mix of the two approaches.

Breaking the components down into a strict logical model, we might see these groupings:

Powertrain
- engine
- transmission

Exhaust
- manifold
- muffler
- turbo charger

Electrical
- spark plugs
- battery

Environmental
- passenger compartment
- climate control
- user preferences

Things get a bit more complicated when we begin to consider the more intangible resources a car might possess:
- a list of driver preferences for cabin temperature and seat position
- a list of pre-programmed radio stations

If we use a strict physical containment, these categories may not seem to fit in very neatly. Is a preferred radio station really "contained" within the passenger compartment? It may be. The radio can be considered part of the passenger compartment, and a natural location to hold a list of radio stations might be within the modelled radio.

Components have another feature which must be considered when analyzing the system: *cardinality,* or how many of a item are present in a system. In our car example, there is only one engine, but many cylinders inside that engine. The engine has a cardinality of one, while the cylinders have a cardinality of eight in a car equipped with a V8 engine. In SNMP parlance, this denotes whether an item is single instanced or multi-instanced. Whether an item is single or multi-instanced will become important when we are actually writing the declarations for the objects and trying to express the relationships between them.

7.4 Attributes

Attributes are the fairly static properties of the device or system we are modelling. If we were asked to describe the attributes of an automobile, we might list off items such as: color, weight, length, height, chassis type, and horsepower. The same holds true for a network device—we might wish to know the board capacity of a chassis, the number of fans in a router, or the version number of a firmware chip on a network interface card. The words "fairly static" shouldn't be stretched too far—these don't include things such as the temperature inside the device, the date a user logged on to a mail server, etc. These are dynamic attributes which fall into other categories.

Attributes can be further refined into related groups, and a good starting place is the component groups developed earlier. We could create new groups to hold the attributes, but grouping attributes such as the horsepower rating with the color of the car will result in the tendency to "bubble-up" attributes into one grouping. This organization results in a top-heavy MIB, which is difficult to maintain over time. A more structured approach is to use the same component categories developed earlier and enumerate specific attributes associated with each one. Building on the earlier example, we might have:

Engine
- horsepower rating

Powertrain

- drive type: 4 or 2 wheel
- transmission type: manual, automatic, and number of speeds

Chassis

- fabrication date

Passenger compartment

- seat type: bench or bucket

Electrical system

- electrical capacity

Climate control system

- thermal rating in BTUs

Another important attribute of any object within a system is that of *identity*. If more than one instance (cardinality is greater than one) of an object can reside in a system, there must be some way to uniquely identify that object. For example, suppose that our car is equipped with the usual four wheels. If we are writing software to manage these wheels, we need some way of identifying exactly which wheel we are discussing. There are two ways to approach this problem:

- determine the identity of the object by an attribute of that object
- assign an arbitrary identity

Take the example of the chassis and doors. On a 4-door sedan there are two attributes of a door which define its location: side of the car (*left* or *right*), and position relative to the front of the car (*front* or *rear*). These attributes can be used to uniquely identify a door when attempting to manage the car. The tuple (*front*, *right*) unambiguously identifies a particular door on a car.

A second approach identifying an instance of an object is to assign an arbitrary identity to the object. If we choose to treat the door to the engine compartment (the hood) and the door to the luggage storage compartment (the trunk) of the car as "doors" and want to mange them as such, our earlier model of basing identity on location relative to the side of the car falls apart. (Note that some cars have the engine located in the rear of the car and the storage compartment located in the front of the car.) To allow an arbitrary number of doors on a car to be identified, we could simply number the doors in any particular order, and let the other attributes of the doors show their "real" identity. In this case, we would have doors named with some arbitrary number, one through six in our example:

1. Right Front
2. Left Front
3. Right Rear
4. Left Rear
5. Engine
6. Storage

These two approaches are quite similar, but have a very important difference in the way their identities are assigned. Our first approach determined identity based on one or more attributes of the object, while our second approach ignored the attributes, and simply assigned an identity. There are advantages to each approach, but neither is appropriate to all situations. In fact, attribute-based identity assignment may not even be possible in all situations. Some sets of objects simply may not have an attribute or a set of attributes that a management system can use to distinguish one entry from another. The radio in the car might be a good example. There is no attribute or combination of attributes of a radio's pre-set stations that uniquely identifies that button. While unlikely, all buttons could be programmed to the same radio station, so the setting of a button cannot identify it. Instead, we can simply number the buttons with a unique number and identify them that way.

7.5 Actions

Actions are the verbs of management. Actions might be something as complex as "*run a diagnostic routine on the board in slot number 3*," or as simple as "*reboot the device*." Actions can prove quite frustrating if you are new to SNMP. Since SNMP has no concept of an explicit action (in other words, there is no ACTION operation), all actions are represented in terms of *implicit* actions which do their work through side effects. With implicit actions, the manager does not send a request that states "reboot the device." Instead, the manager must send a request to set the value of a MIB object to a *trigger value*. This trigger value is recognized by the agent as a request to perform some action.

When designing actions for a system, it is important to distinguish between *action steps* and *action goals*. While the action steps represent discrete manipulations of a system object, goals are the higher level design ambitions for the MIB. In other words, the action goals answer the question "what does a management station need to be able to do to this device?" while action steps answer the question "how does it do it?" Designing actions for SNMP involves taking a high level goal and decomposing it into a series of discrete steps that we wish to expose to a manager. Actions are not easy to model, since it is usually not clear when to start or stop decomposing the action into smaller steps. Take, for example, the high-level goal *throw the ball*. At first glance, it is obvious what we mean by this, but this neglects the implicit sub-actions such as:

1. Pick up the ball
2. Face the catcher
3. Swing your arm back
4. Rapidly bring your arm forward
5. Release the ball

Of course, some people don't wish to be concerned with details such as these — they just want the ball thrown. Other people, however, might wish to have complete control over the entire process so that they can alter such items as: which ball is thrown (that is, *pick up the red ball*), or how hard the ball is thrown (that is, *bring your arm forward with all your might*).

Management applications need to be considered when designing these actions. Providing actions that are too low-level is cumbersome for the application and the user, while control levels that are too high can lead to applications which are too inflexible.

Returning to something more concrete, let's say that we have a central email server where users can log on and read their messages. A short list of the type of actions we might wish to make available through SNMP would be:

- Restart the server
- Start and stop the email service

Now we have to think about the implications of these actions. Do we want the server to reboot if users are logged in? If not, an application would have to terminate all user sessions one by one, and then reboot the server. Otherwise, the reboot action can be designed to have the side effect of first terminating all user sessions before rebooting the server. Depending on your goals for this system, either approach could be desired.

Refining our email server example a bit further, let's examine some possible action steps that help us meet our high-level goals. In order to properly reboot the server, we need to perform this list of actions:

1. Terminate the sessions of all users
2. Shutdown the email service
3. Reboot the server

Here is where design turns into an iterative process. We need to make certain that we have exposed the manipulated objects as *components* of the system. When we performed a component analysis of the system, we may have overlooked sets of objects required for these actions. Taking each of the actions we identified above, which objects do they affect? (See Table 7–1)

Table 7–1 Actions and Affected Objects

Step	Manipulates
Terminate users' sessions	A list of user sessions
Shutdown the email service	A list of services
Reboot the server	A central server object

Now we have almost all the pieces we need. The last critical piece we need to consider is exposing the details of any errors we may encounter. Remember that SNMP can't tell us that the specific reason we were unable to set a variable to a specific value, so we must provide an error-tracking variable to indicate the reason for the failure. SNMP is capable of indicating the rough details of why a request failed: there was no such object, you don't have access to that object, the value you requested was legal, but not right now, etc., but the protocol itself cannot tell you the specific reason an agent was unable to perform a request. Once again we should return to our list of steps and list exactly what sort of errors we might encounter. (See Table 7–2)

Table 7–2 Actions and Possible Errors

Step	Errors
Terminate users' sessions	<no error possible>
Shutdown the email service	users still using service
Reboot the server	email service still active

Some rules of thumb to keep in mind when you are modelling actions:

1. Don't create actions that are complex composite actions. That is, don't confuse action goals and action steps.
2. Don't expose a sub-state without exposing an error for it.
3. Don't over-decompose an action.

Perhaps the best rule of thumb comes from Albert Einstein who counsels us to

"Make things as simple as possible, but no simpler."

In other words, do not expose items just because you can. If there is a legitimate need to enable a manager to control the exact speed at which a ball is thrown, then by all means—create that MIB object. Otherwise, remember that brevity is the greatest virtue a MIB can have.

With SNMP, since it uses a connectionless transport service, we have a few additional concerns that must be addressed. First, messages may be dropped (discarded or lost) by the network, or by a busy agent or manager. Thus, a manager must track the length of time that no response has been received to each request. After a configured amount of time without receiving a response, a manager assumes that the request or response was dropped and retries. If the request was dropped, then the situation is normal. However, if the response was dropped, then the manager has made the same request twice. The MIB objects must be designed to accommodate such situations. Also, if a manager needs to make several requests, and does so one after the other without waiting for a response from each one before making the next request, the network and/or agent may reorder the requests. This must also be accommodated in the MIB design. Finally, there may be multiple managers that are concurrently making requests to an agent. A MIB design must provide the mechanisms to allow multiple managers to compete for resources without becoming deadlocked.

7.6 Statistics

Statistics are performance data which the manager can use to determine what a device has been doing during a specified interval. Statistics are a record of the interesting events which occurred since a specific point in time. Typically, this is a record of the events since the device was last powered up and put into an operational state. Statistics also record the "high water marks" of a system. These high water marks identify peaks in system resource utilization. It is important to note that there is a clear distinction between statistics and the category we will examine next, state. Statistics are a record of the past, not a reflection of the present. Recording the number of transmission upshifts is a statistic, while the currently engaged gear is a state. Once more returning to the initial components analysis of the system, the systems and sub-systems identified there are a good starting point for defining the statistics. Taking each item within the component collection, what sort of events surround its activity? Does it perform some action on a regular basis that is interesting from a performance or fault management point of view?

For our automobile, the interesting statistics are:

Engine

- peak horsepower requirement
- highest RPMs
- total RPMs

Powertrain

- number of upshifts
- number of downshifts

Electrical system

- peak electrical requirements

An easy way to remember the difference between a statistic and a state is to recall that statistics do not represent fluctuating items such as: the current load on the electrical system, the current RPMs of the engine, or even the current speed of the automobile. Statistics are counters that advance but never retreat and the high water marks of system resource usage.

Before we leave this topic, we should consider one last aspect of statistics: lifetime. All statistics are considered valid only for a specific period of time known as the epoch. The beginning of the epoch is typically the time at which the monitored system last started operation, and ends at the present time. For instance, a statistic representing the number of transmission upshifts is valid for the time period beginning with the starting of the car, and ending with the time in which the counter is sampled. Let's examine how the lifetime of a counter works. In Figure 7–1, we have an example of a counter that tracks the number of times the transmission has been upshifted from when the car was started. At the time beginning of the epoch, the time the car starts, the value of the statistic is zero. After a while, the car is put through two upshifts, increasing the counter to two. At the same moment as the second shift, the manager issues a request for the value of the counter. The agent takes the current value of the counter, two, and returns it to the manager. This event constitutes the end of the epoch.

That is, the value of the counter that the manager receives is valid for the period from the car's start until the agent returns the requested value to the manager.

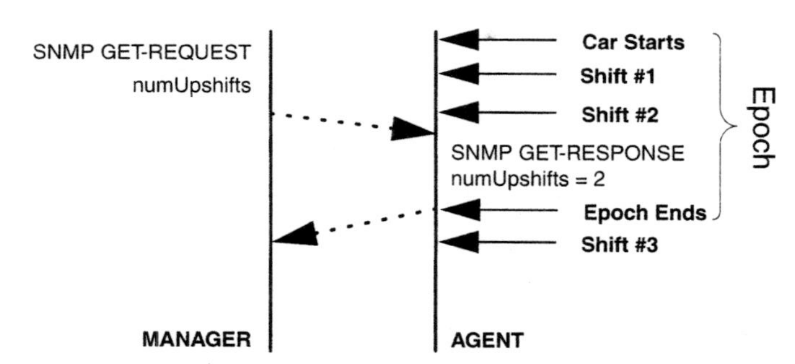

Figure 7–1 Statistical Epochs

Of course, the end of the epoch does not mean that the counter stops counting. After the manager has received the value, the transmission continues to be shifted, and the corresponding counter is increased. We cannot assume that a counter always has a value of zero at the beginning of an epoch. Consider computing the number of upshifts needed to drive from a stoplight in downtown Saratoga, CA on highway 9 to the stop sign at the Skyline Boulevard intersection. We could shut off the car to restart the counter, but the preferable approach is to sample the counter at the stoplight and use that value to "adjust" the upshift counts that we retrieve from the agent during our drive to the intersection.

This counter reverts to zero when the car is shut off. There are other counters whose value is preserved even while the car is shut off. One example is the odometer. When the car is restarted, it picks up just where it left off. These statistics are termed *persistent counters*, as their values persist between restarts of the network management system. Whichever style of statistics a system provides, it is important to note the epoch of the variables, as the network management programs will need this information so that it can correctly interpret the data.

7.7 State

The state of a component provides insight into the current condition of an entire system. While *attributes* are the static properties of components, and *statistics* are a picture of the past, *state* represents dynamic properties. State indicates stages of operation of a component, and can be as simple as *On/Off* or as complex as a series of failure indicators which can aid in problem diagnosis. State variables also represent properties such as resource allocation: the gas tank is half full, or the engine is at 3000 RPMs. At first glance, these may seem to be statistics, but this is more of an insight into the present condition of a system. Statistics, meanwhile, represent the past more than they represent the present. For our automobile example, a statistical object would be the total fuel consumed, while a state object would be the current consumption rate expressed in gallons per minute. Our automobile example might have the following state indicators on these sub-systems:

Engine

- stopped/starting/running/failed
- engine speed in RPMs
- oil pressure
- fuel consumption rate

Powertrain

- 2-wheel drive engaged/4-wheel drive engaged.
- current gear selection

Chassis

- door open/door closed
- window open/window closed

Electrical system

- OK/shorted
- battery charge

Climate control system

- engaged/off-line

We can see from these examples that state variables come in two forms: discrete stages of operation, and fluctuating values. A variable representing discrete stages lets us know exactly what a system is doing at the present time: stopped/started/running/failed. A fluctuating value is a sort of yardstick we use to measure usage and allocation within the system: battery charge, oil pressure. These variables do not report a small set of discrete values. Rather, they track the up and down movement of some aspect of the system.

Now that state has been introduced, a companion topic, *control*, needs to be discussed. States which can be sub-divided into discrete operational stages (*Stopped/Started/Running/Failed*) can be further sub-divided into two classes:

- *desired*, the state we want a component to be in
- *current*, the state the component is actually in

The desired states are termed the *control objects* for a system. These control objects are exposed to the outside world for manipulation. For the engine component, the states {*Stopped* and *Running*} represent the *desired* states, while {*Stopped*, *Starting*, *Running* and *Failed*} represent possible *current* states.

Several different methods can be used to visualize state changes in a managed device or service, but for our purposes we will stick with one: state graphs. These are also called *finite state machines*, but we will relax some of the usual formality associated with them for our purposes. A finite state machine consists of a set of *states* and a set of *inputs* which alter the states, driving the machine from one state to another. A good example of an implementation of a state machine is a vending machine. A vending machine has three major states:

- waiting for money (the machine is expecting coins to be inserted)
- waiting for selection (the machine is expecting a button to be pushed)
- dispensing selection (the machine is delivering the selection)

Each state requires certain inputs to transition to another state. You must insert coins before the machine allows you to select a drink, and you must select a drink before it is delivered. The coins and the selection are the external inputs which drive the machine and transition it from one state to another. When you first walk up to a vending machine, it is in the *waiting for money* state. After you insert money (the input expected at this state), the machine transitions to the *waiting for selection* state. Supplying the next anticipated input, the selection, transitions the machine through the *dispensing selection state* and back to the *waiting for money* state.

Many devices are a bit more complicated than this. Some states will accept any of several inputs, each of which will drive the machine to different states. For instance, our vending machine example ignored the *coin return* input which would return the user's money, and drove the machine back to the *waiting for money* state. We will use these same principles in constructing actions for our MIBs. Each action we design has a logical sequence of states which may be partially or fully controllable through external inputs.

To help visualize the states and inputs to a machine, it is often useful to diagram the transitions in a formal state graph. In our state machine notation, states are represented by labeled nodes of a graph, and inputs by directed arcs connecting the nodes to each other or themselves. The labels of the arcs represent an input to the state as well as any error outputs the input may produce.

Figure 7–2 demonstrates the state graph of the engine component. In this example, the

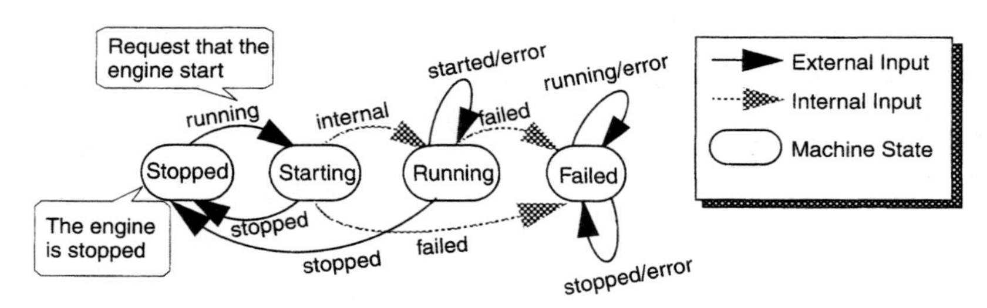

Figure 7–2 State graph for an engine

four states fall into two categories: those which external inputs may cause (the solid arcs), and those which represent internal transitions (the light arcs). An important point to notice about this state machine is that there are no dead-end states. A dead-end state in a machine is one in which no external input can drive the machine to another state. The *failed* state appears to be a dead-end state, but is reached only by some internal catastrophic event unrelated to any external inputs. If the example did not have the state and transition *stopped*, it would be impossible to escape the *started* or *running* states. We end up with a car we are unable to turn off! Designing these sets of transitions is quite important, and until you get a feel for designing actions and states, this is a useful exercise.

7.8 Translating a Model into a MIB

Now that we have all of the pieces for modelling a system, we can try to fit these together in a structured manner using a worksheet, and then translate that worksheet into a MIB. For the moment we will concentrate on organizing components, attributes, states and statistics, and return to the topic of control later. Once you have some experience writing a few MIBs, you probably won't need to bother with this step, but for a first time MIB writer it is often useful to practice this technique.

The first step in organizing a system is breaking down the major components into the attributes, statistics, and states. An easy way to accomplish this is to fill out a simple worksheet. Don't worry about including everything in the sub-system on the first pass; this is definitely an iterative process and you can always make new worksheets to fill in the missing pieces.

In the worksheet used for this process, we have four columns representing the various aspects of a component we are attempting to model: cardinality, attributes, statistics, and state. We begin by selecting a component to model. (Once again, don't worry if you are not certain if this is a component or not. This exercise will help you decide if it is). For each sub-component identified within that component, characterize them with respect to these categories.

Once you have a worksheet for a component completed, the translation to MIB syntax should be fairly mechanical if you follow these rules:

- Sub-components with a cardinality greater than 0 should be part of a table.
- Statistics representing increasing values are counter types: Counter (SNMPv1) or Counter32 (SNMPv2).
- Statistics representing high or low water marks are integer types: INTEGER (SNMPv1), or Integer32 and Unsigned32 (SNMPv2).
- States representing discrete stages of operation use an enumerated INTEGER. Each enumerated value is one of the states mentioned.
- States that have fluctuating values are gauge types: Gauge (SNMPv1) or Gauge32 (SNMPv2).
- Attributes of an object can take on two forms: OCTET STRINGS can be used to represent items such as human readable text descriptions or binary data, and integer types are used to represent measurable quantities such as horsepower rating.

These rules may seem somewhat simplistic, but they should emphasize an important point: constructing a structure is the most critical part of MIB development. Declaring the actual MIB objects, meanwhile, tends to be more of a task of translation than a labor of design.

7.9 Example Object Analysis

Returning to our automobile example, we can now organize the object analysis into a worksheet. Let's take the engine component first. We begin the worksheet by placing all the sub-components contained within the engine (pistons, spark plugs, cylinders, and fuel injectors) in the worksheet. (See Table 7–3)

Table 7–3 Object Analysis Worksheet

Component	Cardinality	Attributes	Statistics	States
ENGINE	1			
Pistons	1 to number of cylinders	Size		
Spark Plugs	1 to number of cylinders	Size and Manufacturer		(Fouled, OK) and Firing Rate
Cylinders	1 to number of cylinders			
Fuel Injectors	1 to number of cylinders	Capacity	Consumed	(Fouled, OK) and Consumption rate

Using this worksheet, we should be able to construct a first pass at a MIB declaration for the engine component. First, we can see that there is only 1 engine whose components all have a cardinality between 1 and the number of cylinders contained within that engine. Since the cardinality of these components varies with the number of cylinders, we must use a table indexed by cylinder number to identify them.

```
engCylTable OBJECT-TYPE
        SYNTAX          SEQUENCE OF EngCylEntry
        MAX-ACCESS      not-accessible
        STATUS          current
        DESCRIPTION
                "This table represents the sub-components of an engine that are dependent
                on the number of cylinders in the engine."
        ::= { engine 1 }

engCylEntry OBJECT-TYPE
        SYNTAX          EngCylEntry
        MAX-ACCESS      not-accessible
        STATUS          current
        DESCRIPTION
                "A row in the engine cylinder table. Rows cannot be created or deleted
                via direct SNMP operations."
        INDEX           { engCylIndex }
        ::= { engCylTable 1 }
```

Since the table is indexed by the cylinder number, it is the first column in our table. For this example, we will first add the columnar objects to the SEQUENCE construct for the table, and then later create OBJECT-TYPE definitions for them.

```
EngCylEntry ::= SEQUENCE {
        engCylIndex                Unsigned32
}
```

Looking back at the worksheet, we can see that each cylinder contains a piston, a spark plug, and a fuel injector. Adding the attributes of these items, the sequence becomes:

```
EngCylEntry ::= SEQUENCE {
        engCylIndex                Unsigned32,
        engCylPistonSize           Unsigned32,
        engCylSparkPlugSize        Unsigned32,
        engCylSparkPlugVendor      OBJECT IDENTIFIER,
        engCylInjectorCapacity     Unsigned32
}
```

Next, we add in our statistical objects:

```
EngCylEntry ::= SEQUENCE {
        engCylIndex                Unsigned32,
        engCylPistonSize           Unsigned32,
        engCylSparkPlugSize        Unsigned32,
        engCylSparkPlugVendor      OBJECT IDENTIFIER,
        engCylInjectorCapacity     Unsigned32,
        engCylFuelConsumed         Counter32
}
```

And finally, our state objects:

```
EngCylEntry ::= SEQUENCE {
        engCylIndex                Unsigned32,
        engCylPistonSize           Unsigned32,
        engCylSparkPlugSize        Unsigned32,
        engCylSparkPlugVendor      OBJECT IDENTIFIER,
        engCylInjectorCapacity     Unsigned32,
        engCylFuelConsumed         Counter32,
        engCylSparkPlugState       INTEGER,
        engCylSparkPlugSparkRate Gauge32,
        engCylInjectorState        INTEGER,
        engCylInjectorFuelRate     Gauge32
}
```

Now we can define the objects:

```
engCylIndex OBJECT-TYPE
        SYNTAX          Unsigned32
```

```
        MAX-ACCESS    not-accessible
        STATUS        current
        DESCRIPTION   "The cylinder number."
        ::= { engCylEntry 1 }

engCylPistonSize OBJECT-TYPE
        SYNTAX        Unsigned32
        UNITS         "Millimeters"
        MAX-ACCESS    read-only
        STATUS        current
        DESCRIPTION   "The diameter of the piston head"
        ::= { engCylEntry 2 }

engCylSparkPlugSize OBJECT-TYPE
        SYNTAX        Unsigned32
        UNITS         "Millimeters"
        MAX-ACCESS    read-only
        STATUS        current
        DESCRIPTION   "The size of the spark plug"
        ::= { engCylEntry 3 }

engCylSparkPlugVendor OBJECT-TYPE
        SYNTAX        OBJECT IDENTIFIER
        MAX-ACCESS    read-only
        STATUS        current
        DESCRIPTION   "The identification of the vendor of the spark plug"
        ::= { engCylEntry 4 }

engCylInjectorCapacity OBJECT-TYPE
        SYNTAX        Unsigned32
        UNITS         "ounces per hour"
        MAX-ACCESS    read-only
        STATUS        current
        DESCRIPTION   "The total fuel capacity of the injector"
        ::= { engCylEntry 5 }

engCylFuelConsumed OBJECT-TYPE
        SYNTAX        Counter32
        UNITS         "ounces"
        MAX-ACCESS    read-only
        STATUS        current
        DESCRIPTION   "Total fuel passed into this cylinder"
        ::= { engCylEntry 6 }

engCylSparkPlugState OBJECT-TYPE
        SYNTAX        INTEGER { fouled(1), ok(2) }
```

```
        MAX-ACCESS    read-only
        STATUS        current
        DESCRIPTION   "The current state of the spark plug"
        ::= { engCylEntry 7 }

engCylSparkPlugSparkRate OBJECT-TYPE
        SYNTAX        Gauge32
        UNITS         "sparks per second"
        MAX-ACCESS    read-only
        STATUS        current
        DESCRIPTION   "The current spark rate of the plug"
        ::= { engCylEntry 8 }

engCylInjectorState OBJECT-TYPE
        SYNTAX        INTEGER { fouled(1), ok(2) }
        MAX-ACCESS    read-only
        STATUS        current
        DESCRIPTION   "The current state of the injector"
        ::= { engCylEntry 9 }

engCylInjectorFuelRate OBJECT-TYPE
        SYNTAX        Gauge32
        UNITS         "ounces per hour"
        MAX-ACCESS    read-only
        STATUS        current
        DESCRIPTION   "The current rate of fuel consumption of the injector"
        ::= { engCylEntry 10 }
```

It's as simple as that. We've gone from a description of a problem to MIB declarations to object declaration in only a few steps. If you are new to writing MIBs, you may have to go through the worksheet exercise a few times before you become accustomed to analyzing a system with SNMP in mind. And once you've written a few, this process should become a bit easier.

CHAPTER 8

Practical Considerations in Building and Maintaining MIBs

This chapter focuses on the practical side of MIB building: MIB organization, OID space organization and the modelling of real world actions, states, statistics, components and attributes, as well as the mechanics of writing and maintaining a MIB.

8.1 The Big Question: SNMPv1 or SNMPv2?

As this chapter focuses on pragmatics, we want to address the one question that should concern most MIB writers: should I write my MIBs in SNMPv1 or SNMPv2 SMI syntax? If you are writing a MIB for an IETF working group, you don't have a choice. All IETF-produced MIBs must be in SMIv2 syntax. However, if you are writing a MIB for a private vendor things aren't as clear-cut. SNMPv1, for better or worse, enjoys much more widespread deployment, and is more likely to be understood by management station software and human network managers. Additionally, many companies have invested heavily in development tools which may not yet have been enhanced to support SMIv2 syntax. Given these conditions, deciding that your MIBs will be written in SMIv2 syntax may not seem to be the wisest decision. SNMPv1 is the only management protocol that is currently an Internet Standard, so it would seem that it would be the safest bet. However, SNMPv2 is clearly the future direction for SNMP. As off-the-shelf network management systems begin supporting SNMPv2, the pressure for vendors to provide SNMPv2 MIBs will certainly increase. SMIv2 offers a richer, more precise syntax for defining MIBs, so writers may find that they don't feel as "confined" when writing for SMIv1 syntax. The SMIv2 syntax, in spite of any shortcomings it may have, is a vast improvement over the SMIv1 syntax.

One approach to solving this problem is to write new MIBs using SMIv2 syntax, and simply translate the MIBs into SMIv1 syntax. Fortunately, SNMPv2 MIBs are easily transformed into SNMPv1 MIBs. In most cases, this task can be handled automatically by a MIB compiler, so the translation to SMIv1 syntax can be done quite accurately. This will preserve the investment you may have in SNMPv1 software and tools, while providing a transition plan for a move to SMIv1 format MIB modules.

Don't be mislead. You can use the SMIv2 syntax for MIB modules to define management information used by SNMPv1 agents and management applications.

8.2 Converting an SNMPv1 MIB to SNMPv2

Once you have decided to write new MIB modules using the SMIv2 syntax, you may decide to convert older SNMPv1 MIBs to the SMIv2 syntax as well. We strongly recommend that you do! The process is very straightforward, and requires only a few steps:

1. Change the IMPORTS section to reference the SNMPv2-SMI module instead of modules RFC1155-SMI and RFC-1212, and change any imported types to their SNMPv2 equivalents. Remember to take advantage of any special textual conventions SNMPv2 provides. DisplayString, for instance, is typically imported from MIB-II by a great many SNMPv1 MIBs. However, an SNMPv2 MIB should import this type from SNMPv2-TC.

```
SPRINKLECO-CONTROLLER-MIB DEFINITIONS ::= BEGIN
IMPORTS
        Counter, Gauge
                FROM RFC1155-SMI
        DisplayString
                FROM RFC1213-MIB
        OBJECT-TYPE
                FROM RFC-1212;
```

Changes to:

```
SPRINKLECO-CONTROLLER-MIB DEFINITIONS ::= BEGIN
IMPORTS
        Counter32, Gauge32, OBJECT-TYPE
                FROM SNMPv2-SMI
        DisplayString
                FROM SNMPv2-TC;
```

2. Add a MODULE-IDENTITY construct after the altered IMPORTS section, and add MODULE-IDENTITY to the IMPORTS for items from SNMPv2-SMI. We now have:

```
SPRINKLECO-CONTROLLER-MIB DEFINITIONS ::= BEGIN
        IMPORTS
                Counter32, Gauge32, OBJECT-TYPE, MODULE-IDENTITY
                        FROM SNMPv2-SMI
                DisplayString
                        FROM SNMPv2-TC;

        sprinklecoControllerMibModule MODULE-IDENTITY
                . . .
                ::= { . . . }
```

3. The SMIv2 states that hyphens are not allowed in the identifiers for objects or for labels on enumerated integer values. However, hyphens are allowed in the original SNMP framework. Thus, it is common practice to allow hyphens. It's your choice. We recommend that you leave in hyphens, and, do not change the identifiers. If you want to follow the "hyphen rule" of SMIv2, then remove all hyphens contained in the identifiers for objects and for labels of enumerated integer values.[1] Generally, the letter after the removed hyphen is changed to uppercase. Even though you are not allowed to alter an identifier name as part of normal MIB maintenance, this is seen as "correcting past mistakes," and is thus allowed in this case. Note that changing the identifier for objects will require that all other modules that import those objects be updated.

```
        pc-current-state OBJECT-TYPE
                SYNTAX          INTEGER { self-test(1), running(2) }
        ...
```

Changes to:

```
        pcCurrentState OBJECT-TYPE
                SYNTAX          INTEGER { selfTest(1), running(2) }
        ...
```

4. The type INTEGER, when not used for enumerated integers, is called Integer32. Change each use of INTEGER, when not followed by enumerated values ("{"... "}") to Integer32. Add a range clause if needed. (For example, add a range clause if the values cannot be negative.)

```
        allowableErrorRate OBJECT-TYPE
                SYNTAX          INTEGER
        ...
```

1. The hyphen purge has interesting roots. Hyphens were removed from the SNMPv2 SMI to make life more convenient for MIB tool developers, who wanted to make expression languages for objects, and the hyphens looked like minus signs. The hyphen, interestingly enough, is specifically allowed in pure ASN.1.

Changes to

```
allowableErrorRate OBJECT-TYPE
          SYNTAX          Integer32 (0..2147483647)
...
```

And

```
monthDay OBJECT-TYPE
          SYNTAX          INTEGER (1..31)
```

Changes to

```
monthDay OBJECT-TYPE
          SYNTAX          Integer32 (1..31)
```

This object is not changed:

```
sprinklerState OBJECT-TYPE
          SYNTAX          INTEGER { open(1), closed(2) }
          ...
```

5. The type Counter is called Counter32 and type Gauge is called Gauge32. Change the names of these types in your MIB module.

6. The meaning of the access specification on an object has changed. The name of the clause has also changed from ACCESS to MAX-ACCESS. First, change the keyword to MAX-ACCESS. Every table and row object should have access value of *not-accessible*. If not, then change them to *not-accessible*. The access value of *write-only* is not allowed in SMIv2. Any objects defined with this access value must be changed to value *read-write*. In SMIv1, it was never perfectly clear if an access level of *read-only* meant a minimum or a maximum value. One interpretation was that a value of *read-only* meant that it was the lowest acceptable implementation level, and it was legal to implement the object as *read-write*. Another interpretation was that the value *read-only* meant the maximal allowed access. If an access level of *read-only* was intended as a minimum, then the value for the translated MAX-ACCESS clause should be *read-write*. Otherwise, leave as *read-only*. For each table that allows rows to be created via SNMP SET operations, the access value for writable objects is changed to *read-create*.

7. Update the values for the STATUS clause to use the new types. The value *mandatory* should be changed to *current*. The value *optional* is no longer allowed. RFC 1908, the SNMPv2 document on coexistence, instructs translators to change the value to *obso-*

lete. This instruction should be looked at with a certain amount of skepticism, and probably be modified to "change the value to *current*, if the definition is still valid, or change the value to *obsolete*, if the definition is no longer valid." (See Chapter 3 on changing the value of a STATUS clause.)

8. Add an INDEX or AUGMENTS clause to any row that does not already have one. Add the IMPLIED qualifier if you have incorrectly implemented indexing using varying length strings or OBJECT IDENTIFIERs in SNMPv1.

9. Add a DESCRIPTION clause to all objects that do not already have one.

10. Add a UNITS clause to any object, where appropriate.

11. Since the type *NetworkAddress* is not part of SMIv2, any object using this type must be changed to *IpAddress*. Additionally, any row object which uses an object defined with this type as all or part of its INDEX must be updated. RFC 1908, the SNMPv2 document on coexistence, instructs the translator to mark the table, row, and contained columnar objects as *obsolete*.[2] Another approach is to create a new not-accessible index columnar object that is defined to always have a value of one. This object is then added to the INDEX clause before the object previously with syntax of NetworkAddress. For example:

    INDEX { atIfIndex, **atNetAddress** }

    would be changed to:

    INDEX { atIfIndex, **atNetType**, **atNetAddress** }

12. SMIv2 does not allow a DEFVAL clause for an object whose type is OBJECT IDENTIFIER to be expressed as a collection of sub-identifiers. The only legal value is a single identifier. For example:

```
moduleType OBJECT-TYPE
        SYNTAX          OBJECT IDENTIFIER
        ACCESS          read-only
        STATUS          mandatory
        DESCRIPTION     " ..."
        DEFVAL          { { vendorRegistration 1 } }
        ::= { modules 1 }
```

    would be changed to:

2. This should be a fairly obscure case. We conducted a survey of 241 MIB modules taken from both vendors and IETF working groups and found this in only 3 modules.

```
-- Add definition of the OID value
unknownModule OBJECT-IDENTITY
        STATUS          current
        DESCRIPTION     "An unknown module"
        ::= { vendorRegistration 1 }

moduleType OBJECT-TYPE
        SYNTAX          OBJECT IDENTIFIER
        MAX-ACCESS      read-only
        STATUS          current
        DESCRIPTION     " ... "
        DEFVAL          { unknownModule }
        ::= { modules 1 }
```

13. All of your events, which are defined with the TRAP-TYPE construct in SMIv1, must be converted to use the NOTIFICATION-TYPE construct in SMIv2. For each value that you have specified in the ENTERPRISE clause, define an OID value with an additional component (sub-identifier) value of zero. Use this value extended by the trap value as the OID value for the event. Change the VARIABLES clause into an OBJECTS clause, add a STATUS clause, and you are done. For example:

```
sprinklerLowPressureEvent TRAP-TYPE
        ENTERPRISE      sprinklecoControllerEvents
        VARIABLES       { sprinklerPressure, sprinklerLowPressure }
        DESCRIPTION
          "The pressure has dropped below the value of sprinklerLowPressure. The
          current pressure is returned as the value of sprinklerPressure, with the
          instance identifying the zone and sprinkler."
        ::= 1
```

Changes to:

```
sprinklecoControllerEventsV2 OBJECT-IDENTITY
        STATUS          current
        DESCRIPTION     "The events for sprinkler controllers."
        ::= { sprinklecoControllerEvents 0 }

sprinklerLowPressureEvent NOTIFICATION-TYPE
        OBJECTS         { sprinklerPressure, sprinklerLowPressure }
        STATUS          current
        DESCRIPTION
          "The pressure has dropped below the value of sprinklerLowPressure. The
          current pressure is returned as the value of sprinklerPressure, with the
          instance identifying the zone and sprinkler."
        ::= { sprinklecoControllerEventsV2 1 }
```

14. SMIv2 requires that all objects defined in a MIB module be contained in at least one object group. It also requires that all notifications be contained in at least one notification group. You must create groups to show the logical grouping of objects and notifications.

That's it. After you have completed these steps, you should have a fully compliant SNMPv2 style MIB.

Additional Optional Changes

There are a few more tasks that aren't strictly required, but will let you take advantage of some of the new syntax.

1. Change existing textual conventions to use the new TEXTUAL-CONVENTION construct.

```
SprinklerState ::= INTEGER { on(1), off(2) }
```

Changes to:

```
SprinklerState ::= TEXTUAL-CONVENTION
        STATUS          current
        DESCRIPTION     "The current operational state of the sprinkler"
        SYNTAX          INTEGER { on(1), off(2) }
```

2. Change existing OBJECT IDENTIFIER value assignments to use the new OBJECT-IDENTITY construct.

```
-- Model 101 Super Lawn Sprinkler
sprinklerModel101 OBJECT IDENTIFIER ::= { sprinklers 1 }
```

Changes to:

```
sprinklerModel101 OBJECT-IDENTITY
        STATUS          current
        DESCRIPTION     "Model 101 Super Lawn Sprinkler"
        ::= { sprinklers 1 }
```

Not Allowed Changes

Finally, there are some things you may not do. SMIv2 suggests that you specify the access of index objects as *not-accessible*. When you convert a MIB module, do not change the access value of index objects from *read-only* to *not-accessible*. You must leave them as *read-only*. (Of course if they are specified as *read-write*, you should change them to *read-only*.)

8.3 Converting an SNMPv2 MIB to SNMPv1

Even though there are a number of excellent tools for converting a module written in SMIv2 syntax into the SMIv1 syntax, we need to examine exactly what is involved in this process.

1. Translate the IMPORT statements to refer to the appropriate SMIv1 types and modules. Typically, this will be RFC1155-SMI and RFC-1212.
2. Translate the OBJECT-TYPE statements to the SMIv1 format using these rules:
   - Replace AUGMENTS with INDEX.
   - Comment out any UNITS clauses.
   - Replace the ACCESS value *read-create* with *read-write*.
   - Replace the STATUS value *current* with *mandatory*.
   - Replace every SYNTAX value of *Counter32* with *Counter*, *Gauge32* with *Gauge*, and *Unsigned32* with *Gauge*.
3. Comment out any OBJECT-TYPE whose SYNTAX value is *Counter64*. As this type has no equivalent in SNMPv1, objects of this type can't be properly translated. It would be nice if there were an alternative, but there is no agreed upon way to get around this restriction.
4. Translate the definitions that follow into simple OID assignments, and comment out all other clauses: MODULE-IDENTITY, OBJECT-IDENTITY, OBJECT-GROUP, NOTIFICATION-GROUP, MODULE-COMPLIANCE, and AGENT-CAPABILITIES. Here's what we mean by this:

```
mdmMIB MODULE-IDENTITY
        LAST-UPDATED "9406120000Z"
        ORGANIZATION "IETF Modem Management Working Group"
        CONTACT-INFO
                " Steven Waldbusser
                Postal: Carnegie Mellon University
                5000 Forbes Ave
                Pittsburgh, PA, 15213
                US
                Tel: +1 412 268 6628
                Fax: +1 412 268 4987
                email: waldbusser@cmu.edu"
        DESCRIPTION
                "The MIB module for management of dial-up modems."
        ::= { mdmMib 1 }
```

Converting this into a simple assignment and the fields commented out:

```
mdmMIB OBJECT IDENTIFIER ::= { mdmMib 1 }
-- MODULE-IDENTITY
-- LastUpdated
--   9406120000Z
-- OrgName
--   IETF Modem Management Working Group
-- ContactInfo
--          Steven Waldbusser
--    Postal: Carnegie Mellon University
--          5000 Forbes Ave
--          Pittsburgh, PA, 15213
--          US
--
--      Tel: +1 412 268 6628
--      Fax: +1 412 268 4987
--    email: waldbusser@cmu.edu
-- Descr
--   The MIB module for management of dial-up modems.
```

5. Translate NOTIFICATION-TYPE to a TRAP-TYPE using these rules:
   - Change the OBJECTS clause to VARIABLES
   - Comment out the STATUS clause
   - SNMPv2 notifications are designed with SNMPv1 Proxy compatibility in mind by requiring that they are registered as *oidVal.0.id*. Some older notification specifications use a form which omits the 0 sub-identifier: *oidVal.id*. If the notification being translated is in this format, then the ENTERPRISE clause of the new TRAP-TYPE is *oidval*, and the value of the trap is *id*. For notifications registered as *oidval.id*, the ENTERPRISE clause is *oidval*.

For example:

```
upsTrapOnBattery NOTIFICATION-TYPE
        OBJECTS {
                upsEstimatedMinutesRemaining, upsSecondsOnBattery,
                upsConfigLowBattTime }
        STATUS  current
        DESCRIPTION
                "The UPS is operating on battery power.  This trap is
                persistent and is re-sent at one minute intervals until
                the UPS either turns off or is no longer running on
                battery."
        ::= { upsTraps 1 }
```

Changes to:

```
psTrapOnBattery TRAP-TYPE
        ENTERPRISE upsTraps
        VARIABLES {
                upsEstimatedMinutesRemaining, upsSecondsOnBattery,
                upsConfigLowBattTime }
--      STATUS current
        DESCRIPTION
                "The UPS is operating on battery power. This trap is
                persistent and is re-sent at one minute intervals until
                the UPS either turns off or is no longer running on
                battery."
        ::= 1
```

6. Translate TEXTUAL-CONVENTION to a simple type assignment, and comment out the fields.

For example:

```
PhysAddress ::= TEXTUAL-CONVENTION
        DISPLAY-HINT    "1x:"
        STATUS          current
        DESCRIPTION
                "Represents media- or physical-level addresses."
        SYNTAX          OCTET STRING
```

Changes to:

```
PhysAddress ::= OCTET STRING
--      DISPLAY-HINT    "1x:"
--      STATUS          current
--      DESCRIPTION
--              "Represents media- or physical-level addresses."
```

8.4 A Roadmap for MIB Development

At this point, designing a MIB may still seem like a daunting task. There are several steps you will need to follow in creating an information framework, and it isn't always clear when you need to perform a specific step, or what exactly is involved in each stage of development, so let's take a look at a roadmap for developing a MIB. Shown across the top of Figure 8–1 are the steps needed to "design a MIB." (We use the term MIB here to mean the collection of documents that define infrastructure, objects, and notifications needed to manage one or more products.) Underneath each step are the documents that will be generated at that step. Note that what is not shown is the iteration that most certainly occurs during actual MIB design.

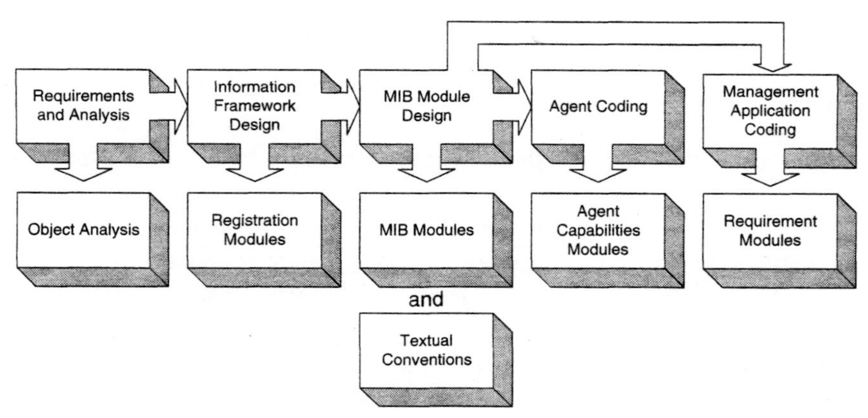

Figure 8–1 MIB Development Roadmap

At each stage, we have a specific set of documents that need to be produced. The first, and most important, is the requirements and analysis phase. As we outlined in the chapter on object analysis, this is where we produce a document describing the manageable objects we are trying to model in the MIB.

The second phase, framework design, is the process of laying out the overall information framework, and then deciding how to organize the object definitions into one or more MIB modules. This phase yields a module which captures the layout of our OID infrastructure.

The third phase, MIB module design, is where the fun begins. This is where we (finally) create the managed object definitions in what most people think of when they hear the word MIB. The agent and management application implementation phase may not appear to be part of the MIB writing process, but it does produce information modules that are responses to the MIB.

We left off the final phase of maintaining the MIB with edits, additions, and deletions of objects. Maintenance is easy, since we have put together an infrastructure before we started defining objects. Now that we have some idea of the development flow of the MIB creation process let's take a closer look at what we mean by a "module."

8.4.1 Types of Modules

The rules specified in the SMI documents are reasonably clear on the mechanics of producing MIB modules, but they never give any guidance on exactly what to put in them. Some people mistakenly believe that MIB modules contain only managed object definitions. While this is true for the vast majority of modules produced throughout the last few years of SNMPv1 development, it is certainly not a requirement. It is perfectly legal to write a MIB module that does not contain a single definition of a managed object. Modules that do not contain definitions of managed objects have been called *Information Modules*. Such modules may contain definitions for only the following items:

- OID registrations
- shared textual conventions
- implementation requirements
- implementation profiles
- SNMPv1 traps or SNMPv2 notifications

On the other hand, a MIB module may contain any of these items, plus definitions of managed objects. The key here is that we want to separate our definitions into smaller modules instead of one large module. These modules, as a group, form an *information framework*. By distributing the information into several modules, the entire framework is much more maintainable. The SNMPv2 framework is a good example of this approach. It contains module SNMPv2-TC that consists solely of textual convention definitions. Other modules simply import these textual conventions from this central module. This is really no different than importing a textual convention from an arbitrary MIB module. However, importing a textual convention from some unrelated module now makes the second module dependent on the first, even when there is no logical relationship. This places a burden on maintenance and the understanding of these modules. Simply put, organize your definitions into modules to ease maintenance and improve clarity. If a textual convention is widely useful, you should place it in a module containing widely used textual conventions instead of burying it in a module containing object definitions.

A suggested minimum set of modules you will need for a complete information framework is shown in Table 8–1.

Table 8–1 Modules in an Information Framework

Module Name	Purpose	Number
<enterprise>-TC	Shared textual conventions for an enterprise	1
<enterprise>-REG	Central registry of OIDs for an enterprise	1
<enterprise>-<area>-MIB	Managed object, and, possibly, event definitions for an enterprise in a particular area	Many
<enterprise>-<area>-PROF	Agent implementation profiles for an enterprise in a particular area such as a product line	Many
<enterprise>-<area>-REQ	Management application requirements for an enterprise in a particular area such as a product line	Many

Remember, that there are absolutely no set rules on how you must structure the information. You could just as easily combine common textual conventions with the central registry of OIDs into one module. We have even seen some MIB writers who place every bit of information into a single module. While we don't recommend this practice, it does show that there are a number of ways to go about this.

Let's look at an example. Suppose a vendor of lawn sprinklers, SprinkleCo, has set up an OID infrastructure, defined two MIB modules, and has two different agent implementations for their products, and has a simple set of management applications. Their information framework might look something like that shown in Table 8–2.

Of course, the numbers and content of your modules will vary according to your needs. For writers first starting to develop a framework, there is a tendency to shove everything into one module: registrations, managed object definitions, textual conventions, etc. While this is convenient, it gets very awkward very quickly.

Table 8–2 Information Framework for SprinkleCo

Module Name	Description
SPRINKLECO-TC	Shared Textual Conventions
SPRINKLECO-REG	Definitions for the OID infrastructure and other registrations
SPRINKLECO-SPRINKLER-MIB	Objects for the sprinkler controller
SPRINKLECO-TIMER-MIB	Objects for the programmed timer
SPRINKLECO-BASIC-PROF	The basic agent capabilities
SPRINKLECO-ADV-PROF	The advanced agent capabilities
SPRINKLECO-BASIC-REQ	The requirements for the basic applications

8.5 OID Infrastructure Organization

In this phase, we layout the object identifier structure of the information framework for an organization. If you are writing MIBs for a company or organization (we will use the word *enterprise* from now on), you will eventually face the problem of name space management, and it is easier to design a flexible OID infrastructure from the outset than it is to expand a poorly designed one. Name space management involves structuring and allocating the OID space "owned" by a particular enterprise. The structure of the upper branches of the universal OID tree is fixed, but control over the OID area for enterprise is entirely up to the framework designer. How to structure this space isn't always obvious, but careful planning will avoid problems later. In general, there are six categories to be concerned with when mapping out an assigned namespace as shown in Table 8–3.

Table 8–3 OID Infrastructure Layout

Category	Purpose
Registration	Identification of modules, and logical and physical components
Generic	Objects and events used by multiple products
Product	Objects and events associated with specific products
Capabilities	Agent implementation profiles
Requirements	Management application managed object requirements
Experimental	Objects and events under development

Each of these areas can be directly mapped to a sub-tree beneath the OID assigned to the enterprise. Even in a small enterprise, each of these sub-trees will probably require further branching to allow for uncrowded growth. For instance, the *product* sub-tree shouldn't have the definitions for a product at that level. Be optimistic! Assume that you will have a great many products, and place them in a structured manner underneath that sub-tree. This applies not only to MIB writers in corporations, but to writers producing MIBs for vendor consortiums and standards bodies as well.

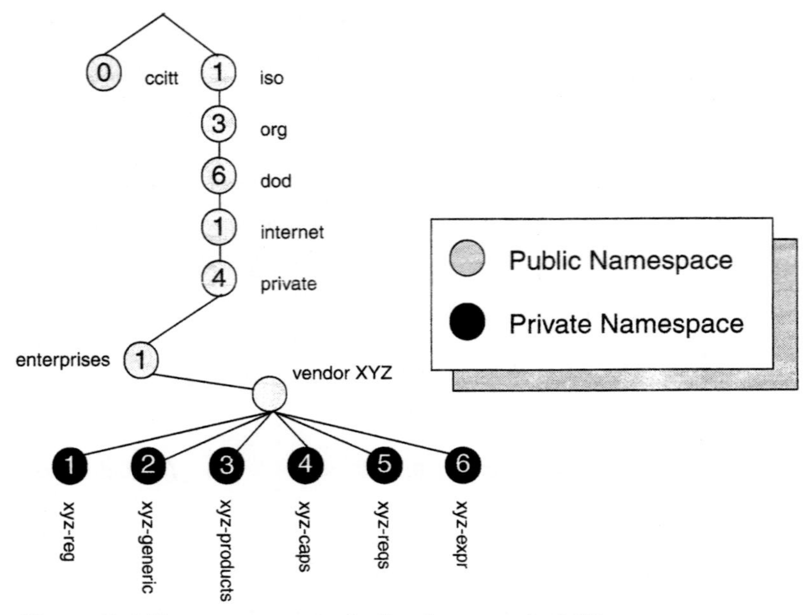

Figure 8–2 Namespace organization for a vendor MIB

Figure 8–2 shows an OID infrastructure layout for an example vendor within the context of the global object identifier namespace. This space is where all the OID assignments reside; items cannot be added to the public namespace by private parties.[3] In this example, we numbered the sub-trees with the registrations 1 through 6: xyz-req(1), xyz-generic(2), xyz-products(3), xyz-caps(4), xyz-reqs(5), and xyz-expr(6). While assigning a sub-tree the value 0 is not forbidden, it typically is not used as a node within the OID infrastructure. In fact, when we start defining objects, using 0 as the last component in an OID to identify an object type is forbidden by the SMI. So, in general, it is best to avoid using 0. Other than zero, there are no real rules on the values for assignments you can make at this level of the OID infrastructure. We could have assigned these values as: xyz-req(1), xyz-generic(10), xyz-products(100), xyz-caps(1000), xyz-reqs(10000), and xyz-expr(100000).

The top level registrations for the enterprise are:

```
vendorXYZ OBJECT-IDENTITY
          STATUS          current
```

3. Instructions for requesting a vendor identifier are in Appendix D.

```
        DESCRIPTION
                "The root of the OID sub-tree assigned to vendorXYZ by the
                Internet Assigned Numbers Authority (IANA)."
        ::= { enterprises X } -- Here we would actually use a number

xyz-reg OBJECT-IDENTITY
        STATUS          current
        DESCRIPTION     "Sub-tree for registrations"
        ::= { vendorXYZ 1 }

xyz-generic OBJECT-IDENTITY
        STATUS          current
        DESCRIPTION     "Sub-tree for common object and event definitions"
        ::= { vendorXYZ 2 }

xyz-products OBJECT-IDENTITY
        STATUS          current
        DESCRIPTION     "Sub-tree for specific object and event definitions"
        ::= { vendorXYZ 3 }

xyz-caps OBJECT-IDENTITY
        STATUS          current
        DESCRIPTION     "Sub-tree for agent profiles"
        ::= { vendorXYZ 4 }

xyz-reqs OBJECT-IDENTITY
        STATUS          current
        DESCRIPTION     "Sub-tree for management application requirements"
        ::= { vendorXYZ 5 }

xyz-expr OBJECT-IDENTITY
        STATUS          current
        DESCRIPTION     "Sub-tree for experimental definitions"
        ::= { vendorXYZ 6 }
```

Of course, had this been an SMIv1 example, we would have used the OID value assignment syntax such as:

```
vendorXYZ OBJECT IDENTIFIER
        ::= { enterprises X } -- Here we would actually use a number


xyz-reg OBJECT IDENTIFIER
        -- Sub-tree for registrations
        ::= { vendorXYZ 1}
```

```
xyz-generic OBJECT IDENTIFIER
        -- Sub-tree for common object and event definitions
        ::= { vendorXYZ 2 }

xyz-products OBJECT IDENTIFIER
        -- Sub-tree for specific object and event definitions
        ::= { vendorXYZ 3 }

xyz-caps OBJECT IDENTIFIER
        -- Sub-tree for agent profiles
        ::= { vendorXYZ 4 }

xyz-reqs OBJECT IDENTIFIER
        -- Sub-tree for management application requirements
        ::= { vendorXYZ 5 }

xyz-expr OBJECT IDENTIFIER
        -- Sub-tree for experimental definitions
        ::= { vendorXYZ 6 }
```

Of course, you are free to use the SMIv1 style of simple OID value assignments to register the object identifiers in an SMIv2 MIB module. There is no strict requirement that you use either one. However, the OBJECT-IDENTITY construct permanently registers an OID value, but a simple OID value does not. Thus, if you use OID value assignments, you might mistakenly reuse an OID value. This is the biggest of all MIB rules:

Caution

NEVER RE-USE AN OBJECT IDENTIFIER VALUE

Reusing an OBJECT IDENTIFIER will be the source of endless frustration for all parties involved (application developers, agent developers, customers, etc.) After you have obtained a registered enterprise tree, you have an infinite number of sub-trees, so don't try to practice MIB ecology and re-cycle them.

8.5.1 Registration

The registration area does not contain definitions of objects and events—it is an area where the identity of products, product components, and MIB related items are registered, such as the identities we assign to all the modules created by the enterprise. These items are never queried by a network management station. Instead, these object identifiers may be returned as the values of queries. Once more returning to the example enterprise, let's say that it has the following product lines shown in Table 8–4.

Table 8–4 Example Product Lines

Product Line	Products
Laser Printers	Model 101 Model 201
Font Cartridges	Cartridge A01 Cartridge A02
Repeaters	Chassis C1000 Chassis C2000
Boards	Ethernet Board 1000 Ethernet Board 2000 Management Board 1000 Management Board 2000
Modems	Model M100

In the registration sub-tree, we create branches for sub-trees for each product line for registrations of these products and their sub-components. We use the OBJECT-IDENTITY construct in SMIv2, or a simple OID assignment for SMIv1 for registration. The resulting registration sub-tree is shown in Figure 8–3.

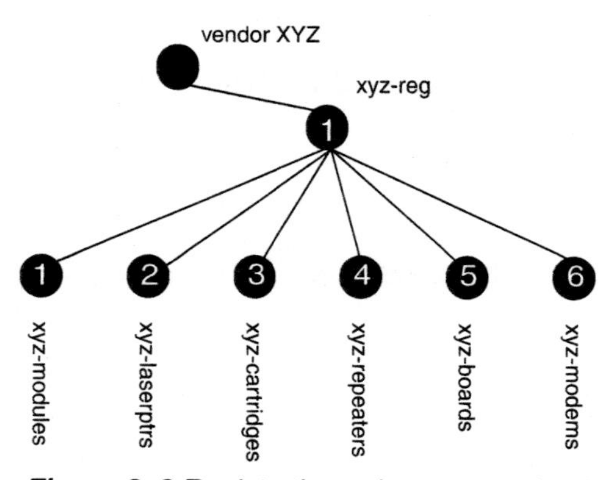

Figure 8–3 Registration sub-tree organization

The registrations for the items in this sub-tree are:

```
xyz-modules OBJECT-IDENTITY
        STATUS          current
        DESCRIPTION     "Sub-tree to register the values assigned to modules
                         with the MODULE-IDENTITY construct"
        ::= { xyz-reg 1}

xyz-laserptrs OBJECT-IDENTITY
        STATUS          current
        DESCRIPTION     "Laser Printers"
        ::= { xyz-reg 2 }
```

```
        -- The laser printer product line
        xyz-laserPrinter101 OBJECT-IDENTITY
                STATUS          current
                DESCRIPTION     "Laser Printer Model 101"
                ::= { xyz-laserptrs 1}

        laserPrinter201 OBJECT-IDENTITY
                STATUS          current
                DESCRIPTION     "Laser Printer Model 201"
                ::= { xyz-laserptrs 2 }


xyz-cartridges OBJECT-IDENTITY
        STATUS          current
        DESCRIPTION     "Font Cartridges"
        ::= { xyz-reg 3 }

        -- The font cartridge product line
        xyz-fontCartridgeA01 OBJECT-IDENTITY
                STATUS          current
                DESCRIPTION     "Font Cartridge Model A01"
                ::= { xyz-cartridges 1 }

        xyz-fontCartridgeA02 OBJECT-IDENTITY
                STATUS          current
                DESCRIPTION     "Font Cartridge Model A02"
                ::= { xyz-cartridges 2 }


xyz-repeaters OBJECT-IDENTITY
        STATUS          current
        DESCRIPTION     "Ethernet and Token Ring Repeaters"
        ::= { xyz-reg 4 }

        -- The repeater product line
        xyz-chassisC1000 OBJECT-IDENTITY
                STATUS          current
                DESCRIPTION     "Chassis Model C1000"
                ::= { xyz-repeaters 1 }

        xyz-chassisC2000 OBJECT-IDENTITY
                STATUS          current
                DESCRIPTION     "Chassis Model C2000"
                ::= { xyz-repeaters 2 }
```

```
xyz-boards OBJECT-IDENTITY
        STATUS          current
        DESCRIPTION     "Boards for repeaters"
        ::= { xyz-reg 5 }

        xyz-ethernet12 OBJECT-IDENTITY
                STATUS          current
                DESCRIPTION     "Ethernet Repeater 12 port Board"
                ::= { xyz-boards 1 }

        xyz-ethernet24 OBJECT-IDENTITY
                STATUS          current
                DESCRIPTION     "Ethernet Repeater 24 port Board"
                ::= { xyz-boards 2 }

        xyz-management1000 OBJECT-IDENTITY
                STATUS          current
                DESCRIPTION     "Management Module Model 1000"
                ::= { xyz-boards 3 }

        xyz-management2000 OBJECT-IDENTITY
                STATUS          current
                DESCRIPTION     "Management Module Model 2000"
                ::= { xyz-boards 4 }

xyz-modems OBJECT-IDENTITY
        STATUS          current
        DESCRIPTION     "Digital Modems"
        ::= { xyz-reg 6 }

        -- The modem product line
        xyz-modem100            OBJECT-IDENTITY
                STATUS          current
                DESCRIPTION     "The Model 100 Modem"
                ::= { xyz-modems 1 }
```

8.5.2 The Generic and Products Sub-trees

The *generic* and *products* sub-trees contain the OIDs for definitions of objects and events. The only difference between the two sub-trees is that the items in the *generic* sub-tree are general purpose to be used by many products of the enterprise, where those in the *products* are for specific services or device categories. For example, let's say the vendor of laser printers has a broad product line, some having unique features. All the printers share a certain set of actions such as: the ability to remotely power cycle, test the print engine, print a test page, etc. Grouping these common items in one (or more sub-trees) has made life easier for a number of people: the management application developers can write generic code fragments that tests the print engine or cycles the power on any printer; and the agent developers can write code to be put in a library and shared by all products. While it is true that it is perfectly legal for one product to implement the objects and events defined for another product, this should be taken as a sign that the items in question should probably be moved to the generic sub-tree.

A large enterprise is very likely to sub-divide these sub-trees further—perhaps for divisions or business units. For a vendor with a product line that includes 802.3 repeaters, laser printers and modems, a *products* sub-tree would look something like that shown in Figure 8–4.

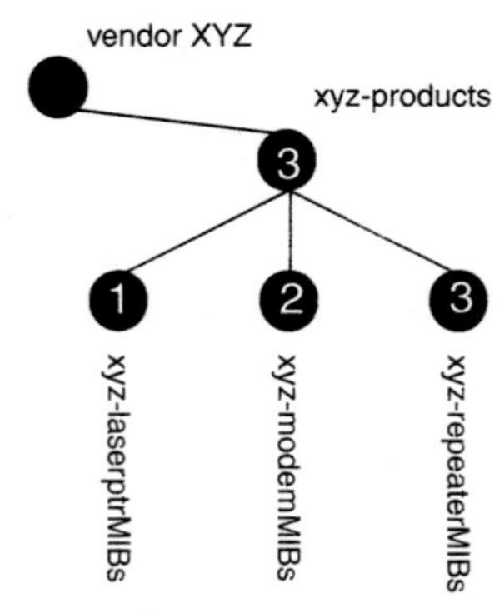

Figure 8–4 Products sub-tree organization

The registrations for these sub-trees are:

```
xyz-laserptrMIBs OBJECT-IDENTITY
        STATUS          current
        DESCRIPTION     "Sub-tree for objects and events in laser printer MIBs"
        ::= { xyz-products 1 }

xyz-modemMIBs OBJECT-IDENTITY
        STATUS          current
        DESCRIPTION     "Sub-tree for objects and events in modem MIBs"
        ::= { xyz-products 2 }

xyz-repeaterMIBs OBJECT-IDENTITY
        STATUS          current
        DESCRIPTION     "Sub-tree for objects and events in chassis-based
                        repeater MIBs"
        ::= { xyz-products 3 }
```

8.5.3 Capabilities

The *capabilities* sub-tree is used to register the identity of agent implementation profiles (defined with an AGENT-CAPABILITIES construct). These profiles are associated with chunks of code, which can include a complete agent. However, they are most often associated with libraries of code used to put together agents.

8.5.4 Requirements

The *requirements* sub-tree is used to register the identity of management application requirement specifications (defined with a MODULE-COMPLIANCE construct). These requirement specifications detail the objects and events used by a functional area of a management application.

8.5.5 Experimental

The *experimental* sub-tree is exactly what the name implies. This is the area where objects and events in MIBs under development can be placed without fear of conflicting with other MIBs. Registering items here solves several potential problems. For those vendors who expose their MIBs to customers, whether in shipping products or pre-release versions, items registered here serve as a warning sign: "*This is apt to change! Don't count on it being here in the next release.*" When the items rooted under an experimental sub-tree are ready for release (to be "frozen"), all that need be done is to re-attach the sub-tree under a permanent branch (in other words, change the initial OBJECT IDENTIFIER of the sub-tree from { xyz-expr X } to { xyz-products X }).

Vendors are often faced with the dilemma of what to do when an IETF working group is in the process of defining a MIB module and a version has been made available for review by posting it in the internet-drafts repository, which the vendor wants to use in a shipping product. If the "internet-draft" version is used in a product, the vendor will be at risk that several months down the road the MIB will change, before being published as an RFC, causing their implementation to be rendered retro-actively non-compliant. An experimental sub-tree of a vendor can serve as a suitable registration point for that MIB.

You may recall that in the IETF-controlled namespace, there is a sub-tree with the same name. Its purpose is the same as it is here. IETF working groups requiring an object identifier to use for early MIB development are assigned one from the experimental sub-tree controlled by the IETF.

8.6 Module Naming

As simple as this topic sounds, this is an important decision. The SNMPv1 framework documents gave very little guidance in this area, so MIBs were written with a wide style of names. Some vendors altered the names of their modules whenever they released a new version. For example, ROUTER-MIB became ROUTER-MIB-R2 in the second release, even if the second release only added objects to the MIB. Even the IETF was guilty of this mistake. Every time a MIB working group published a MIB under a new RFC number, the module name of the MIB changed to match that number. Here are a few things you can do to keep your module names from getting too confusing:

- Use only uppercase letters in the module name. Even though the first letter is the only one required to be uppercase, this is a widely accepted convention.
- Use a three part naming convention for your modules: <ORGANIZATION>-<NAME>-<TYPE>. Begin the module name with the name of your organization or company. This is especially helpful when IMPORTING items into a module. SPRINKLECO-SCHEDULE-MIB indicates exactly where a module came from and exactly what it is. The second part is the actual name of this module: SCHEDULE, COMMON, REPEATER, etc. The final part is the type of module: *MIB*, definitions of managed objects; *REG*, OID registrations; *TC*, textual conventions; *TRAP*, SNMPv1 traps; *NOTI*, SNMPv2 NOTIFICATIONS; *CAP*, agent implementation profiles; and *REQ*, requirements specifications.
- Don't change the name of a module between releases. SNMPv2 modules aren't allowed to do this, and it's a good idea to follow the same convention in SNMPv1 modules. Noting that changes have been made to a module is the responsibility of the MODULE-IDENTITY construct, and should be noted there.

8.7 Module Layout

Now that we have planned the structure of our overall information framework, the OID infrastructure, and decided on our module names, we need to lay out the modules themselves.

8.7.1 Modules for Managed Objects and Events

These modules have six major sections:

- imports
- MODULE-IDENTITY specification
- definitions of any local textual conventions
- registrations of the top level structure of the MIB
- definitions of managed objects and, optionally, notifications
- a series of compliance statements

Just as we took the OID space that we were assigned and carved it up into several sub-trees, we need to do the same thing with a sub-tree for object and event definitions. This is what we mean by "registering the top level structure of the MIB." Each MIB module typically follows the same registration pattern, and MIB writers usually document that pattern like this:

- Each functional area is assigned its own sub-tree, so a module may have as few as one or as many as a dozen functional sub-trees registered. Objects that profile one particular aspect of a managed system are usually kept together underneath the same sub-tree.
- Conformance statements, which include OBJECT-GROUP, NOTIFICATION-GROUP, and MODULE-COMPLIANCE constructs have their own sub-tree.

- Events (defined with the NOTIFICATION-TYPE construct) are registered under a sub-tree which follows this seemingly odd rule: Under the sub-tree chosen to hold the events, another sub-tree is registered as the value 0. This is the sub-tree under which the events themselves are actually registered. This rule isn't really so arbitrary. Registering events this way is part of the interoperability agreement between SNMPv1 and SNMPv2. Some older SNMPv2 MIBs may have events that aren't registered in this way, but they were written before this rule was set in place, so they should not be used as a model of the correct way of assigning OID values to events.

What we end up with is a structure that looks like Figure 8–5:

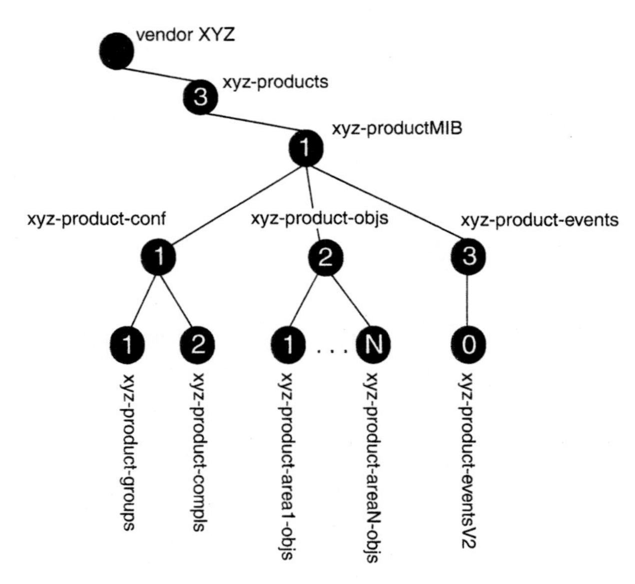

Figure 8–5 MIB organization for a vendor

Let's look at a simple MIB module to see how these sections fit together:

```
-- The module name:
SPRINKLECO-CONTROLLER-MIB DEFINITIONS ::= BEGIN

-- 1) The imports
-- The items in this IMPORTS construct are the ones typically used.
IMPORTS
        MODULE-IDENTITY, OBJECT-TYPE, OBJECT-IDENTITY,
        NOTIFICATION-TYPE, Integer32, Gauge32, Counter32
                FROM SNMPv2-SMI
        TEXTUAL-CONVENTION, DisplayString
                FROM SNMPv2-TC
```

```
        MODULE-COMPLIANCE, OBJECT-GROUP, NOTIFICATION-GROUP
                FROM SNMPv2-CONF
        sprinklecoModules, sprinklecoControllerMIB
                FROM SPRINKLECO-GLOBAL-REG;

-- 2) The module identification
sprinklecoControllerMibModule MODULE-IDENTITY
        LAST-UPDATED            "9511080000Z"
        ORGANIZATION            "SprinkleCo"
        CONTACT-INFO            "..."
        DESCRIPTION             "..."
        REVISION                "9511080000Z"
        DESCRIPTION             "The initial revision of this module"
        ::= { sprinklecoModules 5 }

-- 3) Local textual conventions.
-- This section is entirely optional, as you may not have defined
-- any textual conventions, or you may have imported them from a central source
SprinklerState ::= TEXTUAL-CONVENTION
        STATUS          current
        DESCRIPTION     "..."
        SYNTAX          INTEGER { on(1), off(2) }

-- 4) Registrations for the top level structure of the MIB
-- Most MIB writers use this section to define all the sub-trees where the objects will reside.
-- You may use the OBJECT-IDENTITY production, but
-- it's not illegal to make a simple OID assignment.
sprinklecoControllerConf OBJECT IDENTIFIER
        ::= { sprinklecoControllerMIB 1 }

        sprinklecoControllerGroups OBJECT IDENTIFIER
                ::= { sprinklecoControllerConf 1 }
        sprinklecoControllerCompls OBJECT IDENTIFIER
                ::= { sprinklecoControllerConf 2 }

sprinklecoControllerObjs OBJECT IDENTIFIER
        ::= { sprinklecoControllerMIB 2 }

        sprinklecoControllerValveObjs OBJECT IDENTIFIER
                ::= { sprinklecoControllerObjs 1 }

sprinklecoControllerEvents OBJECT IDENTIFIER
        ::= { sprinklecoControllerMIB 3 }

        sprinklecoControllerEventsV2 OBJECT IDENTIFIER
                ::= { sprinklecoControllerEvents 0 }
```

```
-- 5) The managed objects, and any notifications, go here:
sprinklecoControllerValveControl OBJECT-TYPE
        SYNTAX          SprinklerState
        MAX-ACCESS      read-write
        STATUS          current
        DESCRIPTION     "This is the control object for the valve"
        ::= { sprinklecoControllerValveObjs 1 }


sprinklecoControllerValveFailure NOTIFICATION-TYPE
        OBJECTS         { ... }
        STATUS          current
        DESCRIPTION     " ... "
        ::= { sprinklecoControllerEventsV2 1 }


-- 6) Finally, the compliance statements for the module, including groups
sprinklecoControllerBasicGroup OBJECT-GROUP
        OBJECTS         { sprinklecoControllerValveControl }
        STATUS          current
        DESCRIPTION     "The objects to control valves"
        ::= { sprinklecoControllerGroups 1 }


sprinklecoControllerBasicEvents NOTIFICATION-GROUP
        NOTIFICATIONS   { sprinklecoControllerValveFailure }
        STATUS          current
        DESCRIPTION     "The events for valves"
        ::= { sprinklecoControllerGroups 2 }


sprinklecoControllerComplianceV1 MODULE-COMPLIANCE
        STATUS          current
        DESCRIPTION     "All controllers should provide this level of support"
        MODULE  -- this module
                MANDATORY-GROUPS { sprinklecoControllerBasicGroup,
                                   sprinklecoControllerBasicEvents }
        ::= { sprinklecoControllerCompls 1 }

END
```

That's it. Short though it may be, this is a complete MIB module. A module involving managed objects is typically the most complex, and the other types of modules are fairly simple.

8.7.2 Other Modules

All other modules (registration, textual conventions, profiles, and requirements) take a much simpler form. They have only three sections:

- imports
- MODULE-IDENTITY specification
- definitions

The definitions section is the bulk of the module. This is where we define the textual conventions, OID registrations, implementation profiles, or requirements. Let's look at some samples. First, a registration module looks like this:

```
-- The module name:
SPRINKLECO-GLOBAL-REG DEFINITIONS ::= BEGIN

-- 1) The imports
-- Notice that this statement is much smaller than the one we used for a module to
-- define objects and events. We only need the two identity constructs and the
-- enterprises registration in this module.
IMPORTS
        MODULE-IDENTITY, OBJECT-IDENTITY,
        enterprises
                FROM SNMPv2-SMI;

-- 2) The module identification
sprinklecoGlobalRegModule MODULE-IDENTITY
        LAST-UPDATED          "9511080000Z"
        ORGANIZATION          "SprinkleCo"
        CONTACT-INFO          " ... "
        DESCRIPTION           " ... "
        REVISION              "9511080000Z"
        DESCRIPTION           "The initial revision of this module"
        ::= { sprinklecoModules 1 }

-- 3) OID registrations
-- Here, we register the top level of our OID sub-tree
sprinklecoRoot OBJECT-IDENTITY
        STATUS          current
        DESCRIPTION     "The root of the OID sub-tree assigned to SprinkleCo by the
                        Internet Assigned Numbers Authority (IANA)"
        ::= { enterprises X } -- a real number should be used here

sprinklecoReg OBJECT-IDENTITY
        STATUS          current
        DESCRIPTION     "Sub-tree for registrations"
        ::= { sprinklecoRoot 1 }
```

```
sprinklecoModules OBJECT-IDENTITY
        STATUS          current
        DESCRIPTION     "Sub-tree for module registrations"
        ::= { sprinklecoReg 1 }

sprinklecoGeneric OBJECT-IDENTITY
        STATUS          current
        DESCRIPTION     "Sub-tree for common object and event definitions"
        ::= { sprinklecoRoot 2 }

sprinklecoProducts OBJECT-IDENTITY
        STATUS          current
        DESCRIPTION     "Sub-tree for specific object and event definitions"
        ::= { sprinklecoRoot 3 }

sprinklecoCaps OBJECT-IDENTITY
        STATUS          current
        DESCRIPTION     "Sub-tree for agent profiles"
        ::= { sprinklecoRoot 4 }

sprinklecoReqs OBJECT-IDENTITY
        STATUS          current
        DESCRIPTION     "Sub-tree for management application requirements"
        ::= { sprinklecoRoot 5 }

sprinklecoExpr OBJECT-IDENTITY
        STATUS          current
        DESCRIPTION     "Sub-tree for experimental definitions"
        ::= { sprinklecoRoot 6 }

END
```

Next, we have a capabilities module:

```
-- The module name:
SPRINKLECO-CONTROLLER-CAP DEFINITIONS ::= BEGIN

-- 1) The imports
-- We need the capability construct and linkage from the top level registrations
IMPORTS
        MODULE-IDENTITY
                FROM SNMPv2-SMI
        AGENT-CAPABILITIES
                FROM SNMPv2-CONF
        sprinklecoCaps, sprinklecoModules
                FROM SPRINKLECO-GLOBAL-REG;
```

```
-- 2) The module identification
sprinklecoControllerCapModule MODULE-IDENTITY
        LAST-UPDATED        "9511080000Z"
        ORGANIZATION        "SprinkleCo"
        CONTACT-INFO        " ... "
        DESCRIPTION         " ... "
        REVISION            "9511080000Z"
        DESCRIPTION         "The initial revision of this module"
        ::= { sprinklecoModules 25 }

-- 3) An AGENT-CAPABILITIES construct
-- We use groups sprinklecoControllerBasicGroup and sprinklecoControllerBasicEvents
-- to indicate the level of support that an implementation has for items in module
-- SPRINKLECO-CONTROLLER-MIB.
-- Note that sprinklerBasicGroup is not imported, since the SUPPORTS clause defines a
-- scope for items specified in the INCLUDES clause.
-- Also note that the PRODUCT-RELEASE clause documents the release of the library of
-- code to support these items and not the release of an agent, since more than one
-- agent may use the library.
sprinklecoControllerBasicCap AGENT-CAPABILITIES
        PRODUCT-RELEASE     "Sprinkler Controller Support Library, Release 1.0"
        STATUS              current
        DESCRIPTION         " ... "
        SUPPORTS            SPRINKLECO-CONTROLLER-MIB
        INCLUDES            { sprinklecoControllerBasicGroup,
                                  sprinklecoControllerBasicEvents }
        ::= { sprinklecoCaps 1 }
END
```

Next, we have a requirements module:

```
-- The module name:
SPRINKLECO-CONTROLLER-REQ DEFINITIONS ::= BEGIN

-- 1) The imports
-- We need the requirements construct and linkage from the top level registrations
IMPORTS
        MODULE-IDENTITY
                FROM SNMPv2-SMI
        MODULE-COMPLIANCE
                FROM SNMPv2-CONF
        sprinklecoReqs, sprinklecoModules
                FROM SPRINKLECO-GLOBAL-REG;
```

```
-- 2) The module identification
sprinklecoControllerReqModule MODULE-IDENTITY
        LAST-UPDATED            "9511080000Z"
        ORGANIZATION            "SprinkleCo"
        CONTACT-INFO            " ... "
        DESCRIPTION             " ... "
        REVISION                "9511080000Z"
        DESCRIPTION             "The initial revision of this module"
        ::= { sprinklecoModules 32 }

-- 3) A MODULE-COMPLIANCE construct
-- We use groups sprinklecoControllerBasicGroup and sprinklecoControllerBasicEvents
-- to indicate the level of support that is required for an implementation of items in module
-- SPRINKLECO-CONTROLLER-MIB.
-- Note that sprinklerBasicGroup is not imported, since the MODULE clause defines a
-- scope for items specified in the MANDATORY-GROUPS clause.
sprinklecoControllerBasicReq MODULE-COMPLIANCE
        STATUS                  current
        DESCRIPTION             " ... "
        MODULE                  SPRINKLECO-CONTROLLER-MIB
        MANDATORY-GROUPS        { sprinklecoControllerBasicGroup,
                                        sprinklecoControllerBasicEvents }
        ::= { sprinklecoReqs 1 }
END
```

8.8 Designing Agent Implementation Profiles

Back in Chapter 3, where we described the AGENT-CAPABILITIES construct, it was noted that this construct had evolved during its definition. The result has been some confusion in the SNMP community as to the meaning and use of the agent implementation profiles specified by the AGENT-CAPABILITIES construct. An agent profile was originally meant to completely describe the implementation of an agent. When an agent supports a small number of objects in a closed and dedicated system, and is implemented as a monolithic chunk of code, this model of an agent profile works. However, as agents have evolved to support hundreds (and even thousands) of objects and/or events, and are implemented as modular chunks of code from several sources, the single description profile model does not work. What is needed in this case is a set of profiles for an agent, each describing a chunk of code. The implementation of a chunk of code is what the AGENT-CAPABILITIES construct is suppose to describe. However, the definition and description of the AGENT-CAPABILITIES was not completely reworked. Thus, the source of confusion.

Also, in open and general purpose systems (and in dynamically configurable systems), the chunks of code that make up an agent may change as software and/or hardware sub-systems of the managed system are reconfigured during agent operation. The number of different combinations of these chunks of agent code can be quite high. This is another reason that the profiles are for chunks of code, and not for the complete agent. Note that profiles are not meant to describe the dynamics of the system being managed. For example, a table describing network connections will be empty when there are no network connections to the managed system, and have entries when there are connections. You do not create a profile for a table containing no instances and another for the table when it contains instances.

Putting together a profile is pretty easy. Just remember to be complete and honest in your description. If you are not, then the profile has little value and might even be a liability. The steps are:

1. Review your chunk of agent code to construct a list of all the objects and events that you have implemented.
2. Group the objects and events by the modules where they are defined.
3. Look in the modules to find the object and event (notification) groups.
4. Find the groups that best describe the objects and events that you have implemented.
5. For each object and event, check its definition and your implementation to determine if you have fully implemented all behaviors.
6. For each item not fully implemented, describe the behaviors actually implemented.
7. For columnar objects, if you have any implementation limits on the number of instances, then describe them. (For example, in the RMON MIB there are several control tables. If you allow only a small fixed maximum number of instances to be created, then you must describe this in your profile.)

That's all there is to it. Let's walk through a small example to show how it is done.

Step 1, construct a list of implemented objects and events:

objects: xyz1, xyz2, xyz3, pqr1, pqr2, pqr4, abc1, abc2, abc20, abc21, and abc22
events: efg1, efg2, and stu3

Step 2, group the items by module:

objects: module M1-MIB contains xyz1, xyz2, xyz3, pqr1, pqr2, and pqr4;
module M2-MIB contains abc1, abc2, abc20, abc21, and abc22.
events: module M3-MIB contains efg1, efg2, and stu3

Step 3, list the groups in the modules:

module M1-MIB has groups xyzGroup and pqrGroup
module M2-MIB has groups abcGroup and hijGroup
module M3-MIB has groups efgEvents and stuEvents

Step 4, identify the groups that best describe our items:

xyzGroup, pqrGroup, abcGroup, efgEvents, and stuEvents

Step 5, check implementation and definition of items:

All items in xyzGroup implemented fully
All items except pqr3 in pqrGroup implemented fully (pqr3 is not implemented)
All items except abc1 in abcGroup implemented fully (abc1 has limited implementation)
All items in efgEvents implemented fully
Only item stu3 in stuEvents implemented fully (stu1 and stu2 are not implemented)

Step 6, describe actual implementation (for items not implementing all behaviors):

Item abc1 has read-only access, instead of read-write access

Step 7, describe implementation limits, if any for columnar objects:

Columnar objects abc20, abc21, and abc22 in table abcTable allow a maximum of 10 instances to exist at any time

The resulting AGENT-CAPABILITIES definition is the following:

```
-- name the profile something meaningful
alphabetCap AGENT-CAPABILITIES
        PRODUCT-RELEASE      "Soup library, Release 2.0"
        STATUS               current
        DESCRIPTION          " ... "

-- specify each module, and each group from that module
        SUPPORTS        M1-MIB
                INCLUDES        { xyzGroup, pqrGroup }
-- specify variations, if needed
                VARIATION       pqr3
                        ACCESS          not-implemented
                        DESCRIPTION     "not supported by chipset"

        SUPPORTS        M2-MIB
                INCLUDES        { abcGroup }
-- specify variations, if needed
                VARIATION       abc1
                        ACCESS          read-only
                        DESCRIPTION     "value in ROM and cannot be changed"
                VARIATION       abcTable
                        DESCRIPTION     "table can contain, at most, 10 rows"
```

```
SUPPORTS            M3-MIB
        INCLUDES           { efgEvents, stuEvents }
-- specify variations, if needed
        VARIATION          stu1
                ACCESS              not-implemented
                DESCRIPTION         "didn't have time to implement before
                                    the code was frozen"
        VARIATION          stu2
                ACCESS              not-implemented
                DESCRIPTION         "could not get this to work, so the
                                    code was disabled for this release"

::= { alphabetCaps 1 }
```

Writing the VARIATIONS turns out to be the most difficult part of writing a profile. The next section contains detailed explanations of the sub-clauses to the VARIATION clause. Before moving on, we need to describe how the profiles are meant to be used. The following describes the ideal "agent developer"/"management application developer" scenario:

1. MIB module authors specify collections of related objects using OBJECT-GROUP constructs and events using NOTIFICATION-GROUP constructs. These are used in one or more compliance specifications to specify what the MIB module author believes should be the implementation requirements for the MIB module.
2. Agent developers profile each chunk of their implemented code using an AGENT-CAPABILITIES construct. Each profile is registered with a unique OID.
3. Developers of management application software use these implementation profiles, if available, to help structure the applications to use only those objects and events implemented by agent developers.
4. At run time, a management station retrieves the entries in the *sysORTable* table, each of which contains an OID value corresponding to an implementation profile defined with an AGENT-CAPABILITIES construct.
5. The management application may then alter its behavior to reflect the management information available from the agent.

Another use of the profiles is by users to assist in deciding which managed devices and management applications to purchase. The following steps describe the ideal "system evaluation" scenario:

1. The user gathers profiles from each vendor of the managed devices that are being considered.
2. The user gathers requirement specifications for each management application.
3. The profiles and requirement specifications are compared to determine which management applications and devices will potentially interoperate.

8.8.1 Specifying Variations

Quite often, it is unrealistic for the implementation for a particular agent to conform exactly to a given MIB specification. Hardware or software system limitations are usually the culprit here, and these architectural features preclude a full implementation. Whatever the cause, these variations must be carefully documented. In SMv1, it is difficult to document these limitations in any commonly useful way. Writers of the management software must depend on the written comments accompanying an agent implementation to know what, exactly, is different about that agent. SMIv2, thankfully, allows the agent writers to clearly define how their implementation differs from the standard by using the VARIATION clause in the AGENT-CAPABILITIES construct.

Suppose we have an agent that supports this object:

```
sprinklecoControllerAdminState OBJECT-TYPE
        SYNTAX          INTEGER { running(1), stopped(2), testing(3), resetting(4) }
        MAX-ACCESS      read-write
        STATUS          current
        DESCRIPTION
                "The administrative state of this controller. Set these values to the
                desired state:
                running(1)          Normal operational mode
                stopped(2)          Stop the unit from normal operation
                testing(3)          Initiate a self-test
                resetting(4)        Initiate a reset, the equivalent of a power-cycle"
        ::= { ... }
```

Let's suppose that a hardware limitation prevents our agent from supporting the *testing(3)* enumeration. The agent must always return the SNMP error code *badValue* whenever a request arrives to set this object to that value. What we want to document is that the agent does not support this value at all. Here's a sample AGENT-CAPABILITIES statement we can use for our agent:

```
sprinklecoAgent101Cap AGENT-CAPABILITIES
        PRODUCT-RELEASE         "Model 101 Controller"
        STATUS                  current
        DESCRIPTION             "..."
        SUPPORTS                SPRINKLECO-CONTROLLER-MIB
        INCLUDES                { sprinklecoControllerGroup }
                VARIATION       sprinklecoControllerAdminState
                WRITE-SYNTAX  INTEGER { running(1), stopped(2), resetting(4) }
                DESCRIPTION
                        "The Model 101 sprinkler has no self-test feature support
                        in the underlying hardware"
        ::= { sprinklecoCaps 34 }
```

In this example, we used the WRITE-SYNTAX clause of the VARIATION production to indicate that managers should never attempt to write this value to the object. If you will recall from our discussion in Chapter 3, there are several other types of variations we can specify. These are shown in Table 8–5.

Table 8–5 Types of Variations

VARIATION	Purpose
SYNTAX	Indicates the sub-set of the original values an object supports when the object is read (and, potentially, written if clause WRITE-SYNTAX is not present)
WRITE-SYNTAX	Indicates the sub-set of the original values an object supports when the object is written
ACCESS	Indicates the lowered level of access for this object, or the fact that it is not supported at all.
CREATION-REQUIRES	Lists the objects required to create an instance of a row in a single SET operation.
DEFVAL	Indicates that a different default value will be used when creating an instance of a columnar object

These variation types can even be used in combination. The SYNTAX and WRITE-SYNTAX variations are especially useful in combination. By using both of these, the agent writer can specify that the object supports a different set of values for GET and SET operations.

ACCESS is used to indicate one of two things: the lowered level of access to the object or that the object is not implemented at all. Just to be clear: you cannot use this variation to "promote" the access level of an object. That is, if the MIB indicates that the MAX-ACCESS level of an object is *read-only*, then you can't specify here that an agent supports the object at the *read-write* level. Returning once again to our example, suppose that we could not support the controllerAdminState object at all. We would use this VARIATION:

```
VARIATION     sprinklecoControllerAdminState
        ACCESS          not-implemented
        DESCRIPTION
                "The Model 101 cannot support this object"
```

Our last two variations, CREATION-REQUIRES, and DEFVAL, are used exclusively for rows and columns within a row. CREATION-REQUIRES allows you to specify the minimum set of columns a manager must provide in order to create an instance of that row. Suppose that we are writing an agent to support a MIB with this particular row definition:

```
-- row object
programEntry OBJECT-TYPE
        SYNTAX          ProgramEntry
        MAX-ACCESS      not-accessible
        INDEX           { programIndex }
        DESCRIPTION     " ... "
        ::= { programTable 1 }

-- sequence for row
ProgramEntry ::= SEQUENCE {
        programIndex    Unsigned32,
        programType     INTEGER,
        programStart    DateAndTime,
        programStop     DateAndTime,
        programNotify   INTEGER,
        programOptions  BITS
        }
```

In our agent, a manager is required to supply values for *programStart*, and *programStop* to create a new instance. We can reflect this fact with this VARIATION statement:

```
VARIATION       programEntry -- this must be a row object
        CREATION-REQUIRES
                { programStart, programStop }
        DESCRIPTION
                "Row creation requires values to be specified for
                objects programStart, and programStop"
```

The items specified in the CREATION-REQUIRES clause that are columns in the table, may only be those with access of *read-create*. You cannot specify those with access of *not-accessible* or *read-only*. Here's the only tricky part about CREATION-REQUIRES: the SNMPv2 specification allows you the freedom to name "unrelated" objects as values. You can name objects in other tables in addition to (or instead of) columnar objects of the row in question. Unfortunately, the specifications aren't very clear on when or how this should be used, so this aspect is still up for interpretation.

The DEFVAL clause is fairly straightforward. It indicates that a default value different from that specified in the object's definition is used. Returning to our last example, suppose that we had this definition:

```
programType OBJECT-TYPE
        SYNTAX          INTEGER { daily(1), weekly(2), monthly(3) }
        MAX-ACCESS      read-create
        STATUS          current
        DESCRIPTION
                "The type of program for this entry:
```

```
                        daily      The program is executed every day
                        weekly     The program is executed every week
                        monthly    The program is executed every month"
            DEFVAL                 { daily }
    ::= { programEntry 2 }
```

This tells us that if the manager does not supply a value for *programType*, the agent should use the value *daily* by default. Our agent uses a different default value and we must specify this with the VARIATION:

```
    VARIATION      programType
            DEFVAL              { weekly }
            DESCRIPTION
                        "The Model 101always uses weekly programs by default"
```

At first glance, it might seem that this specifies a "change in behavior" for the object. Our agent will create a program that runs every week, while the MIB specifies that the programs should run every day. DEFVAL is a weak statement in a MIB. The SNMPv2 framework surrounds the discussion of DEFVAL with phrases such as "an acceptable value which may be used," and "might use." Consequently, specifying a different default value in a VARIATION isn't really considered a behavioral change, as the DEFVAL phrase in a MIB is really nothing more than a suggestion.

8.9 Information Module Maintenance

Almost all modules require maintenance over time. Technologies evolve and MIBs must keep pace, or MIBs might not work as well in practice as they do in design. Whatever the reason, you may find yourself wanting to change a MIB's structure, delete some of the objects contained within the MIB, add objects to an existing MIB, or change the way the objects within the MIB work. Each one of these activities has certain restrictions on it, and MIBs require careful maintenance to ensure that management stations are not inadvertently confused when a change is made.

There are a few items you can update without fear of doing anything wrong. Adding or updating any of the optional clauses in an object definition (DEFVAL, REFERENCE, and UNITS) can be done without restriction. Updating the DESCRIPTION clause is also allowed, as long as the updates are purely for editorial reasons. Clarifying remarks are allowed, but any type of edit that would indicate a change in an object's behavior is strictly forbidden.

8.9.1 Adding an Object

To add an item to the MIB, simply choose an unused OID, and define the new object using an unused identifier (object descriptor). For vendors, there is no restriction that an identifier must be globally unique. However, MIBs defined within the IETF must use unique identifiers. Note that the identifiers for siblings registered under a parent in the OID tree should be unique. See the section in Chapter 2 on object identifiers if this is not clear.

Getting back to adding an object, suppose we had a MIB containing these definitions:

```
errorsLarge OBJECT-TYPE
...
        ::= { genericErrors 1 }

errorsSmall OBJECT-TYPE
...
        ::= { genericErrors 2 }
```

And we wanted to add another item named *errorsMedium*. If the sub-identifier 3 has not been used beneath *genericErrors*, we can claim that OID to create:

```
errorsLarge OBJECT-TYPE
...
        ::= { genericErrors 1 }

errorsMedium OBJECT-TYPE
...
        ::= { genericErrors 3 }

errorsSmall OBJECT-TYPE
...
        ::= { genericErrors 2 }
```

Of course, this does not look as neat as it could be, but this keeps the MIB compatible with previous versions and implementations already fielded. If we changed the OID values for the object to this:

```
-- Warning! Bad technique follows!
errorsLarge OBJECT-TYPE
...
        ::= { genericErrors 1 }

errorsMedium OBJECT-TYPE
...
        ::= { genericErrors 2 }

errorsSmall OBJECT-TYPE
...
        ::= { genericErrors 3 }
```

then the object *errorsSmall* that previously had OID value { genericErrors 2 } now has OID value { genericErrors 3 } and object *errorsMedium* has OID value { genericErrors 2 }. Adding the *errorsMedium* object this way will be extremely confusing to a management application, as it is impossible to determine if the OID value { genericErrors 2 } refers to object *errorsMedium* or *errorsSmall*. Definitions of objects, for lack of a better word, are *forever*. Once you have published a definition, the assignment can't be changed.

Adding an object to a table can be done using the same technique, but tables have some special restrictions that you must keep in mind. The one item in a table definition that can never be modified is the INDEX clause. You cannot add to or delete from this clause, so adding an item to a table with the intention of extending the INDEX clause is not allowed. The only way to alter an INDEX clause of a table is to create a new table.

8.9.2 Modifying an Object

Modifying an object is a delicate operation. Once a MIB has been published, it is a contract between agent developers and management station software developers. Changing the contract will cause problems for either side. A good rule of thumb is that clarifying behaviors for an object is fine, but modifying the behavior of an object is not. The only type of item that can be altered is the list of enumerations on an INTEGER object when the enumerations are a list of things, such as network interface types. In general, we can add new values for an attribute, but we can not add new states since this is a change of behavior. Also, SMIv2 allows the labels on enumerated values to be changed. All other changes are illegal such as changing the underlying type of the object, changing the range restrictions on an INTEGER, changing the size of an OCTET STRING, etc.

Let's look at an example where we want to alter an object. Suppose that we had an object that specified the exterior color of a car:

```
carExteriorColor OBJECT-TYPE
        SYNTAX          INTEGER { black(1), white(2), blue(3), red(4) }
        MAX-ACCESS      read-only
        STATUS          current
        DESCRIPTION     "The exterior color of the car"
        ::= { carAttributes 3 }
```

Suppose that two new colors are now supported, and one of them is a shade of blue. To clarify the shades of blue, we also decide to rename the current *blue* to *darkBlue*. We can do this by updating the SYNTAX clause of the object to:

```
        SYNTAX          INTEGER { black(1), white(2), darkBlue(3), red(4),
                                        green(5), lightBlue(6) }
```

By adding these enumerations, the MIB doesn't interfere with any previous implementations. On the contrary, if we had re-declared the object this way (change the values):

```
SYNTAX          INTEGER { black(1), white(2), red(3), green(4),
                          darkBlue(5), lightBlue(6) }
```

management applications talking to older agents would mistakenly believe that dark blue cars were red. When you change the labels of the enumerations, doing so must only be done for clarification, not as reorganization.

It is perhaps easiest to think of enumerated integers as buttons on a control panel. Changing the behavior of a button can lead to unexpected results. For enumerated integers, the integer value of an object is the critical piece. The names such as *darkBlue* and *lightBlue* are primarily for clarity.

8.9.3 Deleting an Object

In Chapter 3, the STATUS clause was fully described. This clause is used to "delete" an object. Note that you can not simply delete an object by removing it from a MIB module. You delete an object from a MIB module by changing the status from *current* (in SMIv2) or *mandatory* (in SMIv1) to *obsolete*, and note this change in the object's DESCRIPTION clause. You must also update the status of other items that reference the deleted object such as rows, object groups, and events. You will also, most likely, want to create new versions of these other items and requirement specifications. The status of agent profiles and requirement specifications are not updated when the status of a referenced item is changed. You only create a new profile when you change your agent implementation. You only create new requirements specifications when your requirements change. The actions for agent developers and management application developers on a change of status are specified in Chapter 3. Remember from Chapter 3, a status value of *deprecated* means that an object is valid in limited circumstances and has been replaced by another object. A status value of *obsolete* means the definition is not valid, since it was found to be flawed, could not be implemented, was redundant or not useful, or is no longer relevant.

Do not remove the definition so that it does not exist in any MIB module, as once an OBJECT IDENTIFIER is assigned, we never want to reuse it. While the old definitions in the MIB take up space, they are actually serving as placeholders to prevent reuse of their identifiers. You may want to create a new MIB module to hold obsoleted objects when you have obsoleted many objects and they would clutter up the original module.

To delete a scalar object:

```
gallonsSprayed OBJECT-TYPE
        SYNTAX          Counter32
        UNITS           "gallons"
        MAX-ACCESS      read-only
        STATUS          current
        DESCRIPTION
```

```
                "Measures the gallons sprayed out of this zone
                since the start of this sprinkler cycle. The start of
                the sprinkler cycle is given by sprinklerCycleTime."
        REFERENCE       "Sprinkler 2000 Manual Pg 100"
        ::= { xxxGroup 1}
```

To delete the gallonsSprayed object, change *current* to *obsolete* and note the change in the DESCRIPTION clause:

```
    gallonsSprayed OBJECT-TYPE
        SYNTAX          Counter32
        UNITS           "gallons"
        MAX-ACCESS      read-only
        STATUS          obsolete -- change the status
        DESCRIPTION
                "Measures the gallons sprayed out of this zone
                since the start of this sprinkler cycle. The start of
                the sprinkler cycle is given by sprinklerCycleTime.

                This object is obsolete. It could not be measured." -- note the change
        REFERENCE       "Sprinkler 2000 Manual Pg 100"
        ::= { xxxGroup 1}
```

8.9.4 Special Considerations for Tables

There are special considerations you should keep in mind when planning to delete items from a table. You cannot delete an object from a table if it is referenced in the INDEX clause. The only way to delete an object that is contained within an INDEX clause is to delete the entire table, and recreate it with a new index clause.

To delete an entire table from the MIB, change the status of the table, row, and all columnar objects in the table to *obsolete*. All other tables which use any of the INDEX fields or augment the table must be also deleted.

The process of deleting a table is relatively straightforward: simply follow the procedures for deleting an object for every object within the table, and also delete the table and row objects. Here is an example of a table that has been completely deleted:

```
    -- A table of outstanding alarm events
    -- Note that this table is obsolete, and is no longer in current use.
    alarmTable OBJECT-TYPE
        SYNTAX          SEQUENCE of AlarmTableEntry
        MAX-ACCESS      not-accessible
        STATUS          obsolete
        DESCRIPTION     "..."
        ::= { alarmObjs 4 }
```

```
alarmTableEntry OBJECT-TYPE
        SYNTAX          AlarmTableEntry
        MAX-ACCESS      not-accessible
        STATUS          obsolete
        DESCRIPTION     "..."
        INDEX           { alarmSource }
        ::= { alarmTable 1 }

AlarmTableEntry ::= SEQUENCE {
        alarmSource     INTEGER,
        alarmType       INTEGER,
        ...
        }

alarmSource OBJECT-TYPE
        SYNTAX          INTEGER { windowUnit(1), doorUnit(2) }
        MAX-ACCESS      not-accessible
        STATUS          obsolete
        DESCRIPTION     "..."
        ::= { alarmTableEntry 1 }

alarmType OBJECT-TYPE
        SYNTAX          INTEGER { high(1), low(2) }
        MAX-ACCESS      not-accessible
        STATUS          obsolete
        DESCRIPTION     "..."
        ::= { alarmTableEntry 2 }
```

When deleting a table you must keep in mind some of the special relationships that a table might have with other tables. If a second table is related to the deleted table by the AUGMENTS clause, or by using all or part of the deleted table's INDEX clause, it too must be deleted. Failing to do so would result in a table that referenced objects that no longer exist.

Unfortunately, there is no way of knowing in advance that deleting a table may pose problems for tables in other MIBs. To tell if this is the case, you must manually search through all other MIBs to ensure that there are no dependencies.[4] Here we see one of the subtle traps of the MIB framework. Module authors have no control over which objects are exported for use by other MIB modules. As a result, the author cannot predict which objects may be in use by other MIBs.

4. Of course, the definition of "all" is dependent on the type of organization for which you are writing the MIB. If you are writing MIBs for a private company, you would check all MIBs defined by that company. If you are writing a MIB for an IETF or industry consortium working group, you have a very difficult task! Its not possible for you to check all MIBs. You must rely on others that reference these MIBs to complete your task.

8.9.5 Documenting Changes

After you make any change to a module, you must update the LAST-UPDATED field of the MODULE-IDENTITY construct. Additionally, a new REVISION/DESCRIPTION pair should be added to document the date and nature of the change made. In practice, of course, most authors make several changes at once rather than documenting each individual edit. Taking our previous example of adding the *errorsMedium* object. The module identity would need to be revised to:

```
testMibModule MODULE-IDENTITY
        LAST-UPDATED  "9601270240Z"    -- 12 Jan 96 2:40 AM UTC
        ORGANIZATION  " ... "
        CONTACT-INFO  " ... "
        DESCRIPTION   "A Sample Module"
        -- Revision history
        -- Remember to put these in reverse chronological order
        REVISION      "9601270240Z"
        DESCRIPTION   "Added errorsMedium object"

        REVISION      "9509080000Z"
        DESCRIPTION   "The initial revision of this module"
        ::= { testModules 56 }
```

You may have noticed that in every MODULE-IDENTITY we have examined thus far there is a REVISION statement that indicates the initial revision of the module. Even though SMIv2 doesn't explicitly require it,[5] and the vast majority of MIB modules we reviewed in preparing this book do not include one (even those from IETF working groups), doing so aids in tracking the history of a module. Without it, it's hard to tell when a module was first released.

If the only change you make to a MIB module is a simple edit such as the addition of some text into a description clause, updating the MODULE-IDENTITY clause is the only documentation required. The addition or deletion of objects or events requires some additional steps. You must create new groupings and requirements. In other words, we need to be able to indicate that there are new implementation requirements for agents. This is accomplished by using the OBJECT-GROUP and NOTIFICATION-GROUP constructs to create new groups, and by using the MODULE-COMPLIANCE construct to create new requirements specifications. The same rule applies to groups and requirements specifications as objects: you may not change the semantics (i.e., add or remove items to/from a group), you may only clarify existing definitions and create new ones.

Suppose that our alarm example used this OBJECT-GROUP statement before we made the addition of the *alarmMedium* object:

5. Actually, the standard does make a somewhat subtle reference to including a REVISION clause in the initial version of a module, but it is never stated as an absolute requirement.

```
alarmGroup OBJECT-GROUP
        OBJECTS         { alarmLarge, alarmSmall }
        STATUS          current
        DESCRIPTION     " ... "
        ::= { alarmGroups 1 }
```

Since we have created a new object that is related to objects *alarmLarge* and *alarmSmall*, we must create a new group containing all of these objects. This new object group must use a different identifier and different OID value. Its definition is:

```
alarmGroup2 OBJECT-GROUP
        OBJECTS         { alarmLarge, alarmSmall, alarmMedium }
        STATUS          current
        DESCRIPTION     "..."
        ::= { alarmGroups 9 }
```

Note that this new group is registered with OID value { alarmGroups 9 }. We follow the same rules for adding an object group as we do for adding an object — we never re-use an object identifier, but we are free to claim any unused one underneath the alarmGroups registration sub-tree.

The final documentation step is creating a new compliance specification using a MODULE-COMPLIANCE construct that references the newly-created object group. As we did with the *alarmGroup*, we use an existing compliance specification as a model for the new one. Suppose that we had this compliance specification as part of the original MIB:

```
sprinkleControllerComplianceV1 MODULE-COMPLIANCE
        STATUS          current
        DESCRIPTION     " ... "
        MODULE          -- this MIB
                MANDATORY-GROUPS { alarmGroup }
        ::= { sprinklecoControllerCompls 1 }
```

The new compliance statement referencing *alarmGroup2*, which we will call sprinkleControllerComplianceV2, and registered with OID value { sprinkleControllerCompls 2 }, would be:

```
sprinkleControllerComplianceV2 MODULE-COMPLIANCE
        STATUS          current
        DESCRIPTION     " ... "
        MODULE          -- this MIB
                MANDATORY-GROUPS { alarmGroup2 }
        ::= { sprinklecoControllerCompls 2 }
```

For both the new object group and compliance, it is important to remember that they are not replacements for the original versions. Rather, these new statements are additions to the module. The original statements remain in the MIB, as agent implementations already in current use still claim conformance to the first versions.

8.10 Statistics

There is little doubt that statistics provided by SNMP agents can help network managers maintain network connectivity and services. However, modelling statistics is where many MIBs tend to get bogged down. Ever fearful of not providing enough information, or providing information just because they can, MIB writers will invariably overload a MIB with too many statistical items. This can have several negative effects: network managers are forced to wade through "useless" statistics, and agent developers are forced to implement them. Before any statistical item is added, it should be carefully justified. Some questions which the MIB writer should ask for every statistic include:

- Who benefits from this variable? (Is it the vendor or the user?)
- Does this variable provide information which cannot be obtained elsewhere?
- Is this statistic actually useful? (Can a user take action based on this?)
- Can the agent implement this statistic at a reasonable cost?
- Is the meaning of this statistic clear to agent developers and users?

If a statistic is useful for the user, and the user can take some action based on a value, then a statistic is probably worthwhile. If this seems fairly obvious, it is. MIB writers frequently ignore this simple dictum and define items which are of dubious value. Even some of the MIBs written by the standards bodies are challenges for developers and users alike. Defining objects that show the number of unused memory buffers on an internal queue might help developers, but does the user little good. This is not to discourage the development of MIBs solely for in-house debugging, but mixing statistics useful to the end user with statistics useful only to developers is poor form. Statistics that require too much bandwidth from the agent should be avoided.

8.10.1 Counters

Once you have arrived at a set of items that are to be modelled as statistics, you need to also consider the time boundaries surrounding items. As we have discussed before, the counter types (*Counter* for SNMPv1 and *Counter32*/*Counter64* for SNMPv2) represent a value relative to an epoch indicator. To review, the *epoch* indicator, which uses the *TimeTicks* type, denotes the point in time when the agent began gathering information about a particular event or set of events. For the vast majority of these counters, the start of the epoch is indicated by the MIB-II variable *sysUpTime*, which represents the time since the agent portion of a device or service last re-initialized. This may or may not represent the last time a device rebooted; counters may be *persistent* across reboots. That is to say, a device can have a counter that does not lose its value when the power is cycled — it simply picks up counting where it left off. However, there is no requirement that the *sysUpTime* epoch be used as a reference point for all counters. In some situations, it is useful, or required, to have another epoch indicator that can be reset without having to reset all statistics. Generally, all statistics in a table need a time stamp columnar object that records when the instance of a row came into existence. Without such a columnar object, a manager may not be able to determine if the counter values are for a previous or a new instance of the row. This is why it is always a good idea to retrieve the epoch variable each time a counter is retrieved—otherwise the values can be mis-interpreted. Whatever the epoch, the DESCRIPTION field of the statistic should explicitly identify the variable used for this purpose.

32 Bit Counters or 64 Bit Counters?

In addition to the epoch, a statistic should have useful units of measurement, and a reasonable size for the counter (32 versus 64 bits). On certain types of LANs, for instance, 32 bit packet counters can roll over (the number of events counted reaches 2^{32}-1 and returns to 0) in under an hour. The Counter64 uses this rule as a condition of use: if a counter does not roll in under an hour, Counter32 should be used instead. Even though the MIBs defined for it use 32 bit counters, 10 megabit Ethernet is an example of this—an object counting the total number of bytes sent on an interface transmitting packets continuously will wrap in about 57 minutes. Here's how we arrived at that figure:

Calculating Counter Rollover for 10 MB Ethernet

$$\frac{2^{32} - 1\,\text{Events}}{(10^7\,\text{Bits Per Sec}) / (8\,\text{Bits Per Byte})} \div (60\,\text{Sec/Min}) \cong 57.27\,\text{Min}$$

We want to determine how long it will take the interface to generate 2^{32}-1 events. The counter is counting each byte transmitted, so an interface transmitting 10^7 bytes per second will create $10^7 \div 8$ events per second. This means that the counter will reach its maximum value in 3435.97 seconds, or approximately 57.27 minutes. This Ethernet octet counter seems to be a clear candidate for using Counter64, but it still uses the 32 bit version. This is partly pragmatic, partly historical. At the time this counter was defined, the 64 bit counter did not exist, so its use is somewhat of an historical holdover from the SNMPv1 MIB framework. From a pragmatic point of view our analysis above ignored the fact that Ethernet requires a small gap between each packet transmitted. When these inter-packet gaps are taken into consideration, the counter will roll in slightly over one hour. The 32 bit counter serves the purposes of Ethernet quite well, but it doesn't hold up well to higher speed networks. Consider the traffic counter requirements of other media, shown in Table 8–6.

Table 8–6 Counter Rollover Times for Various Media

Media/Speed	Counter32	Counter64
802.3 Ethernet /10 MB	57 Minutes	28,077,236 Years
802.5 Token Ring / 16 MB	36 Minutes	292,471 Years
FDDI / 100 MB	5.7 Minutes	46,795 Years

Table 8–6 Counter Rollover Times for Various Media (Continued)

Media/Speed	Counter32	Counter64
T3 / 145 MB	3.9 Minutes	32,272 Years
OC3 / 155 MB	3.7 Minutes	30,190 Years
OC12 / 622 MB	0.9 Minutes	7,523 Years

So it should be clear from this that certain technologies require this very large counter. However, aside from items such as general traffic counts on high speed networks, very few things actually occur quickly enough to justify use of 64 bit counters. Consider this: an event would need to occur more than 1,193,046 times per second over the course of an hour to qualify for using the 64 bit counter. If it sounds as if we are discouraging the use of 64 bit counters, we are. They should be used very sparingly, and only in situations where they are truly needed. Even so, use of these counters can be avoided simply by choosing different measurement units. When dealing with events of this magnitude, a count of individual events is sometimes awkward. When evaluating the traffic flow on a high speed back-end network (let's say a bandwidth of 1 gigabit per second), is it really necessary to report every packet or every octet? Probably not. In fact, at this rate, millions of packets or octets is probably the correct unit. For the case of an octet counter, this causes the counter to wrap in about 8 years instead of 0.25 seconds when a 32 bit counter is used.

8.10.2 Gauges

In general, gauges are used to model three general categories: resource consumption, resource availability, and rates of change. Some modelled objects represent finite resources: memory usage, processor usage, queue lengths, database handles, etc. The usage level of these objects changes continually, going up and down as resources are consumed and returned to the system. Other modelled objects represent rates such as: speed, volume or intensity. Contrast this with the counter types which model increasing values, and you can see that each has a very different use. Deciding whether to use a counter or gauge is actually quite simple. If the value can ever decrease, use a gauge.

Let's examine some items that can be modelled using a gauge type. Suppose that we want to construct an object that reveals the amount of free memory in a system. A simple version might look like this:

```
freeMemory OBJECT-TYPE
        SYNTAX          Gauge32
        UNITS           "1024 bytes"
        MAX-ACCESS      read-only
        STATUS          current
        DESCRIPTION     "The amount of free memory"
        ::= { memory 1 }
```

This simple declaration works well enough, but this object alone doesn't supply some required information. As this object represents a finite resource, we need to supply some context in order to place the value in its proper perspective. The context needed here is what the maximum value of the gauge can be. As simple as this sounds, quite a few MIBs don't have any sort of range around the values a gauge can report. We could simply put boundaries on the declaration like this:[6]

```
freeMemory OBJECT-TYPE
        SYNTAX          Gauge32(0..10240)
...
```

This would indicate that the gauge can vary between 0 (no free memory) and 10240 KB (all free memory). This will work fine for one specific system with a fixed memory configuration, but systems where the installed memory will vary can't use this definition. To solve this problem, we need to declare a companion object which reveals the total amount of memory on the system.

```
totalMemory OBJECT-TYPE
        SYNTAX          Unsigned32
        UNITS           "1024 bytes"
        MAX-ACCESS      read-only
        STATUS          current
        DESCRIPTION     "The total amount of installed memory"
        ::= { memory 1 }

freeMemory OBJECT-TYPE
        SYNTAX          Gauge32
        UNITS           "1024 bytes"
        MAX-ACCESS      read-only
        STATUS          current
        DESCRIPTION     "The amount of free memory, which ranges
                        between 0 and totalMemory"
        ::= { memory 2 }
```

There are several problems you may encounter with gauges. As with the counters, gauges can potentially document resources that exceed the capacity of a 32 bit value. For example, a database server might wish to indicate available disk space, and have this level rise and fall as records are added and deleted. Expressing these values in terms of bytes might exceed the 4 gigabyte capacity. Expressing the value in terms of more logical units such as 1024 byte sectors or megabytes is the only choice here, as there is no 64 bit type available to us that has the behavior we need.

6. In the original SNMP framework, it was never clear if it was legal to provide range restrictions on a Gauge type. The SNMPv2 framework clears this up by explicitly stating that doing so is allowed.

A second problem surrounding gauges is that they can only represent unsigned values, so we can't have declarations such as this one:

```
-- Warning! Illegal declaration
currentTemperature OBJECT-TYPE
        SYNTAX          Gauge32 (-212..212) -- illegal
        MAX-ACCESS      read-only
        STATUS          current
        DESCRIPTION     "The current outside temperature in degrees Fahrenheit"
        ::= { temperature 1 }
```

Unfortunately, there is little that can be done in this situation. One solution is to select a different scale for our temperature object, but this is not always possible:

```
currentTemperature OBJECT-TYPE
        SYNTAX          Gauge32 (0..373)
        MAX-ACCESS      read-only
        STATUS          current
        DESCRIPTION     "The current outside temperature in degrees Kelvin"
        ::= { temperature 1 }
```

We could also choose to use a type other than Gauge or Gauge32 for the object. The signed integer types, INTEGER (in SMIv1) and Integer32 (in SMIv2) can express the values we want, but they don't have the behavior we require. That is, they can express negative values, but they don't latch at maximum (or in our case, minimum) values. (See Chapter 2 for a description of this behavior for gauges.) In this situation, the best approach would be to provide your own type, expressed as a TEXTUAL-CONVENTION, based on an integer:

```
SignedGauge ::= TEXTUAL-CONVENTION
        STATUS          current
        DESCRIPTION
                "This type behaves like a gauge, but is expressed as an Integer32.
                Its value can latch at either a negative number or a positive
                number"
        SYNTAX          Integer32

currentTemperature OBJECT-TYPE
        SYNTAX          SignedGauge (-212..212)
        MAX-ACCESS      read-only
        STATUS          current
        DESCRIPTION     "The current outside temperature in degrees Fahrenheit"
        ::= { temperature 1 }
```

8.11 Components

Translating an object analysis into a MIB is, as we mentioned in Chapter 7, is a fairly mechanical process. The one issue where we have seen many MIB writers back themselves into an analytical corner is the identification of components within a managed system. Suppose that we have a MIB where we are attempting to identify the types of network interface boards inserted into a device. We could use an enumerated INTEGER, and simply identify all the possible types of interface boards at the time we write the MIB. Let's examine this MIB fragment, where we have defined a board identification table.

```
BoardEntry ::= SEQUENCE {
        boardSlot           Integer32,
        boardType           INTEGER,
        ...
        }


boardSlot OBJECT-TYPE
        SYNTAX              Integer32(1..24)
        MAX-ACCESS          not-accessible
        STATUS              current
        DESCRIPTION
                "The slot number where this board resides"
        ::= { boardEntry 1 }


boardType OBJECT-TYPE
        SYNTAX              INTEGER {
                                    ethernet12(1),
                                    ethernet24(2),
                                    tokenRing10(3),
                                    tokenRing20(4)
                            }
        MAX-ACCESS          read-only
        STATUS              current
        DESCRIPTION         "The type of the board occupying this slot"
        ::= { boardEntry 2 }
```

This looks as if it will be very workable, and has some very attractive features. We can look at this one definition, and see all of the possible board types that we may encounter. Simple integers are easy to manipulate programmatically, so both agent and management station software writers will find this table easy to use. However, there are some hidden limitations to this approach that can have a big impact on maintenance. Each time we need to account for new module types, we must add new enumerations:

```
boardType OBJECT-TYPE
        SYNTAX          INTEGER {
                                ethernet12(1),
                                ethernet24(2),
                                tokenRing10(3),
                                tokenRing20(4),
                                fddi10(5),
                                ethernet48(6)
                        }
        MAX-ACCESS      read-only
        STATUS          current
        DESCRIPTION     "The type of the board occupying this slot"
        ::= { boardEntry 2 }
```

While this is perfectly legal, identifying physical objects in this manner means that we are constantly updating MIB modules to reflect the new devices. A better approach is to use OID values to identify items. Thus, we will never have to update the object's definition.

8.12 States

As we saw in Chapter 7, the concept of state changes is an important component of network management. State represents the current condition of a logical or physical component of a device or service, and can be further sub-divided into *desired* and *current* states. If the state variable represents a *control* object, that is, we want to create a variable which a management station can manipulate, we are concerned with both of these types of states. There are two ways to approach this problem: collect all possible states into a single variable, or create separate *current* and *desired* state variables.

Take the example of a device which has a multi-stage start-up sequence. We might wish to expose the start-up sequence through a state variable:

```
state OBJECT-TYPE
        SYNTAX          INTEGER {
                        stopped(1),
                        selfTesting(2),         -- sub-stage for start-up
                        initializing(3),        -- sub-stage for start-up
                        started(4),
                        shuttingDown(5) }       -- sub-stage for shutdown
        MAX-ACCESS      read-write
        STATUS          current
        DESCRIPTION
                "The values stopped(1) and running(4) are control values which will
                cause the entity to start or stop. All other values are sub-state indicators,
                and may be read, but not written."
        ::= { xxxGroup 1 }
```

It is not clear from this declaration exactly which values are intended as the control values (values an application can write), and which are intended as indicators (values the agent uses to indicate the current state). We can document the semantics behind each of the stages in the DESCRIPTION field, and while doing so is always a good idea, it does not help applications to understand which values are legal to write and which are not. The allowable values can also be outlined with a MODULE-CONFORMANCE specification using the WRITE-SYNTAX/SYNTAX clauses. However, this is somewhat of a misuse of this construct; it is intended to specify implementation requirements and is not intended as a mechanism to define the behaviors of managed objects.

We can clear up this confusion by making a clear distinction between the controls and indicators. Returning to our previous example, we can split the object into two new objects:

```
desiredState OBJECT-TYPE
        SYNTAX          INTEGER {
                                  stop(1),          -- stop the entity
                                  start(4) }        -- start the entity
        MAX-ACCESS      read-write
        STATUS          current
        DESCRIPTION     "..."
        ::= { xxxGroup 1 }

currentState OBJECT-TYPE
        SYNTAX          INTEGER {
                                  stopped(1),
                                  selfTesting(2),
                                  initializing(3),
                                  started(4),
                                  shuttingDown(5) }
        MAX-ACCESS      read-only
        STATUS          current
        DESCRIPTION     "..."
        ::= { xxxGroup 2 }
```

Under this scenario, the object *currentState* serves as an indicator of the current operation stage of the device. Applications can control the state through manipulating the variable *desiredState*, and see the results in *currentState*.

There are a few stylistic notes about this example. Transient states are represented by gerunds (verbs ending in *ing*), while terminal states are represented by past tense verbs. Obviously, this is not always possible, but using a consistent naming scheme makes these objects much easier to read. Also remember that enumerated integers need not be contiguous values. If a particular state appears on both the desired and actual state list, it should have the same value.

8.13 Actions

Actions are closely linked to state. Upon closer analysis, an action is really nothing more than a request by a manager for a state change in the agent:

notTransferringFile ⇒ transferingFile
active ⇒ shutDown

This is not just a coincidence. Since SNMP is only capable of dealing with implicit actions, this is actually the only choice possible. Actions must be designed such that they have a series of states which can be monitored and manipulated by the requesting manager.

Take the example of designing a file transfer action between your computer and a remote computer. We need to have the following attributes:

Local File	(Name of file on your computer)
Remote File	(Name of file on the remote computer)
Server Address	(Address of the remote computer)
Direction	(Directional indicator (To/From))
Transfer Trigger	(A way to start the transfer)
Error Indicator	(Last error encountered)

The *local* and *remote* file names are just *DisplayString*s. The *server address* will depend on the underlying protocols; this example will assume an IP address and the Trivial File Transfer Protocol (TFTP). The *direction* indicator is an enumerated integer with two possible values *to*(1) and *from*(2). Now that we have the attributes specified, we need the action trigger. This comes in the form of another enumerated integer representing a state variable.

Desired State - Not transferring, Transferring

To initiate a transfer, a manager would set the attributes, and then initiate the transfer by setting the transfer state variable to the desired state, *transferring*. This implicit action request causes the agent to begin the file transfer. When the agent has completed the file transfer, it can signal this by changing the state variable back to *notTransferring*. The manager, of course, must poll this variable to determine when the file transfer has completed.

Putting all of this together we have the following MIB fragment:

```
-- The transfer objects
xferLocalFile OBJECT-TYPE
        SYNTAX          DisplayString
        MAX-ACCESS      read-write
        STATUS          current
        DESCRIPTION     "The name of the local file. Cannot be changed if the value
                        of xferState is 'transferring'"
        ::= { xfer 1 }
```

```
xferRemoteFile OBJECT-TYPE
        SYNTAX          DisplayString
        MAX-ACCESS      read-write
        STATUS          current
        DESCRIPTION     "The name of the remote file. Cannot be changed if the value
                        of xferState is 'transferring'"
        ::= { xfer 2 }

xferServer OBJECT-TYPE
        SYNTAX          IpAddress
        MAX-ACCESS      read-write
        STATUS          current
        DESCRIPTION     "The TFTP server address. Cannot be changed if the value
                        of xferState is 'transferring'"
        ::= { xfer 3 }

xferDirection OBJECT-TYPE
        SYNTAX          INTEGER { to(1), from(2) }
        MAX-ACCESS      read-write
        STATUS          current
        DESCRIPTION     "The direction of the transfer. Cannot be changed if the value
                        of xferState is 'transferring'"
        ::= { xfer 4 }

xferState OBJECT-TYPE
        SYNTAX          INTEGER { transferring(1), notTransferring(1) }
        MAX-ACCESS      read-write
        DESCRIPTION
                "The trigger to begin a file transfer. If this agent is already
                in the transferring state, setting this value to 'notTransferring'
                will abort the transfer in progress and setting to 'transferring'
                will not affect the current transfer."
        ::= { xfer 5 }

xferError OBJECT-TYPE
        SYNTAX          INTEGER {
                                noError(1),
                                timeout(2),
                                noSuchFile(3)}
        MAX-ACCESS      read-only
        STATUS          current
        DESCRIPTION     "Error status of transfer"
        ::= { xfer 6 }
```

This is a simple, workable solution. However, it neglects the very large (and very real) problem of multiple managers accessing the file transfer function and the situation of dropped or duplicated messages. Two managers can clash with each other's attempts at two different points when using this service: transfer setup and results retrieval. Transfer setup will almost take care of itself, since the setup objects are defined to not allow their values to be changed during transfer. This resource is first-come-first-serve, so the first manager to change the setup objects and start the transfer will block the modification of the setup objects until the transfer completes. (The managers must use a single SET request to modify the setup objects and start a transfer.) If manager application *A* successfully requests a transfer, manager application *B* will get an appropriate error when it requests a transfer (as the agent is already in the *transferring* state). The second point of contention is more problematic. If manager *A*'s file transfer finishes and the agent transitions back to the *notTransferring* state, manager B can now begin a transfer, thus destroying *A*'s results.

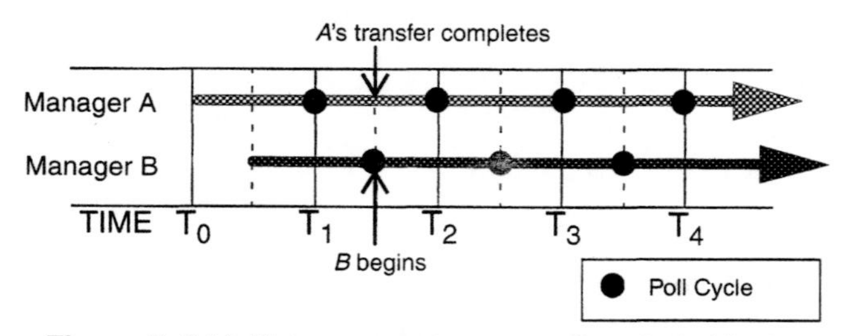

Figure 8–6 Multiple manager access of control objects

In Figure 8–6, we have two managers which begin file transfer attempts at two different times: manager *A* at time T_0, and manager *B* at time $T_{0.5}$. Manager *A* is first to claim the transfer resource, so B is blocked out, but continues retrying the resource every unit of time T. *A*, meanwhile, is also polling the progress of transfer every T units. If *A*'s transfer completes at time $T_{1.5}$, *B* has the opportunity to claim (steal, really) the transfer resource from *A*. If this happens, *A* may not even be aware of what transpired, and blissfully unaware of the situation, will happily poll the progress of what is actually *B*'s file transfer.

There are several solutions to this situation, yet none of them are without problems. Perhaps the easiest to implement is a simple *lifetime* value for the result. This is a timer which begins a countdown after the requested operation has completed. When the timer reaches 0, other managers can access the resource. This is used to preserve the results until the original manager has a chance to retrieve the transfer results. Adding

```
xferResultLifetime OBJECT-TYPE
        SYNTAX          TimeTicks
        MAX-ACCESS      read-write
        STATUS          current
        DESCRIPTION     "The lifetime of the results. Cannot be changed if the value
                        of xferState is 'transferring'"
        ::= { xfer 8 }
```

to the original definition allows the management application to specify a lifetime value for the results of the transfer request. Using this scheme, manager *A* in the previous file transfer example could have specified an *xferResultLifetime* of 3T. In doing so, it has provided a window larger than its polling cycle to insure that it has adequate time to retrieve the results. This approach has the distinct disadvantage that the resource will be unavailable for that length of time. For simple applications this is the easiest approach.

8.14 Tables

In designing tables, there are two overriding concerns for the MIB designer: index selection and row creation. Index selection governs how the rows will be sorted, as well as what data can be represented by the rows. Row creation dictates how much information must be supplied to an agent to create some resource or activate a service.

Even though this book is not about implementing an SNMP agent or manager, it is important to understand what goes on behind the scenes when creating and destroying rows so that you can design useful and implementable tables.

8.14.1 Row Creation

Some MIBs have tables that represent dynamic resources which can be created, suspended, or destroyed. These are the tables that need to utilize a standard row creation and deletion technique. The first question to ask when considering row creation and deletion via SNMP operations is if it is even needed. Row creation via an SNMP operation occurs by a SET request of a remote manager to an instance of one or more columnar objects that do not exist. If a manager can never logically create an instance of a row in a table, then formal row creation is simply not needed. For instance, new instances cannot be created via SNMP operation in a table representing a series of network interface boards. The only way to "create" a row in this table is to physically insert a board, at which time the SNMP agent instantiates a row automatically. Likewise, an SNMP manager cannot create a row in a table of network connections. This can only occur via protocol operations.

The history of a formal row creation concept in a standards document dates back to the original work on the RMON MIB. This MIB introduced a textual convention known as *EntryStatus*, which helped define a formal row creation agreement between a manager and agent. This convention used an enumerated integer to specify the states in creating, deleting, and activating a row.

SMIv2 improved this concept for its "standard" row creation technique. Before we delve into the specifics of row creation in the SNMPv2 framework, let's examine the types of operations a manager will need in order to manage row existence in an agent, and how those operations relate to a managed system. There are five key areas we need to address when manipulating rows:

1. *Determining which row to create.* We need to decide how the manager will determine which row is to be created. In many instances, this can be determined entirely by the management station without consulting the agent. In these cases, the indices of the table in question are attributes that identify the row.
2. *Creating the row itself.* We need to have a technique by which the manager can insert a new row that resolves concurrency issues between multiple managers.
3. *Filling in the values of the row.* After a new row has been created, the manager needs to be able to supply all the values that will make the row "make sense" before the row can be made "active."
4. *Activating and suspending the row.* After the row is filled with the required information, the manager needs to be able to notify the agent that it should activate (or place into service) that row. In some cases the manager may need to request that the agent temporarily suspend a row from service.
5. *Destroying the row.* When a resource instance is no longer needed, the manager needs a mechanism to cause the agent to remove that instance from the system.

There is no formal, enforced mechanism to address the first requirement, so we will examine some options for addressing that requirement shortly. For now, let's focus on SNMPv2's answer to the last three requirements: a textual convention known as *RowStatus*.

```
RowStatus ::= TEXTUAL CONVENTION
        DESCRIPTION    " ... "
        STATUS         current
        SYNTAX         INTEGER {
                              active(1),
                              notInService(2),
                              notReady(3),
                              createAndGo(4),
                              createAndWait(5),
                              destroy(6) }
```

To indicate that new rows can be created by a manager, you simply declare an object that uses this textual convention as its SYNTAX clause, and include that object as part of the row definition.

The row creation mechanism in the SNMPv2 framework does not use the pure "desired state"/"current state" model we have discussed previously. Instead, it uses three action states: *createAndGo*, *createAndWait*, and *destroy*, combined with two desired states: *active* and *notInService*, and a current state: *notReady*. There are two keys to understanding this model. The first is that creation of the instance of one column in a new row does not necessarily create instances of all columns in the row. The second is that there is a distinction between row existence and row activation. Multiple SNMP SET operations may be used to create columns of the row until there is some minimum sub-set in existence which allows the row to become active. The process of "filling in" the values of columns in a row is called "row construction."

The *action* states can be written, but not read.

- *createAndGo* indicates that the agent should accept the row values specified, create items within the row and place the row into service (or activate it).
- *createAndWait* indicates that the agent should accept the values specified (if any) and, create items within the row, but not place the row in service.
- *destroy* indicates that the agent should remove the row from service and then delete it.

The *desired* states can be written and read.

- *notInService* indicates that the row has been suspended. That is, the instance modelled by the row does not exist.
- *active* indicates that the instance of the resource modelled by the row exists.

The *current* state can only be read.

- *notReady* indicates that the row does not contain values for all columnar objects in the row needed for an instance of the resource modelled by the row to be created.

Figure 8–7 demonstrates the states which the RowStatus variable can traverse. This is an example of a fairly well-designed state machine. It demonstrates the following properties.

- There are no dead-end states.
- An illegal request (e.g., one that produces an SNMP error) does not cause the machine to change state.

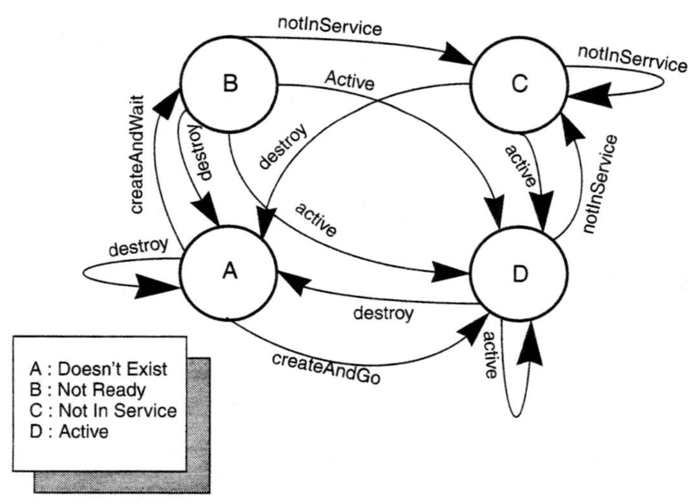

Figure 8–7 State Diagram of RowStatus interaction

The process of row creation/activation actually takes on two forms which, for lack of better terms, we will call: *one-shot* and *dribble* mode. In the one-shot mode, a manager must specify all the values required to activate a row in a single SET operation along with an assignment of the status variable to *createAndGo*. If all requirements are satisfied and an instance of the resource is created, then the status of the row transitions to *Active* (noted by

A ⇒ D). This is the simplest form of row creation and activation using the RowStatus model. The interaction between a manager and agent using one-shot mode can be visualized by Figure 8–8.

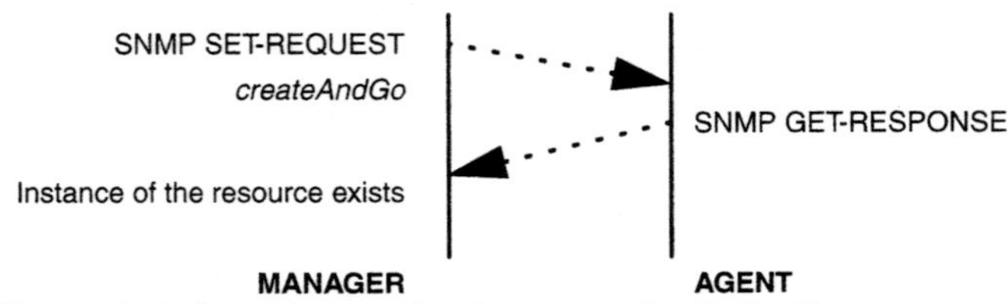

Figure 8–8 One-shot mode of row creation/activation

Of course, if the values for the row do not make sense, or there were not enough values specified in the SET request to fill in the row, the agent returns an error code. In this case, the only appropriate error code is *inconsistentValue* (in SNMPv2) or *badValue* (in SNMPv1).

In dribble mode, creating the row, filling it with values, and activating it are carried out in discrete steps. To create the row, the manager specifies a value of *createAndWait* for the status variable. This SET request may contain values of other columnar objects in the row, but this is not required. More often, the values for the other columnar objects are specified in additional SET requests. After each SET operation, the status variable takes on the value *notReady* or *notInService*. The status variable takes on the value *notReady*, if the row does not have the values for all items required to place the row into service. Once all required values are received for the row, the row is automatically transitioned by the agent to *notInService*, indicating that it is ready to be placed into service. To place this row into service, the manager requests that the status variable transition to the *active* state. A sample interaction of dribble mode row creation is given in Figure 8–9.

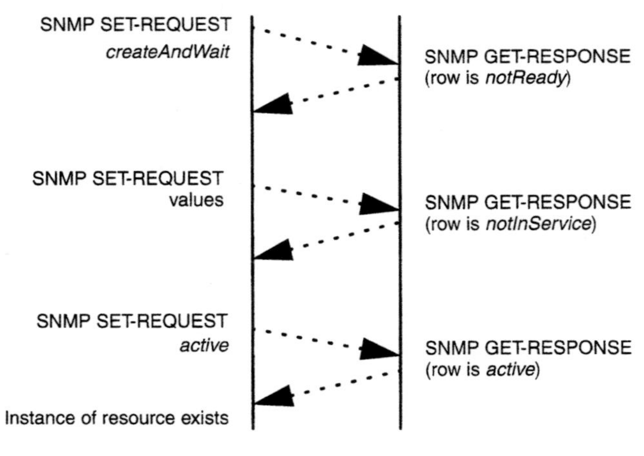

Figure 8–9 Dribble mode row creation/activation

Both row creation techniques have advantages and disadvantages in terms of operational difficulties, but our concern here is the relationship between row creation and MIB design.

Some of the issues surrounding row creation are a bit more complex than they appear. To begin with, let's examine the somewhat subtle difference between creating, activating, and suspending a row, and what implications these areas have for a managed system. At this point, we have carefully ignored the key phrase "place the row into service," so let's examine exactly what this means to a managed system. If you will recall from our discussions of what goes on inside a managed system, the agent portion of a system is usually separate from the managed entity itself. This separation can be a problem for row manipulation. Consider where a row under manipulation "exists" during the various stages during creation. While the row has a status of *notReady* or *notInService*, it exists only in the agent. The managed entity (the email server, the lawn sprinkler controller, the database server) does not have access to the row. When the agent "places the row into service," it requests that the underlying managed entity should create a new resource with the values specified in the row. Taking a row "out of service," or suspending it, means that the agent deletes the instance of the resource, after which the row exists only in the agent itself. Even though we have been showing traffic diagrams like those in Figure 8–9, a more accurate picture might be that shown in Figure 8–10.

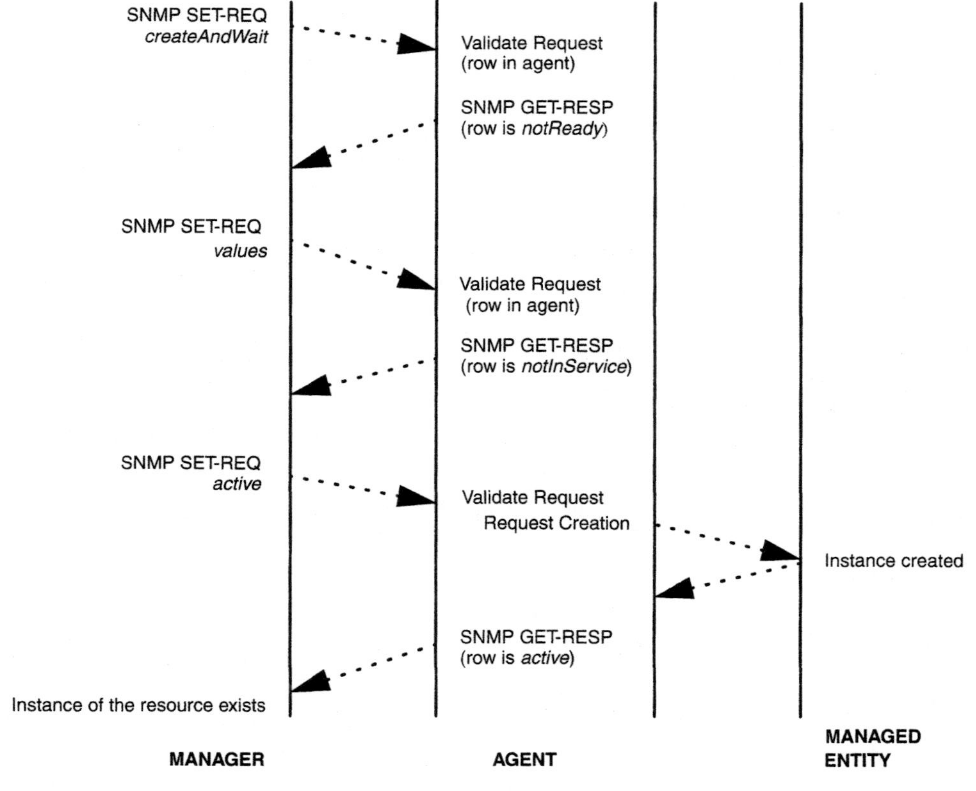

Figure 8–10 Interaction between Manager, Agent, and Managed Entity

In this scenario, the agent saves a copy of the values in the row, and only communicates with the managed entity when the row status is set to active. At that time, the agent requests the managed entity to create an instance of the resource modelled by the row.

It is also possible for an agent to communicate with a managed entity during row construction. This is shown in Figure 8–11.

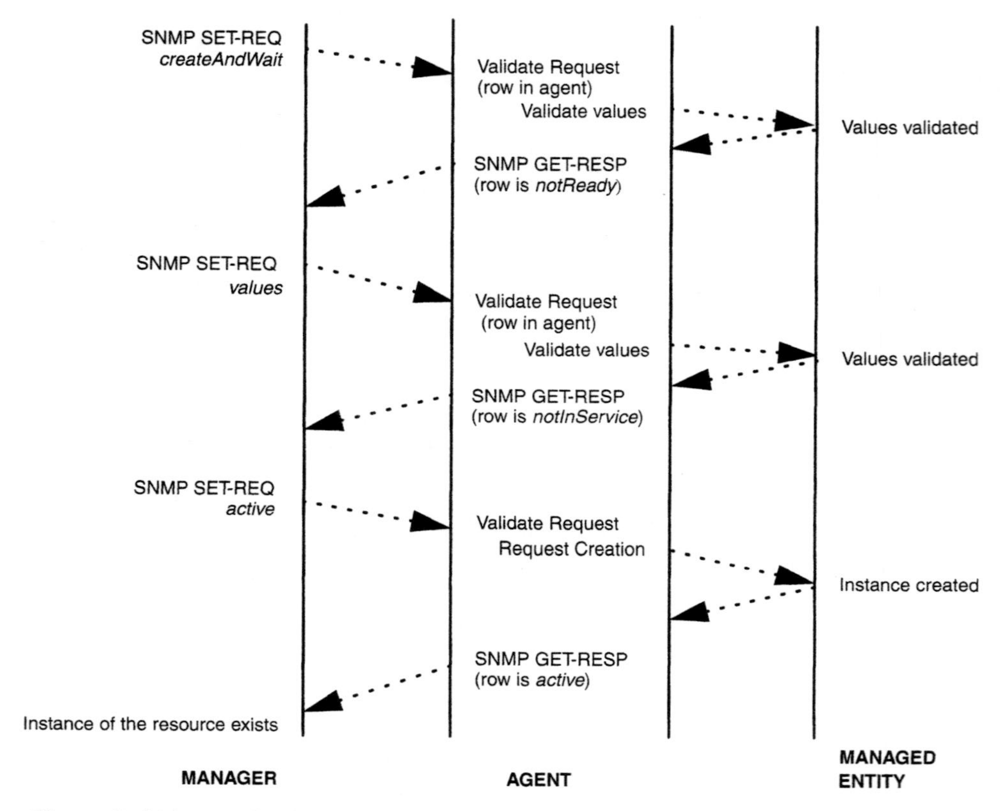

Figure 8–11 Interaction between Agent and Managed Entity During Construction

In this scenario, the agent communicates with the managed entity to confirm that the values requested by the manager are valid. The managed entity is not necessarily instructed to create a new resource until the row is marked as *active*. Now, all of these interactions seem quite reasonable, but they may have some implications that may have an impact on MIB design and implementation strategies for MIBs. The dribble mode of interaction makes the assumption that the agent is tightly coupled with the managed entity. That is, the agent is able to converse with the managed entity to confirm that the row it is holding is valid. If this were not the case, the agent would not discover that the row values where invalid until it attempted to place the row in service.

If you find that your agent implementation is unable to support the dribble mode creation sequence reliably, you should document this in your agent profile:

```
VARIATION        sprinklerProgramRowStatus
        WRITE- SYNTAX            INTEGER {
                                         createAndGo(4),
                                         destroy(6) }
                                         }
        DESCRIPTION     "Can only support one-shot creation and deletion"
```

There are several items to note about these interactions. Since SNMP implementations are not required to support PDU lengths of greater than 484 octets, not all rows can be created using the one-shot method. When designing a table, you should certainly keep this limitation in mind. Specifying rows with large numbers of required objects, or simply large objects will require management applications to use the more complex row creation technique. Consider a rough estimate of the requirements for encoding a PDU with 20 items whose OIDs are 15 sub-identifiers long. Assuming that all items are integers, we have a worst case scenario of 140 octets for the items and 340 octets for the OID values, which brings the total length to 480 octets. This does not even include the overhead of the SNMP header information, so this size is definitely greater than the minimum requirement. While this may not seem that bad, remember that the dribble-mode method of creation is completely optional. A good design goal for a row is:

Design rows that can be created in only one PDU.

Even in some situations where the items being modelled are inserted by an SNMP manager, row creation is not always needed. Take the example of a device that has a limited list of tasks which it can perform at some interval: a lawn sprinkler system, for instance. This lawn sprinkler controller can have five programs, of which zero or more are active. For this device, it is doubtful that it could ever feature support for an arbitrary number of programs—the number is simply fixed at five. In the MIB for this device, we want to have a group dealing with the creation of a watering schedule. Does full support of dynamic row creation make sense for this device? Doubtful. Does it make sense to have a table with five fixed entries each having a state variable indicating if the program was active? Probably. The key here is that the resources are fixed at a small manageable number, not dynamic ones which can be created at any time. The RowStatus syntax makes the somewhat naive assumption that agents have infinite resources, forcing the manager to guess at the reason for a row creation failure. If the lawn sprinkler controller implements a RowStatus variable, it does not have a clear way of communicating to the manager "*I can only implement five watering schedules, please don't ask to create a sixth one.*" By adding a column to the table with the syntax of

```
ProgramStatus ::= TEXTUAL CONVENTION
        STATUS          current
        SYNTAX          INTEGER { active(1), inActive(2) }
        DESCRIPTION
                "This column indicates whether or not a sprinkler
                program is currently in use or not"
```

each entry can state whether or not is being used by the sprinkler controller. If a sprinkler management program wants to create a new program, it can simply look for an entry that has a status of *inActive*.

The observant reader will note that another way to accomplish this is to have a column with the syntax of RowStatus, and have five initial entries, all with the current value of *notIn-Service*. The agent will accept only the desired states *notInService* and *active*. This approach will work, but many MIB readers will assume that using the RowStatus convention means that the agent allows dynamic creation of entries.

8.14.2 Resolving Concurrency Issues

Tables can also aid in resolving concurrency issues over use of a single resource. Let's return to the file transfer example we used in the previous section. One problem we tried to solve was associated with multiple managers accessing the transfer objects and inadvertently overwriting each other's transfer results. While our first approach to solving this was to add a small delay before the transfer object could be used again, we can use tables in a different approach that will be a bit more efficient. If we think of each requested transfer as an entry in a table, we can completely avoid the problem associated with managers interfering with one another. Before we begin re-designing our transfer objects, we should consider how we want the system to behave.

To complete a transfer:

- The manager creates a row with the parameters required for the transfer: the address, the file names, the direction.
- After setting up the parameters, the manager sets the row status to active to request the transfer.
- The agent, when resources become available, changes the state object to *transferring*, and begins the transfer.
- Upon completion, the agent sets the state object to *success* or one of the errors.
- The manager polls the state object to see the result from the transfer request.
- If needed, the manager can take the row out of service to change any of the transfer parameters, and then set the row status back to active to request a new transfer.
- When done, the manager requests that the agent delete the row associated with the transfer.

Now we can re-design our MIB fragment to accommodate this behavior:

```
xferNextIndex OBJECT-TYPE
        SYNTAX          Unsigned32(0..65535)
        MAX-ACCESS      read-only
        STATUS          current
        DESCRIPTION
                "Identifies a hint for the next value of xferIndex to be used in
                 a row creation attempt for the xferTable table. If no new rows
                can be created, this object will have a value of 0"
        ::= { xfer 1 }

xferTable OBJECT-TYPE
        SYNTAX          SEQUENCE of XferEntry
        MAX-ACCESS      not-accessible
        STATUS          current
        DESCRIPTION
                "The current list of in-progress and completed file transfer requests."
        ::= { xfer 2 }

xferEntry OBJECT-TYPE
        SYNTAX          XferEntry
        MAX-ACCESS      not-accessible
        STATUS          current
        DESCRIPTION
                "An entry in the transfer table. Rows are created by an SNMP
                SET request setting the value of xferRowStatus to 'createAndGo'
                or 'createAndWait'. Rows are deleted by an SNMP SET request
                setting the value of xferRowStatus to 'destroy'."
        INDEX           { xferIndex }
        ::= { xferTable 1 }

XferEntry ::= SEQUENCE {
        xferIndex           Unsigned32,
        xferLocalFile       DisplayString,
        xferRemoteFile      DisplayString,
        xferServer          IpAddress,
        xferDirection       INTEGER,
        xferState           INTEGER,
        xfeRowStatus        RowStatus }

xferIndex OBJECT-TYPE
        SYNTAX          Unsigned32(1..65535)
        MAX-ACCESS      not-accessible
        STATUS          current
        DESCRIPTION     "The row index"
        ::= { xferEntry 1 }
```

```
xferLocalFile OBJECT-TYPE
        SYNTAX          DisplayString
        MAX-ACCESS      read-create
        STATUS          current
        DESCRIPTION     "The name of the local file. Cannot be changed if the value
                        of xferRowStatus is active"
        ::= { xferEntry 2 }

xferRemoteFile OBJECT-TYPE
        SYNTAX          DisplayString
        MAX-ACCESS      read-create
        STATUS          current
        DESCRIPTION     "The name of the remote file. Cannot be changed if the value
                        of xferRowStatus is active"
        ::= { xferEntry 3 }

xferServer OBJECT-TYPE
        SYNTAX          IpAddress
        MAX-ACCESS      read-create
        STATUS          current
        DESCRIPTION     "The TFTP server address. Cannot be changed if the value
                        of xferRowStatus is active"
        ::= { xferEntry 4 }

xferDirection OBJECT-TYPE
        SYNTAX          INTEGER{ to(1), from(2) }
        MAX-ACCESS      read-create
        STATUS          current
        DESCRIPTION     "The direction of the transfer. Cannot be changed if the value
                        of xferRowStatus is active"
        ::= { xferEntry 5 }

xferState OBJECT-TYPE
        SYNTAX          INTEGER {
                                waitingToTransfer(1),
                                transferring (2),
                                sucess(3),
                                timeout(4),
                                noSuchFile(5) }
        MAX-ACCESS      read-only
        DESCRIPTION
                "The state of the transfer request"
        ::= { xferEntry 6 }
```

```
xferRowStatus OBJECT-TYPE
        SYNTAX          RowStatus
        MAX-ACCESS      read-create
        STATUS          current
        DESCRIPTION     "The status of the row"
        ::= { xferEntry 7 }
```

You may have noticed one unexpected item we placed in this MIB: *xferNextIndex*. To simplify things, we have indexed this table by a single integer value, *xferIndex*. When a management station is preparing to create an entry in the table, it needs to know the value of the of the index information it should use in the attempt. As this value cannot be known in advance, it has two choices: choose a value at random, and see if it can create a row using that value; or ask the agent which value it should use. Choosing a value at random may work, but the manager will always run the risk of choosing a value already selected by another manager. By letting the agent help this selection, we can ensure that this will not happen. The value of *xferNextIndex* is a hint by the agent of an index that is not currently used. The agent should ideally return a different value for each request for this object's value.

Let's examine the SNMP conversation between a manager and agent using this MIB as shown in Figure 8–12.

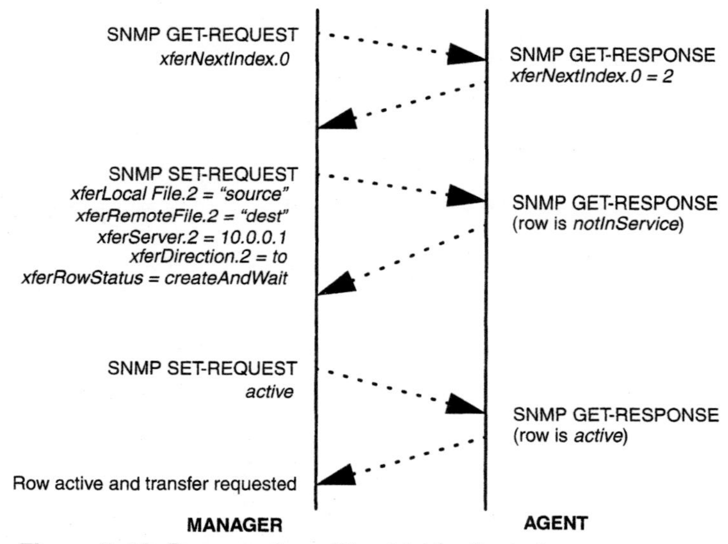

Figure 8–12 Row creation, with a hint for the index

In this example, the manager first asks the agent for a hint of a row index to use. The manager should attempt to create that row. If the row already exists, then the manager should ask for another hint.

8.14.3 INDEX SELECTION

As you will recall, when an application sweeps a table with the SNMP GET-NEXT operation, rows are returned in the order of the values of the variables specified in the INDEX clause for the table. If the field *sprinklerNumber* is the only field mentioned in the INDEX clause, a table sweep would return the entries in the order shown in Table 8–7.

Table 8–7 Single Index Table - INDEX { sprinklerNumber }

sprinklerNumber	sprinklerZone	sprinklerRate
1	3	5
2	1	7
3	2	4
4	2	6
5	3	2
6	3	9

However, indexing in this manner places a restriction on the table—the table can never represent two entries with the same *sprinklerNumber*, even if we wish to state that the sprinkler handles two different zones. If the indexing was changed to "INDEX { sprinklerZone, sprinklerNumber }", then we could have multiple sprinklers with the same number as long as they were in different zones. This indexing (after reassignment of sprinkler number) (see Table 8–8) would be more understandable than one with unique sprinkler numbers across all zones.

Table 8–8 Double Index Table - INDEX { sprinklerZone, SprinklerNumber }

sprinklerZone	sprinklerNumber	sprinklerRate
1	1	7
2	1	4
2	2	6
3	1	5
3	2	2
3	3	9

This creates a "doubly-indexed" table which is sorted by the tuple (*sprinklerZone, sprinklerNumber*).

Selecting the fields in a row which are used as the INDEX clause for a row sometimes involves trade-offs between the needs of management applications and management agents. There is a delicate balance between selecting what is semantically correct and what is practical to implement. In the previous examples, we have not had this problem. The indices selected were selected for good reasons. There are instances where the choice is not as obvious for somewhat hidden reasons.

The IETF defined Bridge MIB contains a table which contains forwarding information about media (MAC) addresses of devices. MAC addresses are represented by a 6 octet OCTET STRING to correspond to a 48 bit IEEE address. The details of how MAC layer bridges operate isn't important here. Suffice it to say that a bridge searches for the address of an incoming packet in an internal forwarding table. Based on the results of this lookup, it may forward the packet to another network. This is where agent implementors are caught in a pinch. The INDEX clause of the forwarding table is defined as:

```
INDEX { macAddress }
```

which indicates that the table must be sorted by MAC address. This sounds innocent enough until some important factors are examined:

- Bridges may have tens of thousands of entries in this table.
- Bridges do not necessarily store the entries in sorted order. Chances are, they are hashed.

This innocuous looking index statement has made life quite difficult for the agent implementor. It represents exactly what a management application wants, that is, making it easy to present a sorted list of addresses to the user. Agent implementations are left with two choices in this situation, and neither of them are acceptable: return the entries out of order, or sort the table. Returning the entries out of order would violate the SNMP GET-NEXT operator, so that approach should not be used. Sorting the table will invariably result in loss of performance for the device itself, as CPU time will be taken up maintaining the sorted list.

When faced with problems such as this, a good rule of thumb is to favor the device with the lowest resources: the agent.

If the table were indexed by an arbitrary integer instead of the address, it would be quite a bit easier to implement on the agent side, while causing management applications to spend a greater amount of time digesting the data (sorting it). This represents an equally onerous problem for the manager. If the table is sorted by an arbitrary integer, a manager cannot depend on the same integer representing a given address on two different bridges.

Moving on to other problem indices, tables indexed by object identifiers can be quite ungainly to manage. These tables, thankfully, are not that common.[7] They are quite difficult to implement efficiently and are best avoided. However, for some situations they are quite elegant. Let's look at an example of a MIB fragment where we have a legitimate need for this structure. This fragment is taken from the SMUX MIB. SMUX was an attempt to create a standard framework where a master SNMP agent could communicate with one or more sub-agents. The master agent dispatches incoming requests to sub-agents registered to process them by considering the registered priority of each sub-agent. Of course, here we are inter-

7. Out of approximately 100 MIBs, we could find only four situations where object identifiers were used as all or part of a table index.

ested in how this relationship was demonstrated in the MIB rather than the details of the actual architecture. The MIB sub-tree (an OBJECT IDENTIFIER), along with the sub-agent's priority, is registered in this table:

```
smuxTreeEntry  OBJECT-TYPE
        SYNTAX          SmuxTreeEntry
        ACCESS          not-accessible
        STATUS          mandatory
        DESCRIPTION     "An entry in the SMUX tree table."
        INDEX           { smuxTsubtree, smuxTpriority }
        ::= { smuxTreeTable 1}

SmuxTreeEntry ::= SEQUENCE {
                smuxTsubtree        OBJECT IDENTIFIER,
                smuxTpriority       INTEGER,
                smuxTindex          INTEGER,
                smuxTstatus         INTEGER
                }

smuxTsubtree   OBJECT-TYPE
        SYNTAX          OBJECT IDENTIFIER
        ACCESS          read-only
        STATUS          mandatory
        DESCRIPTION     "The MIB sub-tree being exported by a SMUX peer."
        ::= { smuxTreeEntry 1 }

smuxTpriority OBJECT-TYPE
        SYNTAX          INTEGER (0..'7fffffff'h)
        ACCESS          read-only
        STATUS          mandatory
        DESCRIPTION     "The SMUX peer's priority when exporting the MIB sub-tree."
        ::= { smuxTreeEntry 2 }
```

In this table, the *smuxTsubtree* is defined as part of the index so that we are assured that no two sub-agents can register to process the same MIB sub-tree at the same priority. There's really no better way to express this relationship. If we were to choose an arbitrary integer type as the index, we would open the door to conflicting registrations.

Now, we aren't claiming that tables containing object identifier indices are inherently bad. Rather, they bring up a few problems you may encounter. First, many implementations of them are either wrong, slow, or both. Some agents we've encountered have great difficulty processing the GET-NEXT operation on a table sorted by OIDs. Second, the instance information required to reference an object indexed by an object identifier can be equal to or greater than the name of the object itself! In some extreme instances, this indexing is not workable, since it would cause the 128 sub-identifier limit to be exceeded.

8.15 Event Design

Events are one of the topics within the network management community which will elicit one of two responses: scorn, "*They aren't reliable, so don't use them;*" or pragmatic appreciation, "*Gee, it would be useful if the device could try to tell me that it just caught on fire.*" This section will assume that you are of the second opinion. However limited they are, events reported by the TRAP operation are part of the management framework, and must be used carefully and sparingly to be effective. There are three general categories to keep in mind when defining events:

- *informational*, which represents non-critical conditions
- *warning*, which indicates pending failure or unexpected events
- *error*, which indicate that a catastrophic condition has occurred

Unfortunately, the category of an event is not absolute, but relative to other conditions that are occurring on the managed system and/or managed network. An event of "network interface down" is critical on a file server with one network interface. However, on a file server with multiple interfaces, the situation is not so critical. If the interface is connected to a shared medium and there is a problem with the medium, there is a critical network problem, but not a critical problem with the server's network interface. Just remember to view our categories as relative and not as absolute.

Informational events help management stations track the current state of a normally operating device. For instance, an event can indicate to a manager that a configuration has changed on a network interface. This may or may not represent an operational problem. *Warning* events are a bit more serious. They indicate that some monitored service has an unexpected condition which may have serious results. Examples of these events might be: an internal temperature reading exceeds the manufacturer's recommendation, or a user at the console of a device typed the wrong password three consecutive times. *Error* events indicate critical conditions for the monitored service. While SNMPv1 and SNMPv2 do not support these categories directly, it is a good idea to describe the importance level of the event in its definition.

If you will recall from the SNMP introduction, traps are messages initiated by the device or service. They are not a response to a request from the manager, although they may be a side effect of a request made by the manager. Perhaps it is a good idea to cover some situations where you would *not* use events. Since events are, by definition, not associated with any manager request, they should not be used to acknowledge operations.

It is tempting to use an event to acknowledge the completion of some manager requested operation (i.e., a file transfer), and we have seen some MIBs which mis-use events in this way. Remember that an event causes a trap to be sent to all managers configured to receive traps from an agent. Sending a *fileTransferFinished* trap to 20 different managers is useless traffic. Even though we pictured one manager and one agent in the protocol exchanges in the SNMP introduction, Figure 8–13 presents a more realistic example of what actually happens when an agent issues a trap.

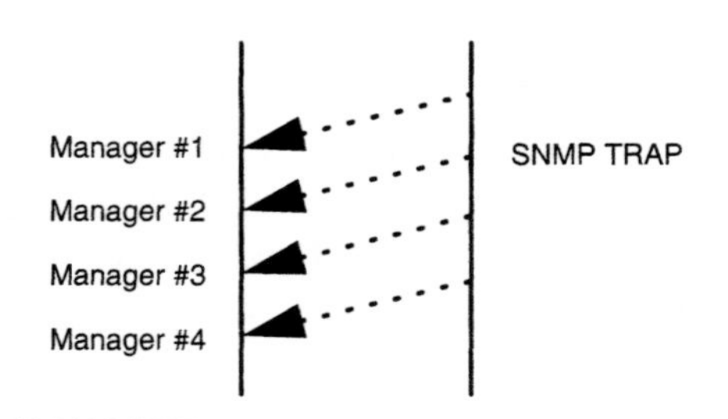

Figure 8–13 Issuing traps to multiple managers

Events are best used in aiding a management station in searching for unusual or alarming conditions. They should not be used as a substitute for a management station polling for critical information. For instance, management applications may query network devices to make sure that their network interfaces are up, but if the device can send a trap to the network management station indicating that a network cable has been disconnected from the interface, the problem will be spotted much sooner. This is the key criteria for defining an event: what problem or condition does it help diagnose? If you can't answer this question, the event in question isn't a good idea. Good event design should address these three questions.

- *"In what context did the condition occur?"*
- *"What is the problem?"*
- *"When is it appropriate to inform the manager?"*

Let's take the context problem first. A shortcoming of many events is that they force management stations to do too much detective work after a trap has been received. Fair examples of providing context are *linkDown/linkUp* events. These events are issued when a device's network interface fails or is returned to service. These events identify the interface whose state changed. Issued without any information, these events would force the manager to determine which interface actually changed state. Unless the management station had stored the previous state of the device, it would be difficult, if not impossible, to determine which interface changed state. Unfortunately, these events do not include other needed information, such as *ifOperStatus* and *ifAdminStatus*. The context is provided by the MIB objects listed in the VARIABLES clause of an SMIv1 TRAP-TYPE construct or the OBJECTS clause of an SMIv2 NOTIFICATION-TYPE construct.

Determining what problem to solve is a bit more difficult, and will depend on the managed system. Unfortunately, it is difficult to give guidance in this area, as the problems addressed by events are so varied. In general, it is best to use events only for those problems deemed mission-critical. Events only speed up the process of finding a problem in a managed system. They are not a substitute for monitoring.

Perhaps the most important point to consider when designing events is when the manager will be informed. This subject is not quite as simple as it first appears. A first reaction to this requirement is: *whenever the triggering event occurs, the agent should issue a trap*. On the surface, this seems to make perfect sense. If a device detects that one of its network interfaces has failed, it should attempt to inform the network management station. However, we need to consider some scenarios where this simplistic approach will actually cause more problems than it will solve. Suppose that the triggering event was something that could occur quite frequently: every time a certain type of network packet was seen, or every time a car's spark plug failed to fire. In situations such as these, a management station would be flooded with traps, and may spend more time accepting them than it does tracking down the cause of the problem. To prevent these situations, it is important to design in some sort of flow control function. There are two approaches we can use for providing this sort of flow control over an agent's unsolicited messages: management station suppression and agent rate limiting. With management station suppression, the technique is quite simple: the agent is instructed to refrain from issuing certain traps until further notice. With trap rate limiting, the process of issuing a trap takes into account the number, type, and frequency of traps issued in the recent past. If too many traps have been issued in a short span of time, the agent may choose not to send one at all in an attempt to relieve (or avoid) trap congestion.

8.16 Learn by Doing

In this chapter we've tried to provide some nuts-and-bolts suggestions for getting work done, but we probably haven't answered every problem you may be facing as a MIB writer. It's important to remember that you aren't alone. If you have questions on how to tackle a particular problem, you should see if someone else has already solved it, or is at least working in the same area. Try some of the resources listed in resource Appendix D: "Guide to SNMP Resources."

CHAPTER 9

Advanced Techniques: Data Structures and Data Types

This chapter deals with advanced techniques in MIBs, especially in dealing with tables in MIBs. The only data structure "built into" the SNMPv1 and SNMPv2 frameworks is the list contained within the table. Fortunately enough, the table can be used as a building block for higher level structures. Additionally, we will also cover some techniques for improving table access speed and retrieval efficiency. Finally, we will examine several techniques for defining types not present in SNMPv1 or SNMPv2.

9.1 Tables within Tables

The SNMP SMI does not allow a MIB writer to state that an object in a table is an array (an ASN.1 sequence). This restriction is known as the problem in the SNMP community. This restriction, known as "no table in a table" in the SNMP community, is a frequent source of frustration for beginning SNMP MIB designers. For software engineers accustomed to using complex data structures, an array within a table would seem to be a simple, straightforward approach to solving certain modelling problems.

Consider the following definitions in a C program for a table called *t1* containing an array called *ai*:

```
struct {
        int i;
        int ai[20];
} t1[40];
```

You might try to create the following MIB definitions for the table:

```
t1Table OBJECT-TYPE
        SYNTAX          SEQUENCE OF T1Entry
        . . .

t1Entry OBJECT-TYPE
        SYNTAX          T1Entry
        . . .
        INDEX           { t1Index }
        . . .

T1Entry ::= SEQUENCE {
        t1Index   Unsigned,
        t1I       Integer32,
        t1A1      SEQUENCE OF Integer32 -- not allowed by SNMP SMI
        }


t1Index OBJECT-TYPE
        SYNTAX          Unsigned32(1..40)
        MAX-ACCESS      not-accessible
        . . .

t1I OBJECT-TYPE
        SYNTAX          Integer32,
        . . .

t1A1 OBJECT-TYPE
        SYNTAX          SEQUENCE SIZE(1..20) -- not allowed by SNMP SMI
                                  OF Integer32
```

If you remember from Chapter 3, only a table object may be defined with SYNTAX value of “SEQUENCE OF <type>”. Thus the definition of object t1Ai is not valid. A valid definition is the following:

```
t1Table OBJECT-TYPE
        SYNTAX          SEQUENCE OF T1Entry
        . . .

t1Entry OBJECT-TYPE
        SYNTAX          T1Entry
        . . .
        INDEX           { t1Index }
        . . .
```

```
T1Entry ::= SEQUENCE {
        t1Index             Unsigned,
        t1I                 Integer32
        }

t1Index OBJECT-TYPE
        SYNTAX              Unsigned32(1..40)
        MAX-ACCESS          not-accessible
        . . .

t1I OBJECT-TYPE
        SYNTAX              Integer32,
        . . .

t1A1Table OBJECT-TYPE
        SYNTAX              SEQUENCE OF T1A1Entry
        . . .

t1A1Entry OBJECT-TYPE
        SYNTAX              T1A1Entry
        . . .
        INDEX               { t1Index, t1A1Index }
        . . .

T1A1Entry ::= SEQUENCE {
        t1A1Index           Unsigned32,
        t1A1                Integer32
        }

t1A1Index OBJECT-TYPE
        SYNTAX              Unsigned32(1..20)
        MAX-ACCESS          not-accessible
. . .

t1A1 OBJECT-TYPE
        SYNTAX              Integer32
```

As you can see, the transformation is straightforward. You just create a second table that takes the indices of the first table and adds one more. You may also notice that it takes many more lines in a MIB module to express a definition written in the C programming language.

In general, when we have a situation where there is a list (an SNMP table) and for each item in the list we want to specify zero, one, or more records of another type, then we use a base table and an expansion table. The expansion table contains the new record types and is indexed from the indices of the base table plus those additional indices needed to identify records in the expansion table. This is shown in Figure 9–1.

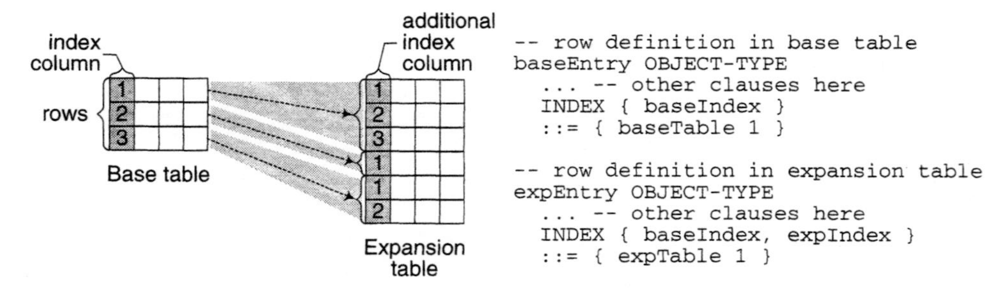
index column
rows
1
2
3
Base table
additional index column
1
2
3
1
1
2
Expansion table
-- row definition in base table
baseEntry OBJECT-TYPE
... -- other clauses here
INDEX { baseIndex }
::= { baseTable 1 }
-- row definition in expansion table
expEntry OBJECT-TYPE
... -- other clauses here
INDEX { baseIndex, expIndex }
::= { expTable 1 }

Figure 9–1 Solution to table within a table problem

9.2 Linked Lists

Before we examine some of the advanced techniques used with tables, we need to introduce *linked lists*. The MIB tables we have discussed thus far have represented simple sorted lists of information. A related technique familiar to many programmers is that of a linked list. A somewhat simplistic difference between the two would be: a linked list allows an application to traverse the data in an order independent of the order in which it is stored, while simple sorted lists are always traversed in their storage order. This definition isn't completely accurate, but it will do for our purposes.

Consider a simple sorted list of six numbers as in Table 9–1.

Table 9–1 A Simple Sorted List

Index	Number
1	34
2	456
3	645
4	765
5	867
6	868

Using SNMP, there is only one way to traverse this list: reading one item at a time, proceeding to the next one in the order they are stored within the table.[1] This works fine as long as the storage order is the same as the sorting order, but this becomes a problem when the storage order differs from the sorting order, as shown in Table 9–2:

1. Note that by traversal, we do not mean *retrieval*. SNMPv2's GET-BULK operation is a fast retrieval mechanism, not a fast traversal algorithm.

Table 9–2 An Unsorted List

Index	Number
1	546
2	324
3	645
4	987
5	867
6	868

To separate the sorting order of a table from the storage order, we need to convert the table into a linked list. With a linked list, we use a separate field, a *next* pointer, to indicate the next item in the table, rather than depending on the storage order to indicate the next item. We use the value zero to indicate a NULL pointer (i.e., no next item). This is shown in Table 9–3.

Table 9–3 A Linked List

Index	Number	Next
1	546	3
2	324	1
3	645	5
4	987	0
5	867	6
6	868	4

To find the number that follows 645, for instance, we would look at the *next* field associated with that entry. In this case, the value is 5. The next field in the sorting order is 867. To find the first item in the linked list, we need a scalar object whose value is the index of the first item in the list, or zero to show the list is empty.

We will use the linked list concept in several places in the next few sections by showing how to improve table access speed and designing tables that are more flexible in their data representation. The key concept here is that tables must be designed to be both logically stored and efficiently retrieved. The indexing mechanism supplied by the SMI may not always meet both goals, so it is up to the MIB designer to correct this shortcoming.

9.3 Fast Table Lookups

Table traversal is arguably the most time and bandwidth consuming aspect of SNMP based management. An application might not know the identification of a particular instance of interest. As a result, it may be forced to sift through hundreds or thousands of entries to locate the specific one of interest. SNMPv2's GET-BULK operation is not necessarily a solution to the problem of speeding up table access. While GET-BULK is helpful in fetching large chunks of a table very quickly, it isn't helpful in locating objects in a table. To significantly speed up certain operations, the manager must be able to access the exact items required in the fewest possible exchanges between the manager and agent. The fundamental problem with the MIB structure is that rows in tables are indexed by what makes them unique, not by what makes lookups easier. In some tables, of course, the index meets both goals, but that is not always the case. When an application uses SNMP's GET-NEXT operation to retrieve items from a table, the concept of the "next" item is determined by the content of the indices. If the indices do not contain the data of interest to the management station, the data must be examined row by row. A further drawback of the way SNMP orders table entries is that the indices are in a fixed order. That is, secondary indices provide a sorting order relative only to the *first* index.

If a table is to be traversed by order of a secondary index, the entire table must be retrieved and sorted on the management station. This is neither efficient nor fast. Relational databases solve this problem by allowing secondary indices on a table, and MIBs can use a similar technique. One simple way to speed up table access without altering a table structure is to provide a secondary table with indices into the original table. Consider the following case as in Table 9–4.

Table 9–4 Sprinkler Table

Sprinkler ID	FlowRate
1	2
3	3
12	1
20	1
21	5
22	4

In this table, the minimum index field would be *sprinklerId*, since that row item disambiguates each row. However, suppose that a management application needed to present data in terms of certain *flowRates*. It would be convenient to have the table ordered by this secondary index as well. Giving the table the INDEX clause

INDEX { sprinklerID, flowRate }

does not sort the table as the application needs. In fact, in the above example, the row order is not affected. Consequently, the management software is still required to retrieve the entire table to find the flow rate needed. What this table needs is a separate index field, either internal to the table or defined within a separate table.

To define another internal index, we can simply add another field to the table which indicates the next *sprinklerID* in the order of increasing flow rates as in Table 9–5.

Table 9–5 Sprinkler Table with Auxiliary Index

Sprinkler ID	FlowRate	RateIndex
1	2	3
3	3	22
12	1	20
20	1	1
21	5	0
22	4	21

Finding the head of the flow rate list is a bit more difficult in this situation. To allow the management software to do this, we need to define a separate object which contains the *sprinklerID* of the head of the list sorted by *rateIndex*.

```
rateIndexHead OBJECT-TYPE
        SYNTAX          SprinklerID        -- INTEGER (1..100)
        MAX-ACCESS      read-only
        STATUS          current
        DESCRIPTION     "Defines the head of the list sorted by FlowRate"
        ::= { sprinklers 5 }
```

In the previous example, this variable would have the value *20*.

Placing this list internal to the table is convenient, but a bit demanding on agents. Another approach is to define this as a separate table with only the secondary index information in it. (See Table 9–6)

Table 9–6 Secondary Index Table

RateID	RateIndex
1	3
2	22
3	20
4	1
5	0
6	21

9.3.1 Index Computation

A third approach that can be used to speed up table access is *index computation*. This technique can be used to speed up table access where the "interesting" columns in the row do not form part of the index, yet applications need to access rows keyed on those columns. Earlier we outlined some reasons why the interesting data cannot always easily be contained within the index. The MAC addresses contained within a 802.1d bridge, for example, are sometimes stored in a data structure known as hash tables, not in sorted lists. Consequently, the agent must transform the native data structure, the hash table, to the SNMP table structure, the sorted MIB table.

Requiring that the agent maintain a list of sorted MAC addresses is at odds with many MAC layer bridge implementations, and might be an unreasonable burden to the agent or the underlying bridging software. Indexing the table by a simple integer makes an agent implementation a bit easier, but now the management software has a difficult time finding the entries needed. Since all entries are stored by an arbitrary index, such as a single INTEGER, looking up the entry associated with a particular MAC address requires a worst case retrieval of all table entries. To allow for speedier access in this case, we can create an object which, given the MAC address of interest, will return the index associated with that address. Indexing the table by a simple integer means that, in the worst case, all entries must be examined before finding the entry of interest (O(n) in algorithms analysis parlance). By adding an index computation object, we regain the constant search time for the table traversal that we had with the original design (O(1)).

To see how this object can be added, let's take the example of the table holding MAC addresses. This is the original specification for the table.

```
macEntry OBJECT-TYPE
        SYNTAX          MacEntry
        MAX-ACCESS      not-accessible
        STATUS          current
        DESCRIPTION     "An example entry"
        INDEX           { macAddress }
        ::= { mac 1 }
```

where macAddress is a 48 bit OCTET STRING:

```
macAddress OBJECT-TYPE
        SYNTAX          OCTET STRING (SIZE(6))
        MAX-ACCESS      not-accessible
        STATUS          current
        DESCRIPTION     "The MAC address"
        ::= { macEntry 1 }
```

This requires an agent implementation to have access to a sorted list of MAC addresses, or to sort them when requested to perform a GET-NEXT operation. To ease this requirement, we can declare the table this way:

```
macEntry OBJECT-TYPE
        SYNTAX          MacEntry
        MAX-ACCESS      not-accessible
        STATUS          current
        DESCRIPTION     "An example entry"
        INDEX           { macIndex }
        ::= { mac 1 }
```

where *macIndex* is a simple integer.

```
macIndex OBJECT-TYPE
        SYNTAX          Unsigned32(1..65535)
        MAX-ACCESS      not-accessible
        STATUS          current
        DESCRIPTION     "The index of the table"
        ::= { macEntry 1 }

macAddress OBJECT-TYPE
        SYNTAX          OCTET STRING (SIZE(6))
        MAX-ACCESS      read-only
        STATUS          current
        DESCRIPTION     "The MAC address"
        ::= { macEntry 2}
```

Declaring the table this way has eased the burden on agents. It can keep the MAC addresses in any order it chooses. However, the management station now has a difficult time locating specific entries. Using only these objects, the manager will be forced to retrieve the entire table just to find the entry corresponding to a particular MAC address. To avoid this inefficiency, we can declare a new control object that will accept a search address and add the results to a secondary table, which is indexed as the management station would like.

First we create a new table:

```
macSecondaryEntry OBJECT-TYPE
        SYNTAX          MacSecondaryEntry
        MAX-ACCESS      not-accessible
        STATUS          current
        DESCRIPTION     "An example entry"
        INDEX           { macSecondaryAddress }
```

```
MacSecondaryEntry ::= SEQUENCE {
        macSecondaryAddress        MACAddress
        macSecondaryIndex          Unsigned32
        macSecondaryRowStatus      RowStatus
}

macSecondaryAddress OBJECT-TYPE
        SYNTAX          MACAddress
        MAX-ACCESS      not-accessible
        STATUS          current
        DESCRIPTION     "The MAC address"
        ::= { macSecondaryEntry 1 }

macSecondaryIndex OBJECT-TYPE
        SYNTAX          Unsigned(1..65535)
        MAX-ACCESS      read-only
        STATUS          current
        DESCRIPTION
                "Specifies the value of the index field in the macTable
                corresponding to the macSecondaryAddress. A value of
                zero indicates that no such entry with the specified
                MAC address exists"
        ::= { macSecondaryEntry 2 }
```

And a new row status and creation object:

```
macSecondaryRowStatus OBJECT-TYPE
        SYNTAX          RowStatus
        MAX-ACCESS      read-create
        STATUS          current
        DESCRIPTION
                "This object controls creation of an entry in the
                macTableSecondary table"
        :: { macSecondaryEntry 3 }
```

If a manager is trying to find the entry in the *macTable* which corresponds to a particular MAC address, it can follow these steps:

1. Look in the *macSecondaryTable* table to see if there is an entry for that MAC address. Another manager may have already requested a lookup of this address.
2. If the entry is not found, create a row in the *macSecondaryTable* table indexed by the the MAC address in question. The agent will supply the value for *macSecondaryIndex* when the row is created.
3. Get the value of *macSecondaryIndex*. If the value is not zero, then use it to index the row in table *macTable*. Otherwise, the MAC address is not in table *macTable*.

Providing this secondary table has an additional advantage: it functions as a cache of lookup items. Frequently referenced items are made available to all stations, so this further increases the efficiency of the agent.

9.4 Hash Tables

Hashing is a common storage technique in which a program organizes large data sets into smaller, more manageable sets. Retrieving a specific data item is typically a two-step process: locating the smaller data set, and then searching that data set for the record. Hashing computes the storage location of a data record using a *key*, a member of the actual record, and a *hash function*, an algorithm which performs some mathematical manipulation of the key. By applying the hash function to the key, a program can determine the storage location, called a *bucket*, of the entire data record. The bucket typically contains a number of records, and is searched sequentially for the desired record. This technique is quite similar to index computation. In fact, the index computation example is really just a form of hashing. The twist that we will add here is that we will use a hybrid technique of index computation and linear search to retrieve entries from the table.

By using a hybrid of the technique used earlier with the bridge table and a linear search of the table, we can model hash tables in a MIB.

Using linked lists, we can easily define hash tables which form internal sort lists or external secondary indices. Let's take a simple example of a hash scheme where some function $F(x)$ computes a hash bucket B for the item x, and uses an index i within the bucket to indicate the location of x within that bucket.

We can declare the hash table itself as:

```
hashTable OBJECT-TYPE
        SYNTAX          SEQUENCE OF HashEntry
        MAX-ACCESS      not-accessible
        STATUS          current
        DESCRIPTION     "..."
        ::= { hash 1 }


hashEntry OBJECT-TYPE
        SYNTAX          HashEntry
        MAX-ACCESS      not-accessible
        STATUS          current
        DESCRIPTION     "..."
        INDEX           { hashBucket, hashIndex }
        ::= { hashTable 1 }
```

```
HashEntry ::= SEQUENCE {
        hashBucket        HashValue,
        hashIndex         HashIndex
        hashData1         Integer32,
        hashData2         Integer32
        }

hashBucket OBJECT-TYPE
        SYNTAX            HashValue
        MAX-ACCESS        not-accessible
        STATUS            current
        DESCRIPTION
                "This indicates the bucket number of the data item"
        ::= { hashEntry 1 }

hashIndex OBJECT-TYPE
        SYNTAX            HashIndex
        MAX-ACCESS        not-accessible
        STATUS            current
        DESCRIPTION
                "This indicates the linear position of the data item within
                the hash bucket"
        ::= { hashEntry 2 }


hashData1 OBJECT-TYPE
        SYNTAX            Integer32
        MAX-ACCESS        read-only
        STATUS            current
        DESCRIPTION       "The first data point"
        ::= { hashEntry 3 }


hashData2 OBJECT-TYPE
        SYNTAX            Integer32
        MAX-ACCESS        read-only
        STATUS            current
        DESCRIPTION       "The second data point"
        ::= { hashEntry 4 }
```

We can also create index computation objects to allow the management stations to quickly locate an item by value. (See Table 9–7)

Table 9–7 Hash Table

Bucket	Index	Data1	Data2
1	1	132	3
2	1	512	12
2	2	642	34
3	2	711	34
4	1	1035	23
4	2	1053	12

9.5 Binary Trees

A binary tree is a data structure commonly used for holding collections of ordered data. Within the tree, we have a special object known as the *root* object. The root object forms the base of the tree, and for our purposes, it is the starting point of any tree traversal we perform. The remaining objects of the tree are divided into two sets, known as children. Each child, usually referred to as either the *left* or *right* child, forms its own binary tree. If you examine a graphical representation of a binary tree, you will quickly see how it gets its name: each node on the graph has two children hanging from it. The nodes without children, known as the *leaf* nodes, form the base of the tree. The binary tree has levels associated with each "row" of objects. Looking at Figure 9–2, you can see that the tree forms a pyramid. The top of the tree, the *root*, is known as level 0. The lower levels are numbered increasingly from 1 to *n*, where the *n* row forms the base of the tree. A *complete* binary tree is one in which every row except row *n* has objects with both left and right children.

A binary tree representation in a MIB is a simple addition to the linked list concept. Let's say that we wanted to represent the following tree of values:

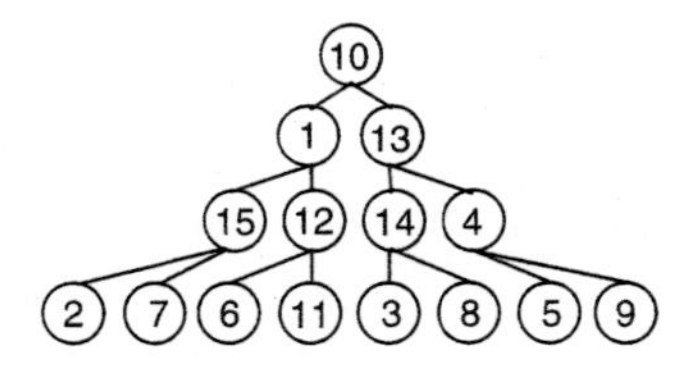

Figure 9–2 A binary tree

These values can be represented by adding a left and right field as additional row objects to form Table 9–8. Note that NULL pointers have the value zero in the table.

Now for the clincher: this can be defined without any additional objects. The *left* and *right* columns in the table are not even required. By taking the index number *N* of an item, the

Table 9–8 Binary Tree Table Representation

Index	Value	Left	Right
1	10	2	3
2	1	4	5
3	13	6	7
4	15	8	9
5	12	10	11
6	14	12	13
7	4	0	0
8	2	0	0
9	7	0	0
10	6	0	0
11	11	0	0
12	3	0	0
13	8	0	0
14	5	0	0
15	6	0	0

index of the left child can be obtained by $2N$ and the right by $2N+1$. For instance, the right child of node at index 2 (value 1) is 2*2 = 4. The left child is (2*2) + 1 = 5.

Currently, this relationship cannot be expressed in the MIB declaration, so it is a good idea to explain this in the DESCRIPTION clauses of the table and index object declaration.

9.6 Multi-Dimensional Arrays

The indexing schemes introduced in the previous section can be extended into multiple dimensions. Most tables are indexed such that they model a simple one dimensional array, commonly called a list. To model such concepts as a two dimensional array, a matrix, we need to structure the indices a bit differently. In this instance, we can introduce additional fields into the INDEX clause to model the new dimensions. Given simple INTEGER index fields, we can use an index clause similar to:

```
rowEntry OBJECT-TYPE
        SYNTAX          RowEntry
        MAX-ACCESS      not-accessible
        STATUS          current
        DESCRIPTION     "An example entry"
        INDEX           {row, column, depth }
```

Figure 9–3 demonstrates the organization of this table, and shows the instance information associated with each cell. In this index clause, we are declaring a three dimensional array.

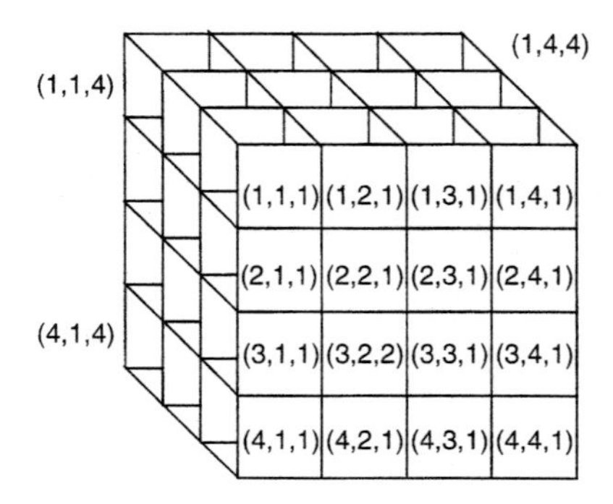

Figure 9–3 Multidimensional Array

Management software utilizing this table can quickly traverse in any dimension desired simply by increasing or decreasing the correct index (This assumes a dense table; we will cover sparse tables shortly). To traverse across a row, a manager must increment the *column* portion of the index: (n,1,n), (n,2,n), (n,3,n), (n,4,n). To traverse down a column, the manager increments the *row* portion of the index: (1,n,n), (2,n,n), (3,n,n), (4,n,n). Finally, to traverse the table in Z order (front to back), the *depth* field can be incremented. Structuring a table like this allows very efficient table traversals using the GET-NEXT operation. The techniques covered thus far can be used in conjunction with each other to form arbitrarily complex relationships such as: a three dimensional table with the cell contents a reference to another table.

9.7 Floating Point Numbers

In the current SMI there is no way to represent floating point numbers directly. ASN.1 does define a REAL type, but the SMI does not allow us to use this type when defining MIBs. To help us solve this problem, let's look at the definition for a REAL in ASN.1 for some ideas. A real number consists of three components: a mantissa, a numeric base, and an exponent. A floating point number can be described using this expression:

$$\textit{Number value} = \textit{Mantissa} * \textit{Base}^{\textit{Exponent}}$$

Thus, the number 123.204 can be expressed as $123204 * 10^{-3}$. Before we present some solutions, the terms precision and range need to be defined:

- Precision—the number of digits that have significance in the mantissa
- Range—the difference between the smallest and largest value of the exponent

9.7.1 Fixed Range Numbers

When the range of the numbers is fixed, but the numbers cannot be expressed as an integer, our solution is quite simple: choose the units carefully, and represent every value as an integer. For example, suppose you are defining a MIB object that measures electrical current, and need to represent values such as 12.34 volts or 56.89 volts. If the values are represented as millivolts (thousandths of a volt) instead of volts, we can avoid the use of floating numbers altogether. In this case, the value would be 1234 millivolts. The *base* and *exponent* described above are constants in this equation. Managers wishing to display the value in volts can legitimately convert the value to the desired units.

```
voltageLevel OBJECT-TYPE
        SYNTAX          Unsigned32
        UNITS           "millivolts"
        MAX-ACCESS      read-only
        STATUS          current
        DESCRIPTION     "The current output level"
        ::= { voltage 1 }
```

9.7.2 Varying Range Numbers

Representing variable range numbers is more of a challenge. In this case we need to provide at least two of the required components: the mantissa and the exponent. The base can be assumed to be 10, but we are, of course, free to provide that as well.

```
-- These objects represent pieces of the equation M * B^E
voltageLevelMantissa OBJECT-TYPE
        SYNTAX          Unsigned32
        UNITS           "volts"
        MAX-ACCESS      read-only
        STATUS          current
        DESCRIPTION
                "The current output level expressed in volts. This number is
                actually the mantissa M of the equation M * B^E"
        ::= { voltage 1 }


voltageLevelBase OBJECT-TYPE
        SYNTAX          INTEGER { two(2), ten(10), sixteen(16) }
        MAX-ACCESS      read-only
        STATUS          current
        DESCRIPTION     "The base (B) of the value"
        ::= { voltage 2 }
```

```
voltageLevelExponent OBJECT-TYPE
        SYNTAX          Integer32
        MAX-ACCESS      read-only
        STATUS          current
        DESCRIPTION     "The exponent (E) to which the base is raised"
        ::= { voltage 3 }
```

This technique is obviously expensive, as it requires three MIB objects to represent one value, but it may be required in some cases.

9.7.3 Displayable Strings

Another technique you can employ to represent floating point numbers is to use displayable strings to encode them. Returning once again to our voltage example, here is a declaration for an object using octet strings to encode floating point numbers:

```
voltageLevel OBJECT-TYPE
        SYNTAX          DisplayString (SIZE (12))
        UNITS           "volts"
        MAX-ACCESS      read-only
        STATUS          current
        DESCRIPTION
                "The current output level expressed in volts. The value is expressed as
                the ASCII representation of the floating point value in format
                   sD.DDDDDEsDD
                Where 's' is a plus or minus sign, 'D' is a digit, and 'E' is the letter 'E'.
                Examples are: -3.17234E+00 and +5.00234E-12"
        ::= { voltage 1 }
```

Just to be clear: the value contained within the voltage level object is the printable ASCII values for the numbers, not the numeric values. These values must be converted back into a some native format to be of use to either the manager or the agent. The size of the octet string is determined by the precision of the floating point number. Our example showed a "single precision" floating point number.

9.7.4 Float in Opaque Wrappers

An alternative approach, especially useful if you are in control of both the agent as well as the management software, is to use of the *Opaque* type to add single and double precision numbers encoded in the IEEE format. Any time that we use the SNMP Opaque type, we must realize that generic management applications, such as MIB browsers and trenders, will have no idea of how to unwrap these objects. Of course, this also applies when the values are encoded as displayable strings or as mantissa and the exponent. The description of the Opaque type in Chapter 2 contained an example of how to use this type to encode 64-bit counters for use in SNMPv1. The same approach can also be used to encode values in the

IEEE format. We don't suggest that the ASN.1 REAL type be used, since it requires extra processing to encode and decode it and provides no advantages over the IEEE format.

Single precision floating point using IEEE encoding:

```
-- The textual convention for an Opaque based single precision floating point
Float ::= Opaque (SIZE(. . .)) -- important details left out

voltageLevel OBJECT-TYPE
        SYNTAX          Float
        UNITS           "volts"
        MAX-ACCESS      read-only
        STATUS          current
        DESCRIPTION
                "The current output level expressed in volts."
        ::= { voltage 1 }
```

Double precision floating point using IEEE encoding:

```
-- The textual convention for an Opaque based double precision floating point
Double ::= Opaque (SIZE(. . .)) -- important detail left out

voltageLevel OBJECT-TYPE
        SYNTAX          Double
        UNITS           "volts"
        MAX-ACCESS      read-only
        STATUS          current
        DESCRIPTION
                "The current output level expressed in volts."
        ::= { voltage 1 }
```

9.8 64 and 32 Bit Counters

One of the problems with using the SNMPv2 type Counter64 in a MIB definition is the lack of SNMPv1 interoperability. Since SNMPv1 does not have the Counter64 type, any MIB defined using it can't be implemented using SNMPv1.[2] There are several techniques we can use to allow these agents to model data found only in 64 bit counters.

9.8.1 Splitting the Data

Since SNMPv1 can implement the Counter32 type, a fairly simple solution is to split the Counter64 object into two 32 bit counters. These two new counters model the high and low order 32 bits of the original object, as Figure 9–4 demonstrates.

2. SNMPv1 agents must return *NoSuchName* when queried for that object's value.

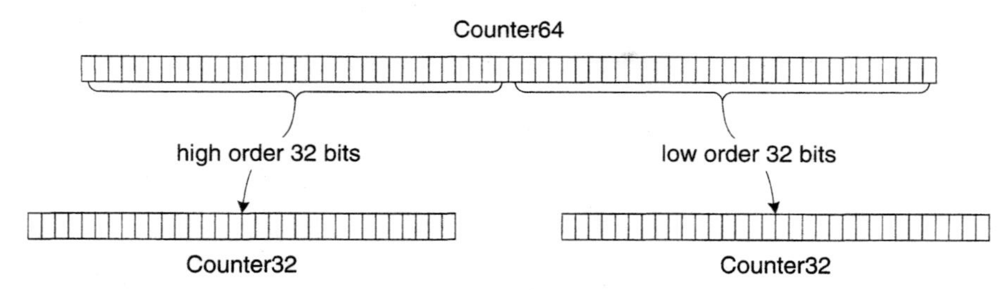

Figure 9–4 Splitting a Counter64 into two Counter32s

The original value is represented by this equation:

Reconstructing a 64 Bit Counter

$$Counter64 = (High\ order\ Counter32 * 2^{32}) + (Low\ order\ Counter32)$$

Of course, the disadvantage of this technique is that applications must have built-in knowledge of the splitting algorithm to reconstruct the actual value of the counter. This is not to say that other applications cannot use the data, although it is easy to misinterpret. To an application examining only the lower order Counter32, it appears to be a counter that wraps more often than it should. This begins to be a problem when faced with a counter that increases at an extremely high rate.

Here's an example of some counters declared using this technique:

```
-- First, declare a textual convention for the two Counters
C64LOW          TEXTUAL-CONVENTION
        STATUS          current
        DESCRIPTION     "This counter represents the low order 32 bits of
                        a 64 bit counter. Objects declared using this type
                        should have a corresponding object of type
                        C64LOW. These two objects should always
                        be retrieved in the same SNMP operation. Even so, there is
                        no guarantee that the value of the other object did not change
                        in between retrieval operations."
        SYNTAX          Counter32

C64HIGH         TEXTUAL-CONVENTION
        STATUS          current
        DESCRIPTION     "This counter represents the high order 32 bits of
                        a 64 bit counter. Objects declared using this type
                        should have a corresponding object of type
                        C64HIGH. These two objects should always
```

```
                          be retrieved in the same SNMP operation. Even so, there is
                          no guarantee that the value of the other object did not change
                          in between retrieval operations."
        SYNTAX            Counter32

packetCounterLow OBJECT-TYPE
        SYNTAX            C64LOW
        ACCESS            read-only
        STATUS            current
        DESCRIPTION
                          "This counter contains the lower 32 bits of the actual
                          value of the packet counter"
        ::= { trafficCounters 1 }

packetCounterHigh OBJECT-TYPE
        SYNTAX            C64HIGH
        ACCESS            read-only
        STATUS            current
        DESCRIPTION
                          "This counter contains the higher 32 bits of the actual
                          value of the packet counter"
        ::= { trafficCounters 2}
```

9.8.2 64-Bit Counters in Opaque Wrappers

An alternative approach, especially useful if you are in control of both the agent as well as the management software, is to use of the *Opaque* type to add the SNMPv2 type Counter64 to SNMPv1. Any time that we use the SNMP Opaque type, we must realize that generic management applications, such as MIB browsers and trenders, will have no idea of how to unwrap these objects. Of course, this also applies when the values are split into upper and lower values. The description of the Opaque type in Chapter 2 contained an example of how to use this type to encode 64-bit counters for use in SNMPv1. The opaque type has historically been underutilized, partially due to uncertainty about its proper use, but primarily due to the fact that opaque objects are not terribly useful for simple applications such as MIB browsers. Whatever the reasons for the low usage of the type, it is perfectly legal to use it in SNMPv1 MIB modules.

If you will recall from our earlier discussions of Opaque, it can be used to "double-wrap" an item. While the original SNMPv1 framework did not clearly state so, this type is intended to encapsulate only BER encoded objects. It is not intended as a general wrapper mechanism for "foreign" encodings such as XDR, or even plain ASCII. Some sources have incorrectly reported that these other encodings are acceptable.

Using an opaque wrapper, we can allow an SNMPv1 agent to implement the Counter64 type by hiding it in an opaque wrapper. We would declare the double wrapped counter this way:

```
-- The textual convention for an Opaque based Counter64
C64 ::= Opaque (SIZE(. . .)) -- important details left out

packetCounter    OBJECT-TYPE
        SYNTAX          C64
        ACCESS          read-only
        STATUS          current
        DESCRIPTION
                "This value indicates the total number of packets that have been sent
                from this interface"
        ::= { trafficCounters 1 }
```

9.8.3 Scaling

A very simple approach to providing SNMPv1 access to a large counter is to provide a roughly equivalent counter using a different scale. That is, instead of counting every single packet, the scaled object would count in units of thousands or even hundreds of thousands of packets. In this respect, you may be able to avoid the use of Counter64 altogether. We would declare the *packetCounter* this way:

```
packetCounter OBJECT-TYPE
        SYNTAX          Counter32
        UNITS           "100,000 packets per count"
        ACCESS          read-only
        STATUS          current
        DESCRIPTION
                "The number of packets transmitted.
                The value is expressed in 100,000 packet units."
        ::= { packetStats 1 }
```

The advantage of this technique is that it avoids any sort of MIB ‘trickery’ that requires the management station to perform some special operation to interpret the values. The disadvantage, of course, is that the object now lacks the fine granularity the Counter64 provides. It would take a large amount of traffic to cause this counter to move at all, so this approach may not be desirable in all cases.

9.8.4 Displayable String 64-Bit Counters

As we saw with floating point numbers, values that are not directly supported by the underlying SMI framework can be encoded in displayable strings. To provide a solution that will hold the printable values for the number, we would declare the object as follows:

```
-- The textual convention for a DisplayString based Counter64
```

```
Display64 ::= DisplayString (SIZE (1..20))

packetCounter OBJECT-TYPE
        SYNTAX          Display64
        ACCESS          read-only
        STATUS          current
        DESCRIPTION
                "The number of packets transmitted. The value is
                expressed in ASCII"
        ::= { packetStats 1}
```

9.9 Summary

We've covered a wide variety of techniques in this chapter, but we've only begun to scratch the surface. Our real intent here is to show that if the SNMPv1 or SNMPv2 frameworks don't have a solution for a particular situation, you can always invent a new technique within the existing framework.

CHAPTER 10

MIB Design Choices in Standard MIBs

This chapter examines several MIB modules on the IETF standards track to highlight some interesting design issues. Our goal is not to show you how to use the MIB modules for management, but to give you background about design choices so you will feel confident in making difficult design choices in your MIB modules.

Previous chapters have covered the syntax of MIB modules, object modelling, name space organization, and techniques for creating tables. The designers of MIB modules must understand and master these areas. Master MIB designers must also know when to use particular techniques and approaches, and how to build complex MIB modules that are simple to understand and use. Becoming a master MIB designer requires experience both writing MIB modules and evaluating MIB modules written by others. Looking at the works of others, you may discover constructs and techniques that you may wish to *borrow*, and also the ones that you should not use.

10.1 Selection Criteria

We found it difficult to choose example MIB modules for this chapter, since we had conflicting goals. We used the following factors to choose the MIB modules analyzed in this chapter:

- Widespread potential of use — we wanted to choose MIB modules that a large number of our readers would use or would understand. Thus, we hope to reduce (or eliminate) the pain of learning the basics of the technology to be managed, which must be accomplished, before the MIB module can be understood.
- Software preferred to hardware — there are many MIB modules for dedicated network devices and network interfaces. However, writing an agent that implements the objects in these modules usually requires modification of the source code to device driver software, which is generally available only to the device vendors. We believe that many

new network services will be written in the future, and access to the source code or management interfaces will be easier to obtain and use than that for device drivers.

- An interesting MIB module — some MIB modules are pretty straightforward and demonstrate no unique design considerations. We wanted to show the MIB modules containing an unusual technique or approach.
- Technology that we knew quite well — there are many areas covered by IETF SNMP MIB modules. We know the technology in many areas, but not all.

Using the list of factors, we made an initial list consisting of the following MIB modules:

- RFC 1213 — MIB-II
- RFC 1493 — Bridge
- RFC 1516 — Ethernet Repeater
- RFC 1514 — Host Resources
- RFC 1565 — Network Services
- RFC 1566 — Mail Transport Service
- RFC 1567 — X.500 Directory Service
- RFC 1573 — Interfaces
- RFC 1611 — Domain Name Server
- RFC 1697 — Relational Database Management Server
- RFC 1757 — Remote Monitoring Probe (RMON)
- RFC 1513 — Token ring extensions for RMON

We decided not to cover RMON and the token ring extensions to RMON, since these MIB modules are covered by other sources. The MIB modules for Bridges and Interfaces, while known to many, were too focused on hardware and we wanted to cover the Repeater MIB in depth. We also decided to combine the Network Services, Mail Transport Service, X.500 Directory Service, Domain Name Server, and Relational Database Management Service MIB modules into one analysis. Remember, our aim is to present a few important MIB design examples, and not the details of individual constructs.

10.2 Aspects of MIB Analysis

We have analyzed MIBs for our employers, MIBs for IETF working groups in which we were not actively participating, and MIBs from other sources. We have developed a list of topics to be included in a MIB module analysis. However, the goals for a MIB module analysis vary quite a bit. Many of the reviews of IETF WG MIB modules were primarily for "look and feel" consistency with other IETF produced MIB modules. The results from this type of review were suggestions for changes to a MIB module. Other reviews were done to assist agent and management application developers in understanding a MIB module. The results from this type of review consisted of technology overviews, diagrams of tables, and suggestions for management applications. Several of the authors of SNMP books such as Rose and McCloghrie in "How to Manage Your Network Using SNMP," Feit in "SNMP: A Guide to Network Management," and Stallings in "SNMP SNMPv2 and RMON" include analyses of MIBs. All of these are different due to the differences in goals.

In general, Table 10–1 lists aspects of a "complete" analysis of a MIB module. Some of these may be done by a consultant, book writer, or in published description by a vendor of its MIB module. However, we are providing a limited analysis so that we can show MIB design issues. Thus, we will present only brief parts of a complete MIB analysis.

Table 10–1 Aspects of MIB Analysis

Item	Preferred Source
Background on the technology	White paper or chapter in a book
Description of the resources being modelled	Section in a book chapter or an informational RFC (or functional specification for a proprietary MIB module)
High level structuring of definitions in the module	Description in the RFC containing the MIB module (or functional specification for a proprietary MIB module)
How this MIB module relates to other MIB modules	Description in the RFC containing the MIB module (or functional specification for a proprietary MIB module)
How the object definitions map to the resources	A product's design specification
Indexing for each table	A white paper or section in a book (or functional specification for a proprietary MIB module)
How the tables are related to other tables	The DESCRIPTION clauses for the tables in MIB module, the description in the RFC containing the MIB module, a white paper, section in a book (or functional specification for a proprietary MIB module)
What are the requirements for row creation and deletion via SNMP operations	The DESCRIPTION clause for each row in the MIB module
A categorization of the objects and events with respect to configuration, monitoring, control, action, statistics, state, components, and attributes	A white paper or Informational RFC (or functional specification for a proprietary MIB module)
A list of the top applications that can be done using the definitions in the MIB module (i.e., what problems can be solved, what can be done using the objects/traps which could not be done without SNMP management, etc.)	A white paper, Informational RFC, section of a book (or functional specification for a proprietary MIB module)

10.3 RFC1213: MIB-II the Core Definitions

To bootstrap the use of the SNMP-based management framework, a core set of definitions was created and called MIB-I. It was updated after some experience and called MIB-II. This MIB module contains definitions for both end systems and routers using the Internet protocol suite. We have chosen this MIB module to show organization aspects of MIB design. Note that we have included very brief sections covering all aspects of MIB analysis to give you a sample of what each section covers.

10.3.1 Technology Background

Each system on a network must have at least one interface that it uses to transmit and receive data from the network. The Internet protocol suite contains many protocols with IP and ICMP required by all systems, and UDP and TCP used by most end systems to communicate with other end systems. One routing protocol, EGP, was a popular protocol when the MIB module was designed.

10.3.2 Modelled Resources

This MIB module views a system as having one or more network interfaces using the Internet protocol suite. Each system has a few key attributes. Each network interface on the system can provide traffic statistics. The device responds to one or more IP addresses. There is a mapping between IP addresses and "physical" addresses for each interface. There is a routing table to determine which interface and, if needed, which router to use for forwarding. The statistics about any of the following protocols used on the system are available: ICMP, IP, TCP, UDP, EGP, and SNMP. Additionally, for TCP there is a list of current TCP connections, and for EGP there is a list of information about each current EGP neighbor.

10.3.3 Structuring of the Definitions

Definitions in the MIB module are grouped into functional areas. (See Table 10–2) An

Table 10–2 Functional Areas of MIB-II

Functional area	OID value for Sub-tree	Description
system	1.3.6.1.2.1.1	Definitions for managing the system.
interfaces	1.3.6.1.2.1.2	Definitions for managing network interfaces.
at	1.3.6.1.2.1.3	Definitions for translation of network address to sub-network address.
ip	1.3.6.1.2.1.4	Definitions for managing the IP protocol.
icmp	1.3.6.1.2.1.5	Definitions for managing the ICMP protocol.
tcp	1.3.6.1.2.1.6	Definitions for managing the TCP protocol.
udp	1.3.6.1.2.1.7	Definitions for managing the UDP protocol.
egp	1.3.6.1.2.1.8	Definitions for managing the EGP protocol.
cmot	1.3.6.1.2.1.9	A placeholder for definitions for use with the CMOT protocol.
transmission	1.3.6.1.2.1.10	A placeholder for definitions, which are contained in other MIB modules, for managing transmission media.
snmp	1.3.6.1.2.1.11	Definitions for managing the SNMP protocol.

OID sub-tree contains the definitions in each functional area. (Within the *interfaces*, *ip*, *tcp*, *udp*, and *egp* sub-trees are definitions of both scalar and columnar objects. The *system*, *icmp*, and *snmp* sub-trees contain definitions of only scalar objects, and the *at* sub-tree contains the definition of only columnar objects, all in one table.)

10.3.4 Description of Tables

The following tables are defined in the MIB module: ifTable, atTable, ipAddrTable, ipRouteTable, ipNetToMediaTable, tcpConnTable, udpTable, and egpNeighTable. (See Figure 10–1) Table ifTable is indexed by a number chosen arbitrarily by the managed system.

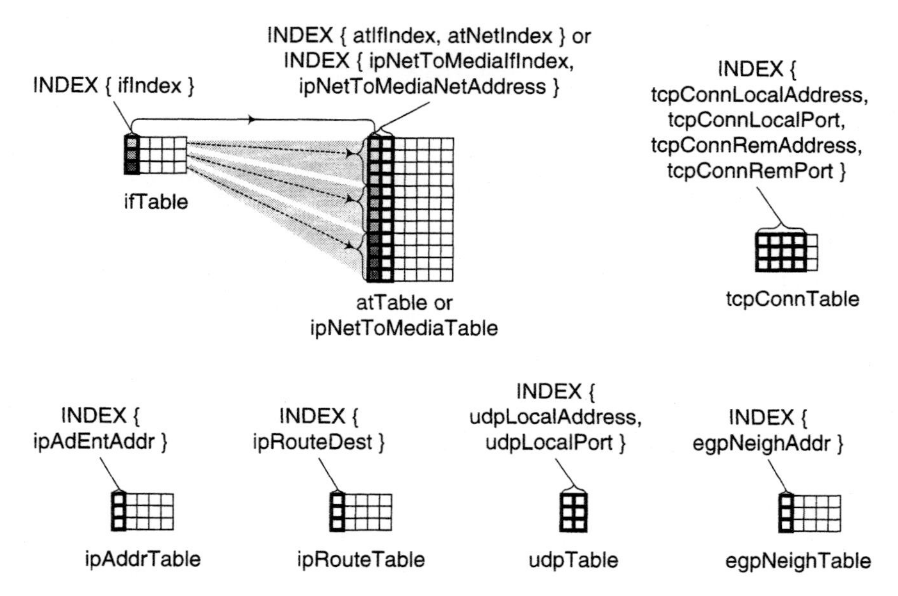

Figure 10–1 Tables in MIB-II

There is an entry in this table for each network level interface. The table contains statistics, state, attributes, and control mechanisms for the interfaces. Table atTable is indexed by network interface number and network address. This table was designed to show the mapping between network address and physical address for each interface. Table ipAddrTable is indexed by IP address. Each row corresponds to an IP address assigned to the system. The table contains configuration information about each IP address. Table ipRouteTable is indexed by an IP address. Each row contains route configuration information for a destination IP address known by the system. Table ipNetToMediaTable is a replacement for table atTable, but contains only IP addresses. It is indexed by network interface number and IP address. Table tcpConnTable is indexed by the source and destination IP and port addresses on each end of a TCP connection. Rows in this table specify the state of each TCP connection from the system. Table udpTable is indexed by IP address and port number. It has an entry for each UDP listener on the managed system. Table egpNeighTable is indexed by an IP address that is the address of each EGP neighbor. Rows contain state, statistics, configuration, and control information for each EGP neighbor.

10.3.5 Interesting Design Issue

This MIB module shows how to organize a large collection of definitions. This module was the first example of definitions for SNMP-based management. There are many good design choices in the organization of definitions of this MIB module. We will step you through these choices and show how you can apply these in the design of your MIB modules.

The first decision is how to structure and manage the OID sub-tree that has been assigned for your use. For an organization or enterprise, there are some top level OID organizational issues that need to be resolved, independent from the issues for a particular MIB module. For SNMP, these are addressed by administrative assignments of OID value in the SMI module. We assume that you have resolved your top level OID organizational issues, either by following our recommendations (see Chapter 8), or by choosing another approach. For a MIB module, you need to choose an OID organization that is both flexible and abstract, but is easy to understand and use. With MIB-I (and MIB-II) the working group needed to define a MIB module that had enough items defined so that systems could be managed, but small and simple enough so that it would see widespread implementation. Too much organization for this first version could have resulted in confusion instead of implementation. The approach taken was to use a minimal amount of organization. The core set of definitions were specified within one MIB module. The OID tree was used to structure definitions into broad areas. Instead of one MIB module, the definitions could have been split into separate modules. Using a single module was appropriate in 1988, but now, separate modules are a better choice. We will show you why.

Separate MIB Modules

Instead of putting all your definitions into a single MIB module, it is better to split your definitions into areas and put them in separate MIB modules. These modules can be contained in the same document, or in separate documents. The separation allows each area to be maintained independently of the others. (See Figure 10–2)

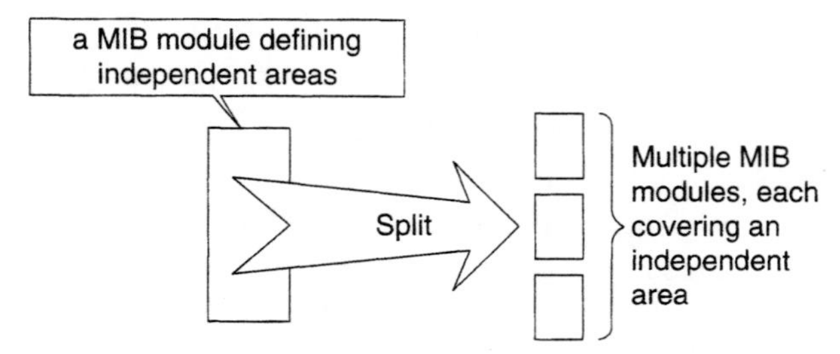

Figure 10–2 Split independent areas into separate MIB modules

However, separation taken to an extreme can increase maintenance costs and make the definitions harder to understand. Finding a good balance between long term goals (such as ease of maintenance) and short term goals (such as ease of understanding) is a hard problem for MIB designers. The following are guidelines to help you in choosing how to split your definitions:

- Base the split on logical grouping, don't split MIB modules due to implementation of your agent. (For example, don't put the definitions for all the objects implemented by an agent in one MIB module.) The AGENT-CAPABILITIES construct is used to specify implementation characteristics.
- Consider how the definitions would be used (or re-used) in other systems and split the definitions to enhance maximum reuse. For example, definitions for a common sub-system, which may be an option on many of the systems developed by your organization, are best split into separate MIB modules, instead of being included in a MIB module containing definitions for the first product that uses the sub-system.
- Split your definitions based on your prediction of the stability of the definitions. That is, when you put together a MIB module, some of the definitions model technology or configurations that are relatively stable, and other definitions are for new technology or new approaches to system configuration. By putting the definitions for the "stable stuff" in one MIB module, and definitions for the "changing stuff" in another MIB module, you allow parallel product development to occur.
- Don't split a MIB module to show implementation requirements. The OBJECT-GROUP, NOTIFICATION-GROUP, and MODULE-COMPLIANCE constructs are used to specify implementation requirements.
- Remember that you cannot have two modules that depend on each other (i.e., they each have an IMPORTS clause that names the other). For large or complex collections of definitions, create a MIB module containing common textual conventions. Also, consider creating a *core* MIB module containing definitions referenced by other modules.

Grouping Within a MIB Module

Within a MIB module, the OID tree should be used to create hierarchical groupings for related definitions. Columnar objects are already grouped by table definitions. However, scalar objects also need to be grouped.

Let's review the objects for managing the TCP protocol in MIB-II. (See Figure 10–3)

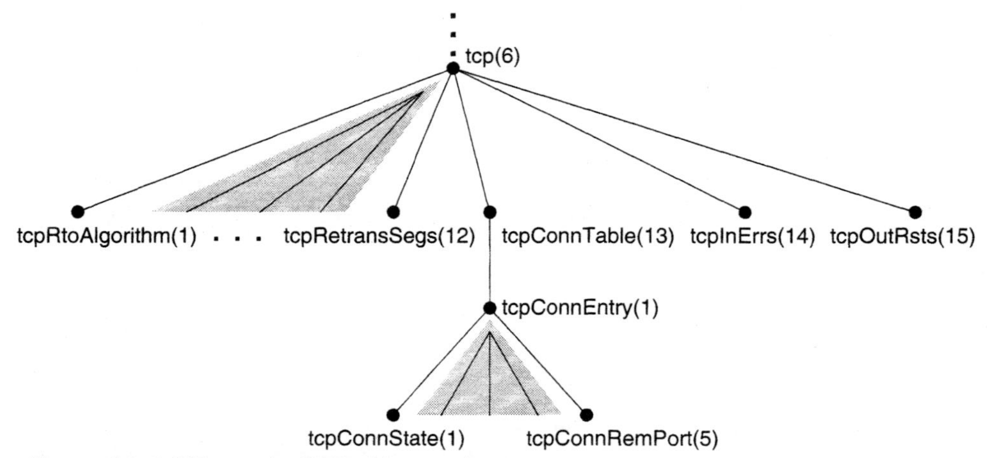

Figure 10–3 OID tree for TCP object assignments

Both scalar objects and the TCP connection table are defined directly under the root of the *tcp* sub-tree (i.e., 1.3.6.1.2.1.6). Twelve of the scalars were defined in the first version, and two of the scalars were added in a later version.

This results in most of the scalar objects assigned OID values before the table *tcp-ConnTable*, but scalar objects *tcpInErrs* and *tcpOutRsts* have assigned OID values after the table. These assignments are completely valid. However, most likely a reader of the MIB module will have difficulty realizing that objects *tcpInErrs* and *tcpOutRsts* logically belong with the other scalar objects in the *tcp* sub-tree. A better organization of the OID tree for objects to manage the TCP protocol is shown in Figure 10–4.

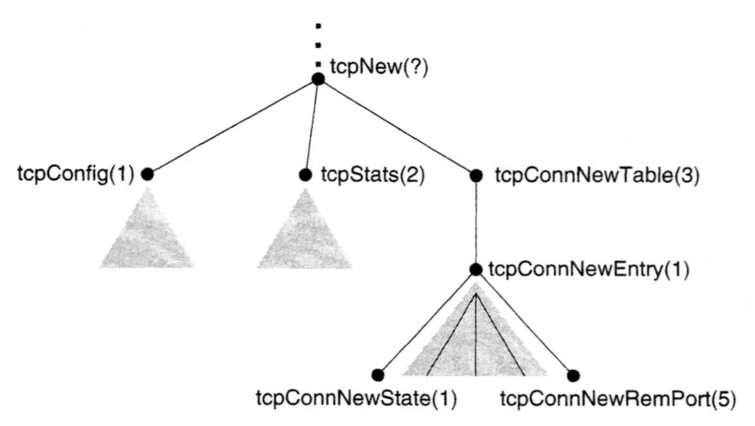

Figure 10–4 Reorganization of TCP OID assignments

In this organization, the scalars are split into two collections. The first collection is called *tcpConfig* and contains the scalar objects that represent the global configuration of the TCP protocol. The second collection is called *tcpStats* and contains the scalar objects that report global statistics for the TCP protocol. The table tcpConnNewTable remains the same structure as before. (Note: if the reorganization was applied, new identifiers and OID assignments would be needed for all of the objects. Remember, OID values cannot be reused. Also, remember that all identifiers for items defined across all IETF standard track MIB modules must be unique.)

Many of the same guidelines for splitting MIB modules apply to organizing definitions within a MIB module. In general, organizing should be done to aid maintenance and improve understanding. However, over-organization can increase maintenance costs and make the definitions harder to understand. The following guidelines will help you choose how to organize the definitions inside your MIB modules:

- Organize definitions into logical groups and sub-groups. Don't just add definitions to a MIB module as you think of them. Plan ahead and organize your definitions so it will be easy to add new ones later.
- Consider splitting a table that has many columns into several tables with one designated as the base table and the others as augmenting tables. For example, split a table that has configuration and statistics into a base table with configuration and an augmenting

table with statistics. Or, if you have much configuration, consider using three tables. The first would contain basic configuration, the second would contain statistics, and the third would contain advanced configuration.

- Generally, don't assign OID values for scalar objects and tables under the same parent OID value.

Design Issue Summary

In MIB-II (RFC 1213) we have looked at two important issues in MIB design. The first is determining when and how to split definitions from one to several MIB modules. The second is how to organize definitions within a MIB module.

10.4 RFC 1516: Ethernet Repeaters

Ethernet repeaters are found in most LANs using the Ethernet or IEEE 802.3 technology. An excellent overview of this technology can be found in "How to Manage Your Network Using SNMP" by Rose and McCloghrie. The technology background that we provide has been quite simplified. We have chosen this MIB module primarily to show how to choose the indexing for tables.

10.4.1 Technology Background

Sending data using ethernet technology requires a network interface connected to a transmission medium. When data is ready to be sent, the network interface first listens for transmissions from others. When no other transmissions are occurring, then the interface may begin transmission. The transmission may be heard by all network interfaces connected to the transmission medium. A collision occurs when more than one transmission is attempted simultaneously. A network interface must listen for collisions during transmission. There are rules to specify what must occur if a collision is detected during transmission.

There are several types of transmission media, each with characteristics of maximum lengths and number of interfaces which may be attached. An ethernet repeater is a device to connect together transmission media to extend the span and/or mediate between different media types. A repeater can be logically pictured as a star. (See Figure 10–5) Bit level data

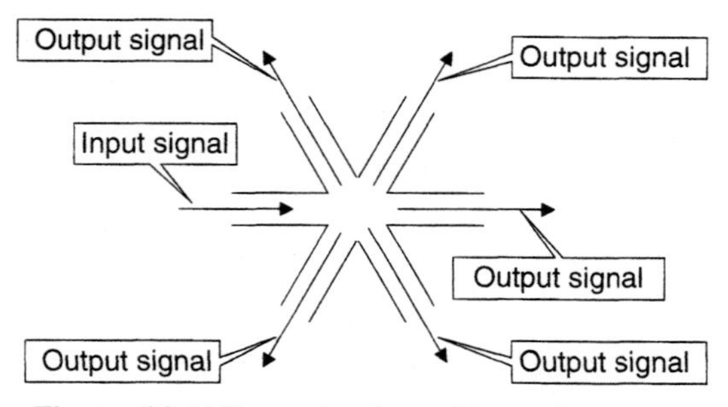

Figure 10–5 Example six port repeater

received on any port of a repeater is transmitted out the other ports of the repeater. If data is received simultaneously on two or more ports, or a collision is received, then the repeater transmits a jamming signal out on all ports. When a port is disabled, it does not transmit nor receive. When a port is partitioned, it does not receive.

There are many ways that ethernet repeaters can be packaged into products. The first and simplest is a non-modular box with a fixed number of ports. For flexibility, a repeater can be packaged as a box with plug-in modules. (See Figure 10–6) The number of ports on a

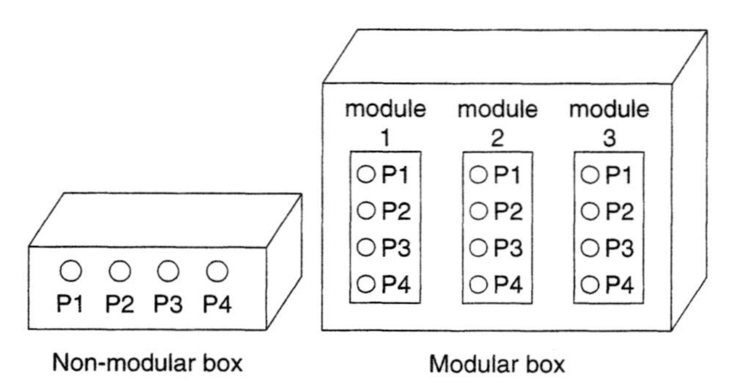

Figure 10–6 One or more logical repeaters in a non-modular or modular box

plug-in module may vary, or the ports may support different transmission medium such as fiber, twisted wires, or coaxial cable. Additionally, multiple repeaters may be packaged into the same physical box. In such systems, a logical repeater (or *repeater unit*) consists of all the ports on the box that are interconnected together. The interconnection of the ports may be controlled by the design of the box, by physically changing switches or jumpers on the box, or through electronic control of the box. Early designs of physical systems had all ports on a plug-in module restricted to be a member of the same repeater unit. Current designs allow any set of ports to be interconnected together. Designs with more flexibility of the interconnection of the ports carry a higher cost.

10.4.2 Modelled Resources

The device modelled by the MIB module contains a single repeater unit. That is, all the ports are interconnected together. The device may consist of one or more collections of ports. A collection of ports is called a *group* in the MIB module. A group is meant to correspond to a physical module in the device. However, this is not a requirement. Ports are identified by the group index and the port index. There is information at the repeater level, at the group level, and at the port level. The information includes configuration, state, and statistics. This model is quite simple and easily maps to devices that are designed as a single repeater unit.

In devices that are designed to support multiple repeater units, the model does not easily map. (See Figure 10–7) At the minimum, the information at the repeater level needs to be indexed. What may not be so clear is how indexing should be done at the group and port level. Remember, a "repeater unit" is the collection of ports connected together, and there is no requirement that these collections correspond to physical plug-in modules.

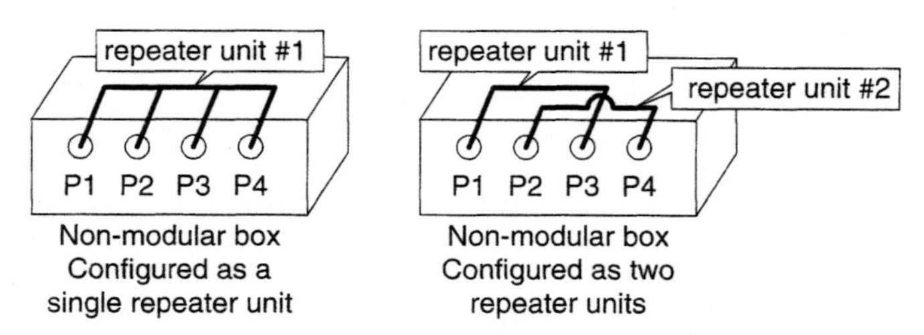

Figure 10–7 A physical box configured as a single repeater unit, or as two repeater units

10.4.3 MIB Module Structuring

The object definitions are structured into three areas organized as separate sub-trees. Within each sub-tree, the information is further divided into information at the repeater level, group level, and port level. (See Figure 10–8) The first sub-tree is labelled as *rptrBasicPackage*. It contains configuration information for the physical device, state information, and a few control objects. The second sub-tree is labelled as *rptrMonitorPackage*. It contains statistics such as the number of frames received, the number of bytes in the valid frames, and error counts. The last sub-tree is labelled as *rptrAddrTrackPackage*. It contains information about source addresses seen in received frames.

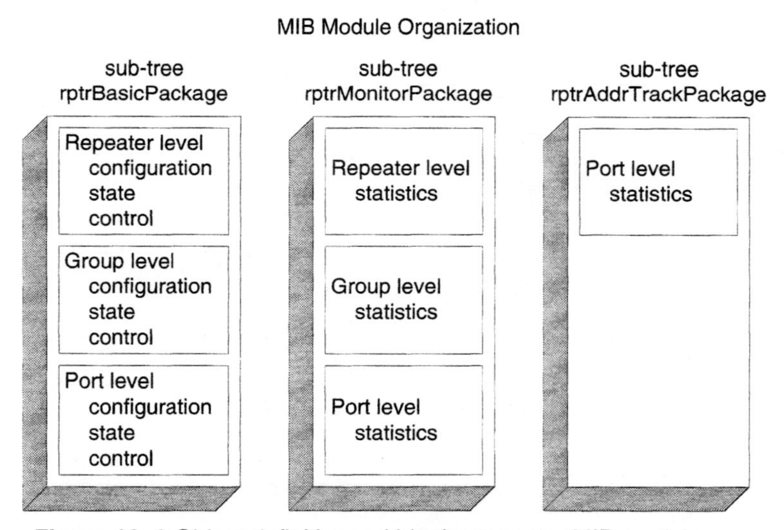

Figure 10–8 Object definitions within the repeater MIB module

10.4.4 Description of Tables

The tables in the MIB module are rptrGroupTable, rptrPortTable, rptrMonitorGroupTable, rptrMonitorPortTable, and rptrAddrTrackTable. (See Figure 10–9) The two tables for groups, rptrGroupTable and rptrMonitorGroupTable, have the identical number of entries. The MIB module designers could have combined the two tables into a single one. However, the object definitions were split to show the logical grouping of the information, and to allow ease of showing the MIB designer's choices for implementation requirements. The first table, rptrGroupTable, is meant to be required, and the second table, rptrMonitorGroupTable, is meant to be optional. This MIB module was written using a *conservative* approach to index specification. Since there is a one-to-one relationship between the rows in the two tables and the MIB was written using SMIv1, the second (and optional) table, rptrMonotorGroupTable, could have used the indices from the first table. That is, the INDEX clause for the definition of rptrMonitorGroupEntry could have been specified as "INDEX { rptrGroupIndex }" instead of "INDEX { ptrMonitorGroupIndex }". Also, the definition of object rptrMonitorGroupIndex is not needed with the change of indexing. If written using SMIv2, the AUGMENTS clause is used when two tables have a one-to-one relationship with rows, which these tables have. Thus, the INDEX clause for rptrMonitorGroupEntry could have been replaced by "AUGMENTS { rptrGroupEntry }". The three tables for ports have identical number of rows. Just like the group tables, the port definitions were split into three tables to highlight the different uses of the information and to allow the MIB designer's choices for implementation requirements to be easily specified.

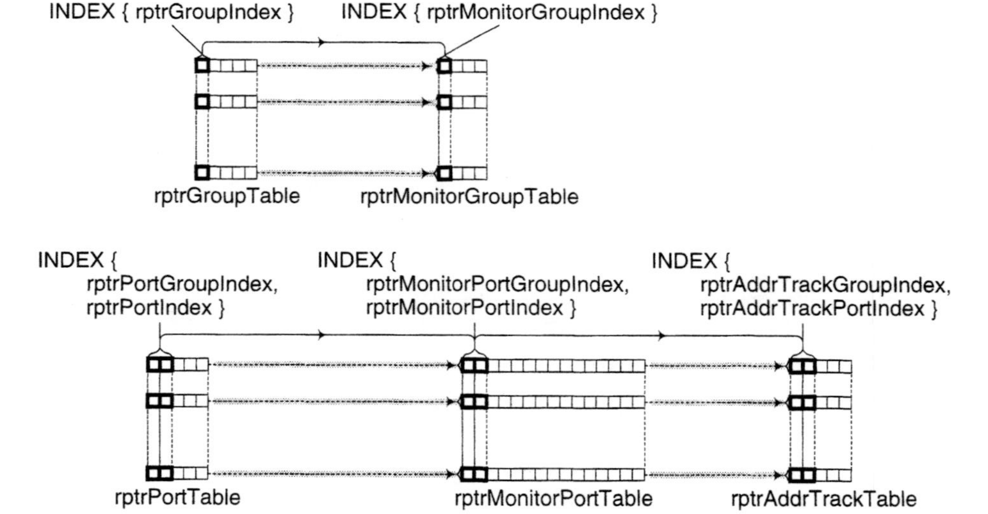

Figure 10–9 Tables and their relationships

The three port tables are indexed by a group and port index. Just like the indexing for the group tables, the port table could have been written so that the INDEX clause for the second and third tables was "INDEX { rptrPortGroupIndex, rptrPortIndex }". The INDEX clause would be replaced with "AUGMENTS { rptrPortTable }" using SMIv2. Each row in the port table must have an associated row in the group table. Thus, the INDEX clause for rptrPortEntry could have been changed from "INDEX { rptrPortGroupIndex, rptrPortIndex }" to "INDEX { rptrGroupIndex, rptrPortIndex }" and the definition of object rptrPortGroupIndex is no longer needed. (See Figure 10–10) Writing the INDEX clause this way is the clearest way to show a linkage between the group table and port table.

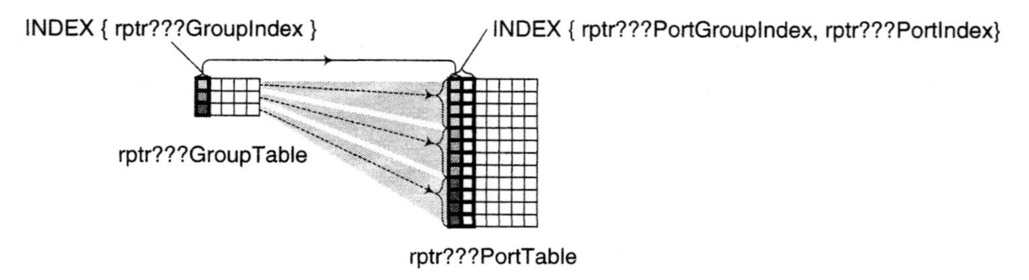

Figure 10–10 Relationship between tables for groups and tables for ports

Table 10–3 summarizes the changes that could have been made, and should be done in new MIB modules. (We cannot go back and "fix" the repeater MIB module. Such a change is not valid.)

Table 10–3 Index Changes

Table	Original Specification	A Better Specification
rptrGroupTable	INDEX { rptrGroupIndex }	-- no change needed --
rptrMonitorGroupTable	INDEX { rptrMonitorGroupEntry }	AUGMENTS { rptrGroupEntry }
rptrPortTable	INDEX { rptrPortGroupIndex, rptrPortIndex }	INDEX { rptrGroupIndex, rptrPortIndex }
rptrMonitorPortTable	INDEX { rptrMonitorPortGroupIndex, rptrMonitorPortIndex }	AUGMENTS { rptrPortEntry }
rptrAddrTrackTable	INDEX { rptrAddrTrackGroupIndex, rptrAddrTrackPortIndex }	AUGMENTS { rptrPortEntry }

10.4.5 Interesting Design Issue

The objects in the repeater MIB module are cleanly organized and specified. However, as pointed out earlier, the MIB maps well to some devices, but does not to others. We will look at several approaches to solve this problem and point out the one we think is the best. The problem with the current MIB module design is the following:

Devices that are designed to support more than one "repeater unit" cannot be directly supported by the definitions in the MIB module.

The information at the repeater level is not indexed. That is, the objects are defined as scalars, which means there is a single instance of each object. However, there are devices with multiple "repeater units" managed by a single SNMP agent. Thus, the information at the repeater level needs to be defined as columnar objects. This is an easy fix to make, once it is realized that a device can contain more than one repeater unit. That is, organize the repeater level information into tables indexed by repeater index. (Note: since this MIB module has been published, the definitions in it cannot be changed. The fix requires that new definitions be created.)

Repeater Index for All Tables

As currently specified in the MIB module, the objects within the tables are defined to specify information "within the repeater." If new group and port tables were created that had index clauses of "INDEX { rptrIndex, rptrGroupIndex }" and "INDEX { rptrIndex, rptrGroupIndex, rptrPortIndex }", the result would be multiple entries for groups which contained ports as members of different repeaters. Figure 10–11 shows a device that is first configured as one repeater unit containing a single group and then re-configured as two repeater units each containing a single group.

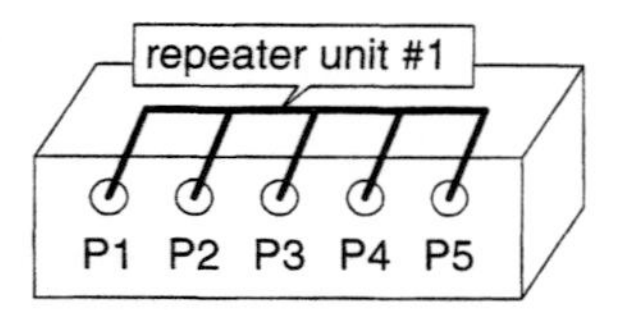

1 repeater unit containing
1 group containing 5 ports

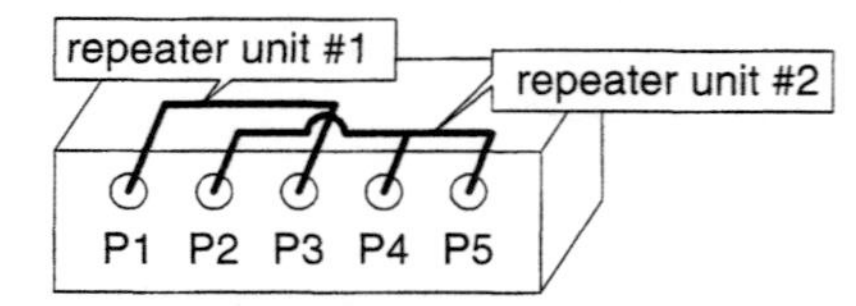

2 repeater units with the first containing 1 group containing 2 ports, and the second containing 1 group containing 3 ports

Figure 10–11 Two configurations of a device with repeater unit indexing of ports and groups

In the first configuration, there would be one entry in the repeater table, one entry in the group tables, and five entries in the port tables. (See Figure 10–12) In the second configura-

group table indexing - first configuration

rptrIndex	rptrGroupIndex
1	1

group table indexing - second configuration

rptrIndex	rptrGroupIndex
1	1
2	2

port table indexing — first configuration

rptrIndex	rptrGroupIndex	rptrPortIndex
1	1	1
1	1	2
1	1	3
1	1	4
1	1	5

port table indexing — second configuration

rptrIndex	rptrGroupIndex	rptrPortIndex
1	1	1
1	1	3
2	1	2
2	1	4
2	1	5

Figure 10–12 Indexing for two configurations of a device

tion, there would be two entries in the repeater table, two entries in the group tables, and five entries in the port tables. This indexing is somewhat unnatural, since the identification of a group or port depends on the configuration of the "repeater units" in the device.

Repeater Index only for Repeater Tables

If the indexing for the group and port tables is left unchanged, then the number of entries for groups would remain unchanged as the configuration of "repeater units" in the device was changed. However, with this approach, each definition of a group or port object would have to be written so that identification of groups and ports was independent of the configuration of the repeater units in the device. Figure 10–13 shows a device that is first configured as one repeater unit containing a single group and then re-configured as two repeater units each containing a single group.

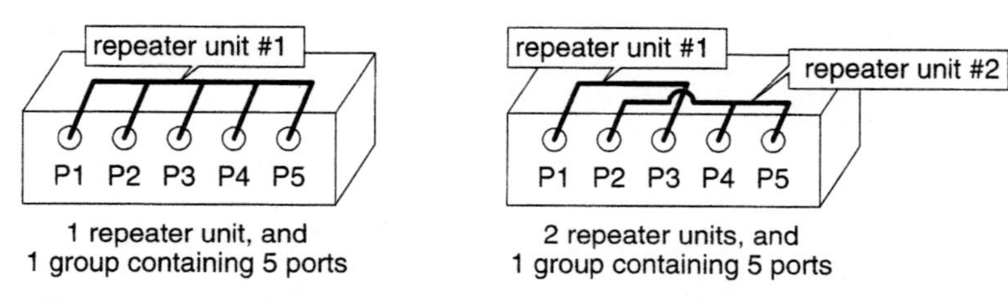

Figure 10–13 Two configurations of a device with indexing of ports and groups independent of repeater unit

In the first configuration, there would be one entry in the repeater table, one entry in the group tables, and five entries in the port tables. (See Figure 10–14) In the second configuration, there would be two entries in the repeater table, one entry in the group tables, and five entries in the port tables. This indexing seems natural, since the identification of a group or port corresponds to the physical configuration of the group or port, and is independent of the configuration of the "repeater units" in the device.

group table indexing

rptrGroupIndex
1

port table indexing

rptrGroupIndex	rptrPortIndex
1	1
1	2
1	3
1	4
1	5

Figure 10–14 Indexing that is independent of configuration of "repeater units" in a device

Community String Indexing

The original MIB module designers believed that the SNMPv1 community string would be the mechanism to access each repeater unit. This approach has the undesirable aspect of duplicate group entries identical to the approach of adding a repeater index to all tables, plus it runs into the global problem of community string management in SNMP. (There is no standard method to manage community strings or associate instances of objects to a particular view.) The result has been that few vendors have used this approach without modification. Thus, there are interoperability problems for those vendors who have used a community string to access information in devices containing multiple repeater units. Figure 10–15 shows the two views of a device configured to contain two repeater units.

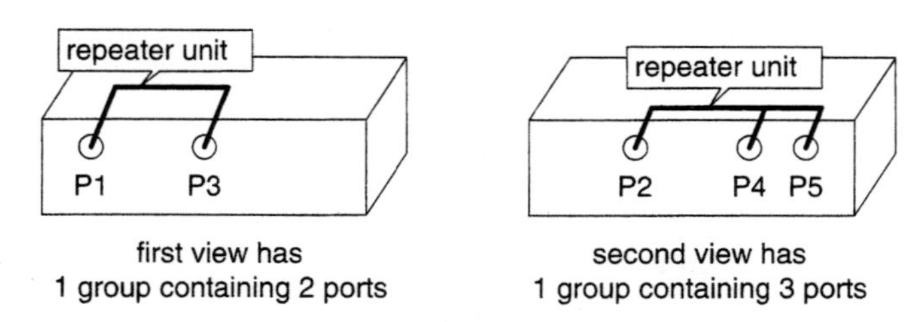

Figure 10–15 Views using community strings for a device configured as two repeater units

In the first view, there would be one entry in the group tables, and two entries in the port tables. In the second view, there would be one entry in the group tables, and three entries in the port tables. The indexing is shown in Figure 10–16. This indexing is somewhat unnatural since the identification of a group or port depends on the configuration of the "repeater units" in the device.

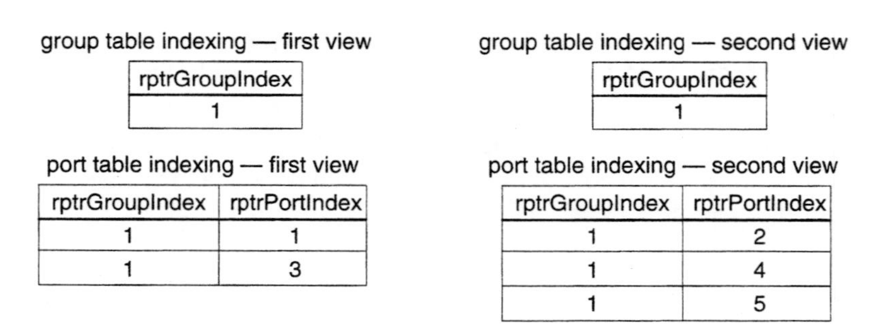

group table indexing — first view

rptrGroupIndex
1

group table indexing — second view

rptrGroupIndex
1

port table indexing — first view

rptrGroupIndex	rptrPortIndex
1	1
1	3

port table indexing — second view

rptrGroupIndex	rptrPortIndex
1	2
1	4
1	5

Figure 10–16 Table contents based on community string views

Design Issue Summary

The indexing of management information is one of the most difficult design choices for MIB authors. This example has shown only one aspect of several which may be faced by a MIB designer. In the repeater MIB module, the choice of indexing is between that based on function versus that based on physical representation. No one approach can be used for all situations. Sometimes an approach based on a blend is needed. Our preferred approach for the repeater MIB is one where the groups and ports are identified by indices that correspond to physical characteristics, independently from repeater unit.

10.5 RFC 1514: Host Resources

Systems that primarily originate and receive application level data are called *end systems* or *network hosts*. Examples include workstations, personal computers, time-shared mini-computers and mainframes, and dedicated file and WEB servers. There are many aspects of these systems that are not directly related to networking that can be managed through the SNMP-based management framework. The Host Resources MIB specification contains definitions of only a core set of these characteristics, which are not related to networking. We examine this MIB module to show how an extensible set of definitions can be created.

10.5.1 Technology Background

Most *hosts* are general purpose computer systems consisting of a CPU, memory, disk drive, and network interface. A host primarily used by a single person also has a display, keyboard, and, optionally, a pointing device. Other sub-systems or attached devices that are found in many systems include: printers, audio playback and recording devices, modems, tape drives, and CD-ROM drives. (See Figure 10–17) The list seems endless, and changes as new technology becomes productized. Also, it seems as though each hardware and operating system vendor appears to use different terminology and approaches for the same capabilities. However, there is a core set of items that are consistent across all host systems, even if they are given different names.

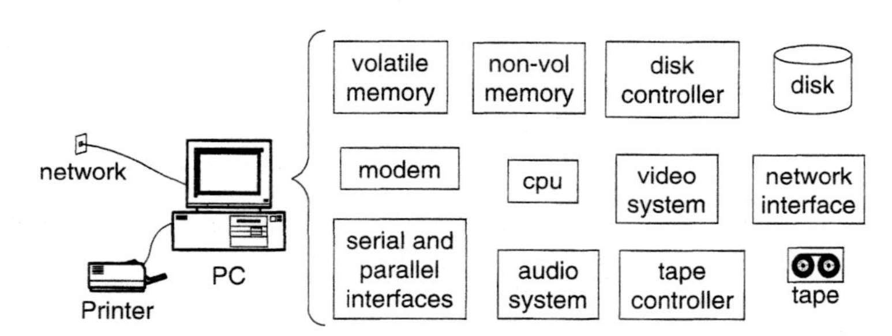

Figure 10–17 Typical devices in or controlled by a network host

Each device in or controlled by a host has a common set of attributes, including device type, product ID, status, and count of detected errors. Additionally, devices may have attributes specifically for their type. For example, attributes of a CPU include firmware version and percentage that the CPU was idle over the last minute. Attributes of network interfaces are specified in table *ifTable,* defined in RFC 1213 (i.e., MIB-II), and updated in RFC 1573. Common attributes of printers controlled by a host include a refined status when running (i.e., printing, idle, or warming up), and error and warning indicators (i.e., low paper, no paper, low toner, no toner, door open, feeder jammed, turned off-line, and service requested). Common attributes for disk-type devices include media access (read-only or read-write), disk type (i.e., hard disk, floppy disk, CD-ROM, ram-disk, etc.), indication if media is removable, and capacity of the media. Each disk may be partitioned into one or more sections that are used for different purposes. A partition may be used for a file system, swap space, or a boot loader program. Some operating systems may support several types of file systems. Also, some operating systems allow a file system to be constructed from multiple partitions that are located on the same or different disk drives.(See Figure 10–18)

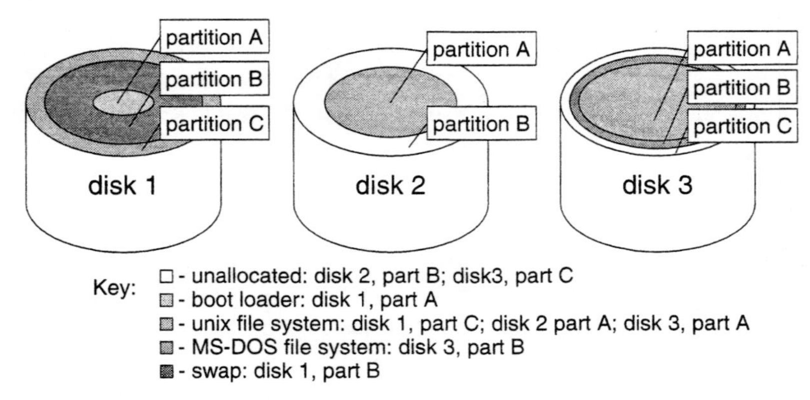

Figure 10–18 Three partitioned disks with combined storage spaces

Besides disks, a system may sub-divide and/or combine other physical devices to create logical storage areas. For example, non-volatile memory may be used as a logical storage area to hold configuration information.

Many systems support multiple file systems. Operating systems almost universally use hierarchical naming of files. Some systems model each file system as an independent sub-tree. Other systems support a single file naming tree and require file systems to be grafted to a branch in the tree. The name of this grafting location is called a mount point. Network operating systems allow a complete or a portion of a remote file system to be accessed as a local file system. (See Figure 10–19)

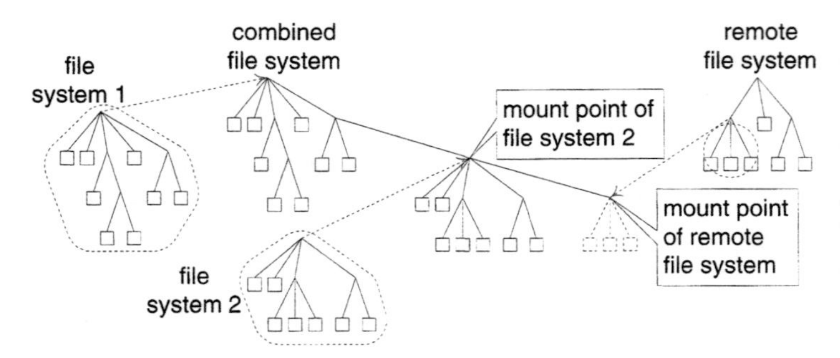

Figure 10–19 File systems with mounting

All host systems execute programs. Operating systems manage the execution of programs. At any point, there may be programs executing (or running), ready to execute (runnable), or waiting for an event to occur (pended or blocked). These are called *loaded* programs. Some systems track the execution time and amount of processor memory allocated for each loaded program. Before a program may be executed, it must be installed on a system or installed on another system from which it can be loaded. Programs stored on long term storage local to the system are called *installed* programs. (See Figure 10–20) Tracking the software installed on a system allows it to be inventoried, and can assist with diagnosing incompatibilities between various versions of software and/or hardware in the system.

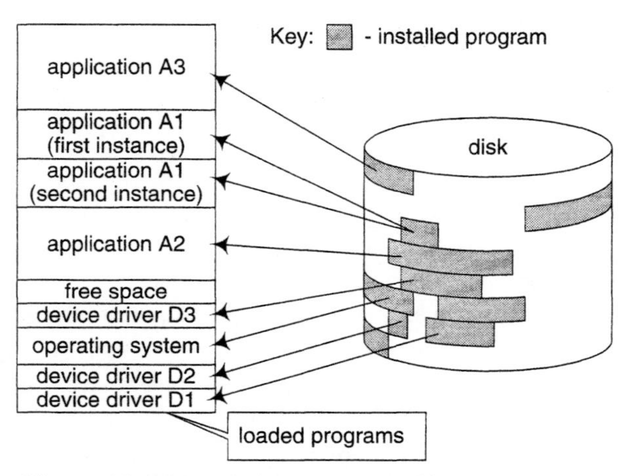

Figure 10–20 Loaded programs and installed programs

10.5.2 Modelled Resources

The MIB module models a host system as having a few global attributes, a list of contained or controlled devices, a list of storage areas, a list of file systems, a list of loaded programs, and a list of installed programs. (See Figure 10–21) There are additional tables for CPUs, network interfaces, directly controlled printers, and disk drives that provide informa-

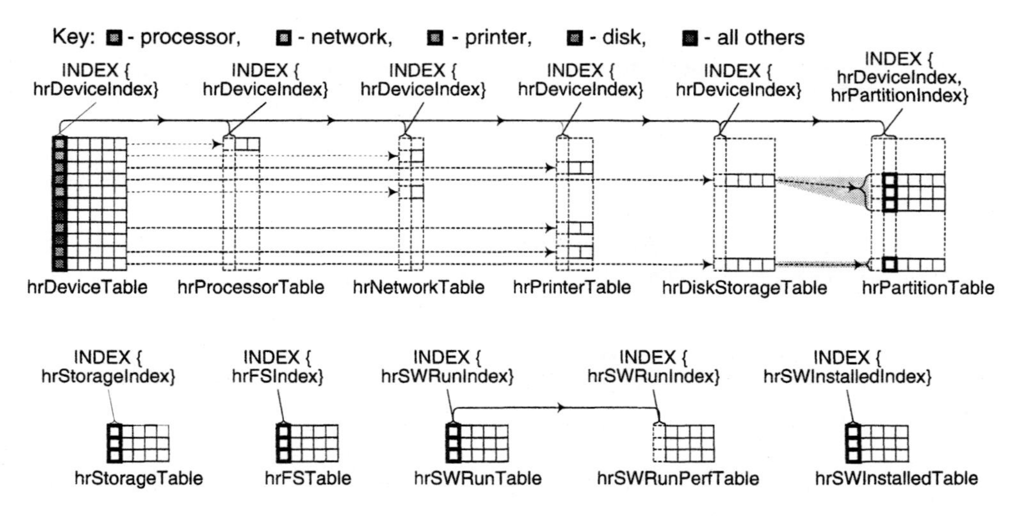

Figure 10–21 Tables and their relationships

tion which is specific to those devices. These tables extend the list of devices. For disk drives, there is a table that provides partition information. There is also a table that augments the list of loaded programs with CPU and memory usage information.

10.5.3 Description of the Tables

The MIB module contains several families of related tables, which is shown in Figure 10–21. The first family is the device related tables. The second family is the storage table. The third family is the file system table. The fourth family is the loaded and installed program tables.

Device Tables

The key table of this MIB module is *hrDeviceTable*, the host device table. It is indexed by an arbitrary number, *hrDeviceIndex*, that is assigned by the management sub-system. This table contains generic information for any type of device contained or directly controlled by the host. (The devices in the table are chosen by the implementor of the management sub-system!) Devices are broadly classified into categories such as processor (CPU), network interface, video, or disk. Specific devices are further identified by a textual description and OID. The textual description should specify the device manufacturer and revision, and optionally the serial number. However, there is no requirement for this information, nor any format specified for the information.[1] The table also has columns that report status of the device and record detected errors. Extending the device table are tables *hrProcessorTable*, *hrNetworkTable*, *hrPrinterTable*, and *hrDiskStorageTable*. These tables are indexed by the index of the device table (i.e., *hrDeviceIndex*), but only have entries for the class of the device associated with each table.

The processor table includes columns to report the product ID of the firmware associated with the CPU, and the percentage over the last minute that the processor was not busy. The network table has a column to report the value of object *ifIndex* for the network interface. Thus, the interfaces table, *ifTable*, can be used to determine attributes of the network interface. The printer table has columns to report the current status of directly connected printers, and to report specific error and warning conditions for each printer. The disk storage table describes the attributes of the disk drive or media in drives with removable media. The columns in this table report allowed access to the media, whether the media is removable from the drive, the type of drive, and the storage capacity of the drive.

The partition table, *hrPartitionTable*, further extends the disk storage table with partition information for each drive. The table is indexed by *hrDeviceIndex* and *hrPartitionIndex*. This additional index is an arbitrary number assigned by the management sub-system. The partition table contains columns that report a textual description of the partition, an ID for the responsible operating system, the size of the partition, and an index into the file system table. This index, if not zero, indicates which file system uses the partition.

1. We believe that objects such as this one are pretty useless! They are GREAT for demos, but for processing by a program, you can't depend on their content and you may not be able to extract the information that you may need, even if it is there, since the format and placement of the information is not specified.

Storage Table

The storage table, *hrStorageTable*, describes each logical area of storage that is allocated and has fixed resource limits. This table is indexed by an arbitrary number chosen by the management sub-system. The entries in the table are quite generic and can be used for file systems, primary memory, or swap space. The primary purpose is to report the total amount of storage space, used storage space, and count of allocation failures.

File System Table

The file system table, *hrFSTable*, describes the file systems available on the host system. This table is indexed by an arbitrary number chosen by the management sub-system. The information reported about each file system include a local mount point, information on remote mounts (if used), the type of the file system (i.e., MS-DOS, Macintosh, etc.), allowed access (read-write or read-only), indication if bootable, date and time of backup, and index into the storage table. This index, if not zero, specifies the entry in the storage table for the file system.

Program Tables

There are three tables in the programs family. The loaded programs table, *hrSWRunTable*, describes the programs that are loaded or running. This table is indexed by an arbitrary number chosen by the management sub-system, which, if possible, should match that used by the operating system on the host. The columns of the table report, for each program, a description, a unique identification, location from where loaded, parameters when loaded, and current status. The program performance table, *hrSWRunPerfTable*, augments the loaded programs table with columns that report, for each program, the amount of processor time used and memory allocated to the program. The installed programs table, *hrSWInstalledTable*, describes the programs that are installed on local long-term storage on a host. This table is indexed by an arbitrary number chosen by the management sub-system. The columns of the table report, for each program, a description, a unique identification, type, and modification date/time.

10.5.4 Interesting Design Issue

This MIB module demonstrates how to create an extensible set of definitions. The device table contains definitions of attributes common to all devices. The processor table, network interface table, printer table, and disk storage table extend the device table with device type specific information. The partition table further extends the disk storage table. These are the current tables in this MIB module. Additional tables could be added for other devices in a future version of this MIB module or in another MIB module. The Printer MIB module, defined in RFC 1759, contains an extensive list of definitions that extend the device table.

The installed applications and running applications tables provide core definitions that can be extended. Unfortunately, these definitions are not used in the Network Services, Mail Transport Service, X.500 Directory Service, Domain Service, and Relational Database Management Service MIB modules. Sadly, missed opportunities for coordination occur in both standards organizations and in private enterprises.

10.6 Server Management

Application programs that run on host computers and perform some work for other programs are called *servers*. Examples of servers include the programs that provide electronic mail service, programs that provide network directory service, or programs that provide network data service. The SNMP-based management framework has long been used to manage network devices. Current trends show it moving to manage network services to integrate management of the "utilities" provided by a computer network. There are MIB modules on the standards track that contain definitions to manage network services. These have not, to date, seen much implementation. They are:

- RFC 1565: Network Services
- RFC 1566: Mail Transport Service
- RFC 1567: X.500 Directory Service
- RFC 1611: Domain Name Server
- RFC 1697: Relational Database Management Service

We will describe these MIB modules at a high level so that you can use some of the techniques from them to create definitions to manage your services.

10.6.1 Technology Background

A *server* program waits for a service request from a *client* program. When a request is received, the service is performed, and a response is sent to the client. After sending the response, the server program waits for the next request. This pattern is quite simple, but complicated by the details. As described, the two programs have different roles. A client initiates the interaction in this model. However, one program may perform many different roles, and also, some application protocols allow either program to initiate interaction. Many application protocols allow one server program to interact with another server program in a *peer* relationship. (See Figure 10–22)

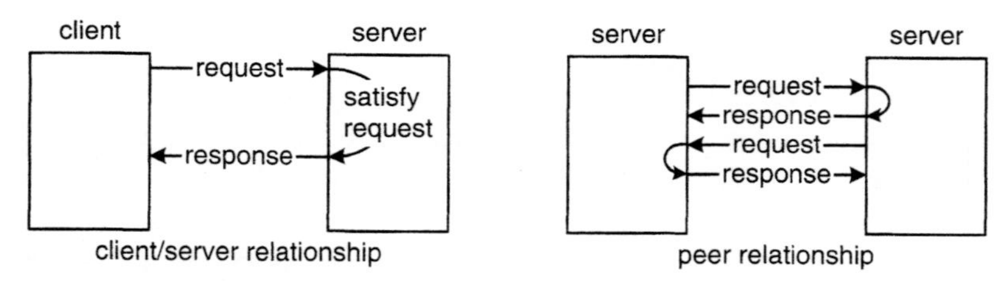

Figure 10–22 Relationships between programs

Applications need a transport service to communicate. Depending on the requirements, either or both of a connection-less or connection-oriented transport mechanism can be possible. For each there are details that must be specified for addressing and connection establishment. For long-lived interactions, it is useful to establish defaults that can be used throughout the interaction. Otherwise, each interaction would carry the overhead of specifying the needed information. Such a long-lived interaction is called an *association* between the two programs. Depending on the application protocol, an association may allow interaction which is initiated by only one of the two programs of the association, or allow interaction initiation by either program. Additionally, an application protocol may require a connection-oriented transport service to establish an association.

A server program may need resources on the local machine and/or resources on other machines to satisfy a service request. (See Figure 10–23) Tracking the use of these resources, controlling access to resources, and efficiently using the resources are important aspects of most server programs. Also, most server programs that require resources must be able to concurrently process many service requests. For complex servers, the actual service function may be performed by many programs working cooperatively.

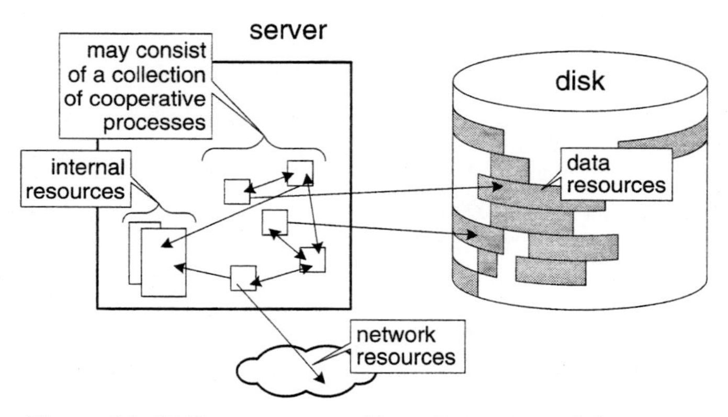

Figure 10–23 Resources used by a Server to satisfy a request

10.6.2 Interesting Design Issue

There are many aspects of network servers. Each can be complicated, and taken together, you end up with a highly complex management problem.

One response to cope with this level of complexity is to tackle one server at a time to limit the amount and scope. (See Figure 10–24) With this approach you will focus on designing a management solution for one server at a time, complete the design, and move to the next one. Also, while you are working on the design for one server, someone else can work on the design for another server. Thus, if you are lucky, you may be able to cut the time of your schedule in half by doubling your resources. You will certainly reduce the risk with this approach, but you will most likely end up with a management system that has cost much to develop and has a different look-and-feel to manage each network server.

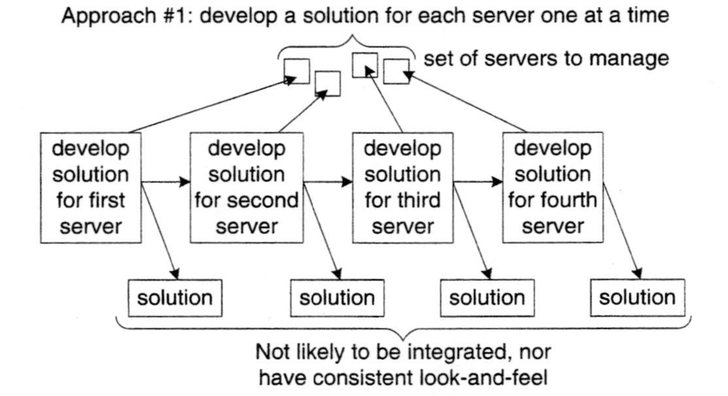

Figure 10–24 Point solution approach to solving complex problem

On the other hand, you can try to develop a design that uses common elements for all network servers. (See Figure 10–25) However, with this approach you may not be able to develop such a design due to the extreme complexity that must be mastered. If you were able to quickly find and develop such a design, you could potentially use less resources and complete sooner than the first approach. Also, the resulting management system should have a higher consistency of look-and-feel than the first system.

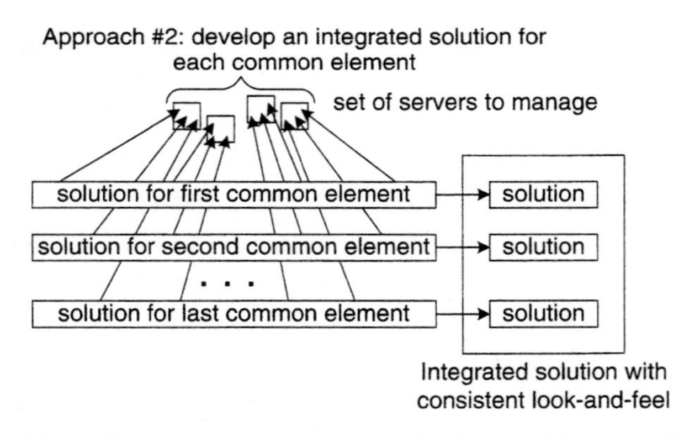

Figure 10–25 Common element approach when solving complex problem

Unfortunately, there is not a single correct answer to the question of "which approach should be used." If you look at how design is done in the IETF organization, you will see that a two phase approach is generally used. (See Figure 10–26) The first phase is designing solutions for small and isolated problems. Only after experience has been gained with "point solutions," and these solutions have not scaled for bigger problems, or have not meshed with other solutions, does an IETF WG attempt to design a "system solution."

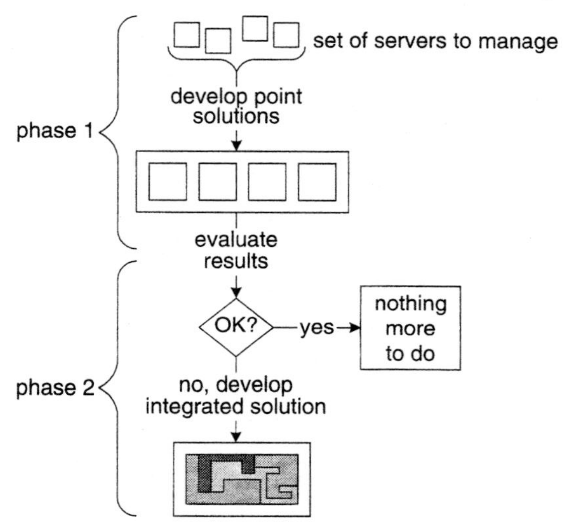

Figure 10–26 Two-phase approach when solving complex problem

With this buildup, it may not be surprising to learn that the Network Servers, Mail Transport Server, X.500 Directory Server, Domain Name Server, Relational Database Management Server, and the Host Resources MIB modules are not fully integrated and aligned. Of these, the Network Servers, Mail Transport Server, and X.500 Directory Server show the closest integration. (They should, since they were developed by the same working group!) The Relational Database Management Server MIB module has some integration with the Network Servers MIB module since it was developed after work was started on the Network Servers MIB module. The Domain Name Server MIB module has no integration with the Network Servers MIB module since it was completed before work started on the Network Servers MIB module (even though it was published later).

CHAPTER 11

MIB Compilers

MIB compilers tend to be greatly misunderstood tools. This term is usually applied to a MIB syntax checker authors use to ensure that their MIBs are written in the correct form, but it also applies to an entire class of tools that perform functions as diverse as drawing tree representations of a MIB, to automatically generating C code for a management application or agent.

This chapter covers the structure and operation of MIB compilers, and shows how to use a compiler for MIB development. Later in this chapter, we will also introduce the compilers for the more popular network management platforms. Finally, we will use a MIB compiler in a project.

11.1 Introduction to MIB Compilers

MIB compilers, simply put, are just translators. They take one form of a MIB, for instance, the SMI form we have spent most of this book discussing, and produce a different form. This second form might be a report, some data structures, or a MIB description language appropriate for a network management station.

MIB compilers address the needs of two groups of users. The MIB writer needs a tool which helps ensure that a MIB is syntactically correct. The management application and management agent writers, on the other hand, need tools to simplify code production. There are, of course, dozens of other uses for MIB compilers, but these are the most common. Many commercial SNMP development packages use MIB compilers as the basis for development of both management and agent software.

A MIB compiler system is structured much like a C or Pascal programming language compiler. It is important to keep in mind that the word *compiler* is a bit more flexible than when used in many situations. We often refer to a compiler when we are speaking of a piece of software that translates high-level user code (a C or Pascal program) into a machine executable. Of course, most language compilers are not monolithic; they break up the various tasks of compilation into several phases and several pieces of software. Each of these phases performs a distinct function and may produce output. One phase might perform a syntax analysis on the input, while another might produce an intermediate output, such as assembly language. The same is true of MIB compiler systems. Each phase of a MIB compiler serves a different purpose.

For our discussion, we will divide the phases into *front-end* and *back-end* compilers. These two compiler sets work together in a system like that shown in Figure 11–1:

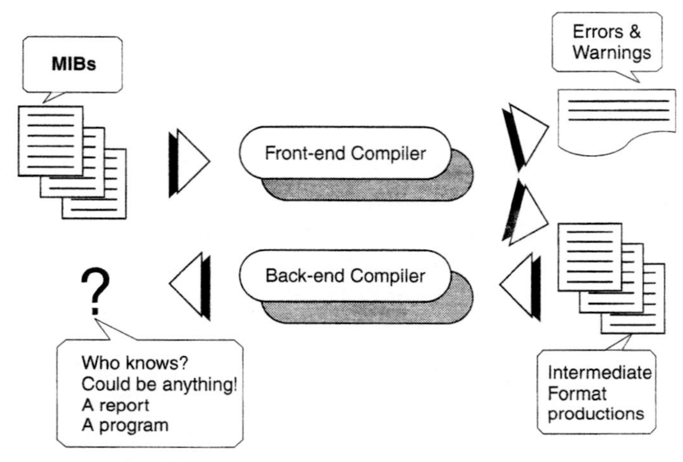

Figure 11–1 A MIB compiler system

In Figure 11–1, we can see the flow of information through the compiler system. The front-end compilers translate a MIB into a form more easily processed by the back-end compiler. The back end is responsible for performing the specific task of the compiler system.

11.2 Front-end compilers

Front-end compilers take MIBs as input and produce another processed format as output. This processed output is sometimes termed *intermediate* format, as it is usually processed by another phase of the compiler, and is rarely seen by humans. These compilers have at least two distinct phases: syntax analysis and intermediate code production. Some more sophisticated systems also include a pre-processing phase before these two phases. The pre-processing phase is much like the pre-processing phase of a C compiler. It allows the author to include files, add and subtract compilation options, and define macro definitions. The pre-processor typically has no specific knowledge of MIBs or network management. In the syntax analysis phase, the compiler checks the MIB for conformance to the standard MIB structure and notes any errors. Most MIB authors are interested in this phase, as they want to produce a MIB that is understandable by management applications. The MIB compiler helps the author by flagging errors, warning of non-standard practices, and suggesting revisions.

The second phase, which is not always present, is intermediate code production. This phase may produce a secondary form of the contents of the MIB. (Just like some programming language compilers, some MIB compilers provide no access to an intermediate form.) There is no standard for an intermediate output for MIB compilers, just as there is no standard for the output of phases from a C compiler. The format could be simple ASCII text or as complex as database records. The key here is that the compiler translates the MIB into a form more easily processed by the back-end compilers within the overall system. Until now, we have discussed a MIB compiler system as if it were responsible for only one function, i.e., it produces a report, or generates some C code. While this is certainly the case in some simple systems, many compilers have multiple functions. In these situations, one front-end compiler services several back-end compilers, as shown in Figure 11–2.

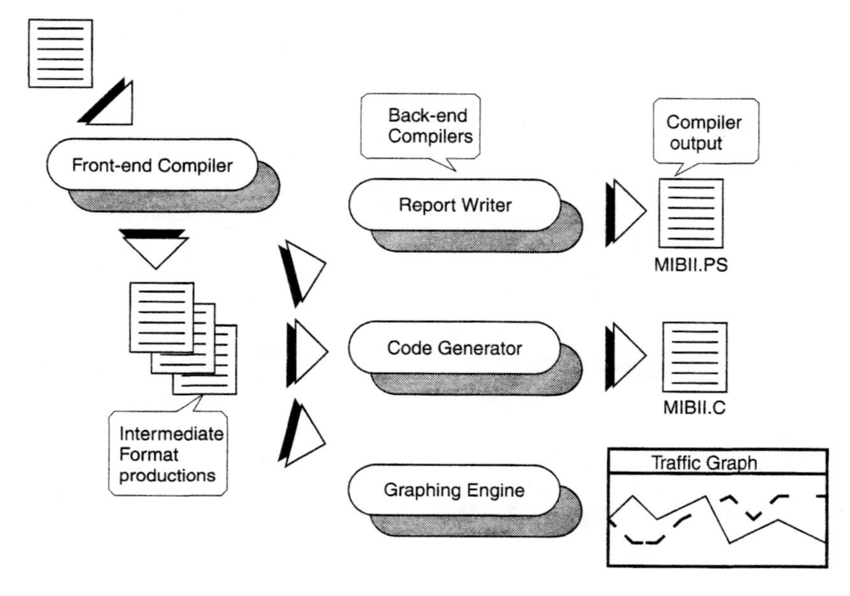

Figure 11–2 Multiple back-end compilers

Let's look at a few examples. Given a MIB declaration such as:

```
ifNumber        OBJECT-TYPE
        SYNTAX          INTEGER
        ACCESS          read-only
        STATUS          mandatory
        DESCRIPTION
                "The number of network interfaces (regardless of their
                current state) on this system"
        ::= { interfaces 1 }
```

If the compiler recognizes that this declaration is correct, it can translate this into something that is a bit easier for other programs to understand. Let's say that the format our applications really need is a list of object declarations, with one object per line. We can have the compiler generate:

```
# Example intermediate output for ifNumber
# Strip away the MIB keywords, and assume a column based scheme
# In addition, form the fully qualified OID name
OBJECT interfaces.ifNumber INTEGER read-only mandatory 1.3.6.1.2.1.2.1
```

Programs that use MIB definitions at run-time can now read this simplified output much faster than parsing the full MIB syntax. The output format preserves the information we need, but frees the back-end programs from recognizing the keywords associated with MIB declarations. As already mentioned, the format of this intermediate output varies greatly between compiler systems, and not all compilers preserve enough of the information needed by possible back-end compilers. In the previous example, for instance, we lost the DESCRIPTION clause.

Another related compiler system is an ASN.1 compiler. MIBs are written in an adapted sub-set of ASN.1. MIB compilers recognize only the sub-set of ASN.1 and the adaptations specified in the SMI. ASN.1 compilers, on the other hand, recognize the entire ASN.1 language, and do not recognize the SNMP adaptations. Using an ASN.1 compiler to check the syntax of a MIB is not a good idea. An ASN.1 compiler will allow ASN.1 syntax that is not allowed in SMNP MIBs and will not allow the SNMP adaptations.

11.3 Back-end compilers

Back-end compilers take the intermediate format produced by the front-end compiler as input and perform some specialized function on it. As the front-end compiler performs all necessary syntactical checks on the MIB, this phase does not require much, if any, syntax checking of the intermediate format. The function of the back-end is to perform some higher level, special purpose function on the target MIBs. These varied functions might include:

- drawing a graphical overview of the MIB
- creating C structures to be used in the production of manager or agent code
- code production for a manager or agent
- some run-time use by a management application

Some management applications such as *MIB browsers* have back-end compilers embedded within them. The term MIB browser refers to a class of generic management applications that are used to query an agent for MIB variables, and display those variables to the user for possible modification. These MIB browsers need to access the MIB definitions of an object very quickly, but parsing a MIB can be quite time consuming. Reading the format produced by the front-end compiler, on the other hand, is usually quite inexpensive, and can be done at run-time by the applications.

Let's suppose we have this style of output from the front-end compiler processing the interface description table from MIB-II:

OBJECT ifEntry.ifIndex INTEGER read-only mandatory
OBJECT ifEntry.ifDescr OCTET_STRING read-only mandatory
OBJECT ifEntry.ifType INTEGER read-only mandatory
OBJECT ifEntry.ifMtu INTEGER read-only mandatory
OBJECT ifEntry.ifSpeed INTEGER read-only mandatory
OBJECT ifEntry.ifPhysAddress OCTET_STRING read-only mandatory
OBJECT ifEntry.ifAdminStatus INTEGER read-write mandatory
OBJECT ifEntry.ifOperStatus INTEGER read-only mandatory
OBJECT ifEntry.ifLastChange TimeTicks read-only mandatory
OBJECT ifEntry.ifOutQLen Gauge32 read-only mandatory
OBJECT ifEntry.ifSpecific OBJECT_IDENTIFIER read-only mandatory
OBJECT ifEntry.ifInOctets Counter read-only mandatory
OBJECT ifEntry.ifUcastOkts Counter read-only mandatory
OBJECT ifEntry.ifNUcastPkts Counter read-only mandatory
OBJECT ifEntry.ifInDiscards Counter read-only mandatory
OBJECT ifEntry.ifInErrors Counter read-only mandatory
OBJECT ifEntry.ifInUnknownProtos Counter read-only mandatory
OBJECT ifEntry.ifOutOctets Counter read-only mandatory
OBJECT ifEntry.ifOutUcastPkts Counter read-only mandatory
OBJECT ifEntry.ifOutNucastPkts Counter read-only mandatory
OBJECT ifEntry.ifOutDiscards Counter read-only mandatory
OBJECT ifEntry.ifOutErrors Counter read-only mandatory

A back-end compiler can transform this into a C structure using the following translations for a system where a *long* is at least 32 bits wide. (See Table 11–1)

Table 11–1 SMI to C Type Translation

SMI Type	C Type
OBJECT IDENTIFIER	typedef struct _snmpoid { unsigned int numSubIds; unsigned long *pSubIds; } SNMPOID;
INTEGER/Integer32	typedef long SNMPI32;
OCTET STRING/Opaque/ BITS	typedef struct _snmpocts{ unsigned int numOctets; unsigned char *pOctets; } SNMPOCTS;
IpAddress	typedef struct _snmpipaddr { unsigned char val[4]; } SNMPIPADDR;
Unsigned32/Gauge/Gauge32/ TimeTicks/Counter/Counter32	typedef unsigned long SNMPU32;
Counter64	typedef struct _snmpu64 { unsigned long highPart; unsigned long lowPart; } SNMPU64;

```
/*
** A structure for the ifEntry row
*/
struct SNMPIFENTRY {
        SNMPI32         SNMPifIndex;
        SNMPOCTS        SNMPifDescr;
        SNMPI32         SNMPifType;
        SNMPI32         SNMPifMtu;
        SNMPU32         SNMPifSpeed;
        SNMPOCTS        SNMPifPhysAddress;
        SNMPI32         SNMPifAdminStatus;
        SNMPI32         SNMPifOperStatus;
        SNMPU32         SNMPifLastChange;
        SNMPU32         SNMPifOutQLen;
        SNMPOID         SNMPifSpecific;
        SNMPU32         SNMPifInOctets ;
        SNMPU32         SNMPifUcastOkts;
        SNMPU32         SNMPifNUcastPkts;
        SNMPU32         SNMPifInDiscards;
        SNMPU32         SNMPifInErrors;
        SNMPU32         SNMPifInUnknownProtos;
        SNMPU32         SNMPifOutOctets Counter;
        SNMPU32         SNMPifOutUcastPkts;
        SNMPU32         SNMPifOutNucastPkts;
        SNMPU32         SNMPifOutDiscards;
        SNMPU32         SNMPifOutErrors;
};
```

We will return to the subject of back-end compilers in a later section, where we will demonstrate some other uses for them. For now, let's take a detailed look at some of the popular front-end MIB compiler systems.

11.4 SMIC

The SNMP Management Information Compiler, or *SMIC,* is a freely available front-end MIB compiler from Bay Networks. An updated and improved version called *SMICng* is available from David T. Perkins. This version runs on a number of operating systems including: Sun Solaris 1 and Solaris 2, IBM AIX and OS/2, Hewlett-Packard HP-UX, Microsoft DOS and NT, and Linux. It parses both SNMPv1 and SNMPv2 MIBs. *SMIC* is the most "feature rich" compiler available to developers. It checks not only for correct syntax of the MIB module language, but also checks for most of the semantic rules of the MIB module language stated in the SMI documents. *SMIC* differs from many other MIB compilers in using a pre-processing phase before any syntax analysis is done. This pre-processing phase means that

SMIC does not read MIBs directly. Rather, it reads a "MIB include file," a sort of control file specifying the names of the MIB files to process, as well as compiler options.

11.4.1 Basic Usage[1]

SMIC has numerous command line options that fall into two major categories: relaxing some of the syntax and semantic rules, and intermediate output format options. *SMIC* has several outputs, which are easy to parse.

11.4.2 Limitations

Since *SMIC* is not directly associated with a network management platform, its output is not immediately usable by these applications. *SMIC's* best use is as a MIB development tool. This is not to meant to imply that *SMIC* cannot or should not be used with these platforms. Indeed, by writing the appropriate back-end compilers, *SMIC* can be integrated into other management systems.

SMIC does not compile MIBs directly, rather it processes a special "wrapper file," which includes the actual MIB module.

11.5 ISODE

The MIB compiler supplied with the ISO Development Environment (ISODE) is called *MOSY. MOSY* accepts SNMPv1 or SNMPv2 MIBs, and generates a simple intermediate format suitable for use by back-end compilers. It is easy to write a back-end parser that uses this output. MOSY has historically been used as a "proof of correctness" test for MIB modules published by IETF working groups. MIBs must pass through this MIB compiler with no errors before being considered for advancement along the standards-track. However, this is no longer the case, since SMIC (and its updated version, SMICng) provide much better analysis and are now being used by IETF working groups.

11.5.1 Basic Usage

The command line syntax of MOSY is:

```
mosy [ -o <file-name> ] [-s ] <mib>
```

The -o option renames the intermediate output file to be <file-name>.

The -s option indicates silent operation.

11.5.2 Intermediate file format

The intermediate file format has two types of entries:

- registration entries that define the OBJECT IDENTIFIER tree
- object definitions

1. For detailed instructions on using SMIC, see "SMIC User's Guide" on page 423.

The registration entries have the following format:

<branch-name> <parent-branch>.<subtree-branch>

For example:

```
mib-2        mgmt.1
system       mib2.1
interfaces   mib2.2
```

The *parent-branch* production is the name of the MIB registration directly above this level in the tree. These entries are mapped directly from the OBJECT IDENTIFIER registrations we find at the front part of a MIB. The registrations in this example came from these lines in the original MIB

```
mib-2 ::= OBJECT IDENTIFIER { mib-2 1 }
system ::= OBJECT IDENTIFIER { mib-2 1 }
interfaces ::= OBJECT IDENTIFIER { mib-2 1 }
```

Object definitions have the following format:

<object-name> <parent-branch>.<subtree-branch> <type> <access> <status>

Where:

<type> is one of:
- *OctetString*
- *ObjectId*
- *TimeTicks*
- *Gauge* or *Gauge32*
- *INTEGER* or *Integer32*
- *Aggregate*
- *Counter*, *Counter32* or *Counter64*

<access> is one of:
- *read-only*
- *read-write*
- *read-create*
- *not-accessible*

<status> is one of:
- *mandatory*
- *deprecated*
- *current*

Some of the *type* fields are close to, but not exactly like their ASN.1 equivalents, and we also see a new keyword, *Aggregate.* The small changes in the names of the data types make it a bit easier to parse the intermediate format. A program scanning the output never needs to read a mix of two-part and one-part type names. That is, the type OCTET STRING becomes OctetString, and the keyword *Aggregate* represents the ASN.1 production *SEQUENCE OF*, as shown in Table 11–2.

Table 11–2 Mosy Types

MOSY Type	SMI Type
OctetString	OCTET STRING
object-id	OBJECT IDENTIFIER
TimeTicks	TimeTicks
Gauge	Gauge
Gauge32	Gauge32
Counter	Counter
Counter32	Counter32
Counter64	Counter64
Integer32	Integer32
INTEGER	INTEGER
Aggregate	SEQUENCE OF
Counter	Counter

Let's take a small example where we can see the result of a simple translation. Suppose that we take a MIB object from MIB-II:

```
ifNumber        OBJECT-TYPE
        SYNTAX          INTEGER
        ACCESS          read-only
        STATUS          mandatory
        DESCRIPTION
                "The number of network interfaces (regardless of their
                current state) on this system"
        ::= { interfaces 1 }
```

MOSY translates this object into this single line:

```
ifNumber        interfaces.1        INTEGER        read-only  mandatory
```

Mosy also uses a series of productions delimited with "%" to note some special items within MIB (See Table 11–3)

Table 11–3 Mosy Output Directives

Directive	Meaning
%n0	OBJECT IDENTIFIER registration
%tc	Textual Convention Definition
%ev	Enumerated Values
%ei	Index Clause
%er	Range on INTEGER or OCTET STRINGs

Let's take a look at a few examples of these productions. A TEXTUAL CONVENTION that had this original declaration:

```
PositiveInteger ::= TEXTUAL-CONVENTION
        STATUS          current
        DESCRIPTION     "A positive Integer"
        SYNTAX          Integer32 (0..'7FFFFFFF'h)
```

becomes

```
%tc     PositiveInteger     Integer32           ""
```

Enumerated INTEGER based values declared like this:

```
Status ::= TEXTUAL-CONVENTION
        STATUS          current
        DESCRIPTION     "Status of the Interface"
        SYNTAX          INTEGER { enabled(1), disabled(2) }
```

would become:

```
%ev     Status     enabled  1
%ev     Status     disabled 2
```

INTEGER based values with restricted ranges declared as:

```
currentTemperature OBJECT-TYPE
        SYNTAX          INTEGER(0..100)
        MAX-ACCESS      read-only
        STATUS          current
        DESCRIPTION     "Current Internal Temperature"
        ::= { chassis 1 }
```

would become:

```
currentTemperature      chassis.1            INTEGER        read-only current
%er                     currentTemperature 0                100
```

11.5.3 Limitations

The simplicity of MOSY's intermediate output comes at a price: some of the information contained within the original MIB is not retained. Comments and default values, for example, are not present in the processed output, so you may run into a few problems if you are planning on using MOSY for development of certain types of back-end compilers.

MOSY has no options to control its checking of MIBs. You are stuck with what the programmer for MOSY decided are syntax and semantic rules for MIB modules. Unfortunately, MOSY doesn't check many of the semantic rules for the SMIv2 constructs.

MOSY's biggest deficiency is its lack of checking of the dependencies between MIB modules. Thus, an IMPORT statement may refer to non-existing items. Also, the values of imported items are not known, and, thus, the intermediate output leaves the values of these items unresolved.

11.6 Using SMIC to Write a MIB

As any good MIB compiler should, SMIC can help write a MIB by pointing out syntactic errors in your MIBs. Unlike other MIB compilers, however, SMIC analyzes your MIB for following the semantic rules and several "well-known" writing conventions. Most MIB compilers only check that a MIB follows a sub-set of the correct syntax for MIB modules. What many MIB compilers miss are the rules for MIB semantics that are in the SMI documents. One example is:

> *If any columnar object in a conceptual row has "read-create" as its maximal level of access, then no other columnar object of the same conceptual row may have a maximal access of "read-write".*

There are dozens of these rules scattered throughout the SMI documents, and SMIC tries to check them all. Some MIBs that pass other MIB compiler checks may not pass through SMIC without errors or warnings, so using SMIC can be a bit irritating at first. Fortunately, SMIC is quite flexible with its checks, since you can vary the degree of its checking. As we have already mentioned, the complete user's guide to the SMIC system is included as an appendix at the end of this book.

11.7 Understanding SMIC's Back-end Format

To create your own back-end MIB compilers using SMIC, you need to have a firm grasp of intermediate productions from SMIC. Fortunately, the productions are quite simple, and you won't need an in-depth compiler background to get useful work done. Additionally, it is quite easy to write a back-end compiler for SMIC that processes only those productions of interest, and ignoring any others. We won't cover all the productions in this section, just some of the basic ones that occur most frequently.

11.7.1 Format Tags

SMIC output consists of one or more tagged productions, each terminated by a semicolon. This production, for instance:

```
nlFileVer 1
 sDate 14 "19950617124820"
 sCompilerId 61 "SMIC (the next generation) version 1.6.32, December 28, 1994.";
```

is at the head of every file SMIC generates. It identifies the version of the compiler, and the date of the compilation. The tag *nlFileVer* tells us what will follow: *a number*, the version of the file format; *sDate*, the compilation date of the MIB; and *sCompilerId*, an identification of the version of SMIC that produced this file. Each of the tags SMIC generates has one or more lowercase letter prefixes that indicate what sort of information will follow. (See Table 11–4)

Table 11–4 Prefixes for SMIC's Intermediate Output

Prefix	Meaning	Example
w	A simple word	ifIndex
s	A length plus a string	5 "A Dog"
n	A simple number	45
m	A two words separated by a period	RFC1213-MIB.system
d	An OID value in dotted format	1.2.3.4
c	A list in curly braces	{ nId 3 }
l	A list ending with a semicolon	ONE TWO ;

For example, the keyword *wnTest* indicates that the two arguments that follow will be a simple word, indicated by the *w*, and a number, indicated by the *n*.

```
wnTest SIMPLE 23
```

11.7.2 Production Tags

SMIC uses these tags to produce the higher level structures it uses to describe MIBs. Before we describe these higher level structures, we need to look at a few of the basic ones used throughout the output.

Locations

SMIC identifies the location of MIB items through the *nnLoc* production. This production is quite simple, but occurs so frequently in the SMICng output that it warrants special mention. As the name of the production tells us, it is simply two numbers: the line and column number, respectively.

```
nnLoc 13 15       -- Indicates line 13 column 15
```

OBJECT IDENTIFIERS

OBJECT IDENTIFIERS are expressed by two different productions: *cOIDval*, and *dOIDval*. The *dOIDval*, as the "d" format tag implies, is simply an OID written in the familiar dotted form: 1.3.6.1.2.1.1. The *cOIDval* production, on the other hand, is a bit more complex. The "c" tag indicates that the value will be a list enclosed in { }s. The members of this list will be one or more of these productions, plus a location identifier for each production. (See Table 11–5)

Table 11–5 Tags for OIDs

Tag	Example
nSUBid <number>	2
wnSUBid <name> <number>	org(3)
wSUBid <name>	ifEntry
mSUBid <name> "." <name>	RFC1213-MIB.ifIndex

For example:

```
wSUBid ifEntry nnLoc 32 15 nSUBid 1 nnLoc 32 22 is { ifEntry 1 }
```

SMIC uses quite a few supporting keywords to build up more complex productions. By far the most frequent is the production covering the OBJECT-TYPE macro.

OBJECT-TYPE

The production representing the OBJECT-TYPE from the SMI is called *wlOT* in the SMIC output. By the name, we know that the values following this tag will be a single word (w) and a list of additional productions followed by a terminating semicolon (l). Here is an example of what we can expect (the line numbers have been provided only for later discussion):

```
wlOT ifIndex                                              1
nnLoc 266 11                                              2
wStatus mandatory                                         3
wOTtype leaf                                              4
cInst { INTEGER }                                         5
cSyntax { SYNint nnLoc 267 23 }                           6
cRsyntax { SYNint nnLoc 267 23 }                          7
wAccess read-only                                         8
sDescr 255 "A unique value for each interface.  Its value 9
```

```
ranges between 1 and the value of ifNumber. The                            10
value for each interface must remain constant at                            11
least from one re-initialization of the entity's                            12
network management system to the next re-                                   13
initialization."                                                            14
cOIDval { wSUBid ifEntry nnLoc 277 21 nSUBid 1 nnLoc 277 29 }               15
dOIDval 1.3.6.1.2.1.2.2.1.1 ;                                               16
```

Here's the original MIB specification:

```
ifIndex OBJECT-TYPE
        SYNTAX          INTEGER
        ACCESS          read-only
        STATUS          mandatory
        DESCRIPTION
                "A unique value for each interface. Its value
                ranges between 1 and the value of ifNumber. The
                value for each interface must remain constant at
                least from one re-initialization of the entity's
                network management system to the next re-
                initialization."
        ::= { ifEntry 1 }
```

Let's look at this production line-by-line. Line 1 begins the production and tells us that we will see a name, *snmpAlarmTable*, and a list, the remaining productions. Line 2 indicates the location in the MIB the object declaration occurred. The STATUS from the original production is reflected in line 3. The values are what you would expect: current, obsolete, mandatory, and deprecated. Line 4 indicates what sort of object we are examining. There are only three types of objects SMIC considers: leaf, table, and row. A leaf node is an object that actually represents data. The *cInst* production given in line 5 demonstrates how an application can form the instance information for this object. Lines 6 and 7 describe (respectively) the syntax as it appears in the MIB, and the "resolved" syntax. In this example, they happen to be the same, but if this object used a textual convention, the original name would be given by *cSyntax*. The *cRsyntax* production, on the other hand, contains the underlying type of the textual convention. The ACCESS or MAX-ACCESS clause is stated by the *wAccess* production in line 8. The values here correspond directly to the legal values used in a MIB. Lines 8 through 15 contain the original description clause.

11.8 MIB2HTML: Publishing MIBs on the World Wide Web

To show that MIB compilers are useful for tasks other than code production and syntax checking, we wanted to include a project that was a bit different than those you may have encountered before. We want to construct a tool that will automatically produce MIBs that, for lack of a better word, are not quite so "MIB-like." Even though most of this book has been concerned with reading and writing MIBs in their ASN.1 form, it is this form that makes them inaccessible to many readers. This ASN.1 form of a MIB is intended more for machine processing than it is for human processing, and we hope to correct this shortcoming with this tool.[2]

In this project, we will create a back-end compiler that re-formats a MIB in a format suited for the World Wide Web (WWW). WWW documents use a language known as Hypertext Markup Language (HTML) to format a document and to aid in organizing related documents. Hypertext documents allow users to traverse documents in a non-linear fashion. That is, users can quickly jump from topic to topic without having to open multiple documents and manually search for an item of interest. There is nothing terribly complex about HTML, so don't be intimidated by the concept. HTML, like other markup languages such as Adobe's Postscript, or Knuth's $\TeX$, simply provide formatting directives to the document output device. In the case of Postscript or $\TeX$, however, the output device is typically a printer, whereas HTML documents on the WWW are usually viewed by users on screen. These formatting directives control how the document appears: the fonts, the justification of the margins, the interline spacing, etc. In addition to providing formatting directives, HTML offers some special capabilities that have nothing to do with how the document is to be displayed. This is where the hypertext concept appears. HTML allows a document author to specify the location of a special type of cross-reference known as a hypertext link. These links allow the users to make the jumps between documents.

Users view HTML documents using an application known as a *browser.* Browsers are special client applications that retrieve hypertext documents from a document server, and display them according to the HTML formatting directives found within the document itself. WWW browsers usually indicate these "jump points" with highlighted or underlined text, giving the user a hint that more information hides behind the word or phrase.

MIBs are rarely self-contained in one neat document. Increasingly, MIBs are dependent on one another. A good example of this is the *interfaces* table from MIB-II. This table models that physical and logical network interfaces on a system. Many of the network protocol MIBs use this MIB as a building block by augmenting this table. These cross references are good candidates for these hypertext links, and there are certainly other excellent links as well: the IMPORTS section of a MIB is a good candidate as well.

Before we begin, let's take a look at what we eventually want to produce: Figure 11–3 shows an example from the IETF 802.5 (Token Ring) MIB, formatted with the MIB2HTML back-end compiler. The words *Counter, transmission*, and *OBJECT-TYPE* represent links to other documents containing the details of their declaration. If the user clicks on them with the mouse, the documents defining them are automatically brought up. Local OBJECT IDENTIFIERS, those that are declared in this MIB module, are organized into a table where their complete values are given. Of course, we usually express the value of an OBJECT IDENTIFIER symbolically, i.e., interfaces.3 or mgmt.2, but in this table we have the complete values specified.

2. This tool is included on the CD-ROM included with this book.

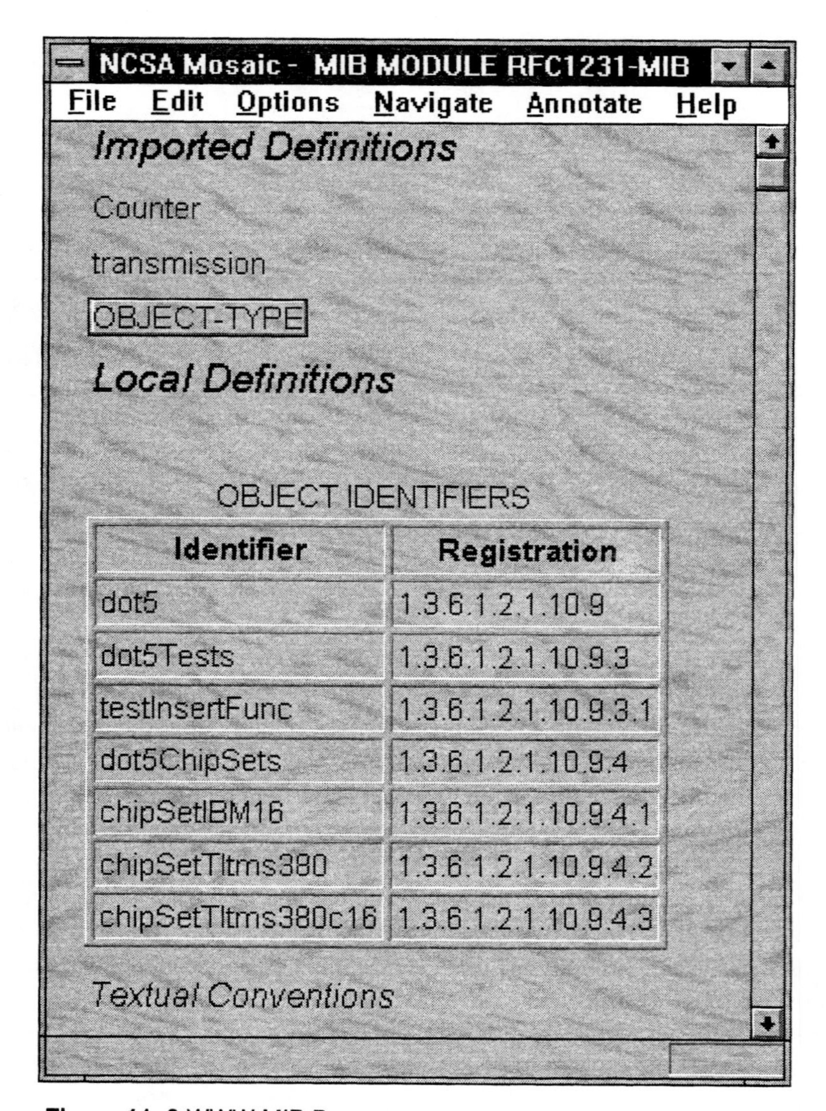

Figure 11–3 WWW MIB Browser

Now let's come up with a list of what types of links we want to provide in our documents:

- links between each imported item and its original definition
- links between each use of a textual convention and its definition
- links between a central registration document and each MIB we compile

Of course, HTML also provides general format specifications, so we can also format the MIB objects to make the important aspects of a MIB easier to identify:

- format a table composed of all object identifier registrations
- condense MIB table declarations into a table of the vital information: types, access, status, etc.
- indicate special fields, such as indices, by putting them in bold or italics

Looking at this as a complete system, we can see that we have several components working together to produce these formatted MIBs. (See Figure 11–4)

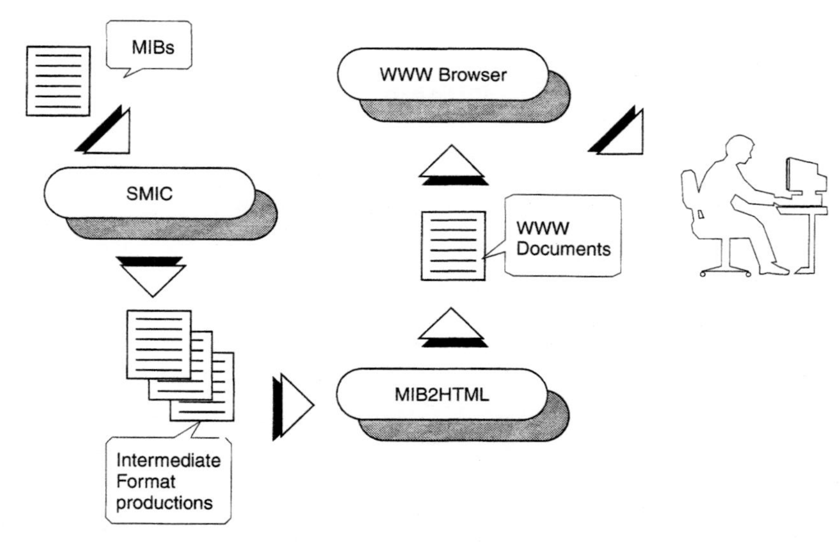

Figure 11–4 WWW Document Production System

11.9 A Development Kit

Now that you've gotten an introduction to what a MIB compiler system can do, you might wish to try to develop some tools of your own. On the CD-ROM accompanying this book, we've included these items:

- versions of the SMIC compiler for several popular operating systems
- the MIB to HTML formatting back-end compiler
- all MIBs produced by the IETF working groups

With these tools and your favorite programming language, you will be set to create a complete MIB processing framework.

CHAPTER 12

Development of a MIB

In this chapter, we will examine a complete example of organizing an information framework for a mythical manufacturer. As SNMP is creeping into non-network oriented applications, we wanted to examine a problem where you would not miss the important details because you were not familiar with the fundamental technology. So this chapter will examine a topic familiar to many readers: lawn sprinklers.[1] Even if you aren't familiar with them, we are confident that you can pick up the details without too much trouble. We have taken a few liberties with the topic, however. Sprinkler systems as sophisticated as the ones we are describing may not exist, but we needed to make them a bit more interesting to demonstrate some of the techniques discussed so far.

12.1 Problem Statement

Our task is to create an information framework for a supplier of irrigation and sprinkler systems. We will call this vendor *SprinkleCo*. SprinkleCo has two product lines: commercial, intended for applications in industrial landscaping, parks and athletic fields; and residential, intended for consumer landscaping. The product lines are actually quite sophisticated and include such advanced features as:

- soil moisture detection
- flow rate monitoring
- pressure monitoring
- leak detection

The goal of all our work, of course, is to make it possible to create a line of sprinkler management software that exploits these key features.

1. Not that you asked, but this chapter was written as one of the authors was attempting to install his own lawn sprinkler system. Give an engineer a simple task, and he is sure to over-design it.

12.1.1 Sprinklers In General

As an introduction, let's look at sprinkler systems in general. The overall concept of a sprinkler system is quite simple: a user-controlled valve releases water into a pipe, allowing it to flow from multiple openings onto the landscaping. There are five components of a sprinkler system we will be concerned with in this example:

- runs of pipe that carry water throughout the system
- valves that allow water to flow into runs of pipe
- emitter heads that allow water to flow out of the pipe
- sensors that report information on soil conditions
- a control device that runs the system by engaging valves

A typical installation would look something like Figure 12–1:

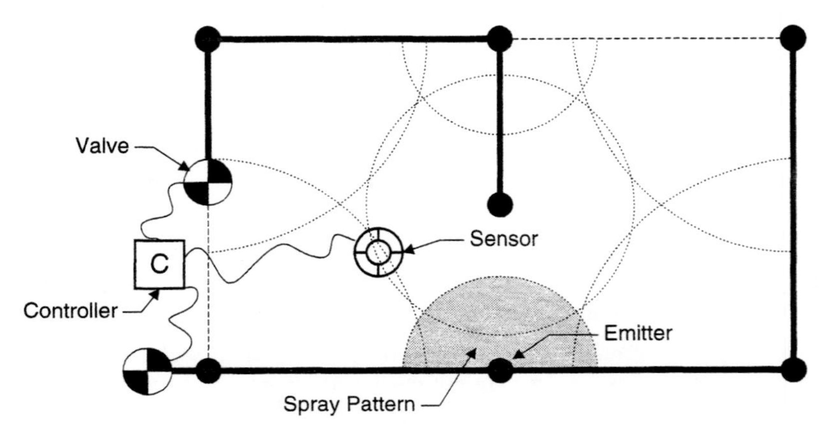

Figure 12–1 A sprinkler installation

12.1.2 Valves

The valves in this system come in two flavors: continuous adjustment, and simple on/off. The continuous adjustment valves allow the controller module to dictate how much water is allowed to flow through. The controller can allow the pipe a high volume of water. The simple valves just open and close on demand. (See Figure 12–2)

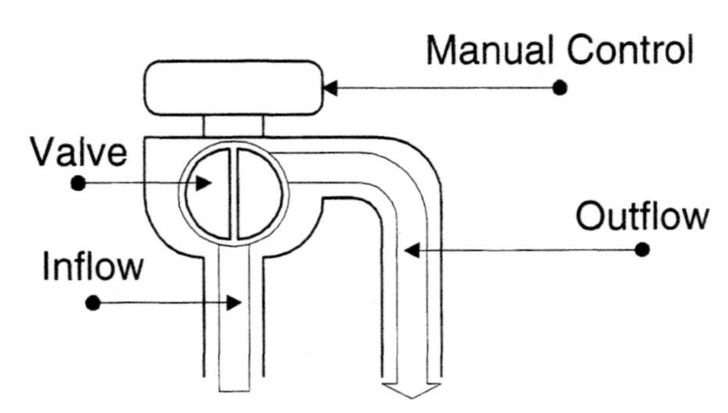

Figure 12–2 Valve cross-section

Both types of valves can be activated manually, just like turning on a water spigot. Valves report the following to the controller:

- the current pressure of the water in the pipe
- the current flow rate of the water in the pipe
- the number of gallons that have flowed through this pipe
- the number of times the valve has been opened and closed

12.1.3 Emitters

The emitters, or spray-heads, are the delivery points for the system. (See Figure 12–3) Water leaves the pipes at this point to rain down on the thirsty plants. The emitter valves in the industrial units are individually controllable. The residential units do not have this feature; when water enters the pipe, the sprinkler emitters open.

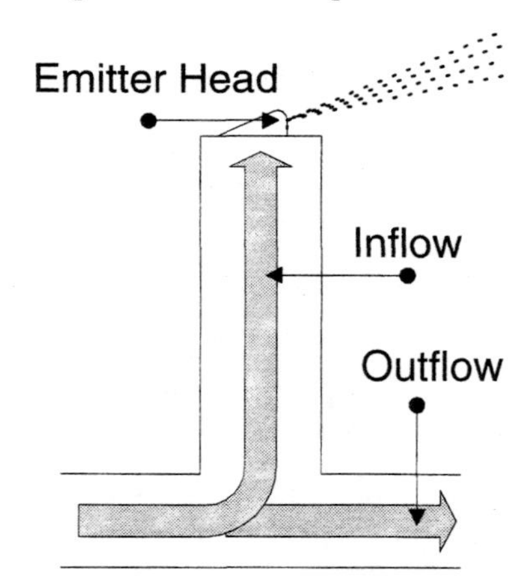

Figure 12–3 Emitter cross-section

12.1.4 Sensors

The sensors allow a user to monitor the moisture content of the soil. An installation can have any number of sensors, although few sites will have more sensors than the number of valves. The controller receives a continuous reading from the sensors indicating the level of water saturation in the soil. This level varies from 0 (dry) to 100 (swampy).

12.1.5 Control Device

The control device is where the agent implementing our MIB resides. The control device sends the signals to the emitters and valves, as well as collecting information from the sensors. Controllers have the following features:

- a real-time clock that can be set from a management station
- on-demand diagnostics
- the ability to schedule watering plans on a regular basis
- report significant events: soil moisture exceeded an allowable range, component controlled by the device has failed

12.1.6 Programmed Watering

The industrial controllers can be programmed with a series of watering schedules. Each schedule has the following attributes:

- the valve to be opened
- the time of day to activate the program
- the duration of the program
- the interval between activations of the program

12.2 Framework Requirements

Before we push forward with developing MIBs, we need to have a firm grasp on exactly what we are trying to accomplish with this framework. Let's draw up a short list of exactly what we want to do:

- determine what sort of components are present in the system: emitters, valves, sensors, and controllers
- examine the attributes of each component
- control each component: turn them on and off, run diagnostics etc.
- create schedule watering plans
- monitor resource levels: flow rates, pressure levels, moisture saturation, etc.
- examine statistical data: total water flow through a component, numbers of valve failures
- be notified if a catastrophic event occurs: a valve is clogged, or a leak is detected

Using this list as a starting point, we should be able to focus on solving these problems.

12.3 Object Analysis

Now that we are familiar with sprinkler systems, we need to take a closer look at the attributes of the components in the system, and identify those we want to monitor or control.

Pipe

Since they can't grow smaller or larger on demand, the pipes have no dynamic properties we can monitor or manage. However, the pipes form the basis for our watering system, so we want to monitor them for leaks and usage levels.

Emitters

Emitters have two major properties: flow rates, expressed in gallons per minute (GPM); and flow patterns. The flow rate of an emitter is, of course, a function of the water pressure applied to it, so this will vary between systems. The flow pattern is a static property of the object, which we know from the model number of the emitter.

Valves

Valves have two properties with which we are concerned: maximum flow rate and current flow rate. The maximum flow rate is, of course, a static property. This rate is built into the device at design time. Current flow rate, on the other hand, is a dynamic property we need to be able to monitor and manage. The industrial valves allow for "infinite-adjustment." The controller can request that the valve open wide, allowing high pressure in the line, or open only a small amount, allowing low pressure in the line. Higher pressure results in greater water delivery at the emitters, so this adjustment is crucial to the entire system.

Moisture Sensors

The moisture sensors do what their name implies: detect the moisture level in the soil. There are no control objects for the sensors; the sensors simply report the amount of moisture in the surrounding soil.

The components of the sprinkler systems have some clear-cut numeric relationships:

- a system has one or more runs of pipe
- every run of pipe has one valve
- every run of pipe has one or more emitter heads

Using this information, we can organize the lawn system into the matrix introduced in Chapter 7. (See Table 12–1)

Table 12–1 Sprinkler Object Analysis Worksheet

Component	Cardinality	Attributes	Statistics	State
Emitters	1 to number of emitters	flow rate	Gallons	open, closed
Pipes	1 to number of runs	Diameter	Flow rate	
Valves	1 to number of runs	Capacity	Flow rate	open, closed
Valves	1 to number of runs	Capacity	Flow rate, Pressure	percent open
Sensors	1 to number of sensors			moisture level

12.4 Using Standard MIBs

The IETF and vendor consortiums have, together and separately, defined a vast number of MIBs ready for use by vendors of networking equipment, software, and services.[2] Perhaps the best approach to MIB design is to decide which MIBs not to design. MIBs produced by standards bodies are not always the closest fit for a particular product, but they often have the benefit of a great many well experienced MIB designers. Our case is a bit different; as of this writing, there isn't a vendor consortium of sprinkler manufacturers defining a MIB. Consequently, we will do most of the ground breaking design here. Ordinarily, you should search for any work already done on the subject, and use that as a starting point for your own designs.

2. See "Mailing Lists" on page 485.

The SNMPv2 framework defines a MIB module which all agents should implement: SNMPv2-MIB.[3] The suggested groups every agent should implement are:

- snmpGroup, which describes network management traffic into and out of the device
- snmpSetGroup, which allows managers to coordinate access to an agent and resources controlled by that agent
- systemGroup, which describes general agent information
- snmpBasicNotificationsGroup, which contains the events an agent should implement

12.5 Framework Design

Our first task is the design of the OID infrastructure for our information framework. First, we must obtain a MIB registration point from the central naming authority.[4] For our fictitious company, we will use a branch beneath the authors' sub-tree, which is { *enterprises* 1194 }. We have registered this branch as:

{ enterprises mibs4you(1194) sprinkleCo(1) }, or { 1 3 6 1 4 1 1194 1 }

Following the model we outlined in Chapter 8, we will allocate six sub-trees to hold the top level registrations of our company:

```
-- the root of the sub-tree for SprinkleCo
sprinklecoRoot          OBJECT IDENTIFIER ::= { enterprises mibs4you(1194) 1 }

-- sub-tree for registrations, which includes modules
sprinklecoReg           OBJECT IDENTIFIER ::= { sprinklecoRoot 1 }
  sprinklecoModules     OBJECT IDENTIFIER ::= { sprinklecoReg 1 }

-- sub-tree for company-wide objects and events
sprinklecoGeneric       OBJECT IDENTIFIER ::= { sprinklecoRoot 2 }

-- sub-tree for product-specific objects and events
sprinklecoProducts      OBJECT IDENTIFIER ::= { sprinklecoRoot 3 }

-- sub-tree for agent profiles
sprinklecoCaps          OBJECT IDENTIFIER ::= { sprinklecoRoot 4 }

-- sub-tree for requirement specifications
sprinklecoReqs          OBJECT IDENTIFIER ::= { sprinklecoRoot 5 }

-- sub-tree for experiments
sprinklecoExpr          OBJECT IDENTIFIER ::= { sprinklecoRoot 6 }
```

3. This MIB module replaces the system and snmp groups found in RFC1213, better known as MIB-2.
4. See "Requesting an Enterprise Identifier" on page 483.

Now we can begin work on the registration tree. This tree holds the OBJECT IDENTIFIERs we will use to identify pieces of hardware as well as logical items such as agent resources. To make our registration points more self-identifying, we have added "Reg" to the end of the name. You can use any convention you wish, but choosing a consistent style will help avoid confusion when faced with similar looking names.

```
-- product families
industrialProducts          OBJECT IDENTIFIER ::= { sprinklecoReg 2 }
-- industrial product lines
   industrialValvesReg      OBJECT IDENTIFIER ::= { industrialProducts 1 }
   industrialEmitterReg     OBJECT IDENTIFIER ::= { industrialProducts 2 }
   industrialDetectorReg    OBJECT IDENTIFIER ::= { industrialProducts 3 }
   industrialControllerReg  OBJECT IDENTIFIER ::= { industrialProducts 4 }

consumerProducts            OBJECT IDENTIFIER ::= { sprinklecoReg 3 }
-- consumer product lines
   consumerValvesReg        OBJECT IDENTIFIER ::= { consumerProducts 1 }
   consumerEmitterReg       OBJECT IDENTIFIER ::= { consumerProducts 2 }
   consumerDetectorReg      OBJECT IDENTIFIER ::= { consumerProducts 3 }
   consumerControllerReg    OBJECT IDENTIFIER ::= { consumerProducts 4 }

-- registrations for the actual hardware
superValve101Reg            OBJECT IDENTIFIER ::= { consumerValvesReg 1 }
superValve201Reg            OBJECT IDENTIFIER ::= { consumerValvesReg 2 }
superValve301Reg            OBJECT IDENTIFIER ::= { consumerValvesReg 3 }
superEmitter101Reg          OBJECT IDENTIFIER ::= { consumerEmitterReg 1 }
superEmitter102Reg          OBJECT IDENTIFIER ::= { consumerEmitterReg 2 }
superEmitter103Reg          OBJECT IDENTIFIER ::= { consumerEmitterReg 3 }
superController101Reg       OBJECT IDENTIFIER ::= { consumerControllerReg 1 }
```

Now let's put these registrations into a registration module.

```
SPRINKLECO-GLOBAL-REG DEFINITIONS ::= BEGIN
IMPORTS
        MODULE-IDENTITY, OBJECT-IDENTITY,
        enterprises
                FROM SNMPv2-SMI;

sprinklecoGlobalRegModule MODULE-IDENTITY
        LAST-UPDATED            "9609080000Z"
        ORGANIZATION            "SprinkleCo"
        CONTACT-INFO
                "Evan McGinnis
                email: bem@3com.com"
        DESCRIPTION
                "The SprinkleCo central registration module"
        ::= { sprinklecoModules 1 }
```

```
-- the root of the sub-tree for SprinkleCo
sprinklecoRoot            OBJECT IDENTIFIER ::= { enterprises mibs4you(1194) 1 }

-- sub-tree for registrations, which includes modules
sprinklecoReg             OBJECT IDENTIFIER ::= { sprinklecoRoot 1 }
  sprinklecoModules       OBJECT IDENTIFIER ::= { sprinklecoReg 1 }

-- sub-tree for company-wide objects and events
sprinklecoGeneric         OBJECT IDENTIFIER ::= { sprinklecoRoot 2 }
-- sub-tree for product-specific objects and events
sprinklecoProducts        OBJECT IDENTIFIER ::= { sprinklecoRoot 3 }
-- sub-tree for agent profiles
sprinklecoCaps            OBJECT IDENTIFIER ::= { sprinklecoRoot 4 }
-- sub-tree for requirement specifications
sprinklecoReqs            OBJECT IDENTIFIER ::= { sprinklecoRoot 5 }
-- sub-tree for experiments
sprinklecoExpr            OBJECT IDENTIFIER ::= { sprinklecoRoot 6 }

-- Product families
industrialProducts        OBJECT IDENTIFIER ::= { sprinklecoReg 2 }
-- Industrial product lines --
  industrialValvesReg     OBJECT IDENTIFIER ::= { industrialProducts 1 }
  industrialEmitterReg    OBJECT IDENTIFIER ::= { industrialProducts 2 }
  industrialDetectorReg   OBJECT IDENTIFIER ::= { industrialProducts 3 }
  industrialControllerReg OBJECT IDENTIFIER ::= { industrialProducts 4 }

consumerProducts          OBJECT IDENTIFIER ::= { sprinklecoReg 3 }
-- Consumer product lines
  consumerValvesReg       OBJECT IDENTIFIER ::= { consumerProducts 1 }
  consumerEmitterReg      OBJECT IDENTIFIER ::= { consumerProducts 2 }
  consumerDetectorReg     OBJECT IDENTIFIER ::= { consumerProducts 3 }
  consumerControllerReg   OBJECT IDENTIFIER ::= { consumerProducts 4 }

-- Products
-- the registrations for the actual hardware
superValve101Reg          OBJECT-IDENTITY
       STATUS             current
       DESCRIPTION        "The Super Valve Model 101"
       ::= { consumerValvesReg 1 }

superValve201Reg          OBJECT-IDENTITY
       STATUS             current
       DESCRIPTION        "The Super Valve Model 201"
       ::= { consumerValvesReg 2 }
```

```
superValve301Reg          OBJECT-IDENTITY
        STATUS            current
        DESCRIPTION       "The Super Valve Model 301"
        ::= { consumerValvesReg 3 }
superEmitter101Reg        OBJECT-IDENTITY
        STATUS            current
        DESCRIPTION       "The Super Emitter Model 101"
        ::= { consumerEmitterReg 1 }

superEmitter102Reg        OBJECT-IDENTITY
        STATUS            current
        DESCRIPTION       "The Super Emitter Model 102"
        ::= { consumerEmitterReg 2 }

superEmitter103Reg        OBJECT-IDENTITY
        STATUS            current
        DESCRIPTION       "The Super Emitter Model 103"
        ::= { consumerEmitterReg 3 }

superController101Reg     OBJECT-IDENTITY
        STATUS            current
        DESCRIPTION       "The Super Controller Model 101"
        ::= { consumerControllerReg 1 }
END
```

The OID values for the items defined in this MIB module are:

```
1.3.6.1.4.1.1194.1 OVA: sprinklecoRoot
1.3.6.1.4.1.1194.1.1 OVA: sprinklecoReg
1.3.6.1.4.1.1194.1.1.1 OVA: sprinklecoModules
1.3.6.1.4.1.1194.1.1.1.1 MI: sprinklecoGlobalRegModule
1.3.6.1.4.1.1194.1.1.2 OVA: industrialProducts
1.3.6.1.4.1.1194.1.1.2.1 OVA: industrialValvesReg
1.3.6.1.4.1.1194.1.1.2.2 OVA: industrialEmitterReg
1.3.6.1.4.1.1194.1.1.2.3 OVA: industrialDetectorReg
1.3.6.1.4.1.1194.1.1.2.4 OVA: industrialControllerReg
1.3.6.1.4.1.1194.1.1.3 OVA: consumerProducts
1.3.6.1.4.1.1194.1.1.3.1 OVA: consumerValvesReg
1.3.6.1.4.1.1194.1.1.3.1.1 OI: superValve101Reg
1.3.6.1.4.1.1194.1.1.3.1.2 OI: superValve201Reg
1.3.6.1.4.1.1194.1.1.3.1.3 OI: superValve301Reg
1.3.6.1.4.1.1194.1.1.3.2 OVA: consumerEmitterReg
1.3.6.1.4.1.1194.1.1.3.2.1 OI: superEmitter101Reg
1.3.6.1.4.1.1194.1.1.3.2.2 OI: superEmitter102Reg
1.3.6.1.4.1.1194.1.1.3.2.3 OI: superEmitter103Reg
1.3.6.1.4.1.1194.1.1.3.3 OVA: consumerDetectorReg
```

```
1.3.6.1.4.1.1194.1.1.3.4 OVA: consumerControllerReg
1.3.6.1.4.1.1194.1.1.3.4.1 OI: superController101Reg
1.3.6.1.4.1.1194.1.2 OVA: sprinklecoGeneric
1.3.6.1.4.1.1194.1.3 OVA: sprinklecoProducts
1.3.6.1.4.1.1194.1.4 OVA: sprinklecoCaps
1.3.6.1.4.1.1194.1.5 OVA: sprinklecoReqs
1.3.6.1.4.1.1194.1.6 OVA: sprinklecoExpr
```

Our top-level registration work is done. Now we are ready to create some objects that will help us manage the sprinkler system.

12.6 MIB Modules Layout

First, let's layout the top level structure of our MIB to get an idea of the work ahead. Looking at our previous analysis, we first assign a value for the root and create sub-trees for the conformance area, which includes groups and compliances:

```
-- root for items in the controller MIB module
sprinklecoControllerMIB    OBJECT IDENTIFIER ::= { sprinklecoProducts 1 }

-- conformance area, containing groups and compliance specifications
sprinklecoControllerConfs  OBJECT IDENTIFIER ::= { sprinklecoControllerMIB 1 }
sprinklecoControllerGroups OBJECT IDENTIFIER ::= { sprinklecoControllerConfs 1 }
sprinklecoControllerCompl OBJECT IDENTIFIER ::= { sprinklecoControllerConfs 2 }
```

There are three major categories we need to model: the controller itself, the valves, and the watering programs. Here, we create a sub-tree for the objects, and the sub-trees for each functional area:

```
-- sub-tree for objects, and for each functional area
sprinklecoControllerObjs    OBJECT IDENTIFIER ::= { sprinklecoControllerMIB 2 }
sprinklecoControllerControllerObjs OBJECT IDENTIFIER ::= { sprinklecoControllerObjs 1 }
sprinklecoControllerValveObjs OBJECT IDENTIFIER ::= { sprinklecoControllerObjs 2 }
sprinklecoControllerProgramObjs OBJECT IDENTIFIER ::= { sprinklecoControllerObjs 3 }
```

Finally, we create a sub-tree for events. So the events can be easily translated to SNMPv1 traps, we create an additional branch with value of zero:

```
-- sub-tree for events
sprinklecoControllerEvents  OBJECT IDENTIFIER ::= { sprinklecoControllerMIB 3 }
sprinklecoControllerEventsV2 OBJECT IDENTIFIER ::= { sprinklecoControllerEvents 0 }
```

12.7 Controller Group

Now we are ready to concentrate the object declarations for the sprinkler controller. We need to expose these properties of the controller: the current time of day maintained by the real-time clock, the controller model, and the state of the controller. First, let's take care of identifying the controller. Remember that we will implement the *system* group from the SNMPv2-MIB module. Many management applications depend on using *sysObjectId* from this group to identify a device:

```
sysObjectID OBJECT-TYPE
        SYNTAX          OBJECT IDENTIFIER
        ACCESS          read-only
        STATUS          mandatory
        DESCRIPTION
                "The vendor's authoritative identification of the
                network management sub-system contained in the
                entity.  This value is allocated within the SMI
                enterprises sub-tree (1.3.6.1.4.1) and provides an
                easy and unambiguous means for determining 'what
                kind of box' is being managed.  For example, if
                vendor 'Flintstones, Inc.' was assigned the
                sub-tree 1.3.6.1.4.1.4242, it could assign the
                identifier 1.3.6.1.4.1.4242.1.1 to its 'Fred
                Router'."
        ::= { system 2 }
```

This is the object where we use the registration tree we built earlier. If a management station requested the value of sysObjectId of a consumer controller model #101, the agent would return the value *superController101Reg*, which we defined in the SPRINKLECO-GLOBAL-REG as *{ consumerControllerReg 1 }*.

Next, we need to identify the version of software currently running on the controller. When the definition of sysObjectID was published, most developers interpreted it to identify a piece of hardware. However, some agent implementors interpreted sysObjectID to identify the software as well. The description clause above certainly seems to imply that hardware identification is the proper use of this object, but some vendors use this object to identify the software version of the SNMP agent software by attaching version information at the end of the hardware identifier. Suppose, for example, that we had software release 4.1 of the controller software. The value returned for sysObjectID would be:

```
-- The sysObjectID of the superController101Reg with 4.1 software
1.3.6.1.4.1.1194.1.1.3.4.1.4.1
```

The meaning of sysObjectID was clarified during an SNMP WG meeting—it only identifies a device type and does not specifiy a software version. Also, a version number appended to the end can cause problems with management applications, since they may have trouble identifying devices using this approach. We use sysObjectID to identify the hardware, and identify the software in separate objects. Here, we can use two integers to identify the major and minor release numbers:

```
controllerMajorVersion OBJECT-TYPE
        SYNTAX          Unsigned32
        MAX-ACCESS      read-only
        STATUS          current
        DESCRIPTION
                "The major release of the controller software.
                In the release identifier 4.1, the 4 is the major release
                number"
        ::= { sprinklecoControllerControllerObjs 1 }

controllerMinorVersion OBJECT-TYPE
        SYNTAX          Unsigned32
        MAX-ACCESS      read-only
        STATUS          current
        DESCRIPTION
                "The minor release number of the controller software.
                In the release identifier 4.1, the 1 is the minor release
                number"
        ::= { sprinklecoControllerControllerObjs 2 }
```

That leaves us with the time of day and the controller state object. The MIB-2 object *sysUpTime* isn't the sort of time object we need for this device. SysUpTime doesn't tell us anything about the current time. Rather, it is an indication of the time since the last re-initialization of the SNMP agent. We need a representation of a real-time clock using a fixed epoch. In other words, we need to be able to retrieve and set the time of day. There are several ways to approach this.

We can represent the time as a DisplayString and use a standard format for the representation:

```
controllerTime OBJECT-TYPE
        SYNTAX          DisplayString(SIZE(8))
        MAX-ACCESS      read-write
        STATUS          current
        DESCRIPTION
                "The current time as a 24 hour clock. The value is in the
                format hh:mm:ss. The time is expressed as a 24 hour
                clock. Some examples of legal strings are:
                02:03:33 and 14:59:59."
        ::= { sprinklecoControllerControllerObjs 3 }
```

Using the DisplayString makes displaying the time quite simple. Management applications need only fetch the value and display it. Another approach is representing time as a count of the number of seconds since midnight.

```
controllerTime OBJECT-TYPE
        SYNTAX          Unsigned32(0..86400) -- number of seconds in a day
        MAX-ACCESS      read-write
        STATUS          current
        DESCRIPTION     "The current time expressed in seconds past midnight"
        ::= { sprinklecoControllerControllerObjs 3 }
```

This approach is a bit more compact, as it will use the smallest possible number of octets once encoded using BER. There's one more approach to this problem we should consider. We can take the numeric values for the hours, minutes, and seconds, and pack them into an OCTET STRING:

```
controllerTime OBJECT-TYPE
        SYNTAX          OCTET STRING(SIZE (3))
        MAX-ACCESS      read-write
        STATUS          current
        DESCRIPTION
                "The current time, with the octets holding these values:
                Octet     Value               Range
                --------  --------            ---------
                1         hour                0..23
                2         minutes             0..59
                3         seconds             0..60"
        ::= { sprinklecoControllerControllerObjs 3 }
```

Of course, there is no one right answer. For our MIB, we will stay with expressing the time in a DisplayString.

Our final objects for the controller are the diagnostic and state control system. Let's take the state control objects first. As we have seen before, we can distinguish between the *desired* state (the administrative state), and the *current* (the operational state). Doing this, we get these two objects:

```
controllerOperState OBJECT-TYPE
        SYNTAX          INTEGER { running(1), resetting(2), diagnosing(3),
                                  stopped(4), failed(5) }
        MAX-ACCESS      read-only
        STATUS          current
        DESCRIPTION
                "The current state of the controller. The values are:
                running(1)        The controller is currently operating
                resetting(2)      The controller is being restarted
                diagnosing(3)     The controller is performing self-diagnostics
                stopped(4)        The controller has been halted
                failed(5)         The controller halted itself. See the
                                  controllerDiagnostics object for details."
        ::= { sprinklecoControllerControllerObjs 4 }
```

```
controllerAdminState OBJECT-TYPE
        SYNTAX          INTEGER { run(1), reset(2), diagnose(3), stop(4) }
        MAX-ACCESS      read-write
        STATUS          current
        DESCRIPTION
                "The desired state of the controller. Setting the value of this
                object to these values will have the following actions:
                run(1)              The controller will enter the run state
                reset(2)            The controller will restart
                diagnose(3)         Will activate the diagnostic routines
                stop(4)             Will halt the controller"
        ::= { sprinklecoControllerControllerObjs 5 }
```

Now we need an object to hold the results of the diagnostic operation.

```
controllerDiagnostics OBJECT-TYPE
        SYNTAX          INTEGER { noResults(1), passed(2),
                                        hardwareFault(3), softwareFault(4) }
        MAX-ACCESS      read-only
        STATUS          current
        DESCRIPTION
                "Indicates the results of the last diagnostic routine performed
                noResults(1)        No diagnostic has yet been performed
                passed(2)           The diagnostics has been passed
                hardwareFault(3)    Hardware fault
                softwareFault(4)    Software fault"
        ::= { sprinklecoControllerControllerObjs 6 }
```

12.8 Valves

The next group we need to consider is the basis for the entire system: the valves. We will have multiple runs of pipe in our system with a valve controlling each one, so we need to represent the valves as entries within a table. It is often helpful for management applications to know the numbers of table entries in advance, so we can declare an object that provides this information:

```
valveCount OBJECT-TYPE
        SYNTAX          Unsigned32
        MAX-ACCESS      read-only
        STATUS          current
        DESCRIPTION     "The total number of valves in the system"
        ::= { sprinklecoControllerValveObjs 1 }
```

Now we can begin the table declaration. If we look back at our object analysis, we can see that there is no one attribute of a valve that can uniquely identify it. So, the easiest way to identify a valve (and thus index the table) will be simple integer, *valveIndex*. This simple integer will uniquely identify each physical valve.

```
valveTable OBJECT-TYPE
        SYNTAX          SEQUENCE OF ValveEntry
        MAX-ACCESS      not-accessible
        STATUS          current
        DESCRIPTION     "A table of valves within the sprinkler system"
        ::= { sprinklecoControllerValveObjs 2 }


valveEntry OBJECT-TYPE
        SYNTAX          ValveEntry
        MAX-ACCESS      not-accessible
        STATUS          current
        DESCRIPTION     "A row in the valve table. Entries cannot
                        be created or deleted via SNMP operations"
        INDEX           { valveIndex } -- this column will identify a valve
        ::= { valveTable 1 }
```

Before we look at the syntax of the *valveEntry*, let's examine what we have thus far. We have declared that *valveTable* is a list of *ValveEntry*, and that each entry in the list (*valveEntry*) has at least one unique value (*valveIndex*). Here is where table declarations can be a bit confusing: each *valveEntry* object uses the syntax *ValveEntry*. We haven't yet defined the type *ValveEntry*, so we need to do that now. If we look back at our analysis sheet, we can see that we have several properties of the valves to model: type, capacity, state, and pressure.

```
ValveEntry ::= SEQUENCE {
                valveIndex          Unsigned32,         -- INDEX Item
                valveType           OBJECT IDENTIFIER,
                valveCapacity       Unsigned32,
                valveAdminState     INTEGER,
                valveState          INTEGER,
                valvePressure       Gauge32
        }
```

This type definition indicates that each entry has five columns: *valveIndex*, the value by which a row is identified; *valveType*, the type of valve; *valveCapacity*, the maximum flow rate of the valve; *valveState*, the current condition of the valve; and *valvePressure*, the current pressure rating of the valve outflow. The next step is to define the syntax of each of these objects.

```
valveIndex OBJECT-TYPE
        SYNTAX          Unsigned32(1..65535)
        MAX-ACCESS      not-accessible
        STATUS          current
        DESCRIPTION     "The unique value which identifies this valve"
        ::= { valveEntry 1 }


-- The value of the valveType object will be one of the registrations declared in
-- the SPRINKLECO-GLOBAL-REG module
valveType OBJECT-TYPE
        SYNTAX          OBJECT IDENTIFIER
        MAX-ACCESS      read-only
        STATUS          current
        DESCRIPTION     "The type of valve"
        ::= { valveEntry 2 }

valveCapacity OBJECT-TYPE
        SYNTAX          Unsigned32(1..100)
        UNITS           "gallons per minute (GPM)"
        MAX-ACCESS      read-only
        STATUS          current
        DESCRIPTION
                "The rated flow capacity of this valve"
        ::= { valveEntry 3 }

valveState OBJECT-TYPE
        SYNTAX          INTEGER { off(1), on(2) }
        MAX-ACCESS      read-write
        STATUS          current
        DESCRIPTION
                "The current state of the valve.
                Setting this value to off(1) requests that the valve be shut off.
                Setting this valve to on(2) requests that the valve be turned on"
        ::= { valveEntry 4 }


valvePressure OBJECT-TYPE
        SYNTAX          Gauge32
        UNITS           "Pounds per square inch (PSI)"
        MAX-ACCESS      read-only
        STATUS          current
        DESCRIPTION
                "The current outlet pressure of the valve"
        ::= { valveEntry 5}
```

This completes our first attempt at the table definition, and it isn't a bad start. We can use this table to check on the current running status of the valves, and to turn valves on and off. The table lacks, however, statistics and a more coherent control model. The control object for the valve, *valveState*, needs some work. A more powerful concept for this object is the desired state/current state model. The current definition ignores the case of someone manually engaging the valve. To allow for this case, we can split this object into two objects:

```
valveAdminState OBJECT-TYPE
        SYNTAX          INTEGER { off(1), on(2), down(3) }
        MAX-ACCESS      read-write
        STATUS          current
        DESCRIPTION
                "The desired state of the valve.
                Setting this value to off(1) requests that the valve be shut off.
                Setting this valve to on(2) requests that the valve be turned on.
                Setting this valve to down(3) requests that the valve be marked
                        administratively down"
        ::= { valveEntry 4 }

valveOperState OBJECT-TYPE
        SYNTAX          INTEGER {
                                off(1),
                                on(2),
                                fault(3),
                                manualOn(4),
                                manualOff(5)}
        MAX-ACCESS      read-only
        STATUS          current
        DESCRIPTION     "The current state of the valve.
                        off(1)     indicates that the valve is currently shut
                        on(2)      indicates that the valve is currently open
                        fault(3)   indicates that the valve is down due to a fault
                        manualOn(4) indicates that the valve was manually open
                        manualOff(5) indicates that the valve was manually closed"
        ::= { valveEntry 5 }
```

Using these states, a valve which had been turned on manually would have a value for *valveOperState* of *manual*On(4), yet would have a value for *valveAdminState* of *off*(1).

Our current table also lacks any statistical objects. For now, we will add just two items: a measure of the total number of gallons of water that have passed through this valve, and the number of times the valve has been opened and closed.

```
valveOutFlow OBJECT-TYPE
        SYNTAX          Counter32
        UNITS           "Gallons"
        MAX-ACCESS      read-only
        STATUS          current
        DESCRIPTION
                "The volum of water that has passed through this valve"
        ::= { valveEntry 7 }

valveOpens OBJECT-TYPE
        SYNTAX          Counter32
        MAX-ACCESS      read-only
        STATUS          current
        DESCRIPTION
                "The number of times this valve has been opened"
        ::= { valveEntry 8 }
```

If we put all of this together into an example system we would have something like that shown in Table 12–2:

Table 12–2 Example values for the valve table

valveIndex	valveCapacity	valveAdminState	valveOperState	valuePressure	valveOutFlow	valveOpens
1	4	off	off	0	30	12
2	4	off	off	0	34	12
3	5	on	on	40	50	15
4	5	on	on	40	50	15
5	3	off	off	0	0	0

12.9 Event Definitions

Now that we have our basic MIB components defined, we need to consider the events that can occur at the controller. If you will recall from the introduction to the product lines, the valves have the ability to:

- perform self tests and report error conditions
- report line pressure
- indicate the current running status of the valve

Using these characteristics, we can define the following events for our system:

- valve malfunction, the valve failed a self test
- manual start, someone engaged a valve manually
- manual stop, someone disengaged a valve manually
- zero line pressure, the valve has detected no water pressure

When defining any type of event, we need to consider the objects that provide the details about the event. That is to say, the event needs to tell the management station not only what is wrong (valve malfunction, zero line pressure), but who is at fault (valve #27). Of course, events aren't required to specify any MIB variables. In those instances where the subject matter of the event is unambiguous, perhaps when the event concerns the agent itself, and not resources controlled by the agent, the list can be empty.

For each of our potential events, the valve needs to be identified. Also, we need to include the desired and the current state of the valve—variables *valveAdminState* and *valveOperState*. Since these objects are indexed by the valve number, the *valveIndex* variable does not need to be included with the event. (Also, since the access for *valveIndex* is *not-accessible*, it cannot be specified as included with the event.) The management station knows exactly which valve by the index of variables valveAdminState and valveOperState. Here are the definitions for the events:

```
valveMalfunction NOTIFICATION-TYPE
        OBJECTS         { valveAdminState, valveOperState, valvePressure }
        STATUS          current
        DESCRIPTION     "A valve failed a self test. The index of the
                        objects identify the valve"
        ::= { sprinklecoControllerEventsV2 1 }

valveManualChange NOTIFICATION-TYPE
        OBJECTS         { valveAdminState, valveOperState }
        STATUS          current
        DESCRIPTION     "A valve was manually turned on or off. The index of
                        the objects identity the valve"
        ::= { sprinklecoControllerEventsV2 2 }

valveZeroLinePressure NOTIFICATION-TYPE
        OBJECTS         { valveAdminState, valveOperState }
        STATUS          current
        DESCRIPTION     "A valve detected a complete drop in line pressure. The
                        index of the objects identity the valve"
        ::= { sprinklecoControllerEventsV2 3 }
```

12.10 Schedules

Each controller can be programmed with a pre-set schedule to follow, and we want to be able to control these schedules through SNMP. Each sprinkler "program" turns on a particular valve at a specific time for a specific length of time. After an interval between one day and one week has passed, the program is activated again. The sprinkler programs have the following items we need to model:

- the valve controlled by this program
- the time of day to start the valve
- the duration of the program
- the interval between invocations of the program

We will need a table to contain these items, as a controller can have several programs to run over time. The objects we just described should be easy to model:

```
programValveIndex OBJECT-TYPE
        SYNTAX          Unsigned32(1..65535)
        MAX-ACCESS      not-accessible
        STATUS          current
        DESCRIPTION     "The valve number corresponding to valveIndex
                        controlled by this program item"
        ::= { programEntry 1 }

programStartTime OBJECT-TYPE
        SYNTAX          DisplayString (SIZE(8))
        MAX-ACCESS      read-create
        STATUS          current
        DESCRIPTION     "The time of day to start the valve"
        ::= { programEntry 2 }

programStopTime OBJECT-TYPE
        SYNTAX          DisplayString (SIZE(8))
        MAX-ACCESS      read-create
        STATUS          current
        DESCRIPTION     "The time of day to stop the valve. The value must be
                        greater than the value of programStartTime"
        ::= { programEntry 3 }

programInterval OBJECT-TYPE
        SYNTAX          Unsigned32(1..7)
        MAX-ACCESS      read-create
        STATUS          current
        DESCRIPTION     "The number of days between invocations of this program"
        ::= { programEntry 4 }
```

The programStartTime and programStopTime objects use the same time of day technique we used for the controller time of day object. We can make this a bit more readable by creating a TEXTUAL-CONVENTION, and using it wherever we have a time of day related object:

```
TimeOfDay ::= TEXTUAL-CONVENTION
        STATUS          current
        DESCRIPTION
                "A value in the format hh:mm:ss. The time is expressed as a 24 hour clock.
                Some examples of legal values are: 02:03:33 and 14:59:59"
        SYNTAX          DisplayString(SIZE(8))
```

Now, we can define programStartTime and programStopTime like this:

```
programStartTime OBJECT-TYPE
        SYNTAX          DisplayString (SIZE(8))
        . . .

programStopTime OBJECT-TYPE
        SYNTAX          DisplayString (SIZE(8))
        . . .
```

We have the basic objects for our table, but we still don't have them organized. We need to decide on an indexing scheme for the table. As each valve can be included in only one program at a time, *programValveIndex* makes a logical choice to be part of the index. At this point, you should see that we've made one important mistake: we should have simply used *valveIndex* instead of creating the *programValveIndex* object.

We don't want this to be the only index, since then a valve could be present in only one program. To allow for a valve to be present in more than one program, we can use *valveStartTime* as a secondary index. This leaves us with the following definition for the row of the program table:

```
programEntry OBJECT-TYPE
        SYNTAX          ProgramEntry
        MAX-ACCESS      not-accessible
        STATUS          current
        DESCRIPTION     "A row in the table of programmed watering cycles"
        INDEX           { valveIndex, programStartTime }
        ::= { programTable 1 }

ProgramEntry ::= SEQUENCE {
                programStartTime  TimeOfDay,
                programStopTime   TimeOfDay,
                programInterval   Unsigned32,
        }
```

The table is starting to take shape now, but we have forgotten one important item: the management application needs to be able to create, delete and suspend sprinkler programs. Hopefully, the answer to this problem is obvious by now — we can use the SNMPv2 standard row creation. To indicate this in our MIB, we need to declare one more object:

```
programRowStatus OBJECT-TYPE
        SYNTAX          RowStatus
        MAX-ACCESS      read-create
        STATUS          current
        DESCRIPTION     "The row status"
        ::= { programEntry 4 }
```

12.11 Conformance Statements

In a small enterprise, you may feel that you don't need compliance specifications in MIB modules. Compliance statements are always a good idea. These specifications state what the MIB module designer believes are the acceptable implementation requirements for the MIB module. Since the designer of a MIB module is usually a team of agent and management application developers, the compliance specifications form an "implementors agreement" between these developers. If you are writing a MIB for a situation where the agent and management application developers are two separate groups and not directly involved in the MIB design process, these statements will help avoid misunderstandings. In our case, the only optional items in the MIB are the objects for scheduling programs. We create a group for these objects, but do not include the group in the MANDATORY-GROUPS clause. You can include compliance specifications within a MIB module containing definitions of objects and events, or in separate modules (perhaps with compliance statements for other MIBs).

First, we need to organize the objects into groups:

```
valveGroup OBJECT-GROUP
        OBJECTS         { -- Note that object valveIndex is NOT included, since
                          -- it is not-accessible
                        valveCount,
                        valveType,
                        valveCapacity,
                        valveAdminState,
                        valveOperState,
                        valvePressure,
                        valveOutFlow,
                        valveOpens
                        }
        STATUS          current
        DESCRIPTION     "The objects for controlling valves"
        ::= { sprinklecoControllerGroups 1 }
```

```
controllerGroup OBJECT-GROUP
        OBJECTS         {
                        controllerMajorVersion,
                        controllerMinorVersion,
                        controllerTime,
                        controllerOperState,
                        controllerAdminState,
                        controllerDiagnostics
                        }
        STATUS          current
        DESCRIPTION     "The objects for managing a valve controller"
        ::= { sprinklecoControllerGroups 2 }

programGroup OBJECT-GROUP
        OBJECTS         {
                        programStopTime,
                        programInterval,
                        programRowStatus
                        }
        STATUS          current
        DESCRIPTION     "The objects for providing scheduled watering capabilities"
        ::= { sprinklecoControllerGroups 3 }
```

We also organize the events into a group:

```
controllerEventGroup NOTIFICATION-GROUP
        NOTIFICATIONS {
                        valveMalfunction,
                        valveManualChange,
                        valveZeroLinePressure
                        }
        STATUS          current
        DESCRIPTION     "The events for a controller"
        ::= { sprinklecoControllerGroups 4 }
```

Now we define a compliance specification:

```
sprinklecoControllerBasicComplV1 MODULE-COMPLIANCE
        STATUS          current
        DESCRIPTION     "The basic implementation requirements for the Controller MIB"
        MODULE          -- This module
        -- the group programGroup is not required for a minimal implementation
                MANDATORY-GROUPS    { valveGroup, controllerGroup,
                                      controllerEventGroup }
        ::= { sprinklecoControllerCompl 1 }
```

Now we have half of our conformance work done. We've stated what the minimum requirements are, but we haven't specified what a full implementation should be. To do this, we define another compliance specification that includes the scheduled program objects:

```
sprinklecoControllerAdvancedComplV1 MODULE-COMPLIANCE
        STATUS          current
        DESCRIPTION     "The advanced implementation requirements for the
                        Controller MIB"
        MODULE          -- This module
                MANDATORY-GROUPS        { valveGroup, controllerGroup,
                                        programGroup, controllerEventGroup }
        ::= { sprinklecoControllerCompl 2 }
```

12.12 Assembling the MIB Module

The past few sections have presented the MIB in bits and pieces, so let's take a look at what the complete MIB module looks like:

```
SPRINKLECO-CONTROLLER-MIB DEFINITIONS ::= BEGIN
IMPORTS
        MODULE-IDENTITY, OBJECT-TYPE,
        NOTIFICATION-TYPE, Unsigned32, Gauge32, Counter32
                FROM SNMPv2-SMI
        TEXTUAL-CONVENTION, DisplayString, RowStatus
                FROM SNMPv2-TC
        MODULE-COMPLIANCE, OBJECT-GROUP, NOTIFICATION-GROUP
                FROM SNMPv2-CONF
        sprinklecoProducts, sprinklecoModules
                FROM SPRINKLECO-GLOBAL-REG;

sprinklecoControllerMibModule MODULE-IDENTITY
        LAST-UPDATED            "9609080000Z"
        ORGANIZATION            "SprinkleCo"
        CONTACT-INFO
                "Evan McGinnis
                email: bem@3com.com"
        DESCRIPTION
                "The SprinkleCo controller MIB"
        REVISION                "9609080000Z"
        DESCRIPTION             "The initial revision of this module"
        ::= { sprinklecoModules 2 }

-- root for items in the controller MIB module
sprinklecoControllerMIB     OBJECT IDENTIFIER ::= { sprinklecoProducts 1 }
```

```
-- conformance area, containing groups and compliance specifications
sprinklecoControllerConfs  OBJECT IDENTIFIER ::= { sprinklecoControllerMIB 1 }
sprinklecoControllerGroups OBJECT IDENTIFIER ::= { sprinklecoControllerConfs 1 }
sprinklecoControllerCompl OBJECT IDENTIFIER ::= { sprinklecoControllerConfs 2 }

-- sub-tree for objects, and for each functional area
sprinklecoControllerObjs    OBJECT IDENTIFIER ::= { sprinklecoControllerMIB 2 }
sprinklecoControllerControllerObjs OBJECT IDENTIFIER ::= { sprinklecoControllerObjs 1 }
sprinklecoControllerValveObjs OBJECT IDENTIFIER ::= { sprinklecoControllerObjs 2 }
sprinklecoControllerProgramObjs OBJECT IDENTIFIER ::= { sprinklecoControllerObjs 3 }

-- sub-tree for events
sprinklecoControllerEvents  OBJECT IDENTIFIER ::= { sprinklecoControllerMIB 3 }
sprinklecoControllerEventsV2 OBJECT IDENTIFIER ::= { sprinklecoControllerEvents 0 }

-- textual conventions
TimeOfDay ::= TEXTUAL-CONVENTION
        STATUS          current
        DESCRIPTION
                "A value in the format hh:mm:ss. The time is expressed as
                a 24 hour clock. Some examples of legal values are:
                02:03:33 and 14:59:59"
        SYNTAX          DisplayString(SIZE(8))

-- the controller objects
controllerMajorVersion OBJECT-TYPE
        SYNTAX          Unsigned32
        MAX-ACCESS      read-only
        STATUS          current
        DESCRIPTION
                "The major release number of the controller software.
                In the release identifier 4.1, the 4 is the major release
                number"
        ::= { sprinklecoControllerControllerObjs 1 }

controllerMinorVersion OBJECT-TYPE
        SYNTAX          Unsigned32
        MAX-ACCESS      read-only
        STATUS          current
        DESCRIPTION
                "The minor release number of the controller software.
                In the release identifier 4.1, the 1 is the minor release
                number"
        ::= { sprinklecoControllerControllerObjs 2 }
```

```
controllerTime OBJECT-TYPE
        SYNTAX          TimeOfDay
        MAX-ACCESS      read-write
        STATUS          current
        DESCRIPTION
                "The current time as a 24 hour clock"
        ::= { sprinklecoControllerControllerObjs 3 }

controllerOperState OBJECT-TYPE
        SYNTAX          INTEGER {
                                running(1),
                                resetting(2),
                                diagnosing(3),
                                stopped(4),
                                failed(5)
                                }
        MAX-ACCESS      read-only
        STATUS          current
        DESCRIPTION
                "The current state of the controller. The values are:
                running(1)          The controller is currently operating
                resetting(2)        The controller is being restarted
                diagnosing(3)       The controller is performing self-diagnostics
                stopped(4)          The controller has been halted
                failed(5)           The controller halted itself. (See the
                                    controllerDiagnostics object for details)"
        ::= { sprinklecoControllerControllerObjs 4 }

controllerAdminState OBJECT-TYPE
        SYNTAX          INTEGER {
                                run(1),
                                reset(2),
                                diagnose(3),
                                stop(4)
                                }
        MAX-ACCESS      read-write
        STATUS          current
        DESCRIPTION
                "The desired state of the controller. Setting the value of this
                object to these values will have the following actions:
                run(1)              The controller will enter the run state
                reset(2)            The controller will restart
                diagnose(3)         Will activate the diagnostic routines
                stop(4)             Will halt the controller"
        ::= { sprinklecoControllerControllerObjs 5 }
```

```
controllerDiagnostics OBJECT-TYPE
        SYNTAX          INTEGER {
                                noResults(1),
                                passed(2),
                                hardwareFault(3),
                                softwareFault(4)
                                }
        MAX-ACCESS      read-only
        STATUS          current
        DESCRIPTION
                "Indicates the results of the last diagnostic routine performed
                noResults(1)        No diagnostic has yet been performed
                passed(2)           The diagnostics has been passed
                hardwareFault(3)    Hardware fault
                softwareFault(4)    Software fault"
        ::= { sprinklecoControllerControllerObjs 6 }

-- the valve objects
valveCount OBJECT-TYPE
        SYNTAX          Unsigned32
        MAX-ACCESS      read-only
        STATUS          current
        DESCRIPTION     "The total number of valves in the system"
        ::= { sprinklecoControllerValveObjs 1 }

valveTable OBJECT-TYPE
        SYNTAX          SEQUENCE OF ValveEntry
        MAX-ACCESS      not-accessible
        STATUS          current
        DESCRIPTION     "A table of valves within the sprinkler system"
        ::= { sprinklecoControllerValveObjs 2 }

valveEntry OBJECT-TYPE
        SYNTAX          ValveEntry
        MAX-ACCESS      not-accessible
        STATUS          current
        DESCRIPTION     "A row in the valve table. Entries cannot
                        be created or deleted via SNMP operations"
        INDEX           { valveIndex } -- this column will identify a valve
        ::= { valveTable 1 }

ValveEntry ::= SEQUENCE {
                valveIndex          Unsigned32, -- INDEX Item
                valveType           OBJECT IDENTIFIER,
                valveCapacity       Unsigned32,
                valveAdminState     INTEGER,
```

```
            valveOperState     INTEGER,
            valvePressure      Gauge32,
            valveOutFlow       Counter32,
            valveOpens         Counter32
    }


valveIndex OBJECT-TYPE
        SYNTAX          Unsigned32(1..65535)
        MAX-ACCESS      not-accessible
        STATUS          current
        DESCRIPTION     "The unique value which identifies this valve"
        ::= { valveEntry 1 }


-- The value of the valveType object will be one of the registrations declared in
-- the SPRINKLECO-GLOBAL-REG module
valveType OBJECT-TYPE
        SYNTAX          OBJECT IDENTIFIER
        MAX-ACCESS      read-only
        STATUS          current
        DESCRIPTION     "The type of valve"
        ::= { valveEntry 2 }

valveCapacity OBJECT-TYPE
        SYNTAX          Unsigned32(1..100)
        UNITS           "gallons per minute (GPM)"
        MAX-ACCESS      read-only
        STATUS          current
        DESCRIPTION
                "The rated flow capacity of this valve"
        ::= { valveEntry 3 }

valveAdminState OBJECT-TYPE
        SYNTAX          INTEGER { off(1), on(2), down(3) }
        MAX-ACCESS      read-write
        STATUS          current
        DESCRIPTION
                "The desired state of the valve.
                Setting this value to off(1) requests that the valve be shut off.
                Setting this valve to on(2) requests that the valve be turned on.
                Setting this valve to down(3) requests that the valve be marked
                        administratively down"
        ::= { valveEntry 4 }
```

```
valveOperState OBJECT-TYPE
        SYNTAX          INTEGER {
                                off(1),
                                on(2),
                                fault(3),
                                manualOn(4),
                                manualOff(5)}
        MAX-ACCESS      read-only
        STATUS          current
        DESCRIPTION     "The current state of the valve.
                        off(1)      indicates that the valve is currently shut
                        on(2)       indicates that the valve is currently open
                        fault(3)    indicates that the valve is down due to a fault
                        manualOn(4) indicates that the valve was manually open
                        manualOff(5) indicates that the valve was manually closed"
        ::= { valveEntry 5 }

valvePressure OBJECT-TYPE
        SYNTAX          Gauge32
        UNITS           "Pounds per square inch (PSI)"
        MAX-ACCESS      read-only
        STATUS          current
        DESCRIPTION
                "The current outlet pressure of the valve"
        ::= { valveEntry 6 }


valveOutFlow OBJECT-TYPE
        SYNTAX          Counter32
        UNITS           "Gallons"
        MAX-ACCESS      read-only
        STATUS          current
        DESCRIPTION
                "The volum of water that has passed through this valve"
        ::= { valveEntry 7 }


valveOpens OBJECT-TYPE
        SYNTAX          Counter32
        MAX-ACCESS      read-only
        STATUS          current
        DESCRIPTION
                "The number of times this valve has been opened"
        ::= { valveEntry 8 }
```

```
-- the programmed watering objects
programTable OBJECT-TYPE
        SYNTAX          SEQUENCE OF ProgramEntry
        MAX-ACCESS      not-accessible
        STATUS          current
        DESCRIPTION     "A table of programmed watering cycles for
                        each valve"
        ::= { sprinklecoControllerProgramObjs 1 }

programEntry OBJECT-TYPE
        SYNTAX          ProgramEntry
        MAX-ACCESS      not-accessible
        STATUS          current
        DESCRIPTION     "A row in the table of programmed watering cycles.
                        Entries can be created and deleted via SNMP SET operations.
                        Creation requires a SET request containing at least
                        programStopTime and programRowStatus.
                        The values of programStopTime and programInterval cannot
                        be modified while the row is active"
        INDEX           { valveIndex, programStartTime }
        ::= { programTable 1 }

ProgramEntry ::= SEQUENCE {
                programStartTime  TimeOfDay,
                programStopTime   TimeOfDay,
                programInterval   Unsigned32,
                programRowStatus  RowStatus
        }

programStartTime OBJECT-TYPE
        SYNTAX          TimeOfDay
        MAX-ACCESS      not-accessible
        STATUS          current
        DESCRIPTION     "The time of day to start the valve"
        ::= { programEntry 1 }


programStopTime OBJECT-TYPE
        SYNTAX          TimeOfDay
        MAX-ACCESS      read-create
        STATUS          current
        DESCRIPTION     "The time of day to stop the valve. The value must be
                        greater than the value of programStartTime"
        ::= { programEntry 2 }
```

```
programInterval OBJECT-TYPE
        SYNTAX          Unsigned32(1..7)
        MAX-ACCESS      read-create
        STATUS          current
        DESCRIPTION     "The number of days between invocations of this program"
        ::= { programEntry 3 }

programRowStatus OBJECT-TYPE
        SYNTAX          RowStatus
        MAX-ACCESS      read-create
        STATUS          current
        DESCRIPTION     "The row status"
        ::= { programEntry 4 }


-- the controller events
valveMalfunction NOTIFICATION-TYPE
        OBJECTS         { valveAdminState, valveOperState, valvePressure }
        STATUS          current
        DESCRIPTION     "A valve failed a self test. The index of the
                        objects identify the valve"
        ::= { sprinklecoControllerEventsV2 1 }

valveManualChange NOTIFICATION-TYPE
        OBJECTS         { valveAdminState, valveOperState }
        STATUS          current
        DESCRIPTION     "A valve was manually turned on or off. The index of
                        the objects identity the valve"
        ::= { sprinklecoControllerEventsV2 2 }

valveZeroLinePressure NOTIFICATION-TYPE
        OBJECTS         { valveAdminState, valveOperState }
        STATUS          current
        DESCRIPTION     "A valve detected a complete drop in line pressure. The
                        index of the objects identity the valve"
        ::= { sprinklecoControllerEventsV2 3 }


-- Object and Event groups
valveGroup OBJECT-GROUP
        OBJECTS         {
                        valveCount,
                        valveType,
                        valveCapacity,
                        valveAdminState,
                        valveOperState,
```

```
                        valvePressure,
                        valveOutFlow,
                        valveOpens
                        }
        STATUS          current
        DESCRIPTION     "The objects for controlling valves"
        ::= { sprinklecoControllerGroups 1 }


controllerGroup OBJECT-GROUP
        OBJECTS         {
                        controllerMajorVersion,
                        controllerMinorVersion,
                        controllerTime,
                        controllerOperState,
                        controllerAdminState,
                        controllerDiagnostics
                        }
        STATUS          current
        DESCRIPTION     "The objects for managing a valve controller"
        ::= { sprinklecoControllerGroups 2 }


programGroup OBJECT-GROUP
        OBJECTS         {
                        programStopTime,
                        programInterval,
                        programRowStatus
                        }
        STATUS          current
        DESCRIPTION     "The objects for providing scheduled watering capabilities"
        ::= { sprinklecoControllerGroups 3 }


controllerEventGroup NOTIFICATION-GROUP
        NOTIFICATIONS {
                        valveMalfunction,
                        valveManualChange,
                        valveZeroLinePressure
                        }
        STATUS          current
        DESCRIPTION     "The events for a controller"
        ::= { sprinklecoControllerGroups 4 }
```

```
-- the compliance specifications
sprinklecoControllerBasicComplV1 MODULE-COMPLIANCE
        STATUS          current
        DESCRIPTION     "The basic implementation requirements for the Controller MIB"
        MODULE          -- This module
        -- the group programGroup is not required for a minimal implementation
                MANDATORY-GROUPS        {
                                        valveGroup,
                                        controllerGroup,
                                        controllerEventGroup
                                        }
        ::= { sprinklecoControllerCompl 1 }

sprinklecoControllerAdvancedComplV1 MODULE-COMPLIANCE
        STATUS          current
        DESCRIPTION     "The advanced implementation requirements for the
                        Controller MIB"
        MODULE          -- This module
                MANDATORY-GROUPS        {
                                        valveGroup,
                                        controllerGroup,
                                        programGroup,
                                        controllerEventGroup
                                        }
        ::= { sprinklecoControllerCompl 2 }

END
```

The OID values for the items defined in this MIB module are:

```
1.3.6.1.4.1.1194.1.1.1.2 MI: sprinklecoControllerMibModule
1.3.6.1.4.1.1194.1.3.1 OVA: sprinklecoControllerMIB
1.3.6.1.4.1.1194.1.3.1.1 OVA: sprinklecoControllerConfs
1.3.6.1.4.1.1194.1.3.1.1.1 OVA: sprinklecoControllerGroups
1.3.6.1.4.1.1194.1.3.1.1.1.1 OG: valveGroup
1.3.6.1.4.1.1194.1.3.1.1.1.2 OG: controllerGroup
1.3.6.1.4.1.1194.1.3.1.1.1.3 OG: programGroup
1.3.6.1.4.1.1194.1.3.1.1.1.4 OG: controllerEventGroup
1.3.6.1.4.1.1194.1.3.1.1.2 OVA: sprinklecoControllerCompl
1.3.6.1.4.1.1194.1.3.1.1.2.1 MC: sprinklecoControllerBasicComplV1
1.3.6.1.4.1.1194.1.3.1.1.2.2 MC: sprinklecoControllerAdvancedComplV1
1.3.6.1.4.1.1194.1.3.1.2 OVA: sprinklecoControllerObjs
1.3.6.1.4.1.1194.1.3.1.2.1 OVA: sprinklecoControllerControllerObjs
1.3.6.1.4.1.1194.1.3.1.2.1.1 SOT: controllerMajorVersion syn: Unsigned32 acc: ro
1.3.6.1.4.1.1194.1.3.1.2.1.2 SOT: controllerMinorVersion syn: Unsigned32 acc: ro
1.3.6.1.4.1.1194.1.3.1.2.1.3 SOT: controllerTime syn: TimeOfDay acc: rw
```

1.3.6.1.4.1.1194.1.3.1.2.1.4 SOT: controllerOperState syn: ENUM{
    running(1) resetting(2) diagnosing(3) stopped(4) failed(5) } acc: ro
1.3.6.1.4.1.1194.1.3.1.2.1.5 SOT: controllerAdminState syn: ENUM{
    run(1) reset(2) diagnose(3) stop(4) } acc: rw
1.3.6.1.4.1.1194.1.3.1.2.1.6 SOT: controllerDiagnostics syn: ENUM{
    noResults(1) passed(2) hardwareFault(3) softwareFault(4) } acc: ro
1.3.6.1.4.1.1194.1.3.1.2.2 OVA: sprinklecoControllerValveObjs
1.3.6.1.4.1.1194.1.3.1.2.2.1 SOT: valveCount syn: Unsigned32 acc: ro
1.3.6.1.4.1.1194.1.3.1.2.2.2 TOT: valveTable
1.3.6.1.4.1.1194.1.3.1.2.2.2.1 ROT: valveEntry index{ valveIndex }
1.3.6.1.4.1.1194.1.3.1.2.2.2.1.1 COT: valveIndex syn: Unsigned32(1..65535) acc: na
1.3.6.1.4.1.1194.1.3.1.2.2.2.1.2 COT: valveType syn: OID acc: ro
1.3.6.1.4.1.1194.1.3.1.2.2.2.1.3 COT: valveCapacity syn: Unsigned32(1..100) acc: ro
1.3.6.1.4.1.1194.1.3.1.2.2.2.1.4 COT: valveAdminState syn: ENUM{
    off(1) on(2) down(3) } acc: rw
1.3.6.1.4.1.1194.1.3.1.2.2.2.1.5 COT: valveOperState syn: ENUM{
    off(1) on(2) fault(3) manualOn(4) manualOff(5) } acc: ro
1.3.6.1.4.1.1194.1.3.1.2.2.2.1.6 COT: valvePressure syn: Gauge32 acc: ro
1.3.6.1.4.1.1194.1.3.1.2.2.2.1.7 COT: valveOutFlow syn: Counter32 acc: ro
1.3.6.1.4.1.1194.1.3.1.2.2.2.1.8 COT: valveOpens syn: Counter32 acc: ro
1.3.6.1.4.1.1194.1.3.1.2.3 OVA: sprinklecoControllerProgramObjs
1.3.6.1.4.1.1194.1.3.1.2.3.1 TOT: programTable
1.3.6.1.4.1.1194.1.3.1.2.3.1.1 ROT: programEntry index{ valveIndex programStartTime }
1.3.6.1.4.1.1194.1.3.1.2.3.1.1.1 COT: programStartTime syn: TimeOfDay acc: na
1.3.6.1.4.1.1194.1.3.1.2.3.1.1.2 COT: programStopTime syn: TimeOfDay acc: rc
1.3.6.1.4.1.1194.1.3.1.2.3.1.1.3 COT: programInterval syn: Unsigned32(1..7) acc: rc
1.3.6.1.4.1.1194.1.3.1.2.3.1.1.4 COT: programRowStatus syn: RowStatus acc: rc
1.3.6.1.4.1.1194.1.3.1.3 OVA: sprinklecoControllerEvents
1.3.6.1.4.1.1194.1.3.1.3.0 OVA: sprinklecoControllerEventsV2
1.3.6.1.4.1.1194.1.3.1.3.0.1 NT: valveMalfunction
1.3.6.1.4.1.1194.1.3.1.3.0.2 NT: valveManualChange
1.3.6.1.4.1.1194.1.3.1.3.0.3 NT: valveZeroLinePressure

12.13 Capabilities Modules

Now we need to turn our attention to documenting our agent implementation. As we indicated earlier, the ability to program a watering schedule is the major difference between the residential and industrial controllers. To reflect this, we need to provide two capabilities statements:

```
-- A capabilities module for SprinkleCo agents
SPRINKLECO-CONTROLLER-CAP DEFINITIONS ::= BEGIN
IMPORTS
        MODULE-IDENTITY
                FROM SNMPv2-SMI
        AGENT-CAPABILITIES
                FROM SNMPv2-CONF
        sprinklecoCaps, sprinklecoModules
                FROM SPRINKLECO-GLOBAL-REG;

sprinklecoControllerCapModule MODULE-IDENTITY
        LAST-UPDATED            "9609080000Z"
        ORGANIZATION            "SprinkleCo"
        CONTACT-INFO
                        "Evan McGinnis
                        email: bem@3com.com"
        DESCRIPTION             "The SprinkleCo Capabilities module"
        REVISION                "9609080000Z"
        DESCRIPTION             "The initial revision of this module"
        ::= { sprinklecoModules 3 }

sprinklecoBasicAgentV10 AGENT-CAPABILITIES
        PRODUCT-RELEASE         "Basic Sprinkler agent 1.0"
        STATUS                  current
        DESCRIPTION             "Lawn Sprinkler agent for 200 series"
        SUPPORTS                SNMPv2-MIB
                INCLUDES        {
                                snmpGroup,
                                snmpSetGroup,
                                systemGroup,
                                snmpBasicNotificationsGroup
                                }
        SUPPORTS                SPRINKLECO-CONTROLLER-MIB
                INCLUDES        {
                                controllerGroup,
                                valveGroup,
                                controllerEventGroup
                                }
        ::= { sprinklecoCaps 1 }

sprinklecoAdvancedAgentV10 AGENT-CAPABILITIES
        PRODUCT-RELEASE         "Advanced Sprinkler agent 1.0"
        STATUS                  current
        DESCRIPTION             "Lawn Sprinkler agent for 300 series"
        SUPPORTS                SNMPv2-MIB
                INCLUDES        {
```

```
                                   snmpGroup,
                                   snmpSetGroup,
                                   systemGroup,
                                   snmpBasicNotificationsGroup
                                   }
        SUPPORTS                   SPRINKLECO-CONTROLLER-MIB
              INCLUDES             {
                                   controllerGroup,
                                   valveGroup,
                                   programGroup,
                                   controllerEventGroup
                                   }
        ::= { sprinklecoCaps 2 }

    END
```

12.14 Maintenance of Modules

If SprinkleCo has some popular products and begins to expand their product lines, we may be faced with expanding or changing the MIB. Suppose that the company wants to phase a new product into the product line: an automatic liquid fertilizer/liquid insecticide dispenser. This is typical of many situations the MIB writer faces—how do I use an existing MIB to represent new product concepts? We must be extremely careful when adding new capabilities to MIBs. We don't want to cause problems for older network management stations simply because we are enhancing the MIB. In this section, we will try to add these new MIB objects so that they fit with the existing scheme.

12.14.1 Liquid Fertilizer

The liquid fertilizer dispenser is an add-on system for the current valves. The system has a 64 ounce reservoir of liquid fertilizer to be injected into the outflow water from the valve. (See Figure 12–4)

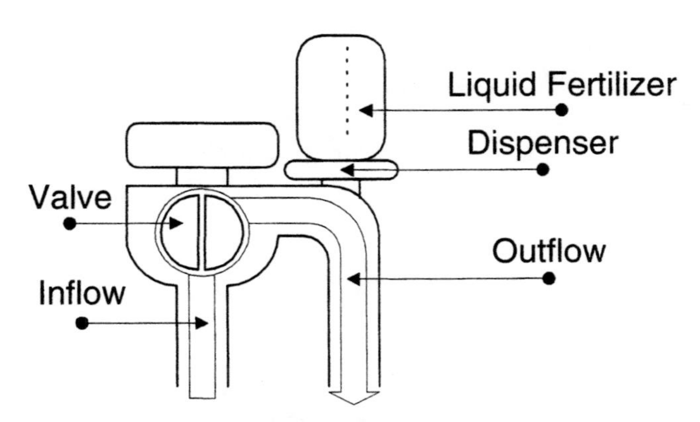

Figure 12–4 Control Valve with fertilizer option

The system dispenses a fluid at a specified rate (measured in ounces per gallon). The valve can also report back the following items:

- the level of fluid in the reservoir
- the number of ounces of fluid dispensed by this system

Only newer models of controllers can manage these systems; older models simply ignore the new hardware if it is installed.

This new sub-system may not be present on all valves, so we need to find a way to indicate this in the MIB. We could simply add new objects to the valve table. Consider this definition of a *ValveEntry*:

```
-- One possible way to add the liquid fertilizer dispenser
ValveEntry ::= SEQUENCE {
        valveIndex          Unsigned32, -- INDEX Item
        valveType           OBJECT IDENTIFIER,
        valveCapacity       Unsigned32,
        valveAdminState     INTEGER,
        valveOperState      INTEGER,
        valvePressure       Gauge32,
        valveOutFlow        Counter32,
        valveOpens          Counter32,
        valveDispenserState INTEGER -- the new valve
    }
```

In this attempt, we have added a new column, *valveDispenserState*. As you can see from the example entries in Table 12–3, if a system has just a few valves with the new subsystem, the table contains wasted space. As we add other columns to control and monitor the dispensers, we make this problem worse. Make no mistake—this arrangement will work; it simply won't work as well as it could with another arrangement.

Table 12–3 Example valve table with added column for dispenser state

valveIndex	valveCapacity	valveAdminState	valveOperState	valuePressure	valveOutFlow	valveOpens	valveDispenser-State
1	4	off	off	0	30	12	**notPresent**
2	4	off	off	0	34	12	**notPresent**
3	5	on	on	40	50	15	**open**
4	5	on	on	40	50	15	**closed**
5	3	off	off	0	0	0	**notPresent**

A better approach to this problem is adding another table to control the dispensers. If you will recall from our previous discussion on the relationships between tables, this is an example of a one-to-one, sparse relationship. That is, for every entry in the valve table, there is at most one corresponding entry in the fertilizer dispenser table. Of course, there may be no corresponding entry, hence the table is sparse. In this situation, the tables might look like Figure 12–5:

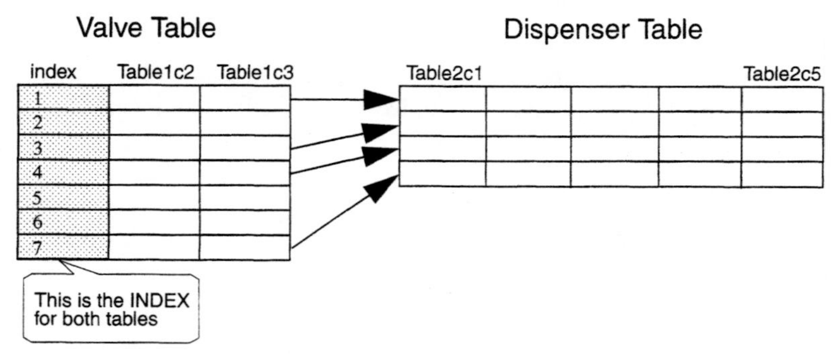

Figure 12–5 Valve Table and Dispenser Table

For this new dispenser table, we can use the same index the valve table uses, *valveIndex*. The new table is declared as:

```
-- First, we create a new sub-tree for the objects:
sprinklecoControllerDispenserObjs OBJECT IDENTIFIER ::= { sprinklecoControllerObjs 4 }

-- the despenser objects
dispenserCount OBJECT-TYPE
        SYNTAX          Unsigned32
        MAX-ACCESS      read-only
        STATUS          current
        DESCRIPTION     "The total number of liquid dispensers"
        ::= { sprinklecoControllerDispenserObjs 1 }


dispenserTable OBJECT-TYPE
        SYNTAX          SEQUENCE OF DispenserEntry
        MAX-ACCESS      not-accessible
        STATUS          current
        DESCRIPTION
                "A table of fertilizer dispensers. The number of entries
                is between zero and the number of valves. Since a valve
                may not contain a dispenser, there may not be an entry
                in this table for each valve in the valve table"
        ::= { sprinklecoControllerDispenserObjs 2 }
```

```
dispenserEntry OBJECT-TYPE
        SYNTAX          DispenserEntry
        MAX-ACCESS      not-accessible
        STATUS          current
        DESCRIPTION
                "A row in the fertilizer dispenser table. Entries cannot
                be created of deleted with SNMP operations"
        INDEX               { valveIndex }
        ::= { dispenserTable 1 }

DispenserEntry ::= SEQUENCE {
        dispenserAdminState         INTEGER,
        dispenserOperState          INTEGER,
        dispenserFluidLevel         Gauge32,
        dispenserDelivered          Counter32,
        dispenserDeliverRate        Unsigned32
        }

dispenserAdminState OBJECT-TYPE
        SYNTAX          INTEGER { off(1), on(2), down(3) }
        MAX-ACCESS      read-write
        STATUS          current
        DESCRIPTION
                "The desired state for the dispenser.
                Setting the value to off(1) requests the dispenser to close.
                Setting the value to on(2) requests the dispenser to begin injecting
                        liquid into the outflow.
                Setting this valve to down(3) requests that the dispenser be marked
                        administratively down"
        ::= { dispenserEntry 1 }

dispenserOperState OBJECT-TYPE
        SYNTAX          INTEGER { off(1), on(2), fault(3), manualOn(4), manualOff(5) }
        MAX-ACCESS      read-only
        STATUS          current
        DESCRIPTION     "The current state of the dispenser"
        ::= { dispenserEntry 2 }

dispenserFluidLevel OBJECT-TYPE
        SYNTAX          Gauge32(0..64)
        UNITS           "fluid ounces"
        MAX-ACCESS      read-only
        STATUS          current
        DESCRIPTION     "The level of the fluid present in the reservoir"
        ::= { dispenserEntry 3 }
```

```
dispenserDelivered OBJECT-TYPE
        SYNTAX          Counter32
        UNITS           "fluid ounces"
        MAX-ACCESS      read-only
        STATUS          current
        DESCRIPTION     "The amount of fluid delivered by the dispenser"
        ::= { dispenserEntry 4 }

dispenserDeliverRate OBJECT-TYPE
        SYNTAX          Unsigned32(1..4)
        UNITS           "ounces per gallon"
        MAX-ACCESS      read-write
        STATUS          current
        DESCRIPTION     "The desired rate of delivery by the dispenser"
        ::= { dispenserEntry 5 }
```

The values for *dispenserAdminState* and *dispenserOperState* should look familiar—they are exact copies of the values defined for *valveOperState* and *valveAdminState*. The other control object in this sub-system is *dispenserDeliverRate*. This object controls the rate at which to inject liquid fertilizer into the outflow.

Now let's look at some of the statistical objects needed in this table. We need to have a measure of the fluid level in the holding tank, and *dispenserFluidLevel* provides this. We have defined this object as a gauge. The fluid level will rise when more fertilizer is added to the reservoir, and fall as liquid is injected into the outflow stream.

That takes care of the definitions of the objects themselves. Now we have three more tasks to perform: add new OBJECT GROUP and MODULE-COMPLIANCE statements to the controller MIB, create a new AGENT-CAPABILITIES to reflect the new implementation, and update the MODULE-IDENTITY of both information modules we have changed.

First, let's take care of adding the new OBJECT-GROUP:

```
dispenserGroup OBJECT-GROUP
        OBJECTS         {
          dispenserCount,
                        dispenserAdminState,
                        dispenserOperState,
                        dispenserFluidLevel,
                        dispenserDelivered,
                        dispenserDeliverRate
                        }
        STATUS          current
        DESCRIPTION
                "The objects for managing despensers"
        ::= { sprinklecoControllerGroups 5 }
```

Now for the new compliance specifications. Since the dispensers will be used in both the industrial and consumer products, we update our existing compliance specifications. We change the status on them to *deprecated* to show that they are still valid, but are replaced by another:

```
sprinklecoControllerBasicComplV1 MODULE-COMPLIANCE
        STATUS          deprecated
        DESCRIPTION     "The basic implementation requirements for the Controller MIB.
                        This specification is replaced by
                        sprinklecoControllerBasicComplV2"
        . . .

sprinklecoControllerAdvancedComplV1 MODULE-COMPLIANCE
        STATUS          deprecated
        DESCRIPTION     "The advanced implementation requirements for the
                        Controller MIB.
                        This specification is replaced by
                        sprinklecoControllerAdvancedComplV2"
        . . .
```

We must create replacement compliance specifications with new identifiers and register them with unused OID values. These replacements are the same as the old, except we have included the dispenser group:

```
sprinklecoControllerBasicComplV2 MODULE-COMPLIANCE
        STATUS          current
        DESCRIPTION
                "The basic implementation requirements for the controller MIB"
        MODULE          -- This module
        -- The schedules group is not required for a minimal implementation
        MANDATORY-GROUPS        {
                                valveGroup,
                                controllerGroup,
                                controllerEventGroup,
                                dispenserGroup
                                }
        ::= { sprinklecoControllerCompl 3 }


sprinklecoControllerAdvancedComplV2 MODULE-COMPLIANCE
        STATUS          current
        DESCRIPTION
                "The advanced implementation requirements for the controller MIB"
        MODULE          -- This module
        MANDATORY-GROUPS        {
```

```
                            valveGroup,
                            controllerGroup,
                            programGroup,
                            controllerEventGroup,
                            dispenserGroup
                            }
    ::= { sprinklecoControllerCompl 4 }
```

Next, we need to document the new capabilities. There are two different ways we can approach this. The existing two AGENT-CAPABILITIES statements reflected the two types of agents a controller might possess: the basic agent without the ability to schedule a watering program, and an advanced agent that does support programmed watering. We could simply define a new capabilities statement that would indicate that the new agent supported all OBJECT-GROUPs supported by the older agents plus the one, *dispenserGroup*, we just defined. Since the code to implement the dispenser objects is a separate chunk from the code for the other objects, we should define a capabilities specification just for the dispenser objects. This is the following:

```
sprinklecoDispenserCapV1 AGENT-CAPABILITIES
    PRODUCT-RELEASE        "Dispenser objects library 1.0"
    STATUS                 current
    DESCRIPTION            "Support for the dispenser objects"
    SUPPORTS               SPRINKLECO-CONTROLLER-MIB
          INCLUDES         {
                           dispenserGroup
                           }
    ::= { sprinklecoCaps 3}
```

The only task we have left is documenting our changes to the SPRINKLECO-CONTROLLER-MIB and SPRINKLECO-CONTROLLER-CAP modules.

```
sprinklecoControllerMibModule MODULE-IDENTITY
    LAST-UPDATED           "9611080000Z"
    ORGANIZATION           "SprinkleCo"
    CONTACT-INFO
          "Evan McGinnis
          email: bem@3com.com"
    DESCRIPTION
          "The SprinkleCo controller MIB"

    REVISION        "9611080000Z"
    DESCRIPTION     "Added the objects for the management of
                    the fluid dispenser system"

    REVISION        "9609080000Z"
    DESCRIPTION     "The initial revision of this module"
    ::= { sprinklecoModules 2 } -- value not changed
```

12.15 What's Next?

In this chapter, we've examined a relatively simple example of an information framework. Chances are, either as a reader or author of MIBs, you will be confronted with much more complex frameworks. Indeed, some frameworks are complex enough to warrant an entire book. After reading and understanding this book, you now have the knowledge to analyze these frameworks. So the next step, especially for new MIB readers and writers, is to examine some of the high quality MIBs produced by IETF working groups, independent vendors of networking equipment and services, and academic research products. Be careful, however! In the course of preparing this book, we have examined hundreds of MIBs, and the quality varies widely. Tucked inside some of those hundreds of MIBs, though, are some very interesting techniques that you may be able to use in your own framework. Be sure to look at the MIB Resources appendix for some pointers on locating MIBs.

APPENDIX A

ASN.1 and BER

This appendix contains a minimal introduction to the Basic Encoding Rules (BER) defined by the International Standard ISO 8825. This is not a general reference for BER, but provides only the information needed specifically for the SNMP protocol.

A.1 What is ASN.1?

ASN.1 is a machine independent data description language borrowed from the OSI suite of protocols. Only a small sub-set of ASN.1 is used to define the SNMP protocol, and only that small sub-set is covered in this appendix.

The language of ASN.1 has the following properties:

- Comments are begun by two hyphens "--" and terminated either by another set of hyphens or the end of line character
- Identifiers of the language begin with a letter, and may contain letters, digits, and hyphens, but may not end with a hyphen or contain two consecutive hyphens
- A module of the language contains definitions for types and definitions of values
- The identifier for a type must start with an uppercase letter
- The identifier for a value must start with a lowercase letter
- Reserved keywords are all uppercase

The character set used by ASN.1 is limited to:

- A to Z
- a to z
- 0 to 9
- : ; | = , { } < . ( ) [ ] - ' "

Characters outside this set may be used within the values of strings, and in comments, but all keywords, identifiers, and punctuation must use this set.

The ASN.1 keywords are shown in Table A–1:

Table A–1 ASN.1 Keywords

BOOLEAN	INTEGER	BIT	STRING	OCTET
NULL	SEQUENCE	OF	SET	IMPLICIT
CHOICE	ANY	EXTERNAL	OBJECT	IDENTIFIER
OPTIONAL	DEFAULT	COMPONENTS	UNIVERSAL	APPLICATION
PRIVATE	TRUE	FALSE	BEGIN	END
DEFINITIONS	EXPLICIT	ENUMERATED	EXPORTS	IMPORTS
REAL	INCLUDES	MIN	MAX	SIZE
FROM	WITH	COMPONENT	PRESENT	ABSENT
DEFINED	BY	PLUS-INFINITY	MINUS-INFINITY	TAGS

ASN.1 has only one "operation" (if it can be called such), the assignment statement, which uses the "::=" operator.

A.1.1 ASN.1 Type Definition

An ASN.1 type definition has the following syntax:

```
<newType> "::=" <typeSpecification>
```

A.1.2 ASN.1 Value Definition

An ASN.1 value definition has the following syntax:

```
<newValue> <type> "::=" <valueSpecification>
```

A.2 ASN.1 Fundamental Types

ASN.1 has the following fundamental types which are used in the definition of the SNMP management protocol:

A.2.1 INTEGER

The type INTEGER represents any negative or non-negative value, no matter how large. In SNMP, all uses of this type are restricted to a specified range.

A.2.2 OCTET STRING

The OCTET STRING type represents an unbounded sequence of 8-bit bytes (octets) of binary information. In SNMP, all uses of this type are restricted to a specified range.

A.2.3 OBJECT IDENTIFIER

The OBJECT IDENTIFIER type represents an unbounded sequence of non-negative integers of unbounded range. Values of this type are used to uniquely identify items for all space and time. In SNMP, the length of the sequence is limited to a maximum of 128 elements, and the maximum value of any element is 2^{32}-1 (4294967295).

A.2.4 NULL

The NULL type represents a placeholder.

A.3 ASN.1 Structured Types

ASN.1 has the following structured types which are used in the definition of the SNMP management protocol:

A.3.1 SEQUENCE

The SEQUENCE type represents a list of specified types. This is roughly analogous to a *struct* in C.

A.3.2 SEQUENCE OF

The SEQUENCE OF <type> type represents an array of a specified type.

A.3.3 CHOICE

The CHOICE type represents a list of alternatives.

A.4 Basic Concepts of BER

The Basic Encoding Rules specify a series of procedures for the *Transfer Syntax* of types specified with ASN.1. A transfer syntax, simply put, is the actual representation of octets to be sent from one network entity to another.

All ASN.1 values can be translated using the basic encoding rules into a series of: tag (what ASN.1 type is it?), length (how long is the payload?), and value (the payload). (See Figure A–1)

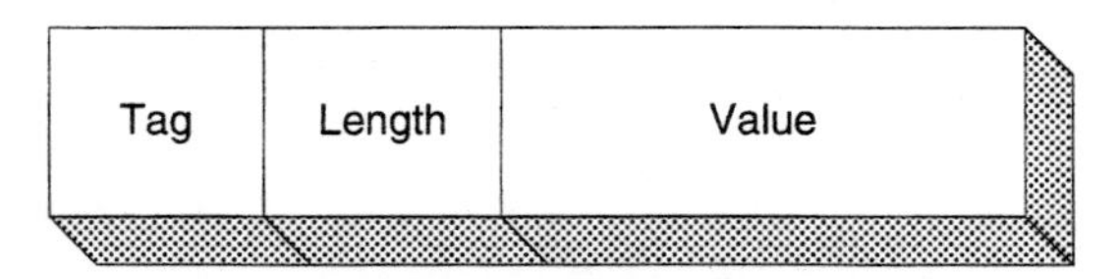

Figure A–1 Fields of a BER encoded ASN.1 value

A.4.1 TAGs

All ASN.1 types have an associated tag. The format of the first, and most likely, only, octet of a BER encoded tag is shown in Figure A–2:

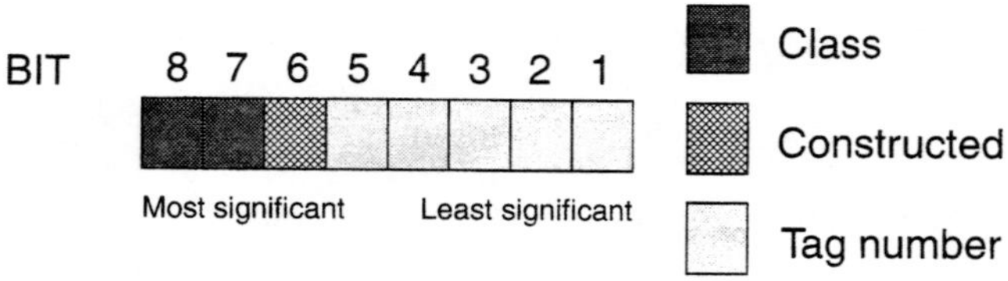

Figure A–2 BER Tag format

The tag field has three sub-fields:

- Class — indicates the class of the tag, as given in Table A–2
- Constructed — indicates whether the encoding is *primitive* (0) or *constructed*(1)
- Tag value — as given in Table A–3

Table A–2 Class subfield values

CLASS	Bit 8	Bit 7	Comment
Universal	0	0	Built-in types
Application	0	1	SNMP defined types
Context-Specific	1	0	Used in context
Private	1	1	Not used in the SNMP protocol

Table A–3 Tag values for SNMP types

Type	SNMPv1 protocol	SNMPv2 protocol	ASN.1 Tag	Tag Number	Tag Value
INTEGER/Integer32	✔	✔	UNIVERSAL 2	0x02	0x02
OCTET STRING	✔	✔	UNIVERSAL 4	0x04	0x04
NULL	✔	✔	UNIVERSAL 5	0x05	0x05
OBJECT IDENTIFIER	✔	✔	UNIVERSAL 6	0x06	0x06
SEQUENCE	✔	✔	UNIVERSAL 16	0x10	0x30
IpAddress	✔	✔	APPLICATION 0	0x00	0x40
Counter/Counter32	✔	✔	APPLICATION 1	0x01	0x41
Gauge/Gauge32	✔	✔	APPLICATION 2	0x02	0x42
TimeTicks	✔	✔	APPLICATION 3	0x03	0x43
Opaque	✔	✔	APPLICATION 4	0x04	0x44
Counter64		✔	APPLICATION 6	0x06	0x46

A.4.2 Length

The length field specifies the length of the payload, not the overall length of an item. There are two forms of the length field: short and long. In the short form, the length is a single octet where bit 8 is always 0 and bits 7 through 1 are used to specify the length of the value. This allows lengths of 0 to 127 to be represented. Figure A–3 shows a short form length encoding where the length of the value is 1100110_2 (or 102).

Value | 0 | 1 | 1 | 0 | 0 | 1 | 1 | 0 | = 102

☐ Short/Long form indicator

Figure A–3 Short form length

In the long form, the length is specified in multiple octets. The first octet has bit 8 set to 1 and bits 7 through 1 specify the number of remaining octets to specify the length. The only exception the standard makes is that this value may not be all 1s (11111111_2). Consequently, the length of the length can range from 1 to 126 octets. These octets specify the length of the value. This length is interpreted as an unsigned integer. Figure A–4 shows a long form length encoding where the length of the length is 3, and the length of the value is $011100110101100110110101_2$ (or 7559605).

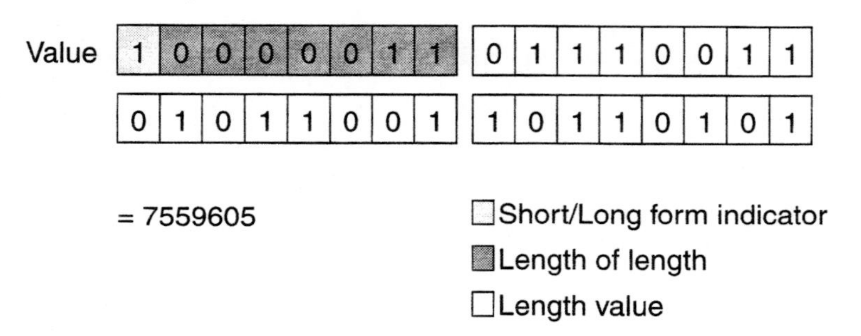

Figure A–4 Long form length

Lengths in this form can range from 1 to an astounding $2^{(126*8)}$, so this should cover all cases required by SNMP. When encoding using this form, it is perfectly acceptable to use more octets than the minimum required. Another legal encoding of 7559605 could use 4 octets with the first octet set to all 0s, instead of 3 octets as shown in Figure A–4.

It is perfectly legal to always use the long form when encoding lengths, even for values which would otherwise be encoded using the short form (0..127). Some implementations may, in fact, use the long form exclusively, or use the long form exclusively for certain types such as sequences.

A.5 Encoding of Values Used in the SNMP Protocol

A.5.1 INTEGER and Integer32

Integer values are represented by a twos-complement form of the value. This value is interpreted as follows:

1. Number the bits sequentially starting with bit 1 of the last octet as 0 and continuing through bit 8 of the first octet.
2. Assign each bit position the value 2^n, where n is the number of the bit assigned in step 1.
3. Add up all values assigned in step two for bits whose value is 1 (except bit 8 of the first octet).
4. If bit 8 of the first octet is 1, subtract the numeric value represented by this bit (e.g., the value is 2^n) from the value obtained in step 3.

In Figure A–5, the twos-complement value is calculated by:
$2^{12} + 2^{10} + 2^9 + 2^7 + 2^5 + 2^4 + 2^2 + 2^0 = 5813 - 2^{15} = -26955$

BIT	8	7	6	5	4	3	2	1	8	7	6	5	4	3	2	1
Position	15	14	13	12	11	10	9	8	7	6	5	4	3	2	1	0
Value	1	0	0	1	0	1	1	0	1	0	1	1	0	1	0	1
Position	2^{15}			2^{12}		2^{10}	2^9		2^7		2^5	2^4		2^2		2^0

□Sign bit

Figure A–5 INTEGER 2s Complement Encoding

To form the value of a positive number, say 255, follow these simple steps:

1. Write down the number without any leading zero binary digits.

1	1	1	1	1	1	1	1

2. Add, if needed, leading zero binary digits so that the number of digits is a multiple of eight. (In this case, no additional digits are needed.)
3. Otherwise, add eight leading binary digits of zero.

0	0	0	0	0	0	0	0	1	1	1	1	1	1	1	1

Remember that the leading binary digit indicates the sign of the value.

0	0	0	0	0	0	0	0	1	1	1	1	1	1	1	1

□Sign bit

To form the value of a negative number, say -26955, follow these simple steps:

1. Write down the number as if it is positive, using the smallest number of octets possible (i.e. no extra leading octets of all 0's).

2. Invert the bits (All 1's become 0's and all 0's become 1's.

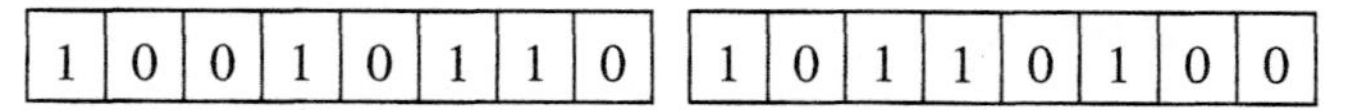

3. Add 1 to the result.

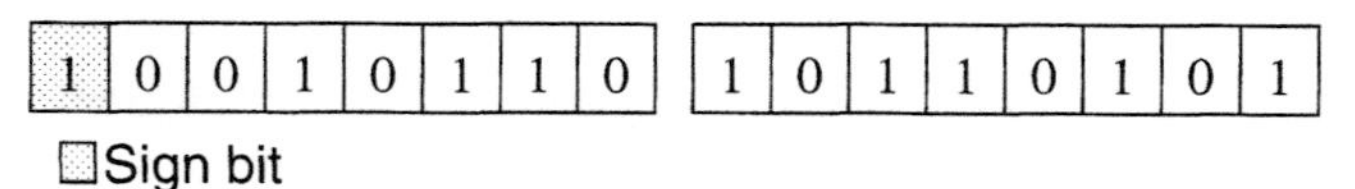

Figure A–6 shows a full encoding of this integer.

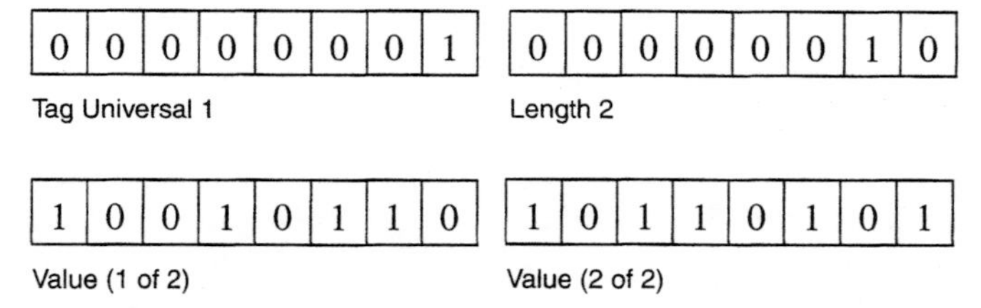

Figure A–6 INTEGER encoding

A.5.2 OCTET STRING

The OCTET STRING is quite simple to encode. The value is simply the octets of the value itself. (See Figure A–7)

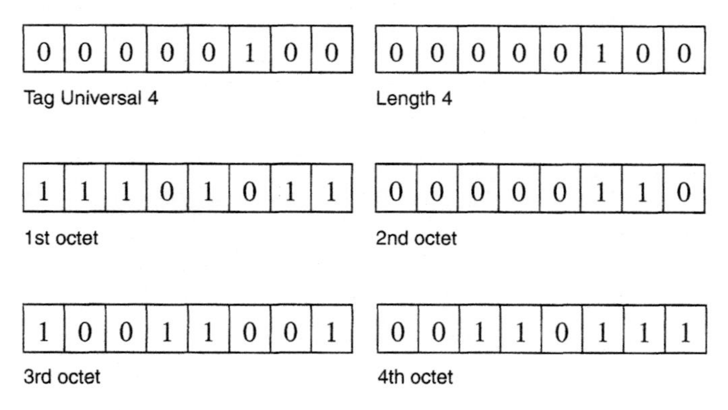

Figure A–7 OCTET STRING encoding

A.5.3 NULL

An encoded NULL type has no value octets — just a tag and a length of 0. (See Figure A–8)

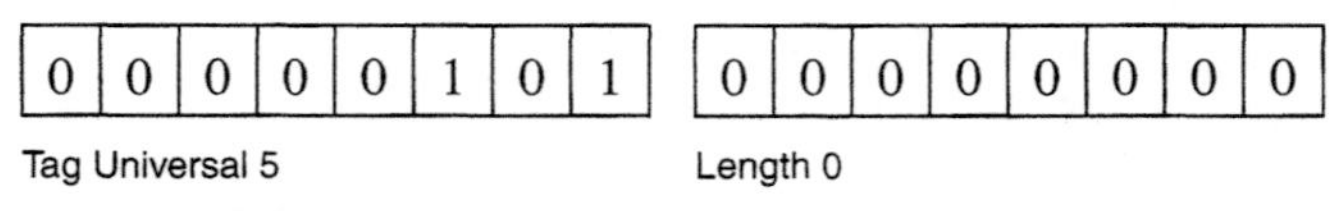

Figure A–8 NULL encoding

A.5.4 OBJECT IDENTIFIER

An encoded OBJECT IDENTIFIER consists of each sub-identifier in the original value encoded and concatenated. Each sub-identifier is encoded as a series of octets, which is as follows:

- Bit 8 in each octet indicates if it is the last octet of the sub-identifier by setting this bit to 0
- Bits 7 through 1 in the octets, when concatenated, form the value of the sub-identifier
- The first octet in the sub-identifier may not have the value 80_{16}. This ensures that the smallest number of octets are used for the encoding. A value of 80_{16} would indicate that more octets follow, but the value bits (7-1) are set to zero

The encoding of the first two sub-identifiers, however, does not follow these rules. In the interests of the smallest possible encoding, the first sub-identifier encoding takes advantage of the fact that the top two layers of the OBJECT IDENTIFIER tree are fixed at a small set of values, namely: *ccitt*(0), *iso*(1), and *joint-iso-ccitt*(2). The subtrees beneath these are also limited, so the first two sub-identifiers are represented by a single octet computed by the formula:

(X*40) + Y
X = the value of the first sub-identifier (0, 1 or 2)
Y = the value of the second sub-identifier

An OBJECT IDENTIFIER { 1 3 } would have an encoded value of: 43_{10}. Note that this encoding technique places a restriction on OBJECT IDENTIFIER values: the length of the shortest identifier is two. Also remember that the SMI restricts each sub-identifier to 2^{32}- 1, so the maximum number of octets required to encode a sub-identifier is 5. (Remember that only seven bits of a value are encoded per octet. Four octets can encode value upto 2^{28}- 1 and five octets can encode a value upto 2^{35}- 1.) Figure A–9 shows an encoding of the OBJECT IDENTIFIER value { 1 3 6 3255 }. The first octet of the value is 40*1 + 3, or 43_{10}, which is 0101011_2. The second octet of the value is 6_{10}, which is 0000110_2. The third and fourth octets of the value encode 3255_{10}, which is 00110010110111_2. Since this value takes two octets to encode, the first of the two octets has a leading binary digit of one to indicate it is not the last to encode the sub-identifier's value. The second of the two octets has a leading binary digit of zero to indicate that it is the last to encode the sub-identifier's value.

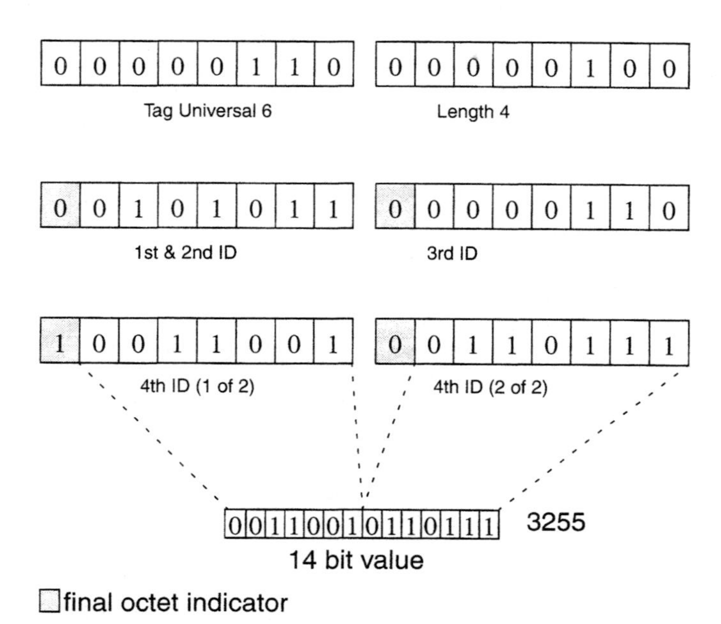

Figure A–9 OBJECT IDENTIFIER encoding

A.5.5 IpAddress

The underlying type of an IpAddress is a four octet OCTET STRING, and is encoded just as a regular OCTET STRING. The only difference is the tag, which is APPLICATION 0. Figure A–10 shows an encoding of the IP address 129.213.224.111.

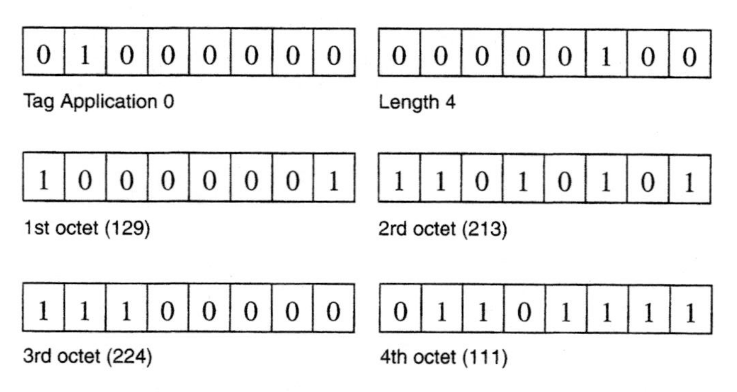

Figure A–10 IpAddress encoding 129.213.224.111

A.5.6 Counter and Counter32

The underlying type of the counters is the INTEGER, and the value portion is encoded in the same manner. The tag for this encoding is APPLICATION 1. Figure A–11 shows an encoding of value 4.

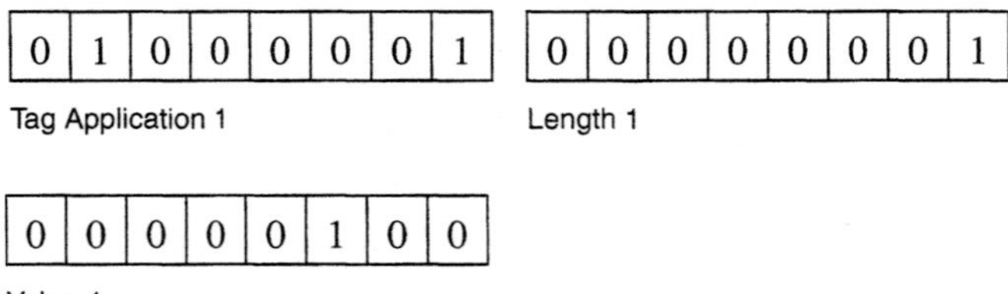

Figure A–11 Counter and Counter32 encoding for 4

A.5.7 Gauge, Gauge32, and Unsigned32

The underlying type of the gauge and unsigned types is the INTEGER, and it is encoded in the same manner. The tag for this encoding is APPLICATION 2. Figure A–12 shows an encoding of value 3.

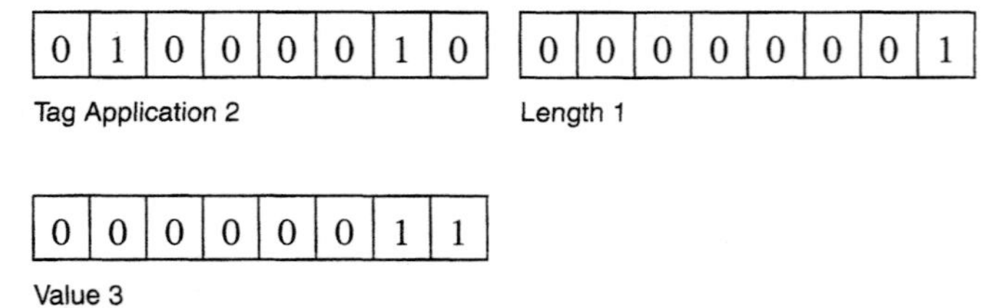

Figure A–12 Gauge, Gauge32, and Unsigned32 encoding for 3

Figure A–13 shows an encoding of 2147483648.

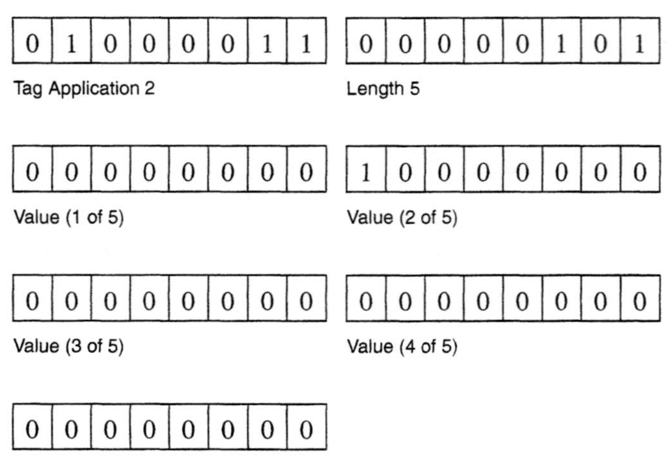

Figure A–13 Gauge, Gauge32, and Unsigned encoding for 2147483648

A.5.8 TimeTicks

The underlying type of the TimeTicks type is INTEGER, and is encoded in the same manner. The tag for this encoding is APPLICATION 3. An example encoding for the value 2476949835 of this type is given in Figure A–14.

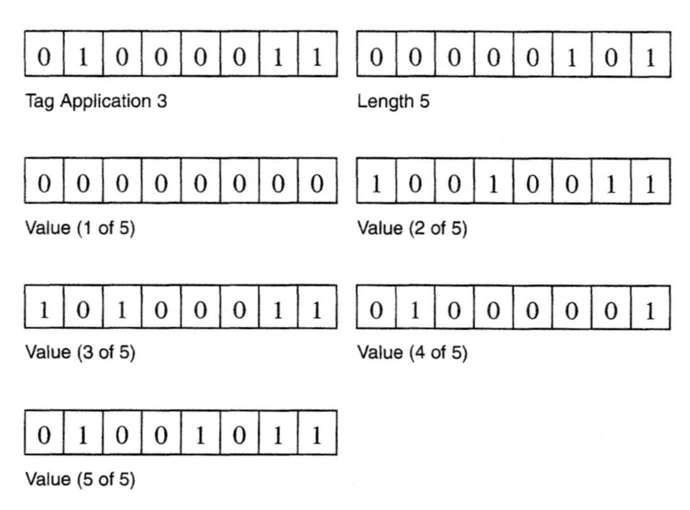

Figure A–14 TimeTicks encoding for 2476949835

A.5.9 Opaque

The Opaque type has an underlying type of OCTET STRING, and is encoded using the same rules. The tag, however, is APPLICATION 4. Figure A–15 shows an encoding of a gauge value of 3. Note that the value is first encoded in BER and this is encoded again. The original value 3 is “double wrapped.”

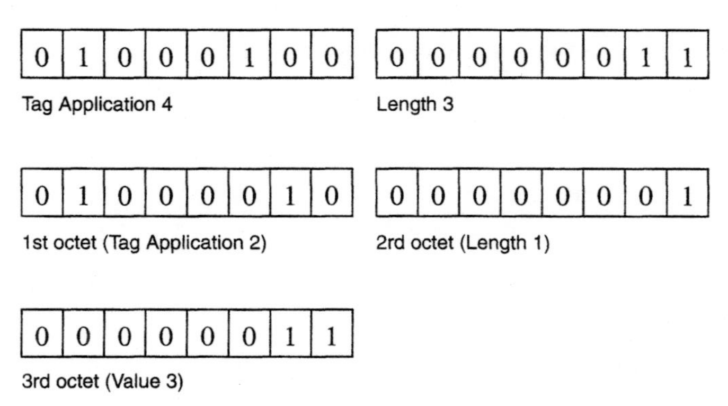

Figure A–15 Opaque encoding

A.5.10 Counter64

The Counter64 type has an underlying type of INTEGER, and is encoded using the same rules. The tag, however, is APPLICATION 6. In Figure A–16, an example encoding of a 64 bit counter is shown. Notice that the encoding will never need more than 9 value octets. For values in the range of 2^{63}-1 to 2^{64}-1, the first octet is set to all 0s.

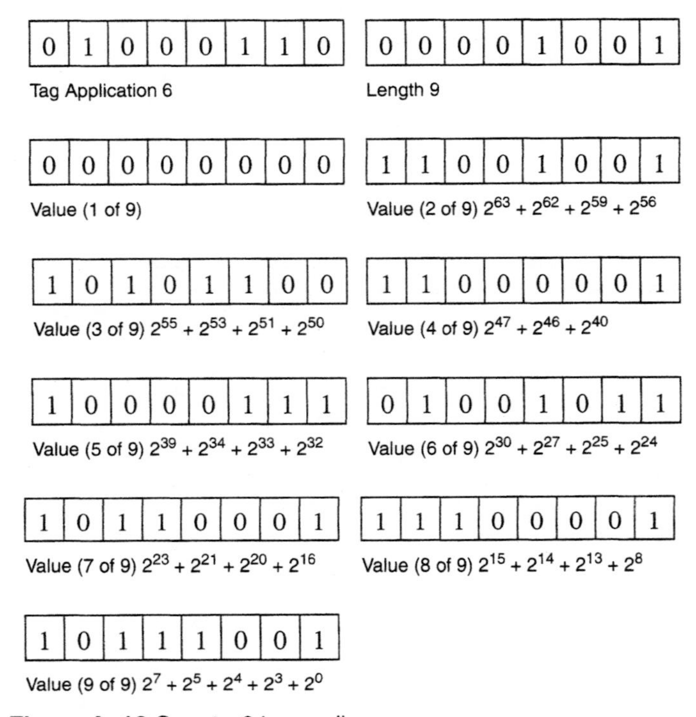

Figure A–16 Counter64 encoding

A.5.11 SEQUENCE

The only other encoding we need to discuss is for type SEQUENCE. The BER encoding for this type is actually quite simple. The values contained in a sequence are concatenated, and treated as one value for a SEQUENCE wrapper. Let's say we have the following SEQUENCE definition:

```
Message ::= SEQUENCE {
                version INTEGER { version-1(0)},
                community OCTET STRING
        }
```

And a value of:

```
sampleMessage ::= { 0, 'EB069937'h }
```

The INTEGER is encoded as shown in Figure A–17:

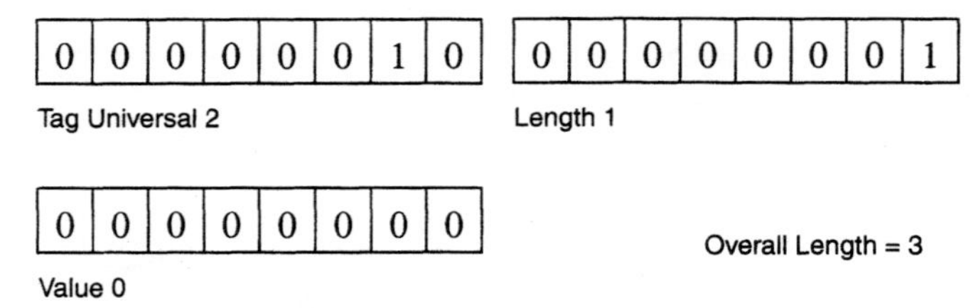

Figure A–17 INTEGER encoding

The OCTET STRING is encoded as shown in Figure A–18:

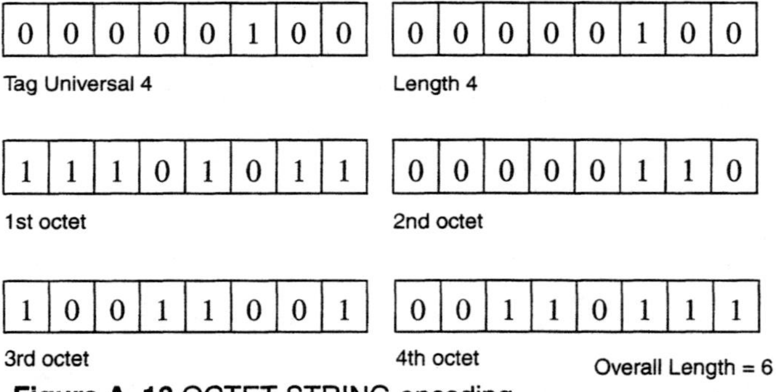

Figure A–18 OCTET STRING encoding

Putting these two values together in a SEQUENCE encoding to form a single value of length 9 yields the encoding shown in Figure A–19:

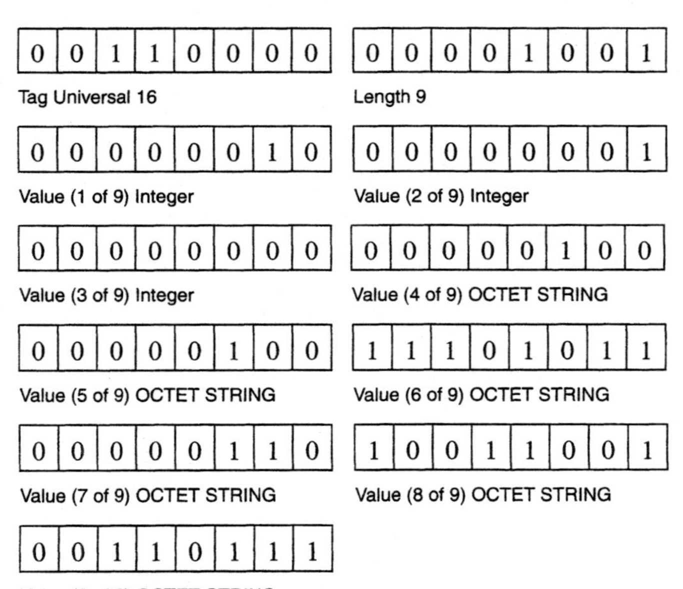

Figure A–19 SEQUENCE encoding

A.6 Minimum/Maximum Encodings

In designing tables, it is a good idea to consider the best and worst case of an encoding of all items in a row. Table A–4 shows the boundaries on the encoded types. This table assumes that the long form of the length is used only when needed, otherwise the short form is used.

Table A–4 Minimum and Maximum Encoded Lengths

Type	Value	Length of encoded value	Minimum length of length	Length of tag, length, value
INTEGER/Integer32	0	1	1	3
	2147483647	4	1	6
OCTET STRING	"" (zero length string)	0	1	2
	string of length 1024	1024	3	1028
	string of length 65535	65535	3	65539
NULL	NULL	0	1	2
OBJECT IDENTIFIER	{ 0 0 }	1	1	3
	{ 1 3 6 1 2 1 1 1 }	7	1	9
IpAddress	1.2.3.4	4	1	6
Counter/Counter32/ Unsigned32	0	1	1	3
	4294967295	5	1	7
Gauge/Gauge32	0	1	1	3
	4294967295	5	1	7
TimeTicks	0	1	1	3
	4294967295	5	1	7
Opaque	'0500'h	2	1	4
	'420103'h	3	1	5
	string of length 65535	65535	3	65539
Counter64	0	1	1	3
	18446744073709551615	9	1	11

APPENDIX B

SNMP Protocol

The specifications of the SNMPv1 and SNMPv2 protocols are described in this appendix. The ASN.1 definitions of the message format are given, followed by diagrams, and the textual descriptions of the message semantics.

B.1 SNMPv1

The following sections are a concise reference specification and clarification of the SNMPv1 protocol based on the definitions from RFCs 1157 and 1155.

B.1.1 SNMPv1 Protocol

```
SNMPv1-Message ::= SEQUENCE {
    version       -- the version of the message format
        INTEGER {
            version-1(0)
            },
    community     -- community name
        OCTET STRING(SIZE(0..65535)),
    pdu           -- one of the request, response, or trap PDUs
        CHOICE {
            get-request       [0] IMPLICIT V1-RR-PDU,
            getnext-request   [1] IMPLICIT V1-RR-PDU,
            get-response      [2] IMPLICIT V1-RR-PDU,
            set-request       [3] IMPLICIT V1-RR-PDU,
            trap              [4] IMPLICIT V1-TRAP-PDU
            }
    }
```

```
V1-RR-PDU ::= SEQUENCE { -- a request or response PDU
    request-id        -- a value specified in a request and
                      -- returned in the response to a request
        INTEGER(-2147483648..2147483647),
    error-status      -- value not used in requests (but should be
                      -- set to zero)
        INTEGER {
            noError(0),
            tooBig(1),
            noSuchName(2),
            badValue(3),
            genErr(5)
            },
    error-index       -- value not used in requests (but should be
                      -- set to zero)
        INTEGER(0..65535),
    variable-bindings -- a list of pairs, each consisting of an OID,
                      -- which is an identity (or approximation) and the
                      -- value (or a placeholder) of an object instance
        V1-VarBindList
    }

V1-TRAP-PDU ::= SEQUENCE { -- an SNMPv1 trap PDU
    enterprise        -- the value of object sysObjectID for "generic"
                      -- traps, otherwise the value specified in a
                      -- TRAP-TYPE construct
        OBJECT IDENTIFIER,
    agent-addr        -- the IP address of the agent sending the trap
                      -- or IP address 0.0.0.0
        [APPLICATION 0] IMPLICIT OCTET STRING(SIZE (4)),
    generic-trap      -- generic trap type
        INTEGER {
            coldStart(0),
            warmStart(1),
            linkDown(2),
            linkUp(3),
            authenticationFailure(4),
            egpNeighborLoss(5),
            enterpriseSpecific(6)-- this value indicates a specific trap,
                         -- which is identified by the values of the
                         -- "enterprise" and "specific-trap" fields
            },
    specific-trap     -- specific code (should be zero for generic traps)
        INTEGER(0..2147483647),
    time-stamp        -- the value of object sysUpTime when the
                      -- event occurred
        [APPLICATION 3] IMPLICIT INTEGER(0..4294967295),
    variable-bindings -- "interesting" information
        V1-VarBindList
    }
```

```
V1-VarBind ::= SEQUENCE {
    identity          -- identity (or approximation for GETNEXT PDUs)
                      -- of an object instance
        OBJECT IDENTIFIER,
    value
        CHOICE {
            placeholder  NULL,
            int32        INTEGER(-2147483648..2147483647),
            string       OCTET STRING(SIZE(0..65535)),
            oid          OBJECT IDENTIFIER,
            ipAddress    [APPLICATION 0] IMPLICIT OCTET STRING(SIZE (4)),
            counter32    [APPLICATION 1] IMPLICIT INTEGER(0..4294967295),
            uint32       [APPLICATION 2] IMPLICIT INTEGER(0..4294967295),
            timeTicks    [APPLICATION 3] IMPLICIT INTEGER(0..4294967295),
            opaque       [APPLICATION 4] IMPLICIT
                                        OCTET STRING(SIZE(2..65535))
            }
    }

V1-VarBindList ::= SEQUENCE SIZE(0..65535) OF V1-VarBind
```

B.1.2 SNMPv1 Messages

Figure B–1 is a diagram of an SNMPv1 message. The tag for the PDU depends on the PDU type.

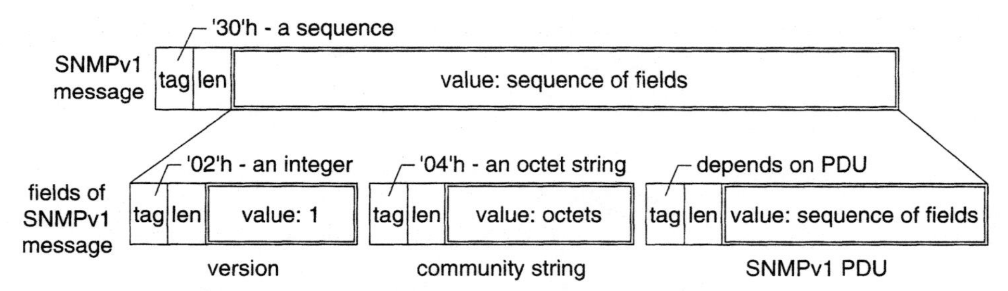

Figure B–1 BER encoding of an SNMPv1 message

Table B–1 lists the tag values for each SNMPv1 PDU type.

Table B–1 Tag values for SNMPv1 PDUs

PDU type	Tag value
get-request	'a0'h
getnext-request	'a1'h
get-response	'a2'h
set-request	'a3'h
trap	'a4'h

B.1.3 SNMPv1 Request or Response PDU

Figure B–2 is a diagram of an SNMPv1 request or response PDU.

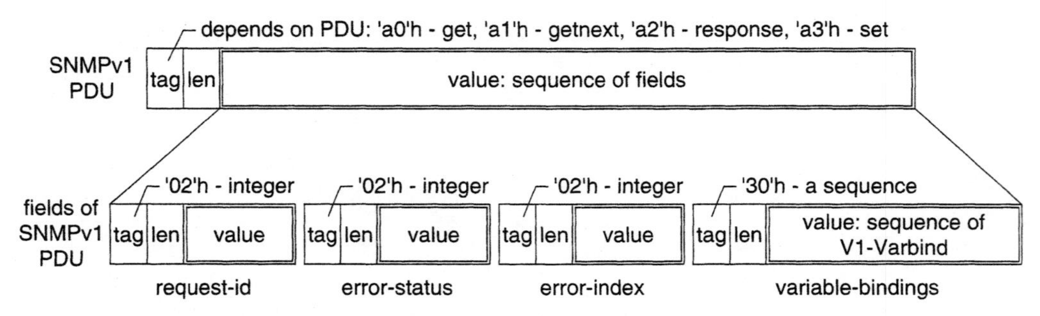

Figure B–2 BER encoding of an SNMPv1 request or response PDU

B.1.4 SNMPv1 Trap PDU

Figure B–3 is a diagram of an SNMPv1 trap PDU.

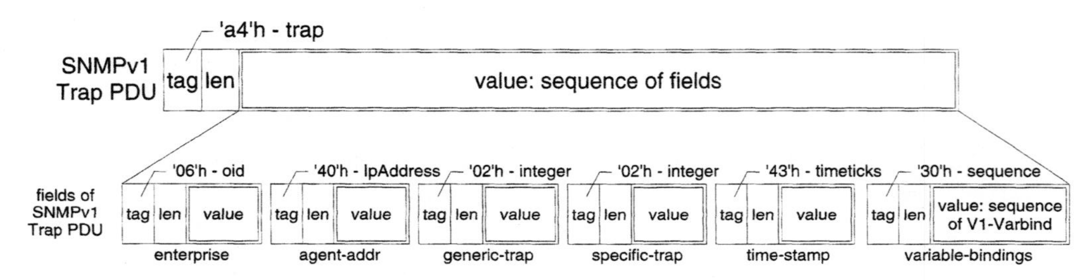

Figure B–3 BER encoding of an SNMPv1 trap PDU

B.1.5 SNMPv1 Variable-bindings

Figure B–4 is a diagram of SNMPv1 variable-bindings.

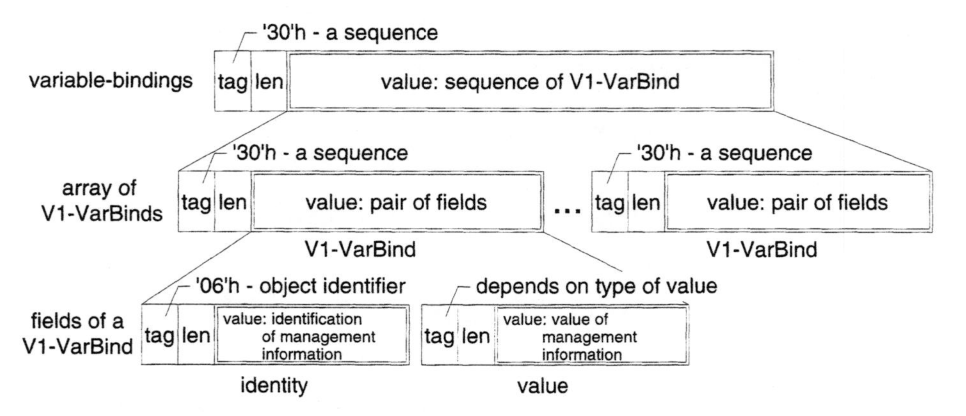

Figure B–4 BER encoding of an SNMPv1 variable-bindings

Remember, the variable-bindings is an array of SNMPv1 varbinds that may have zero, one, or several elements. The tags of data values for variables are listed in Table B–2. (Note: also included is the tag for NULL, which is used only as a placeholder.)

Table B–2 Tag values for SNMPv1 data values

Data Type	Tag value
placeholder (NULL)	'05'h
INTEGER	'02'h
OCTET STRING	'04'h
OBJECT IDENTIFIER	'06'h
IpAddress	'40'h
Counter	'41'h
Gauge (Unsigned integer)	'42'h
TimeTicks	'43'h
Opaque	'44'h

B.1.6 SNMPv1 Message Semantics

The descriptions that follow illustrate actions to process SNMPv1 messages. The implementation of the protocol is not constrained to these actions. The only constraint is that the same results must be achieved as those described below.

The designer of an SNMP management application chooses the variables needed in GET, SET, and GETNEXT operations. The designer typically uses an SNMP function library from an SNMP technology vendor to construct SNMP messages, send them, receive responses, and decode them. It is beyond the scope of this book to describe any of these function libraries. In general, an application must construct a request VarBindList and then call a function specifying the agent identity, the operation, and security information. The function implements the operation and returns to the application a response VarBindList, and the values of the fields error-status and error-index.

B.1.7 SNMPv1 Message Processing

Sending a Request

The top level actions for a manager to send a request message are as follows:

1. The appropriate PDU is constructed based on the VarBindList and the operation type.
2. The PDU, security information, and agent identity are input to a security mechanism to apply authentication and encryption to the PDU. Note that this step does nothing, since no mechanism was defined for SNMPv1. The result is just the PDU, but is conceptually an encrypted and signed PDU.

3. The result from the security mechanism and the community string (an element of the security information) are used to generate an SNMPv1 message.
4. The message is then serialized, using the basic encoding rules of ASN.1, and sent using a transport service to the specified SNMP agent.

Receiving a Request

The top level actions for an agent to receive a request message are as follows:

1. It first increments the value of variable snmpInPkts and then de-serializes the incoming transport message, using the basic encoding rules of ASN.1, to construct an ASN.1 object. (The source transport address is saved.) Next it performs a rudimentary parse of the ASN.1 object (an SNMPv1 message). If the parse fails, it increments the value of variable snmpInASNParseErrs, discards the message, and performs no further actions.
2. It then verifies the version number of the SNMP message. If there is a mismatch, it increments the value of variable snmpInBadVersions, discards the message, and performs no further actions.
3. The community name, security information, and the data (the conceptually encrypted and signed PDU) found in the SNMPv1 message are input to a security mechanism. The PDU is conceptually decrypted and authenticated. Either an ASN.1 object (an SNMPv1 PDU) and profile identity are returned, or an authentication failure is signaled. In the latter case, the agent increments the value of variable snmpInBadCommunityNames, (possibly) generates a trap, discards the message, and performs no further actions.
4. The agent then performs a rudimentary parse on the ASN.1 object returned from the security service to build an ASN.1 object corresponding to an SNMPv1 PDU object. (The the value of request-id is saved.) If the parse fails, it increments the value of variable snmpInASNParseErrs, discards the datagram, and performs no further actions. Otherwise, using the profile identity returned from the security mechanism, the PDU is processed.

Sending a Response

The top level actions for an agent to send a response message are as follows:

1. It first constructs a GET-RESPONSE PDU using as input the saved request-id value and the values for error-status, error-index, and VarBindList returned from processing the request.
2. The PDU, security information, and agent identity are input to a security mechanism to apply authentication and encryption to the PDU. Note that this step does nothing, since no mechanism was defined for SNMPv1. The result is just the PDU, but is conceptually an encrypted and signed PDU.
3. The result from the security mechanism and the community string (an element of the security information) are used to generate an SNMPv1 message.
4. The message is then serialized, using the basic encoding rules of ASN.1, and then sent using a transport service to the manager address from the request.

Receiving a Response

The top level actions for a manager to receive a response message are as follows:

1. The incoming transport message is de-serialized using the basic encoding rules of ASN.1, to construct an ASN.1 object. Next a rudimentary parse of the ASN.1 object (an SNMPv1 message) is done. If the parse fails, the message is discarded and no further actions are done.
2. It then verifies the version number of the SNMP message. If there is a mismatch, it discards the message and performs no further actions.
3. The community name, security information, and the data (the conceptually encrypted and signed PDU) found in the SNMPv1 message are input to a security mechanism. The PDU is conceptually decrypted and authenticated. Either an ASN.1 object (an SNMPv1 PDU) and profile identity is returned, or an authentication failure is signaled. In the latter case, the message is discarded and no further actions are done.
4. The manager then performs a rudimentary parse on the ASN.1 object returned from the security service to build an ASN.1 object corresponding to an SNMPv1 PDU object. If the parse fails, it discards the datagram, and performs no further actions. Otherwise, using the profile identity returned from the security mechanism and the request-id value, the PDU is processed.

B.1.8 SNMPv1 GET Request Processing

A GET request is first processed according to any applicable rule in the list below:

1. If, for any object instance identity in the variable-bindings array, the identity does not exactly match the identity of some object instance available for GET operations in the relevant MIB view, then the agent sends to the manager a GetResponse-PDU of identical form, except that the value of the error-status field is *noSuchName*, and the value of the error-index field is the index of the object instance identity in the variable-bindings array.
2. If the size of the GetResponse-PDU generated as described below would exceed any local constraints, then the agent sends to the manager a GetResponse-PDU of identical form, except that the value of the error-status field is *tooBig*, and the value of the error-index field is zero.
3. If, for any object instance identity in the variable-bindings array, the value of the object instance cannot be retrieved for reasons not covered by any of the foregoing rules, then the agent sends to the manager a GetResponse-PDU of identical form, except that the value of the error-status field is *genErr* and the value of the error-index field is the index of the object instance identity in the variable-bindings array.

If none of the foregoing rules apply, then the agent sends to the manager a GetResponse-PDU such that, for each element of the variable-bindings array of the received message, the corresponding element of the variable-bindings array for the GetResponse-PDU contains the identity and value of that object instance. The value of the error-status field of the GetResponse-PDU is *noError* and the value of the error-index field is zero. The value of the request-id field of the GetResponse-PDU is that of the received message.

B.1.9 SNMPv1 GETNEXT Request Processing

A GETNEXT request is first processed according to any applicable rule in the list below:

1. If, for any object instance identity approximation in the variable-bindings array, that identity does not lexicographically precede the identity of some object instance available for GET operations in the relevant MIB view, then the agent sends to the manager a GetResponse-PDU of identical form, except that the value of the error-status field is *noSuchName*, and the value of the error-index field is the index of the object instance identity approximation in the variable-bindings array.
2. If the size of the GetResponse-PDU generated as described below would exceed any local constraints, then the agent sends to the manager a GetResponse-PDU of identical form, except that the value of the error-status field is *tooBig*, and the value of the error-index field is zero.
3. If, for any object instance identity approximation in the variable-bindings array, the value of the lexicographical successor to the identity cannot be retrieved for reasons not covered by any of the foregoing rules, then the agent sends to the manager a GetResponse-PDU of identical form, except that the value of the error-status field is *genErr* and the value of the error-index field is the index of the object instance identity approximation in the variable-bindings array.

If none of the foregoing rules apply, then the agent sends to the manager a GetResponse-PDU such that, for each element in the variable-bindings array of the received message, the corresponding element in the variable-bindings for the GetResponse-PDU contains the identity and value of that object instance whose identity is, in the lexicographical ordering of the identities of all object instances available for get operations in the relevant MIB view the immediate successor to object instance identity approximation specified in the request. The value of the error-status field of the GetResponse-PDU is *noError* and the value of the error-index field is zero. The value of the request-id field of the GetResponse-PDU is that of the received message.

B.1.10 SNMPv1 SET Request Processing

A SET request is first processed according to any applicable rule in the list below:

1. If, for any object instance identity in the variable-bindings array, the object instance is not available for SET operations in the relevant MIB view, then the agent sends to the manager a GetResponse-PDU of identical form, except that the value of the error-status field is *noSuchName*, and the value of the error-index field is the index of the object identity in the variable-bindings array.

2. If, for any value in the variable-bindings array, that value is not consistent with that required for the object instance, then the agent sends to the manager a GetResponse-PDU of identical form, except that the value of the error-status field is *badValue*, and the value of the error-index field is the index of the value in the variable-bindings array.
3. If the size of the Get Response type message generated as described below would exceed any local constraints, then the agent sends to the manager a GetResponse-PDU of identical form, except that the value of the error-status field is *tooBig*, and the value of the error-index field is zero.
4. If, for any object instance identity in the variable-bindings array, the value of the object instance cannot be altered for reasons not covered by any of the foregoing rules, then the agent sends to the manager a GetResponse-PDU of identical form, except that the value of the error-status field is *genErr* and the value of the error-index field is the index of the object instance identity in the variable-bindings array.

If none of the foregoing rules apply, then for each object instance identified in the variable-bindings array of the received message, the corresponding value is assigned to the object instance. Each object instance value assignment specified by the SetRequest-PDU should be effected as if simultaneously set with respect to all other assignments specified in the same message. The agent then sends to the manager a GetResponse-PDU of identical form except that the value of the error-status field of the generated message is *noError* and the value of the error-index field is zero.

B.2 SNMPv2

The following sections are a concise reference specification and clarification of the SNMPv2 protocol based on the definitions from RFCs 1902, 1905, and 1906.

B.2.1 SNMPv2 Protocol

```
SNMPv2-Message ::= SEQUENCE {
    -- contents not yet defined
    }


SNMPv2-PDU ::= CHOICE {
        get-request       [0] IMPLICIT V2-RR-PDU,
        getnext-request   [1] IMPLICIT V2-RR-PDU,
        response          [2] IMPLICIT V2-RR-PDU,
        set-request       [3] IMPLICIT V2-RR-PDU,
        getbulk-request   [5] IMPLICIT V2-GB-PDU,
        inform-request    [6] IMPLICIT V2-RR-PDU,
        trap              [7] IMPLICIT V2-RR-PDU,
        report            [8] IMPLICIT V2-RR-PDU
        }
```

```
V2-RR-PDU ::= SEQUENCE { -- a request, response, trap, or report PDU
    request-id        -- a value specified in a request and
                      -- returned in the response to a request
        INTEGER(-2147483648..2147483647),
    error-status      -- value not used in requests (but should
                      -- be set to zero)
        INTEGER {
            noError(0),
            tooBig(1),
            noSuchName(2),
            badValue(3),
            readOnly(4),
            genErr(5),
            noAccess(6),
            wrongType(7),
            wrongLength(8),
            wrongEncoding(9),
            wrongValue(10),
            noCreation(11),
            inconsistentValue(12),
            resourceUnavailable(13),
            commitFailed(14),
            undoFailed(15),
            authorizationError(16),
            notWritable(17),
            inconsistentName(18)
            },
    error-index       -- value not used in requests (but should
                      -- be set to zero)
        INTEGER(0..65535),
    variable-bindings -- a list of pairs, each consisting of an OID,
                      -- which is an identity (or approximation) and the
                      -- value (or a placeholder) of an object instance
        V2-VarBindList
    }

V2-GB-PDU ::= SEQUENCE { -- a getbulk PDU
    request-id        -- a value specified in a request and
                      -- returned in the response to a request
        INTEGER(-2147483648..2147483647),
    non-repeaters     -- number of non-repeaters in varBind list
        INTEGER(0..65535)
    max-repetitions  -- number of repetitions
        INTEGER(0..65535),
    variable-bindings -- a list of pairs, each consisting of an OID,
                      -- which is an approximation of the identity and a
                      -- placeholder for the value of an object instance
        V2-VarBindList
    }
```

```
V2-VarBind ::= SEQUENCE {
    identity         -- identity (or approximation for GETNEXT PDUs)
                     -- of an object instance
        OBJECT IDENTIFIER,
    value
        CHOICE {
            placeholder      NULL,
            noSuchObject     [0] IMPLICIT NULL,
            noSuchInstance   [1] IMPLICIT NULL,
            endOfMibView     [2] IMPLICIT NULL,
            int32        INTEGER(-2147483648..2147483647),
            string       OCTET STRING(SIZE(0..65535)),
            oid          OBJECT IDENTIFIER,
            ipAddress    [APPLICATION 0] IMPLICIT OCTET STRING(SIZE (4)),
            counter32    [APPLICATION 1] IMPLICIT INTEGER(0..4294967295),
            uint32       [APPLICATION 2] IMPLICIT INTEGER(0..4294967295),
            timeTicks    [APPLICATION 3] IMPLICIT INTEGER(0..4294967295),
            opaque       [APPLICATION 4] IMPLICIT
                                     OCTET STRING(SIZE(2..65535)),
            counter64    [APPLICATION 6] IMPLICIT
                                     INTEGER(0..18446744073709551615)
            }
    }

V2-VarBindList ::= SEQUENCE SIZE(0..65535) OF V2-VarBind
```

B.2.2 SNMPv2 Messages

Figure B–5 is a diagram of an SNMPv2 message.

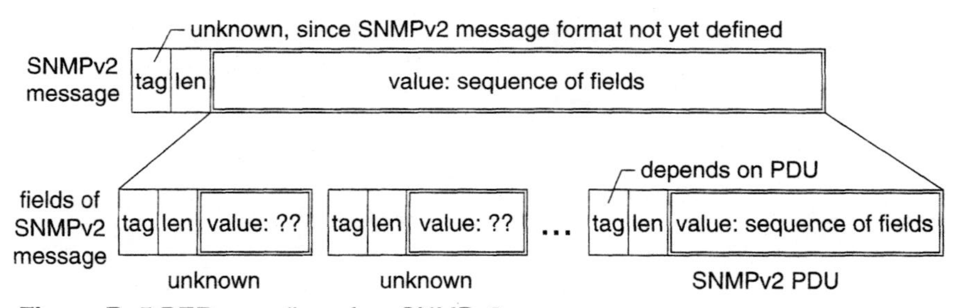

Figure B–5 BER encoding of an SNMPv2 message

(The diagram is incomplete, since there is currently no standards-track definition of an SNMPv2 message.) The tag for the PDU depends on the PDU type.

Table B–3 lists the tag values for each SNMPv2 PDU type.

Table B–3 Tag values for SNMPv2 PDUs

PDU type	Tag value
get-request	'a0'h
getnext-request	'a1'h
get-response	'a2'h
set-request	'a3'h
getbulk-request	'a5'h
inform-request	'a6'h
v2-trap	'a7'h
v2-report	'a8'h

B.2.3 SNMPv2 Request, Response, Trap, or Report PDU

Figure B–6 is a diagram of an SNMPv2 request, response, trap, or report PDU.

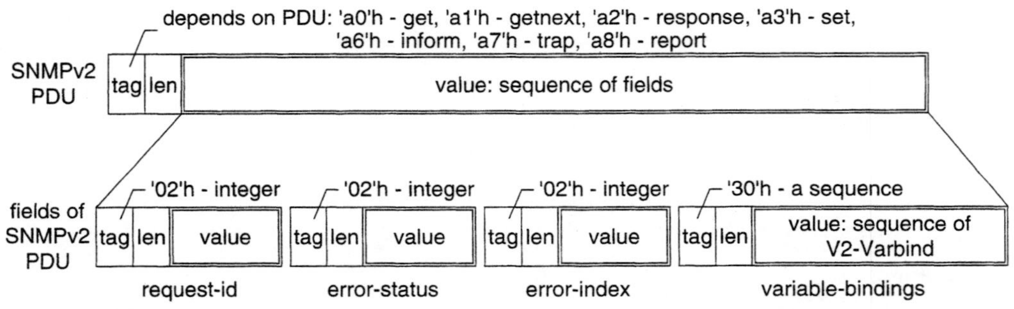

Figure B–6 BER encoding of an SNMPv2 request, response, trap, or report PDU

B.2.4 SNMPv2 Getbulk PDU

Figure B–7 is a diagram of an SNMPv2 getbulk PDU.

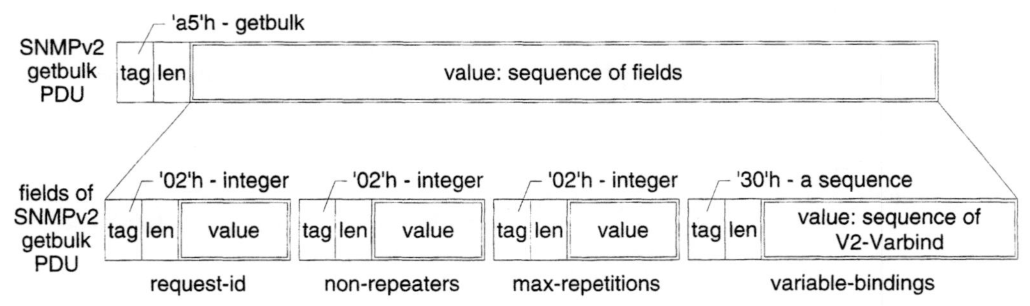

Figure B–7 BER encoding of an SNMPv2 getbulk PDU

B.2.5 SNMPv2 Variable-bindings

Figure B–8 is a diagram of SNMPv2 variable-bindings.

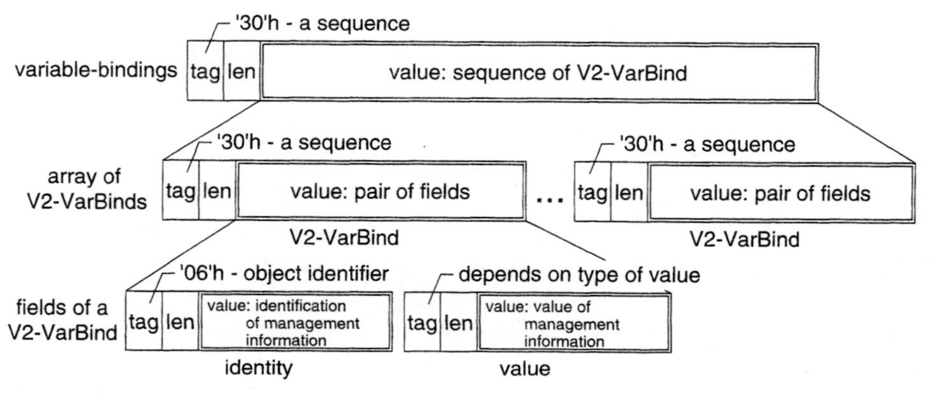

Figure B–8 BER encoding of an SNMPv2 variable-bindings

Remember, the variable-bindings is an array of SNMPv2 varbinds that may have zero, one, or several elements. The tags of data values for variables are listed in Table B–4. (Note: also included are the tags for NULL, which is used only as a placeholder, and for the exception values.)

Table B–4 Tag values for SNMPv2 data values

Data Type	Tag value
placeholder (NULL)	'05'h
noSuchObject exception	'80'h
noSuchInstance exception	'81'h
endOfMibView exception	'82'h
INTEGER	'02'h
OCTET STRING	'04'h
OBJECT IDENTIFIER	'06'h
IpAddress	'40'h
Counter32	'41'h
Gauge32 (Unsigned integer)	'42'h
TimeTicks	'43'h
Opaque	'44'h
Counter64	'46'h

B.2.6 SNMPv2 Message Semantics

Complete descriptions cannot be presently provided on how SNMPv2 messages are processed, since there is no standards-track definition. What is provided illustrates the actions to process SNMPv2 messages. The implementation of the protocol is not constrained to these actions. The only constraint is that the same results must be achieved as those described below.

The designer of an SNMP management application chooses the variables needed in GET, SET, GETNEXT, and GETBULK operations. The designer typically uses an SNMP function library from an SNMP technology vendor to construct SNMP messages, send them, receive responses, and decode them. It is beyond the scope of this book to describe any of these function libraries. In general, an application must construct a request VarBindList and then call a function specifying the agent identity, the operation, and security information. The function implements the operation and returns to the application a response VarBindList, and the values of error-status and error-index fields.

B.2.7 SNMPv2 Message Processing

Sending a Request

The top level actions for a manager to send a request message are as follows:

1. The appropriate PDU is constructed based on the VarBindList and the operation type.
2. The PDU, security information, and agent identity are input to a security mechanism to apply authentication and encryption to the PDU. Note that the output from this step is currently undefined.
3. The result from the security mechanism and, possibly, additional parameters are used to generate an SNMPv2 message. Note that the output from this step is currently undefined.
4. The message is then serialized, using the basic encoding rules of ASN.1, and sent using a transport service to the specified SNMP agent.

Receiving a Request

The top level actions for an agent to receive a request message are as follows:

1. It first increments the value of variable snmpInPkts and then de-serializes the incoming transport message, using the basic encoding rules of ASN.1, to construct an ASN.1 object. (The source transport address is saved.) Next it performs a rudimentary parse of the ASN.1 object (an SNMPv2 message). If the parse fails, it increments the value of variable snmpInASNParseErrs, discards the message, and performs no further actions.
2. It extracts, decrypts, and authenticates an SNMPv2 PDU from the message. Note that how this is done is currently undefined.
3. The agent then performs a rudimentary parse on the ASN.1 object returned from the security service to build an ASN.1 object corresponding to an SNMPv2 PDU object. (The request-id value is saved.) If the parse fails, it increments the value of variable

snmpInASNParseErrs, discards the datagram, and performs no further actions. Otherwise, using the profile identity returned from the security mechanism, the PDU is processed.

Sending a Response

The top level actions for an agent to send a response message are as follows:

1. It first constructs a GET-RESPONSE PDU using as input the saved request-id value and the values of error-status, error-index, and VarBindList returned from processing the request.
2. The PDU, security information, and agent identity are input to a security mechanism to apply authentication and encryption to the PDU. Note that the output from this step is currently undefined.
3. The result from the security mechanism and, possibly, additional parameters are used to generate an SNMPv2 message. Note that the output from this step is currently undefined.
4. The message is then serialized, using the basic encoding rules of ASN.1, and then sent using a transport service to the manager address from the request.

Receiving a Response

The top level actions for a manager to receive a response message are as follows:

1. The incoming transport message is de-serialized using the basic encoding rules of ASN.1, to construct an ASN.1 object. Next a rudimentary parse of the ASN.1 object (an SNMPv2 message) is done. If the parse fails, the message is discarded and no further actions are done.
2. It extracts, decrypts, and authenticates an SNMPv2 PDU from the message. Note that how this is done is currently undefined.
3. The manager then performs a rudimentary parse on the ASN.1 object returned from the security service to build an ASN.1 object corresponding to an SNMPv2 PDU object. If the parse fails, it discards the datagram, and performs no further actions. Otherwise, using the profile identity returned from the security mechanism and the request-id, the PDU is processed.

B.2.8 SNMPv2 GET Request Processing

Upon receipt of a GET request, an agent processes each of the elements of the variable-bindings array to produce a Response-PDU. All fields of the Response-PDU have the same values as the corresponding fields of the received request except as indicated below. Each element of the variable-bindings array is processed as follows:

1. If the object instance identity exactly matches the identity of an object instance accessible by this request, then the value field of the variable-bindings array element is set to the value of the identified object instance.

2. Otherwise, if a prefix of the object instance identity does not exactly match the identity of any (potential) object type accessible by this request, then the value field of the variable-bindings array element is set to *noSuchObject*.
3. Otherwise, the value field of the variable-bindings array element is set to *noSuchInstance*.

If the processing of any element of the variable-bindings array fails for a reason other than listed above, then the Response-PDU is re-formatted with the same values in the request-id and variable-bindings fields as the received GetRequest-PDU, with the value of the error-status field set to *genErr*, and the value of the error-index field is set to the index of the failed variable-bindings array element.

Otherwise, the value of the error-status field in the Response-PDU is set to *noError*, and the value of the error-index field is set to zero.

The generated Response-PDU is then encapsulated into a message. If the size of the resultant message is less than or equal to both any local constraints and the maximum message size of the manager, the message is transmitted to the manager.

Otherwise, an alternate Response-PDU is generated. This alternate Response-PDU is formatted with the same value in the request-id field as the received GetRequest-PDU, with the value of the error-status field set to *tooBig*, the value of the error-index field set to zero, and zero elements in the variable-bindings array. This alternate Response-PDU is then encapsulated into a message. If the size of the resultant message is less than or equal to both any local constraints and the maximum message size of the manager, it is transmitted to the manager. Otherwise, the snmpSilentDrops variable is incremented and the resultant message is discarded.

B.2.9 SNMPv2 GETNEXT Request Processing

Upon receipt of a GetNextRequest-PDU, the agent processes each element of the variable-bindings array to produce a Response-PDU. All fields of the Response-PDU have the same values as the corresponding fields of the received request except as indicated below. Each element of the variable-bindings array is processed as follows:

1. The object instance is located from the lexicographically ordered list of the object instances that are accessible by this request and whose identity is the first lexicographic successor of the object instance identity approximation in the incoming GetNextRequest-PDU. The identity and value fields for the element of the variable-bindings array in the Response-PDU are set to the identity and value of the located object instance.
2. If the requested object instance identity approximation does not lexicographically precede the identity of any object instance accessible by this request, i.e., there is no lexicographic successor, then the element of the variable-bindings array produced in the Response-PDU has the value field set to *endOfMibView*, and the identity field set to the value of the identity field in the request.

If the processing of any element of the variable-bindings array fails for a reason other than listed above, then the Response-PDU is re-formatted with the same values in its request-id and variable-bindings fields as the received GetNextRequest-PDU, with the value of its error-status field set to *genErr*, and the value of its error-index field is set to the index of the failed element of the variable-bindings array.

Otherwise, the value of the Response-PDU's error-status field is set to *noError*, and the value of its error-index field to zero.

The generated Response-PDU is then encapsulated into a message. If the size of the resultant message is less than or equal to both a local constraint and the maximum message size of the manager, it is transmitted to the manager.

Otherwise, an alternate Response-PDU is generated. This alternate Response-PDU is formatted with the same values in its request-id field as the received GetNextRequest-PDU, with the value of its error-status field set to *tooBig*, the value of its error-index field set to zero, and zero elements in the variable-bindings array. This alternate Response-PDU is then encapsulated into a message. If the size of the resultant message is less than or equal to both a local constraint and the maximum message size of the manager, it is transmitted to the manager. Otherwise, the snmpSilentDrops variable is incremented and the resultant message is discarded.

B.2.10 SNMPv2 GETBULK Request Processing

Upon receipt of a GetBulkRequest-PDU, the agent processes each element of the variable-bindings array to produce a Response-PDU with its request-id field having the same value as in the request. Processing begins by examining the values in the non-repeaters and max-repetitions fields. If the value in the non-repeaters field is less than zero, then the value of the field is set to zero. Similarly, if the value in the max-repetitions field is less than zero, then the value of the field is set to zero. The successful processing of each element of the variable-bindings array from the request generates zero or more elements of the variable-bindings array for the Response-PDU. That is, the one-to-one mapping between the elements of the variable-bindings array of the GetRequest-PDU, GetNextRequest-PDU, and SetRequest-PDU types and the resultant Response-PDUs does not apply for the mapping between the elements of the variable-bindings array of a GetBulkRequest-PDU and the resultant Response-PDU. The values of the non-repeaters and max-repetitions fields in the request specify the processing requested. One element of the variable-bindings array in the Response-PDU is requested for the first N elements in the request, and M elements are requested for each of the R remaining elements in the request. Consequently, the total number of requested elements communicated by the request is given by $N + (M * R)$, where N is the minimum of: (a) the value of the non-repeaters field in the request, and (b) the number of elements in the variable-bindings array from the request; M is the value of the max-repetitions field in the request; and R is the maximum of: (a) number of elements in the variable-bindings array from the request minus N, and (b) zero. The agent produces a Response-PDU with up to the total number of requested elements communicated by the request. If N is greater than zero, the first through the (N)-th elements of the of variable-bindings array for the Response-PDU are each produced as follows:

1. The object instance is located from the lexicographically ordered list of the object instances that are accessible by this request and whose identity is the first lexicographic successor of the object instance identity approximation in the incoming GetBulkRequest-PDU. The identity and value fields for the element of the variable-bindings array in the Response-PDU are set to the identity and value of the located object instance.
2. If the requested object instance identity approximation does not lexicographically precede the identity of any object instance accessible by this request, i.e., there is no lexicographic successor, then the element of the variable-bindings array produced in the Response-PDU has the value field set to *endOfMibView*, and the identity field set to the identity field in the request.

If M and R are non-zero, the (N + 1)-th and subsequent elements of the variable-bindings array for the Response-PDU are each produced in a similar manner. For each iteration i, such that i is greater than zero and less than or equal to M, and for each repeated element, r, such that r is greater than zero and less than or equal to R, the (N + ((i-1) * R) + r)-th element of the variable-bindings array for the Response-PDU is produced as follows:

1. The object instance is located from the lexicographically ordered list of the object instances that are accessible by this request and whose identity is the (i)-th lexicographic successor of the (N + r)-th object instance identity approximation in the incoming GetBulkRequest-PDU. The identity and value fields for the element of the variable-bindings array in the Response-PDU are set to the identity and value of the located object instance.
2. If there is no (i)-th lexicographic successor, then the element of the variable-bindings array produced in the Response-PDU has the value field set to *endOfMibView*, and the identity field set to either the identity of the last lexicographic successor, or if there are no lexicographic successors, to identity field of the (N + r)-th element in the request.

While the maximum number of elements in the variable-bindings array for the Response-PDU is bounded by N + (M * R), the response may be generated with a lesser number of elements (possibly zero) for either of three reasons.

1. If the size of the message encapsulating the Response-PDU containing the requested number of elements would be greater than either a local constraint or the maximum message size of the manager, then the response is generated with a lesser number of elements. Elements are removed from the end of the variable-bindings array until the message encapsulating the Response-PDU is approximately equal to but no greater than

either a local constraint or the maximum message size of the manager. Note that the number of variable bindings removed has no relationship to the values of N, M, or R.

2. The response may also be generated with a lesser number of elements if for some value of iteration i, such that i is greater than zero and less than or equal to M, that all of the generated elements have the value field set to *endOfMibView*. In this case, the variable-bindings array may be truncated after the (N + (i * R))-th element.
3. In the event that the processing of a request with many repetitions requires a significantly greater amount of processing time than a normal request, then the agent may terminate the request with less than the full number of repetitions, providing at least one repetition is completed.

If the processing of any element of the variable-bindings array fails for a reason other than listed above, then the Response-PDU is re-formatted with the same values in its request-id and variable-bindings fields as the received GetBulkRequest-PDU, with the value of its error-status field set to *genErr*, and the value of its error-index field set to the index of the failed element of the variable-bindings array.

Otherwise, the value of the Response-PDU's error-status field is set to *noError*, and the value of its error-index field to zero.

The generated Response-PDU (possibly with no elements in the variable-bindings array) is then encapsulated into a message. If the size of the resultant message is less than or equal to both a local constraint and the maximum message size of the manager, it is transmitted to the manager. Otherwise, the snmpSilentDrops variable is incremented and the resultant message is discarded.

B.2.11 SNMPv2 SET Request Processing

Upon receipt of a SetRequest-PDU, the agent determines the size of a message encapsulating a Response-PDU having the same values in its request-id and variable-bindings fields as the received SetRequest-PDU, and the largest possible sizes of the error-status and error-index fields. If the determined message size is greater than either a local constraint or the maximum message size of the manager, then an alternate Response-PDU is generated, transmitted to the manager, and processing of the SetRequest-PDU terminates immediately thereafter. This alternate Response-PDU is formatted with the same values in its request-id field as the received SetRequest-PDU, with the value of the error-status field set to *tooBig*, the value of the error-index field set to zero, and zero elements in the variable-bindings array. This alternate Response-PDU is then encapsulated into a message. If the size of the resultant message is less than or equal to both a local constraint and the maximum message size of the manager, it is transmitted to the manager. Otherwise, the snmpSilentDrops variable is incremented and the resultant message is discarded. Regardless, processing of the SetRequest-PDU terminates.

Otherwise, the agent processes each element of the variable-bindings array to produce a Response-PDU. All fields of the Response-PDU have the same values as the corresponding fields of the received request except as indicated below.

The elements of the variable-bindings array are conceptually processed as a two-phase operation. In the first phase, each element is validated; if all validations are successful, then each object instance is altered in the second phase. Of course, implementors are at liberty to implement either the first, or second, or both, of these conceptual phases as multiple implementation phases. Indeed, such multiple implementation phases may be necessary in some cases to ensure consistency.

The following validations are performed in the first phase on each element of the variable-bindings array until they are all successful, or until one fails:

1. If the object instance identity specifies an existing or non-existent object instance to which this request is or would be denied access because it is or would not be in the appropriate MIB view, then the value of the Response-PDU's error-status field is set to *noAccess*, and the value of its error-index field is set to the index of the element of the variable-bindings array.
2. Otherwise, if a prefix of the object instance identity matches the identity of an object type and instances of that object type cannot be created or modified no matter what new value is specified, then the value of the Response-PDU's error-status field is set to *notWritable*, and the value of the error-index field is set to the index of the failed element of the variable-bindings array.
3. Otherwise, if the value field specifies a type which is inconsistent with that required for the object type identified by a prefix of the object instance identity, then the value of the error-status field of the Response-PDU's is set to *wrongType*, and the value of the error-index field is set to the index of the failed element of the variable-bindings array.
4. Otherwise, if the value field specifies a length which is inconsistent with that required for the object type identified by a prefix of the object instance identity, then the value of the error-status field of the Response-PDU is set to *wrongLength*, and the value of the error-index field is set to the index of the failed element of the variable-bindings array.
5. Otherwise, if the value field contains an ASN.1 encoding which is inconsistent with that field's ASN.1 tag, then the value of the error-status field of the Response-PDU is set to *wrongEncoding*, and the value of the error-index field is set to the index of the failed element of the variable-bindings array. (Note that not all implementation strategies will generate this error.)
6. Otherwise, if value field specifies a value which could under no circumstances be assigned to the object instance, then the value of the error-status field of the Response-PDU is set to *wrongValue*, and the value of the error-index field is set to the index of the failed element of the variable-bindings array.
7. Otherwise, if the identity specifies an object instance which does not exist and could not ever be created (even though some object instances of the object type might under some circumstances be able to be created), then the value of the error-status field of the Response-PDU is set to *noCreation*, and the value of the error-index field is set to the index of the failed element of the variable-bindings array.

8. Otherwise, if the identity specifies an object instance which does not exist but cannot be created under the present circumstances (even though it could be created under other circumstances), then the value of the error-status field of the Response-PDU is set to *inconsistentName*, and the value of the error-index field is set to the index of the failed element of the variable-bindings array.
9. Otherwise, if the identity specifies an object instance which exists but cannot be modified no matter what new value is specified, then the value of the error-status field of the Response-PDU is set to *notWritable*, and the value of the error-index field is set to the index of the failed element of the variable-bindings array.
10. Otherwise, if the value field specifies a value that could under other circumstances be assigned to the object instance, but is presently inconsistent or otherwise unable to be assigned to the object instance, then the value of the Response-PDU's error-status field is set to *inconsistentValue*, and the value of its error-index field is set to the index of the failed element of the variable-bindings array.
11. When, during the above steps, the assignment of the value specified by the value field to the specified object instance requires the allocation of a resource which is presently unavailable, then the value of the Response-PDU's error-status field is set to *resourceUnavailable*, and the value of its error-index field is set to the index of the failed element of the variable-bindings array.
12. If the processing of the element fails for a reason other than listed above, then the value of the Response-PDU's error-status field is set to *genErr*, and the value of its error-index field is set to the index of the failed element of the variable-bindings array.
13. Otherwise, the validation of the element succeeds.

At the end of the first phase, if the validation of all elements succeeded, then the value of the Response-PDU's error-status field is set to *noError* and the value of its error-index field is zero, and processing continues as follows.

For each element of the variable-bindings array in the request, the identified object instance is created if necessary, and the specified value is assigned to it. Each of these object instance value assignments occurs as if simultaneously with respect to all other assignments specified in the same request. However, if the same object instance is specified more than once in a single request, with different associated values, then the actual assignment made to that object instance is implementation-specific.

If any of these assignments fail (even after all the previous validations), then all other assignments are undone, and the Response-PDU is modified to have the value of its error-status field set to *commitFailed*, and the value of its error-index field set to the index of the failed element of the variable-bindings array.

If and only if it is not possible to undo all the assignments, then the Response-PDU is modified to have the value of its error-status field set to *undoFailed*, and the value of its error-index field is set to zero. Note that implementations are strongly encouraged to take all possible measures to avoid use of either *commitFailed* or *undoFailed* — these two error-status codes are not to be taken as license to take the easy way out in an implementation.

Finally, the generated Response-PDU is encapsulated into a message, and transmitted to the manager.

APPENDIX C

SMIC User's Guide

C.1 List of Acronyms

- ASN.1: Abstract Syntax Notation One
- BER: Basic Encoding Rules
- BNF: Backus-Naur Form
- IETF: Internet Engineering Task Force — the organization that creates the standards for the Internet suite of protocols
- IP: Internet Protocol
- ISO: International Organization for Standardization
- TC: Textual convention
- MIB: Management Information Base
- MOSY: Managed Object Syntax compiler (YACC based)
- OID: Object Identifier
- OSI: Open Systems Interconnection
- OVA: Object identifier Value Assignment
- RFC: Request for Comments — the documents published by the IETF

- SMI: Structure of Management Information
- SMIC: SNMP Management Information Compiler
- SMICng: SMIC Next Generation
- SNMP: Simple Network Management Protocol
- SNMPv1: SNMP version 1
- SNMPv2: SNMP version 2
- TCP: Transmission Control Protocol

C.2 Conventions

Due to the constraints of formatting, some examples of input and output to and from SMICng could not be fitted on one line. When a single line has to be broken, the plus (+) character is specified as the first character of the continuation lines. Below shows a contiguous line and the same line broken into two pieces.

```
An example long line before splitting.

An example long line that
+            shows continuation after splitting.
```

C.3 Introduction

This document describes a compiler for SNMP MIBs written in either the SNMPv1 format or the SNMPv2 format. (These formats are documented in RFC 1155, RFC 1212, and RFC 1215 for SNMPv1 and RFC 1442, RFC 1443, and RFC 1444 for SNMPv2.) This compiler is called SMICng. This is short for SNMP MIB Information Compiler the "next generation". The first version of this compiler, simply called SMIC (or SMIC classic), has been freely available to the IETF community since August of 1992. This new version has been extensively re-engineered and extended to support both SNMPv1 and SNMPv2.

SMICng is written in portable C code and is available on several hardware and operating system platforms including MS-DOS, OS/2, and UNIX.

SMICng is designed for use by MIB developers, agent implementors, management station implementors, management station users, managed device vendors, and users of managed devices.

SMICng can be used alone to check the syntax of a SNMP MIB or as part of a system of programs used to generate MIB representations in other formats. These formats include those used in management station MIB schema files, the data structures and code used for the development of SNMP agents, and the data structures and code used to develop network management applications. The other programs are not supplied as part of this SMICng package.

SMICng has the capability to check MIBs at varying levels of strictness. The checking level is controlled with command line switches, compiler directives, or with options specified in an environment variable. Output from SMICng is specified with command line switches and includes the following: internal data structures used for debugging or analysis by sophisticated MIB developers; an intermediate file to be used by other programs; MOSY version 7.1 output, both .defs and .tcl files (MOSY is a popular SNMP MIB compiler); a list of object name to object identifier assignments and a list of defined traps; a list of object identifier to name assignments, and an SNMPv1 MIB from an SNMPv2 MIB. Programs can be easily written to read one of the outputs from SMICng and then create a new output format.

C.4 Overview

SMICng provides the following features:

- can read multiple input files
- parses MIBs written in the syntax defined by SNMPv1 SMI, concise MIB, and trap format documents (RFC 1155, RFC 1212, and RFC 1215)
- parses MIBs written in the syntax defined by SNMPv2 SMI, SNMPv2 Textual Conventions, and SNMPv2 conformance documents (RFC 1442, RFC 1443, and RFC 1444)
- parses multiple MIB modules in one input stream
- checks the validity of IMPORTS clauses
- resolves textual conventions and checks that their usage is valid
- supports use of extended ASN.1 size/range constructs
- can create SNMPv1 MIBs from SNMPv2 MIBs
- can create MOSY v7.1 .defs and .tcl files
- alias assignments for modules and object names
- has selective checking of MIB constructs
- has extensive MIB syntax checking and can continue syntax checking after most syntax errors
- has extensive checking of MIB consistency
- runs on many platforms including MS-DOS and UNIX
- has multiple output options
- can unregister an item's OID registration
- has conditional compiling of MIB modules based on need
- can exclude imported MIB modules from outputs
- uses environment variable to locate "included" files
- uses environment variable to specify default checking options
- has extensive help via command line options

SMICng is NOT a general purpose ASN.1 parser. Thus, it lacks the capability to compile arbitrary ASN.1 macros or any ASN.1 construct not needed for parsing SNMPv1/SNMPv2 MIBs.

The SMICng package includes:

- A MIB compiler, SMICng, for several different platforms
- A MIB stripper (or extraction tool), MSTRIP, for several different platforms
- Source files and makefiles for SMICng and MSTRIP
- This documentation
- Stripped and "corrected" MIBs from RFCs

C.5 Use of SMICng

To use SMICng, perform the following six tasks, which are explained in the following sections:

1. Select and prepare the MIBs to be compiled.
2. Set the environment variable SMICINCL to name the directories containing MIBs.
3. 3Set the environment variable SMICOPTS to specify the default values for the command line options.
4. Create a "MIB include file".
5. Run SMICng and correct errors in the MIBs.
6. Generate output(s).

C.5.1 Select and Prepare MIBs

To use SMICng, first obtain the MIBs (i.e., the ASN.1 modules) to be compiled. A MIB may be contained in a document, such as an RFC. In this case, the text before and after the MIB module, and the page breaks within the MIB module must be stripped from the document. The resulting MIB module (or modules) can now be read by SMICng.

The stripping process can be done manually in a text editor; with a script for a text processing language such as AWK, Perl, or TCL; or with the help of a MIB stripper program. A stripper program and all of the standard MIBs are provided with the SMICng package. Typically, standard MIBs are placed in a directory and made read-only, proprietary MIBs are placed in another directory and also made read-only, and MIBs under development or testing are placed in yet another directory.

C.5.2 Set SMICINCL Environment Variable

For SMICng to locate the files that it reads, the value of the environment variable named SMICINCL must be set to a list of names of directories to be searched (after the current directory) for files. The names in the list must be separated by semicolons (;) in DOS or OS/2, and by colons (:) or spaces in UNIX. For example, the following shows how to set up the environment variable to search two directories for both UNIX and DOS:

- in UNIX (using the C Shell):
  setenv SMICINCL "/pub/mibs/rfc /pub/mibs/draft"
  or
  setenv SMICINCL /pub/mibs/rfc:/pub/mibs/draft
- in UNIX (using the Bourne shell):

SMICINCL="/pub/mibs/rfc /pub/mibs/draft"
or
SMICINCL=/pub/mibs/rfc:/pub/mibs/draft
and
export SMICINCL

- in DOS and OS/2:
SET SMICINCL=C:\MIBS\RFC;C:\MIBS\DRAFT

C.5.3 Set SMICOPTS Environment Variable

SMICng has many command line options. Most control the level of checking for various MIB constructs. The desired level of checking can be specified via the SMICOPTS environment variable so that these options need not be specified on the command line or in a "MIB Include file". For example, by default SMICng terminates ASN.1 comments in MIBs with only an end of line, instead of either an end of line or a pair of dashes. (This makes "commenting out" a section of a MIB quite easy.) If strict checking of termination of ASN.1 comments is desired, then the "CH" option can be used on the command line, or specified as the value of the SMICOPTS environment variable. This is shown below for the latter:

- in UNIX (using the C shell):
setenv SMICOPTS "-CH"
or
setenv SMICOPTS -CH
- in UNIX (using the Bourne shell):
SMICOPTS="-CH"
or
SMICOPTS=-CH
and
export SMICOPTS
- in DOS and OS/2:
SET SMICINCL=-CH

C.5.4 Create a "MIB Include File"

The next step is to construct a "MIB include file". This can be done using a text editor, a program, or a script to a text processing program such as AWK, Perl, or TCL. This file contains a "condInclude" directive to specify to the name of a "MIB include file" for each unique module specified in an IMPORTS clause, MODULE clause in a MODULE-COMPLIANCE macro, or SUPPORTS clause in a AGENT-CAPABILITIES macro. It also contains a "condInclude" directive for the file containing MIB modules selected in the first step.

The "MIB include file" may also contain other directives to specify compile options, create aliases, or unregister items defined in other MIB modules.

SMICng requires that all MIB modules containing definitions used by MIB modules selected in the first step be compiled together and before the selected MIB modules. The "MIB include file" specifies MIB modules on which the selected MIB modules are directly dependent. However, these MIB modules may be dependent on other MIB modules. With proper setup and usage, the conditionally included "MIB include files" will include exactly those files that they depend on recursively. An example of a simple "MIB include file" is shown below (all the directives are explained later in this document):

```
-- file: mymib.inc - an example MIB include file
-- IMPORTS:
#condInclude "rfc1442.inc" -- SNMPv2-SMI
#condInclude "rfc1443.inc" -- SNMPv2-TC
#condInclude "rfc1444.inc" -- SNMPv2-CONF
#condInclude "rfc1213.inc" -- RFC1213-MIB

-- MIB module
#condInclude "mymib.mi2" -- MY-MIB
#condExcludeModule MY-MIB 0 -- exclude module MY-MIB from
                 -- output if used for IMPORTs
```

The "condInclude" directive is not available in SMIC classic. It has only the "include" directive. With only this directive, the complete list of files containing MIB modules on which the selected MIB is dependent must be specified in the "MIB include file" and ordered so that all items are defined before they are needed by other modules. For example, MIB-II (module RFC1213-MIB) from RFC 1213 depends on definitions from RFC 1155 and RFC 1212. These MIBs must be included before RFC 1213. (With the "condInclude" directive, only the files containing MIB modules on which the selected MIB modules are directly dependent need be specified in the "MIB include file".) SMICng supports both the "include" and "condInclude" directives. A "MIB include file" using this approach to compile the simple file would look like the following:

```
-- file: mymib.inc - an example MIB include file
-- IMPORTS:
#include "rfc1442.sm2" -- SNMPv2-SMI
#excludeModule SNMPv2-SMI
#include "rfc1443.sm2" -- SNMPv2-TC
#excludeModule SNMPv2-TC
#include "rfc1444.sm2" -- SNMPv2-CONF
#excludeModule SNMPv2-CONF
#include "rfc1155.smi" -- RFC1155-SMI
#excludeModule RFC1155-SMI
#include "rfc1212.smi" -- RFC-1212
#excludeModule RFC-1212
#include "rfc1213.mib" -- RFC1213-MIB
#excludeModule RFC1213-MIB
```

```
-- MIB module
#include "mymib.mi2" -- MY-MIB
```

The powerful conditional include mechanism is available only in SMICng (as well as the module exclude and conditional module exclude directives) and not in SMIC. Constructing the "MIB include file" for a new MIB module is easier, since only the IMPORTS clause, the MODULE clause in MODULE-COMPLIANCE macros, and the SUPPORTS clause in AGENT-CAPABILITIES macros of the new MIB module need to be consulted, and not the recursive dependencies of all of the modules specified in these clauses.

C.5.5 Run SMICng

SMICng has a multitude of options that can be chosen when it is executed. Running SMICng with the "H" option, with no arguments, or with invalid arguments will result in SMICng providing instruction on how to get help. For example, the following can be used:

```
smicng -h
```

There is help available on the syntax of the command line, help on directives in "MIB include files", help with the environment variables, help with the format of the error and warning messages, and help with setting up and using SMICng.

The command line options are prefixed with either a slash (/) or hyphen (-) character in MS-DOS and OS/2, and a hyphen (-) in Unix. There are single character and double character options. The options can be specified in either upper or lower case.

Typically the command to execute SMICng will be very simple, but it can contain many arguments, depending upon the level of checking desired. In most cases, the following command is sufficient to check the syntax of a MIB:

```
smicng mymib.inc
```

C.5.6 Output

When compiling a new MIB, several passes may be needed to correct all the errors in the MIB found by SMICng. When all errors have been eliminated, the next step is to select output from SMICng. However, SMICng does allow the "dump outputs" to be generated even when errors are present. Other outputs such as MOSY or SNMPv1 MIBs are available only when no errors are present. Other than errors and warnings, output from SMICng is specified via command line switches. The details on these and the format of error and warning messages are shown later in this document.

C.6 MIB Stripper

A simple program is provided along with SMICng to strip an RFC to reveal a MIB module. This program, called MSTRIP, uses form feed (e.g., page break) characters to determine the footer and header lines in a document. If form feeds are not used, MSTRIP will not be able to remove header and footer lines. These will have to be removed with a text editor. The program is very simple, and does not do sophisticated blank line elimination. Thus, the resulting MIB module, while being compilable, may have extra blank lines in the quoted strings which are used in DESCRIPTION and REFERENCE clauses. These must be fixed with a text editor, if desired. Running MSTRIP is simple. The one and only argument is the name of the document to be stripped. The output from MSTRIP is on standard out. This must be redirected to a file. The following shows how to run MSTRIP:

```
mstrip rfcDocument >mibModule
```

C.7 SMICng Environment Variables

SMICng uses two environment variables. The value of the SMICINCL environment variable is a list of names of directories to search for files. These directories are searched after the current directory when a file is opened for input. The directory names in the list must be separated by semicolons (;) in DOS or OS/2, and by colons (:) or spaces in UNIX.

The second environment variable is SMICOPTS. Its value is the default set of command line options for SMICng. An option specified here can be turned off on the command line by adding an “o” suffix to the option. For example, to check comments for strict compliance to ASN.1, the “CH” option can be specified as the value for SMICOPTS. To turn off the option, the “turn off” format of the “CH” option, which is “CHO”, can be specified on the command line. Alternatively, the *#removeOpt “H”* directive can be specified in the “MIB include file”.

C.8 Command Line Arguments to SMICng

The command line arguments to SMICng are the options, which are not required, followed by the name of one or more input files. The syntax is shown below:

```
smicng [<options>] <inputFile>...
```

C.8.1 Command Line Options

There are many options for SMICng because of its versatility. The options are prefixed with either a slash (/) or hyphen (-) character in MS-DOS and OS/2, and a hyphen (-) in Unix. There are single character and double character options. The options can be specified in either upper or lower case. An option can be turned off by specifying an “o” as the suffix. (The “turn off” is useful for turning off options that were specified in the environment variable SMICOPTS.) There are four classes of options. The “help options” have “H” as the first character. The "dump options" have "D" as the first character. The "checking options" have "C" as the first character. The other options are a single letter.

C.8.2 Command Line Options Detailed

Help Options

- HC - print help on the command line syntax
- HD - print help on directives
- HE - print help on the environment variables
- HG - print help on the format of error and warning messages
- HS - print help on setup to run SMICng
- HA - print help on all areas
- H - print a list of the help options
-
- Dump Options
- DS - dump string table
- DP - dump TRAP-TYPE & NOTIFICATION-TYPE definitions
- DO - dump OBJECT-TYPE definitions
- DT - dump IMPORT definitions
- DK - dump SMI definitions
- DG - dump OBJECT-GROUP definitions
- DM - dump module definitions
- DF - dump AGENT-CAPABILITIES definitions
- DE - dump MODULE-COMPLIANCE definitions
- DA - dump alias definitions
- DQ - dump SEQUENCE definitions
- DV - dump textual convention definitions
- DL - dump object value assignments (OVAs) and OBJECT-IDENTITY definitions
- DB - dump a list of all filenames
- DU - dump resource usage statistics
- DD - dump all

Miscellaneous Options

- F <file> - name of the output file (this is also used for the dump options)
- 1 - print copyright notice and right to use license
- 2 - print version information
- I - print names of input files during compilation
- Y - ignore module exclude directives and include all MIB modules in outputs
- X - suppress strings in scanner
- T - set the preferred version to SNMPv2. SMICng has an auto-version determination mechanism built into it. If however, there are no IMPORTS, then the value of the "preferred version" is used to determine which set of rules (either SNMPv1 or SNMPv2) to use

- M <count> - sets the maximum number of error or warning messages that when exceeded will cause SMICng to terminate early. For example, if the value is 10, then on the eleventh message, SMICng will terminate. Set to a value of zero, means that an unlimited number of messages is allowed (The default value is 100)
- Q - causes SMICng to auto re-register OBJECT-TYPE, OBJECT-IDENTITY, & NOTIFICATION items. Only those items that have identical descriptors (i.e., names) and OID values will be auto re-registered. The preferred mechanism is via the #unregister directive
- 0 - sets the message(and error) file to output file (i.e., sets stderr to stdout)

Output options - for the output options below, SMICng will generate the requested output only when there are no errors in parsing the input file(s) and only for the items that are not in excluded modules.

- V - output an SNMPv1 MIB for each MIB module
- Z - output information on the parsed MIB modules in "intermediate format". This is an easy to parse format that can be used by other programs
- 8 - output information on each module in the same format as the .defs files produced by MOSY v7.1
- 9 - output information on each module in the same format as the .tcl files produced by MOSY v7.1
- A - constrain the MOSY outputs, specified with the "8" or "9" options, to be identical to that output by MOSY. By default, SMICng outputs "corrected" versions of MOSY .defs and .tcl files
- K - output a list of the names of all defined items in sorted order
- N - output an OID tree and defined traps (this output will always be generated even when there are errors in parsing)

Checking Options

- C4 - allow (in SNMPv1) non-standard value for ACCESS for leaf OBJECT-TYPE items of "write-only" or "not-accessible". (In SNMPv2, "write-only" is not a valid value for ACCESS, and items used for table indices and those for use in notifications may have ACCESS of "not-accessible")
- C5 - allow (in SNMPv1) the value of "optional" for STATUS. (In SNMPv2, the values for STATUS were changed and "optional" is not one of the choices)
- CJ - allow (in SNMPv1) a DEFVAL on Counters. (In SNMPv2, this practice is explicitly not allowed)
- CR - check (in SNMPv1) that INDEX objects have ACCESS value of "read-only". (In SNMPv2, INDEX objects have ACCESS values of either "read-only" or "not-accessible")
- CK - allow (in SNMPv1) zero valued enumerations. This is standard practice, even though explicitly disallowed in SNMPv1. (In SNMPv2, the values for enumerations can be from -2147483648 to 2147483647)

- CL - allow (in SNMPv1) negative valued enumerations. (In SNMPv2, the values for enumerations can be from -2147483648 to 2147483647)
- C3 - allow (in SNMPv1) an INDEX clause on objects. (In SNMPv2, this discouraged practice in SNMPv1 (which was added for backwards compatibility), is not allowed)
- C9 - don't allow duplicate OID values to be assigned to OVAs. By default, multiple OVAs may be assigned the same OID value.
- CG - allow unused IMPORTs and unused textual conventions. Usually, there is a problem if an item is imported and not used, or a textual convention is defined and not used. When not specified, SMICng will generate warning messages for the unused items
- C6 - do not check that the names for table, row, sequences are all related. The convention that is followed in standard MIBs is to use "Table" as the suffix on table names, and use the suffix "Entry" on rows and sequences. All three use the same prefix with the identical case of all letters except the first which must be in uppercase for sequences (this is an ASN.1 rule), and lowercase for tables and rows (this is also an ASN.1 rule)
- CC - check that all OBJECT-TYPE items that have syntax of INTEGER have a range, and items that have syntax of OCTET STRING have a size specified
- CW - disallow in SEQUENCEs a syntax of INTEGER with a range or a syntax of OCTET STRING with a size
- CH - strict ASN.1 for comments. By default, SMICng only terminates ASN.1 comments by the end of the line. When specified, this option allows both end of line and a pair of dashes to terminate a comment. SMICng's default behavior is to allow blocks of ASN.1 to be easily "commented out"
- C7 - restrict positive INTEGER values to be less than or equal 2G-1 (2147483647). In SNMPv1, there was no explicit limit on the range of INTEGERs. By default, SMICng allows the following ranges for INTEGERS: (-2147483648..2147483647), (0..4294967295), and any sub-ranges of these. With the "C7" option, only (-2147483648..2147483647) and sub-ranges are allowed
- CU - allow underbars in names. ASN.1 does not allow the underbar character. This option relaxes that rule
- CE - allow the syntax of SEQUENCE items to match the syntax of the referenced OBJECT-TYPE item when the syntax specified in the SEQUENCE is the base type defined by the textual convention used as the syntax of the OBJECT-TYPE. For example, this option would allow a syntax of "OCTET STRING" to be specified in a sequence for an OBJECT-TYPE item defined with syntax of DisplayString
- CB - a check is done that all index items with a base syntax of INTEGER have a range specified, and all with a base syntax of OCTET STRING have a size specified
- CO - allow (in SNMPv2) hyphens in enumerated value names, even though they are explicitly disallowed in the SMI. (In SNMPv1, hyphens are allowed)
- CP - allow (in SNMPv2) hyphens in descriptors (i.e., the names of items), even though they are explicitly disallowed in the SMI. (In SNMPv1, hyphens are allowed)

- CS - require (in SNMPv2) that items in compliances (MODULE-COMPLIANCE and AGENT-CAPABILITIES) be specified in the IMPORTS clause of the module containing the compliances. Strict ASN.1 requires that any item defined in another module and used in the current module to be specified in the IMPORTS clause for the current module. This results in essentially a "double-import". By default, SMICng uses the context specified in MODULE-COMPLIANCE or AGENT-CAPABILITIES macros to uniquely identify items. (In SNMPv1, there is no comparable construct)
- CT - no check (in SNMPv2) of the value for ACCESS of items in OBJECT-GROUPs. The definition of the OBJECT-GROUP macro specifies that no members may have an ACCESS value of "not-accessible". (In SNMPv1, there is no comparable construct)
- CM - no check (in SNMPv2) that all leaf OBJECT-TYPE items defined in a module are members of at least one OBJECT-GROUP. This check, done by default, is important to make sure that an oversight didn't occur. Only OBJECT-GROUPs and their members can be specified in MODULE-COMPLIANCE macros. (In SNMPv1, there is no comparable construct)
- CV - allow (in SNMPv2) an SNMPv1 OID value or an OBJECT-TYPE item to be used in a MODULE-COMPLIANCE or AGENT-CAPABILITIES macro as if it were an SNMPv2 OBJECT-GROUP. (In SNMPv1, there is no comparable construct)
- CA - allow (in SNMPv2) a module to be defined without a MODULE-IDENTITY macro. SNMPv2 requires that all information modules contain a MODULE-IDENTITY as their first definition

C.8.3 Command Line Input File

The <inputFile> to SMICng is the name of a file or is a hyphen (-) specify "stdin". One or more files may be specified on the command line. These can be the names of files containing MIBs, or more likely, these are the names of "MIB include files". If the filename is not an absolute path (i.e., does not start with a drive letter (C:) or back slash (\) in DOS and OS/2, or start with a slash (/) in UNIX), SMICng first tries to open the file in the "current directory". If the file is not found, then SMICng tries to locate the file in the directories specified by the value of the SMICINCL environment variable. Using the earlier example MYMIB, the following command lines cause the same set of MIBs to be compiled:

```
smicng mymib.inc
    or
smicng rfc1442.inc rfc1443.inc
+                 rfc1444.inc rfc1213.inc mymib.mi2
    or
smicng - < mymib.inc
    or
cat mymib.inc | smicng -
```

C.9 SMICng Input

The inputs to SMICng are MIB modules and "compiler directives". Typically, as shown in the earlier examples, a "MIB include file" is constructed that either conditionally includes files (#condInclude), this is the preferred method, or explicitly includes files (#include). There are also other directives such as those to define aliases, or those to change the command line option settings. Directives can be contained within a "MIB include file" or a "MIB file". In all cases, they must be placed only between MIB modules.

C.9.1 MIB Modules

SMICng can parse both SNMPv1 and SNMPv2 MIB modules. SMICng uses auto-version recognition based on SMI items specified in the IMPORTS clause used in a module. The SMI items include the macros, such as the OBJECT-TYPE and TRAP-TYPE from SNMPv1, and the ones from SNMPv2 including OBJECT-IDENTITY, MODULE-IDENTITY, OBJECT-TYPE, TEXTUAL-CONVENTION, NOTIFICATION-TYPE, OBJECT-GROUP, MODULE-COMPLIANCE, or AGENT-CAPABILITIES. Also included are the syntax types such as Counter, NetworkAddress, IpAddress, Gauge, TimeTicks, and Opaque from SNMPv1 and Integer32, IpAddress, Counter32, Gauge32, TimeTicks, Opaque, NsapAddress, Counter64, and UInteger32 from SNMPv2. All SMI items specified in the IMPORTS clause for a module must be from the same version of SNMP. That is, it is illegal to import OBJECT-TYPE from RFC 1212 (an SNMPv1 macro) and Gauge32 from RFC 1442 (an SNMPv2 syntax type) into the same MIB module. Special versions of the MIB modules defining the SMI items are supplied with the SMICng package. These must be used since SMICng does not parse MACRO definitions or type definitions, and uses a proprietary mechanism instead.

SMICng parses "SNMP ASN.1" modules. "SNMP ASN.1" is a subset of the full 1987 version of the ASN.1 language (with a few extensions).

C.9.2 Directives

Directives are commands to the compiler to control its operation. All directives start with the "#" character (which is not a valid character in an ASN.1 identifier). The directives are case independent. For example, "#include" and "#INCLUDE" are both recognized by SMICng. Each directive has zero, one, or several operands. Directives must come in-between MIB modules.

Directives:

- #include "<fileName>" - process an include file
- #condInclude "<fileName>" - include a file if the file has not already been included
- #aliasModule <module> <alias> - alias a module
- #aliasItem <module> <item> <aliasModule> <aliasItem> - alias an item
- #excludeModule <module> - exclude a module from outputs
- #condExcludeModule <module> <level> - exclude module based on include level

- #unregister <module> <item> - unregister an item from its OID value
- #pushOpt - push compile checking options
- #popOpt - pop compile checking options
- #setOpt "<options>" - set checking options to those specified
- #addOpt "<options>" - add one or more options to the current set of checking options
- #removeOpt "<options>" - remove one or more options from the current set of checking options
- #printOpt - print current set of checking options
- #SNMPv1 - set the current parsing preference to SNMPv1 SMI rules
- #SNMPv2 - set the current parsing preference to SNMPv2 SMI rules

Include and CondInclude Directives

Typically, a SNMP MIB module is dependent on definitions of items from other MIB modules. SMICng, unlike other MIB compilers, checks that the items specified in the IMPORTS clause of a module exist and that their use is valid. For example, if an item is imported and used to specify an OID value, SMICng checks that the item is defined and has an OID value. To be able to implement the checks, SMICng requires that all the MIB modules on which the original MIB module depends to be compiled with and specified before the original MIB module.

The combining and specifying of the MIB modules is done with the #include or #condInclude directive. These directives are specified in a "MIB include file". This approach is used so that the ASN.1 specifications defining MIBs is kept separate from the directives used by SMICng. This allows the files containing the MIBs to be used by other systems or to be printed without any changes. The alias feature (which is explained later) may also be required to accomplish the goal of never having to modify the ASN.1 specifications defining MIBs.

The operand to these directives is the name of a file which is enclosed in quotes. The format of the filename is operating system dependent. The "#include" directive instructs SMICng to open the file unconditionally. The "#condInclude" directive instructs SMICng to only open the file if it has not previously been opened. If the filename is not an absolute path (i.e., does not start with a drive letter (C:) or backslash (\) in DOS and OS/2, or does not start with a slash (/) in UNIX), SMICng first tries to open the file in the "current directory". If the file is not found, then SMICng tries to locate the file in the directories specified by the value for the SMICINCL environment variable. Shown below are examples of the "include" directive.

in both UNIX and DOS
#include "filename"
in UNIX
#include "../../filename"
or

```
#include "/pub/mibs/rfc/filename"

in DOS
#include "C:\MIBS\RFC\filename"
        or
#include "\MIBS\RFC\filename"
        or
#include "..\..\filename"
```

Even though absolute and relative file names are allowed, experience has shown that the most effective way to use SMICng is to specify filenames without any path specifiers and use the SMICINCL environment variable to name the directories. This allows reorganization of directory structure and transfer between DOS and Unix.

The conditional include directive is new to SMICng. It was not present in SMIC. It is now the preferred mechanism to use.

The "include level" is the nesting level of the include or conditional include files. There can be up to 10 levels of nesting of includes. Files named on the command line or in the SMICOPTS environment variable are at include level zero. The files they include are level 1.

Alias Directives

The alias directives allow an alternative name to be defined for items in IMPORTS statements. This includes both the object and textual convention names as well as the "FROM" module name. In the past, these names could change as the defining document was evolved as it moved through the standards process. For example, consider a MIB written with the following IMPORTS:

```
IMPORTS
    ...
    OwnerString FROM RFC1271-MIB
    ... ;
```

If RFC 1271 were republished with a new RFC number, say RFC 9999, the module name would be changed to RFC9999-MIB. To process this new version without changing any other MIB files that import items defined in it, the "MIB include file" must be modified by changing the include directive to use the new version of the file instead of the old, and a "moduleAlias" directive should be added to map the old module name to the new name. The following shows the directive to be added:

```
#moduleAlias RFC9999-MIB  RFC1271-MIB
             ^            ^
```

```
            |          |
            \-Real name  \-Old name (i.e., alias)
```

If the name of the textual convention was also changed, to say "OwnerStringXXX", the following directive would also be needed:

```
#aliasItem RFC9999-MIB OwnerStringXXX \
            ^          ^    RFC9999-MIB OwnerString
            |          |    ^           ^
            \-Real Name-/   |           |
                            \--Old name--/
                             (i.e., alias)
```

As shown, these alias directives can eliminate changes to MIBs due to changes of the names of IMPORTed items. Without the alias facility, the references would be left dangling. A module or symbol may have multiple aliases.

The good news is that the convention for naming MIB modules has changed so that the name of the module is a label for the technology described by the objects in the MIB. Thus, names of standard MIB modules will not be changed as the RFC containing them is updated and revised.

Exclude Directives

The exclude module (#excludeModule) and conditional exclude module (#condExcludeModule) are used to exclude the specified module from the output generated by SMICng. This is useful when only one module is of interest such as when generating MOSY .defs or .tcl files. The exclude module directive takes a single operand which is the name of the module to unconditionally exclude. The conditional exclude module directive has two operands. The first is the module name and the second is the depth of the include stack. If the current depth in the include stack is greater than the specified number, then the module is excluded. A value of zero is used in the example and in the "MIB include files" supplied with the SMICng package. This causes the MIB modules whose "MIB include file" is not specified on the command line to be excluded from the output. (If it is desired to include all MIB modules in the output, then the "Y" option can be used to override the module exclude directives.) If the output that is desired should include a MIB module, then the "MIB include file" for that MIB module should be specified on the command line to SMICng before any other files that reference it directly or indirectly via conditional includes. For example, suppose one wanted to see the OID values defined in a new MIB module and the OID values defined in RFC 1442 (the SNMPv2 SMI). (Note that the option to output an OID tree is "N".) For this, the command line to SMICng might look like the following:

```
smicng -n rfc1442.inc mymib.inc
```

Unregister Directive

The unregister directive (#unregister) has operands of module and item within the module. The item must be defined by one of the following SNMPv1 or SNMPv2 macros: OBJECT-IDENTITY, MODULE-IDENTITY, OBJECT-TYPE, NOTIFICATION-TYPE, OBJECT-GROUP, MODULE-COMPLIANCE, or AGENT-CAPABILITIES. These macros, as a side effect, register the item being defined to an OID value. An object identifier value assignment (OVA) (i.e., "a OBJECT IDENTIFIER ::= { par 1 }") assigns a value but does not do a "registration". The difference between the macros and the OVA is that one and only one item can be registered to any OID value. Thus, many OVAs can specify the same OID value, but only one item defined with a macro can specify a particular OID value. One consistency check done by SMICng is to make sure there is only one registration per OID value. (Not all registrations of OID values are for SNMP MIB items. SMICng has no mechanism to gain the knowledge of these external registrations. These external registrations may be documented via the OBJECT-IDENTITY macro.)

There are limited cases where an OID value needs to be unregistered from an item. One case is when items from a MIB are moved to another MIB and the original MIB is not updated to reflect this change. For example, consider MIB module M1 containing definitions for object types a, b, and c. A decision is made to create a new module, say M2, that contains object type c. To compile both MIBs with SMICng, an unregister directive must be specified between the modules. Without it, SMICng will give an error of two items being registered with the same OID value. The following abbreviated example shows the unregister:

```
M1 DEFINITIONS ::= BEGIN
  ...
 a OBJECT-TYPE ...
 b OBJECT-TYPE ...
 c OBJECT-TYPE ...
END

#unregister M1 c

M2 DEFINITIONS ::= BEGIN
  ...
 c OBJECT-TYPE ...
END
```

The preferred method to accomplish the movement of objects from one module to another is to update original module to removed the objects that have been moved. Also, all modules that specify the objects in an IMPORT statement must be updated. This may not be possible in some cases. This is why the unregister and alias directives are provided.

Option (or checking) Directives

The "option directives" are used to manage the settings of the options that are used for MIB checking. When processing MIBs, the amount of checking is determined by the settings of the checking options. The initial settings of options is specified in the value of the SMICOPTS environment variable. These option values are augmented or modified by the options on the command line to SMICng. The "option directives" allow the options to be modified while SMICng is processing its input. The directives may be processed before and after processing each MIB module. Instead of strictly changing the options (the #setOpt directive), there are directives to save settings (the #pushOpt directive) and restore settings (the #popOpt directive), and directives to selectively change individual options without affecting the other options (the #addOpt and #removeOpt directives). The #printOpt directive may be used to print the current option settings. (Also, the option settings for each module are shown with the intermediate format output, and with the dump module output.)

The argument to #setOpt, #addOpt, and #removeOpt is a character string of zero, one, or more letters identifying the options. In the SMICOPT environment variable and on the command line, the options are prefixed with the letter "C". As elements of the string, only a single character is used for each option. Optionally, the characters may be separated by spaces. For example, the string "H T O" is used to specify the option for strict ASN.1 comments, for no check of ACCESS for items in OBJECT-GROUPs, and to allow hyphens in names of enumerated values. Two special characters are also allowed. These are "X" to suppress strings in the scanner and "Q" for auto-registration.

These directives have proved to be quite useful when compiling MIBs from different sources, or that were developed years apart from each other. For example, suppose a new MIB module was to be developed and it was desired to use the most strict MIB checking rules for it. However, this MIB depends on IETF standard MIBs which were written before standard practices and conventions were worked out (and before SMIC or SMICng were available). They require somewhat relaxed MIB checking rules to compile without errors or warnings. A "MIB include file" would be set up to include the standard MIBs and the new MIB under development. If the most strict checking was specified on the command line to SMICng, many warnings and errors would be generated by the standard MIBs. To get around the generation of these errors, the checking options should be saved and modified before parsing the standard MIB, and restored afterwards. All the "MIB include files" distributed with SMICng follow the same pattern. They conditionally include the files containing the modules that are specified as imports to the module for which the "MIB include file" is being written. The MIB file of interest is bracketed with directives to save the options and restore the options. Inside the bracketing, the options are modified to those needed to compile the MIB without errors. The following shows two "MIB include files" where the directives are used to eliminate errors:

```
-- file: rfc1442.inc - SNMPv2-SMI

-- MIB Module
```

```
#pushOpt     -- Save checking options
#addOpt "A"  -- No check for MODULE-IDENTITY
#SNMPv2      -- Use SNMPv2 rules

#condInclude "rfc1442.sm2" -- SNMPv2-SMI
#condExcludeModule SNMPv2-SMI 0
#popOpt      -- Restore checking options
```

And another example...

```
-- file: rfc1443.inc - SNMPv2-TC

-- IMPORTS
#condInclude "rfc1442.inc" -- SNMPv2-SMI

-- MIB Module
#pushOpt     -- Save checking options
#addOpt "A"  -- No check for MODULE-IDENTITY
#addOpt "G"  -- Allow unreferenced TCs
#SNMPv2      -- Use SNMPv2 rules
#condInclude "rfc1443.sm2" -- SNMPv2-TC
#condExcludeModule SNMPv2-TC 0
#popOpt      -- Restore checking options
```

Use of the option directives are not limited to the above examples. The directives can also be used to change the settings for multiple MIB modules.

(NOTE: The conventions for writing MIBs have changed over the years. The "rules" have "changed" as experienced has been gained by writing MIBs. It is expected that the older MIBs will be updated to use the modern conventions which will make them easier to understand. Until then, SMICng will have options for specifying which rules to use.)

Version Directives

There are two options (#SNMPv1 and #SNMPv2) to set the current preferred version of SNMP SMI rules to use. SMICng, without the "T" option specified in the environment or on the command line, defaults to SNMPv1 MIB rules. However, SMICng has an auto-version determination mechanism built into it. Thus, for MIBs with the IMPORTS correctly specified, there is no need to use these directives (except for the SMI modules which are supplied with SMICng).

C.10 Output from SMICng

Output from SMICng is caused by errors or warnings during compiling and by command line switches. The following sections detail each output.

C.10.1 Format of Error/Warning Messages

Error and warning messages from SMICng are tagged with the best estimate of the location of the problem. The formats of the messages are:

```
"W:" [ "f(" <file> ")," ] "(" <line> "," <column> ")"
                                    <message>
   and

"E:" [ "f(" <file> ")," ] "(" <line> "," <column> ")"
                                    <message>
```

Where:

W - warning
E - error
<file> - name of file
<line> - line number in file
<column> - column in line
<message> - text indicating the problem

SMICng uses multiple passes to process a MIB module. The first pass does a loose check using an extended version of the syntax. The extensions include many common problems seen by the author of SMICng while reviewing MIBs. During this pass, locations of elements of the MIB are saved along with their values. The subsequent passes are used to complete the syntax checking and to check the semantic values for consistency to the highest level that can be done through a compiler. (Maybe SMIC the future version (SMICfv) will be able to read description text and give suggestions to the MIB author. This is left as an exercise to the next person to work on SMIC and is either a joke or challenge which is left to the reader to decide.)

SMICng prints the message “Syntax error” during the first pass to indicate that the MIB module contains one or more errors from which SMICng could not recover based on its first level of error parsing heuristics. This causes SMICng to fall back to its second level of error recovery. When this occurs, SMICng may not be able to correctly synchronize back to parsing the remaining valid constructs in the MIB. The failure to resynchronize may result in a cascade of meaningless errors. The original error should be fixed before spending too much time trying to resolve the errors that follow. A few errors may cause SMICng to either skip over the remaining constructs in a MIB, or to even immediately abort the parsing of a MIB.

One difficult error for SMICng is malformed quoted strings. These are missing beginning or ending quotes, and “embedded” quotes in a quoted string. Consider a quoted string with a missing ending quote. Since there are no stated limits on the size of a string, SMICng can only end a quoted string by an ending quote or end-of-file. When this occurs, an error is reported at an “unusual” place. This may misdirect the search for the real error. If an error message specifies an end-of-file in a string or locates an error at the beginning of a string, then the MIB should be searched back to the last quote used and then forward to find the location to put the missing quote.

The same confusion, except limited to one line, can occur with ASN.1 comments. The "strict" ASN.1 rules allow comments to be ended with a pair of dashes and not just end of line. Thus, if a line of dashes is used to separate sections of a MIB or multiple dashes are used to create drawings in comments, surprising errors can occur when a comment is "ended" prematurely.

In general, the messages generated during the subsequent passes after the first, identify the source exactly, or identify the item containing a problematic clause. Sometimes these passes will generate many bogus errors from one true error. For example, an error in a definition of a row OBJECT-TYPE could lead to additional errors, which will be eliminated when the error with the row is corrected.

Experience in writing and correcting MIBs is the best teacher in determining whether to spend time looking at a long list of errors, or to simply correct the first error and recompile.

The "M <count>" option may be used to terminate SMICng early when an excessive number of messages are generated. This is useful in scripts for automated compiling when the output needs to be limited.

C.10.2 Dump Outputs

SMICng has many "Dump Outputs". Many of them were added to help verify that SMICng was correctly capturing all the MIB information building internal data structures. However, a few of these are quite useful in gaining in-depth insight about the MIBs that were compiled.

String table

The "string table" is a balanced binary tree. Dumping it prints each item in the tree with the associated level and left or right tag. The string table is also traversed "in-order" which causes all the items to be printed in sorted order.

TRAP-TYPE & NOTIFICATION-TYPE definitions

TYPE definition is printed with the value of each field. After the traps, a table is printed that lists the traps for each unique value of the ENTERPRISE field. Each notification is printed with the values for each field.

OBJECT-TYPE definitions

Each OBJECT-TYPE definition is printed with the value of each field. Additionally, each leaf and row object have the "instance" encodings printed. Also, for leaf items with syntax value based on textual conventions, the resolved syntax is printed.

IMPORT items

Both a list of imported items and the modules specified in the FROM clause of the imported are printed.

SMI items

A list of all SMI items (defined types and macros) is printed. SMICng does not "hard-code" the name of modules containing definitions of SMI items. But, SMICng does not parse ASN.1 macro definitions or type definitions. Instead, a special extension is used to define these items. This allows the definitions to be placed in any module and allows the IMPORT linkages to be checked.

Module definitions

A list of modules that were compiled is printed. For each module, a quite useful list of information is printed. This includes the SMI format of the module, the SMICng checking options, a list of imported items, a list of exported items (which should always be empty), and, if used, the values of fields associated with the the module-identity macro.

OBJECT-GROUP definitions

A list of all object-groups is printed with the value of each field.

AGENT-CAPABILITIES definitions

A list of all agent-capabilities is printed with the value of each field.

Alias definitions

A list of all aliases is printed. This includes both item aliases and module aliases.

SEQUENCE definitions

A list of sequences is printed including the items defined as members.

Textual convention definitions

A list of textual conventions, both those defined with the TEXTUAL-CONVENTION macro and via an assignment, is printed with the values for all fields.

OVA and OBJECT-IDENTITY definitions

A list of object value assignments (OVAs) and OBJECT-IDENTITY definitions is printed with the values for all fields.

File names

A list is printed for all files opened by SMICng. With each file is printed its source - named in environment variable SMICOPTS, named on the command line, or included from another file.

Usage Statistics Output

A list of the space used by all data structures in SMICng is printed. This output can be used to see the usage count for each type of item that may be contained in a MIB. The following is the output from compiling MIB-II (from RFC 1213) and the standard SNMP traps (from RFC 1215):

```
Statistics:
  String Space: 65520
```

Strings: 600 527(12000)
File names: 15 11(270)
File name bytes: 471
Modules: 5 5(430)
Import From lists: 8 4(192)
Import Modules: 5 4(360)
Import items: 20 11(320)
Imports: 20 11(1160)
Sub Ids: 450 428(11700)
OID tree Nodes: 210 210(7140)
SMI items: 8 8(416)
OVA items: 30 22(1860)
OT items: 210 190(20160)
  Table: 8
   Row: 8
   Leaf: 174
SYN items: 280 266(8400)
SR items: 20 14(480)
Enum items: 100 89(2200)
Index items: 20 14(680)
Sequences: 10 8(580)
Sequence members: 80 69(1920)
Text conv: 5 2(320)
Traps: 20 6(1360)
Trap vars: 20 3(480)
Trap ents: 5 1(60)
Dynamic memory used: 138479

On each line with three values, the first value is the number of items allocated, the second is the number actually used, and the third, (in parenthesis) is the amount of memory used (which is based on the number allocated). The following is a description for each possible line:

- "String space" is the memory used to store all of the symbol names and strings used by SMICng. Most memory usage for MIB objects is typically for the "DESCRIPTION" and "REFERENCE" strings. (The "X" option can be used to suppress all strings used.)
- "Strings" is the number of items in the "string space".
- "File Names" is the number of files read compiling.
- "File name bytes" is the amount of space taken up by the file names.
- "Modules" is the number of modules defined.
- "Exports" is the number of items in export lists.

- “Import From Lists” and
- “Import Modules”, which have the same value in valid MIBs, is the number of modules named in IMPORTS.
- “Import items” and “Imports”, which have the same value in valid MIBs, is the total number of items specified in all IMPORT statements.
- “Aliases” is the number of aliases, both module and item, that are defined.
- “Sub Ids” is the number of sub-identifiers used in OID specifications.
- “OID tree Nodes” is the number of nodes in the OBJECT IDENTIFIER tree built by SMICng.
- “Extra OID TN items” is the number of additional nodes in the OID tree that were created when more than one item has the same OID value.
- “SMI items” is the number of SMI data types and macros that are enabled.
- “OVA items” is the total number of OID value assignments.
- “OT items” is the number of OBJECT-TYPE definitions. These are further broken down into counts for “Tables”, “Rows”, and “Leaves”. “Table” and “Row”, which have the same value in valid MIBs, is the total number of SNMP tables/rows. “Leaf” is the total count of “columnar” and “simple” objects.
- “SYN items” is the number of syntax specifications used in defining MIB items.
- “SR items” is the number of size or range specifications used in syntax specifications.
- “DV items” is the number of DEFVAL, default value, specifications in MIB items.
- “Enum items” is the total number of values for enumerated and bit string syntax objects.
- “Index items” is the number of items, both SNMP objects and syntax names, used in all INDEX clauses.
- “Sequences” is the total number of sequences, and is the same as the number of tables and rows in valid MIBs.
- “Sequence members” is the total number of items in sequences.
- “Text conv” is the total number of textual conventions including those defined with the TEXTUAL-CONVENTION macro, and those defined via an assignment.
- “Traps” is the total number of traps.
- “Trap vars” is the total number of variables specified for traps and in notifications.
- “Trap ents” is the number of unique values for the enterprise clause for all traps.
- “Module Idents” is the number of MODULE-IDENTITY definitions.
- “Module Revisions” is the number of revision clauses used in MODULE-IDENTITY macros.
- “Notifications” is the number of NOTIFICATION-TYPES defined.
- “Object Groups” is the number of OBJECT-GROUPS defined.
- “Module Compls” is the number of MODULE-COMPLIANCE definitions.
- “Modules in Module Compls” is the number of modules specified in MODULE-COMPLIANCE macros.
- “Mandatory Groups” is the number of mandatory groups in MODULE-COMPLIANCE macros.

- "Compl Group or Object" is the number of groups and objects specified in MODULE-COMPLIANCE macros.
- "Agent Caps" is the number of AGENT-CAPABILITIES definitions.
- "Modules in Agent Caps" is the number of modules in AGENT-CAPABILITIES macros.
- "Included Groups" is the number of included groups in AGENT-CAPABILITIES macros.
- "Agent cap variations" is the number of variations in AGENT-CAPABILITIES macros.
- "Dynamic memory used" is the sum of the memory allocated for SMICng's internal data structures. (NOTE: this is less than the "real" amount of dynamic data used by SMICng, since most runtime library implementations of "malloc" also allocate additional space to track the allocated memory.)

Note: An easy way to determine the number of objects in a private MIB is the following:

1. determine the number of objects in the MIBs that are IMPORTed by the private MIB (i.e., get the statistics from compiling only the standard MIBs).
2. determine the total number of objects in all of the MIBs (i.e., get the statistics from compiling both the standard and private MIBs)
3. subtract the counts to determine the difference which is number of objects defined in the private MIB.

All

When this is selected, then all dump options are enabled.

Other Outputs

Only the modules that have not been excluded will have information output for these options. Modules are excluded with the exclude or conditional exclude directive. The "Y" option can be used to override the excludes so that all modules are included.

These outputs are the most interesting and can be used by other programs (supplied by the user).

SNMPv1 MIB

The "V" option is used to output an SNMPv1 MIB for each module that has not been excluded. Normally, all modules except one are excluded. The conversion works for most constructs.

Conversion restrictions

1. The conversion of SMI types and macros is "hard coded". The chosen mapping may cause problems in some systems, not so with SMIC or SMICng. The table of conversions is specified after this table.
2. ASN.1 syntax rules allow modules to be identified in the IMPORT clause with their

OID value. If this is done, the conversion does not use this information.

3. The conversion ignores aliases. That is, it uses the name specified in the MIB and does not substitute in the resolved alias value.
4. The conversion correctly substitutes an INDEX clause for an AUGMENTS clause. However, the IMPORTs, if needed, are not done.
5. The conversion converts notifications to traps. If the OID value of the notification has a value of zero as the next to last sub-identifier, then the mapping is reversible. SMICng handles both reversible and non-reversible mappings.

Conversion Rules

Rules for IMPORTs:

SNMPv2-SMI - below shows each item and the translation that will occur (and what MOSY does):

internet -
SMICng - IMPORTS from SNMPv2-SMI-v1
MOSY - IMPORTS from RFC1155-SMI
directory -
SMICng - IMPORTS from SNMPv2-SMI-v1
MOSY - IMPORTS from RFC1155-SMI
mgmt -
SMICng - IMPORTS from SNMPv2-SMI-v1
MOSY - IMPORTS from RFC1155-SMI
experimental -
SMICng - IMPORTS from SNMPv2-SMI-v1
MOSY - IMPORTS from RFC1155-SMI
private -
SMICng - IMPORTS from SNMPv2-SMI-v1
MOSY - IMPORTS from RFC1155-SMI
enterprises -
SMICng - IMPORTS from SNMPv2-SMI-v1
MOSY - IMPORTS from RFC1155-SMI
security -
SMICng - IMPORTS from SNMPv2-SMI-v1
MOSY - no change
snmpV2 -
SMICng - IMPORTS from SNMPv2-SMI-v1
MOSY - no change
snmpDomains -
SMICng - IMPORTS from SNMPv2-SMI-v1
MOSY - no change
snmpProxys -

SMICng - IMPORTS from SNMPv2-SMI-v1
MOSY - no change
snmpModules -
SMICng - IMPORTS from SNMPv2-SMI-v1
MOSY - no change
MODULE-IDENTITY -
SMICng - drops
MOSY - drops
OBJECT-IDENTITY -
SMICng - drops
MOSY - drops
Integer32 -
SMICng - IMPORTS from SNMPv2-SMI-v1
MOSY - drops
IpAddress -
SMICng - IMPORTS from SNMPv2-SMI-v1
MOSY - IMPORTS from RFC1155-SMI
Counter32 -
SMICng - IMPORTS from SNMPv2-SMI-v1
MOSY - renames to Counter and
IMPORTS from RFC1155-SMI
Gauge32 -
SMICng - IMPORTS from SNMPv2-SMI-v1
MOSY - renames to Gauge and
IMPORTS from RFC1155-SMI
TimeTicks -
SMICng - IMPORTS from SNMPv2-SMI-v1
MOSY - IMPORTS from RFC1155-SMI
Opaque -
SMICng - IMPORTS from SNMPv2-SMI-v1
MOSY - IMPORTS from RFC1155-SMI
NsapAddress - (NOTE: there is no such type in SNMPv1)
SMICng - IMPORTS from SNMPv2-SMI-v1
MOSY - no change
Counter64 - (NOTE: there is no such type in SNMPv1)
SMICng - IMPORTS from SNMPv2-SMI-v1
MOSY - no change
UInteger32 - (NOTE: there is no such type in SNMPv1)
SMICng - IMPORTS from SNMPv2-SMI-v1
MOSY - no change
OBJECT-TYPE -
SMICng - IMPORTS from RFC-1212

MOSY - IMPORTS from RFC-1212
NOTIFICATION-TYPE -
SMICng - changes to TRAP-TYPE and
IMPORTS from RFC-1215
MOSY - changes to TRAP-TYPE and
IMPORTS from RFC-1215

SNMPv2-TC - below shows each item and the translation that will occur (and what MOSY does):

TEXTUAL-CONVENTION -
SMICng - drops
MOSY - drops
DisplayString -
SMICng - IMPORTS from SNMPv2-TC-v1
MOSY - IMPORTS from RFC1213-MIB
PhysAddress -
SMICng - IMPORTS from SNMPv2-TC-v1
MOSY - IMPORTS from RFC1213-MIB
MacAddress -
SMICng - IMPORTS from SNMPv2-TC-v1
MOSY - IMPORTS from RFC1286-MIB
TruthValue -
SMICng - IMPORTS from SNMPv2-TC-v1
MOSY - IMPORTS from RFC1253-MIB
TestAndIncr -
SMICng - IMPORTS from SNMPv2-TC-v1
MOSY - no change
AutonomousType -
SMICng - IMPORTS from SNMPv2-TC-v1
MOSY - IMPORTS from RFC1316-MIB
InstancePointer -
SMICng - IMPORTS from SNMPv2-TC-v1
MOSY - IMPORTS from RFC1316-MIB
RowStatus -
SMICng - IMPORTS from SNMPv2-TC-v1
MOSY - no change
TimeStamp -
SMICng - IMPORTS from SNMPv2-TC-v1
MOSY - no change
TimeInterval -
SMICng - IMPORTS from SNMPv2-TC-v1
MOSY - no change

DateAndTime -
SMICng - IMPORTS from SNMPv2-TC-v1
MOSY - no change

SNMPv2-CONF - below shows each item and the translation that will occur (and what MOSY does):
OBJECT-GROUP -
SMICng - drops
MOSY - drops
MODULE-COMPLIANCE -
SMICng - drops
MOSY - drops
AGENT-CAPABILITIES -
SMICng - drops
MOSY - drops

Rules for MACROs:

Below shows the translation for each MACRO:

- MODULE-IDENTITY - goes to OID value assignment and comments for clauses.
- OBJECT-IDENTITY - goes to OID value assignment and comments for clauses.
- OBJECT-TYPE - translated to RFC 1212 format; AUGMENTS turned into INDEX; IMPLIED is a problem; UNITS goes to a comment; SYNTAX is not changed; new syntax types cause problems; access "read-create" goes to "read-write"; and status "current" goes to "mandatory".
- NOTIFICATION-TYPE - translated to TRAP-TYPE; if OID value is format "enterprise.0.trapId", then value for ENTERPRISE clause is "enterprise" and value for trap is "trapId" (this is a reversible trap/notification); if OID value is "oidVal.trapId", then value for ENTERPRISE clause is "oidVal" and value for trap is "trapId" (this is a non-reversal trap); and STATUS clause is turned into a comment.
- TEXTUAL-CONVENTION - goes to type assignment and comments for clauses.
- OBJECT-GROUP - goes to OID value assignment and comments for clauses.
- MODULE-COMPLIANCE - goes to OID value assignment and comments for clauses.
- AGENT-CAPABILITIES - goes to OID value assignment and comments for clauses.

Output Intermediate format

SMICng was designed to thoroughly check MIB modules written in ASN.1. Parsing a MIB module is quite a difficult task due to the flexibility of ASN.1 and the required checking of the SNMP SMI semantic rules. To allow other programs to have available the complete set of information found in a MIB module without requiring them to include a complex parser and checker, SMICng can output the MIB information in a pre-digested and easy to parse format. This is called the "intermediate format". (The format of this file has been completely redesigned from that output from SMIC classic.) Programs that use this information are called "back-ends" since they are run after SMICng. These programs can be used to select MIB objects of interest and perform desired analysis and/or output the data in any desired format. (However, no back-ends are supplied with the SMICng package.) The format of SMICng's intermediate file was designed so that it could be easily parsed with a very simple top down parser. The syntax of the intermediate file is self-describing. However, a simple set of rules are given below that show how to parse it. In fact, the format of the intermediate file has the property that it can be extended so that parsers for the old format will be able to read the extended format and skip over the new additions. (This was not the case with the SMIC classic intermediate file, and one of the main reasons for its replacement.) Details of the intermediate file format are given at the end of this document.

Output MOSY v7.1 ".defs" file format

MOSY is a popular MIB compiler written by Marshall Rose. It is part of the ISO Development Environment (ISODE) package. The output from MOSY has been used by some privately developed MIB tools. SMIC classic was designed to have an output identical to MOSY version 6.0 to allow continued use of MOSY output tools. SMICng has been updated to have an output identical to the latest version of MOSY (version 7.1). This is different than the previous version of MOSY. SMIC classic has an option to output "extended MOSY format". This format is not provided in SMICng. (The new "intermediate format" output by SMICng should provide all that is needed and more.)

Even the latest version of MOSY does not output all the information that it gathers about a MIB, and it appears to have several short comings. SMICng, by default, outputs a "corrected" version of the .defs file. The "A" option can be specified (with the "8" option) to cause the .defs file to be "identical" to that output by MOSY v7.1. It should be noted that, by convention, the files input and output by MOSY are named using the name of the MIB module with an extension. (MOSY also requires that a file contain only one MIB module.) MOSY uses the ".my" extension for files containing MIB modules and the ".defs" extension for definitions output. For example, MOSY would expect the file containing MIB module RFC1213-MIB to be named "RFC1213-MIB.my" and would create output file "RFC1213-MIB.defs". SMICng runs in environments (such as DOS) where the file name is limited in length and is not case sensitive and thus can not be made to match the module name. It is up to the user of SMICng to specify the names of the input files and to choose the proper file name to use with the "F" option for the output.

Below are the differences between SMICng and MOSY .defs files:

- ranges - for items that include a syntax specification such as an OBJECT-TYPE, if a single range is given, then MOSY will print this information. However, if a single value is specified, or more than one range, then MOSY does not output any range information. For example, for "INTEGER (1..23)" or "INTEGER(2..2)" MOSY will output the range. But for "INTEGER (2)" or "INTEGER (1..23 | 30..40)", MOSY does not output any information. SMICng outputs all ranges specified.

- sizes - for items that include a syntax specification such as for an OBJECT-TYPE, if a size specification is given, then MOSY will print only the first (or only) size. For example, for "OCTET STRING (SIZE(1..3))", "OCTET STRING (SIZE(6))", or "OCTET STRING (SIZE(6..6))" MOSY will output the size information. But for "OCTET STRING (SIZE(1..2 | 12..20))", MOSY will only output information on "1..2". SMICng outputs all sizes specified.
- TC definitions - MOSY only outputs information about textual conventions defined with the TEXTUAL-CONVENTION macro. SMICng outputs information about textual conventions defined via the macro and defined via a type assignment.
- TC size/ranges - MOSY does not output information about a size or range specified in a TC definition. (Only for enumerated integers and bit strings is information output.) SMICng outputs information for sizes, ranges, enumerated integers, and bit strings.
- TC resolution - the name of a textual convention may be specified in a MIB module anywhere a base ASN.1 type or SNMP SMI defined type (other than SEQUENCE) may be specified. Examples include the SYNTAX clause of the OBJECT-TYPE and TEXTUAL-CONVENTION macros, and a textual convention type assignment. The .defs file contains the value of the syntax for object types and textual conventions. SMICng always substitutes the "resolved syntax" in the output. MOSY has a complex procedure. If the TC is imported, then MOSY can not resolve it, so the name of the TC is output. If the TC is defined in the current module as a macro, then its name is output. If the TC is a local type assignment, then MOSY substitutes the definition and starts the resolution procedure again. (TCs can be defined as refinements to other TCs.) Any sub-typing specified is ignored by MOSY in this process for locally defined TCs.
- Traps - MOSY does not output any information about traps defined in MIB modules. SMICng outputs the name of each trap, the trap value, the value of the enterprise clause, and a list of the variables returned by the trap.

Below are a few MOSY format (using SMICng "corrections") output fragments from MIBs from RFCs:

```
-- MOSY format from
--   SMIC (the next generation) version x.x.x, <date>.

-- Module RFC1155-SMI
--   from file: rfc1155.smi
ccitt           0
null            ccitt.0
iso             1
org             iso.3
dod             org.6
internet        dod.1
```

```
directory          internet.1
mgmt               internet.2
experimental       internet.3
private            internet.4
enterprises        private.1

 ...

-- Module RFC1213-MIB
--   from file: rfc1213.mib
mib-2              mgmt.1
system             mib-2.1
interfaces         mib-2.2
at                 mib-2.3
ip                 mib-2.4
icmp               mib-2.5
tcp                mib-2.6
udp                mib-2.7
egp                mib-2.8
transmission       mib-2.10
snmp               mib-2.11

%tc          DisplayString   OctetString   ""
%tc          PhysAddress     OctetString   ""

sysDescr        system.1     OctetString read-only    mandatory
%er          sysDescr       0          255
sysObjectID     system.2     ObjectID read-only       mandatory
sysUpTime       system.3     TimeTicks read-only      mandatory

-- Module RFC1215-TRAP
--   from file: rfc1215.trp
%trap coldStart 0 snmp
%trap warmStart 1 snmp
%trap linkDown 2 snmp { ifIndex }
%trap linkUp 3 snmp { ifIndex }
%trap authenticationFailure 4 snmp
%trap egpNeighborLoss 5 snmp { egpNeighAddr }
```

The output from SMICng is slightly different than MOSY's output. This is due to SMICng being able to resolve all imported items. Thus a reference to a textual convention in the syntax clause for an item is resolved to the base type instead of a reference to the TC.

Output MOSY v7.1 .tcl file Format

MOSY version 7.1 added the creation of .tcl files. These files were designed to work with the APIs described in the book, "How to Manage Your Network Using SNMP" by Rose & McCloghrie. The output from SMICng is identical to that from MOSY except for one part. MOSY "hard codes" a directory name in one clause of the created .tcl files. SMICng by default uses a TCL variable to name the directory. The "A" option used with the "9" option causes SMICng to output identical files as MOSY.

It should be noted that, by convention just like the .defs files, the files input and output by MOSY are named with the name of the MIB module. (MOSY requires that a file contain only one MIB module.) SMICng runs in environments (such as DOS) where the file name is limited in length and is not case sensitive and thus can not be made to match the module name. It is up to the user of SMICng to specify the names of the input files and to choose the proper file name to use with the "F" option for the output.

Output a list of MIB items sorted by Name

The "K" option is used to output the MIB items sorted by name. All the "descriptors" in IETF standard MIBs must be unique. However, experimental or private MIBs may have items whose descriptors are not unique. Each line of output contains the name of the item followed by its type. The types are the following: "module", "oid-value-assignment", "object-type", "sequence", "tcMacro", "tcAssignment", "trap-type", "SMI-item", "alias", "module-identity", "object-identity", "notification-type", "object-group", "module-compliance", and "agent-capabilities". Items that have duplicate names are marked with the phrase "**Dup" on the right end of the line. The following shows a few fragments using MIBs from RFCs:

```
Names of items
AGENT-CAPABILITIES(SNMPv2-CONF):     SMI-item
APPLICATION-MIB:                     module
ATM-MIB:                             module
Aal5VccEntry(ATM-MIB):               sequence
AarpEntry(RFC1243-MIB):              sequence
AclEntry(SNMPv2-PARTY-MIB):          sequence **Dup
AclEntry(RFC1353-MIB):               sequence **Dup
AlarmEntry(RFC1271-MIB):             sequence
ApplEntry(APPLICATION-MIB):          sequence
AreaID(RFC1253-MIB):                 tcAssignment

 ...

snmpParties(SNMPv2-PARTY-MIB):       oid-value-assignment **Dup
snmpParties(RFC1353-MIB):            oid-value-assignment **Dup
snmpProxys(SNMPv2-SMI):              oid-value-assignment
snmpRisingAlarm(SNMPv2-M2M-MIB):     notification-type
snmpSecrets(RFC1353-MIB):            oid-value-assignment
snmpSet(SNMPv2-MIB):                 oid-value-assignment
```

```
snmpSetGroup(SNMPv2-MIB):               object-group
snmpSetSerialNo(SNMPv2-MIB):            object-type

 ...

snmpViews(SNMPv2-PARTY-MIB):            oid-value-assignment
sonetCompliance(SONET-MIB):             module-compliance
sonetCompliances(SONET-MIB):            oid-value-assignment
sonetConformance(SONET-MIB):            oid-value-assignment

 ...

viewEntry(SNMPv2-PARTY-MIB):            object-type **Dup
viewEntry(RFC1353-MIB):                 object-type **Dup
viewIndex(SNMPv2-PARTY-MIB):            object-type
viewMask(SNMPv2-PARTY-MIB):             object-type **Dup
viewMask(RFC1353-MIB):                  object-type **Dup
viewParty(RFC1353-MIB):                 object-type
viewStatus(SNMPv2-PARTY-MIB):           object-type **Dup
viewStatus(RFC1353-MIB):                object-type **Dup

 ...

zip(RFC1243-MIB):                       oid-value-assignment
zipEntry(RFC1243-MIB):                  object-type
zipTable(RFC1243-MIB):                  object-type
zipZoneIndex(RFC1243-MIB):              object-type
zipZoneName(RFC1243-MIB):               object-type
zipZoneNetEnd(RFC1243-MIB):             object-type
zipZoneNetStart(RFC1243-MIB):           object-type
zipZoneState(RFC1243-MIB):              object-type
**end of item names**
```

Output an OID tree and Traps

The "N" option is used to output the elements of the selected MIB(s) in OID order and to also output the traps in "enterprise" order. Two tables are output. The first contains a line for each item (that has an associated OID value) consisting of the OID value, the item's name, and the type of the item. The types are the following: "module", "oid-value-assignment", "object-type", "module-identity", "object-identity", "notification-type", "object-group", "module-compliance", and "agent-capabilities". The second table is a list of traps organized by the value of the "enterprise" clause. Below are a few fragments using MIBs from RFCs:

```
OID tree
0.0  null(RFC1155-SMI): oid-value-assignment
```

```
1.3  org(RFC1155-SMI): oid-value-assignment
1.3.6  dod(RFC1155-SMI): oid-value-assignment
1.3.6.1  internet(RFC1155-SMI): oid-value-assignment
1.3.6.1  internet(SNMPv2-SMI): oid-value-assignment
1.3.6.1.1  directory(RFC1155-SMI): oid-value-assignment
1.3.6.1.1  directory(SNMPv2-SMI): oid-value-assignment
1.3.6.1.2  mgmt(RFC1155-SMI): oid-value-assignment
1.3.6.1.2  mgmt(SNMPv2-SMI): oid-value-assignment
1.3.6.1.2.1  mib-2(RFC1213-MIB): oid-value-assignment
1.3.6.1.2.1.1  system(RFC1213-MIB): oid-value-assignment
1.3.6.1.2.1.1.1  sysDescr(RFC1213-MIB): object-type
1.3.6.1.2.1.1.2  sysObjectID(RFC1213-MIB): object-type
1.3.6.1.2.1.1.3  sysUpTime(RFC1213-MIB): object-type
1.3.6.1.2.1.1.4  sysContact(RFC1213-MIB): object-type
1.3.6.1.2.1.1.5  sysName(RFC1213-MIB): object-type
1.3.6.1.2.1.1.6  sysLocation(RFC1213-MIB): object-type
1.3.6.1.2.1.1.7  sysServices(RFC1213-MIB): object-type
1.3.6.1.2.1.2
+          interfaces(RFC1213-MIB): oid-value-assignment
1.3.6.1.2.1.2.1  ifNumber(IF-MIB): object-type
1.3.6.1.2.1.2.1  ifNumber(RFC1213-MIB): object-type
1.3.6.1.2.1.2.2  ifTable(IF-MIB): object-type
1.3.6.1.2.1.2.2  ifTable(RFC1213-MIB): object-type
1.3.6.1.2.1.2.2.1  ifEntry(IF-MIB): object-type
1.3.6.1.2.1.2.2.1  ifEntry(RFC1213-MIB): object-type
1.3.6.1.2.1.2.2.1.1  ifIndex(IF-MIB): object-type
1.3.6.1.2.1.2.2.1.1  ifIndex(RFC1213-MIB): object-type

...

1.3.6.1.6.3.1.1.5
+           snmpTraps(SNMPv2-MIB): oid-value-assignment
1.3.6.1.6.3.1.1.5.1
+             coldStart(SNMPv2-MIB): notification-type
1.3.6.1.6.3.1.1.5.2
+             warmStart(SNMPv2-MIB): notification-type
1.3.6.1.6.3.1.1.5.3
+                linkDown(IF-MIB): notification-type
1.3.6.1.6.3.1.1.5.3
+              linkDown(SNMPv2-MIB): notification-type
1.3.6.1.6.3.1.1.5.4
+                 linkUp(IF-MIB): notification-type
```

```
1.3.6.1.6.3.1.1.5.4
+               linkUp(SNMPv2-MIB): notification-type
1.3.6.1.6.3.1.1.5.5
+     authenticationFailure(SNMPv2-MIB): notification-type
1.3.6.1.6.3.1.1.5.6
+         egpNeighborLoss(SNMPv2-MIB): notification-type

...

1.3.6.1.6.3.2
+            snmpM2M(SNMPv2-M2M-MIB): module-identity
1.3.6.1.6.3.2.1
+     snmpM2MObjects(SNMPv2-M2M-MIB): oid-value-assignment
1.3.6.1.6.3.2.1.1
+         snmpAlarm(SNMPv2-M2M-MIB): oid-value-assignment
1.3.6.1.6.3.2.1.1.1
+         snmpAlarmNextIndex(SNMPv2-M2M-MIB): object-type
1.3.6.1.6.3.2.1.1.2
+            snmpAlarmTable(SNMPv2-M2M-MIB): object-type
1.3.6.1.6.3.2.1.1.2.1
+            snmpAlarmEntry(SNMPv2-M2M-MIB): object-type
1.3.6.1.6.3.2.1.1.2.1.1
+            snmpAlarmIndex(SNMPv2-M2M-MIB): object-type
1.3.6.1.6.3.2.1.1.2.1.2
+          snmpAlarmVariable(SNMPv2-M2M-MIB): object-type

...

1.3.6.1.6.3.3.3
+     partyMIBConformance(SNMPv2-PARTY-MIB):
+                           oid-value-assignment
1.3.6.1.6.3.3.3.1
+     partyMIBCompliances(SNMPv2-PARTY-MIB):
+                           oid-value-assignment
1.3.6.1.6.3.3.3.1.1
+      unSecurableCompliance(SNMPv2-PARTY-MIB):
+                             module-compliance
1.3.6.1.6.3.3.3.1.2
+      partyNoPrivacyCompliance(SNMPv2-PARTY-MIB):
+                             module-compliance
1.3.6.1.6.3.3.3.1.3
+      partyPrivacyCompliance(SNMPv2-PARTY-MIB):
```

```
+                          module-compliance
1.3.6.1.6.3.3.3.1.4
+    fullPrivacyCompliance (SNMPv2-PARTY-MIB):
+                          module-compliance
1.3.6.1.6.3.3.3.2
+    partyMIBGroups(SNMPv2-PARTY-MIB):
+                        oid-value-assignment
1.3.6.1.6.3.3.3.2.1
+        partyMIBGroup(SNMPv2-PARTY-MIB): object-group

**end of oid tree**

Traps
 enterprise: { iso(1) org(3) dod(6) internet(1) mgmt(2)
+             mib-2(1) snmp(11) }
  trap: coldStart(RFC1215-TRAP), value 0
  trap: warmStart(RFC1215-TRAP), value 1
  trap: linkDown(RFC1215-TRAP), value 2
  trap: linkUp(RFC1215-TRAP), value 3
  trap: authenticationFailure(RFC1215-TRAP), value 4
  trap: egpNeighborLoss(RFC1215-TRAP), value 5
 enterprise: { iso(1) org(3) dod(6) internet(1) mgmt(2)
+             mib-2(1) rmon(16) }
  trap: risingAlarm(DRAFT-RMON-TRAP-MIB), value 1
  trap: fallingAlarm(DRAFT-RMON-TRAP-MIB), value 2
  trap: packetMatch(DRAFT-RMON-TRAP-MIB), value 3
 enterprise: { iso(1) org(3) dod(6) internet(1) mgmt(2)
+            mib-2(1) transmission(10) frame-relay(32)}
  trap: frDLCIStatusChange(RFC1315-MIB), value 1
 enterprise: { iso(1) org(3) dod(6) internet(1) mgmt(2)
+             mib-2(1) transmission(10) x25(5) }
  trap: x25Restart(RFC1382-MIB), value 1
  trap: x25Reset(RFC1382-MIB), value 2
 enterprise: { iso(1) org(3) dod(6) internet(1) mgmt(2)
+             mib-2(1) dot1dBridge(17) }
  trap: newRoot(BRIDGE-MIB), value 1
  trap: topologyChange(BRIDGE-MIB), value 2
 enterprise: { iso(1) org(3) dod(6) internet(1) mgmt(2)
+             mib-2(1) snmpDot3MauMgt(26) }
  trap: rpMauJabberTrap(MAU-MIB), value 1
  trap: ifMauJabberTrap(MAU-MIB), value 2
 enterprise: { iso(1) org(3) dod(6) internet(1) mgmt(2)
```

```
+              mib-2(1) snmpDot3RptrMgt(22) }
   trap: rptrHealth(SNMP-REPEATER-MIB), value 1
   trap: rptrGroupChange(SNMP-REPEATER-MIB), value 2
   trap: rptrResetEvent(SNMP-REPEATER-MIB), value 3
**end of TRAPs**
```

C.11 MIBs with SMICng

The SMICng package comes complete with corrected versions of MIBs from RFCs. All the files are named based on the RFC number and not the module name. This allows the files to be used in Unix and DOS/Windows environments. The extensions of the files are based on the conventions shown below:

.inc - MIB include file
.mib - SNMPv1 MIB
.mi2 - SNMPv2 MIB
.smi - SNMPv1 SMI with extensions for SMICng
.sm2 - SNMPv2 SMI with extensions for SMICng
.trp - SNMPv1 MIB containing only traps

There are "MIB include files" for all MIB modules. These use the conditional include directive so that only the MIBs specified in the IMPORTS clause, those in the MODULE clause of MODULE-COMPLIANCE macros, and those in the SUPPORTS clause of AGENT-CAPABILITIES macros need be specified. For those MIBs that caused errors or warnings to be reported in SMICng, the MIB include file specifies the options so no messages will be reported. Some errors were corrected. If so, they are described in header lines in the MIB files.

C.12 Compiler Extensions and Limitations

SMICng has a support for several constructs that are suppose to be legal in SNMP MIBs but have not yet been added to MIBs on the standards track. The support is either lacking or not available at all in other MIB compilers. These items are described below as extensions, even though they have always been "legal" in both the SNMPv1 and SNMPv2 SMIs. However, writing MIBs using them could result in difficulties with other compilers that do not recognize the constructs.

C.12.1 Sub-typing Extensions

The first is the support for sub-typing for ranges of integer based types and sizes for octet string based types. The allowed sub-typing is a sub-set of the full set of sub-typing from ASN.1. The sub-set does not include the less-than or greater-than operators; the "INCLUDES" construct; nor the "FROM" construct. Also the use of named values is not allowed. The resulting syntax for this "rational sub-set" is shown below:

Syntax:

<integerSubType>
= <empty>
| "(" <range> ["|" <range>]... ")"

<octetStringSubType>
= <empty>
| "(" "SIZE" "(" <range> ["|" <range>]... ")" ")"

<range> = <value> | <value> ".." <value>

<value> = "-" <number> | <number> | <hexString>
| <binString> | "MAX" | "MIN"

where
<empty> is the empty string
<number> is a non-negative integer
<hexString> is a hexidecimal string (i.e. 'xxxx'H)
(Note: this is interpreted as an unsigned integer)
<binString> is a binary string (i.e. 'xxxx'B)
(Note: this is interpreted as an unsigned integer)

The values for the ranges have the following restrictions:

1. any <value> used in a SIZE clause must be non-negative.
2. when a pair of values is specified, the first value must be less than the second value.
3. when multiple ranges are specified, the ranges may not overlap but may touch. For example, (1..4 | 4..9) is invalid, where (1..4 | 5..9) is valid
4. the ranges must be included by the base type. For type Integer32 the max value is 2gig-1, but for UInteger32 the max value is 4gig-1. Thus the range "(0..3000000000)" is valid for UInteger32, but not for Integer32.

Examples:
INTEGER (-20..100)
INTEGER (0..100 | 300..500)
INTEGER (0 | 2 | 4 | 6 | 8 | 10)
OCTET STRING (SIZE(0..100))
OCTET STRING (SIZE(0..100 | 300..500))
OCTET STRING (SIZE(0 | 2 | 4 | 6 | 8 | 10))
Integer32 (1000..MAX)
Integer32 (MIN..-1 | 1..MAX)

```
DisplayString (SIZE(0 | 100..MAX))
  note: since DisplayString is defined as a
      textual convention with max size of 255,
      then the specification "100..MAX" above
      is equivalent to "100..255"
```

C.12.2 OID Support on Imports

The following feature is supported by SMICng but should not be used since it is not well known by the SNMP community nor supported by other MIB compilers.

The ASN.1 language allows for different modules to have the same name. In other uses of ASN.1, MIB modules must be assigned OID values to guarantee uniqueness. In SNMPv1, this was not done. In SNMPv2, the MODULE-IDENTITY macro is used to register an OID value for a module. Once this is done, it is possible to refer to two different modules by OID value instead of by name in the IMPORTS clause. This must be done if items from modules with the same name are imported into a third module. An example of this is shown below:

```
-- First module named M1
M1 DEFINITIONS ::= BEGIN
  ...
  m1 MODULE-IDENTITY
    ...
  ::= { myModules 1 }
  ...
  myA OBJECT-TYPE ...
END

-- Second module named M1
M1 DEFINITIONS ::= BEGIN
  ...
  m1 MODULE-IDENTITY
    ...
  ::= { yourModules 1 }
  ...
  yourA OBJECT-TYPE ...
END

-- Third module with interest in items myA and yourA
M2 DEFINITIONS ::= BEGIN
  IMPORTS
    ...
    myA FROM M1-my { ... myModules(1) 1 }
```

```
    yourA FROM M1-your { ... yourModules(1) 1 };
  ...
END
```

The above may seem a little contrived. However, duplicate module names can occur. The convention for naming standard MIB modules has changed from names based on RFC numbers to names based on the functional area covered by the items in the MIB. An enterprise, another standards organization, or an industry consortium using the same convention could name a MIB module with a conflicting name. Thus a common scenario where this naming collision could occur is the creation of a MIB module containing instances of AGENT-CAPABILITIES that depended on items from the two identically named MIB modules.

C.12.3 Imported Items with Duplicate Names

The ASN.1 language allows for items defined in different modules to have the same name. It requires that all items defined within one module to have a unique name. The SNMPv1 and SNMPv2 SMIs require that the names of all items defined in standard MIB modules to be unique. However, an enterprise, another standards organization, or an industry consortium could quite innocently choose a name for an item duplicating one from a standard MIB module. ASN.1 provides for this to occur. It allows two different items with the same name to be imported into a third MIB module, and it allows an item to be created in a MIB module with the same name as an imported item. When either of these occur, ASN.1 requires that the name of the item to be prefixed by the module name every where an imported item is specified in the module where it is imported. An example of these two cases is shown below:

```
-- First module with item "a"
M1 DEFINITIONS ::= BEGIN
  ...
  a OBJECT-TYPE ...
END

-- Second module with item "a"
M2 DEFINITIONS ::= BEGIN
  ...
  a OBJECT-TYPE ...
END

-- Third module with interest in items named "a"
M3 DEFINITIONS ::= BEGIN
  IMPORTS
    ...
    a FROM M1
```

```
    a FROM M2;
  ...
  b ... ::= { M1.a 1 }
END

-- Fourth module with interest in imported item
--   named "a", and item defined in module named "a"
M4 DEFINITIONS ::= BEGIN
  IMPORTS
    ...
    a FROM M1;
  ...
  b ... ::= { M1.a 1 }
  a ... ::= { c 1 }
  d ... ::= { a 1 }
END
```

C.12.4 ASN.1 OIDs

The “Zen” of OIDs has long been a mystery. The author of SMIC and SMICng didn’t reach the highest level of understanding until work on SMICng was underway. The level of support that SMICng provides for OIDs may seem like an extension, but it is really just that which is required by the ASN.1 language. In ASN.1, an OID value is specified in curly braces (i.e., “{“ and “}”). The first item inside the curlys may be a number, a name-and-number, a “well-known” name, or the name of an item defined in or imported into the MIB module that has an OID value. The remaining items in the curlys may be either numbers or name-and-numbers. The next is key. When a name-and-number are specified as an item, the name is purely commentary! That is, the name is purely to help the reader of the MIB and does not do any “registration” or “assignments”. Below is the syntax for OIDs and a few examples:

```
Syntax:

<oidValue> = "{" <firstItem> [<item>]... "}"

<firstItem> = <number>
        | <nameNumber>
        | <wellKnownName>
        | <itemWithOIDvalue>

<nameNumber> = <name> "(" <number> ")"

<item> = <number>
```

```
    | <nameNumber>

where
  <number> is a non-negative integer
  <name> is any valid ASN.1 identifier starting with
      a lower case letter
  <wellKnownName> is "ccitt", "iso",
      or "joint-iso-ccitt"
  <itemWithOidvalue> is an item defined in or
      imported into the module

Examples:

{ iso org(3) dod(6) }
{ 1 3 6 }

sysObjectID ... ::= { system 2 }
sysObjectID ... ::= { system sysObjectID(2) }

Each of the above pairs specify the same value!
```

In ASN.1, one and only one item can be registered with an OID value. Registration is not done through "normal" value assignments in ASN.1. For example, the line below shows a value assignment and not a registration:

```
a OBJECT IDENTIFIER ::= { system 1 }
```

Several of the macros defined in the SNMPv1 and SNMPv2 SMIs do registration as a "side-effect". Thus the OID value assignment for "a" above is valid, but defining "a" with the OBJECT-TYPE macro to have the same OID value as item sysDescr is not valid. This is because sysDescr is defined with the OBJECT-TYPE macro and thus the OID value "{ system 1 }" has already been registered and can not be re-registered for "a". In SMIC classic, the distinction between registration and value assignment was not correctly understood and implemented. SMIC classic incorrectly assumed type assignments were also registrations.

SMICng has no way to know of registrations other than through the macros defined in the SNMP SMIs. The OBJECT-IDENTITY macro in SNMPv2 SMI can be used to document registrations done outside SNMP's framework.

It should be noted that other MIB compilers impose limitations on OID values. The most common one is limiting the number of items in the curly to two. This is generally not a problem since OID value assignments can be written to split up an OID value consisting of a list of items. Below is an example of this:

```
Original OID value:
internet OBJECT IDENTIFIER ::= { iso 3 6 1 }

Rewritten value:
org OBJECT IDENTIFIER ::= { iso 3 }
dod OBJECT IDENTIFIER ::= { org 6 }
internet OBJECT IDENTIFIER ::= { dod 1 }
```

C.12.5 ASN.1 Macros

SMICng does not parse ASN.1 macros nor parse the complete allowed syntax for type definitions! It is not a general purpose ASN.1 compiler. (To support these features would probably resulted in a doubling or tripling of SMICng's size!) However, one of SMICng's design goals was to allow SNMP's macros and types to be defined in any MIB module (i.e., no "hard-coding" of module names to fake up the resolving of the IMPORTS linkages). SMICng uses an extension to "define" an SMI items, that is the macros and types used in SNMP MIB modules. The SMICng package provides replacements for the original "SMI modules" with the macro and type definitions "commented out" and replaced by the SMICng definition mechanism. The user of SMICng has no need to modify these files. The user has only the requirement to use these modified versions instead of the originals.

C.12.6 Error Recovery

SMICng has extensive error recovery in it. However, it is not all knowing. The allowed syntax for ASN.1 and the SNMP extensions make for difficult situations to always recover. SMICng does a better job than SMIC classic by remembering to location of clauses as it parses a MIB so that when it later checks the syntax parsed MIB module, if errors are found, it can output the exact location of the problem (or at least the location of the item containing the problem).

C.12.7 Forward References

SMICng has no limits on forward references within a MIB module. However, SMICng does require that all imported items must be previous defined. Thus, all MIBs that are of interest and are referenced directly or indirectly through the IMPORTS clause, the MODULE clause in MODULE-COMPLIANCE macros, or the SUPPORTS clause in an AGENT-CAPABILITIES macro must be compiled. SMICng does not use a library of previously compiled MIBs to resolve these linkages. Therefore all of the MIBs must be compiled together. Since a referenced item must already be defined, it is impossible for a pair of MIB modules to reference items from each other. This does not cause any problem since this practice is not valid in SNMP MIB modules.

C.13 Acknowledgments

Many people have helped with testing SMICng to make sure that it really "does the right thing." The key people include:

Evan McGinnis at 3Com
Jeff Case and associates at SNMP Research
Bert Wijnen and associates at IBM
Greg Foster and all my other colleagues at Bay Networks (the merged SynOptics and Wellfleet)

Its been a long year working on the upgrade of SMIC classic to SMICng. This would not have been possible without the support from SMP and the entertainment provided by IMMER.

And finally, please send me bugs, suggestions, fixes, enhancements from using SMICng so that I can put them into the next version.

Enjoy using this tool and let us know how it works
for you. Your friend...

David T. Perkins

C.14 Format of SMIC Intermediate file

Design Goals

1. All information from compile process is captured
   with the execption of ASN.1 comments.
2. The intermediate file is easy to parse. It can be done with no lookahead, and with C library fscanf calls.
3. The intermediate file can be easily read by a person.
4. The data structures built from the compiler will be identical to those built using an intermediate file parser.
5. The format has the flexibility so that additional clausescan be added without requiring old versions to be updated.

All items in the intermediate file follow the same pattern.

This is a "keyword" followed by its arguments. The prefix of the keyword specifies the type of the arguments. The prefix can be one or more of the following with the constraint that only one type of list is allowed per keyword and the list must be the last argument for the keyword. Parsers of the intermediate file should assume that new types of items can be added to semicolon terminated lists. Thus, if an item is encountered in the list, a default parser should be called to parse and discard the item.

Below are are prefixes and their meaning:

- w - WORD (i.e., a simple name), example: ifIndex
- s - LENGTH STRING (i.e., string length followed by string), example: 5 "a dog"
- n - NUMBER, example: 45; NOTE: all numbers are unsigned.
- c - curly braced list, example: { nSUBid 1 nnLoc 12 34 }
- l - list terminated with semicolon, example: FIRST SECOND ;
- d - dotted numbers, example: 1.2.3.4.5
- m - words separated with a dot, examples: MOD1.itemA or MOD2.ItemB

Below is the syntax of SMICng intermediate files:

```
ifile =
   "nlFileVer" NUMBER
      "sDate" LENGTH STRING
      "sCompilerId" LENGTH STRING ";"
      itemDef...
-- ifile is definition of an intermediate file
-- where NUMBER is the version of the file format
-- where STRING (from sDate) is the date that
--   the module was compiled
-- where STRING (from sCompilerId) is the ID of the compiler


itemDef =
   moduleStart | moduleEnd | importFrom | exportDef |
   smiDef | ovaDef | otDef | seqDef | ttDef | tcDef |
   miDef | oiDef | ntDef | ogDef | mcDef | acDef


moduleStart =
   "wlModule" NAME
      "sFile" LENGTH STRING
      [ "sRfile" LENGTH STRING ]
      loc
      [ "cOIDval" oidValue
        [ "dOIDval" dottedOidValue ] ]
      "nSMIver" NUMBER
      "sOptions" LENGTH STRING ";"
-- moduleStart starts the definition of a module
-- where NAME is name of module
-- where STRING (for sFILE) is the name of the
```

```
--   file containing the module
-- where STRING (for sRfile) is the full name of the file
-- where loc is the line and column where the module starts
-- where oidValue is the OID value of the module,
--   if one is specified
-- where dottedOidValue is dotted form of OID value,
--   if one is specified
-- where NUMBER (for nSMIver) is 1 for SNMPv1 or
--   2 for SNMPv2
-- where STRING (for sOPTIONS) is the options used
--   to parse the module


loc =
   "nnLoc" NUMBER NUMBER
-- loc is the location of an element of the MIB
-- where the first NUMBER is the line number and
--   the second number is the column number

oidValue =
   "{" oidItemList "}"

oidItemList =
   { oiditem
     loc }...

oidItem =
   { "SUBidbad" } |
   { "nSUBid" NUMBER } |
   { "wnSUBid NAME NUMBER } |
   { "wSUBid NAME } |
   { "mSUBid NAME "." NAME }

dottedOIDOidValue =
   NUMBER { "." NUMBER }...

moduleEnd =
   "End"
-- moduleEnd ends the list of defintions in a module


importFrom =
```

```
  "wlIMPORTfrom" NAME
     loc
     [ "cOIDval" oidValue
       [ "dOIDval" dottedOidValue ] ]
     "cIEitems" "{" ieItemList "}" ";"
-- importFrom is the name of a module and items
--   imported from it
-- where NAME (for lwIMPORTfrom) is the name of the module
-- where loc (after lwIMPORTfrom) is the line & column
--   of the module
-- where oidValue is the OID value of the module,
--   if one is specified
-- where dottedOidValue is dotted form of OID value,
--   if one is specified
-- where ieItemList is a list of imported items
--   from the module


ieItemList =
  { "wItem" NAME
     loc }...
-- ieItemList is a list of items in an import or export
-- where NAME is the name of an item
-- where loc is the line and column of the item


exportDef =
  "lEXPORTS"
     "cIEitems" "{" ieItemList "}" ";"
-- exportDef is a list exported items
-- where ieItemList is a list of exported items
--   from a module


smiDef =
  "wlSMI" NAME
     loc ";"
-- smiDef is the name of a SMI item
--   (i.e., OBJECT-TYPE or Counter)
-- where NAME is the name of SMI item
```

```
-- where loc is the line & column of the item


ovaDef =
   "wlOVA" NAME
      loc
      "cOIDval" oidValue
      [ "dOIDval" dottedOidValue] ";"
-- ovaDef is the name of an Object Value Assignment
-- where NAME is the name of the OVA
-- where loc is the line & column where it is defined
-- where oidValue is the OID value of the OVA
-- where dottedOidValue is dotted form of OID value,
--   if resolved


otDef =
   "wlOT" NAME
      loc
      "wStatus" NAME
      "wOTtype" NAME
      [ "cInst" instanceEncoding ]
      "cSyntax" syntax
      "cRsyntax" syntax
      [ "sUnits" LENGTH STRING ]
      {{ "wAccess" NAME } |
       { "wMaxAccess" NAME }}
      [ "sDescr" LENGTH STRING ]
      [ "sRefer" LENGTH STRING ]
      [ { "cIndex" indexItemList } |
        { augmentsRow } ]
      [ "cDefVal" "{" defval loc "}" ]
      "cOIDval" oidValue
      [ "dOIDval" dottedOidValue ] ";"
-- otdef is an OBJECT-TYPE definition
-- where NAME (for lwOT) is the name of the OBJECT-TYPE
-- where loc if the line & column of the OBJECT-TYPE
-- where NAME (for wStatus) is the status
-- where NAME (for wOTtype) is the type
--   (i.e., table, row, or leaf)
-- where instanceEncoding specifies how the
--   instances are encoded
```

```
-- where syntax (for cSyntax) is the syntax of
--   the OBJECT-TYPE
-- where syntax (for cRSyntax) is the resolved syntax
--   (which may be the same as the syntax)
-- where STRING (for sUnits) is the units, if present
-- where NAME (for wAccess or wMaxAccess) is the
--   access or max-access
-- where STRING (for sDescr) is the description text,
--   if present
-- where STRING (for sRefer) is the reference text,
--   if present
-- where indexItemList is a list of index items
-- where augmentsRow is the row name if the AUGMENTS
--   clause was used
-- where defval is the default value
-- where oidValue is the OID value of the OBJECT-TYPE
-- where dottedOidValue is dotted form of OID value,
--   if resolved


instanceEncoding =
   "{" { "ZERO" | instanceItem... } "}"
-- instanceEncoding specify the rules for instances
--   of the object
-- where ZERO is used for scalar items
-- where a list of instanceItem is specified for
--   columnar items

instanceItem =
   "UNKNOWN" |              -- unknown encoding
   "INTEGER" |              -- integer
   "IVSTRING" |             -- implied varying string
                    --   with no size
   "VSTRING" |              -- varying string with no size
   { "nIVSTRING" NUMBER } | -- implied varying string with
                    --   min and no max
   { "nVSTRING"  NUMBER } | -- varying string with min
                    --   and no max
   { "nnIVSTRING" NUMBER NUMBER } | -- implied varying
                       --   string with size
   { "nnVSTRING" NUMBER NUMBER } | -- varying string with
                       --   size
```

```
    { "nFSTRING" NUMBER } | -- fixed length string
                          --  (with size)
    "IOID" |              -- implied OID
    "OID" |               -- OID
    "NADDR" |             -- network address
    "IP" |                -- IP address
    "NSAP"                -- NSAP


syntax =
    "{" syntaxItem
      loc "}"

syntaxItem =
    "SYNbad" | synInt | synOctstr | "SYNoid" | "SYNnull" |
    "SYNnaddr" | "SYNipAddr" | "SYNcntr" | synGauge |
    "SYNticks" | "SYNopaque" | synEnum | synSeqOf |
    synSeq | synTc | synBitstr | synInt32 | "SYNcntr32" |
    synGauge32 | "SYNnsap" | "SYNcntr64" | synUint32

synInt =
    "SYNint" |
    { "cSYNint" "{" rangeList "}" }
-- INTEGER syntax


synOctstr =
    "SYNoctstr" |
    { "cSYNoctstr" "{" rangeList "}" }
-- OCTET STRING syntax


synGauge =
    "SYNgauge" |
    { "cSYNgauge" "{" rangeList "}" }
-- Gauge Syntax


synENUM =
    "cSYNenum" "{" enumList "}"
-- Enumerated integer syntax
```

```
synSeqOf =
   "wSYNseqof" NAME
-- SEQUENCE OF syntax


synSeq =
   "wSYNseq" NAME
-- SEQUENCE syntax


synTc =
   { "wSYNtc" NAME } |
   { "mSYNtc" NAME "." NAME } |
   { "wcSYNtcR" NAME "{" rangeList "}" } |
   { "wcSYNtcS" NAME "{" rangeList "}" } |
   { "mcSYNtcR" NAME "." NAME "{" rangeList "}" } |
   { "mcSYNtcS" NAME "." NAME "{" rangeList "}" }
-- Textual convention specified as name of syntax


synBitstr =
   "cSYNbitstr" "{" enumList "}"
-- BIT STRING syntax


synInt32 =
   "SYNint32" |
   { "cSYNint32" "{" rangeList "}" }
-- Integer32 syntax


synGauge32 =
   "SYNgauge32" |
   { "cSYNgauge32" "{" rangeList "}" }
-- Gauge32 syntax


synUint32 =
   "SYNuint32" |
```

```
  { "cSYNuint32" "{" rangeList "}" }
-- UInteger32 syntax


rangeList =
  { range
   loc }...

range =
  "SRbad" |
  { "nSRneg" NUMBER } |        -- negative number
  { "nSRpos" NUMBER } |        -- non-negative number
  { "nnSRpp" NUMBER NUMBER } | -- two non-negative numbers
  { "nnSRnp" NUMBER NUMBER } | -- negative and
                    --  non-negative number
  { "nnSRnn" NUMBER NUMBER } | -- two non-negative numbers
  { "nnSRpn" NUMBER NUMBER } | -- non-negative and
                    --  negative number
  { "SRmin" } |               -- MIN
  { "SRmax" } |               -- MAX
  { "nSRminn" NUMBER } |      -- MIN and negative number
  { "nSRminp" NUMBER } |      -- MIN and positive number
  { "nSRnmax" NUMBER } |      -- negative number and MAX
  { "nSRpmax" NUMBER } |      -- positive number and MAX
  { "SRmm" }                  -- MIN to MAX

enumList =
  { enum
   loc }...

enum =
  { "wENUMbad" NAME } |
  { "wnENUMneg" NAME NUMBER } | -- name and negative
                    --  number
  { "wnENUMpos" NAME NUMBER }  -- name and non-negative
                    --  number


indexItemList =
  "{" { indexItem
      loc }... "}"
```

```
indexItem =
  { "wIndexIimp" NAME } |
  { "wIndexI" NAME } |
  { "mIndexIimp" NAME "." NAME } |
  { "mIndexI" NAME "." NAME } |
  { "cIndexIimp" "{" syntax "}" } |
  { "cIndexI" "{" syntax "}" }

augmentsRow =
  { wAugRow NAME loc } |
  { mAugRow NAME "." NAME loc }

defval =
  { "DVbad" } |
  { "wDVname" NAME } |
  { "mDVname" NAME "." NAME } |
  { "sDVstr" LENGTH STRING } |
  { "sDVbstr" LENGTH STRING } |
  { "sDVhstr" LENGTH STRING } |
  { "nDVpos" NUMBER } |
  { "nDVneg" NUMBER } |
  { "cDVbit" dfBit } |
  { "dDVip" IPADDRESS } |
  { "wDVenum" NAME } |
  { "wDVoid" NAME defvaloid } |
  { "mDVoid" NAME "." NAME defvaloid } |
  { "cDVoid" oidValue defvaloid }

defvaloid =
  { "dDVoid" dottedOidValue }

dfBit =
  "{" bitItem "}"

listItem =
  { bitElement
   loc }...

bitElement =
  { "BITelBad" } |
  { "wBITna" NAME }
```

```
seqDef =
  "wlSEQ" NAME
    loc
    "cSEQIL" "{" seqItemList "}" ";"
-- seqDef is a SEQUENCE definition

seqItemList =
  { seqItem
   loc }...

seqItem =
  { "wcSeqI" NAME syntax }


ttDef =
  "wlTT" NAME
    loc
    "cOIDval" oidValue
    [ "dOIDval" dottedOidValue]
    [ "cVar" "{" varList "}" ]
    [ "sDescr" LENGTH STRING ]
    [ "sRefer" LENGTH STRING ]
    "nTrapVal" NUMBER ";"
-- ttDef is a TRAP-TYPE definition


varList =
  { varItem
   loc }...

varItem =
  { "wVarI" NAME } |
  { "mVarI" NAME "." NAME }


tcDef =
  "wlTC" NAME
```

```
        loc
        [ "wStatus" NAME ]
        [ "sDescr" LENGTH STRING ]
        [ "sRefer" LENGTH STRING ]
        [ "TCmacro" ]
        [ "sDspHint" LENGTH STRING ]
        "cSyntax" syntax
        [ "cRsyntax" syntax ] ";"
-- tcDef is a type assignment (a v1 textual convention) or
-- is a TEXTUAL-CONVENTION definition

miDef =
    "wlMI" NAME
        loc
        "sLastUpdate" LENGTH STRING
        "sOrgName" LENGTH STRING
        "sContactInfo" LENGTH STRING
        "sDescr" LENGTH STRING
        [ "cRevL" "{" revList "}" ]
        "cOIDval" oidValue
        [ "dOIDval" dottedOidValue ]
        [ "sRefer" LENGTH STRING ] ";"
-- miDef is a MODULE-IDENTITY definition

revList =
    { "sRev" LENGTH STRING
      "sDescr" LENGTH STRING }...

oiDef =
    "wlOI" NAME
        loc
        "wStatus" NAME
        "sDescr" LENGTH STRING
        [ "sRefer" LENGTH STRING ]
        "cOIDval" oidValue
        [ "dOIDval" dottedOidValue ] ";"
-- oiDef is an OBJECT-IDENTITY definition


ntDef =
    "wlNT" NAME
        loc
```

```
      "wStatus" NAME
      [ "cVarL" "{" varList "}" ]
      "sDescr" LENGTH STRING
      [ "sRefer" LENGTH STRING ]
      "cOIDval" oidValue
      [ "dOIDval" dottedOidValue ] ";"
-- ntDef is a NOTIFICATION-TYPE definition


ogDef =
   "wlOG" NAME
      loc
      "wStatus" NAME
      [ "cVarL" "{" varList "}" ]
      "sDescr" LENGTH STRING
      [ "sRefer" LENGTH STRING ]
      "cOIDval" oidValue
      [ "dOIDval" dottedOidValue ] ";"
-- ogDef is an OBJECT-GROUP definition


mcDef =
   "wlMC" NAME
      loc
      "wStatus" NAME
      "sDescr" LENGTH STRING
      [ "sRefer" LENGTH STRING ]
      [ mcModInfo ]...
      "cOIDval" oidValue
      [ "dOIDval" dottedOidValue ] ";"
-- mcDef is a MODULE-COMPLIANCE definition


mcModInfo =
  { wlMCMOD NAME mcMod ";" } |
  { lMCMOD mcMod ";" }

mcMod =
  { loc
    [ "cOIDval" oidValue
      [ "dOIDval" dottedOidValue ] ]
    [ "cMGR" "{" manGroupList "}" ]
```

```
    [ "cCGO" "{" compGroupObjList "}" ] }

manGroupList =
   { manGroupItem
    loc }...

manGroupItem =
   { "wMGroupI" NAME } |
   { "mMGroupI" NAME "." NAME }

compGroupObjList =
   { compGroupItem |
    compObjItem }...

compGroupItem =
    { { "mlCGroupI" NAME } |
     { "mlCGroupI" NAME "." NAME } }
    loc
    "sDescr" LENGTH STRING  ";"

compObjItem =
    { { "wlCObjI" NAME } |
     { "mlCObjI" NAME "." NAME } }
    loc
    "sDescr" LENGTH STRING
    [ "cSyntax" syntax
     [ "cRsyntax" syntax ] ]
    [ "cWsyntax" syntax
     [ "cWrsyntax" syntax ] ]
    [ "wMinAccess" NAME ] ";"

acDef =
   "wlAC" NAME
     loc
     "sRels" LENGTH STRING
     "wStatus" NAME
     "sDescr" LENGTH STRING
     [ "sRefer" LENGTH STRING ]
     [ acModInfo ]...
     "cOIDval" oidValue
```

```
    [ "dOIDval" dottedOidValue ] ";"
-- acDef is an AGENT-CAPABILITIES definition


acModInfo =
  { "wlACMOD" NAME acMod ";" } |
  { "lACMOD" acMod ";" }

acMod =
  { loc
   [ "cOIDval" oidValue
     [ "dOIDval" dottedOidValue ] ]
   [ "cIGR" "{" groupList "}" ]
   [ "cACV" "{" agentVariationList "}" ] }

groupList =
  { groupItem
    loc }...

groupItem =
  { "wIGroupI" NAME } |
  { "mIGroupI" NAME "." NAME }

compGroupObjList =
  { compGroupItem |
    compObjItem }...

compGroupItem =
  { { "mlCGroupI" NAME } |
    { "mlCGroupI" NAME "." NAME } }
    loc
    "sDescr" LENGTH STRING  ";"

agentVariationList =
  agentVar...


agentVar =
  { { "wlVObjI" NAME } |
    { "mlVObjI" NAME "." NAME } }
    loc
    "sDescr" LENGTH STRING
```

```
[ "cSyntax" syntax
  [ "cRsyntax" syntax ] ]
[ "cWsyntax" syntax
  [ "cWrsyntax" syntax ] ]
[ "wAccess" NAME ]
[ "cCreReq" "{" varList "}" ]
[ "cDefVal" "{" defval loc "}" ]  ";"
```

APPENDIX D

Guide to MIB Resources

This section outlines some useful resources when creating a MIB.

D.1 Requesting an Enterprise Identifier

To obtain an enterprise identifier, contact the Internet Assigned Numbers Authority:

Postal: IANA
USC/Information Sciences Institute
4676 Admiralty Way
Marina del Rey, CA 90292

Phone: +1 310 822-1511

Fax: +1 310 823-6714

Email: iana-mib@isi.edu -- *for enterprise identifiers*
iana@isi.edu -- *for other correspondence*

URL: http://www.iana.org/iana

D.2 Public MIB Repositories

A great many MIBs from both vendors and IETF working groups are available at Internet sites via anonymous FTP. Reading example MIBs is an excellent way of understanding how other groups have solved similar problems you may face. Some vendor MIBs are deposited in the **mib** sub-directory at **venera.isi.edu**. These can be obtained via anonymous FTP or through the IANA Web page.

To obtain a MIB via anonymous FTP:

ftp venera.isi.edu
name (venera.isi.edu:bem) **anonymous**
331: Guest login ok, send your complete email address as password
Password: **<your complete email address>**
230: Guest login ok, access restrictions apply.
ftp> **cd mib**

Many of the MIBs deposited at this site are out of date, so searching here for a MIB from your favorite vendor can be discouraging. Most vendors also maintain private anonymous FTP sites. Contact the vendor directly and inquire about their on-line MIB information.

D.3 Obtaining RFCs

There are many repositories for RFCs. The best starting location to find a site is the IETF Web page:

http://www.ietf.org

D.4 MIB Development Software

The most up-to-date information about the SMICng MIB compiler can be found on the Web page:

http://www.snmpinfo.com

There are MIB compilers included in many popular network management station software, but these usually are limited to translating the MIB into some proprietary format used by that station. Using these special purpose compilers has not proven that a MIB is correct, but that it works with that particular platform.

D.5 SNMP Newsgroups

There are some netnews groups dedicated to SNMP:
comp.protocols.snmp discusses SNMP and MIB questions.
comp.dcom.net-management discusses network management in general.

D.6 SNMP Publications

There is really only one publication dedicated to SNMP: *The Simple Times*. This is available via email in three formats: Postcript, rich-text, and HTML. You can get information on subscribing by sending a note with a subject of "help" to:

st-subscriptions@simple-times.org

D.7 SNMP and MIB World Wide Web Sites

There are several good WWW sites for information about using SNMP, MIBs and network management in general. There are several sites which make a good starting point for your search:

- SNMP Info: **http://www.snmpinfo.com**
- University of New York, Buffalo: **http://netman.cit.buffalo.edu**
- University of Twente: **http://www.snmp.cs.utwentel.nl**
- University of Delft (Netherlands): **http://dnpap.et.tudelft.nl/DNPAP/dnpap.html**
- Technical University of Munich (Germany): **http://www.ldv.e-technik.tu-muenchen.de/forsch/netmanage**
- Simple Times: **http://www.simple-times.org/pub/simple-times/issues**

D.8 Mailing Lists

Standards organizations and vendor consortiums have defined a great number of MIBs that are ready for use. If you have questions about implementation details of a particular MIB, you may be able to get helpful advice from the mailing list. However, the authors have found that list activity drops off precipitously once the bulk of a MIB is written, and it begins its slow trek through the standardization process. You can also retrieve a great deal of information by retrieving the mail archives for these lists.

Working groups are constantly forming and disbanding, so your best bet for tracking down a working group is to check the IETF home page. At this time, the Table D–1 shows the mailing lists regarding SNMP, including MIBs. (Unless otherwise noted, specify one of the following phrases in the body of the email message to subscribe or unsubscribe to the mailing list.)

subscribe <list-name> [your-email-address]
unsubscribe <list-name> [your-email-address]

For example, to subscribe to the snmp mailing list send a message to **snmp-request@psi.com (not snmp@psi.com)** with body:

subscribe snmp

Table D–1 SNMP Related Mailing Lists

Mailing Lists	To Subscribe/Unsubscribe
SNMP topics	snmp-request@psi.com
IETF SNMPv2 WG	snmp2-request@tis.com
IETF 100VG AnyLan MIB WG	vgmib-request@hprnd.rose.hp.com

Table D–1 SNMP Related Mailing Lists (Continued)

Mailing Lists	To Subscribe/Unsubscribe
IETF AToM MIB WG	atommib-request@thumper.bellcore.com
IETF Application MIB WG	applmib-request@emi-summit.com
IETF Bridge MIB WG	bridge-mib-request@pa.dec.com
IETF DS1/DS3 MIB WG	trunk-mib-request@cisco.com
IETF DataLink Switching MIB WG	aiw-dlsw-mib-request@networking.raleigh.ibm.com
IETF Distributed Management MIB WG	majordomo@nexen.com
IETF Entity MIB WG	majordomo@cisco.com
IETF Frame Relay Service MIB WG	frs-mib-request@newbridge.com
IETF IEEE 802.3 MIB WG	hubmib-request@hprnd.rose.hp.com
IETF IPv6 MIB WG	ipv6mib-request@research.ftp.com
IETF ISDN MIB WG	isdn-mib-request@cisco.com
IETF Interfaces MIB WG	if-mib-request@thumper.bellcore.com
IETF Remote Network Monitoring MIB WG	rmonmib-request@cisco.com
IETF SNA DLC Services SDLC & LLC-2 MIB WG	snadlcmib-request@cisco.com
IETF SNA NAU Services PU 2.0 & 2.1 and LU 1,2,3 & 6.2 MIB WG	snanaumib-request@cisco.com
IETF SNMP Agent Extensibility WG	agentx-request@fv.com
IETF Uninteruptible Power Supply MIB WG	ups-mib-request@cs.utk.edu

APPENDIX E

References & Reading List

This book has only covered a small portion of the entire management framework. The sources listed here provide an excellent starting point for an in-depth understanding of SNMP and network management in general.

E.1 ASN.1 Information

1. International Organization for Standardization. 1987. "Information processing systems. Open Systems Interconnection. Specification of Abstract Syntax Notation One (ASN.1)." Reference number ISO 8824 : 1987 (E).
2. International Organization for Standardization. 1987. "Information processing systems. Open Systems Interconnection. Specification of Basic Encoding Rules for Abstract Syntax Notation One (ASN.1)." Reference number ISO 8825 : 1987 (E).
3. Douglas Steedman. Abstract Syntax Notation One (ASN.1): The Tutorial and Reference. Technology Appraisals, Isleworth, Middlesex United Kingdom, 1993. ISBN 1-871802-06-7.

E.2 Recommended SNMP Information

1. Sidnie Feit. SNMP: A Guide to Network Management, McGraw-Hill, New York, NY, 1995. ISBN 0-07-020359-8.
2. Marshall T. Rose. The Simple Book, Prentice Hall (Revised Second Edition), Upper Saddle River, NJ, 1996. ISBN 0-13-451659-1.
3. Marshall T. Rose & Keith McCloghrie. How to Manage Your Network Using SNMP: The Network Management Practicum, Prentice Hall, Englewood Cliffs, NJ, 1995. ISBN 0-13-141517-4.

E.3 Additional SNMP Information

1. Mark A. Miller. Managing Internetworks with SNMP, M&T Books, New York, NY, 1993. ISBN 1-55851-304-3.
2. Gilbert Held. LAN Management with SNMP and RMON, John Wiley & Sons, New York, NY, 1996. ISBN 0-471-14736-2.
3. William Stallings. SNMP, SNMPv2 and RMON: Practical Network Management (Second Edition), Addison-Wesley, Reading, Massachusetts, 1996. ISBN 0-201-63479-1.
4. Mathias Hein & David Griffiths. SNMP: Simple Network Management Protocol Theory and Practice, International Thomson Publishing, Boston, MA, 1995. ISBN 1-850-32139-6.
5. Allan Leinwand & Karen Fang Conroy. Network Management: A Practical Perspective, Addison-Wesley, Reading, MA, 1996. ISBN 0-201-60999-1.
6. Sean J. Harnedy. Total SNMP: Exploring the Simple Network Management Protocol, CBM Books, Horsham, PA, 1994. ISBN 1-878956-33-7.

APPENDIX F

Guide to the CD-ROM

This appendix describes the CD-ROM that accompanies this book. The following platforms are supported: HPUX 9.05 and 10.10, AIX 3.2.1 and 4.01, Solaris 2.4, SunOS 4.1.4, Linux, MSDOS, and Windows 95/NT.

F.1 Contents of the CD-ROM

The CR-ROM contains the following files:

For MS-DOS, Windows95, and NT

- dos16.zip MSDOS executables
- dos32.zip Microsoft Windows 95/NT executables
- html.zip HTML versions of all MIBs
- 32mibs.zip MIBs with long file names
- 32mibsv1.zip MIBs with long file names (SMIv1 versions of SMIv2 MIBs)
- mibsv1.zip MIBs (SMIv1 versions of SMIv2 MIBs)
- 32rfc.zip MIB and Network Management RFCs

For Unix-type systems

- aix.tar IBM AIX executables
- hpux.tar HP HPUX executables
- linux.tar Linux executables
- solaris.tar Sun Solaris 2.x executables
- sunos.tar Sun SunOS 4.x executables
- html.tar HTML versions of all MIBs
- imf.tar SMIC intermediate format of all MIBs
- mibs.tar MIBs
- mibsv1.tar MIBs (SMIv1 versions of SMIv2 MIBs)
- rfc.tar MIB and Network Management RFCs

The ".zip" files can be extracted with the pkunzip and unzip programs. For example, to extract the MSDOS executables, you would type:

```
pkunzip dos16
```

The ".tar" files are intended for use on UNIX workstations. To extract them, use the tar program. For example, to extract the AIX executables, you would type:

```
tar xf aix.tar
```

F.2 Setup and Use

Here's how to set up your MIB development environment:

1. Create a new directory, say *mibs*, and make that your current working directory.
2. Extract all of the MIBs using the tar or unzip program. Note that the supplied MIBs were extracted from RFCs and corrected. Do not use uncorrected MIBs from RFCs.
3. Set up the SMICINCL environment variable to name the directory containing the MIBs.
4. Create a new directory, or use an existing one to hold the executables.
5. Extract the executables for your operating system using the tar or unzip program.
6. Modify your PATH environment variable to specify the directory containing the extracted executables.
7. Test that the executables are installed by entering the command "smicng -1". You should see something like the following:

```
SMICng version 2.0.11(BOOK)(MS-DOS32), October 11, 1996.
Copyright 1996 David T. Perkins. All Rights Reserved.
This software is furnished under a license and may be used and
copied only in accordance with the terms of such license.
David T. Perkins makes no representations about the suitability
of this software for any particular purpose. The software is
supplied "AS IS", and David T. Perkins makes no warranty,
either express or implied, as to the use, operation, condition,
or performance of the software.
David T. Perkins retains all title and ownership in this work.
For assistance or to report bugs send EMAIL to
    dperkins@scruznet.com
```

8. Test that the SMICINCL environment variable is correctly set up by entering the command "smicng rfc1213.inc" to compile MIB-II. The result should be something like the following:

```
Successful parsing
```

and not the message:

```
E: Could not open file "rfc1213.inc" from command line
*** 1 error and 0 warnings in parsing
```

That's all there is to it! You are now ready to begin examining the standard MIBs we have included, or to begin to write your own. Instructions on using SMIC are given in Appendix C.

F.3 WWW MIB Formatter

Another executable that we have provided is a back-end MIB compiler which reformats a MIB into HTML, so that you can publish a MIB in a WWW page. This executable is called mib2html. It is quite easy to use, but it does require, however, that you have used SMIC to generate intermediate files from your MIBs. Here's how to use mib2html:

1. Compile your MIB with SMIC using the "Z" option. This will create an "intermediate" format file that mib2html requires. For example, suppose that you have created a MIB in a file named *mymib.mib* and a SMIC include file named *mymib.inc*. You would enter the following command to produce the intermediate file *mymib.imf*:

   ```
   smicng -Z mymib.imf mymib.inc
   ```

2. Convert your MIB into HTML by telling mib2html to process the intermediate file you created in the previous step. This is done with the command:

   ```
   mib2html mymib.imf
   ```

3. The mib2html program will create two files, each named after the module name of your MIB. For instance, if your MIB module is named SPRINKLER-MIB, the two files created would be SPRINKLER-MIB.html and SPRINKLER-MIB_.html.
4. We've also included two scripts for Unix workstations that will allow you to compile all MIBs into the intermediate format, and then into HTML. The first script is named *create_mibs*, and takes no command line arguments. For each MIB in the current directory, it will create a corresponding file that ends in the *.imf* extension. The second script is named *create_html*, and formats all *.imf* files created in the first step into HTML files.

Index

J

K

L

P